SMALL HOTELS
GUEST HOUSES & INNS
GREAT BRITAIN AND IRELAND
1991

Published by RAC Publishing, RAC House, Bartlett Street,
South Croydon CR2 6XW

ISBN 0 86211 093 9

Typeset by BP Integraphics Ltd, Bath

Printed and bound by The Bath Press, Avon

Advertising Managers:
Kingslea Press Ltd, 137 Newhall St, Birmingham B3 1SF
Telephone: 021-236 8112

Cover picture: Cyfie Farm, Llanfihangel, Llanfyllin

CONTENTS

Introduction

Whether it's a friendly seaside guest house, a budget overnight stay while working away from home, a cheerful country inn or that small hideaway hotel with a touch of luxury—the choice is yours! In response to popular demand for more quality information on such places RAC Publishing brings you the *RAC Guide to Small Hotels, Guest Houses and Inns*.

The guide is also a reflection of the growing success of the RAC Hotel Inspection Scheme. In this sector we now have over 2,000 establishments able to display the RAC sign.

Our famous and comprehensive *RAC Hotel Guide, Great Britain and Ireland*, first published in 1904 is now joined by this brand new guide. The *RAC Guide to Small Hotels, Guest Houses and Inns* has both the space and the scope to do justice to the popular and smaller alternative choice in accommodation in Britain and Ireland.

Places in this guide are special. Unlike so many larger establishments they are not so impersonal, you are the guest. Often you may be treated like a friend. Someone might not only take an interest in your comfort, but also in the pleasure and enjoyment of your stay. Above all, even if the stay is not budget-priced, it should be value-for-money.

Awards

For some years now, the RAC has recognised the very high standards reached by some of their listed hotels by the awards of Highly Acclaimed and Acclaimed status. To gain such recognition an establishment must have a proportion of rooms with en suite bathrooms, decorations and furnishings with a certain degree of elegance and above-average fittings and equipment. Inns, too if they reach high standards can be awarded one to three tankards. Highly Acclaimed hotels and tankard inns are listed on pp 14–16.

Best of the Year—1990

Each year, we will choose what we consider the best small hotel or guest house of the year for each of six regions.

We congratulate the winners for 1990, described on pp 6–11

South-West Region:	Hayne Farm, Black Torrington, Devon
South-East Region :	Langshott Manor, Horley, Surrey
Midland Region :	Lypiatt House, Cheltenham, Gloucestershire
North Region :	Manor House, Beverley, Humberside
Scotland :	Ravenscourt House, Grantown-on Spey, Highland
Wales :	Three Wells Farm, Llandrindod Wells, Powys

Symbols

	English	Français	Deutsche
ℓ	Telephone number	Numéro de téléphone	Telefonnummer
♿	Facilities for the disabled	Aménagements pour handicapés	Einrichtungen für Behinderte
⊨	Information about bedrooms	Renseignements sur les chambres	Informationen über Schlafzimmer
🏠	Facilities at hotel	Aménagements de l'hôtel	Einrichtungen im Hotel
✕	Information about meals	Renseignements sur les repas	Informationen über Mahlzeiten
£	Price information	Renseignements sur les tarifs	Preisinformationen
B&B	Price of single room & breakfast	prix d'une chambre d'une personne + petit déjeuner	Preis für Einzelzimmer und Frühstück

HB	Half-board	Demi-pension	Teilverpflegung
Bk	Breakfast	Petit déjeuner	Frühstück
L	Lunch	Déjeuner	Mittagessen
D	Dinner	Dîner	Abendessen
fr	From	A partir de	von
WB	Short breaks	Mini-vacances	Kurzurlaube
[V]	Vouchers accepted	Tickets/Bons de réduction acceptés	Gutscheine werden angenommen
w/e	Weekends	Week-ends	Wochenende
w/d	Weekdays	Jours de semaine	Wochentage
cc	Credit cards	Cartes de crédit	Kreditkarten
ns	No-smoking areas	Zones non fumeurs	Nichtraucher-Gebiete
NS	No smoking anywhere in hotel	Interdiction de fumer dans l'hôtel	Rauchverbot im ganzen Hotel
tcf	Tea/coffee-making facilities	Equipement pour faire du thé/café dans les chambres	Tee-/Kaffee-Aufgußeinrichtungen
P	Parking	Parking	Parken
G	Garage	Garage	Garage
U	Lock-up garage	Garage fermé	abschließbare Garage
LD	Last dinner time	Dernière heure pour dîner	letzte Abendessenszeit
nr	No restaurant service	Pas de restaurant	keine Restaurantbedienung
✵	Languages spoken	Langue(s) parlée(s)	diese Sprache/n wird/werden gesprochen

Fr French   De German   It Italian   Es Spanish   Po Portuguese   Ja Japanese   Ar Arabic

Prices: Prices given in the Guide are forecasts by hoteliers of what they expect to charge in 1991. As the information is, of necessity, compiled well in advance of publication, varying conditions may have brought about increases in published charges. It is always wise to check with a hotel what the relevant charges are before booking. All prices quoted should include VAT where applicable.

Last dinner may be the last time dinner orders are taken *or* the last time a booking for dinner can be made.

Weekend breaks: please consult the hotel concerned for full details.

Arrival times: Small hotels, guest houses and inns may close for part of the afternoon. It is wise to inform them of your expected arrival time when booking, and courteous to telephone them if you are delayed.

Cancellation of reservations: Should it become necessary to cancel reserved accommodation, guests are advised to telephone at once to the hotel, followed by written confirmation. If rooms which are reserved and not occupied cannot be re-let, the hotel proprietor may suffer loss, and guests may be held legally responsible for part of the cost.

Maps: Map references in the guide are to the relevant square on the maps on pages 17–32.

Establishment entries shown with ᕇ are, in the opinion of their owner or manager, suitable for disabled people. Disabled visitors are recommended to contact the hotel direct and to discuss with the manager whether their particular requirements can be met.

Farms: Short entries shown with *Farm* after the telephone number (except in the Republic of Ireland) are members of the Farm Holiday Bureau, a network of farming families throughout the UK who offer a warm welcome to guests to stay on their farms. The RAC has not inspected these farms, but they have been inspected and approved by the relevant National Tourist Boards.

Discount vouchers: Many establishments are prepared to offer readers of this guide discounts on accommodation prices. They are shown by a [V] at the end of the price section. Use the vouchers at the end of the guide to obtain your discount.

Shortened hotel entries: A number of hotels failed to provide detailed information for the 1991 season. In such cases only the name, address and telephone number appear in the entry.

Licenses: hotels, guests houses and inns serve alcoholic drinks unless they are shown as unlicensed. They may be subject to any of the following limitations.
Restaurant licence (*Rest lic*) A licence whereby the sale of alcoholic drinks is restricted to customers taking meals.
Residential licence (*Resid lic*) A licence whereby the sale of alcoholic drinks is restricted to residents and their friends.
Club licence A licence granted to establishments at which it is necessary to become a member of a club in order to obtain alcoholic drinks. To comply with the law, a period of 24 hours after joining should elapse before such club membership can take effect.
Temperance hotels (*Temp*) do not allow the consumption of alcohol on the premises.
Unlicensed hotels do not sell alcoholic drinks, but guests may bring their own.

5

Hayne Farm Black Torrington

A working farm in the depths of the Devon countryside may seem an unlikely setting for an award winner, but Ivan and Valerie McKee not only raise beef cattle, they also run a most successful guest house. The attractive old farmhouse has a huge inglenook fireplace, said to be one of the biggest in Devon, and has been completely renovated. A recent extension has added two more en suite bedrooms and a dining room where good English food is provided, with puddings a speciality.

Langshott Manor Horley

Langshott Manor needs little introduction. One look at this exquisite Elizabethan manor house, lovingly restored and furnished with care to set off its charms to the best advantage, is all it takes to recognise an outstanding place. Mr and Mrs Noble are to be congratulated on a superb small hotel.

Lypiatt House Cheltenham

Close to the centre of the elegant spa town of Cheltenham, Lypiatt House is a charming Victorian building which has been sympathetically restored and decorated. The Malloys have some lovely pieces of antique furniture, and tastefully chosen carpets and curtains enhance the spacious rooms with their graceful windows and corniced ceilings.

Manor House Beverley

Just outside the ancient city of Beverley, on the edge of the Yorkshire Wolds, the Manor House, a substantial Victorian house, is run with great success by chef-patron Derek Baugh and Lee Crane, who is a skilled pâtissière. And this outstanding small hotel is as notable for the comfort of its beautifully furnished rooms as it is for the excellence of its food.

Ravenscourt House
Grantown-on-Spey

No expense was spared when this former Manse was refurbished recently and it is now an excellent hotel. Set in lovely gardens, it is a solid, stone-built house with spacious rooms carefully planned to provide a relaxing atmosphere; the Orangery, in particular, makes a delightful dining room. Freddie Bartlett and Sammy Bain are courteous and friendly hosts and have added those touches, like the fine original paintings, which make this hotel so extra-special.

Three Wells Farm
Llandrindod Wells

There's a warm Welsh welcome from the Buftons at Three Wells Farm, a working farm with sheep, pedigree Welsh black cattle, ducks, hens and a variety of wild life. There are riding ponies, and a fishing lake right beside the farmhouse, so guests have lots to do. And there are cheerful, well-furnished rooms and good food waiting when you return.

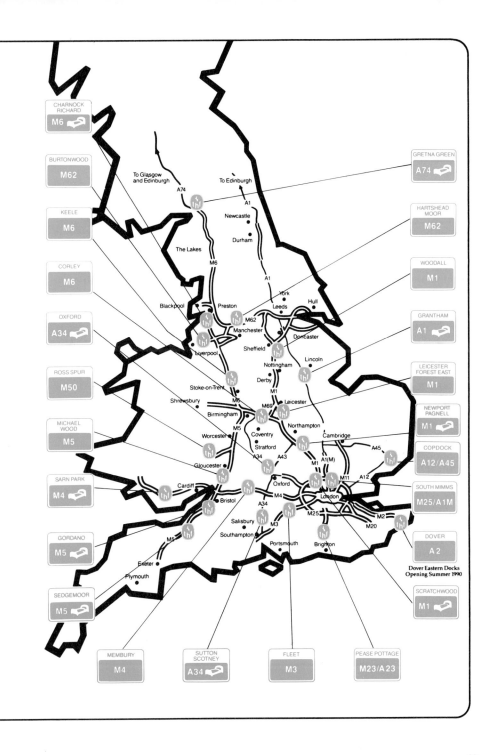

CHARNOCK RICHARD
M6

BURTONWOOD
M62

KEELE
M6

CORLEY
M6

OXFORD
A34

ROSS SPUR
M50

MICHAEL WOOD
M5

SARN PARK
M4

GORDANO
M5

SEDGEMOOR
M5

GRETNA GREEN
A74

HARTSHEAD MOOR
M62

WOODALL
M1

GRANTHAM
A1

LEICESTER FOREST EAST
M1

NEWPORT PAGNELL
M1

COPDOCK
A12/A45

SOUTH MIMMS
M25/A1M

DOVER
A2

Dover Eastern Docks
Opening Summer 1990

SCRATCHWOOD
M1

MEMBURY
M4

SUTTON SCOTNEY
A34

FLEET
M3

PEASE POTTAGE
M23/A23

To Glasgow and Edinburgh
To Edinburgh
A74
A1
Newcastle
Durham
The Lakes
M6
A1
Blackpool
Preston
York
Leeds
Hull
M62
Manchester
Doncaster
Liverpool
Sheffield
Lincoln
Nottingham
Stoke-on-Trent
Derby
Shrewsbury
M1
M6
Leicester
Birmingham
M69
Worcester
M5
Coventry
Northampton
Cambridge
Stratford
A34
A43
A1(M)
A45
Gloucester
M1
A12
Cardiff
Oxford
M11
Bristol
M4
London
A34
M25
A3
M2
Salisbury
M20
Southampton
Portsmouth
Brighton
Exeter
M5
Plymouth

13

Highly Acclaimed Hotels & Guest Houses

England

ALNMOUTH Marine House
AMBLESIDE Gables
  Grey Friar Lodge Country House
AMOTHERBY Greenacres Country
BADMINTON Bodkin House
BAINBRIDGE Riverdale House
BANBURY Easington House
  La Madonette
BATH Bath Lodge
  Brompton House
  Cheriton House
  Dorian House
  Eagle House
  Highways House
  Leighton House
  Lord Nelson Inn
  Oakleigh
  Orchard House
  Tasburgh
BEVERLEY Manor House
BILLINGSHURST Old Wharf
BINGLEY Hallbank
BIRMINGHAM Bridge House
BISHOP AUCKLAND Greenhead Country House
BLACKPOOL Arosa
  Cliff Head
  Lynstead
  Old Coach House
  Sunray
BLAKENEY Lower Viney
BOURNEMOUTH Tudor Grange
BOURTON ON THE WATER Ridge
BRADFORD-ON-AVON Widbrook Grange
BRAMPTON Oakwood Park
BRANSCOMBE Bulstone
BREDWARDINE Bredwardine Hall
BRENDON Millslade
BRIGHTON Adelaide
  Ascott House
  Kempton House
BROADWAY Leasow House
  The Old Rectory
BROCKENHURST Cottage
BRUTON Fryerning
BUXTON Brookfield
  Thorn Heyes
  Westminster
CALDBECK High Greenrigg
  Park End
CAMBORNE Lowenac
CAMBRIDGE Cambridge Lodge
  Lensfield
CANTERBURY Ebury
  Pilgrims

  Thanington
CHAGFORD Thorworthy House
CHELMSFORD Snows Oakland
CHELTENHAM Allards
  Beaumont House
  Cotswold Grange
  Hannaford's
  Lypiatt House
  On the Park
  Regency House
  Stretton Lodge
CHESTER Green Gables
  Redland
CHURCH STRETTON Paddock Lodge
CIRENCESTER La Ronde
  Wimborne
CLITHEROE Harrop Fold Country Farm
COLYTON Swallows Eaves
CONISTON Coniston Lodge
COXLEY VINEYARD Coxley Vineyard
CROMER Westgate Lodge
CROYDE Whiteleafe at Croyde
DOVER East Lee
  Number One
DROXFORD Little Uplands Country Manor
FOWEY Carnethic House
FRESHWATER, IoW Blenheim House
FRINTON-ON-SEA Montpellier
GARBOLISHAM Ingleneuk
GISLINGHAM Old Guildhall
GLOSSOP Wind in the Willows
GLOUCESTER Rotherfield House
GRANGE-OVER-SANDS Elton
HARROGATE Glenayr
  Hadleigh
  Shannon Court
HARROW Lindal
HASTINGS Eagle House
HAYLING ISLAND Cockle Warren Cottage
HEREFORD Collins House
HENLEY-IN-ARDEN Ashleigh House
HILGAY Crosskeys Riverside
HOLT Lawns
HONITON Colestocks House
HORLEY Langshott Manor
HOVE Claremont House
HUBBERHOLME Kirkgill Manor
HUNSTANTON Sunningdale
INGLETON Pines Country
KESWICK Allerdale House
  Dalegarth House
  Gales Country House
  Greystones
  Ravenworth
  Shemara
  Stonegarth
  Swiss Court
  Thornleigh

KETTLEWELL Langcliffe House
KIDDERMINSTER Cedars
KING'S LYNN Russet House
KIRKBY LONSDALE Cobwebs Country
KIRKBY STEPHEN Town Head
KNARESBOROUGH Newton House
KNUTSFORD Longview
LANGPORT Hillards Farm
LEOMINSTER Withenfield
LICHFIELD Oakleigh House
LINCOLN D'Isney Place
  Minster Lodge
LONDON SE3 Vanburgh
LONDON SW7 Alexander
LONDON W2 Byron
LONDON W2 Pembridge Court
LONDON WC1 Academy
LOOE Polraen Country House
LOWESTOFT Lodge
LYNTON Gordon House
  Millslade
MAIDEN NEWTON Maiden Newton
MIDDLESBROUGH Grey House
MILTON KEYNES Linford Lodge
MILTON-UNDER-WYCHWOOD Hillborough
MINEHEAD Alcombe House
  Dorchester
  Mayfair
MORCHARD BISHOP Wigham Farm
MORECAMBE Beach Mount
  Hotel Prospect
  Hotel Warwick
NEWQUAY Porth Enodoc
NORWICH Belmont
  Cavalier
  Wedgewood
NOTTINGHAM Balmoral
NUNEATON Ambion Court
OXFORD Chestnuts
  Cotswold House
  Gables
  Tilbury Lodge
PADSTOW Green Waves
  Woodlands
PENZANCE Estoril
  Tarbert
PLYMOUTH Georgian House
PORTSMOUTH/SOUTHSEA Seacrest
PRESTON Tulketh
RICHMOND Richmond Gate
RYE Jeakes House
ST AUSTELL Nanscawen House
ST IVES Dean Court
ST MARY'S, IoS Brantwood
SALCOMBE Lyndhurst
SANDOWN, IoW Braemar
  St Catherine's
SCARBOROUGH Bay

  Premier
SEASCALE Cottage
SHANKLIN, IoW Apse Manor Country House
  Bay House
  Luccombe Chine
  Osborne House
SHERINGHAM Beacon
  Fairlawns
SHREWLEY Shrewley House
SHREWSBURY Abbots Mead
SOMERTON Lynch Country House
SOUTHEND-ON-SEA Ilfracombe House
SPALDING Stables
STARBOTTON Hilltop Country
STRATFORD-UPON-AVON Melita
  Twelfth Night
SWAFFHAM Horse & Groom
SYMONDS YAT EAST Saracens Head
TAUNTON Meryan House
THAME Essex House
THORALBY High Green House
THORNTON CLEVELYS Victorian House
TORQUAY Glenorleigh
  Haldon Priors
  Robin Hill
UCKFIELD Hooke Hall
UPPINGHAM Old Rectory
VOWCHURCH Croft Country
WARWICK North Leigh
  Park Cottage
WESTCLIFF-ON-SEA West Park
WESTON SUPER MARE Braeside
  Milton Lodge
  Wychwood
WHITBY Kimberley
  York House
WIMBORNE MINSTER Beech Leas
WINDERMERE Blenheim Lodge
  Cranleigh
  Fir Trees
  Glenburn
  Glencree
  Hawksmoor
  Holly Park
  St John's Lodge
  West Lake
  Woodlands
WINDSOR Dorset
WIVELISCOMBE Hurstone Farmhouse
WOOLACOMBE Sunnycliff
WORKINGTON Morven
YARMOUTH, GREAT Trotwood
YORK Arndale

Scotland
ABERFELDY Guinach House
AUCHTERARDER Cairn Lodge
AVIEMORE Balavoulin House

AYR Windsor
BLAIRGOWRIE Rosebank House
CARDROSS Kirkton House
CONTIN Coul House
CULLEN Bayview
CUPAR Redlands Country Lodge
DENNY Topps Farm
DERVAIG, MULL Druimard Country House
EDINBURGH Brunswick
  Cumberland
  Lodge
  Thrums
ELGIN Park House
FORTINGALL Rose Villa
GRANTOWN-ON-SPEY Ravenscourt House
GRETNA Surrone House
HADDINGTON Browns
KIRKBEAN Cavens House
MOFFAT Well View
PITLOCHRY Balrobin
  Knockendarroch
ROTHESAY Ardyne
  St Ebba

Wales
BONTDDU Borthwnog Hall
BRECON Coach
CARMARTHEN Ty Mawr
LLANDRINDOD WELLS Three Wells Farm
LLANWRTYD WELLS Lasswade House
NEW QUAY Park Hall
RHYL Harbour
SOLVA Lochmeyler Farm
SWANSEA Tredillion House
TENBY Harbour Heights
TINTERN Parva Farmhouse

Isle of Man
PORT ERIN Regent House

Channel Islands
Guernsey
L'ANCRESSE Lynton
ST PETER PORT Midhurst House
ST SAVIOUR'S La Girouette Country House

Jersey
ST HELIER Runnymede Court
ST OUEN Hotel des Pierres

Tankard Inns

England

ABBERLEY	Manor Arms	🍺🍺
ASTBURY	Egerton Arms	🍺
ATHERSTONE	Old Red Lion	🍺🍺🍺
BISHOPS CASTLE	Castle	🍺
BLACKBURN	Millstone	🍺🍺🍺
BOROUGHBRIDGE	Crown Inn	🍺🍺
BOURNE	Angel	🍺🍺🍺
BRIGHOUSE	Grove Inn	🍺🍺
BURFORD	Maytime Inn	🍺🍺
BURNT YATES	Bay Horse Inn	🍺🍺
CHARD	George	🍺
CHISELHAMPTON	Coach and Horses	🍺🍺
COALVILLE	Bardon Hall	🍺🍺
COLESBOURNE	Colesbourne	🍺🍺
CONISTON	Black Bull	🍺🍺
CRACKINGTON HAVEN	Combe Barton Inn	🍺🍺
CROYDON	Windsor Castle	🍺🍺
DELPH	Old Bell Inn	🍺🍺
EASTWOOD	Sun Inn	🍺🍺
EVERCREECH	Pecking Mill Inn	🍺🍺
EWEN	Wild Duck Inn	🍺🍺🍺
GLASTONBURY	Red Lion	🍺🍺
GRASSINGTON	Black Horse	🍺🍺
GUISBOROUGH	Fox & Hounds	🍺🍺
HAVERTHWAITE	Dicksons Arms	🍺🍺
HAWKSHEAD	Queens Head	🍺🍺
	Red Lion	🍺🍺
HOLNE	Church House Inn	🍺
KINGSWINFORD	Kingfisher	🍺🍺🍺
KNARESBOROUGH	Yorkshire Lass	🍺🍺🍺
LANCING	Sussex Pad	🍺🍺
LEICESTER	Red Cow	🍺🍺
LELANT	Badger Inn	🍺🍺
LOSTWITHIEL	Royal Oak Inn	🍺🍺
MADELEY	Wheatsheaf Inn	🍺🍺
MARTOCK	White Hart	🍺
MUNGRISDALE	Mill Inn	🍺🍺
SCARBOROUGH	Pickwick Inn	🍺🍺
STANNERSBURN	Pheasant Inn	🍺
TATTENHALL	Pheasant Inn	🍺🍺
TEDBURN ST MARY	Kings Arms Inn	🍺
TELFORD	Hundred House	🍺🍺🍺
TETFORD	White Hart Inn	🍺
THAXTED	Farmhouse Inn	🍺🍺
THELBRIDGE	Thelbridge Cross Inn	🍺🍺🍺
THIRSK	Old Red House	🍺🍺
UPPINGHAM	Crown	🍺🍺
WALKERINGHAM	Brickmakers Arms	🍺🍺
WARWICK-ON-EDEN	Queens Arms Inn	🍺🍺
WHITCHURCH	Crown	🍺
WIGGLESWORTH	Plough Inn	🍺🍺🍺
WINDERMERE	Albert	🍺🍺
WROXHAM	Kings Head	🍺🍺
YELVERTON	Burrator Inn	🍺

Scotland

DALRY	Dalry Inn	🍺🍺
SOUTH QUEENSFERRY	Hawes Inn	🍺

Wales

ABERCRAF	Abercrave Inn	🍺
LLANBEDR	Victoria Inn	🍺🍺

MAP OF GREAT BRITAIN

KEY TO MAP SECTIONS

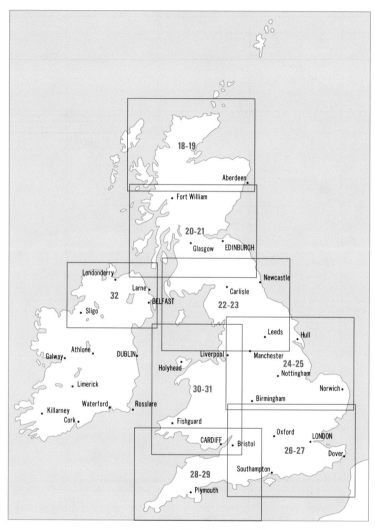

Map pages 18 - 32   Scale 1:1,050,000

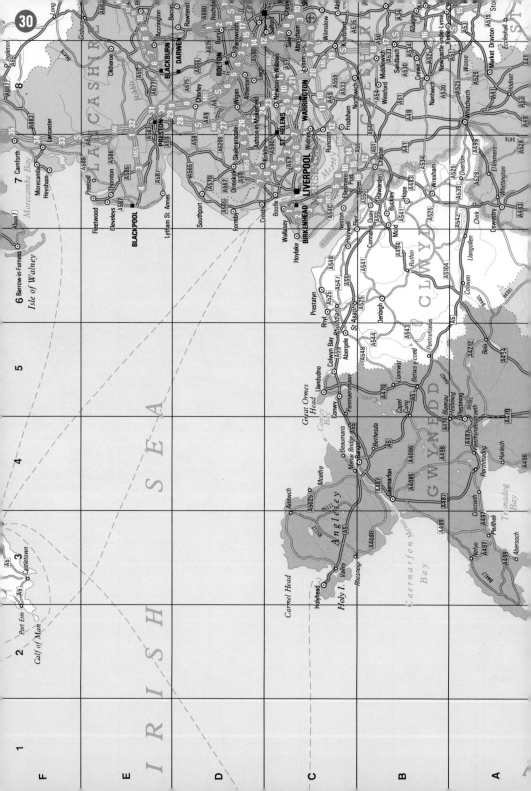

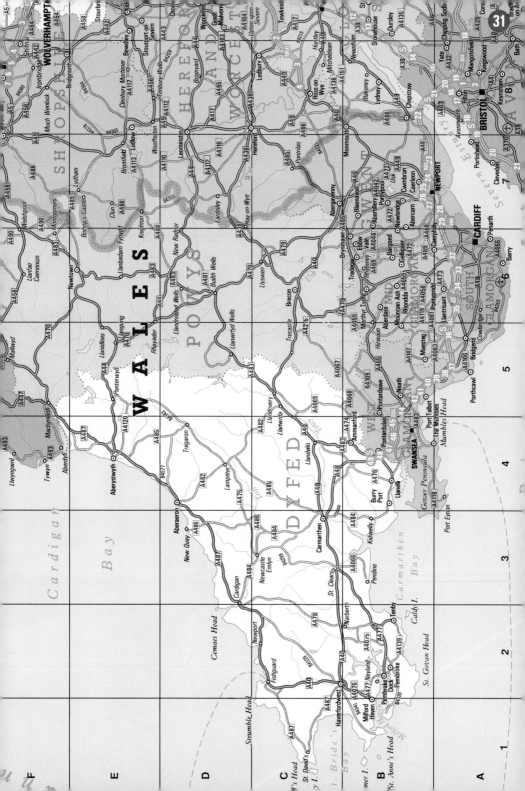

ENGLAND

ABBERLEY Worcestershire. Map 26B9

Manor Arms at Abberley Gt Witley, WR6 6BN (0299) 896507 Tx: 335672.
A 300 year-old inn with bedrooms in a modern extension. Situated in the village centre with rural views.

Church Farm Nr Worcester, WR6 6BP (0299) 896316. *Farm.* Sally and Roy Neath
Sleeps 5,
£ B&B from £14

ABINGER HAMMER Surrey. Map 27A4

Crossways Farm Raikes Lane, Nr Dorking, RH5 6PZ (0306) 730173. *Farm.* Sheila Hughes
Sleeps 6, ns
£ B&B from £14, D £8

ABNEY Map 24C5

Lane End Farm Hathersage, Sheffield, S30 1AA (0433) 50371. *Farm.* Mrs Jill Salisbury
Sleeps 6,
£ B&B from £13–£18

AISLABY North Yorkshire. Map 23E5

Cote Bank Farm Egton Road, Whitby, YO21 1UG (0947) 85314. *Farm.* Barbara Howard
Sleeps 6,
£ B&B from £12·50, D £7

ALDEBURGH Suffolk. Map 27F8

Cotmandene (Acclaimed) 6 Park La, IP15 5HL (0728) 453775. *Guest House.*

ALDWINCLE Northamptonshire. Map 26F1

Peartree Farm Nr Kettering, NN14 3EL (080 15) 614. *Farm.* Mavis Hankins
Sleeps 6,
£ B&B from £13, D from £6·50

ALFRISTON East Sussex. Map 27B2

Riverdale Seaford Rd, Polegate, BN26 5TR (0323) 870397.
5 bedrs, 3 en suite, 1 ba; TV; tcf P 8; no children LD 5, nr lunch. Rest lic

ALKMONTON Derbyshire. Map 24C3

Dairy House Farm (Acclaimed) nr Longford DE6 3DG (0335) 330359.

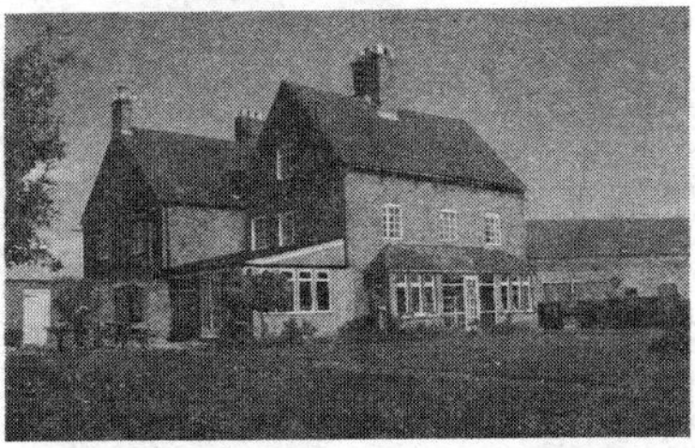

Redbrick farmhouse with oak beamed rooms and inglenook fireplace. Set on an 82 acre working dairy farm. Situated 3 miles north off A50 Derby/Uttoxeter Road from Foston village turnoff. Putting.
7 bedrs, 3 en suite, 1 ba; tcf TV, dogs; ns; P 8; no children under 5 LD 8. Resid lic
£ B&B £14–£17; HB weekly £148–£160; dep.

ALNMOUTH Northumberland. Map 23C9

Marine House (Acclaimed) 1 Marine Rd, NE66 2RW Alnwick (0665) 830349.
From Alnwick follow signs to Alnmouth, turn right at roundabout in the village and left signed 'beach and car park'. Follow road round to Marine House.
11 bedrs, 11 en suite; TV; tcf TV; dogs; ns; P 12; children over 3 LD 7, nr lunch. Resid lic
£ B&B & dinner £29–£33; HB weekly £200–£228; WB £57 (2 nts); [10% V]; dep.

Bilton Barns Alnwick, NE66 2TB (0665) 830427. *Farm.* Dorothy Jackson
Sleeps 6,
£ B&B from £13·50, D £8

ALNWICK Northumberland. Map 23C9

Aln House (Acclaimed) South Rd, NE66 2NZ (0665) 602265. *Guest house.*
8 bedrs, 3 en suite, 1 ba; tcf TV, dogs; P 8; no children Breakfast only. Resid lic

Bondgate House (Acclaimed) 20 Bondgate Without, NE66 1PN (0665) 602025. Fax: (0665) 602554.
A 250-year-old house of character and charm in the bustling market town of Alnwick. Just off the A1, close to the town's entrance gates.
8 bedrs, 3 en suite, 2 ba; TV; tcf TV, ns; P 8,

coach; child facs ✕ LD 4.30, nr Sun. Resid & Rest lic
£ B&B (double) £26–£30; HB weekly £130–£140; D £7; dep.

Aydon House   South Rd, NE66 2NT
☎ (0665) 602218. *Hotel.*

Aindyke Farmhouse   NE66 3PB ☎ (0665) 602193. *Farm.* Mrs Anne Davison
Sleeps 8, ns ☎ (10)
£ B&B from £15, D £9

ALSTON   Cumbria.   Map 23A6

Loatburn Farm   CA9 3LQ ☎ (0434) 381544. *Farm.* Edith Jopling
Sleeps 6, ns ☎
£ B&B from £9, D £5

Middle Bayles Farm   CA9 3BS ☎ (0434) 381383. *Farm.* Mrs Pat Dent
Sleeps 6, 🐾 ns ☎
£ B&B from £11, D £6

ALTRINCHAM   Cheshire.   Map 24B5

Beechmount   Barrington Rd, WA14 1HN
☎ 051-928 4523. Closed 24 Dec–2 Jan.
£ B&B fr £27·60

ALVELEY   Shropshire.   Map 24B1

The Low Farm   Nr Bridgnorth, WV15 6HX
☎ (029 97) 206. *Farm.* Patricia Lawley
Sleeps 6, 🐾 ☎
£ B&B from £10, D £6·50

AMBLESIDE   Cumbria.   Map 22F4

Gables (Highly Acclaimed)   Church Walk, LA22 9DJ ☎ (053 94) 33272.

A Victorian, part-timbered hotel with views over Loughrigg Fell. Family owned and run, and offering a warm welcome. Follow the one way system from the A591 into Ambleside, hotel is set in cul-de-sac leading to parish church. Open Jan–Nov.
🛏13 bedrs, 13 en suite; TV; tcf 📺TV, dogs; P 8; child facs ✕ LD 5, nr lunch. Resid lic
£ B&B £17–£20; HB weekly £189; dep.

Grey Friar Lodge Country House (Highly Acclaimed)   Brathay, LA22 9NE ☎ (053 94) 33158.

Once a vicarage and later a bishop's house, Grey Friar Lodge is a traditional lakeland stone country house set in its own grounds with magnificent views. This family owned and run hotel offers personal service with warm hospitality. Situated 1½ miles west of Ambleside on A593. Open mid Mar–Oct.
🛏8 bedrs, 8 en suite; TV; tcf 📺ns; P 12; children over 12 ✕ LD 7.30, nr lunch. Resid & Rest lic
£ B&B & dinner £29–£37; HB weekly £195–£238; dep.

Lyndhurst (Acclaimed)   Wansfell Rd, LA22 0EG
✆(053 94) 32421.
Victorian lakeland stone hotel in a quiet position with its own garden. Family run with homely atmosphere.
⌂8 bedrs, 8 en suite; TV; tcf �📺P 8; child facs ✕LD 8, nr lunch. Resid lic
£B&B £17·50–£22; HB weekly £175–£205; dep. [10% V Nov–May]

Rysdale Hotel (Acclaimed)   Rothay Rd, LA22 0EE
✆(053 94) 32140.
Family run hotel with magnificent views. On Rothay Road opposite recreation area near St Mary's Church. Open Feb–Nov.
⌂9 bedrs, 4 en suite, (1 sh), 2 ba; TV; tcf �📺ns; P 2; child facs ✕LD 5, nr lunch, Sun dinner; Resid & Rest lic
£ B&B £14–£20; HB weekly £160–£195; [10% V w/d] **cc** Access, B'card/Visa; dep.

Smallwood House (Acclaimed)   Compston Rd, LA22 9DJ ✆(053 94) 32330.
⌂14 bedrs, 3 en suite, 2 ba; TV; tcf �📺TV, dogs; P 13; coach; child facs ✕LD 6; nr lunch & Tue dinner. Resid & Rest lic
£ B&B £14–£17·50; HB weekly £142–£165; D £8; [10% V Oct–Jun]; dep.

Anchorage   Rydal Rd, LA22 9AY ✆(053 94) 32046.
Modern accommodation with beautiful views of surrounding fells. 300 metres from town centre on left side opposite health centre. Open Mar–Oct.
⌂5 bedrs, 2 en suite, 1 ba; TV, tcf �📺TV, ns; P 7; no children under 10 ✕Breakfast only. Unlic
£B&B (double) £30–£40; HB weekly £98–£133; dep.

Hillsdale   Church St, LA22 0BT ✆(053 94) 33174.
⌂8 bedrs, 1 en suite, (4 sh), 1 ba; TV; tcf �📺coach ✕Breakfast only. Unlic

AMESBURY   Wiltshire.   Map 26C4

Druids Motel   2 Countess Rd, SP4 7DW
✆(0980) 22800.

AMPLEFORTH   North Yorkshire.   Map 23E4

Carr House   Shallowdale, York, YO6 4ED
✆(034 76) 526. *Farm*. Mrs Anna Taylor

Sleeps 4, ns ⛟ (7)
£ B&B from £10–£15, D £7·50

ANDOVERSFORD   Gloucestershire.
Map 26C7

Old Comfort (Highly Acclaimed)   Dowdeswell, GL54 4LR ✆(0242) 820349.
Recently refurbished 17th century hotel standing high on the Cotswold Hills with stunning views over the Gloucestershire countryside. On the A436 between Andoversford and Seven Springs.
⌂6 bedrs, 6 en suite; TV; tcf �📺P 10 ✕LD 10, Rest lic
£ B&B £35, B&B (double) £50; L £25, D £41
cc Diners; dep.

ANGMERING-ON-SEA   West Sussex.
Map 27A2

Three Crowns   Sea Rd, BN16 1LS ✆Rustington (0903) 784074.
Close to the sea off the A259.
⌂10 bedrs, 3 ba; TV; tcf �📺TV, dogs, ns; P 60, G 4 ✕LD 7.30
£ B&B £27·50, B&B (double) £50; HB weekly £250; L £7·25, D £13·50; [10% V] **cc** Access, B'card/Visa; dep.

ARNSIDE   Cumbria.   Map 22F3

Willowfield   The Promenade, LA5 0AD
✆(0524) 761354.
⌂9 bedrs, 2 en suite, 2 ba; TV; tcf �📺TV; P 10 ✕nr lunch. Rest lic

ARRATHORNE   North Yorkshire.   Map 23C4

Elmfield House   Bedale, DL8 1NE ✆(0677) 50558. *Farm*. Edith and Jim Lillie   ♿
Sleeps 21, ⛟
£ B&B from £16, D £8·50

ASCOT   Berkshire.   Map 26F5

Highclere (Acclaimed)   Kings Rd, SL5 9AD
✆(0990) 25220 Fax: (0990) 872528.
On A30 from Staines turn left at Sunningdale shops before railway crossing. 2 miles further opposite Ascot post office. Putting.

12 bedrs, 12 en suite; TV; tcf ♠TV, dogs; P 12; child facs ✗LD 9, nr lunch
£B&B £71·50, B&B (double) £79·50; D £15; WB £46; [5% V w/e] cc Access, B'card/Visa.

ASCOTT Warwickshire. Map 26D8

Ascott House Farm   Whichford, nr Long Compton, Shipston-on-Stour, CV36 5PP ☎(0608) 84655. *Farm.* Mrs Janet Haines
Sleeps 6, ♠ ☎
£ B&B from £12–£16

ASHBOURNE Derbyshire. Map 24C4

Home Farm   Norbury, DE6 2ED ☎(033 524) 284/286. *Farm.* Gillyan Prince
Sleeps 6, ns ☎
£ B&B from £10–£12

Sidesmill Farm   Snelston, DE6 2GQ
☎(0335) 42710. *Farm.* Mrs Catherine Brandrick
Sleeps 5, ns ☎ (3)
£ B&B from £10·50–£12·50

ASHBURTON Devon. Map 28G3

Gages Mill (Acclaimed)   Buckfastleigh Rd, TQ13 7JW ☎(0364) 52391.
A small country hotel, formerly a wool mill, set on the edge of Dartmoor National Park. Carefully converted 14th century building. Take A38 from Exeter, turning off at the second exit for Ashburton. Cross the A38 towards Two Bridges, take first left towards Buckfastleigh, and Gages Mill is ¼ mile on the left. Open Mar–Oct.
8 bedrs, 8 en suite; tcf ♠TV; P 10; no children under 5 ✗LD4, nr lunch. Resid & Rest lic
£B&B (double) £31–£37; HB weekly £157·50–£175; dep.

Adams Hele Farm   TQ13 7NW ☎(0364) 52525.
Farm. Dorothy Dent
Sleeps 6, ♠ ☎
£ B&B from £11·50, D £6·50

ASHFORD Kent. Map 27D4

Croft (Acclaimed)   Canterbury Rd, Kennington, TN25 4DU ☎(0233) 622140.
A country style house set in two acres of mature gardens. Take A28 from Ashford towards Canterbury for 1¼ miles—Croft Hotel is on right hand side.
28 bedrs, 28 en suite; TV; tcf ♠TV; dogs; P 30, U 2, coach; child facs ✗LD8, nr lunch; Resid lic
£B&B £34–£44, B&B (double) £45–£55; WB £17·50 cc Access, B'card/Visa.

Downsview   Willesborough Rd, Kennington TN24 9QP. ☎(0233) 621953. *Putting.* (QMH)
21 bedrs, 17 en suite, 4 ba; TV; tcf ♠TV, dogs;

P 20, coach; child facs; con 15 ✗LD8.30, bar meals only lunch. Resid & Rest lic
cc Access, Amex, B'card/Visa, Diners.

ASHFORD-IN-THE-WATER Derbyshire. Map 24C4

Highfield Farm   Bakewell, DE4 1QN
☎(0629) 812482. *Farm.* Jean Brocklehurst
Sleeps 4, ns ☎ (10)
£ B&B from £12

ASHOVER Derbyshire. Map 24D4

Old School Farm   Uppertown S45 0JF ☎(0246) 590813.
Take A632 from Chesterfield towards Matlock, turn onto B5057 Darley Dale road, and take second left to a set of crossroads. Go straight over and continue until reach farm on left. Open Mar–Oct.
4 bedrs, 1 ba ♠TV; P 10; child facs ✗LD 9.30 am, nr lunch. Unlic
£ B&B £9–£12; HB weekly £98–£126; WB £28–£36 (2 nts HB); dep.

ASHPRINGTON Devon. Map 29A3

Sharpham Barton   Totnes, TQ9 7DX ☎(080423) 278. *Farm.* Claire Grimshaw
Sleeps 6, ♠ ns ☎
£ B&B from £15–£18, D £8

ASHTON-UNDER-LYNE Gtr Manchester Map 24B6

Welbeck House   324 Katharine St, OL6 7BD
☎061-344 0751
8 bedrs, 8 en suite; TV; tcf ♠TV, dogs; P 20 ✗LD 9, nr lunch, dinner Fri, Sat or Sun.
£ B&B £40, B&B (double) £50; [5% V] cc Access, Amex, B'card/Visa, Diners; dep.

ASHWORTH VALLEY Lancashire. Map 24B6

Leaches Farm   Rochdale, OL11 5UN ☎(0706) 41116/7 or 228520. *Farm.* Mrs Jane Neave
Sleeps 6, ♠ ☎
£ B&B from £12–£15

ASTBURY Cheshire. Map 24B4

♣ **Egerton Arms**   CW12 4RQ ☎Congleton (026 02) 73946
Period black and white inn opposite Norman church. Large gardens.
7 bedrs, (1 sh), 3 ba; TV; tcf ♠TV, dogs, ns; P 100, coach; child facs ✗LD 9.30
£ B&B £22, B&B (double) £38 cc B'card/Visa, Diners.

ATHERSTONE   Warwickshire.   Map 24D2

🏆 🏆 🏆 **Old Red Lion**   Long St, CV9 1BB
☎ (0827) 713156 Fax: (0827) 711404
Historic inn conveniently situated in main street of town.
🛏 22 bedrs, 22 en suite; TV; tcf 🏠 P 22, coach; child facs ✕ LD 9.45; bar meals only Sun dinner
£ B&B £45, B&B (double) £55–£65; L £8, D £10; [5% V w/e] **cc** Access, Amex, B'card/Visa, Diners.

ATTLEBOROUGH   Norfolk.   Map 25D2

Scales Farm   Old Buckenham, NR17 1PE
☎ (0953) 860324. *Farm*. Mary P Askew
Sleeps 3, 🐾 ns
£ B&B from £12

AUDLEM   Cheshire.   Map 24A4

Little Heath Farm   Crewe, CW3 0HE
☎ (0270) 811324. *Farm*. Hiliary Bennion
Sleeps 6, 🐾
£ B&B from £10, D from £6·50

AUDLEY   Staffordshire.   Map 24B4

The Domvilles Farm   Barthomley Road, Stoke-on-Trent, ST7 8HT ☎ (0782) 720378.
Farm. Mrs Eileen Oulton
Sleeps 10, 🐕 🐾
£ B&B from £12–£14, D £7

AVETON GIFFORD   Devon.   Map 29A2

Court Barton Farmhouse   Kingsbridge, TQ7 4LE
☎ (0548) 550312. *Farm*. John and Jill Balkwill
Sleeps 16, 🐾
£ B&B from £14

Helliers Farm   Ashford, Kingsbridge, TQ7 4ND
☎ (0548) 550689. *Farm*. Christine Lancaster
Sleeps 9, ns 🐾
£ B&B from £12·50

AVON DASSETT   Warwickshire.   Map 26D9

Crandon House   Leamington Spa, CV33 0AA
☎ (029 577) 652. *Farm*. Deborah Lea
Sleeps 6, 🐕 🐾 (8)
£ B&B from £15–£20, D from £9

AWLISCOMBE   Devon.   Map 29B4

Godford Farm   Honiton, EX14 0PW ☎ (0404) 42825. *Farm*. Sally Lawrence
Sleeps 6 + cot, 🐾
£ B&B from £11·50, D £7

BACUP   Lancashire.   Map 24B6

Pasture Bottom Farm   OL13 9UZ
☎ (0706) 873790. *Farm*. Ann Isherwood
Sleeps 4, 🐾 🐕
£ B&B from £12, D £5

BADMINTON, GREAT   Avon.   Map 26B5

Bodkin House (Highly Acclaimed)   A46, GL9 1AF
☎ (045 423) 310 Fax: (0453) 843572.

A delightful old coaching inn situated next to the Badminton estate on the A46 Bath to Stroud road. From junction 18 on M4 hotel is on right hand side at Petty France. Closed Xmas.
🛏 8 bedrs, 8 en suite; TV; tcf 🏠 dogs; P 30, coach ✕ LD 10
£ B&B £40–£45, B&B (double) £60–£70; L £9, D £15; WB £90 (HB 2 nts); [10% V] **cc** Access, Amex, B'card/Visa, Diners; dep.

BAINBRIDGE   North Yorkshire.   Map 23C4

Riverdale House (Highly Acclaimed)   DL8 3EW
☎ Wensleydale (0969) 50311.
Several Dales cottages have been carefully and sympathetically restored and converted into this country hotel in the quiet village of Bainbridge. On the A684 Wensleydale road. Open Mar–Nov.
🛏 15 bedrs, 11 en suite, 4 ba; TV; tcf 🏠 TV, ns; P 4, coach; child facs ✕ LD 8, nr lunch. Resid & Rest lic
£ B&B £24·50, B&B (double) £46; D £13; [10% V]; dep.

BAKEWELL   Derbyshire.   Map 24C4

Lathkil (Acclaimed)   Over Haddon, DE4 1JE
☎ (0629) 812501.
🛏 4 bedrs, 4 en suite; TV; tcf 🏠 dogs, ns; P 24, coach ✕ LD 8.45
cc Access, B'card/Visa, Diners; dep.

Castle Cliff   Monsal Head, DE4 1NL ☎ Gt Longstone (062 987) 258.

BAMPTON   Devon.   Map 29B5

Bridge House (Acclaimed)   24 Luke St, EX16 9NF
☎ (0398) 31298.

Courtyard   19 Fore St, EX16 9NO ☎ (0398) 31536.
🛏 6 bedrs, 3 en suite, 1 ba; TV; tcf 🏠 P 40; child facs ✕ LD 9.30, nr Sun dinner. Resid & Rest lic

BAMPTON   Oxfordshire.   Map 26D6

'Morar', Weald Street, OX8 2HL
☎(0993) 850162 Telex: 83343 ABTELX ref 'Morar'.
Farm. Janet Rouse
Sleeps 6, ns ⌛ (6)
£ B&B from £14·30–£20, D £11·50

BANBURY   Oxfordshire.   Map 26D8

Easington House (Highly Acclaimed)   50 Oxford
Rd, OX16 9AN ☎(0295) 270181.

*A 16th century Grade II listed building, formerly a
royal manor farm house. Recently refurbished, and
only 300 yards from Banbury Cross. Prize winning
gardens. On the A41 in the centre of Banbury, south
of the cross.* Closed Xmas & New Year.
⇔12 bedrs, 10 en suite, 1 ba; TV; tcf
🏠dogs; P 20, G 1; child facs ✕ Dinner by arrang.
Resid lic
£ B&B fr £28–£55, B&B (double) fr £35–£65;
D £8·50; [5% V Sept–Mar] **cc** Access, B'card/Visa;
dep.

La Madonette (Highly Acclaimed)   North
Newington, OX15 6AA ☎(0295) 730212.
*A 17th century mill house peacefully situated in rural
surroundings close to the Cotswolds. From Banbury
Cross take B4035 for 2½ miles, turn right signed
Shutford Newington, and follow for ¼ mile to hotel
entrance on right.* Swimming pool. Closed Xmas &
New Year.
⇔6 bedrs, 6 en suite; TV; tcf 🏠P 20; child facs
✕ Breakfast only. Resid lic
£ B&B £35–£37·50, B&B (double) £45–£55
cc Access, B/card/Visa.

Kelvedon   11 Broughton Rd, OX16 9QB ☎(0295)
263028.
*From Banbury Cross take West Bar Street into
Broughton Road. Hotel 50 yards on left.*
⇔4 bedrs, 1 en suite, 2 ba; TV; tcf 🏠TV, dogs, ns;
P 4; child facs ✕ Breakfast only. Unlic
£ B&B £16–£20, B&B (double) £25–£30; dep.

Tredis   15 Broughton Rd, OX16 9QB
☎(0295) 4632.
⇔11 bedrs, 2 en suite, 3 ba; TV; tcf 🏠ns; P 5,

coach; child facs ✕LD 12 noon, nr lunch & Sat–
Sun dinner. Unlic

BARCOMBE   East Sussex.   Map 27B3

Camoys Farm House   Mill Road, Lewes, BN8
5BH ☎(0273) 400662. *Farm.* Mrs Hedley Cornwell
Sleeps 6
£ B&B from £15, D from £8

BARNARD CASTLE   Durham.   Map 23B5

West Roods Farm   Boldron, DL12 9SW
☎Teesdale (0833) 690116.
*From A66, 2¼ mile W of road to Beldron village. DO
NOT ENTER VILLAGE. 2 miles S Barnard Castle,
signed Lamb Hill, West Roods, Roods House.* Open
Easter–Oct.
⇔3 bedrs, 2 en suite, 1 ba; TV; tcf 🏠dogs, ns;
P 6 ✕LD 6, nr lunch, Mon, Wed & Sun dinner. Unlic
£ B&B £13–£15, B&B (double) £26–£30; HB
weekly £122–£149; [5% V June, Tues–Wed]; dep.

BARNHAM   Norfolk.   Map 25D1

East Farm   Thetford, IP24 2PB
☎(0842) 890231. *Farm.* Margaret Heading
Sleeps 6, �);⌛ (3) ns
£ B&B from £18, D £10

BARNSDALE BAR   North Yorkshire.
     Map 23D1

TraveLodge   Gt North Rd, WF8 3JB ☎Pontefract
(0977) 620711 Tx: 557457
*Main road motel with petrol, restaurant and shops
complex.* (THF) Motor Lodge.

BARNSTAPLE   Devon.   Map 28F5

Muddlebridge House (Acclaimed)   Freminton
EX31 2NQ ☎(0271) 76073.
⇔3 bedrs, 3 en suite, 1 ba; TV; tcf 🏠dogs, ns; P 4;
child facs ✕ Breakfast only. Unlic

Yeodale   Pilton Bridge, EX31 1PG
☎(0271) 42954.
⇔10 bedrs, 2 ba; TV; tcf 🏠TV, dogs; child facs
✕LD 7, nr lunch. Resid lic
£ B&B £15–£18; HB weekly £150·50–£171·50;
D £6·50; [10% V] **cc** Access, B'card/Visa.

Castle Hill Barton   Filleigh, EX32 0RX
☎(05986) 242. *Farm.* Angela Sexon
Sleeps 6, 🐦⌛
£ B&B from £10, D from £5

Higher Churchill Farm   East Down, EX31 4LT
☎(0271) 850543. *Farm.* Mrs Andrea Cook
Sleeps 6, ns ⌛
£ B&B from £12, D £6

Higher Clifton Farm, East Down, EX31 4LX
☎(0271) 850372. *Farm*. Mrs Elizabeth Smyth
Sleeps 6, ☺
£ B&B from £12, D £6

Huxtable Farm West Buckland, EX32 0SR
☎(05986) 254. *Farm*. Barbara and Jackie Payne ♿
Sleeps 12, ns ☺
£ B&B from £15–£17, D £9

Norwood Farm Hiscott, EX31 3JS ☎(0271) 85260
Farm. Belinda Richards
Sleeps 6, 🐕 ns ☺ (12)
£ B&B from £17, D £10

Norwood Farm Hiscott, EX31 3JS ☎(0271) 85260
Farm. Belinda Richards
Sleeps 6, 🐕 ns ☺ (12)
£ B&B from £17, D £10

Waytown Farm Shirwell, EX31 4JN ☎(0271)
850396. *Farm*. Hazel Kingdon
Sleeps 6, ☺
£ B&B from £12–£13, D £5·50

BARTON ON SEA Hampshire. Map 26C2

Old Coastguard (Acclaimed) 53 Marine Dr East,
BH25 7DX ☎New Milton (0425) 612987.

BASSENTHWAITE Cumbria. Map 22E5

Ravenstone CA12 4QG ☎(059681) 240.
Charming dower house built by Earl of Carlisle for Lady Charlotte Howard. Hotel offers panoramic views. From Keswick take A591 Carlisle road for 4½ miles. Snooker. Open Mar–Oct.
🛏14 bedrs, 14 en suite; TV; tcf 🏧dogs; P 25; child facs ✗LD 7.30, nr lunch
£ B&B £22–£25; HB weekly £189–210

BATH Avon. Map 26B5

Bath Lodge (Highly Acclaimed) Norton St Philip,
BA3 6NH ☎(022572) 3737. Fax: (022572) 3193.

A superbly converted former gatehouse, built in the early 19th century complete with towers, battlements and portcullis. Rooms overlook the magnificent natural gardens. Situated 7 miles south of Bath on the A36 near Limpley Stoke.
🛏4 bedrs, 4 en suite; TV; tcf 🏧ns; P 25, G 3; coach; child facs ✗LD 10
£B&B £65, B&B (double) £85–£95 cc Access, Amex, B'card/Visa; dep.

Brompton House (Highly Acclaimed) St Johns
Rd, BA2 6PT ☎(0225) 448423/420972.

Elegant Georgian rectory set in lovely gardens. 5 mins level walk to city. Take A46 to Bath, turn left at traffic lights signed city centre, take immediate right over the Cleveland Bridge. Closed Xmas & New Year.
🛏12 bedrs, 12 en suite, TV; tcf 🏧ns; P12; child facs ✗Breakfast only. Resid lic
£B&B £30–£35, B&B (double) £50–£55
cc Access; dep.

Cheriton House (Highly Acclaimed) 9 Upper
Oldfield Park, BA2 3JX ☎(0225) 429862.
Victorian house with mature gardens in quiet location.
🛏9 bedrs, 9 en suite; TV; tcf 🏧 P9 ✗Breakfast only. Unlic
£ B&B £32–£35, B&B (double) £40–£50; [10% V]
cc Access, B'card/Visa.

Dorian House (Highly Acclaimed) 1 Upper
Oldfield Park, BA2 3JX ☎(0225) 426336.
An elegant and substantial Victorian house with magnificent views of the city and surrounding hills. A family run hotel within easy walking distance of the city. Take A4 to Bath, filter left to ring route following signs to Exeter A367. Leave ring road south of city under rail viaduct. Take A367 Wells Rd for 300 metres to left hand bend. Upper Oldfield Park is immediately after bend on right.
🛏7 bedrs, 7 en suite; TV; tcf 🏧ns; P9, G2, coach; child facs ✗Breakfast only. Resid lic
£B&B £29–£35, B&B (double) £44–£52; [5% V Jan–Mar] cc Access, Amex, B'card/Visa, Diners; dep.

Eagle House (Highly Acclaimed)   Church St, Bathford BA1 7RS ✆(0225) 859946.

A small Georgian mansion with fine, elegant reception rooms and many period features. Set in 1½ acres of garden on the edge of an area of outstanding natural beauty. Take A363 towards Bradford on Avon for 150 yards from A4, then fork left up Bathford Hill for 300 yards. Turn first right into Church St and hotel is 200 yards on the right. Closed Xmas & New Year.
⇄8 bedrs, 8 en suite; TV; tcf 👁dogs; P 10; child facs ✗Breakfast only. Resid lic
£ B&B £26·50–£34·50, B&B (double) £39–£53; [5% V except Sat]

Highways House (Highly Acclaimed)   143 Wells Rd, BA2 3AL ✆(0225) 421238.
A delightful and well-appointed Victorian house with a relaxed and homely atmosphere. Only 10 mins walk to city centre. Situated on A367 Exeter Rd (Wells Rd) on the left about ¼ mile from railway viaduct. Closed Xmas.
⇄7 bedrs, 7 en suite; TV; tcf 👁P8; no children under 5 ✗Breakfast only. Unlic
£B&B £28–£36, B&B (double) £42–£52; dep.

Leighton House (Highly Acclaimed)   139 Wells Rd, BA2 3AL ✆(0225) 314769.
Spacious Victorian house in own grounds on south side of Bath with fine views over the city.
⇄7 bedrs, 5 en suite, (2 sh); TV; tcf 👁P 7; child facs ✗Breakfast only. Unlic
cc Access, B'card/Visa; dep.

Lord Nelson Inn (Highly Acclaimed)   Marshfield, SN14 8LP✆ (0225) 981820.
250 year-old coaching inn in village near Bath.
⇄ 3 bedrs, 3 en suite; TV; tcf; 👁 dogs, ns; P 2; child facs ✗LD 9.30
£ B&B £42, B&B (double) £55–£60; £7, D £10; [5% V w/d] cc Access, Visa.

Oakleigh (Highly Acclaimed)   19 Upper Oldfield Park, BA2 3JX ✆(0225) 315698.
A combination of Victorian elegance and 20th century comfort. From city centre take A367 to Exeter. First turning on right is Oldfield Park.
⇄4 bedrs, 4 en suite; TV; tcf 👁ns; P 4; no children under 18 ✗Breakfast only. Unlic
£B&B £30–£45, B&B (double) £40–£50; WB cc Access, B'card/Visa, dep.

Bath (Avon)

Bath (Avon)

Orchard House (Highly Acclaimed)   Warminster Rd, Bathampton, BA2 6XG ☎(0225) 466115.

A modern hotel built in 1984 to high standards. Situated 1¼ miles from Bath on A36 at Bathampton.
⇥14 bedrs, 14 en suite, 2 ba; TV; tcf 🏠dogs, ns; P16; child facs ✕LD8 nr lunch, Sun dinner. Resid lic
£B&B £41–£45, B&B (double) £53–£60; WB £71; [10% V] **cc** Access, Amex, B'card/Visa, Diners; dep.

Tasburgh (Highly Acclaimed)   Warminster Rd, Bathampton, BA2 6SH ☎(0225) 425096.

Gracious Victorian building set in 7 acres with canal frontage and views of city.
⇥13 bedrs, 8 en suite, 2 ba; TV; tcf 🏠ns; P15; coach; child facs ✕Breakfast only. Resid lic
cc Access, Amex, B'card/Visa, Diners; dep.

Dorset Villa (Acclaimed)   14 Newbridge Rd, BA1 3JZ ☎(0225) 425975.

⇥7 bedrs, 5 en suite, 1 ba; TV 🏠TV, dogs, ns; P6, coach; child facs ✕LD 9, nr lunch. Resid lic
£B&B £26–£31, B&B (double) £36–£41; HB weekly £150–£228; [10% V] **cc** Access, B'card/Visa

Oldfields (Acclaimed)   102 Wells Rd, BA2 3AL ☎(0225) 317984.
Restored, family run Victorian guest house with views and garden.
⇥14 bedrs, 8 en suite, 2 ba; TV; tcf 🏠dogs, P10; child facs ✕Breakfast only. Unlic
£ B&B £25–£40, B&B (double) £35–£52
cc Access, B'card/Visa; dep.

Villa Magdala (Acclaimed)   Henrietta Rd, BA2 6LX ☎(0225) 466329.
Built in 1868, a mixture of French and Italian architecture with fine cast iron, stair balustrades. Set in its own attractive grounds, opposite Henrietta Park just outside the city centre.
⇥17 bedrs, 17 en suite; TV; tcf 🏠ns; P13, U2, coach; no children under 4 ✕Breakfast only. Unlic
£B&B £40, B&B (double) £50–£65; WB £45 (Nov–Mar double) **cc** B'card/Visa; dep.

Wentworth House (Acclaimed)   106 Bloomfield Rd, BA2 2AP ☎(0225) 339193.

Imposing Victorian building surrounded by delightful garden of ¾ acre. Follow A367 and Bloomfield Rd is a right-hand fork ¾ mile from city centre. Swimming pool. Closed Xmas.
⋈20 bedrs, 20 en suite, TV; tcf �📺 TV, dogs; P 20, coach; child facs ✗nr lunch, Sun dinner. Resid lic
£ BB £21–£30, B&B (double) £42–£47; D £10·50
cc Access, B'card/Visa; dep.

Arden 73 Gt Pulteney St, BA2 4DL
✆(0225) 466601 Fax: (0225) 465548.
⋈10 bedrs, 10 en suite; TV; tcf �📺 P 2, coach; child facs ✗nr lunch. Resid & Rest lic
£ B&B £45–£60, B&B (double) £55–£57
cc Access, B'card/Visa; dep.

Arney 99 Wells Rd, BA 2 3AN ✆(0225) 310020.

Avon Bathwick St, BA2 6NX ✆(0225) 446176
Fax: (0225) 447452
Georgian hotel situated on the ring road close to the Roman Baths. Situated 200 yards from fire station on section between A4 and A36.
⋈12 bedrs, 12 en suite; TV; tcf �📺dogs, ns; P 20; child facs ✗Breakfast only. Resid lic
£ B&B £35–£45, B&B (double) £49·50–£65; WB (10% discount); [5% V] cc Access, B'card/Visa.

Cedar Lodge 13 Lambridge, London Rd, BA1 6BJ
✆(0225) 423468.
Detached grade II listed Georgian house.
⋈3 bedrs, 1 en suite, 1 ba; TV �📺 TV, NS; P 6; child

facs ✗ nr lunch. Unlic
£ B&B £25, B&B (double) £33–£45.

Chequers 50 Rivers St, BA1 2QA ✆(0225) 424246
Listed Georgian inn offering comfortable, quiet accommodation. Completely refurbished. Rivers St runs parallel to road running between Circle and Royal Crescent going out of town centre.
⋈4 bedrs, (1 sh), 2 ba; TV; tcf �📺coach; child facs ✗LD 9.45
£ B&B £20–£22·50; [10% V] cc Access, Amex; dep.

County 18 Pulteney Rd, BA2 4DN
✆(0225) 466493.
Situated on the main A36 Pulteney Rd within walking distance of the city.
⋈23 bedrs, 12 en suite, 3 ba; TV; tcf �📺 TV, dogs; P 60, coach; child facs ✗LD 9.30, nr lunch & Sun dinner
£ B&B £42·50–£47·50, B&B (double) £60–£70
cc Access, B'card/Visa; dep.

Edgar 64 Gt Pulteney St, BA2 4DN
✆(0225) 420619.
Situated on the A4 (London Rd) 200 yards towards the city from the A46 junction.

Grove Lodge 11 Lambridge, London Rd, BA1 6BJ ✆(0225) 310860.
⋈8 bedrs, 2 ba; TV �📺NS; child facs ✗Breakfast only. Resid lic
£ B&B £22–£25, B&B (double) £36–£40; [10% V]; dep.

Hotel St Clair 1 Crescent Gardens, Upper Bristol Rd, BA1 2NA ✆(0225) 425543.
Travel south from Royal Crescent on A4; hotel at bottom of Marlborough Lane.
⋈10 bedrs, 3 en suite, 2 ba; TV; tcf �📺ns; coach; children over 3 ✗Breakfast only. Resid lic
£ B&B £18–£24, B&B (double) £28–£40
cc Access, B'card/Visa; dep.

Kennard 11, Henrietta St, BA2 6LL
☎ (0225) 310472 Fax: (0225) 442456.
A building of historical importance set in a quiet Georgian street just off Great Pulteney Street. Close to Henrietta Park.
🛏 12 bedrs, 9 en suite, 2 ba; TV; tcf 🐾 dogs; coach ✕ Breakfast only. Unlic
£ B&B £25–£30, B&B (double) £45–£55; [10% V]
cc Access, B'card/Visa; dep.

Lynwood 6 Pulteney Gdns, BA2 4HG
☎ (0225) 426410.
Situated on A46 on outskirts of city centre.
🛏 12 bedrs, (12 sh), 1 ba; TV; tcf 🐾 P 2 (£1·50); no children under 3 ✕ Breakfast only. Unlic
£ B&B £19·50, B&B (double) £34 **cc** Access, Amex, B'card/Visa, Diners; dep.

Millers 69 Gt Pulteney St, BA2 4DL ☎ (0225) 465798.

Bath (Avon)

Avon Hotel

Bathwick Street, Bath, Avon BA2 6NX
Tel Reservations (0225) 446176 & 422226
Fax: (0225) 447452

The **Avon Hotel** is 830 metres **level** walk★ to the Roman Baths, main tourist areas and shopping centre with easy access to the Ring road and M4 Motorway.

Our **large floodlit car park** is freely available to our guests even after checkout time.

All rooms have en-suite facilities, are centrally heated and equipped with colour TV, alarm radio and welcome tray.

There are several large **ground floor** bedrooms some with **four poster beds** and **family suites** sleeping up to six. Cots and High Chairs are available.

Our "Honeymoon Special", includes four poster ground floor room with fresh flowers and iced Champagne.

We have several rooms specially reserved for *non-smokers*.

Write or phone for brochure and room rates.

★ *We stress LEVEL because the steep hills of Bath are not for the faint hearted!!!!!*

Bath (Avon)

WELCOME TO BATH

Situated on the main Pulteney Road, and walking distance to the city centre, Abbey, Pump Room, Roman Baths, Railway & Coach Stations
COUNTY HOTEL
18/19 Pulteney Road, Bath, BA2 4EZ, Avon. Tel: 466493 & 425003

Built in 1786 and close to city centre. From A4 city ring road, Great Pulteney Street is opposite the Holburne Museum.
🛏14 bedrs, 6 en suite, 3 ba; TV 🛉TV, ns; child facs ✗nr dinner. Sun lunch. Resid lic
£B&B £22–£24, B&B (double) £36–£50; L £9; WB £18; dep.

Oxford, 5 Oxford Row, Lansdown Rd, BA1 2QN
☎ (0225) 314039.
🛏10 bedrs, 2 en suite, (3 sh), 2 ba 🛉TV, ns; no children under 8 ✗Breakfast only. Unlic

Tacoma 159 Newbridge Hill, BA1 3PX
☎(0225)310197.
Leave Bath on A4 to Bristol (Charlotte St), in 1¼ miles turn right at second set of traffic lights onto A431. Hotel is just over ¼ mile on left.
🛏8 bedrs, 2ba; tcf 🛉TV, ns; P5 ✗Breakfast only. Unlic
£B&B £15·50–£17, B&B (double) £26·50–£28; dep.

Waltons 17 Crescent Gardens, Upper Bristol Rd, BA1 2NA ☎ (0225) 426528.

BATTLE East Sussex. Map 27C3

Little Hemingfold (Acclaimed) Telham, TN33 0TT ☎ (042 46) 4338.
17th century farmhouse set in 40 acres of woods and farmland with a 2 acre trout lake. About 1¼ miles south of Battle, farm lane is off A2100 next to bend sign. Tennis, fishing.
🛏13 bedrs, 10 en suite, 2 ba; TV; tcf 🛉dogs, ns; P50; children over 8 ✗LD 7. Rest lic
£ B&B £25–£30, B&B (double) £45–£55; HB weekly £244–£297; L £15, D £16; WB £84; [5% V w/d, Oct–Apr] cc Access, B'card/Visa; dep.

BEAFORD Devon. Map 28F5

Beaford House Winkleigh, EX19 8AB ☎ (080 53) 305. *Swimming pool, putting, tennis.*

BECKERMET Cumbria. Map 22E4

Royal Oak CA21 2XB ☎ (0946) 841551.
£ B&B £35 (w/e £14·50); B&B (double) £35 (w/e £22); WB (HB w/e)

BEDALE North Yorkshire. Map 23C4

Ainderby Myers Farm Nr Hackforth, DL8 1PF
☎(0609) 748668. *Farm.* Mrs Valerie Anderson
Sleeps 6, ns 🛌
£ B&B from £12, D £8

Blairgowrie Nr Crakehall, DL8 1JZ
☎(0748) 811377. *Farm.* Doris Irene Knox
Sleeps 4, ns 🛌 (8)
£ B&B from £14, D £8

Mill Close Farm Patrick Brompton, DL8 1JY
☎(0677) 50257. *Farm.* Mrs P. A. Knox
Sleeps 6
£ B&B £12, D £8

BEDFORD Bedfordshire. Map 26F8

Linden View (Acclaimed) 16 Linden Rd, MK40 2DA ☎(0234) 52795.
🛏11 bedrs, 8 en suite, 1 ba; TV; tcf 🛉TV, ns; P 6, coach; child facs ✗LD 7.30, nr lunch. Resid lic
cc Access, Amex, B'card/Visa; dep.

Kimbolton 78 Clapham Rd, MK41 7PN
☎(0234) 54854
On the A6 at the northern end of the town centre. 5 mins walk from station.
🛏14 bedrs, 14 en suite; TV; tcf 🛉TV, ns; P 18, coach; child facs ✗LD 8.30, nr lunch, dinner Fri–Sun. Resid & Rest lic
£ B&B £36·80–£39·10, B&B (double) £46–£50·60; D £9; WB £25·30 cc Access, Amex, B'card/Visa.

BEESTON Nottinghamshire. Map 24D3

Brackley House 31 Elm Av, NG9 1BU
☎Nottingham (0602) 251787.

BELPER Derbyshire. Map 24D4

Shottle Hall Farm Shottle, DE5 2EB ☎Cowers Lane (077 389) 203. Closed Xmas.
🛏9 bedrs, 1 en suite, 2 ba; tcf 🛉TV, dogs, ns; P30; child facs ✗LD 6, nr lunch. Resid & Rest lic
£B&B £20·50, B&B (double) £36–£50; HB weekly £210; D £10; [5% V]; dep.

Chevin Green Farm Chevin Road, DE5 2UN
☎(0773) 822328. *Farm.* Carl and Joan Postles ♿
Sleeps 11, ns 🛌
£ B&B from £13–£15

BENNIWORTH Lincolnshire. Map 25A5

Skirbeck Farm Panton Road, LN3 6JN ☎(0507) 313682. *Farm.* Kay Olivant
Sleeps 6, 🛌 ns
£ B&B from £13, D £6·50

BERE FERRERS Devon. Map 28F3

Lanterna Yelverton, PL20 7JL ☎Tavistock (0822) 840380.
A 200-year-old former farmhouse built of local stone with many quaint features. Leave Tavistock on A390 towards Liskeard, turn right after 2 miles to Bere Alston. Follow signs for 4 miles, then take Bere Ferrers road. Hotel in centre of village.
🛏5 bedrs, 2 en suite, 1 ba 🛉TV, ns; P8; child facs ✗LD 8. Resid & Rest lic
£B&B £15·50–£18; HB weekly £123–£138; L £5, D £5; [10% V] cc Access, B'card/Visa; dep.

BERKELEY Gloucestershire. Map 26B6

Green Acres Farm Breadstone, GL13 9HF
✆(0453) 810348. *Farm.* Barbara Evans
Sleeps 6, ☎ (10)
£ B&B from £13–£17·50

BERRY POMEROY Devon. Map 29A3

Berry Farm Totnes, TQ9 6LG
✆(0803) 863231. *Farm.* Mrs Geraldine Nicholls
Sleeps 6, ns ☎
£ B&B from £10·50

BETLEY Cheshire. Map 24A4

Adderley Green Farm Heighley Castle Lane, Nr
Crewe, CW3 9BA ✆(0270) 820203. *Farm.*
Mrs Sheila Berrisford
Sleeps 6, ⋔ ☎
£ B&B from £12, D £7

BEVERLEY Humberside (North Humberside).
Map 24F7

Manor House (Highly Acclaimed) Northlands,
Walkington, HU17 8RT ✆(0482) 881645.
Fax: (0482) 866501

*Take B1230 from Walkington to Beverley, turn left
at traffic lights then left, and left again.*
🛏5 bedrs, 5 en suite; TV; tcf 🏠dogs; P 50; no
children under 12 ✕LD 9.15, nr lunch. Resid lic
£ B&B £61·50–£81·50, B&B (double) £88–£113;
D £24·50; [10% V] **cc** Access, B'card/Visa.

BEXHILL-ON-SEA East Sussex. Map 27C3

Dunselma Marina, TN40 1BP ✆(0424) 212988.
🛏11 bedrs, 2 en suite, (1 sh), 2 ba; TV; tcf
🏠TV, dogs; child facs ✕LD 5, nr lunch. Resid lic

Park Lodge 16 Egerton Rd, TN39 3HH
✆(0424) 216547.
🛏10 bedrs, 6 en suite, (2 sh), 1 ba; TV; tcf 🏠ns;
child facs ✕LD 6.30, nr Mon–Sat lunch, Sun
dinner. Resid lic
cc Access, B'card/Visa; dep.

Victoria 1 Middlesex Rd, TN40 1LP
✆(0424) 210382.
🛏10 bedrs, 5 en suite, 3 ba; TV; tcf 🏠TV, dogs, ns;
P 6, coach; child facs ✕LD 5, nr Sun dinner. Temp.

BICKINGTON Devon. Map 29A3

Kellinch Farm Newton Abbot, TQ12 6PB
✆(0626) 821252. *Farm.* Frances Pike
Sleeps 6 + cot, ☎
£ B&B from £10–£12·50, D £7·50

BICKLEY Kent. Map 27B5

Glendevon House 80 Southborough Rd, BR1
2EN ✆081-467 2183.
*A small hotel set in a residential area 1½ miles from
Bromley town centre. Take A21 from Sevenoaks, or
A222 from Chislehurst. Hotel in Bickley station road.*
🛏10 bedrs, 1 en suite, (3 sh), 1 ba; TV; tcf
🏠TV, dogs; P 6 ✕Unlic
£ B&B £18–£19·50, B&B (double) £30–£34;
[10% V] **cc** Access, B'card/Visa; dep.

BILLINGSHURST West Sussex. Map 27A3

Old Wharf (Highly Acclaimed) Newbridge,
Wisborough Green, RH14 0JG ✆(0403) 784096.

*Historic canalside warehouse, recently restored. All
bedrooms have superb canal views, and there is a
sunny walled courtyard. The Old Wharf is off the
A272 between Wisborough Green and Billingshurst.*
🛏4 bedrs, 4 en suite; TV; tcf 🏠TV, NS; P 10; no
children under 12 ✕Dinner on request. Unlic
£ B&B £30, B&B (double) £45–£60 **cc** Access,
Amex, B'card/Visa; dep.

Lannards Okehurst Lane, RH14 9HR
✆(040378) 2692. *Farm.* Betty and Derek Sims
Sleeps 5, ns
£ B&B from £12·50

BILSDALE North Yorkshire. Map 23E4

Hill End Farm Chop Gate, TS9 7JR ✆(043 96)
278. *Farm.* Brenda Johnson
Sleeps 6, ☎ ⋔
£ B&B from £11, D £7·50

Wether Cote Farm Helmsley, YO6 5WF
✆(043 96) 260. *Farm.* Winnie Wood
Sleeps 6, ⋔ ☎
£ B&B from £11, D £7·50

BINGLEY West Yorkshire. Map 23C2

Hallbank (Highly Acclaimed)   Beck La, BD16 4DD
📞 Bradford (0274) 565296.

*Victorian hotel standing in its own grounds high up
with extensive views of the Aire Valley. Near the five
rise locks, ½ mile from Bingley town centre (A650)
off Park Rd. Closed Xmas.*
🛏9 bedrs, 9 en suite; TV; tcf 📺TV, ns; P 20;
children over 5; child facs ✕LD 7.30, nr lunch, Sun
dinner. Resid lic
£ B&B £35, B&B (double) £50; [5% V]

BIRCHER Herefordshire. Map 31D8

Home Farm   Nr Leominster, HR6 0AX
📞(056 885) 525. *Farm.* Doreen Cadwallader
Sleeps 6, 🐾 ns
£ B&B from £12

BIRMINGHAM West Midlands. Map 24C1

Bridge House (Highly Acclaimed)   49 Sherbourne
Rd, Acocks Green, B27 6DX 📞021-706 5900.
*Well-appointed, family run hotel in two linked
Victorian buildings close to railway station. Off main
A45.*
🛏28 bedrs, 25 en suite, (1 sh), 1 ba; TV; tcf 📺TV,
dogs; P 60, coach; child facs ✕nr lunch. Resid lic
£ B&B £25·30, B&B (double) £40·25 **cc** Access,
Amex, B'card/Visa.

Beech House (Acclaimed)   21 Gravelly Hill North,
Erdington, B23 6BT 📞021-373 0620.
*Edwardian, tudor-style house set well back from
road behind beautiful large beech trees. Dining
room boasts art nouveau stained glass landscape
window. Situated on A5127, 500 metres from junc
6 of M6 motorway. Closed 23 Dec–5 Jan.*
🛏9 bedrs, 3 en suite, 2 ba; TV; tcf 📺TV, dogs, ns;
P 10; children over 5 ✕LD 7, nr lunch, Fri–Sun
dinner (by arrangement). Unlic
£B&B £25·30–£32·20, B&B (double) £39·10–£46;
HB weekly £257·60–£305·90 **cc** Access, B'card/
Visa; dep.

Lyndhurst (Acclaimed)   135 Kingsbury Rd,
Erdington, B24 8QT 📞021-373 5695.

*Small hotel with newly refurbished restaurant, 10
mins from city centre. From M6 junction 6 take
A5127 up Gravelly Hill. Turn first right into Kingsbury
Road. Hotel ¼ mile on right.*
🛏14 bedrs, 10 en suite, 3 ba; TV; tcf 📺TV; P 12,
coach ✕LD 8, nr lunch. Resid & Rest lic
£B&B £27·50–£34, B&B (double) £40–£45; HB
weekly £228–£268; D £8·50; [10% V] **cc** Access,
Amex, B'card/Visa, Diners; dep.

Willow Tree (Acclaimed)   759 Chester Rd,
Erdington, B24 0BY 📞021-373 6388.

*Double-fronted 1930s house with attractive
gardens. On A452 close to M6 junction 5.*
🛏7 bedrs, 5 en suite, 1 ba; TV; tcf
📺TV, ns; P 8; child facs ✕LD 8. Resid lic
£ B&B £20–£30; L £10, D £10; [5% V] **cc** Access,
B'card/Visa; dep.

Alexander   44 Bunbury Rd, Northfield, B31 2DW
📞021-475 4341.
🛏12 bedrs, 2 ba 📺TV, dogs; P 12, coach;
child facs ✕LD 6.30, nr lunch, Fri–Sun dinner.
Resid lic

Belmont   419 Hagley Rd, B17 8BL 📞021-429
1663. *Billiards.*

Bristol Court   250 Bristol Rd, Edgbaston, B5 7SL
📞021-472 0078.

Heath Lodge   117 Coleshill Rd, Marston Green,
B37 7HT 📞021-779 2218.
*Hotel is about half way between A452 and A45, ¼
mile from airport and NEC. Closed Xmas & New
Year*
🛏12 bedrs, 6 en suite, 1 ba; TV; tcf 📺TV, dogs;
P 17; child facs ✕LD 8.30, nr lunch. Resid & Rest
lic

£ B&B £26–£35, B&B (double) £37–£45; [10% V] **cc** Access, Amex, B/card/Visa.

Highfield House Holly Rd, Blackheath, Rowley Regls B65 0BH 021-559 1066.

Holyhead 6 Holyhead Rd, Handsworth, B20 0CT 021-554 8560.

Remwick House 13 Bournbrook Rd, Selly Park, B29 7BL 021-472 4640.
From city centre take A38 south west. Close to Pebble Mill BBC, Warwickshire cricket ground and Birmingham University. Closed Xmas.
9 bedrs, 5 en suite, 2 ba; TV; tcf
TV; P 6 Breakfast only. Unlic
£ B&B £15–£20; dep.

Rollason Wood Wood End Rd, Erdington, B24 2BJ 021-373 1230. Fax: 021-382 2578.
Family owned and run hotel a mile from Spaghetti junction on the M6. Take exit to B'ham NE (not A38M), then A5127 for 1 mile. Turn right on A4040.
35 bedrs, 11 en suite, (5 sh), 5 ba; TV; tcf TV, dogs, ns; P 45, coach LD 9, nr lunch. Resid lic
£ B&B £15·60–£32, B&B (double) £26·50–£46; D £6 **cc** Access, Amex, B'card/Visa, Diners.

Tri-Star Coventry Rd, Elmdon, B26 3QR 021-782 1010/6131.
Homely hotel within walking distance of airport and NEC. Situated on A45 Coventry Rd.
15 bedrs, 3 en suite, 5 ba; TV; tcf TV; P 25
LD 8.30, nr lunch, Sun dinner. Resid lic
£ B&B £27·60–£41·40, B&B (double) £34·50–£46; D £10; dep.

Welcome House 1641 Coventry Rd, Yardley, B26 1DD 021-707 3232.
6 bedrs, 1 en suite, 2 ba; TV P 8; no children under 3 Breakfast only. Unlic
cc B'card/Visa; dep.

Wentworth 103 Wentworth Rd, Harborne, B17 9SU 021-427 2839.
Family run hotel within easy reach of city centre. Closed 2 wks Xmas.
16 bedrs, 16 en suite; TV; tcf TV, dogs; P 14, G 1, coach; child facs LD 9, nr lunch. Resid lic
£ B&B £35, B&B (double) £46

Woodlands 379 Hagley Rd, B17 8DL 021-429 3935.
17 bedrs, (6 sh), 3 ba; TV; tcf TV; P 19, coach; child facs LD 7, nr lunch, Fri–Sat dinner. Resid lic
cc Access, Amex, B'card/Visa, Diners; dep.

BISHOP AUCKLAND Durham. Map 23C5

Greenhead Country House (Highly Acclaimed) Greenhead, Fir Tree, Crook DL15 8BL (0388) 763143.

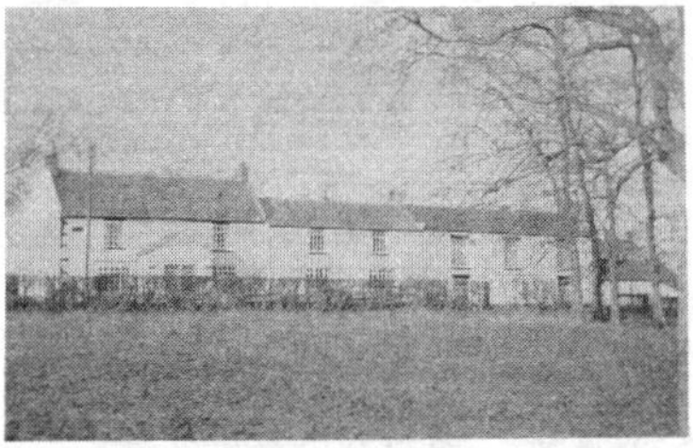

Turn off A1 onto A68 through Fir Tree village; turn right at Fir Tree Inn 500 yards on left.
6 bedrs, 6 en suite; TV; tcf TV; P 12; no children under 14 LD 9, nr Mon–Sat lunch. Resid lic
£ B&B £28, B&B (double) £38 **cc** Access, B'card/Visa; dep.

Greenwell Farm Tow Law, DL13 4PH (0388) 527248. *Farm.* Mike and Linda Vickers
Sleeps 6, ns
£ B&B from £12–£15, D £8·50

BISHOPS CASTLE Shropshire. Map 31E7

P Castle SY9 5DG **℄** (0588) 638403
Early 18th century stone-built hotel on high ground in market square.

BISHOP'S STORTFORD Hertfordshire.
Map 27B7

Brook House 29 Northgate End, CM23 2LD
℄ (0279) 655992 Fax: (0279) 812870.
From junction 8 of the M11 follow signs to A120 Hertford and at next roundabout turn left, then first right. Follow road for 1 ½ miles and hotel is on right.
⊨25 bedrs, 25 en suite; TV; tcf ⊞TV; P 2, G 4; child facs ✕LD 9.30, nr Sun. Resid & Rest lic
£ B&B £37·50–£42·50, B&B (double) £47·50–£52·50; L £3–£5, D £7–£12; WB; [5% V] **cc** Access, Amex, B'card/Visa.

BISPHAM Lancashire. Map 22F2

Garville 3 Beaufort Av, FY2 9HQ **℄** Blackpool (0253) 51004.
⊨7 bedrs, 2 en suite, 1 ba; TV; tcf ⊞TV, dogs, ns; P 5, G 1; child facs ✕LD 1 pm, nr lunch. Resid lic

Langwood 250 Queens Prom, FY2 9HA **℄** (0253) 51370.
Situated on the promenade 2 ½ miles north of Blackpool Tower. Open Mar–Dec.
⊨28 bedrs, 16 en suite, 1 ba; tcf ⊞lift, TV, dogs; P 15, coach; child facs ✕LD6, nr lunch
£B&B £18; HB weekly £148; D£8; WB £45; dep.

BLACKBURN Lancashire. Map 23A2

P P P Millstone Church La, Mellor, BB2 7JR
℄ Mellor (025 481) 3333 Tx: 635309.
Traditional inn in village setting with all modern comforts.
⊨19 bedrs, 19 en suite; TV; tcf ⊞dogs, ns; P 40, coach; child facs ✕LD 9.45, bar meals only Sat lunch
cc Access, Amex, B'card/Visa, Diners.

BLACKCROSS Cornwall. Map 28D2

Home Stake Farm Nr Newquay, TR8 4LU **℄** St Austell (0726) 860423.
Swimming pool, tennis.
(See advertisement under Newquay)

BLACKPOOL Lancashire. Map 22F2

Arosa (Highly Acclaimed) 18 Empress Dr, FY2 9SD **℄** (0253) 52555.
South-facing hotel run by same owners for 15 years. Near Gynn Square and boating pool on the North Shore. Open Easter–Nov, Xmas & New Year.
⊨22 bedrs, 21 en suite, 2 ba; TV; tcf
⊞TV, dogs; P 7, coach; child facs ✕Resid lic
£ B&B £18; D £6; dep.

Cliff Head (Highly Acclaimed) 174 Queens Promenade, Bispham FY2 9JH **℄** (0253) 591086.
Situated 2 ½ miles north of Blackpool tower.
⊨7 bedrs, 7 en suite; TV; tcf ⊞TV, dogs; P 3; child facs

Lynstead (Highly Acclaimed) 40 King Edward Av, FY2 9TA **℄** (0253) 51050. *Private Hotel.*

Old Coach House 50 Dean Street, FY4 1BP
℄ (0253) 44330.
Tudor style detached Victorian house set in gardens with seating areas and conservatory. Situated in the heart of Blackpool. Take Waterloo Road exit off M55, turn left at the traffic lights, left at next lights, and Dean Street is second on the right. Open Jan–Oct.
⊨6 bedrs, 6 en suite; TV; tcf ⊞dogs, ns; P 6; child facs ✕nr lunch. Unlic
£ B&B £18·40–£21, B&B (double) £34·50–£40; HB weekly £148·75–£168·75; [10% V Jan–May]
cc Access, B'card/Visa; dep.

Sunray (Highly Acclaimed) 42 Knowle Av, North Shore, FY2 9TQ **℄** (0253) 51937.
Turn right about 1 ¾ miles north of Tower along promenade. Hotel about 300 yards on left. Closed Xmas & New Year.
⊨9 bedrs, 9 en suite, 1 ba; TV; tcf ⊞TV, dogs; P 6; child facs ✕LD 2, nr lunch. Unlic
£ B&B £20–£27, B&B (double) £40–£50; HB weekly £158–£228; D£10; [10% V]; dep.

Brooklands (Acclaimed) 28 King Edward Av, North Shore, FY2 9TA **℄** (0253) 51479.
Situated 100 yards from Queens Promenade, near Gynn Square.
⊨18 bedrs, 9 en suite, 2 ba; TV; tcf ⊞P 7, coach; child facs ✕LD 5, nr lunch. Resid lic
£ B&B £14–£18; HB weekly £115·50–£136·50; [5% V]; dep.

Burlees (Acclaimed) 40 Knowle Av, Queens Prom, North Shore, FY2 9TQ **℄** (0253) 54535.
Pleasant 1930's-style building with double bays, red brick ground floor and white rendered first floor. South-facing front garden. Travel north along prom to Gynn Square then onto Queens Promenade. Turn right at Uncle Tom's cabin into Knowle Avenue, hotel is about 300 yards on left. Closed Nov–Feb.
⊨10 bedrs, 7 en suite, 1 ba; tcf ⊞TV, P 5; child facs ✕LD 4, nr lunch. Resid lic
£ B&B £14–£20; HB weekly £133–£177
cc Access, B'card/Visa; dep.

Cliftonville (Acclaimed)   14 Empress Dr, FY2 9SE
☎ (0253) 51052.
Off Queens Promenade adjacent to Cliffs Hotel.
Solarium. Open May–Oct.
🛏19 bedrs, 19 en suite, 1 ba; TV, tcf 🛗lift, TV; P 6,
coach; child facs ✕LD 5, nr lunch. Resid lic
£B&B £14·50–£17·50; HB weekly £105–£130
cc Access, B'card/Visa; dep.

Derwent (Acclaimed)   8 Gynn Av, FY1 2LD
☎ (0253) 55194.
🛏12 bedrs, 4 en suite, 2 ba; tcf
🛗TV, dogs; P 4, coach ✕nr lunch. Resid lic

Hartshead (Acclaimed)   17 King Edward Av,
FY2 9TA ☎ (0253) 53133.
🛏10 bedrs, 3 en suite, 2 ba; TV; tcf 🛗TV, dogs, ns;
P 6, coach; children over 3 ✕LD 3.30, nr lunch.
Resid lic

Knowsley (Acclaimed)   68 Dean St, FY4 1BP
☎ (0253) 43414.
🛏14 bedrs, 7 en suite, 1 ba; TV, tcf 🛗TV, dogs;
P 10, U 1, coach; child facs ✕LD 12 noon. Resid
lic
cc Access, B'card/Visa; dep.

Mimosa (Acclaimed)   24A Lonsdale Rd, FY1 6EE
☎ (0253) 41906.

A modern, purpose built hotel close to all amenities.
Lonsdale Rd is the exit from No. 4 Bloomfield car
park near the coach station.
🛏15 bedrs, 15 en suite; TV; tcf 🛗TV, dogs; P 15,
U 2, coach; child facs ✕LD 7.30 (on request only).
Unlic
£ B&B £15–£35, B&B (double) £30–£40; [10% V
w/d in high season] **cc** Access, B'card/Visa; dep.

Surrey House (Acclaimed)   9 Northumberland Av,
FY2 9SB ☎ (0253) 51743.
Personally-run hotel close to the main conference
hotels and Queen's Promenade. At North Shore join
prom at Gynn Square roundabout. Surrey House is
five roads north of Queens Promenade. Open Apr–
Oct.
🛏11 bedrs, 9 en suite, 2 ba; tcf 🛗TV, dogs, ns; P 6,
G 1 (75p); no children under 1; child facs ✕LD
2.30, nr lunch. Unlic
£B&B £11–£17·50; HB weekly £120; dep.

Villa (Acclaimed)   9 Withnell Rd, FY4 1HF ✆ (0253) 43314.

Close to the south prom between the pleasure beach and South Pier. Open Easter–Nov.
🛏19 bedrs, 12 en suite, 2 ba; TV; tcf 🐕dogs, ns; P 9, coach; child facs ✕LD 5.30, nr lunch. Resid lic
£ B&B £13·50–£24, B&B (double) £24–£44; HB weekly £91–£125; [10% V Jun–Aug, w/d Sept/Oct]
cc Access, B'card/Visa; dep.

Ashcroft   42 King Edward Av, FY2 9TA ✆ (0253) 51538.
Small friendly hotel in south facing position off Queen's Promenade. Take third turning on right after Gynn roundabout.
🐕TV; P 4, G 1; no children under 5 ✕LD 2, nr lunch. Resid lic
£ B&B £14; HB weekly £114; dep.

Denely   15 King Edward Av, FY2 9TA ✆ (0253) 52757.
One mile north of tower. Open Jan–Nov.
🛏9 bedrs, 2 en suite, (2 sh), 1 ba; tcf 🐕TV, ns; P 6; child facs ✕LD 3.30, nr lunch. Unlic
£ B&B £12–£18, HB weekly £108·50–£147; dep.

Lyndale   13 Northumberland Av, FY2 9SB ✆ (0253) 54033

Lynwood   38 Osborne Rd, FY4 1HG ✆ (0253) 44628.
Extensively modernised guest house close to South Shore entertainment. Osborne Road is directly opposite Sandcastle Centre. Closed Xmas.
🛏8 bedrs, 6 en suite, 1 ba; TV, tcf 🐕child facs ✕LD 9 am, nr lunch. Unlic
£ B&B £12–£17; HB weekly £112–£140; [5% V]
cc Access, B'card/Visa; dep.

New Esplanade   551 New South Prom, FY4 INF ✆ (0253) 41646.

New Heathcot   270 Queens Prom., Bispham FY2 9HD ✆ (0253) 595130.
Small hotel with views over the Irish sea. Situated on Queens Promenade. Open Easter–Nov.
🛏8 bedrs, 4 en suite, 2 ba; TV; tcf 🐕TV; P 6; child

facs ✕LD 5.30, nr lunch. Resid lic
£ B&B £13·50–£16·50; HB weekly £112–£132; D £6·50; [10% V]; dep.

North Mount   22 King Edward Av, FY2 9TD ✆ (0253) 55937.
Small family-run hotel close to the sea off Queens Promenade. Second turning right after Gynn Square and hotel is on left before crossroads.
🛏8 bedrs, 2 ba; tcf 🐕TV, dogs; P 1, coach; child facs ✕LD 4.30, nr lunch. Resid lic
£ B&B £10–£11·50; HB weekly £92–£110; [5% V Dec–Aug]; dep.

Roker   563 New South Prom, FY4 1NF ✆ (0253) 41853.
Well-placed hotel with sea and beach views, close to all amenities. Within minutes of pleasure beach. Closed 1 Nov–22 Dec, Feb–Apr.
🛏18 bedrs, 4 en suite; tcf 🐕TV; P 12, coach; child facs ✕nr lunch. Resid lic
£ B&B £12·50–£16; HB weekly £108–£125·50
cc Access, B'card/Visa; dep.

Sunny Cliff   98 Queens Promenade, FY2 9NS ✆ (0253) 51155.
Small hotel in a quiet position overlooking sea and cliffs. About 1¼ miles north of the Tower. Open Apr–early Nov and Xmas.
🛏12 bedrs, 2 ba; tcf 🐕TV, dogs; P 2, child facs ✕LD 6, nr lunch. Resid lic
£ B&B £12–£14; HB weekly £110–£120

Woodlaigh   32 King Edward Dr, North Shore, FY2 9TA ✆ (0253) 593624.

BLACK TORRINGTON   Devon.   Map 28F5

Hayne Farm (Acclaimed)   Beaworthy, EX21 5QG ✆ (040923) 449. *Billiards.*
🛏6 bedrs, 3 en suite, 1 ba; tcf 🐕TV, dogs, NS; P 6; child facs ✕LD 7.30, nr Mon–Sat lunch, Sun dinner. Unlic

BLAKENEY   Gloucestershire.   Map 26A6

Lower Viney (Acclaimed)   Viney Hill, GL15 4LT ✆ (0594) 516000.

Spacious Grade II listed period house near the Severn Estuary and on the edge of the Forest of Dean. From Chepstow on A48 2¼ miles out of Lydney. Turn left signed Viney Hill, and property is

*first on the right. From Gloucester turn is ¼ mile
through Blakeney.*
⇥6 bedrs, 6 en suite; TV; tcf 🛉TV, ns; P 10; child
facs ✗LD 5.30, nr lunch, Sat & Sun dinner
£ B&B £15–£18, B&B (double) £28–£35; WB £45
(2 nts HB); D £7·50; [5% V] cc B/card/Visa.

BLAKENEY Norfolk. Map 35B2.

Flintstones Wireton, NR25 7TL ✆(0263) 740337.
⇥3 bedrs, 1 ba; TV; tcf 🛉dogs, ns; P 3; child
facs ✗nr lunch. Resid lic

BLANDFORD FORUM Dorset. Map 29E4

Downwood Vineyards Wimborne Road, DT11
9HN ✆(0258) 454228. *Farm.* David and Jacky Hall
Sleeps 6, 🐎🛆 ♿
£ B&B from £15

BOGNOR REGIS West Sussex. Map 26F2

Homestead 90 Aldwick Rd, PO21 2PD
✆(0243)823443.
*Small hotel just 200 yards from the beach. West
from the pier; Homestead is by the second
crossroad, on the right.*
⇥10 bedrs, 1 en suite, (1 sh), 1 ba 🛉TV, dogs;
P 12; child facs ✗LD 6, nr lunch. Resid lic
£ B&B £10·50–£11; HB weekly £89·50–£92·50;
D £3·50; dep.

BOREHAMWOOD Hertfordshire. Map 27A6

Grosvenor 148 Shenley Rd, WD6 1EQ ✆081-953
3175 Tx: 928868 Fax: 081-207 5500.
*Hotel is located opposite the BBC studios, just past
the turning into Whitehouse Rd. Closed Xmas–New
Year.*
⇥28 bedrs, 10 en suite, (6 sh), 5 ba; TV; tcf 🛉ns;
P 20, coach; child facs ✗LD 10

£ B&B £34–£48, B&B (double) £42–£58; L £10·50;
D £13·50; WB £21·50; [5% V w/d] cc Access,
Amex, B'card/Visa, Diners

BOROUGHBRIDGE North Yorkshire. Map 24D8

📺 📺 **Crown Inn** Roecliff, YO5 9LY ✆(0423)
322578
*Small, busy country inn in tranquil setting
overlooking village green. Excellent, well-equipped
bedrooms.*
⇥6 bedrs, 6 en suite; TV; tcf

Farndale (Acclaimed) Horsefair, YO5 9AH
✆(0423) 323463.
⇥13 bedrs, 4 en suite, (2 sh); 3 ba; TV 🛉TV, dogs;
P 8, coach; child facs ✗LD 9. Resid & Rest lic

BOSCASTLE Cornwall. Map 28D4

Melbourne House New Rd, PL35 0DH ✆(084 05)
650.
*Follow B3266 from Camelford, past signs to
Boscastle Harbour. Melbourne House is 200 yards
on left.*
⇥6 bedrs, 2 en suite, 2 ba; TV; tcf 🛉dogs; P 8; no
children under 10 ✗LD 6, nr lunch. Resid lic
£ B&B £12–£16; HB weekly £119–£145; [5% V]
cc Access, B'card/Visa; dep.

Old Coach House Tintagel Rd, PL35 0AS
✆(084 05) 398.
*Located at junction of B3263 and B3266. Open
Jan–Nov.*
⇥4 bedrs, 4 en suite; TV; tcf 🛉ns; P 6; no children
under 6 ✗LD 10 am, nr lunch. Resid lic
£ B&B £13–£20; HB weekly £132–£176 cc Access,
Amex, B'card/Visa; dep.

BOURNE Lincolnshire. Map 25A3

🝪 🝪 🝪 **Angel** Market Place, PE10 9AE ✆ (0778) 422346 Fax: (0778) 393065
Traditional coaching inn with its coach yard roofed over to provide a small arcade of shops.
🛏14 bedrs, 14 en suite; TV, tcf ⋔P 75, coach; child facs ✗LD 9.30, nr Sun dinner
cc Access, Amex, B'card/Visa.

BOURNHEATH Worcestershire. Map 26B9

Hill Farm Bromsgrove, B61 9HU
✆ (0527) 72403. *Farm.* Lillan Rutter
Sleeps 6, ⛇
£ B&B from £15–£17·50, D £11·50

BOURNEMOUTH and BOSCOMBE Dorset. Map 26C2

Tudor Grange (Highly Acclaimed) 31 Gervis Rd, BH1 3EE ✆ (0202) 291472.
Tudor building with oak panelled reception rooms and original 300-year-old "William and Mary" staircase. The hotel stands in its own grounds just yards from the beach lift. From Lansdowne roundabout take Meyrick Road, turn left at next roundabout into Gervis Road, and Tudor Grange is on the right. Open Mar–Nov
🛏12 bedrs, 11 en suite, 2 ba; TV; tcf ⋔TV, dogs; P 11; child facs ✗LD 7, nr lunch. Resid lic
£ B&B £20–£26; HB weekly £175–£205; D £8·50; [5% V Mar–May, Nov]; dep.

Borodale (Acclaimed) 10 St John's Rd, Boscombe, BH5 1EL ✆ (0202) 35285.

Cransley (Acclaimed) 11 Knyveton Rd, East Cliff, BH1 3QG ✆ (0202) 290067.

Small hotel set in garden in a pine clad road close to the East Cliff and beach. From A338 Ringwood road follow signs to East Cliff. Knyveton Road is first left off slip road past Holdenhurst Road roundabout. Open April–Nov.
🛏12 bedrs, 9 en suite, (1 sh), 1 ba; TV; tcf ⋔TV, dogs; P 10; child facs ✗nr lunch. Resid lic
£B&B £12–£20; HB weekly £90–£139; [10% V Apr–Jun, Sept, Oct] **cc** Access, B'card/Visa; dep.

Croham Hurst (Acclaimed) 9 Durley Rd Sth, West Cliff, BH2 5JH ✆ (0202) 22353.
🛏40 bedrs, 40 en suite; TV; tcf ⋔lift, ns; P30, coach; child facs ✗LD 6.30. Resid & Rest lic
cc Access, B'card/Visa; dep.

East Cliff Cottage (Acclaimed) 57 Grove Rd, East Cliff, BH1 3AT ✆ (0202) 22788.
Quiet, olde world hotel with modern amenities, set on the East Cliff. Grove Road is behind the Carlton Hotel.
🛏10 bedrs, 4 en suite, 2 ba; TV; tcf ⋔TV, dogs; P 10, coach; child facs ✗LD 8, nr Sun dinner. Unlic
£ B&B £17·50–£20; HB weekly £120–£145; D £6·50; WB £40; [10% V Oct–Jun]; dep.

Golden Sands (Acclaimed) 83 Alumhurst Rd, Alum Chine, BH4 8HR ✆ (0202) 763832.
A detached 19th century family house with modern amenities, close to the west undercliff. Situated on the road from Westbourne shopping centre to Alum Chine, west of Bournemouth. Closed Dec & Jan.
🛏11 bedrs, 11 en suite; TV; tcf ⋔ns; P 11; no children under 3 ✗LD 4, nr lunch. Resid lic
£ B&B £24–£28·80, B&B (double) £41–£48; HB weekly £140–£175; WB £18·50; dep.

Highclere (Acclaimed) 15 Burnaby Rd, Alum Chine, BH4 8JF ✆ (0202) 761350.
Follow signs for Westbourne/Alum Chine. Turn left off Alumhurst Rd into Crosby Rd, then left into Burnaby Rd. Hotel 50 yards on left. Solarium. Open Easter–Oct.
🛏9 bedrs, 9 en suite; TV; tcf ⋔TV, dogs; P 7; child facs ✗LD 5, nr lunch. Resid lic
£ B&B £15·75–£17; HB weekly £134–£145; [5% V Apr–Jun, Oct Mon–Thurs]; dep.

Holmcroft (Acclaimed)   5 Earle Rd, Alum Chine, Westbourne, BH4 8JQ ☎(0202) 761289.
Quietly situated, family-run hotel close to wooded chines and sandy beach. Follow signs to Alum Chine, between Bournemouth and Poole. Take fifth turning on left down Alumhurst Road.
➡ 19 bedrs, 19 en suite; TV; tcf 俞dogs, ns; P 14; child facs ✕LD 5, nr lunch. Resid lic
£ B&B £20–£25; HB weekly £154–£175 cc Access, B'card/Visa; dep.

Linwood House (Acclaimed)   11 Wilfred Rd, Boscombe, BH5 1ND ☎(0202) 397818.
A hotel standing in its own grounds in a quiet area near Shelley Park. From Christchurch Road turn into Chessil Avenue, take first right into Wilfred Road and hotel is on the left. Open mid Mar–Oct.
➡ 10 bedrs, 7 en suite, 2 ba; TV; tcf 俞TV, dogs; P 7; no children under 5 ✕nr lunch. Resid lic.
£ B&B (double) £28–£39; HB weekly £93·50–£114·50.

New Dorchester (Acclaimed)   64 Lansdowne Rd, BH1 1RS ☎(0202) 551271.
Victorian villa in gardens of ¼ acre. Closed 25 Dec–1 Jan.
➡ 10 bedrs, 5 en suite, 2 ba; TV; tcf 俞P 10; children over 12 ✕LD 7, nr lunch. Resid lic
£ B&B £16–£30, B&B (double) £30–£40; HB weekly £150–£210 cc Access, Amex, B'card/Visa, Diners; dep.

Ravenstone (Acclaimed)   36 Burnaby Rd, Alum Chine, Westbourne, BH4 8JG ☎(0202) 761047.
Detached white-walled hotel built at the turn of the century. Follow A338 Wessex Way to Westbourne, then follow signs for Alum Chine down Alumhurst Road. Turn into Beaulieu Road on the left, and Burnaby Road is on the right. Open Mar–Oct.
➡ 9 bedrs, 9 en suite; TV; tcf 俞P 5; child facs ✕LD 5, nr lunch. Resid lic
£ B&B £18–£20; HB weekly £136–£165; D £5; WB £21; [5% V Mar–May, Oct]; dep.

Silver Trees (Acclaimed)   57 Wimborne Rd, BH3 7AL ☎(0202) 556040.

Charming Victorian house standing in its own wooded grounds with sweeping lawns and colourful flowers. Take Wessex Way into Bournemouth, then A347 (Wimborne Rd) north.

➡ 8 bedrs, 5 en suite, 2 ba; TV 俞ns; P 12; no children under 2 ✕Breakfast only. Unlic
£ B&B £23–£29, B&B (double) £32–£38
cc Access, B'card/Visa; dep.

Tower House (Acclaimed)   West Cliff Gdns, BH2 5HP ☎(0202) 290742.

Wood Lodge (Acclaimed)   10 Manor Rd, East Cliff, BH1 3EY ☎(0202) 290891.

A late-Victorian house in its own carefully tended grounds in a tree-lined road. Situated midway between Bournemouth and Boscombe piers, about 300 yards from the cliff top. Putting. Open Easter–mid Oct
➡ 15 bedrs, 14 en suite, 1 ba; TV; tcf 俞TV, dogs; P 12; child facs ✕LD 7, nr lunch. Resid lic
£ B&B £18–£27; HB weekly £145–£190; D £9
cc Access, B'card/Visa; dep.

Wychcote (Acclaimed)   2 Somerville Rd, BH2 5LH ☎(0202) 557898.

An elegant Victorian hotel with its own gardens. Leave the A338 Wessex Way at the West Cliff exit, take second exit at next roundabout (Durley Chine Road) and Somerville Road is first on left.
➡ 12 bedrs, 6 en suite, 2 ba; TV; tcf 俞P 12; no children under 5 ✕LD 8.30, nr lunch. Resid lic
£ B&B £14·50–£21·50; HB weekly £120–£195; WB £36; [5% V Oct–Mar] cc Access, B'card/Visa; dep.

Albemarle   123 West Hill Rd, Westcliff, BH2 5PH ☎(0202) 551351.
Centrally situated hotel close to West Cliff and sea front. Follow signs to BIC from Wessex Way. West Hill Road on left after Wessex Hotel.
➡ 11 bedrs, 4 en suite, (1 sh) 2 ba; TV; tcf 俞dogs, ns; child facs ✕LD 4, lunch only Sun. Resid lic
£ B&B £14–£20; HB weekly £120–£160; WB £35; [5% V Oct–Jun] cc Access, B'card/Visa; dep.

Alum Bay   19 Burnaby Rd, Alum Chine, BH4 8JF
✆(0202)761034.
*A detached private hotel near Alum Chine and
sandy beach. From Westbourne follow signs to
Alum Chine along Alumhurst Road turn left into
Crosby Road and left into Burnaby Road. Alum Bay
is fifth building on left.*
⊨12 bedrs, 7 en suite, 1 ba; TV; tcf ♠TV, dogs, ns;
P 10, coach; child facs ✕LD6, nr lunch. Resid lic
£ B&B £14–£25, B&B (double) £34–£46; HB weekly
£147–£180; WB £41·50; [5% V] **cc** Access, B'card/
Visa; dep.

Bay Tree   17 Burnaby Rd, Alum Chine, BH4 8JF
✆(0202) 763807.
*From Westbourne take Alumhurst Rd, turn left into
Beaulieu Rd then right into Burnaby Rd. Bay Tree
is 300 yards on right. Open 1 Jan–28 Dec.*
⊨9 bedrs, 6 en suite, (1 sh), 1 ba; tcf ♠TV, ns; P 9,
coach; child facs ✕LD 4.30, nr lunch. Resid lic
£B&B £13·75–£20·75; HB weekly £125–£155·25;
D £6; [10% V]; dep.

Beechwood   14 Studlands, BH4 8JA
✆(0202)767015

Blinkbonnie Heights   26 Clifton Rd,
Southbourne, BH4 3PA ✆(0202) 426512.
*Family run hotel in its own grounds. Just off the
Overcliff Drive, 80 yards from the sea. Southbourne
is between Christchurch and Boscombe.*
⊨13 bedrs, 7 en suite, 2 ba; TV; tcf ♠TV, dogs;
P 12, coach; children over 3, child facs ✕LD3, nr
lunch. Resid lic
£B&B £10–£18; HB weekly £84–£125; dep.

Boltons   9 Durley Chine Rd, Westcliff, BH2 5JT
✆(0202) 760907.
Swimming pool.
⊨13 bedrs, 5 en suite, (4 sh), 2 ba; TV ♠TV, dogs;
P 12; children over 2, child facs ✕LD 10. Resid &
Rest lic
cc Access, Amex; dep.

Braemar   30 Glen Rd, Boscombe, BH5 1HS
✆(0202)396054.
*Family run hotel in a quiet road near the cliff tops.
From Christchurch Rd take Crabton Close Rd, turn
right into Wilfred Rd and first right into Glen Rd.
Hotel on the right. Open Mar–end Oct & 23–28 Dec.*
⊨11 bedrs, 5 en suite, 2 ba; TV; tcf ♠TV; P6,
coach; child facs ✕nr lunch. Resid lic
£B&B £14–£17; HB weekly £95–£130; [5% V]; dep.

Britannia   40 Christchurch Rd, BH1 3PE
✆(0202)556700.

Cavendish   20 Durley Chine Rd, West Cliff BH2
5LF ✆(0202) 290489.
*Follow signs to West Cliff and BIC. Hotel is on left
side of Durley Chine Rd. Open Easter–Nov.*
⊨17 bedrs, 12 en suite, 2 ba; TV; tcf ♠TV; P 14;

no children under 5   ✕LD 4, nr lunch; Unlic
£ B&B £12–£17·50; HB weekly £100–£150; dep.

Chinebeach   14 Studland Rd, Alum Chine BH4
8JA ✆(0202) 767015.
*Family run hotel with private access to Alum Chine.
From centre of Bournemouth turn into Exeter Rd,
at first roundabout turn right into Priory/Westcliff Rd,
then turn left at second roundabout into Alumhurst
Rd. Turn left into Studland Rd. Swimming pool,
sauna, solarium, gymnasium.*
⊨22 bedrs, 17 en suite, 2 ba; TV; tcf ♠TV, dogs,
ns; P 9, coach; child facs ✕LD noon, nr lunch.
Resid lic
£ B&B £14–£21; HB weekly £130–£180; D £6;
[5% V except Jul & Aug] **cc** Access, B'card/Visa;
dep.

Clifton Court   30 Clifton Rd, Southbourne, BH6
3PA ✆(0202) 427753.
⊨11 bedrs, 7 en suite, 2 ba; tcf ♠TV, dogs; P 12,
coach; child facs ✕LD 10am, nr lunch. Resid lic

Denby   24 Southern Rd, Southbourne, BH6 3SR
✆(0202) 428958.

Derwent House   36 Hamilton Rd, Boscombe,
BH1 4EH ✆(0202) 309102.
*A family run hotel close to the town centre. From
Bournemouth take Christchurch Rd, turn left into
Hamilton Rd past Boscombe Gardens, and hotel is
on right.*
⊨10 bedrs, 4 en suite, (2 sh), 2 ba; TV; tcf ♠TV,
dogs; P 10, coach; child facs ✕LD5, nr lunch.
Resid lic
£B&B £12–£17; HB weekly £80–£132; [5% V]
cc Access, B'card/Visa; dep.

Dorset Westbury   62 Lansdowne Rd North, BH1
1RS ✆(0202) 551811.
Closed 20 Dec–10 Jan.
⊨17 bedrs, 8 en suite, 3 ba; TV; tcf ♠TV, dogs;
P 20, coach; child facs ✕LD 12 noon, nr lunch.
Resid lic
£B&B £14·50–£22; HB weekly £126–£170; [10% V
Oct–Mar, min stay 2 nights] **cc** Access, B'card/
Visa; dep.

Gervis Court   38 Gervis Rd, BH1 3DH
✆(0202)556871.
*A family run hotel standing in its own grounds amid
pine trees. From St Pauls roundabout on Wessex
Way take turning signed to East Cliff. Hotel is in
Gervis Rd towards town centre. Putting. Open Mar–
mid Dec.*
⊨16 bedrs, 10 en suite, 3 ba; tcf ♠TV; P15; child
facs ✕LD7.15, nr lunch. Resid lic
£B&B £18; HB weekly £106–£180; D £6; WB
£26·50 (HB 2 nights); [10% V] **cc** Access, B'card/
Visa; dep.

Glen 12 Rosemount Rd, Alum Chine, BH4 8HB
☎(0202) 763795.
*Detached hotel in quiet cul-de-sac. From A338
Poole to Bournemouth Rd take Alum Chine exit at
Frizzel House roundabout. Follow Alum Chine signs
to Alumhurst Rd, and Rosemount Rd is third on the
left.*
🛏11 bedrs, 4 en suite, 2 ba; tcf 🎬TV, dogs; P 5,
coach; no children under 3 ✕LD 4, nr lunch. Resid
lic
£ B&B £13–£18; HB weekly £113–£135; [10%V
Apr–Jun, Sept–Nov]

Hawaiian 4 Glen Rd, Boscombe, BH5 1BR
☎(0202) 393234.
*A small family hotel 5 mins walk from the beach.
Take the first right hand turn from the pier at
Boscombe, first right into Percy Rd and Glen Rd is
on the left. Open Mar–Nov.*
🛏12 bedrs, 8 en suite, 2 ba; TV; tcf 🎬TV, ns; P 7;
child facs ✕LD6, nr lunch. Resid & Rest lic
£B&B £15–£18; HB weekly £120–£138; D £6;
[10%V Apr–May, Oct, Nov]; dep.

Holme Lacy 32 Florence Rd, Boscombe,
BH5 1HQ ☎(0202) 396933

Ingledene 20 Derby Rd, BH1 3QA ☎(0202)
555433.
*Turn left off Wessex Way by railway/bus station
roundabout, cross next roundabout and turn left into
Knyveton Rd. Turn left into Derby Rd.*
🛏8 bedrs, 6 en suite, 1 ba; TV; tcf 🎬TV, dogs; P 1,
coach; no children under 5 ✕LD6, nr lunch. Unlic
£ B&B £11·40–£15·20; HB weekly £88–£121·50;
[10%V Sept–June]; dep.

Langton Hall 8 Durley Chine Rd, BH2 5JY
☎(0202) 555025.
🛏35 bedrs, 24 en suite; TV; tcf 🎬lift, TV; P 38,
coach; child facs ✕LD 7.30, nr Mon–Sat lunch

Mae Mar 91 West Hill Rd, BH2 5PQ
☎(0202) 553167.
🛏43 bedrs, 27 en suite, 4 ba; TV; tcf 🎬lift, TV,
dogs, ns; coach; child facs ✕LD 5.30. Resid &
Rest lic
£ B&B £15–£25·50; HB weekly £112·50–£168;
L £4·95, D £6; WB fr £35; [10%V except Jul]
cc Access, B'card/Visa; dep.

Naseby-Nye Byron Rd, Boscombe Overcliff, BH5
1JD ☎(0202) 394079. *Hotel.*

Newlands 14 Rosemount Rd, Alum Chine,
BH4 8HB ☎(0202) 761922.
*From Westbourne take Alumhurst Rd to Alum Chine,
then turn left into Rosemount Rd. Open Mar–Oct.*
🛏11 bedrs, (4 sh), 2 ba; tcf 🎬TV; P 5; child
facs ✕LD breakfast time, nr lunch. Resid lic
£ B&B £10–£16; HB weekly £88–£133; dep.

Northover 10 Earle Rd, Alum Chine, BH4 8JQ
☎(0202) 767349.
*Hotel situated 400 yards from sea front at Alum
Chine. Open Mar–Oct & Xmas.*
🛏10 bedrs, 6 en suite, 2 ba; tcf 🎬TV, dogs, ns;
P 10; children over 3 ✕LD5, nr lunch. Rest lic
£ B&B £15–£20; HB weekly £120–£150; WB £15;
[5%V Mar–May & Oct]; dep.

Oak Hall 9 Wilfred Rd, Boscombe, BH5 1ND
☎(0202) 395062.
*Hotel in level position adjacent to Shelley Park.
Follow signs from A35 Boscombe Pier and seafront.
Open Nov–Sept*
🛏13 bedrs, 8 en suite, 2 ba; TV; tcf 🎬TV; dogs, ns;
P 9, coach; child facs ✕LD 4, nr lunch. Resid lic
£ B&B £16–£18·50; HB weekly £113–£152;
D £6·25; WB £64; [10%V Jan–May] **cc** Access,
B'card/Visa; dep.

Parklands 4 Rushton Cres, BH3 7AF
☎(0202) 552529.
*Small detached hotel on the edge of Meyrick Park.
Take Wimborne Rd from Wessex Way (signed
Wimborne) to cemetery junction. Turn left at traffic
lights, and left into Rushton Cres.*
🛏10 bedrs, 7 en suite, 1 ba; TV; tcf 🎬TV; P6; no
children under 10 ✕LD 2, nr lunch.
£ B&B £17–£23; D fr £6·50; WB £17 (HB min 3
nights, Nov–Apr) **cc** Access, B'card/Visa; dep.

Pine Lodge 12 Westbourne Pk Rd, BH4 8HG
☎(0202) 761872.

St Johns Lodge 10 Swithun's Rd South,
BH1 3RQ ☎(0202) 290677.
*From A338 turn left at station roundabout following
signs for East Cliff. Cross next roundabout into St
Swithins Road South, and hotel is 300 yards on the
left. Sauna.*
🛏15 bedrs, 5 en suite, (1 sh), 3 ba; TV, tcf 🎬TV,
ns; P 13; child facs ✕LD 4, nr lunch. Resid lic
£ B&B £15·50–£18·50; HB weekly £115–£159
cc Access, B'card/Visa; dep.

Sea Dene 10 Burnaby Rd, Alum Chine, BH4 8JF
☎(0202) 761372.
*Small hotel 400 yards from beach. Follow Alumhurst
Rd to Alum Chine, take left turn into Crosby Rd and
hotel is on left. Open Mar–Nov.*
🛏7 bedrs, 5 en suite, 1 ba; TV; tcf 🎬TV, dogs; P 4,
coach; no children under 3 ✕LD7.30, nr lunch.
Resid lic
£ B&B £11–£16; HB weekly £110–£145
cc Access, B'card/Visa; dep.

Sea View Court 14 Boscombe Spa Rd, BH5 1AZ
☎(0202) 397197.
🛏17 bedrs, 7 en suite, 2 ba; TV 🎬TV; coach; child
facs ✕LD 3, nr lunch. Resid lic
£ B&B £12–£20; HB weekly £90–£145

ENGLAND

Seaway   30 St Catherines Rd, Southbourne, BH6 4AB ☎(0202) 423636.
➟10 bedrs, 5 en suite, 2 ba; tcf ♠TV, dogs; P 10; child facs ✗LD 6.30, nr lunch. Resid lic

Shoreline   7 Pinecliffe Ave, Southbourne, BH6 3PY ☎(0202) 429654.
Pinecliffe Ave is a turning off Southbourne Overcliff Drive, between Shell House and Commodore Hotel.
➟10 bedrs, 4 en suite, 2 ba; TV; tcf ♠dogs; P 5; no children under 5 ✗LD 7, nr lunch. Resid lic
£B&B £11–£15; HB weekly £95–£135; [10% V Jan 2–May 31, Oct–Dec 23]; dep.

Sorrento   16 Owls Rd, Boscombe, BH5 1AG ☎(0202) 394019.
From A35 Christchurch Rd turn left at traffic lights by St Johns Church into Owls Rd. Hotel is on the left. Solarium, gymnasium. Open 15 Jan–29 Dec.
➟17 bedrs, 12 en suite, (1 sh), 2 ba; TV; tcf ♠TV, dogs; P 19; child facs

Valberg   1a Wollenstonecraft Rd, Boscombe, BH5 1JQ ☎(0202) 394644.
From Boscombe Pier take first right, first right and first left.
➟10 bedrs, 10 en suite; TV; tcf ♠TV, ns; P 7; no children under 4 ✗LD 12.30, nr lunch. Resid lic
£ B&B £13; HB weekly £120–£144; dep.

Washington   3 Durley Rd, West Cliff, BH2 5JQ ☎(0202) 557023
Hotel is in West Cliff area, a turning off West Hill Rd.
➟19 bedrs, 15 en suite, 2 ba, TV; tcf ♠TV, dogs; P 22, coach; child facs ✗LD 6, nr lunch. Resid lic
£ B&B £17·25–£21·50; HB weekly £153–£180; WB £16·50; dep.

Wenmaur House   14 Carysfort Rd, Boscombe, BH1 4EJ ☎(0202) 395081.
➟11 bedrs, (6 sh), 3 ba; TV; tcf ♠TV, dogs; P 9, coach; child facs ✗LD 6.30, nr lunch. Resid lic.
£ HB weekly £95–£140 cc Access, B/card/Visa; dep.

West Bay   West Cliff Gdns, BH2 5HL ☎(0202) 552261.
At A338 roundabout follow signs to West Cliff and BIC, at next roundabout take second left into Durley Chine Rd. At next roundabout take first left and first right into West Cliff Gdns. Closed Dec.
➟12 bedrs, 11 en suite, (1 sh), 1 ba; TV, tcf ♠TV, dogs; P6, coach; child facs ✗LD 6, nr lunch. Resid lic
£B&B £20–£23·50; HB weekly £161–£184; D £6; [5% V Jan–Jun & Oct] cc Access, B'card/Visa; dep.

West Dene   117 Alumhurst Rd, Alum Chine, BH4 8HS ☎(0202) 764843.
From A338 follow signs to Alum Chine, where hotel is situated on sea front. Open Feb–Nov.

➟17 bedrs, 12 en suite, 3 ba; TV; tcf ♠TV; P 17, coach; no children under 4 ✗LD 3.30, nr lunch. Resid lic
£B&B £22·50–£26·50; HB weekly £161–£214; D £14 cc Access, Amex, B'card/Visa, Diners; dep.

Whitley Court   West Cliff Gdns, West Cliff, BH2 5HL ☎(0202) 551302.

Wrenwood   11 Florence Rd, Boscombe, BH5 1HH ☎(0202) 395086.
➟10 bedrs, 10 en suite, 1 ba; TV; tcf ♠ns; P 7; no children under 3 ✗LD 5, nr lunch. Resid lic

BOURTON-ON-THE-WATER   Glos.
Map 26C7

The Ridge   Whiteshoots, GL54 2LE ☎Cotswold (0451) 20660.
On A429, one mile south of Bourton towards Cirencester.
➟5 bedrs, 4 en suite, 1 ba; TV; tcf ♠TV, ns; P 10; children over 6 ✗Unlic
£ B&B £15–£20, B&B (double) £26–£35; D £8

BOX   Wiltshire.
Map 26B5

Hatt Farm   Old Jockey, Nr. Bath, SN14 9DJ ☎(0225) 742989. *Farm.* Mrs Carol Pope
Sleeps 4, ns ⌂
£ B&B from £12·50.

Saltbox Farm   Drewetts Mill, Corsham, SN14 9PT ☎(0225) 742608. *Farm.* Mary Gregory
Sleeps 4, ⌖ ns ⌂
£ B&B from £12·50

BOYLESTONE   Derbyshire.
Map 24C3

Lees Hall Farm   DE6 5AA ☎(0335) 330259. *Farm.* Mavis Wilson
Sleeps 4, ns ⌂
£ B&B from £12–£14

BRACEBRIDGE HEATH   Lincolnshire.
Map 24F5

The Manor House   Manor Farm, Lincoln, LN4 2HW ☎(0522) 520825. *Farm.* Mrs Jill Scoley
Sleeps 6
£ B&B from £12

BRADFORD-ON-AVON   Wiltshire.
Map 29E7

Widbrook Grange (Highly Acclaimed) Trowbridge Rd, BA15 1UH ☎(022 16) 475.

BRADLEY   Derbyshire.
Map 24C4

Common End Farm   Nr Ashbourne, DE6 1PL ☎(0335) 70356. *Farm.* Pat Howson
Sleeps 6, ns ⌂ (12)
£ B&B from £12·50, D £8

New Park Farm   Moorend, Ashbourne, DE6 1LQ
☎ (0335) 43425. *Farm*. Carol Akers   ♿
Sleeps 12, ns ⌖
£ B&B from £10·50–£13·50, D £7·50

Yeldersley Old Hall Farm   Yeldersley Lane,
Ashbourne, DE6 1PH ☎ (0335) 44505. *Farm*. Mrs
Janet Hinds
Sleeps 6, ns ⌖
£ B&B from £11–£13, D £7

BRADNOP   Staffordshire.   Map 24C4

Pool Hall Farm   Nr Leek, ST13 7LZ
☎ (0538) 382774. *Farm*. Barbara and Jim Clowes
Sleeps 6, ⼨ ns ⌖
£ B&B from £10–£12, D £6

BRAILES   Oxfordshire.   Map 26D8

New House Farm   Banbury, OX15 5BD
☎ (060875) 239. *Farm*. Helen Taylor
Sleeps 6, ⼨ ns ⌖ (2)
£ B&B from £12·50–£16, D £7

BRAILSFORD   Derbyshire.   Map 24C2

Shirley Hall Farm   Shirley, DE6 3AS
☎ (0335) 60346. *Farm*. Mrs Sylvia Foster
Sleeps 10, ns ⌖
£ B&B from £11, D £7

BRAMFIELD   Suffolk.   Map 25F1

Broad Oak Farm   Halesworth, IP19 9AB
☎ (098684) 232. *Farm*. Mrs Patricia Kemsley   ♿
Sleeps 6, ⌖ ⼨
£ B&B from £10, D £6

BRAMPTON   Cumbria.   Map 23A7

Oakwood Park (Highly Acclaimed)   Longtown Rd,
CA8 2AP ☎ (069 77) 2436.

*An imposing Victorian house set in 10 acres of
parkland 3 miles from Carlisle Airport. Take junction
43 off M6 to A69 Newcastle Rd. In Brampton turn
right, left onto A6071 Longtown Rd, and hotel is on
right. Tennis.*
🛏4 bedrs, 4 en suite, 1 ba; TV; tcf 📺 P 10; ns; child
facs ✕ LD 8.30, nr lunch. Resid & Rest lic
£ B&B £20, B&B (double) £30–£36; HB weekly
£126; D £8·50; [5% V] **cc** Access, B'card/Visa; dep.

Cracrop Farm   Kirkcambeck, CA8 2BW ☎ (069 78)
245. *Farm*. Marjorie Stobart
Sleeps 6, ns ⌖
£ B&B from £15, D £8

High Rigg   Walton, CA8 2AZ
☎ (069 77) 2117. *Farm*. Margaret Mounsey
Sleeps 6, ns ⌖
£ B&B from £10, D £6

Hullerbank   Talkin, CA8 1LB ☎ (069 76)
668. *Farm*. Sheila Stobbart
Sleeps 6, ⌖
£ B&B from £14·50–£15, D £8

BRANSCOMBE   Devon.   Map 29C4

Bulstone (Acclaimed)   Higher Bulstone, EX12 3BL
☎ (029 780) 446.
*From A3052 take turning signed Bulstone ¾ mile
(ignore all other turnings for Branscombe). Hotel is
near top of hill ¾ mile from junction. Open Feb–Nov.*
🛏12 bedrs, 6 en suite, 3 ba; tcf 📺 TV, dogs, ns;
P 30; child facs ✕ LD 7.30, nr lunch. Resid & Rest
lic
£ B&B £15–£24; HB weekly £183–£215; D £12; WB
£50; dep.

BRAUNTON   Devon.   Map 28F6

Denham   North Buckland, EX33 1HY
☎ (0271) 890297.
*Family-run beef farm of 60 acres close to several
beaches. Recently enlarged to provide further
accommodation. From Braunton on the A361 to
Ilfracombe take second left turn after Knowle village.*
🛏10 bedrs, 10 en suite; TV; tcf 📺 TV; P 10; child
facs ✕ LD 7, nr lunch. Rest lic
£ B&B (double) £34–£38; HB weekly £140–£150;
D £10

BREDONS NORTON   Gloucestershire.
                          Map 26B7

Home Farm   Tewkesbury, GL20 7HA ☎ (0684)
72322. *Farm*. Mike and Anne Meadows
Sleeps 6, ⼨ ⌖
£ B&B from £14–£16; D £9

BREDWARDINE   Hereford & Worcester
(Herefordshire).   Map 31D7

Bredwardine Hall (Highly Acclaimed)   HR3 6DB
☎ Moccas (098 17) 596.
*A charming mid-Victorian manor house set in its own
large wooded grounds close to the River Wye. From
Hereford take A438 Brecon/Hay-on-Wye Rd for 10
miles, turn left on B4352 Bredwardine/Hay-on-Wye
Rd, follow road for 1 ¾ miles over river bridge into
village centre. Open 1 Mar–30 Nov.*
🛏5 bedrs, 5 en suite; TV, tcf 📺ns; P 6; no children
under 10 ✕ LD 4.30, nr lunch

£ B&B £26–£28, B&B (double) £40–£44; HB weekly £198–£212; WB; [10% V]; dep.

Old Court Farm ☎(09817) 375. *Farm.* Sue Whittall
Sleeps 6, ☻
£ B&B from £12, D from £10

BRENDON Devon. Map 28G6

Millslade (Highly Acclaimed) ☎(05987) 322.

A fine 18th century house set in 9 acres of tranquil grounds. From Porlock Hill take the A39 for 7 miles. Turn left into Brendon Valley, and Millslade is at the far end of the valley. Fishing.
⊨6 bedrs, 5 en suite, 2 ba; TV; tcf 🛉TV, dogs; P 40, coach; child facs ✗LD 9.30. Resid & Rest lic
£ B&B £22, B&B (double) £36–£42; HB weekly £224–£434; D £10; WB £74 (3 nights HB)
cc Amex, B'card/Visa, Diners; dep.

BRIDESTOWE Devon. Map 28F4

Linden Glade EX20 4NS ☎(083 786) 236.
Take A30 from Okehampton towards Launceston. 1 ¾ miles past Bridestowe turn off on right. Open May–Sept.
⊨4 bedrs, 1 ba 🛉TV, ns; P 4; children over 10 ✗Breakfast only. Unlic
£ B&B £12

The Knole Farm Okehampton, EX20 4HA ☎(083 786) 241. *Farm.* Mavis Bickle
Sleeps 10, 🐎☻
£ B&B from £10–£12, D £6

Week Farm Okehampton, EX20 4HZ ☎(083786) 221. *Farm.* Margaret Hockridge ♿
Sleeps 16, 🐎☻
£ B&B from £12–£15, D £7·50–£9

BRIDGNORTH Shropshire. Map 31E8

Middleton Lodge Middleton Priors, WV16 6UR ☎(0746 34) 228 & 675.
Take the B4368 Bridgnorth to Ditton Priors, then follow signs to hotel. Closed Xmas & New Year.
⊨3 bedrs, 3 en suite; TV; tcf 🛉NS; P 4; no children under 12 ✗Breakfast only. Unlic
£ B&B £20–£25, B&B (double) £30–£40

BRIDGWATER Somerset. Map 29C6

Cokerhurst Farm 87 Wembdon Hill, TA6 7QA ☎(0278) 422330. *Farm.* Diana Chappell
Sleeps 6, ☻ ns
£ B&B from £15

BRIDLINGTON Humberside (North Humberside). Map 25A8

Bay Ridge (Acclaimed) Summerfield Rd, YO15 3LF ☎(0262) 673425.
Follow south along South Marine Drive, passing station and theatre. Take second right turn into Summerfield Rd.
⊨14 bedrs, 12 en suite, 1 ba; TV, tcf 🛉TV, dogs, ns; P 7, coach; child facs ✗LD 6 (9 Oct–Apr), nr lunch. Resid & Rest lic
£ B&B £15; HB weekly £120; D £6·50; WB £17·50 (HB); [10% V Sep–May]; dep.

Norton Lodge (Acclaimed) 123 Promenade, YO15 2QN ☎(0262) 673489.
⊨12 bedrs, 10 en suite, 1 ba; TV; tcf 🛉TV; P 7, U 1, coach ✗LD 5.30. Resid lic

Glencoe 43 Marshall Ave, YO15 2DT ☎(0262) 676818.
⊨16 bedrs, 4 en suite, 4 ba; tcf 🛉TV, dogs; coach; child facs ✗LD 7. Resid lic

Park View 9 Tennyson Av, YO15 2EH ☎(0262) 672140. *Close to north beach and leisure centre.*
⊨17 bedrs, 4 ba; TV; tcf 🛉TV, dogs; P 8, coach; child facs ✗LD 4, nr lunch. Resid & Rest lic
£ B&B £10–£11; D £4; [10% V]

BRIDPORT Dorset. Map 29C4

Britmead House (Acclaimed) 154 West Bay Road, DT6 4EG ☎(0308) 22941.

An elegant red brick detached house with a charming central staircase, and views over the garden. From Bridport follow signs for West Bay. Britmead is 700 yards south on the A35.
7 bedrs, 5 en suite, 1 ba; TV; tcf 🐾dogs, ns; P8; children over 5, child facs ✗LD5, nr lunch. Resid lic
£B&B £18·50–£26, B&B (double) £28–£40; HB weekly £155·75–£196; WB £22·75 (any 3 days); [10% V] **cc** Access, Amex, B'card/Visa, Diners; dep.

Church Ground Farm Salway Ash, DT6 5JD ✆(030 888) 282. *Farm.* Keith and Judy Lockyer Sleeps 10, ns ☎ (8)
£ B&B from £14–£16, D £8

BRIGHOUSE West Yorkshire. Map 24C7

🅿 🅿 **Grove Inn Motel** 281 Elland Rd, Brookfoot, HD6 2RG ✆(0484) 713049
Two-storied white-painted building, with motel-style bedrooms, in large garden and overlooking its own fishing and boating lake.

BRIGHTON East Sussex. Map 27B2

Adelaide (Highly Acclaimed) 51 Regency Sq, BN1 2FF ✆(0273) 205286 Fax: (0273) 220904.

Beautifully restored Grade II listed Regency building, modernised throughout. Hotel is located on the sea front opposite West Pier. Closed 24 Dec–15 Jan.
12 bedrs, 12 en suite, 1 ba; TV, tcf 🐾ns; child facs ✗LD8.30, nr lunch & Wed & Sun dinner. Resid lic
£B&B £33–£60, B&B (double) £55–£70; HB weekly £285–£290; WB £42·50; [10% V] **cc** Access, Amex, B'card/Visa, Diners.

Ascott House (Highly Acclaimed) 21 New Steine, Marine Parade, BN2 1PD ✆(0273) 688085.

Elegant Regency hotel situated close to Palace Pier. From the pier follow coast road east for 250 yards, and New Steine is on the left.
12 bedrs, 9 en suite, (2 sh), 1 ba; TV; tcf 🐾coach; no children under 3 ✗LD 6, nr lunch. Resid lic
£ B&B £22–£30, B&B (double) £46–£58 **cc** Access, Amex, B'card/Visa, Diners; dep.

Kempton House (Highly Acclaimed) 33 Marine Par, BN2 1TR ✆(0273) 570248.

Seafront Regency style hotel in a convervation area, with sea-facing patio garden. Turn left at Palace Pier roundabout onto Marine Parade, hotel 200 yards on left.
12 bedrs, 12 en suite; TV; tcf 🐾dogs; coach; child facs ✗Dinner by arrangement, nr lunch. Resid lic
£ B&B £30–£50, B&B (double) £40–£54; HB weekly £196–£245 **cc** Access, Amex, B'card/Visa, Diners, dep.

Allendale (Acclaimed) 3 New Steine, BN2 1PB ✆(0273) 675436

Family run Regency hotel, close to seafront and town. Take Marine Parade east from Palace Pier to the first garden square.
13 bedrs, 6 en suite, (2 sh), 2 ba; TV; tcf

ﬁns; coach; children over 7 ✕Breakfast only. Unlic
£ B&B £24–£27, B&B (double) £36–£56; WB £49 (3 nights incl Sun); [10% V Sun–Wed, Jan–Jun]
cc Access, Amex, B'card/Visa.

Amblecliff (Acclaimed)   35 Upper Rock Gdns, BN2 1QF ✆(0273) 681161.

Small, comfortable hotel in elegant Victorian building, recently refurbished. Take A23 to sea front, turn left, and left again at first traffic lights.
⋈11 bedrs, 7 en suite, 2 ba; TV; tcf ﬁTV, ns; P 3 (£1·50); children over 12 ✕Breakfast only. Resid lic
£ B&B £16–£30, B&B (double) £32–£48; [5% V Oct–May] cc Access, Amex, B'card/Visa; dep.

Andorra (Acclaimed)   15–16 Oriental Pl, BN1 2LJ ✆(0273) 21787.
Small elegant hotel in Grade II listed buildings, carefully restored. Two turnings past West Pier in the Hove direction.
⋈20 bedrs, 18 en suite, 1 ba; TV; tcf ﬁdogs; coach; child facs ✕nr lunch. Resid lic
£ B&B £18–£25; HB £126–£175; WB £36; [10% V] cc Access, B'card/Visa; dep.

Arlanda (Acclaimed)   20 New Steine, BN2 1PD ✆(0273) 699300.

200 year old listed Regency building. The first garden square about 400 metres east along Marine Parade.
⋈ 12 bedrs, 12 en suite; TV; tcf
ﬁcoach; child facs ✕LD 4, Resid lic
£B&B £30, B&B (double) £50–£60 cc Access, Amex, B'card/Visa, Diners; dep.

Cavalaire House (Acclaimed)   34 Upper Rock Gdns, BN2 1QF ✆(0273) 696899.
⋈9 bedrs, 2 en suite, (1 sh), 1 ba; TV; tcf
ﬁchildren over 10 ✕Breakfast only. Unlic

Gullivers (Acclaimed)   10 New Steine, BN2 1PB ✆(0273) 695415

Grade II listed Regency building, recently renovated and set in a Brighton seafront square. Towards the marina on the coast road, Gullivers is in the sixth turning past Palace Pier.
⋈9 bedrs, 5 en suite, 1 ba; TV; tcf
ﬁdogs, ns; coach ✕Breakfast only. Unlic
£ B&B £20–£36, B&B (double) £48–£54; [10% V except w/e] cc Access, B'card/Visa; dep.

Le Fleming's (Acclaimed)   12A Regency Sq, BN1 2FG ✆(0273) 27539.

Brighton (East Sussex)

Regency style listed building in period square, with accommodation on three floors. Situated on left of square opposite West Pier.
9 bedrs, 9 en suite; TV; tcf ⓕTV, dogs; coach; child facs ✗Breakfast only. Resid & Rest lic
£B&B £30–£45, B&B (double) £40–£55; WB (10% discount); [10% V] cc Access, Amex, B'card/Visa.

Malvern (Acclaimed)   33 Regency Sq, BN1 2GG
☎(0273) 24302.
Carefully modernised grade II listed Regency building, situated on the seafront opposite West Pier.
12 bedrs, 12 en suite, 1 ba; TV; tcf
✗LD 6, nr lunch, Sun dinner. Resid lic
£ B&B £30–£38, B&B (double) £44–£60; WB £75; [5% V] cc Access, Amex, B'card/Visa, Diners; dep.

Marina House (Acclaimed)   8 Charlotte St, Marine Par, BN2 1AG ☎(0273) 605349 & 679484.

Early Victorian building in Regency style set in Kemp Town area of Brighton. From Palace Pier roundabout take first left onto Marine Parade, then left again in ⅓ mile into Charlotte Street. Hotel on left.
10 bedrs, 7 en suite, 1 ba; TV; tcf ⓕTV; coach; child facs ✗LD 7. Resid & Rest lic
£B&B £12·50–£19, B&B (double) £24–£37; HB weekly £121–£163; L £5, D £7; WB; [10% V] cc Access, Amex, B'card/Visa, Diners.

New Steine (Acclaimed)   12A New Steine, Marine Par, BN2 1PB ☎(0273) 681546.
A small hotel in a quiet lawned square about 200 yards from Palace Pier. From A27 turn left by pier. Closed Dec & Jan.
11 bedrs, 4 en suite, (4 sh), 3 ba; TV, tcf ⓕTV, dogs, ns; children over 8 ✗Breakfast only. Unlic

£ B&B £14–£25, B&B (double) £32–£39; [5% V Feb, Mar, Oct mid-week]; dep.

Regency (Acclaimed)   28 Regency Sq, BN1 2FH
☎(0273) 202690 Fax: (0273) 220438.

Small family-run hotel in grade II listed building. Situated directly opposite the West Pier on north side of Regency Sq.
14 bedrs, 10 en suite, 1 ba; TV; tcf ⓕcoach; child facs ✗LD 5, nr lunch & Sat, Sun dinner
£ B&B £30–£37, B&B (double) £50–£60; HB weekly £210–£280; D £12·50; WB £40 (2 nights); [10% V for 3 nights] cc Access, Amex, B'card/Visa, Diners; dep.

Sutherland (Acclaimed)   9–10 Regency Sq, BN1 2FG ☎(0273) 27055 Fax: (0273) 779192.
Grade II listed building situated close to Conference Centre. Take first turning on right along the seafront past the Metropole Hotel into Preston St, which leads to Regency Sq.
26 bedrs, 20 en suite, (2 sh), 2 ba; TV, tcf ⓕlift, dogs, ns; coach; children over 12 ✗Dinner by arrangement. Resid lic
£ B&B £16–£38, B&B (double) £32–£80; WB; [5% V] cc Access, Amex, B'card/Visa, Diners; dep.

The Twenty One (Acclaimed)   21 Charlotte St, Marine Par, BN2 1AG ☎(0273) 686450.
Early Victorian townhouse off Marine Parade.
7 bedrs, 5 en suite, 1 ba; TV, tcf ⓕTV; children over 12 ✗LD previous day, nr lunch & Sun or Mon dinner. Resid lic
£ B&B £30–£45, B&B (double) £40–£65; [10% V w/d] cc Access, Amex, B'card/Visa; dep.

Trouville (Acclaimed)   11 New Steine, Marine Par, BN2 1PB ☎(0273) 697384.

Tastefully restored Regency hotel in a grade II listed building set in a seafront square. Situated off Marine Parade close to Palace Pier. Open Feb–Dec.
➽9 bedrs, 2 en suite, (2 sh), 2 ba; TV; tcf 📺TV; ns ✗Breakfast only. Resid lic
£ B&B £17, B&B (double) £30–42 cc Access, Amex, B'card/Visa; dep.

Ambassador 22 New Steine, Marine Parade, BN2 1PD ✆(0273) 676869.
Take Marine Parade opposite Palace Pier, turn left into New Steine and hotel is on right side of square.
➽9 bedrs, 9 en suite; TV; tcf 📺TV, ns; coach; child facs ✗Breakfast only. Unlic
£ B&B £23–£25, B&B (double) £40–£50; dep.
cc Access, Amex, B'card/Visa.

Downlands 19 Charlotte St, BN2 1AG
✆(0273) 601203

Fyfield House 26 New Steine, BN2 1PP ✆(0273) 602770.
At Palace Pier turn left into Marine Parade, and New Steine is first square on the left. Closed Xmas & New Year.
➽9 bedrs, 4 en suite, (1 sh), 1 ba; TV; tcf 📺TV, dogs; child facs ✗Breakfast only. Unlic
£ B&B £14–£23; WB (Jan & Feb); [10% V Jan–mid May] cc Access, Amex, B'card/Visa, Diners; dep.

Melford Hall 41 Marine Par, BN2 1PE
✆(0273) 681435.
Situated left at Palace Pier on the seafront. Closed Xmas.
➽12 bedrs, 10 en suite, 2 ba; TV; tcf 📺TV, ns; P 12; no children under 2; child facs ✗Breakfast only. Unlic
£ B&B £17–£32, B&B (double) £34–£50; [10% V]
cc Access, Amex, B'card/Visa, Diners; dep.

Paskins 19 Charlotte St, BN2 1AG ✆(0273) 601203
Hotel close to sea. Follow A23 to sea front, Charlotte Street is 500 yards to east.

Weekend breaks
Please consult the hotel for full details of weekend breaks; prices shown are an indication only. Many hotels offer mid week breaks as well.

Discount vouchers
RAC discount vouchers are at the end of the guide. Establishments with a [V] shown at the end of the price information will accept them in part payment for accommodation bills on the full, standard rate, not against bargain breaks or any other special offers. Please note the limitations shown in the entry: w/e for weekends, w/d for weekdays, and which months they are accepted.

➽18 bedrs, 16 en suite, 1 ba; TV; tcf 📺dogs; child facs ✗LD 9 am, nr lunch. Resid lic
£ B&B £15–£27·50, B&B (double) £27–£47·50; D £8 cc Access, B'card/Visa; dep.

Rowland House 21 St George's Terr, Marine Par, BN2 1JJ ✆(0273) 603639.
➽10 bedrs, (10 sh), 1 ba; TV; tcf 📺dogs; P 1, coach ✗Breakfast only. Resid lic
cc Access, B'card/Visa; dep.

BRIGSTEER Cumbria. Map 23A4

Low Plain Farm LA8 8AX ✆(044 88) 323.
Farm. Stella and John Dicker
Sleeps 6, 🐾 🛏
£ B&B from £10–£12·50, D £5

BRILL Buckinghamshire. Map 26E7

Poletrees Farm Nr Aylesbury, HP18 9TZ ✆(0844) 238276. *Farm.* Anita Cooper
Sleeps 4, ns
£ B&B from £14

BRIMPTON Berkshire. Map 26E5

Manor Farm Reading, RG7 4SQ ✆(0734) 713166. *Farm.* Jean Bowden
Sleeps 4/6, 🛏
£ B&B from £15–£17·50

BRISTOL Avon. Map 29D7

Alandale (Acclaimed) 4 Tyndall's Park Rd, Clifton ✆(0272) 735407.
Formerly a Victorian gentleman's residence now an elegant hotel facing the BBC studios. Set in the leafy suburb of Old Clifton just off the main A4015.
➽17 bedrs, 17 en suite; TV; tcf 📺dogs; P 10 ✗Breakfast only. Resid lic
£ B&B £35, B&B (double) £48; HB weekly 10% discount; [10% V w/e]

Glenroy (Acclaimed) Victoria Sq, Clifton BS8 4EW ✆(0272) 739058 Fax: (0272) 739058.

Detached early Victorian buildings forming part of a gracious Regency square with parkland in the centre. From the Clifton suspension bridge follow route to city centre, and Victoria Square is after 600 yards. Closed Xmas.

50 bedrs, 50 en suite; TV; tcf 🐕dogs; P 16, coach; child facs ✗nr lunch, Fri–Sun dinner. Resid lic
£ B&B £40, B&B (double) £52–£60; D £6; WB £23·50 (double pp, £35 single); [10% V] **cc** Access, B'card/Visa

Washington (Acclaimed)   11 St Paul's Rd, BS8 1LX ✆(0272)733980 Tx: 449075 Fax: (0272)741082.
St Pauls Rd is just off the traffic lights by the BBC studios on Whiteladies Rd. Closed 21 Dec–4 Jan.
43 bedrs, 29 en suite, 6 ba; TV; tcf 🐕dogs; P20, coach; child facs ✗Breakfast only. Resid & Rest lic
£ B&B £26–£45, B&B (double) £45–£61; [10% V w/e] **cc** Access, Amex, B'card/Visa, Diners.

Alcove   508 Fishponds Rd, Fishponds, BS16 3DT ✆(0272) 653886.
From M4 take junction 19 on to M32, exit junction 2, turn left to Fishponds. In 200 yards turn left again, and hotel is at second zebra crossing.
9 bedrs, 1 en suite, 4 ba; TV; tcf 🐕dogs; P 7, G 1, coach ✗Breakfast only. Resid lic
£ B&B £17–£25, B&B (double) £30–£36

Birkdale   10–11 Ashgrove Rd, Redland, BS6 6LY ✆(0272)733635

Cavendish House   18 Cavendish Rd, Henleaze, BS9 4DZ ✆(0272)621017.
Small hotel in a quiet side road. Situated 3 miles from junction 17 of the M5 towards city centre, near Clifton Downs.
8 bedrs, 2 ba; TV 🐕dogs, ns; P 5; child facs ✗Breakfast only. Unlic
£B&B £19, B&B (double) £34; dep.

Chesterfield   3 Westbourne Pl, BS8 1RZ ✆(0272) 734606 Tx: 449075 Fax: (0272) 741082.
On Queens Rd take turning immediately next to Victoria Rooms. Hotel is on left. Closed 2 wks Aug, Xmas & New Year.
13 bedrs, 3 ba; TV; tcf 🐕dogs; coach; child facs ✗Breakfast only. Unlic
£B&B £23, B&B (double) £38 **cc** Access, B'card/Visa.

Downlands   33 Henleaze Gdns, Henleaze, BS9 4HH ✆(0272)621639.
10 bedrs, 1 en suite, 2 ba; TV; tcf 🐕TV, dogs; child facs ✗Breakfast only. Unlic

Downs View   38 Upper Belgrave Rd, Clifton, BS8 2XN ✆(0272) 737046.
Follow signs to zoo from junction 17 of M5. Hotel is just before the zoo.
14 bedrs, 4 en suite, 2 ba; TV; tcf 🐕dogs ✗Breakfast only. Unlic
£ B&B £20–£22, B&B (double) £36–£38; [5% V]

Kingsley   93 Gloucester Rd North, Filton, BS12 7PT ✆(0272) 699947.
About 2 miles from junction 16 of the M5, on A38 in Filton near British Aerospace. Closed 25–31 Dec.
6 bedrs, 2 ba; TV; tcf 🐕P6; child facs ✗Breakfast only. Unlic
£ B&B £14, B&B (double) £27; dep.

Oakdene   45 Oakfield Rd, Clifton, BS8 2BA ✆(0272) 735900.
Off A4018 opposite BBC studios in Whiteladies Rd, Clifton. Closed Xmas & New Year.

Bristol (Avon)

Bristol (Avon)

14 bedrs, 7 en suite, 4 ba; TV; tcf 👪dogs; P 8; child facs ✕Breakfast only. Unlic
£ B&B £22–£28, B&B (double) £34–£40; [10% V w/e]; dep.

Oakfield   52–54 Oakfield Rd, BS8 2BG
☎(0272) 735556. *Hotel.*

Pembroke   13 Arlington Villas, St Paul's Rd, BS8 2EG ☎(0272) 735550. Tx: 449075
Fax: (0272) 741082
From Queens Rd turn right into Pembroke Rd then immediately right into Arlington Villas. Hotel is near the bottom on the left. Closed 2 wks Aug, Xmas & New Year.
14 bedrs, 3 ba; TV; tcf 👪dogs; coach; child facs ✕Breakfast only. Unlic
£ B&B £23, B&B (double) £38 **cc** Access, B'card/Visa.

Westbourne   40–44 St Pauls Rd, Clifton BS8 1LR
☎(0272) 734214

BRIXHAM   Devon.   Map 29A1

Fair Winds   New Rd, TQ5 8DA ☎(0803) 853564

Harbour View   65 King St, TQ5 9TH
☎(0803) 853052.
Former harbour master's house dating back to late 18th century, overlooking Brixham inner harbour.
10 bedrs, (4 sh), 3 ba; TV; tcf 👪P2 ✕LD4.30, nr lunch. Unlic
£ B&B £14·50–£15·50, B&B (double) £28–£33·50; HB weekly £143·50–£166·25 **cc** Access, B'card/Visa; dep.

Raddicombe Lodge   Kingswear Rd, TQ5 0EX
☎(0803) 882125.
A small hotel in its own grounds of lawns and garden overlooking the sea. Midway between Brixham and Dartmouth. Open May–Sept.
9 bedrs, 3 en suite, 2 ba; TV; tcf 👪P 10; child facs ✕Breakfast only
£ B&B £14·30–£25·40, B&B (double) £28·60–£40·60; [5% V May–Sep] **cc** Access, B'card/Visa; dep

Sampford House   57 King St, TQ5 9TH ☎(080 45) 7761.
Situated directly above the inner harbour, 50 yards from the coastguards building. Open Mar–mid-Nov.
6 bedrs, 2 ba; TV; tcf 👪TV, dogs, ns; P 3; child facs ✕LD 10am, nr lunch. Unlic
£ B&B £14, B&B (double) £28–£32; D £6·95; dep.

BROADSTAIRS   Kent.   Map 27F5

Bay Tree (Acclaimed)   12 Eastern Esplanade, CT10 1DR ☎Thanet (0843) 62502.
Well-appointed small hotel on sea front.
11 bedrs, 9 en suite, 1 ba; TV 👪ns; P 11, coach; children over 10 ✕LD 2, nr lunch. Resid lic
cc Access, Amex; dep.

Devonhurst   13 Eastern Esplanade, CT10 1DR
☎(0843) 63010
A family run hotel overlooking a sandy bay and the sea. Follow signs down main road for Bleak House.
9 bedrs, 7 en suite, (2 sh), 1 ba; TV; tcf 👪no children under 5 ✕LD 6.30, nr lunch. Resid lic
£ B&B (double) £33–£41; HB weekly £140–£160; [10% V Sep–May] **cc** Access, Amex, B'card/Visa, Diners; dep.

East Horndon 4 Eastern Esplanade, CT10 1DP
☎ Thanet (0843) 68306.
*A small hotel in a quiet position overlooking the sea.
Situated on the sea front.* Open Mar–Nov.
🛏 11 bedrs, 4 en suite, 2 ba; TV; tcf 🐕dogs; child
facs ✗LD 5, nr lunch. Resid & Rest lic
£ B&B £15; HB weekly £125; D £6·50 **cc** Access,
Amex, B'card/Visa; dep.

Merriland The Vale, CT10 1RB ☎ (0843) 61064.
Guest House.

Rothsay 110 Pierremont Av, CT10 1NT ☎ (0843)
62646 & 602397.
*Seaside hotel 2 mins walk from town centre and
Viking Bay. Turn right off High St into Queens Rd
(by Nat West Bank), turn right after 200 yards. Hotel
is situated on corner.*
🛏 12 bedrs, 12 en suite; TV; tcf 🐕TV, dogs, ns;
coach; child facs ✗LD 10.30. Resid & Rest lic
£ B&B £20–22; L £7, D £8·50; WB; [5% V w/d]
cc Access, B'card/Visa; dep.

Sunnydene 10 Chandos Rd, CT10 1QP ☎ Thanet
(0843) 63347.
*Small hotel with sea views adjacent to the beach.
Opposite Viking Bay, next to Chandos Sq.*
🛏 9 bedrs, 2 ba; TV; tcf 🐕ns; no children
under 3 ✗LD 6, nr lunch. Resid lic
£ B&B £14–£16; HB weekly £117–£130 **cc** B'card/
Visa; dep.

White House 59 Kingsgate Av, CT10 3LW
☎ Thanet (0843) 63315.
*Large white walled house with its own large garden.
From Kingsgate on B2052 take road opposite
nurseries to sea. Hotel on left, between Broadstairs
and Cliftonville.*
🛏 9 bedrs, 4 en suite, 1 ba; TV 🐕TV; P8, coach;
child facs ✗LD6, nr lunch. Resid lic
£ B&B £18–£25·50, B&B (double) £32–£42; HB
weekly £135–£166·25; WB (2 nights B&B £32, 2
nights HB £46); [5% V Jan–Jun, mid Sep–Xmas]
cc Access, B'card/Visa; dep.

BROADSTONE Dorset. Map 26C2

Fairlight (Acclaimed) 1 Golf Links Rd, BH18 8BE
☎ (0202) 694316.
*Edwardian hotel standing in its own grounds in a
peaceful setting near the golf course. From
Wimborne by-pass follow signs to Poole, then local
signs to Broadstone. At roundabout take sports
centre exit (Station Approach), first right into Moor
Rd, then first left into Golf Links Rd. Hotel is on the
left.*
🛏 10 bedrs, 7 en suite, 1 ba 🐕TV, dogs, ns; P8;
child facs ✗LD 7.30, nr lunch. Resid & Rest lic
£ B&B £26–£29, B&B (double) £40–£46; HB weekly
£196–£238; D £15·50; WB (£40 B&B, £80 HB)
cc Access, B'card/Visa; dep.

BROADWAY Hereford & Worcester
(Worcestershire). Map 26C7

Leasow House (Highly Acclaimed) Laverton
Meadows, WR12 7NA ☎ (0386) 73526
Fax: (0386) 73596.

*Grade II listed farmhouse set in quiet countryside
3 miles from Broadway village. From Broadway take
B4632 to Cheltenham, turn right to Wormington and
Dumbleton, and farm is first on left.*
🛏 7 bedrs, 7 en suite; TV; tcf 🐕dogs, ns; P 10;
child facs ✗Breakfast only. Unlic
£ B&B (double) £42–£52; [5% V] **cc** Amex, B'card/
Visa; dep.

Old Rectory (Highly Acclaimed) Church Street,
Willersey, WR12 7PM ☎ (0386) 853729.

*Tudor House in walled garden opposite church.
Take B4632 from Broadway for 1½ miles into
Willersey, turn right into Church St at the Bell Inn,*
Open mid-Jan–mid-Dec.
🛏 6 bedrs, 6 en suite; TV; tcf 🐕ns; P 8, G 2: no
children under 12 ✗Breakfast only. Unlic
£ B&B £49–£85, B&B (double) £59–£95; WB (Nov–
Mar); [10% V w/d] **cc** Access, B'card/Visa; dep

Whiteacres (Acclaimed) Station Rd, WR12 7DE
☎ (0386) 852320.
*A late Victorian house with white exterior and black
oak panels on gable ends. Situated at the junction
of A44 and B4632.* Open Mar–Oct.
🛏 6 bedrs, 6 en suite; TV; tcf 🐕ns; P 6; no children
under 12 ✗Breakfast only. Unlic
£ B&B (double) £36; [10% V Mar–May]

Olive Branch 78 High St, WR12 7AJ
☎ (0386) 853440. Closed Xmas & New Year
🛏 9 bedrs, 5 en suite, 2 ba; TV, tcf 🐕TV, ns; P9,
coach; child facs ✗Breakfast only. Unlic
£ B&B £17·50, B&B (double) £32; [5% V]; dep.

BROAD WOODKELLY   Devon.   Map 28F4

Middlecott Farm   Winkleigh, EX19 8DZ ☎(0837) 83381. *Farm.* June Western
Sleeps 6, ♒ ⛎
£ B&B from £10–£12, D £6

BROCKENHURST   Hampshire.   Map 26D2

The Cottage (Highly Acclaimed)   Sway Rd, SO4 7SH ☎Lymington (0590) 22296.

Delightfully converted forest cottage with oak beams. Follow A337 from Lyndhurst, turn right into Grigg Lane. Continue to crossroads, carry straight over and hotel is 100 yards on right of Sway Rd.
🛏6 bedrs, 6 en suite; TV; tcf 📺ns; P 11; coach; children over 16 ✗LD 9.30. Rest lic
£B&B £38–£40, B&B (double) £58–£64; HB weekly £275–£295; L £5, D £12·50; WB £72 (Nov–Mar)
cc Access, B'card/Visa; dep.

BROMBOROUGH   Merseyside.   Map 30D7

Dresden   866 New Chester Rd, L62 7HF ☎051-334 1331 & 1353.
Family run hotel with Swiss owners. From Liverpool Tunnel take A41 to Bromborough, and hotel is on Eastham side. Open 5 Mar–15 Feb.
🛏6 bedrs, 2 en suite, 2 ba; tcf 📺TV, dogs; P 20, coach; child facs ✗LD 9.30, nr all Mon & Sun dinner. Resid & Rest lic
£B&B £22·50, B&B (double) £39·50; HB weekly £180–£199; L £6, D £7·50; dep.

BROMLEY   Kent.   Map 27B5

Grianan   23 Orchard Rd, BR1 2PR ☎081-460 1795.
Villa St. Philomena   1 Lansdowne Rd ☎081-460 6311.
Lansdowne Rd is off Plaistow Lane, 2 mins walk from Sundridge Park Station.
🛏18 bedrs, 2 en suite, (3 sh), 5 ba; TV 📺TV; P 6, coach

BROOKTHORPE   Gloucestershire.   Map 26B7

Gilbert's   Gilbert's Lane, Nr Gloucester, GL4 0UH ☎(0452) 812364. *Farm.* Jenny Beer
Sleeps 6, ns ⛎
£ B&B from £19

BROSELEY   Shropshire.   Map 31A8

Cumberland   Jackson Av, TF12 5NB ☎Telford (0952) 882301.

BROWSTON   Norfolk.   Map 25F2

Manor Farm Cottage   Great Yarmouth, NR3 9DP ☎(0493) 604557. *Farm.* Mrs J P Hodgkin   ♿
Sleeps 6, ⛎ ns
£ B&B from £13·50

BRUNDISH   Suffolk.   Map 27E8

Woodlands Farm   Nr Woodbridge IP13 8BP ☎(037 984) 444/520. *Farm.* Jill Graham
Sleeps 6, ns ⛎
£ B&B from £13, D £8

BRUTON   Somerset.   Map 29D6

Fryerning (Highly Acclaimed)   Burrowfield Frome Rd, BA10 0HH ☎(0749) 812343

BUCKFAST   Devon.   Map 28G3

Black Rock (Acclaimed)   Buckfast Rd, TQ11 0EA ☎Buckfastleigh (0364) 42343.
Hotel signed from A38 to Buckfast Abbey. Fishing.
🛏10 bedrs, 8 en suite, 2 ba; TV; tcf 📺TV, dogs, ns; P 50; child facs ✗LD 10
£B&B £20; HB weekly £175; L £7, D £10; [10% V]
cc Access, B'card/Visa; dep.

BUCKFASTLEIGH   Devon.   Map 28G3

Rockfield House (Acclaimed)   Station Rd, TQ11 0BU ☎(0364) 43602.
🛏5 bedrs, 2 en suite, 1 ba; TV; tcf 📺dogs; P 5; children over 12 ✗LD 5, nr lunch. Resid lic

Dartbridge Manor   Dartbridge Rd ☎(0364) 43575
🛏10 bedrs, 10 en suite ✗Breakfast only
£B&B £15; WB

Royal Oak   59 Jordan St, TQ11 0AX ☎(0364) 43611.
🛏5 bedrs, 2 en suite, 2 ba; tcf 📺TV, dogs; child facs ✗LD 4.30, nr lunch. Resid lic

Wellpark Farm Bungalow   Dean Prior, TQ11 0LY ☎(0364) 43775. *Farm.* Mrs Rosemarie Palmer
Sleeps 6 + 6 cot, ns ⛎
£ B&B from £11

BUCKNELL   Shropshire.   Map 31B7

Bucknell House   SY7 0AD ☎(054 74) 248. *Farm.* Peter and Brenda Davies
♒ ⛎ (12)
£ B&B from £13·50

The Hall SY7 0AA ☎(054 74) 249. *Farm.* Mrs Christine Price
Sleeps 6, ns ⛄ (7)
£ B&B from £12, D £7

BUDE Cornwall. Map 28E4

Pencarrol 21 Downs View, EX23 8RF
☎(0288) 352478.
Enter Bude from A39, and follow signs from town centre to Crooklets Beach. Downs View is opposite beach car park exit.
⛱8 bedrs, 1 en suite, 2 ba; TV; tcf ℻TV, dogs, P 1; child facs ✖LD 5, nr lunch. Unlic
£ B&B £11–£15; HB weekly £114–£127·50; WB; [5% V]; dep.

BUDLEIGH SALTERTON Devon.
Map 29B4

Long Range (Acclaimed) Vales Rd, EX9 6HS
☎(039 54) 3321.
Attractive, seaside villa hotel with its own garden. Leave Budleigh Salterton on Sidmouth road, and 800 yards from the seafront turn right into Raleigh Rd, and right into Vales Rd. Open Mar–Oct.
⛱7 bedrs, 7 en suite; TV; tcf ℻TV, ns; P 6, U 2 (£1); children over 4 ✖LD 7, nr lunch. Resid & Rest lic
£ B&B 19·50; HB weekly £175; D £9·50

Tidwell House (Acclaimed) Knowle, EX9 7AG
☎(039 54) 2444.
⛱9 bedrs, 7 en suite, 3 ba; tcf ℻TV, dogs; P 20, U 1, G 3; child facs ✖LD 9, nr lunch. Resid & Rest lic

BUDOCK Cornwall. Map 28C2

Higher Kergilliack Falmouth, TR11 5PB ☎(0326) 72271. *Farm.* Jean Pengelly
Sleeps 6, 🐴 ⛄
£ B&B from £12–£15, D £8

BULPHAN Essex. Map 27C6

Bonny Downs Farmhouse Doesgate Lane, Nr Upminster, RM14 3TB ☎(0268) 542129. *Farm.* Rose Newman ♿
Sleeps 6, ns ⛄
£ B&B from £14–£18, D £8

BURFORD Oxfordshire. Map 26C6

🍷 🍷 **Maytime Inn** Asthall, OX8 4HW ☎(099 382) 2068
A centuries-old, Cotswold-stone inn in the little village of Asthall off A40. ☂ Fr
⛱2 bedrs, 2 en suite; annexe 4 bedrs, 4 en suite, TV; tcf ℻dogs; P 100, coach; child facs ✖LD 10
£ B&B £35; B&B (double) £48; L £12·50, D £12·50; WB £62·50 (HB) **cc** Access, Amex, B'card/Visa.

BURNESIDE Cumbria. Map 22F3

Garnett House Farm Kendal, LA9 5SF ☎(0539) 724542. *Farm.* Mrs Sylvia Beaty
Sleeps 10, ⛄
£ B&B from £11–£11·50, D £5·50

Low Hundhowe Farm Kendal, LA8 9AB ☎(0539) 722060. *Farm.* Marjorie Hoggarth
Sleeps 6, ⛄
£ B&B from £11·50, D £6

BURNT YATES North Yorkshire. Map 24D8

🍷 🍷 **Bay Horse Inn** HG3 3EJ ☎Harrogate (0423) 770230
Attractive Georgian coaching inn with motel-type bedrooms adjoining.
⛱6 bedrs, 6 en suite; annexe 10 rooms, 10 en suite; TV, tcf ℻dogs; P 70, coach; child facs ✖LD 9.30; bar meals only Mon–Sat lunch
£ B&B £35–£38, B&B (double) £50–£55; HB weekly £250–£275; L £8·95; D £12·95; WB £65; [5% V w/d]
cc Access, Amex, B'card/Visa.

Buckfast (Devon) ___

BURSCOUGH   Lancashire.   Map 30C7

Brandreth Barn   Brandreth Farm, Tarlscough Lane, Nr Ormskirk, LH0 0RJ ✆(0704) 893510
Farm. Mrs M Wilson   &
Sleeps 14, ❧ ns
£ B&B from £28·75, D £8

BURTON-UPON-TRENT   Staffordshire.
Map 24C3

Delter (Acclaimed)   5 Derby Rd, DE14 1RU
✆(0283) 35115.
🛏5 bedrs, 5 en suite; TV; tcf � TV; P 5; child facs ✗ LD 9.30, nr Sat & Sun dinner. Resid lic
cc Access.

BURWASH   East Sussex.   Map 27C3

Admiral Vernon   Etchingham Rd, TN19 7BJ
✆(0435) 882230.
Situated on A265 at east end of Burwash, 4 miles from Hurst Green.
🛏7 bedrs, 1 ba; TV; tcf �TV, dogs; P 24, U 1, G 1, coach; children over 10 ✗ LD 8.45
£ B&B £22, B&B (double) £35; HB weekly £115; L £7, D £12; [10% V]; dep.

BURY ST EDMUNDS   Suffolk.   Map 27D8

Olde White Hart (Acclaimed)   35 Southgate St, IP33 2AZ ✆(0284) 755547.

A grade II listed Tudor building with many exposed beams, once a public house. From the A45 take

---

En suite rooms
En suite rooms may be bath or shower rooms. If you have a preference, remember to state it when booking a room.

Using RAC discount vouchers
Please tell the hotel when booking if you plan to use an RAC discount voucher (see end of guide) in part payment of your bill. Only one voucher will be accepted per party per stay. Discount vouchers will only be accepted in payment for accommodation, not for food.

---

the Bury St Edmunds (east) exit to the town centre. On the next roundabout take the last exit (unmarked) into Southgate St. Hotel is 300 metres on right.
🛏10 bedrs, 10 en suite; TV; tcf �ns; P 10; child facs ✗ Breakfast only. Resid lic
£ B&B £34–£38, B&B (double) £44–£48
cc Access, Amex, B'card/Visa; dep.

BURYAS BRIDGE   Cornwall.   Map 28B1

Rose Farm   Chyanhal, Penzance, TR19 6AN
✆(0736) 731808. *Farm.* Mrs Penny Lally
Sleeps 6, ❧
£ B&B from £16–£17·50

BUSHTON   Wiltshire.   Map 26C5

Smiths Farm   Swindon, SN4 7PX
✆(0793) 731285. *Farm.* Dee Freeston
Sleeps 6, 🐕 ❧
£ B&B from £13

BUSLINGTHORPE   Lincolnshire.   Map 25A5

East Farm House   Middle Rasen Road, Market Rasen, LN3 5AQ ✆(0673) 842283. *Farm.* Mrs Gill Grant
Sleeps 6, ❧ 🐕
£ B&B from £14, D £7

BUXTON   Derbyshire.   Map 24C5

Brookfield Hall (Highly Acclaimed)   Long Hill SK17 6SU ✆(0298) 24151
Victorian house with large, well-decorated rooms and period furniture set in 10 acres of gardens and woodland. 1 mile out of Buxton on A5004. Riding.
🛏4 bedrs, 4 en suite ✗ dinner Fri–Sun; other meals by arrangement only
£ B&B £35, B&B (double) £55; D £12

Thorn Heyes (Highly Acclaimed)   137 London Rd, SK17 9NW ✆(0298) 23539.
A stone built, former gentleman's residence set in its own attractive gardens. The elegant Victorian hotel has a private house atmosphere. Situated on the London Rd. Closed 2 wks Nov.
🛏11 bedrs, 10 en suite; (1 sh); TV; tcf �dogs, ns; P 12; no children ✗ LD 6, nr lunch & Tue dinner. Resid & Rest lic
£ B&B £17·50, B&B (double) £35; HB weekly £168; D £10; dep.

Westminster (Highly Acclaimed)   21 Broad Walk, SK17 6JR ✆(0298) 23929.

Period building in quiet position overlooking Pavilion Gardens. Open Feb–Nov & Xmas.
📧12 bedrs, 12 en suite; TV; tcf 🛏ns; P 12, coach; child facs ✕LD 3.30, nr lunch Wed dinner. Resid lic
£ B&B £22, B&B (double) £36; HB weekly £165; D £7·50–£8 **cc** Access, Amex, B'card/Visa; dep.

Netherdale (Acclaimed)   16 Green Lane, SK17 9DP ☎ (0298) 23896.

A renovated Edwardian house in a residential area within easy reach of Pooles Cavern Country Park and Buxton town centre. From the Market Place head towards Ashbourne to the London Rd traffic lights, take second right and Netherdale is 300 yards along the road. Snooker. Closed Dec & Jan.
📧10 bedrs, 7 en suite, (1 sh), 1 ba; TV; tcf
🛏ns; P 12, G1 ✕LD 10 am, nr lunch
£ B&B £15–£17·50; HB weekly £165–£186; [10% V Apr, May, Oct, Nov]; dep.

Old Hall (Acclaimed)   The Square, SK17 6BD
☎ (0298) 22841 Fax: (0298) 72437.
📧37 bedrs, 32 en suite, 2 ba; TV; tcf 🛏lift, TV, dogs, ns; coach; child facs ✕LD 10.30
cc Access, Amex, B'card/Visa.

Buxton Lodge   28 London Rd, SK17 9NX
☎ (0298) 23522.
Small, family run hotel on the A515 Buxton to Ashbourne Rd, 5 mins from the town centre.
📧7 bedrs, 3 en suite, 2 ba; TV; tcf 🛏TV, dogs, ns; P 4; child facs ✕LD 6, nr lunch. Resid lic
£ B&B £16·50–£24·50, B&B (double) £29–£33; HB weekly £157·50–£171·50; [5% V Oct–Mar, Mon–Fri]; dep.

Buxton View   74 Corbar Rd, SK17 6RJ ☎ (0298) 79222.
Stone built house in a pleasant garden with a commanding view. From Buxton Pavilion Gardens

*take Whaley Bridge Rd for 300 yards, then second
turning on right into Corbar Rd.* Open Mar–Nov.
⊨5 bedrs, 5 en suite; TV; tcf 🏠TV, dogs, ns; P 5,
G2; child facs ✗LD 7, nr lunch. Unlic
£B&B £20, B&B (double) £32; D £9; dep.

Hawthorn Farm Fairfield Rd, SK17 7ED ✆(0298)
23230.
*Situated on the A6 Manchester–Stockport road,
adjoining High Peak golf course.* Open Apr–Oct.
⊨12 bedrs, 2 ba; tcf 🏠TV dogs; P 12; child facs
✗Breakfast only. Unlic
£B&B £14–£15; [10% V]; dep.

Swanleigh 7 Grange Rd, SK17 6NH ✆(0298)
24588.
*Family guest house in a quiet but central location.
From market place turn left into South Avenue and
right into Grange Rd. Hotel is on the left.*
⊨7 bedrs, 2 ba; TV; tcf 🏠TV, ns; P 4 ✗Breakfast
only. Unlic
£B&B £13–£15; dep.

High House Foxlow Farm, SK17 9LE ✆(0298)
24219. *Farm.* Tina Heathcote
Sleeps 4, ⛺ (5)
£ B&B from £14, D £9

BUXWORTH Derbyshire.   Map 24B5

Cote Bank Farm via Whaley Bridge, SK12 7NP
✆(0663) 750566. *Farm.* Pamela Broadhurst
Sleeps 4, ns ⛺ (6)
£ B&B from £14–£15·50

CALDBECK Cumbria.   Map 22F6

High Greenrigg House (Highly Acclaimed) CA7
8HD ✆(06998) 430.
*Carefully restored 17th-century farmhouse at foot of
Caldbeck Fells. From Caldbeck village take B5299
west for three miles. Turn off where signposted
'Greenhead, Branthwaite, Fellside'. Hotel in half a
mile.*
⊨8 bedrs, 6 en suite, 1 ba 🏠TV, dogs, ns; P 8;
child facs ✗LD noon, nr lunch. Resid & Rest lic
£ B&B £19·50–£24·50; HB weekly £177–£207;
D £10; dep.

Park End (Highly Acclaimed) CA7 8HH ✆(069 98)
494
⊨3 bedrs, 3 en suite; TV; tcf

Swaledale Watch Whelpo, CA7 8HQ ✆(069 98)
409.
⊨3 bedrs, 1 ba; tcf 🏠TV, ns; P 12; child facs
✗LD 2, nr lunch. Unlic

CAMBERLEY Surrey.   Map 26F5

Camberley 116 London Rd, GU15 3TJ. ✆(0276)
24410.
⊨6 bedrs, (4 sh), 2 ba; TV 🏠TV; P 8; child facs
✗Breakfast only. Unlic

CAMBORNE Cornwall.   Map 28C2

Lowenac (Highly Acclaimed) Bassett Rd, TR14
8SL ✆(0209) 719295.

⊨5 bedrs, 5 en suite; TV; tcf 🏠dogs; P 70, U 3,
coach; child facs ✗Bar meals only lunch

CAMBRIDGE Cambridgeshire.   Map 27B8

Cambridge Lodge (Highly Acclaimed) 139
Huntingdon Rd, CB3 0DQ ✆(0223) 352833
Fax: (0223) 355166.
*Attractive mock-Tudor Edwardian house,
charmingly furnished. Situated in lovely gardens. On
A1307 Huntingdon road just north of the city.*
⊨11 bedrs, 8 en suite, (3sh), 1 ba; TV; tcf
🏠dogs, ns; P 24; child facs ✗LD 9.45, nr Sat
lunch. Resid & Rest lic
£ B&B £45–£55, B&B (double) £60–£90; L £14·95,
D £19·95; WB £30 (B&B) **cc** Access, Amex, B'card/
Visa, Diners.

Lensfield (Highly Acclaimed) 53 Lensfield Rd,
CR2 1GH ✆(0223) 355017 Tx: 818183
Fax: (0223) 312022.
*Small and friendly family run hotel, centrally situated
with easy access to colleges.* Closed Xmas & New
Year.
⊨36 bedrs, 32 en suite, (4 sh), 2 ba; TV; tcf
🏠TV; P 5, coach; child facs ✗nr lunch
£ B&B £30–£40, B&B (double) £48–£50; D £7
cc Access, Amex, B'card/Visa, Diners; dep.

Bon Accord (Acclaimed) 20 St Margaret's Sq,
CB1 4AP ✆(0223) 411188 and 246468.
*Small family run guest house in a quiet cul-de-sac
about 1 ½ miles from city centre. From junction 11
of the M11 turn right onto Cambridge ring road. At
second roundabout turn left, then third on left.*

12 bedrs, 1 en suite, 3 ba; TV, tcf NS; P 12, G 2; child facs Breakfast only. Unlic
£ B&B £18–£26, B&B (double) £30–£38
cc Access, B'card/Visa; dep.

Suffolk House (Acclaimed)   69 Milton Rd, CB4 1XA (0223) 352016.

Tudor style hotel, family run and with its own secluded garden. Situated on the A1309, which is off the A10.
8 bedrs, 8 en suite; TV; tcf TV, ns; P 10; no children under 6 nr lunch, Sat, Sun dinner. Resid & Rest lic
£ B&B £45, B&B (double) £55 cc Access, B'card/Visa; dep.

Centennial   63–69 Hills Rd, CB2 1PG (0223) 314652 Tx: 817019.
Family-run hotel opposite botanical gardens. On southern side of the city, close to station. On A1307.
26 bedrs, 21 en suite, 4 ba; TV; tcf

TV; P 28, coach; child facs LD 10
£ B&B £42, B&B (double) £46–£55; HB weekly £238–£269; L £8, D £11 cc Access, Amex, B'card/Visa, Diners; dep.

CAMELFORD   Cornwall.   Map 28D4

Countryman   7 Victoria Rd, PL32 9XA (0840) 212250.
11 bedrs, 2 en suite, (3 sh), 2 ba; TV; tcf TV, dogs; P 16, coach; child facs LD 7. Resid & Rest lic

Warmington House   32 Market Pl, PL32 9PD (0840) 213380.
6 bedrs, (2 sh), 1 ba; TV; tcf P 8, coach; child facs LD 9.45. Resid & Rest lic
cc Access, B'card/Visa; dep.

CANNINGTON   Somerset.   Map 29C6

Blackmore Farm   Bridgwater, TA5 2NE (0278) 653442. *Farm.* Mrs Ann Dyer
Sleeps 6, ns
£ B&B from £14

CANTERBURY   Kent.   Map 27E5

Ebury (Highly Acclaimed)   65 New Dover Rd, CT1 3DX (0227) 768433 Fax: (0227) 459187.

A fine Victorian building with many original features preserved or restored, standing in its own grounds. Leave Canterbury following signs for Dover (A2) and hotel is on left. Indoor swimming pool. Open Jan 14–Dec 24.
➨ 15 bedrs, 15 en suite; TV; tcf 🛏️TV, dogs, ns; P 23; child facs ✕LD 8.30, nr lunch & Sun dinner. Resid & Rest lic
£ B&B £35–£37, B&B (double) £50–£58; HB weekly £200–£220; D £10; WB £60 (double 2 nights); [5% V w/d] **cc** Access, Amex, B'card/Visa, dep.

Thanington (Highly Acclaimed)   140 Wincheap CT1 3RY ✆(0227) 453227.

Tudor style building with modern extension and patio. In Canterbury follow signs for Dover, and hotel is located 200 yards past traffic lights. From the south the hotel is on the main Canterbury approach, about 400 yards before the city walls. Open Jan–6 Nov.
➨ 14 bedrs, 11 en suite, (2 sh), 1 ba; TV 🛏️ns; P 11, U 1 (£5) ✕Breakfast only. Resid lic
£ B&B £39–£47·50, B&B (double) £47·50–£54; [5% V mid Sept–June when open]

Abba   Station Rd West, CT2 8AN ✆(0227) 464771 Fax: (0233) 720758.
Hotel is situated 3 mins walk from Canterbury West station.
➨ 19 bedrs, 3 en suite, (1 sh), 4 ba; tcf 🛏️TV, dogs, ns; P 7, coach; child facs ✕LD 9.45. Resid lic
£ B&B £17·50–£20, B&B (double) £30–£40; HB weekly £150–£170; L £5·75, D £11·25; dep.

Alexandra House   1 Roper Rd, CT2 7EH ✆(0227) 767011.
A quiet family run guest house in the centre of Canterbury. Situated near Westgate Towers, off St Dunstan's Street.
➨ 9 bedrs, (4 sh), 2 ba; TV; tcf 🛏️TV, dogs, ns; P 6, coach; child facs ✕Breakfast only. Unlic
£ B&B £14–£16, B&B (double) £28–£34; [5% V]; dep.

A Grade II listed Georgian building built in 1810 as a farmhouse with a top floor added in 1830. New additions have recently been made. Situated on the A28 Canterbury–Ashford Rd 12–15 mins walk from the cathedral.
➨ 10 bedrs, 10 en suite; TV; tcf 🛏️TV, dogs; P 10 ✕Breakfast only. Unlic
£ B&B £42–£48, B&B (double) £50–£55
cc Access, B'card/Visa.

Ersham Lodge (Acclaimed)   12 New Dover Rd, CT1 3AP ✆(0227) 463174 Fax: (0227) 455482.

Castle Court   8 Castle St, CT1 2QF ✆(0227) 463441.
➨ 12 bedrs, 2 ba 🛏️TV, dogs, ns; P 2; coach ✕Breakfast only. Unlic
£ B&B £15–£18, B&B (double) £26–£30; [10% V Nov–Mar] **cc** Access, B'card/Visa; dep.

Canterbury (Kent)

Highfield Summer Hill, CT2 8NH ☎ (0227) 462772.
A gracious house set in an acre of attractive gardens one mile from the city centre. Entering Canterbury from London direction, hotel is on the right just before the first roundabout. Open Feb–Nov.
⊨8 bedrs, 3 en suite, 2 ba; tcf ♠P10; children over 5 ✗ Breakfast only. Resid lic
£ B&B £22–£24, B&B (double) £32–£47
cc Access, B'card/Visa; dep.

Pointers 1 London Rd, CT2 8LR ☎ (0227) 456846.
Hotel is situated at the junction of St Dunstan's Church, London Rd and Whitstable Rd, facing down to Westgate Towers. Closed 25 Dec–mid Jan.
⊨14 bedrs, 8 en suite, (2 sh), 2 ba; tcf ♠dogs; P10, coach; child facs ✗LD 8.15, nr lunch. Resid & Rest lic
£ B&B £28–£35, B&B (double) £40–£52; HB weekly £168–£217, D£12; WB (£48); [10% V Nov–Jun]
cc Access, Amex, B'card/Visa, Diners; dep.

CARBIS BAY Cornwall. Map 28B2

Tregorran Headland Rd, TR26 2NU ☎ Penzance (0736) 795889.
Spanish style hotel overlooking beaches. Follow St Ives/Carbis Bay signs, and turn right for Carbis Bay beach. Headland Rd is the last turning on the right before beach. Swimming pool, snooker, solarium, gymnasium. Open Easter–Oct.
⊨15 bedrs, 9 en suite, (2 sh), 3 ba; tcf ♠TV, dogs; P20, coach; child facs ✗LD 7.30. Resid lic
£ B&B £13·50–£30; D £6; WB (£15); [5% V]; dep.

White House The Valley, TR26 2QY ☎ Penzance (0736) 797405.
Hotel built around former 18th century Cornish mining cottage with superb seaviews through Brunel viaduct. In Carbis Bay follow signs to beach, cross railway bridge, and hotel is in valley on the left. Closed Nov.
⊨10 bedrs, 10 en suite; tcf ♠TV; P10; child facs ✗LD 8. Resid & Rest lic
£ B&B £18–£25, B&B (double) £30–£40; HB weekly £213·75–£216; D £8; WB; dep.

Please tell the manager if you chose your hotel through an advertisement in the guide.

Using RAC discount vouchers
Please tell the hotel when booking if you plan to use an RAC discount voucher (see end of guide) in part payment of your bill. Only one voucher will be accepted per party per stay. Discount vouchers will only be accepted in payment for accommodation, not for food.

CARLISLE Cumbria. Map 22F6

Angus (Acclaimed) 14 Scotland Rd, Stanwix, CA3 9DG ☎ (0228) 23546.
A cosy Victorian terrace building standing on the site of Hadrians Wall. Leave the M6 at junction 44 and follow A7 into Carlisle. Hotel is on left at fifth set of traffic lights.
⊨9 bedrs, 4 en suite, 2 ba; TV; tcf ♠TV, dogs, ns; G8, coach; child facs ✗LD 7.30, nr lunch, nr Sat & Sun Nov–Apr. Resid & Rest lic
£ B&B £17–£25, B&B (double) £27–£37; D £7
cc Access, B'card/Visa.

East View (Acclaimed) 110 Warwick Rd CA1 1JU ☎ (0228) 22112.
From junction 43 of the M6, head towards town centre and hotel is 1½ miles on the left.
⊨7 bedrs, 7 en suite; TV; tcf ♠dogs, ns; P4, coach; child facs ✗ Breakfast only. Unlic

All Seasons Park Broom, CA6 4QH ☎ (0228) 73696. *Hotel.*

Royal 9 Lowther St, CA3 8ES ☎ (0228) 22103.
Centrally situated hotel on the line of the old city wall. A few minutes walk from bus and railway stations. Sauna.
⊨23 bedrs, 11 en suite, 6 ba; TV; tcf ♠TV, dogs; coach; child facs ✗LD 6.30, nr Sun. Resid & Rest lic
£ B&B £16·50–£26·50, B&B (double) £27·50–£37·50; HB weekly £140–£210; L £3, D£5·50; [10% V] **cc** Access, B'card/Visa; dep.

Bank End Roadhead, CA6 6NU ☎ (069 78) 644. *Farm.* Dorothy Downer
Sleeps 2, ns
£ B&B from £18–£21, D £9

CARNFORTH Lancashire. Map 22F3

Holmere Hall (Acclaimed) Yealand Conyers, LA5 9SN ☎ (0254) 735353

CARPERBY North Yorkshire. Map 23C4

Grayford Nr Leyburn. DL8 4DW ☎ (09693) 517

CASTLE COMBE Wiltshire. Map 26B5

Sevington Farm Yatton Keynell, Chippenham, SN14 7LD ☎ (0249) 782408. *Farm.* Judith and Roger Pope
Sleeps 6, ♠ ns ⌂
£ B&B from £13–£16

CASTLE DONINGTON Leicestershire. Map 24D3

Park Farmhouse (Acclaimed) Melbourne Rd DE7 2KN ☎ (0332) 862409.

Black and white oak-panelled farmhouse, built in the early 17th century. Take the A453 to Isley Walton, turn off for Melbourne, and hotel is ⅓ mile along road.
⋈8 bedrs, 6 en suite, 2 ba; TV; tcf 🏨dogs, ns; P15, coach; child facs ✕LD8, nr lunch. Resid lic
£ B&B £26–£39, B&B (double) £36–£49; [10% V winter w/e] cc Access, Amex, B'card/Visa, Diners; dep.

Four Poster 73 Clapgun St. ☎Derby (0332) 810335 & 812418.
Situated in the centre of Castle Donington in the street behind the Church.
⋈11 bedrs, 3 en suite, 3 ba; TV; tcf 🏨TV, dogs, ns; P 20 ✕Breakfast only. Unlic
£ B&B £15, B&B (double) £30–£50; WB

CATLOWDY Cumbria. Map 22F7

Bessiestown Farm (Acclaimed) Penton CA6 5QP ☎Nicholforest (022877) 219.
Attractive white walled farmhouse on beef and sheep farm overlooking the Scottish Border in a setting of moorland and forests. Leave M6 at junction 44 and follow A7 to Longtown. At Bush Hotel turn right and continue for 6 miles to T junction. Turn right onto B6318 for 1⅓ miles to Catlowdy. Farm is opposite Post Office. Indoor swimming pool.
⋈5 bedrs, 5 en suite; tcf 🏨TV, ns; P 10, coach; child facs ✕LD5, nr lunch & Sun dinner. Resid lic
£B&B £22·50–£25, B&B (double) £35–£40; HB weekly £170–£190

CAWSTON Norfolk. Map 25E3

Grey Gables Country House (Acclaimed) Norwich Rd, Eastgate, NR10 4EY ☎(0603) 871259.

Former rectory built of mellow Norfolk red brick with a slate roof, converted in early Victorian times. From Cawston village take the Norwich road, and bear left past the petrol station. Grey Gables is ⅓ mile out of the village on the left. Tennis, riding. Closed Xmas.

⋈7 bedrs, 6 en suite, 1 ba; TV; tcf 🏨dogs, ns; P 10 ✕lunch by arrangement. Rest lic
£B&B £30–£42, B&B (double) £40–£52; HB weekly £178–£203; L £11, D £16; WB £54 (2 nts HB); [10% V] cc Access, B'card/Visa; dep.

CHADDLEWORTH Berkshire. Map 26D5

Manor Farm Newbury, RG16 0EG ☎(048 82) 215. *Farm.* Mrs Margaret Cooper
Sleeps 4
£ B&B from £15

CHAGFORD Devon. Map 28F4

Thorworthy House (Highly Acclaimed) TQ13 8EY ☎(0647) 433297.
Large Victorian house surrounded by a lovely 2-acre garden. All rooms have magnificent views over Dartmoor National Park. Turn right in Chagford Square, take the left fork to Fernworthy and at the top of the hill take the second right turning to Thornworthy. Follow signs to hotel. Tennis, putting.
⋈7 bedrs, 6 en suite, 2 ba; TV 🏨TV, dogs; P 6; child facs ✕LD 7.45, nr lunch. Rest lic
£ B&B £30, B&B (double) £65; HB weekly £350; D £17·50

Glendarah House TQ13 8BZ ☎(0647) 433270.
White-painted Victorian house with good views situated about ⅓ mile east of centre of Chagford. Open Mar–Dec.
⋈8 bedrs, 1 en suite, 2 ba; TV; tcf 🏨TV, ns; P 9; child facs ✕LD 6·30, nr lunch; Resid & Rest lic
£B&B £14·50–£18·50; HB weekly £161–£189; D £8·50; [5% V]

Frenchbeer Farm TQ13 8EX ☎(0647) 432427. *Farm.* Christine Malseed
Sleeps 6, 🐕 ns 🧒
£ B&B from £14, D £6

CHARD Somerset. Map 29C5

🏆 **George** Fore Street ☎(04606) 3413
A stone and brick inn with a courtyard in town centre opposite the Guildhall.

Watermead (Acclaimed) 83 High St, TA20 1QT ☎(0460) 62834.

Symbols (full details on p. 4)		
⋈ information about bedrooms	nr no restaurant service	*Farms*
🏨 facilities at hotels	🗣 languages spoken	🐕 dogs accepted
✕ information about meals	[V] RAC vouchers accepted	🧒 (4) children accepted (min. age)

Large detached modernised house, quietly situated overlooking open countryside to the rear. Set at the top of the hill forming Chard. High St on the left.
🛏9 bedrs, 6 en suite, 1 ba; TV; tcf 🎬TV, dogs, ns; P 9, U 2; child facs ✗LD 10 am, nr lunch. Resid lic
£B&B £12·50–£15; HB weekly £150; [5% V]

CHARING   Kent.   Map 27D4

Barnfield   Ashford, TN27 0BN ☎(0233) 712421
Farm. Mrs Phillada Pym
Sleeps 6
£ B&B from £16, D from £9·50

CHARLBURY   Oxfordshire.   Map 26D7

Banbury Hill Farm   Enstone Road, OX7 3JH
☎(0608) 810314. *Farm.* Angela Widdows
Sleeps 6, ns 🛇
£ B&B from £14, D available

CHARLTON   Oxfordshire.   Map 26D7

Home Farm   OX7 3BR ☎(0295) 811683
🛏3 bedrs, 3 en suite; TV; tcf 🎬dogs, ns; P 3; no children under 12 ✗Breakfast only. Unlic

CHARLTON MUSGROVE   Somerset.   Map 29D5

Lower Church Farm   Rectory Lane, Wincanton, BA9 8ES ☎(0963) 32307. *Farm.* Alicia Teague
Sleeps 6, 🐾 ns 🛇 (6)
£ B&B from £12

CHARMOUTH   Dorset.   Map 29C4

Newlands House (Acclaimed)   Stonebarrow Lane, DT6 6RA ☎(0297) 60212. Open Mar–Oct.

🛏12 bedrs, 11 en suite, 1 ba; TV; tcf 🎬TV, dogs, ns; P 15; no children under 6 ✗LD midday, nr lunch. Resid & Rest lic
£B&B £17·50–£20·50; HB weekly £171·60–£188; D£9·40; WB; dep.

CHATHILL   Northumberland.   Map 21F2

Doxford Farmhouse   Doxford Farm, NE6 75DY ☎(066 579) 235. *Farm.* Audrey and Douglas Turnbull
Sleeps 6, 🐾 ns 🛇
£ B&B from £12–£15, D £8–£9

CHATTERIS   Cambridgeshire.   Map 25B1

Bramley House (Acclaimed)   15 High St, PE16 6BE ☎(035 43) 5414 or 5580
Built in Georgian times, Bramley House is situated in a conservation area. Hotel is centrally placed in town.
🛏14 bedrs, 14 en suite; TV; tcf 🎬TV, dogs, ns; P 19, coach; child facs ✗Breakfast only. Resid lic
£B&B £15, B&B (double) £25; WB; [10% V]
cc Access, Amex, B'card/Visa, Diners.

CHEADLE   Staffordshire.   Map 24B3

Royal Oak   69 High St, ST10 1AN ☎(0538) 753116

Ley Fields Farm   Leek Road, Stoke-on-Trent, ST10 2EF ☎(0538) 752875. *Farm.* Mrs Kathryn Clowes
Sleeps 6, 🛇
£ B&B from £12–£15, D £7–£8

CHEDDAR   Somerset.   Map 29C6

The Market Cross (Acclaimed)   Church St, The Cross, BS27 3RA ☎(0934) 742264.

A Grade II listed Regency building with original flagstone hallway and marble fireplaces. Take the A38 or the A371 to Cheddar.

En suite rooms
En suite rooms may be bath or shower rooms.
If you have a preference, remember to state it when booking a room.

7 bedrs, 3 en suite, 1 ba; TV TV, ns; P 7; child facs LD 7, nr lunch. Rest lic
£ B&B £16–£17, B&B (double) £28–£37; [5% V Mon–Wed, Feb–Apr & Jun] cc Access; B'card/Visa; dep.

CHEDWORTH Gloucestershire. Map 26B7

Hartpury Farm Nr Cheltenham, GL54 4AL (028 572) 350. *Farm*. Peter and Peggy Booth Sleeps 6,
£ B&B from £10·50–£11·50, D £6·50

CHELMSFORD Essex. Map 27C6

Snows Oaklands (Highly Acclaimed) 240 Springfield Rd, CM2 6BP (0245) 352004 or 260357

A fine old Georgian mansion standing in its own grounds of over ¼ acre. Situated ¾ mile from the town centre near Essex Police HQ.
15 bedrs, 13 en suite, 1 ba; TV; tcf TV, ns; P 14, coach; child facs bar meals only. Resid & Rest lic
£ B&B £28·40, B&B (double) £44·50; [5% V]

Boswell House (Acclaimed) 118–120 Springfield Rd, CM2 6LF (0245) 287587.
A 19th century town house converted in 1980 to a hotel, and furnished throughout with stripped pine. Situated on the A113 in the town centre opposite the leisure centre. Closed Xmas & New Year.
13 bedrs, 13 en suite; TV; tcf TV, ns; P 15, coach; child facs LD 8.30. Resid & Rest lic
£ B&B £33–£38, B&B (double) £51; HB weekly £287–£301; L £3, D £8; [5% V] cc Access, Amex, B'card/Visa, Diners.

Beechcroft 211 New London Rd, CM2 0AJ (0245) 352462.

From A12 follow the B1007 to Chelmsford. Hotel 3 miles from A12. Closed Xmas & New Year.
20 bedrs, 8 en suite, 5 ba; TV; tcf TV, dogs; P 15; child facs Breakfast only. Unlic
£ B&B £24·85–£32, B&B (double) £39·50–£51·50
cc Access, B'card/Visa; dep.

Tanunda 217–219 New London Rd, CM2 0AJ (0245) 354295.
Hotel is situated by the only main traffic light in New London Rd. Closed last wk Aug, first wk Sept & 2 wks Xmas.
20 bedrs, 11 en suite, 3 ba; TV; tcf TV, dogs; P 20 LD 7.25, nr dinner Fri–Sun, nr lunch; Rest lic
£ B&B £22·75–£28·75, B&B (double) £37·50–£46·50; D £6–£9 cc Access, B'card/Visa.

CHELTENHAM Gloucestershire. Map 26B7

Allards (Highly Acclaimed) Shurdington, GL51 5XA (0242) 862498.
Gracious house dating back to 1756, and set in its own 3-acre grounds with superb views of the Cotswold escarpment and the Malvern Hills. On the A46 2 miles south of Cheltenham, a short distance from M5 junction 11.
11 bedrs, 11 en suite, 1 ba; TV; tcf ns; P 15, G 2, coach; child facs LD 7.30, nr lunch. Unlic
£ B&B £19–£20; D £9·50; [5% V] cc Access, B'card/Visa; dep.

Beaumont House (Highly Acclaimed) 56 Shurdington Rd, GL53 0JE (0242) 245986.

An elegant detached listed Victorian building set in its own peaceful, picturesque gardens. Many original features remain. Set on the A46 Stroud road at the Cheltenham end of Shurdington Rd.
18 bedrs, 15 en suite, (2 sh), 1 ba; TV; tcf

TV, dogs, ns; P 22, coach; child facs ✕LD 6.
Resid lic
£ B&B £16–£32, B&B (double) £40–£50; HB weekly
£175–£280; L £3, D £9·50; WB (£19·50); [10% V]
cc Access, B'card/Visa; dep.

Cotswold Grange (Highly Acclaimed)   Pittville
Circus Rd, GL52 2QH ☎(0242) 515119.
*Fine country house built of mellow Cotswold stone
set in a tree-lined avenue. Pleasant garden patio
and ornamental pool. From the town centre follow
signs for Prestbury, turn right at the roundabout on
Prestbury Rd, and hotel is 200 yards on the right.*
25 bedrs, 25 en suite; TV; tcf TV, dogs; P 20,
coach; child facs ✕LD 7.30, nr Sun. Resid & Rest
lic
£ B&B £34, B&B (double) £45; L £6·50, D £12;
[10% V w/e] **cc** Access, B'card/Visa; dep.

Hannaford's (Highly Acclaimed)   20 Evesham Rd.
GL52 2AB ☎(0242) 515181 or 524191.
*Modernised Regency-style hotel, built in 1830 by
Joseph Pitt and retaining much of its original charm.
Leave Cheltenham on the A435 Evesham road, and
Hannaford's is on the left about ¼ mile out of the
town centre.*
10 bedrs, 9 en suite, 1 ba; TV; tcf no children
under 5 ✕LD 7.45, nr lunch, dinner Sun. Dinner
Sat by arrangement. Resid lic
£ B&B £20–£30, B&B (double) £43·50–£46; D £11;
WB (£65) **cc** Access, B/card/Visa; dep.

Lypiatt House (Highly Acclaimed)   Lypiatt Rd,
GL50 2QW ☎(0242) 224994 Fax: (0242) 224996.
*A beautifully restored mid-Victorian house set in its
own grounds, with impressive public rooms. Follow
signs for A40 Gloucester or A46 Stroud. Closed
Xmas & New Year.*
10 bedrs, 10 en suite; TV; tcf ns; P 14; no
children under 12 ✕LD 2, nr lunch Sun dinner.
Resid lic

£ B&B £37–£52, B&B (double) £50–£65; WB;
[10% V w/d] **cc** Access, B'card/Visa.

On the Park (Highly Acclaimed)   38 Evesham Rd,
GL52 2AH ☎(0242) 518898.
12 bedrs, 9 en suite, 2 ba; TV; tcf TV, dogs;
P 10, U 1, coach; child facs ✕LD 8, nr lunch. Resid
& Rest lic
cc Access, B'card/Visa; dep.

Regency House (Highly Acclaimed)   50 Clarence
Sq, GL50 4JR ☎(0242) 582718.
*Hotel is situated off the A435 Evesham road, 5 mins
from the town centre.*
8 bedrs, 7 en suite, (1 sh); TV; tcf
ns; child facs ✕Breakfast only. Resid lic
£ B&B £25; B&B (double) £40 **cc** Access, B'card/
Visa.

Stretton Lodge (Highly Acclaimed)   Western Rd,
GL50 3RN ☎(0242) 528724 Fax: (0242) 570771.
*Gracious Victorian town house, carefully restored
and modernised, and still retaining its period
character. Western Rd, is off St George's Rd which
is off Promenade.*
9 bedrs, 9 en suite; TV; tcf ns; P 6; child facs
✕LD 12 noon, nr lunch. Resid lic
£ B&B £30–£40, B&B (double) £47·50–£55; HB
weekly £230–£330 **cc** Access, Amex, B'card/Visa;
dep.

Abbey (Acclaimed)   16 Bath Parade ☎(0242)
516053 Tx: 437369 Fax: (0242) 227188

Cheltenham (Gloucestershire)

A terraced hotel close to the centre of Cheltenham.
13 bedrs, 7 en suite, (4 sh), 2 ba; TV; tcf
TV; child facs ✗LD 6, nr Sun dinner. Resid &
Rest lic
£ B&B £18–£22, B&B (double) £40; L £6, D £11;
[10% V w/e] cc Access, B'card/Visa, Diners; dep.

Hallery House (Acclaimed)   48 Shurdington Rd,
GL53 0JE ✆(0242) 578450.

*A Victorian listed house, built in 1837 and lovingly
restored by its owners. Situated on the A46 Stroud–
Cheltenham Rd, near the town centre.*
16 bedrs, 10 en suite, 2 ba; TV; tcf dogs, ns;
P 20, U 3 (£1), coach; child facs ✗LD 7, nr lunch.
Resid lic
£ B&B £15–£40, B&B (double) £25–£45; HB weekly
£170–£350; D £10; WB £50 (D, B&B); [10% V]
cc Access, B'card/Visa; dep.

Hollington House (Acclaimed)   115 Hales Rd,
GL52 6ST ✆(0242) 519718 Fax: (0242) 570280.
*A detached Victorian house in its own pleasant
grounds close to the centre of Cheltenham. From
M4/M40 at the first traffic lights after junction A40/
A435 in Cheltenham turn right into Hales Rd. Hotel
700 yards on right. From M5 follow A40 Oxford
signs until London Rd/Old Bath Rd/Hales Rd
crossroads.*
9 bedrs, 8 en suite, 1 ba; TV; tcf ns; P 12; no
children under 3 ✗LD 7; nr lunch or Sun dinner.
Resid lic
£ B&B £28, B&B (double) £38; WB (min 2 persons,
£25pppn); [10% V] cc Access, Amex, B'card/Visa.

Milton House (Acclaimed)   12 Royal Parade,
Bayshill Rd, GL50 3AY ✆(0242) 582601
Fax: (0242) 222326.
*A splendid Regency terrace hotel in a Grade II listed
building retaining original characteristics.*
9 bedrs, 9 en suite; TV; tcf TV, ns; P 4; child
facs ✗LD 9 am, nr lunch. Resid lic
£B&B £28·75–£38, B&B (double) £40–£50
cc Access, Amex, B'card/Visa; dep.

Willoughby (Acclaimed)   1 Suffolk Sq, GL50 2DR
✆(0242) 522798. *Guest House.*

Bowler Hat   130 London Rd, GL52 6HN
✆(0242) 577362. *Hotel.*

Broomhill   218 London Rd, GL52 6HW
✆(0242) 513086.
*Comfortable guest house close to all amenities. On
the A40 London Rd.*
3 bedrs, 1 en suite, 1 ba; TV; tcf
TV, dogs, ns; P 3 ✗Breakfast only. Unlic
£B&B £17·50, B&B (double) £35; [10% V]; dep.

Hilden Lodge   271 London Rd, Charlton Kings,
GL52 6YL ✆(0242) 583242.
*Situated on A40 Oxford Rd, 1 ½ miles from town
centre.*
10 bedrs, 9 en suite, 2 ba; TV; tcf TV, dogs, ns;

Please tell the manager if you chose your hotel
through an advertisement in the guide.

Discount vouchers
RAC discount vouchers are at the end of the
guide. Establishments with a [V] shown at the end
of the price information will accept them in part
payment for accommodation bills on the full,
standard rate, not against bargain breaks or any
other special offers. Please note the limitations
shown in the entry: w/e for weekends, w/d for
weekdays, and which months they are accepted.

Cheltenham (Gloucestershire)

P 10, G 2, coach; child facs ✗LD 10. Rest lic
£ B&B £25, B&B (double) £38; L £6, D £8; [10%V
except Gold Cup wk] **cc** Access, B'card/Visa.

Ivy Dene   145 Hewlett Rd, GL52 6TS
☎(0242)521726. Closed 2 wks Jan.
🛏9 bedrs, 3ba; TV; tcf 🅃TV, dogs; P7; child facs
✗Breakfast only. Unlic
£ B&B £12·50–£15; [10%V]; dep.

Leeswood   14 Montpellier Dr, GL501TX
☎(0242)524813.
*At the junction of the A46/A40 take town centre
route. Montpellier Drive is second turning on the left.*
🛏7 bedrs, 3ba; TV; tcf 🅃TV, dogs; P6
✗Breakfast only. Unlic
£ B&B £16·50–£17·50

Montpellier   33 Montpellier Terr., GL501UX
☎(0242)526009.
🛏10 bedrs, 4en suite, (3 sh), 2ba; TV; tcf
🅃TV, dogs; child facs ✗LD6.45, nr lunch, Sat &
Sun dinner. Resid lic
£ B&B £16–£26, B&B (double) £34–£40; WB (£15)
cc B'card/Visa; dep.

North Hall   Pittville Circus Rd, GL52 2PZ
☎(0242)520589.
*A Regency style hotel in a quiet, tree-lined road.
Situated close to the town centre off Hewlett Rd.*
Closed Xmas & New Year.
🛏20 bedrs, 12en suite, 6ba; TV; tcf 🅃TV, dogs;
P20, coach; child facs ✗LD7.15, nr lunch & Sun
dinner. Resid & Rest lic
£ B&B £18–£27·50, B&B (double) £31–£43·50; HB
weekly £165–£222; D £9·50; WB (£46); [5%V]
cc Access, B'card/Visa.

Old Vineyards   Timbercombe Lane, Charlton
Kings, GL53 8EE ☎(0242) 582893. *Farm.* Closed
Xmas.
🛏5 bedrs, 2 ba; tcf 🅃TV, dogs, ns; P8; child facs
✗Breakfast only. Unlic

Hunting Butts Farm   Swindon Lane, GL50 4NZ
☎(0242) 524982. *Farm.* Jane Hanks   ⅆ
Sleeps 16, 🐂🐃
£ B&B from £12–£15

CHERITON FITZPAINE   Devon. Map 29A4

Brindiwell Farm   Crediton, EX17 4HR
☎(03636) 357. *Farm.* Doreen Lock
Sleeps 6, 🐃
£ B&B from £10, D £6

CHESTER   Cheshire.   Map 30B7

Green Gables (Highly Acclaimed)   11 Eversley Pk,
off Liverpool Rd, CH2 2AJ ☎(0244) 372243.
*Victorian house, elegantly modernised and offering
stylish, comfortable accommodation. Situated off
A5116 Liverpool Rd, about 1 mile from town centre.*
🛏4 bedrs, 4 en suite; TV; tcf 🅃TV, ns; P 8; child
facs ✗Breakfast only. Unlic
£ B&B £20, B&B (double) £33; [5%V winter w/d]

Redland (Highly Acclaimed)   64 Hough Green,
CH4 8JY ☎(0244) 671024.
*Wood-panelled Victorian hotel with large, gracious
reception rooms, set in its own grounds. Situated
off the A549 one mile from the city centre. Snooker,
sauna, solarium.*
🛏11 bedrs, 11 en suite; TV; tcf 🅃dogs, ns; P 14
✗Breakfast only. Resid lic
£ B&B £35, B&B (double) £40–£55; [5%V]; dep.

Weston (Acclaimed)   82 Hoole Rd, CH23NT
☎(0244)326735.
🛏7 bedrs, 4 en suite, 1 ba; TV; tcf 🅃TV; P30,
coach; child facs ✗LD8, nr lunch. Resid & Rest
lic
cc Access, B'card/Visa; dep.

Brookside   12 Brook Lane, CH2 2AP
☎(0244)381943.
*Hotel situated north of the city off A5116 Liverpool
Rd, near Northgate leisure centre. Sauna, solarium,
gymnasium.*
🛏26 bedrs, 26 en suite, 2ba; TV; tcf 🅃TV, dogs;
P 15, coach; child facs ✗LD 9.30, nr lunch. Resid
lic
£ B&B £27, B&B (double) £42; WB (£47); [5%V]
cc Access, B'card/Visa; dep.

Cavendish   42–44 Hough Green, CH4 8JQ
☎(0244)675100.
🛏20 bedrs, 16en suite, 3ba; TV 🅃TV, dogs, ns;
P34, coach; child facs ✗LD 9. Resid lic
cc Access, Amex, B'card/Visa, Diners; dep.

Devonia   33–35 Hoole Rd, CH2 3NH
✆(0244)322236.
🛏10 bedrs, 3 ba; TV; tcf 🏠TV, dogs; P 20, coach; child facs ✕LD 6, nr lunch

Eaton   29–31 City Rd, CH1 3AE ✆(0244)320840.
Situated on the main road from Chester Station to city centre.
🛏22 bedrs, 13 en suite, (9 sh); TV; tcf 🏠dogs, ns; P 10, coach; child facs ✕LD 8, nr lunch. Resid & Rest lic
£ B&B £24·50–£29·50, B&B (double) £37–£42; HB weekly £171·50–£248·50; D £8·95; WB (£49); [10% V] **cc** Access, Amex, B'card/Visa; Diners; dep.

Egerton Lodge   57 Hoole Rd, Hoole, CH2 3NJ
✆(0244) 320712.
A small Victorian hotel situated half a mile from city centre. From M53 follow A56 into Chester, and hotel is about ¼ mile on left. Closed Xmas.
🛏5 bedrs, 3 en suite, 2 ba; TV; tcf
🏠P 4; children over 3 ✕Breakfast only. Unlic
£B&B £15–£19·50, B&B (double) £23–£29; WB (winter); [5% V Apr–Oct] **cc** Access, B'card/Visa; dep.

Eversley   9 Eversley Park, CH2 2AJ ✆(0244) 373744.
Attractive Victorian hotel set in a quiet location ¼ mile north of city on A5116 turn right into Eversley Park, and hotel is on the top left. Closed Xmas & New Year.
🛏11 bedrs, 8 en suite, (1 sh), 1 ba; TV; tcf
🏠TV, ns; P 17, coach; child facs ✕LD 8, nr lunch. Resid lic
£ B&B £20–£25, B&B (double) £36·50–£42; HB weekly £126–£157·50; WB **cc** Access, B'card/Visa; dep.

Gables   5 Vicarage Rd, Hoole, CH2 3HZ
✆(0244)323969.
Pleasant Victorian house in a quiet residential area. From M53 take A56 Hoole Rd, after 1 mile turn left at church into Vicarage Rd. Closed Xmas & New Year.
🛏7 bedrs, 2 ba; TV; tcf 🏠TV, dogs, ns; P7, children over 5 ✕Breakfast only. Unlic

£ B&B £16, B&B (double) £24; [10% V Jan–Jun].

Hamilton Court   5–7 Hamilton St, Hoole, CH2 3A
✆(0244) 345387.
From M53 take A56 Hoole Rd, and Hamilton St is a turning off. Closed Xmas & New Year.
🛏12 bedrs, 6 en suite, 2 ba; TV; tcf 🏠TV, dogs; P 5, G 10, coach; child facs ✕nr lunch. Resid lic
£B&B £16, B&B (double) £31 **cc** Access, B'card/Visa; dep.

Riverside and Recorder   22 City Walls, off Lower Bridge St, CH1 1SB ✆(0244)326580
Fax: (0244)311567
A Georgian hotel on the city walls overlooking River Dee. Approach via Lower Bridge St, left into Duke St, and car park entrance 100 yards on right.
🛏24 bedrs, 24 en suite, 2 ba; TV; tcf 🏠TV, dogs, ns; P 24; child facs ✕LD 9, nr lunch. Resid & Rest lic
£ B&B £35–£42, B&B (double) £44–£55; HB weekly £220–£260; D £9·95; WB £35 (HB 2 nights); [5% V Nov–Feb] **cc** Access, B'card/Visa; dep.

Vicarage Lodge   11 Vicarage Rd, Hoole, CH2 3HZ ✆(0244) 319533
Family-run Victorian guesthouse, off the A56 Hoole Rd 1 mile from city centre.
🛏4 bedrs, 2 en suite, (1 sh), 1 ba; TV; tcf
🏠P 7; child facs ✕LD 7, nr lunch. Unlic
£ B&B £14–£20; dep.

CHEW MAGNA   Avon.   Map 29D7

Woodbarn Farm   Denny Lane, Bristol, BS18 8SZ
✆(0272) 332599. *Farm.* Mrs Judi Hasell
Sleeps 6, ns ☞
£ B&B from £12

CHEWTON MENDIP   Somerset.   Map 29D7

Pantiles   Bathway, Nr Bath, BA3 4ND
✆(076 121) 519. *Farm.* Pat Hellard
Sleeps 6, ♥ ns ☞
£ B&B on application

CHIPPENHAM   Wiltshire.   Map 29E7

Oxford (Acclaimed)   32–36 Langley Rd, SN15 1BX ✆(0249) 652542.

Small hotel situated about ⅓ mile from town centre. On B4069 Lyneham Rd (formerly A420).
⊨13 bedrs, 7 en suite, (1 sh), 1 ba; TV; tcf ↑↑dogs; P 9, U 1, coach; child facs ✗LD 8, lunch & dinner by arrangement. Resid & Rest lic
£ B&B £22–£32, B&B (double) £34–£42; HB weekly £190–£250; L £8·50, D £8·50; WB (£60); [10% V]
cc Access, Amex, B'card/Visa; dep.

CHISLEHAMPTON Oxfordshire. Map 26E6

🍺 🍺 **Coach and Horses** Stadhampton Rd. OX9 7UX ✆ Stadhampton (0865) 890255
Three-storey, Oxford-stone, 16th-century inn of considerable character.
⊨9 bedrs, 9 en suite; TV; tcf ↑↑dogs; P 34 ✗LD 10, nr Sun & Sat lunch
cc Access, Amex, B'card/Visa, Diners; dep.

CHITTLEHAMPTON Devon. Map 28F5

Stowford Cottage Stowford, Umberleigh, EX37 9RX ✆ (076 94) 536. *Farm.* Hugh and Rosemary Smith
Sleeps 6
£ B&B from £14, D from £7

North Newton Farm Umberleigh, EX37 9QS ✆ (07694) 544 [changing to (0769) 540544]
Farm. Mrs Margaret Thomas
Sleeps 6, 🐂
£ B&B from £11–£12·50, D from £6

CHORLEY Lancashire. Map 30D8

Swifts House Farm Bentley Lane, Heskin ✆ (0257) 45490. *Farm.* Mrs Maree Fiddler
Sleeps 6
£ B&B from £13, D from £4

CHRISTCHURCH Dorset. Map 26C2

Pines (Acclaimed) 39 Mudeford, BH23 3NQ ✆ (0202) 475121.
⊨14 bedrs, 8 en suite, 2 ba; TV; tcf ↑↑TV, dogs, ns; P 16; child facs ✗LD 8.45, nr lunch. Rest lic
cc Access, Amex, B'card/Visa, Diners; dep.

Belvedere 59 Barrack Rd, BH23 1PD ✆ (0202) 485978. *Hotel.*

CHURCH STRETTON Shropshire.
Map 31B7

Paddock Lodge (Highly Acclaimed) All Stretton, SY6 6HG ✆ (0692) 723702.
Modern building in very peaceful setting surrounded by the Stretton Hills. From A49 take B4370 to All Stretton. Entrance next to Stretton Hall Hotel.
⊨3 bedrs, 3 en suite, 1 ba; TV; tcf ↑↑TV, dogs, ns; P 5; child facs ✗LD 7.30, nr lunch. Unlic
£ B&B (double) £32; HB weekly £158; dep.

Belvedere (Acclaimed) Burway Rd, SY6 6DP ✆ (0694) 722232.
Detached Edwardian house standing in its own grounds on the lower slopes of the Long Mynd. Turn west from A49 into Church Stretton along Burway Rd. Hotel on right. Closed Xmas & New Year.
⊨12 bedrs, 6 en suite, 4 ba; tcf ↑↑TV, dogs; P 9; child facs ✗LD 6, nr lunch. Resid & Rest lic
£ B&B £15·50–£17; HB weekly £98–£107·10; [10% V]; dep.

Court Farm Cretton, SY6 7HH ✆ (069 43) 219.
Stone Tudor farmhouse with inglenook fireplace, set in very rural area of outstanding natural beauty. From Church Stretton take B4371 towards Much Wenlock for 6 miles, then turn left for Gretton and Cardington. Follow to crossroads, turn right down hill for 300 metres, and farm is third house on right. Open Feb–Nov.
⊨4 bedrs, 2 en suite, 1 ba; tcf ↑↑TV, NS; P 8, U 1; no children under 12 ✗LD 6.30, nr lunch Fri dinner. Unlic
£ B&B £14–£17; HB weekly £155–£168; [5% V]; dep.

Acton Scott Farm SY6 6QN ✆ (069 46) 260. *Farm.* Mary Jones

Symbols (full details on p. 4)

⊨ information about bedrooms	nr no restaurant service	*Farms*
↑↑ facilities at hotels	⁏⁏ languages spoken	↑ dogs accepted
✗ information about meals	[V] RAC vouchers accepted	🐂 (4) children accepted (min. age)

Sleeps 6, 🐾
£ B&B from £10

Rectory Farm Woolstaston, Leebotwood, SY6
6NN ☎(069 45) 306. *Farm*. Jeanette Davis
Sleeps 6, 🐾(12)
£ B&B from £15

CIRENCESTER Gloucestershire. Map 26C6

La Ronde (Highly Acclaimed) 52 Ashcroft Rd,
GL3 1QX ☎(0285) 654611.
*A Cotswold stone Victorian building situated near
the town centre.*
⊨10 bedrs, 10 en suite; TV; tcf 📺dogs, ns; P9
✗LD 9, nr Mon & Sat lunch & all Sun
£ B&B £39·50, B&B (double) £44·50; HB weekly
£299·25; L£7·50, D£12 **cc** Access, B'card/Visa.

Wimborne (Highly Acclaimed) 91 Victoria Rd,
GL7 1ES ☎(0285) 653890.
*Attractive double-fronted Cotswold stone house with
spacious rooms. From market place with church on
left, go straight ahead to traffic lights, turn right into
Victoria Road and Wimborne is on left.*
⊨5 bedrs, 5 en suite; TV; tcf 📺NS; P 5; no children
under 5 ✗nr lunch. Unlic
£ B&B £20–£25, B&B (double) £25–£30; HB weekly
£136–£149; dep.

Raydon House (Acclaimed) 3 The Avenue, GL7
1EH ☎(0285) 653485.
*Well decorated hotel near town centre and market
place. The Avenue runs between Victoria Road and
Watermoor Road.*
⊨10 bedrs, 9 en suite; 1 ba
£ B&B £29–£35, B&B (double) £45–£55; D£10·50

Arkenside 44 Lewis La, GL7 1EB
☎(0285) 653072.
⊨18 bedrs, 4 en suite, 4 ba; tcf 📺TV, dogs; P 14,
coach; child facs ✗nr lunch & weekend

CLAYTON West Yorkshire. Map 23C2

Brow Top Farm Baldwin Lane, Bradford, BD14
6PS ☎(0274) 882178. *Farm*. Margaret Priestley
Sleeps 6, 🐾
£ B&B from £12·50–£15

CLEETHORPES Humberside (South Humberside). Map 25A6

Mallow View 9–11 Albert Rd, DN35 8LX
☎(0472) 691297.
⊨15 bedrs, 2 en suite, (2 sh), 2 ba; TV; tcf
📺TV, dogs; coach; child facs ✗LD7, nr lunch

CLEOBURY NORTH Shropshire. Map 31B8

Charlcotte Farm Bridgnorth, WV16 6RR ☎(074
633) 238. *Farm*. Wendy Green
Sleeps 6, 🐾ns
£ B&B from £12

CLIFTON HAMPDEN Oxfordshire. Map 26E6

Barley Mow (Acclaimed) OX14 3EH ☎(086 730)
7847.
*A 13th century inn on a peaceful backwater of the
River Thames.*
⊨4 bedrs, 1 en suite, 2 ba; TV; tcf
📺ns; P250, coach; child facs ✗LD9.30
£B&B £34·50–£41, B&B (double) £54; L£8·15,
D£8·15; WB £27·50 **cc** Access, Amex, B'card/
Visa, Diners.

CLIFTONVILLE Kent. Map 27F5

Greswolde (Acclaimed) 20 Surrey Rd, CT9 2LA
☎Thanet (0843) 223956.
*Small, elegant Victorian hotel retaining much
original charm and character. Situated about 1 mile
along coast road from Margate opposite Georges
lawns and indoor bowls.*
⊨6 bedrs, 6 en suite; TV; tcf 📺TV, dogs, ns
✗Breakfast only. Resid lic
£B&B £15–£19, B&B (double) £29. **cc** Access,
B'card/Visa; dep.

Falcon Holiday 4 Ethelbert Rd, CT9 1RY
☎Thanet (0843) 223846.
*Modern hotel with large sun terrace. Situated close
to winter gardens and lido. Swimming pool. Open
Apr–Nov & 23–28 Dec.*
⊨30 bedrs; TV; tcf 📺lift, TV; P 12, coach; child facs
✗LD6, nr lunch. Resid & Rest lic

£ B&B £15·50–£18·50; HB weekly £106–£128; D £6; WB (£43); [10% V]; dep.

Riverdale   40–46 Sweyn Rd, CT9 2DF ✆ Thanet (0843) 223628.
Situated on the B2052 Margate/Broadstairs road.
Open Mar–Nov & 24 Dec–New Year.
📞 34 bedrs, 17 en suite, 4 ba; TV; tcf 🏠 coach; child facs ✗ LD 6.30, nr Sat lunch. Resid & Rest lic
£ B&B £17·50–£24·50, B&B (double) £35–£40; HB weekly £118–£157; L £4, D £6 **cc** Access, Amex, B'card/Visa, Diners; dep.

CLITHEROE   Lancashire.   Map 24A7

Harrop Fold (Highly Acclaimed)   Bolton by Bowland, BB7 4PJ ✆ (020 07) 600 Tx: 635562. *Farm.*
📞 7 bedrs, 7 en suite; TV; tcf 🏠 P 15; no children ✗ LD 8.30, nr lunch. Resid lic
cc Access, B'card/Visa; dep.

Brooklyn (Acclaimed)   32 Pimlico Rd, BB7 2AH ✆ (0200) 28268.
An elegant, stone-built Victorian town house with paved forecourt and small walled garden. From Clitheroe centre Pimlico Rd is signed to West Bradford and Grindleton.
📞 8 bedrs, 6 en suite, 1 ba; TV; tcf 🏠 TV, ns; child facs ✗ Dinner by arrangement. Unlic
£ B&B £14–£15·50; HB weekly £140–£155·50; [10% V]; dep.

En suite rooms

En suite rooms may be bath or shower rooms. If you have a preference, remember to state it when booking a room.

Using RAC discount vouchers

Please tell the hotel when booking if you plan to use an RAC discount voucher (see end of guide) in part payment of your bill. Only one voucher will be accepted per party per stay. Discount vouchers will only be accepted in payment for accommodation, not for food.

CLOWS TOP   Worcestershire.   Map 26B9

Clay Farm   Nr Kidderminster, DY14 9NN ✆ (029922) 421. *Farm.* Mike and Ella Grinnall
Sleeps 6, 🐕 🐈 (6)
£ B&B from £13–£15

CLUN   Shropshire.   Map 31B7

New House Farm   Craven Arms, SY7 8NJ ✆ (0588) 638314. *Farm.* Miriam Ellison
Sleeps 6, 🐕 🐈
£ B&B from £12·50, D £7

CLYST ST GEORGE   Devon.   Map 29B4

Marianne Pool   Exeter, EX3 0NZ ✆ (0392) 874939. *Farm.* Janet Bragg
Sleeps 6, 🐈
£ B&B from £10·50–£12·50

COALVILLE   Leicestershire.   Map 24D2

🍴 🍴 **Bardon Hall**   Beveridge La, Bardon Hill ✆ (0530) 81 3644
A country inn situated on A50 west of jn 21 of M1. Several modern bedroom blocks surround the original building.
📞 35 bedrs, 35 en suite; TV; tcf

COCKERMOUTH   Cumbria.   Map 22E5

Crag End Farm   Rogerscale, CA13 0RG ✆ (0900) 85658. *Farm.* Mrs Margaret Ann Steel
Sleeps 6, 🐕 🐈 ns
£ B&B from £14, D £8

High Stanger Farm   CA13 9TS ✆ (0900) 823875. *Farm.* Alison Hewitson
Sleeps 6, 🐈 🐕
£ B&B from £13·50, D £7·50

CODSALL   Staffordshire.   Map 24B2

Moors Farm (Acclaimed)   Chillington Lane, WV8 1QM ✆ (090 74) 2330.
From Codsall to Codsall Wood turn off into Chillington Lane.
📞 6 bedrs, 2 en suite, 2 ba; TV; tcf 🏠 P 20, coach; children over 4; child facs ✗ LD 8, nr lunch. Resid & Rest lic
£ B&B £21–£26, B&B (double) £34–£42; HB weekly £168–£230; D £9; dep.

Clitheroe (Lancashire)

BROOKLYN GUEST HOUSE

32 Pimlico Road, Clitheroe, Lancs BB7 2AH   Tel: 0200 28268
Elegant Victorian townhouse. Annexe opposite. Close to town centre. 8 bedrooms, 6 en-suite. All with colour TV, welcome trays. TV lounge, central heating throughout. Evening meals by arrangement.

COLCHESTER Essex. Map 27D7

Bovills Hall (Acclaimed) Ardleigh, CO7 7RT
📞(0206) 230217.

Comfortable manor house set in 14 acres of
grounds on the edge of Dedham Vale. On the
B1029 Gt. Bromley side of Ardleigh, after the railway
station. Open Feb–Nov.
🛏4 bedrs, 1 en suite, 1 ba, TV; tcf 🏠TV; P6; no
children under 7, child facs ✗Breakfast only. Unlic
£ B&B £18–£23, B&B (double) £28–£35; dep.

COLESBOURNE Gloucestershire. Map 26B7

🍷 🍷 **Colesbourne Inn** Nr Cheltenham, GL55
9NP📞Coberley (024 287) 376.
A 200-year-old, Cotswold-stone coaching inn on the
A435, six miles south of Cheltenham. Bedrooms in
a converted stable block.
🛏10 bedrs, 10 en suite; TV; tcf
🏠dogs; P70, coach; child facs ✗LD 10
£ B&B £25–£28, B&B (double) £40–£48; D £7; WB
£75 (2 nts); [10% V] **cc** Access, Amex, B'card/Visa,
Diners.

COLNE Lancashire. Map 24B7

Higher Wanless Farm Red Lane, BB8 7JP
📞(0282) 865301. Farm. Carole Mitson
Sleeps 5, 🐾 (3)
£ B&B from £15–£20, D from £7·50

Parson Lee Farm Wycoller, BB8 8SU📞(0282)
864747. Farm. Patricia Hodgson
Sleeps 6, 🐶🐾
£ B&B from £10–£14, D £5

COLYTON Devon. Map 29C4

Swallows Eaves (Highly Acclaimed) Colyford,
EX13 6QJ📞(0297) 53184.

Attractive gabled hotel in a natural garden setting
at centre of village. Lovely views over Axe Estuary.
On the A3052 coastal road between Lyme Regis
and Sidmouth, in the village centre opposite the
Post Office.
🛏8 bedrs, 8 en suite; TV; tcf 🏠ns; P10; children
over 12 ✗LD7.30. Resid & Rest lic
£ B&B £22·50–£26·50; HB weekly £224–£245;
L£8·50, D£14·50; WB (£59 w/e); [10% V Nov–Apr]

St Edmunds Swan Hill Rd, Colyford, EX13 6QQ
📞(0297) 52431.
Pleasantly situated detached guest house with
commanding views. ¼ miles inland from Seaton on
A3052. Open Mar–Oct.
🛏7 bedrs, (4 sh), 2ba; tcf 🏠TV, dogs; P8
✗LD 7.30, nr lunch. Resid & Rest lic
£ B&B £12·50–£14, B&B (double) £28–£35; HB
weekly £150–£187; dep.

Smallicombe Farm Northleigh, EX13 6BU
📞(0404) 83310. Farm. Maggie Todd
Sleeps 6, 🐾
£ B&B from £12–£14, D £6·50

Wiscombe Linhaye Southleigh, EX13 6JF📞(040
487) 342. Farm. Sheila Rabjohns ♿
Sleeps 6, 🐾
£ B&B from £11–£16, D £6

COMBE MARTIN Devon. Map 28F6

Blair Lodge (Acclaimed) Moory Meadow, EX34
0DG📞(0271) 882294

Channel Vista (Acclaimed) 2 Woodlands, EX34
0AT📞(027 188) 3514.

Charming Edwardian period house set close to
picturesque cove. On main A399 150 yards from
beach. Open April–Oct.
🛏7 bedrs, 7 en suite; TV; tcf 🏠TV; P8, coach;
children over 3 ✗LD3, nr lunch. Resid lic
£ B&B £17–£18·50; HB weekly £120–£142; WB
£69 (3 nights) **cc** Access, B'card/Visa.

Saffron House (Acclaimed) King St, EX34 0BX
📞(0271 88) 3521.
Family run hotel, built in the 17th century as a
farmhouse with extensive views of surrounding hills
and countryside. Situated on the village street close
to the harbour and beach. Swimming pool.

🛏10 bedrs, 5 en suite, (3 sh), 1 ba; tcf 🛋TV, dogs; P 10, coach; child facs ✕LD 7, nr lunch. Resid lic
£ B&B £13–£20; HB weekly £140–£175
cc Access, B'card/Visa; dep.

Wheel Farm (Acclaimed) Berrydown, EX34 0NT
📞(027 188) 2550.
Take A39 or A399 to Combe Martin. Wheel Farm is 2¾ miles on the Barnstaple Rd.
🛏6 bedrs, 3 en suite, (1 sh), 2 ba; tcf 🛋TV; dogs; P 20; child facs ✕Resid & Rest lic

Firs Woodlands, Seaside, EX34 0AS
📞(027 188) 3404.
🛏9 bedrs, 1 en suite, 2 ba 🛋TV, ns; P 10, coach; child facs ✕LD 3, nr lunch. Resid lic

Woodlands 2 The Woodlands, EX34 0AT
📞(027 188) 2769. *Guest House.*
🛏8 bedrs, (4 sh), 1 ba; TV; tcf 🛋TV; P 7; children over 3, child facs ✕LD 5, nr lunch. Resid lic

Holdstone Farm EX34 0PE 📞(027 188) 3423. *Farm.* Mrs Jayne Lerwill
Sleeps 6, ⮢
£ B&B from £12, D £9

COMBE RALEIGH E. Devon. Map 29B4

Windgate Farm Nr Honiton, EX14 0UJ 📞(0404) 42386. *Farm.* Mrs A E Batty
Sleeps 5, ns ⮢ (10)
£ B&B from £12·50–£15

COMPTON MARTIN Avon. Map 29D7

Herons Green Farm Bristol, BS18 6NL 📞(0272) 333372. *Farm.* Mrs Sandra Hasell
Sleeps 6, ⮢
£ B&B from £12·50

CONGLETON Cheshire. Map 24B4

Sandhole Farm Hulme Walfield, CW12 2JH
📞(0260) 224419. *Farm.* Veronica Worth
Sleeps 14, ns ⮢
£ B&B from £14

CONISTON Cumbria. Map 22F4

🍺 🍺 **Black Bull** Yewdale Rd, CA21 8DU 📞(053 94) 41335
Pleasantly situated 16th century coaching inn at foot of Old Man mountain. 🎾 Fr
🛏7 bedrs, 7 en suite, 1 ba; TV; tcf 🛋TV, dogs, ns; P 15, U1, child facs ✕LD 9
£ B&B £25; L £6·95, D £9·75 cc Access, B'card/Visa; dep.

Coniston Lodge (Highly Acclaimed) Sunny Brow, LA21 8HH 📞(05394) 41201.
Small family-run hotel in beautiful surroundings offering comfortable, cottage-style accommodation. From the crossroads by the garage in village centre, Coniston Lodge is up the hill signed Old Man.
🛏6 bedrs, 6 en suite; TV; tcf 🛋NS; P 3, G 6; no children under 10 ✕LD 7.30, nr lunch, Mon & Sun dinner. Resid & Rest lic
£ B&B £27·50–£35·50; D £13·50; [5% V w/d]
cc Access, B'card/Visa; dep.

Crown LA21 8EA 📞(05394) 41243.
Friendly inn situated in the village centre.
🛏7 bedrs, 2 ba; TV; tcf 🛋dogs; P 30, coach; child facs ✕LD 8.30, nr Sun dinner
£ B&B £17–£18, B&B (double) £30–£36; HB weekly £140–£160; L £6, D £8; WB £35; [10% V]
cc Access, Amex, B'card/Visa; dep.

CONSETT Co Durham. Map 23C6

Bee Cottage Farm Castleside, DH8 9HW
📞(0207) 508224 *Farm.* Liz Lawson ♿
Sleeps 30, 🐾 ns ⮢
£ B&B from £13–£20, D £7

Fairley May Farm Kiln Pit Hill, DH8 9SQ 📞(0434) 682262. *Farm.* Anne Charlton
Sleeps 6, 🐾 ⮢
£ B&B from £13, D £7

COOKLEY Suffolk. Map 25F1

Green Farm Nr Halesworth, IP19 0LH
📞(098 685) 209. *Farm.* Mr & Mrs A. T. Veasy
Sleeps 6
£ B&B from £13, D from £8

CORBRIDGE-ON-TYNE Northumberland.
Map 23B7

Tynedale (Acclaimed) Market Pl, NE45 5AW
📞(043 463) 2149.

🛏7 bedrs, 7 en suite; TV; tcf 🛋TV; no children under 12 ✕Breakfast only
£ B&B £18·50, B&B (double) £32; [10% V]; dep.

CORFE CASTLE   Dorset.   Map 29E4

Knitson Farm   Wareham, BH20 5JB ✆(0929) 422836. *Farm.* Rachel Helfer
Sleeps 6, ✆
£ B&B from £11–£13, D £9

CORHAMPTON   Hampshire.   Map 26D3

Corhampton Lane Farm   Southampton, SO3 1NB ✆(0489) 877506. *Farm.* Mrs Barbara Hall
Sleeps 4, ns
£ B&B from £14–£16

CORSE   Gloucestershire.   Map 26B7

Kilmorie Guest House   Gloucester Road, Staunton, Nr Gloucester, GL19 3RQ ✆(0452) 840224. *Farm.* Sheila Barnfield
Sleeps 11, ✆(5)
£ B&B from £8·50, D £5

CORSHAM   Wiltshire.   Map 26B5

Boyds Farm   Gastard, SN13 9PT ✆(0249) 713146. *Farm.* Dorothy Robinson
Sleeps 6, ns ✆
£ B&B from £12·50

Pickwick Lodge Farm   SN13 0PS ✆(0249) 712207. *Farm.* Gill Stafford
Sleeps 6, ✆ ns ✆
£ B&B from £12–£15, D from £8·50

COUNTISBURY   Devon.   Map 28G6

Coombe Farm   Lynton, EX35 6NF ✆(059 87) 236. *Farm.* Rosemary and Susan Pile
Sleeps 13, ✆ ns ✆
£ B&B from £14·50, D £11·50

COVENTRY   West Midlands.   Map 26D9

Croft   23 Stoke Green, LV3 1FP ✆(0203) 457846. *One mile from city centre on A427 Rugby Rd, adjacent to Stoke Green. Solarium, snooker.*
✆12 bedrs, 1 en suite, (4 sh), 3 ba; TV; tcf
✆TV, dogs; P 20 ✆LD 8.30, nr lunch Mon–Fri. Resid & Rest lic
£ B&B £24–£28, B&B (double) £44; L £4·50, D £7·35 **cc** Access, B'card/Visa.

Discount vouchers
RAC discount vouchers are at the end of the guide. Establishments with a [V] shown at the end of the price information will accept them in part payment for accommodation bills on the full, standard rate, not against bargain breaks or any other special offers. Please note the limitations shown in the entry: w/e for weekends, w/d for weekdays, and which months they are accepted.

Hearsall Lodge   1 Broad La, CV5 7AA ✆(0203) 674543.
✆18 bedrs, 1 en suite, (12 sh), 4 ba; TV; tcf
✆TV, dogs; P 18, child facs ✆LD 7.30, nr lunch & Fri–Sun dinner. Resid lic

Northanger   35 Westminster Rd, Earlsdon CV1 3GB ✆(0203) 226780.
Situated off A429 on entering Coventry.
✆9 bedrs, 3 ba; TV; tcf ✆TV, dogs; coach; child facs ✆Breakfast only. Unlic
£ B&B £15–£16, B&B (double) £26–£28.

COWAN BRIDGE   Lancashire.   Map 22F3

Collingholme Farm   via Carnforth, LA6 2JL ✆(052 42) 71775. *Farm.* Anne and Peter Burrow
Sleeps 5, ns ✆
£ B&B from £10

Garghyll Dyke   Kirkby Lonsdale, Carnforth, LA6 2HT ✆(05242) 71446. *Farm.* Gillian Burrow
Sleeps 4, ✆ ✆
£ B&B from £11·50–£13

COWLEY   Gloucestershire.   Map 26B7

Butlers Hill Farm   Cockleford, Cheltenham, GL53 9NW ✆(024 287) 455. *Farm.* Bridget Brickell
Sleeps 6, ✆(6)
£ B&B from £12·50, D £6

COXLEY VINEYARD   Somerset.   Map 29D6

Coxley Vineyard (Highly Acclaimed)   Nr Wells, BA5 1RQ ✆Wells (0749) 73854.
Modern hotel and restaurant overlooking vineyard on A39 between Glastonbury and Wells.
✆4 bedrs, 4 en suite; TV; tcf ✆P 30; child facs ✆LD 9.30, nr Sat lunch, Sun dinner & all Wed. Resid & Rest lic
cc Access, Amex, B'card/Visa, Diners; dep.

CRACKINGTON HAVEN   Cornwall.
                                                        Map 28D4

✆ ✆ Coombe Barton   EX23 0JG ✆St Gennys (084 03) 345
An extended Georgian building right by the beach in beautiful bay. Open 15 Mar–Oct.
✆7 bedrs, 3 en suite, 2 ba; TV; tcf ✆TV, dogs, ns; P 40; no children under 2 ✆LD 9.30
£ B&B £19–£31·50, B&B (double) £36–£45; [5% V]
cc Access, Amex; dep.

Trevigue Farm   Bude, EX23 0LQ ✆(08403) 418
Farm. Janet Crocker
Sleeps 6, ns ✆(12)
£ B&B from £16–£18, D £11

Treworgie Barton Bude, EX23 0NL ☎ (08403) 233. *Farm.* Pam Mount
Sleeps 6, ☙
£ B&B from £12–£18, D £9

CRANBROOK Kent. Map 27C4

Hallwood Farm TN17 2SP ☎ (0580) 713204. *Farm.* Ann and David Wickham
Sleeps 6, ☞ ns ☙ (5)
£ B&B from £15, D £10

CRANFORD ST ANDREW
Northamptonshire. Map 24F1

Dairy Farm Kettering, NN14 4AQ ☎ (053 678) 273. *Farm.* Audrey Clarke ⅊
Sleeps 6, ☞ ns ☙
£ B&B from £17, D £8.50

CRANTOCK Cornwall. Map 28C3

Crantock Cottage West Pentire Rd, TR8 5SA ☎ (0637) 830232.
Small hotel with fine views over Crantock Bay. From Newquay/Perranporth road follow signs to Crantock. Hotel on right before leaving village.
🛏 9 bedrs, 4 en suite, 2 ba; tcf 📺 TV, dogs, ns; P 10; child facs ✗ LD 6. Resid & Rest lic
£ B&B £15·20–£20; HB weekly £122·50–£154·50; L £4·50, D £6·25; WB £52 (3 nights); dep.

CRAVEN ARMS Shropshire. Map 31B7

Strefford Hall Farm Strefford, SY7 8DE ☎ (0588) 672383. *Farm.* Mrs Caroline Morgan
Sleeps 6, ns ☙
£ B&B from £12·50–£15, D £7·50

CRAWLEY West Sussex. Map 27A4

Barnwood (Acclaimed) Balcombe Rd, Pound Hill, RH10 4RU ☎ (0293) 882709.
🛏 35 bedrs, 35 en suite; TV; tcf 📺 P 50, coach; child facs ✗ LD 9, nr lunch
cc Access, Amex, B'card/Visa, CB, Diners; dep.

CREDITON Devon. Map 29A4

Thatched Cottage (Acclaimed) Barnstaple Cross, EX17 2EW ☎ (036 32) 3115.
🛏 3 bedrs, 3 en suite; TV; tcf 📺 TV, dogs, ns; P 6; child facs ✗ dinner by arrangement. Unlic

Court Barton Lapford, EX17 6PZ ☎ (0363) 83441. *Farm.* Sheila Mather
Sleeps 6 + cot, ns ☙
£ B&B from £13·50, D £7

CROMER Norfolk. Map 25E3

Westgate Lodge (Highly Acclaimed) Macdonald Rd, NR27 9AP ☎ (0263) 512840.

Fully modernised, detached Victorian hotel standing in its own grounds. Opposite the putting greens just off the front at West End. Open Etr–Oct.
🛏 11 bedrs, 11 en suite, 1 ba; TV; tcf 📺 P 12; children over 3 ✗ LD 6.30, nr lunch. Resid lic
£ B&B (double) £42·55; HB weekly £157·55; D £9; dep.

Chellow Dene (Acclaimed) 23 Macdonald Rd, NR27 9AP ☎ (0263) 513251. Open Apr–Oct.
🛏 7 bedrs, 2 ba; TV; tcf 📺 TV, dogs; P 6; child facs ✗ LD 5, nr lunch
£ B&B £14; HB weekly £104; dep.

Sandcliff Runton Rd, NR27 0HJ ☎ (0263) 512888.
Sea front hotel, situated at the junction of McDonald Rd, opposite putting green. Closed Xmas & New Year
🛏 23 bedrs, 15 en suite, 2 ba; TV; tcf 📺 TV, dogs, ns; P 14; coach; child facs ✗ LD 7.30, bar snacks only lunch. Resid lic
£ B&B £18·20–£22·20; dep.

Shrublands Farm Northrepps, NR27 0LN ☎ (0263) 78297. *Farm.* Mrs Ann Youngman
Sleeps 6, ☙ (13) ns
£ B&B from £13.50, D £9

CROPWELL BISHOP Nottinghamshire. Map 24E3

Home Farm NG12 3BU ☎ (0602) 892598
Farm. Mrs K. Barlow
Sleeps 4
£ B&B from £12

CROYDE Devon. Map 28F6

The Whiteleaf (Highly Acclaimed) EX33 1PN ☎ (0271) 890266.
A comfortable 1930s hotel surrounded by lawns and terraces. Furnished and run as a private house. Situated SW of Croyde village on B3231 Croyde/Braunton road.
🛏 5 bedrs, 5 en suite; TV; tcf 📺 dogs; P 10; child facs ✗ LD 7, nr lunch. Resid lic
£ B&B £27–£29, B&B (double) £44–£48; HB weekly £235–£255; WB £115 (3 nights D, B&B) cc Access, B'card/Visa; dep.

Combas Farm EX33 1PH ☎ (0271) 890398
Farm. Mrs Gwen Adams ⅊
Sleeps 12, ☞ ☙
£ B&B from £12–£14, D £5

Weekend breaks
Please consult the hotel for full details of weekend breaks; prices shown are an indication only. Many hotels offer mid week breaks as well.

CROYDE BAY Devon.   Map 28F6

Moorsands House (Acclaimed)   Moor La,
EX33 1NP ✆Croyde (0271) 890781.

*Spacious Victorian hotel, renovated to a high
standard, with garden and sea views. Take B3231
from Braunton to Croyde Post Office. Turn left and
first left into Moor Lane. Open Mar–Oct.*
🛏8 bedrs, 8 en suite, TV; tcf 🛅TV, dogs, ns; P 8;
children over 2 ✕LD 6, nr lunch. Resid lic
£B&B £18–£20, B&B (double) £32–£36; HB weekly
£150·50–£164·50; D £7·50; [10% V] **cc** Access,
B'card/Visa; dep.

CROYDON Surrey.   Map 27B5

♟ ♟ **Windsor Castle**   415 Brighton Rd, CR2
6EJ ✆081-680 4559 Fax: 081-680 4559.
*Modernised Queen Anne coaching inn with recent
extensions of red brick.*
🛏30 bedrs, 30 en suite; TV; tcf
🛅TV, dogs, ns; P 65, coach; child facs

Kirkdale (Acclaimed)   22 St Peter's Rd CR0 1HD
✆081-688 5898 Fax: 081-667 0817.
*Large detached building close to Fairfield Halls and
centre of Croydon.*
🛏18 bedrs, 7 en suite, 2 ba; TV; tcf 🛅P 12; no
children under 3 ✕LD 8, nr lunch & dinner w/e.
Resid lic
£ B&B £23–£28, B&B (double) £37–£42
cc Access, B'card/Visa; dep.

Markington (Acclaimed)   9 Haling Park Rd, South
Croydon, CR2 6NG ✆081-681 6494 Fax: 081-688
6530.
*Late Victorian property skilfully converted into a
hotel with modern furnishings. Situated off the A235.*

*From London take A23, from M25 take junction 7.
Closed Xmas & New Year.*
🛏22 bedrs, 22 en suite, 2 ba; TV; tcf 🛅TV, dogs,
ns; P 19, coach ✕LD 8.30, nr lunch & Fri–Sun
dinner. Resid lic
£B&B £30–£48, B&B (double) £45–£58; D £10; WB
(£50); [10% V w/e] **cc** Access, Amex, B'card/Visa;
dep.

Alpine   16–22 Moreton Rd, CR2 7DL ✆081-
688 6116.
*Pass under railway bridge, Moreton Rd is first left
after S. Croydon station.*
🛏35 bedrs, 29 en suite, 4 ba; TV; tcf 🛅TV; P 40,
coach; child facs ✕LD 9.30. Resid lic
£B&B £33–£42, B&B (double) £42–£48; HB weekly
£260–£324; L £8·50, D £8·50

Beech House   7–11 Beech House Rd, CR0 1JQ
✆081-688 4385 Fax: 081-760 0861. *Private hotel.*
🛏24 bedrs, 20 en suite, (1 sh), 1 ba; TV; tcf
🛅P 10, coach; child facs ✕LD 7.45, nr lunch &
Fri–Sun dinner. Resid lic
£ B&B £38–£45, B&B (double) £45–£58; WB
cc Access, B'card/Visa; dep.

Lonsdale   158 Lower Addiscombe Rd. ✆081-
654 2276 or 5957.
*Family run hotel with well-kept garden. Situated on
A222, a few mins walk from E or W Croydon
stations. Billiards.*
🛏12 bedrs, 2 en suite, 4 ba; TV; tcf 🛅TV; P 10,
coach; child facs ✕LD midday, nr lunch. Resid lic
£ B&B £32–£37, B&B (double) £42–£47·50; HB
weekly £285·50–£321·50; D £11·50; WB (£29);
[10% V w/d, 5% V w/e] **cc** Access, Amex, B'card/
Visa; dep.

CUBLEY Derbyshire.   Map 24C3

South View Farm   Ashbourne, DE6 2FB ✆(0335)
330302. *Farm.* Carol Critchlow
Sleeps 6, 🐕 (6 mths)
£ B&B from £11

CUCKLINGTON Somerset.   Map 29D5

Hale Farm   Wincanton, BA9 9PN ✆(0963)
33342. *Farm.* Pat and Jim David
Sleeps 6, 🐈 ns 🐕 (3)
£ B&B from £13, D £6·50

CULLOMPTON Devon. Map 29B4

Newcourt Barton Langford, EX15 1SE ✆(088 47)
326. *Farm.* Mrs Sheila A Hitt
Sleeps 6, ns ☡ (11)
£ B&B from £10·50–£11·50

Oburnford Farm EX15 1LZ ✆(0884) 32292
Farm. Mrs Gillian Pring
Sleeps 14, ⚲ ☡
£ B&B from £16·50, D £9

DARLASTON West Midlands. Map 24B2

Hotel Petite (Acclaimed) Stafford Rd, WS10 8UA
✆021-526 5482. *Hotel.*

DARSHAM Suffolk. Map 27F8

Priory Farm Saxmundham, IP17 3QD ✆(072 877)
459. *Farm.* Mrs Suzanne Bloomfield
Sleeps 4, ☡ ns
£ B&B from £13, D £8

DAVENTRY Northamptonshire. Map 26E8

Drayton Lodge NN11 4NL ✆(0327)
702449. *Farm.* Ann Spicer
Sleeps 6, ⚲ ns ☡   ♿
£ B&B from £15–£20

DAWLISH Devon. Map 29B3

West Hatch (Acclaimed) 34 West Cliff, EX7 9DN
✆(0626)864211.
*Detached, homely hotel overlooking the sea, close
to the beach. From town centre hotel is up West
Cliff (Teignmouth Rd) on the right.*

⊨11 bedrs, 10 en suite, (1 sh), 1 ba; TV; tcf
TV, ns; P 11; child facs ✗LD 5.30, nr Mon–Sat
lunch & Sun dinner. Resid lic
£ B&B £24–£31·50, B&B (double) £33–£42; HB
weekly £138·50–£172; dep.

Mimosa 11 Barton Ter, EX7 9QH
✆(0626)863283.
*Victorian building just 6 mins walk from the sea.
Situated opposite Manor Gardens and Dawlish
Museum.*
⊨9 bedrs, 1 en suite, 2 ba TV; P 4; no children
under 2 ✗LD 3, nr lunch. Resid lic
£ B&B £10–£11; HB weekly £97–£103; dep.

Lidwell Farm EX7 0PS ✆(0626) 773001. *Farm.*
Alison Thomson
Sleeps 6, ☡
£ B&B from £10–£12, D £7

DEAL Kent. Map 27F4

Sutherland House 186 London Rd, CT14 9PT
✆(0304)362853.
⊨10 bedrs, 10 en suite; TV P 17, no children
under 5 ✗LD 12 noon, nr lunch Sun dinner. Resid
& Rest lic
£ B&B (double) £38; D £14–£20 **cc** Access, Amex,
B'card/Visa, Diners; dep.

DELPH Lancashire. Map 24B6

🍺 🍺 **Old Bell** Huddersfield Rd, Saddleworth,
OL3 5EG ✆Saddleworth (0457) 870130.
*Well-restored 18th-century stone-built inn on edge
of village on A62.* ✗ Fr

10 bedrs, 9 en suite, (1 sh); TV; tcf dogs; P 25; child facs ✕LD 9.30
£ B&B £38·50–£46·50 (w/e £21·80), B&B (double) £54·50; L £7·50, D £10·50; **cc** Access, B'card/Visa.

Globe Farm Huddersfield Road, Nr Oldham, OL3 5LU ☎(0457) 873040. *Farm.* Jean Mayall
Sleeps 6, 🐕
£ B&B from £14, D from £4·50

DENSHAW Greater Manchester. Map 24B6

Boothstead Farm Rochdale Road, Oldham, OL3 5UE ☎(0457) 878622. *Farm.* Mrs Norma Hall
Sleeps 5, 🐕 ns
£ B&B from £15, D £6

DENSTONE Staffordshire. Map 24C3

Manor House Farm Prestwood, Nr Uttoxeter, ST14 5DD ☎(0889) 590415. *Farm.* Chris Ball
Sleeps 6, ns 🐕
£ B&B from £11–£18

DERBY Derbyshire. Map 24D3

Rollz (Acclaimed) 684 Osmaston Rd, DE2 8GT ☎(0332) 41026.
Leave M1 at junction 24 on A6 to Derby. At A11 ring road take A514 Milbourne to Derby road.
14 bedrs, 3 ba; tcf TV; P 3; no children under 3 ✕LD 8.30, nr lunch. Resid lic
£ B&B £18·40; dep.

Rangemoor (Acclaimed) 67 Macklin St, DE1 1LF ☎(0332) 47252.
Head for city centre and St Peters St, into Victoria St, turn left into Becket St and left again into Macklin St.
20 bedrs, 6 ba; TV; tcf TV, dogs; P 18, G 2, coach; child facs ✕Breakfast only. Unlic
£ B&B £21·50, B&B (double) £32

DERSINGHAM Norfolk. Map 25C3

Westdene House (Acclaimed) 60 Hunstanton Rd, PE31 6HQ ☎(0485) 540395.

Victorian house with good facilities and beautiful gardens. Situated on the A149 midway between Kings Lynn and Hunstanton. On right at traffic lights.
5 bedrs, 1 en suite, 1 ba; TV; tcf TV, dogs;

P 15, coach; child facs ✕LD 10. Resid & Rest lic
£ B&B £16–£18, B&B (double) £28–£32; HB weekly £148–£160; L £5·50, D £7·50 **cc** Access, B'card/Visa; dep.

DEVIZES Wiltshire. Map 26C5

Higher Green Farm Poulshot, SN10 4RW ☎(0380) 828355. *Farm.* Marlene Nixon
Sleeps 6, 🐓 ns 🐕
£ B&B from £13

Lower Foxhangers Farm Rowde, SN10 1SS ☎(0380) 828254. *Farm.* Cynthia & Colin Fletcher
Sleeps 6, 🐓 🐕
£ B&B from £12·50

DIDDLEBURY Shropshire. Map 31B8

Glebe Farm (Acclaimed) Nr Craven Arms, SY7 9DH ☎Munslow (058476) 221.
An elegant Elizabethan farmhouse with one wing half-timbered and the other built of mellow sandstone. Gardens with stream and well-kept lawns. Situated east of B4368, 4 miles north east of Craven Arms. Open Mar–Nov.
6 bedrs, 4 en suite, 1 ba; TV; tcf dogs, ns; P 10, G 2; children over 8 ✕LD 6, nr lunch, Mon & Tues dinner Wed–Sun dinner by arrangement. Resid & Rest lic
£ B&B £18–£25; D £12·50; dep.

DINTON Buckinghamshire. Map 26F7

Wallace Farm Nr Aylesbury, HP17 8UF ☎(0296) 748660 Fax: (0296) 748851. *Farm.* Jackie Cook ♿
Sleeps 6, 🐕
£ B&B from £14–£16

DISS Norfolk. Map 25E1

Shimpling Hall Farm IP21 4UF ☎(0379) 741233. *Farm.* Mrs Helen Gowing
Sleeps 6, 🐕 ns
£ B&B from £15

DODDISCOMBSLEIGH Devon. Map 29A4

Whitemoor Farm Nr Exeter, EX6 7PU ☎(0647) 52423. *Farm.* Mrs Barbara Lacey
Sleeps 6, 🐓 ns 🐕 (5)
£ B&B from £12–£14

Please tell the manager if you chose your hotel through an advertisement in the guide.

Weekend breaks
Please consult the hotel for full details of weekend breaks; prices shown are an indication only. Many hotels offer mid week breaks as well.

DONCASTER South Yorkshire. Map 24E6

Almel 20 Christchurch Rd, DN1 2QL ☎(0302) 365230.
Family run hotel in the centre of Doncaster. Christchurch Rd leads of the left hand side of Church Way.
⊨26 bedrs, 4 en suite, (2 sh), 6 ba; TV; tcf
🏠TV, dogs; P8, coach ✕LD 8, nr lunch. Resid & Rest lic
£ B&B fr £17, B&B (double) fr £30; D£3·50
cc Access, B'card/Visa; dep.

DORCHESTER Dorset. Map 29D4

Lower Lewell Farmhouse West Stafford, DT2 8AP ☎(0305) 267169. *Farm.* Marian Tomblin
Sleeps 6, ⛄
£ B&B from £13–£16

Maiden Castle Farm DT2 9PR ☎(0305) 62356. *Farm.* Hilary Hoskin
Sleeps 6, 🐴⛄
£ B&B from £14

Manor Farm Waterston, DT2 7SS ☎(0305) 848210. *Farm.* Ann Bamlet
Sleeps 6, 🐴⛄ (3)
£ B&B from £12–£15

DORSINGTON Warwickshire. Map 26C8

Church Farm CV37 8AX ☎Stratford-upon-Avon (0789) 720471.
⊨7 bedrs, 7 en suite; TV; tcf 🏠TV, ns; P10, coach; child facs ✕LD5.30, nr lunch. Unlic
£B&B fr £11·50

DOVEDALE Derbyshire. Map 24C4

Hillcrest House (Acclaimed) Thorpe, DE6 2AW ☎Thorpe Cloud (033 529) 436.
⊨7 bedrs, 1 ba; tcf 🏠TV, dogs; P12, coach; child facs ✕LD5. Resid & Rest lic

DOVER Kent. Map 27E4

Ardmore (Highly Acclaimed) 18 Castle Hill Rd, CT16 1QW ☎(0304) 205895.
A 200 year old listed family-run hotel with views of harbour and town, set in the leas of Dover Castle, from M2/A2 follow signs to docks and castle. Closed Xmas.
⊨4 bedrs, 4 en suite; TV; tcf
🏠ns; U1 ✕Breakfast only. Unlic
£ B&B (double) £25–£40; WB (Nov–Feb); dep.

East Lee (Highly Acclaimed) 108 Maison Dieu Rd, CT16 1RT ☎(0304) 210176.

EAST LEE
Guest House
108, Maison Dieu Road, DOVER,
Kent CT16 1RT
Tele: DOVER (0304) 210176
Resident Proprietors Mr & Mrs. M. J. Knight

A fine Victorian residence, tastefully restored and decorated in traditional style. From town centre follow signs for docks, and East Lee is on the one-way system.
⊨4 beds, 4 en suite; tcf 🏠TV, NS; P2, G2; child facs ✕Breakfast only. Unlic
£ B&B £25, B&B (double) £28–£34; [5% V]
cc Acccess, B'card/Visa; dep.

Number One (Highly Acclaimed) 1 Castle St, CT16 1QH ☎(0304) 202007.

A charming Georgian town house, built about 1800 and retaining many original features. High walled garden overlooked by Dover Castle. From M20 and A20 follow Castle directions in Dover. From M2 and A2 take Dover bypass to second roundabout, then turn right. Number One at bottom of hill.
⊨5 bedrs, 3 en suite, (2 sh); TV; tcf
🏠ns; P2, U4 (£2) ✕Breakfast only. Unlic
£ B&B £22–£31, B&B (double) £26–£35; [10% V]; dep.

Beaufort House (Acclaimed) 18 Eastcliff Marine Parade, CT16 1LU ☎(0304) 216444 Fax: (0304) 211100.
Listed Georgian building overlooking sea with sunny terrace. On the seafront 150 yards from entrance to Eastern Docks.
⊨26 bedrs, 26 en suite, 3 ba; TV; tcf 🏠TV, dogs, ns; P24, G2, coach; child facs ✕LD 10.30
£ B&B £24–£29, B&B (double) £34–£42; L£3·50, D£5; [5% V] **cc** Access, B'card/Visa

Castle House (Acclaimed) 10 Castle Hill Rd, CT16 1QW ☎(0304) 201656 Fax: (0304) 210197.

Listed building circa 1830 situated at the foot of Dover Castle. Follow signs to castle. Closed Dec.
🛏6 bedrs, 3 en suite, (3 sh); TV; tcf 🏠ns; P3, G1 (£2); no children under 10 ✗nr lunch, Mon dinner. Resid lic
£B&B £23–£26, B&B (double) £28–£34
cc Access, B'card/Visa; dep.

Fleur de Lis (Acclaimed)   9–10 Effingham Cres, CT17 9RH ☎(0304) 206142. *Hotel.*

Gateway Hovertel (Acclaimed)   Snargate St, CT17 9BL ☎(0304) 205479.
Follow Hoverport signs to Snargate St and hotel is on right. Open Feb–Dec.
🛏27 bedrs, 27 en suite; TV 🏠TV; P27, coach; child facs ✗LD 7.30, nr lunch. Resid lic
£B&B £27·50–£32·50, B&B (double) £44–£50; [10% V except Jul & Aug] cc Access, B'card/Visa.

Hubert House (Acclaimed)   9 Castle Hill Rd, CT16 1QW ☎(0304) 202253.

🛏10 bedrs, 3 en suite, (4 sh), 2 ba; TV; tcf 🏠dogs; P8; child facs ✗LD9, nr lunch. Sun dinner. Rest lic
£B&B £22–£25, B&B (double) £34–£38; D £7·75
cc Access, B'card/Visa, Diners; dep.

Palma Nova (Acclaimed)   126 Folkstone Rd, CT17 9SP ☎(0304) 208109.

Family-run guest house in converted town house. Situated on the A20 Dover–Folkestone road. From Eastern Docks follow signs to Folkestone, then turn left at second roundabout into Folkestone Rd. Closed Xmas.
🛏6 beds, 2 ba; TV 🏠TV, dogs, ns; P6 ✗LD 7.30, nr lunch. Unlic
£ B&B £14–18, B&B (double) £22–24; D £6·50; WB (£20); [10% V Dec–Apr]; dep.

Pennyfarthing (Acclaimed)   109 Maison Dieu Rd, CT16 1RT ☎(0304) 205563.
Spacious, comfortable Victorian guest house close to ferries and hoverport.
🛏6 bedrs, 4 en suite, (2 sh); TV; tcf 🏠ns; P6; child facs ✗Breakfast only. Unlic
£B&B £14–£16, WB (mid-Sept–Mar); dep.

Peverell House (Acclaimed)   28 Park Av, CT16 1HD ☎(0304) 202573.

From A2 towards Dover Castle, turn right off Castle Hill Rd, and hotel is halfway down hill on the left.
🛏6 bedrs, 2 en suite, 2 ba; TV; tcf 🏠TV, dogs; P6 (£1); child facs ✗LD 5, nr lunch. Resid lic
£B&B £15–£17, B&B (double) £24–£28; HB weekly fr £150; D £5; dep.

Tower (Acclaimed)   98 Priory Hill, CT17 0AD ☎(0304) 208212.
Converted water tower, fully modernised and with own private entrance and garden. Turn left at traffic lights opposite Town Hall, Tower is the last house on the right up Priory Hill. Closed 24–28 Dec.
🛏5 bedrs, 3 en suite, 1 ba; TV; tcf 🏠dogs, ns; P1, U2; child facs ✗Breakfast only. Unlic
£ B&B £18–£25, B&B (double) £26–£35; [10% V Thurs–Sat]; dep.

Ashmohr   331 Folkestone Rd, CT17 9JG ☎(0304) 205305.

Dover (Kent) _____

Beaufort House

18 East Cliff, Marine Parade, Dover, Kent CT16 1LU
Tel: 0304 216444   Fax: 0304 211100
Ideally located on seafront just 150yds from main port and easily spotted by red canopies. Private secure car park. Wake up calls and early breakfasts arranged. Licensed bar and evening meals available. 26 rooms all en-suite. Credit card and group reservations welcomed.

On main A20 Folkestone to Dover road, 1 mile from town centre.
🛏3 bedrs, 1 ba; tcf 📺TV; P 3 ✗Breakfast only. Unlic
£ B&B (double) £22–£26; [10% V]; dep.

Beulah House   94 Crabble Hill, CT17 0SA
📞(0304) 824615.
Small guest house with riverside gardens. Situated next to Esso garage on A256 Crabble Hill.
🛏8 bedrs, (1 sh), 2 ba; TV 📺TV, ns; P 8, U 1 (£2); child facs ✗Breakfast only. Unlic
£ B&B £18, B&B (double) fr £34; dep.

Byways   247 Folkestone Rd, CT17 9LL 📞(0304) 204514.
Well-fitted family-run hotel. Enter Dover on Folkestone road and Byways is first hotel on right.
🛏15 bedrs, 7 en suite, (2 sh), 2 ba; TV; tcf 📺P 12, coach; no children under 2 ✗nr lunch. Resid & Rest lic
£ B&B £14–£20, B&B (double) £25–£35; [5% V]
cc Access, B'card/Visa; dep.

Continental   Marine Par, East Cliff, CT16 1LZ
📞(0304) 201669.
Regency hotel at foot of the white cliffs. Situated close to Eastern Docks on Dover seafront.
🛏6 bedrs, 6 en suite; TV; tcf 📺P6 ✗LD 9
£ B&B £30–£35, B&B (double) £46–£55; HB weekly £231–£266; L £5, D £10; dep.

Elmo   120 Folkestone Rd, CT17 9SP 📞(0304) 206236.
Situated on the main A20 towards Folkestone, close to Priory Station.
🛏6 bedrs, 2 ba; TV 📺TV; P 6, U 1, coach ✗LD 8, nr lunch, Sun dinner. Unlic
£ B&B £13–£16, B&B (double) £21–£25; [5% V Nov–Mar]

Weekend breaks
Please consult the hotel for full details of weekend breaks; prices shown are an indication only. Many hotels offer mid week breaks as well.

Discount vouchers
RAC discount vouchers are at the end of the guide. Establishments with a [V] shown at the end of the price information will accept them in part payment for accommodation bills on the full, standard rate, not against bargain breaks or any other special offers. Please note the limitations shown in the entry: w/e for weekends, w/d for weekdays, and which months they are accepted.

Linden   231 Folkestone Rd, CT17 9SL 📞(0304) 205449.
On A20 ¾ mile west of town centre.
🛏4 bedrs, 1 ba; tcf 📺TV; P 4; no children under 3 ✗Breakfast only. Unlic
£ B&B £14; [10% V Oct–May]; dep.

St Brelade's   82 Buckland Av, CT16 2NW
📞(0304) 206126.
Conveniently placed guest house close to ferry and docks. From London Rd turn left into Buckland Ave.
🛏8 bedrs, (2 sh), 3 ba; TV; tcf 📺TV, ns; P 6, coach; child facs ✗LD 10, nr lunch. Resid lic
£ B&B £14·50–£18, B&B (double) £25–£35; D £12·50; WB (£13 pp); [5% V Nov–Apr]
cc Access, B'card/Visa; dep.

St Martins   17 Castle Hill Rd, CT16 1QW 📞(0304) 205938.
Grade II listed hotel built in 1830. Situated beside Dover Castle. Closed Xmas.
🛏8 bedrs, (8 sh), 1 ba; TV; tcf 📺ns; child facs ✗Breakfast only. Resid lic
£ B&B £18–£25, B&B (double) £25–£35; dep.

Westbank   239 Folkestone Rd, CT17 9LL 📞(0304) 201061.
Semi-detached Victorian house near docks. Situated on A20 Folkestone Rd.
🛏5 bedrs, 2 en suite, 1 ba; TV; tcf 📺dogs; P 6; child facs ✗LD 6, nr lunch. Resid lic
£ B&B £14–£16, B&B (double) £25–£30; dep.

Whitmore   261 Folkestone Rd, CT17 9LL 📞(0304) 203080.
Small guest house with private car park. On main A20 Folkestone Rd at junction with Elms Vale Rd.
🛏4 bedrs, 1 en suite, 1 ba; TV; tcf 📺dogs; P 4, coach; child facs ✗Dinner by arrangement, nr lunch. Unlic
£ B&B £12–£15, B&B (double) £20–£28; D £6·50; WB

DOVERIDGE   Derbyshire.   Map 24C3

Ley Hill Farm Guest House   DE6 5PA 📞(0889) 564252. *Farm.* Mrs Beverley Poyser
Sleeps 16
£ B&B from £15, D from £7·50

The Beeches Farmhouse   Waldley, Derby, DE6 5LR 📞(0889) 590288. *Farm.* Barbara Tunnicliffe
Sleeps 16, 🐾 🐕
£ B&B from £12·50–£18, D £6·50

DOWN THOMAS Devon. Map 28F2

Gabber Farm Plymouth, PL9 0AW ☎(0752)
862269. *Farm.* Margaret MacBean
Sleeps 12, ⮑ ⋔
£ B&B from £10, D £5

DOWNTON Wiltshire. Map 26C3

The Warren High St, nr Salisbury, SP5 3PG
☎(0725) 20263.
*Part Elizabethan house with large walled garden.
Leave Salisbury by A338 to Downton, turn left at
traffic lights and Warren on left opposite Post Office.
Closed Dec 16–Jan 15.*
🛏6 bedrs, 1 en suite, 3 ba; tcf 🏨TV, dogs, ns; P 8;
no children under 5 ✗Breakfast only. Unlic
£ B&B £25–£30, B&B (double) £40–£43; dep.

DROITWICH Hereford & Worcester
(Worcestershire). Map 26B8

Foxbrook 238a Worcester Rd, WR9 8AY☎(0905)
772414. *Guest House.*

DROXFORD Hampshire. Map 26E4

Little Uplands (Highly Acclaimed) Garrison Hill,
Little Uplands, SO3 1QL ☎(0489) 878507
Fax: (0489) 877853.
*On main A32 Alton Fareham Rd. Swimming pool,
tennis, sauna, solarium, gymnasium, fishing.*
🛏17 bedrs, 17 en suite; TV; tcf 🏨TV, dogs, ns;
P65, G 25, coach; child facs ✗LD 9. Resid & Rest
lic
£ B&B £30, B&B (double) £40; HB weekly £300;
L £3·50, D £7·50; [10% V] **cc** Access, Amex,
B'card/Visa, Diners; dep.

DULVERTON Somerset. Map 29A5

Springfield Farm TA22 9QD ☎(0398)
23722. *Farm.* Tricia Vellacott
Sleeps 4, ⋔ ns ⮑
£ B&B from £11–£13, D £6–£8

DUNMOW, GREAT Essex. Map 27C7

Spicer (Acclaimed) Brick End, Broxted, CM6 2BL
☎(0279) 850047.

DUNSTER Somerset. Map 29B6

Bilbrook Lawns (Acclaimed) Bilbrook, TA24 6HE
☎Washford (0984) 40331.

*Georgian house set behind extensive lawns
bordered on one side by a stream. Situated on A39
3 miles W of Williton on right. Open Mar–Oct &
Xmas.*
🛏7 bedrs, 4 en suite, 1 ba; TV; tcf 🏨dogs, ns; P8;
child facs ✗LD 7.30. Resid & Rest lic
£ B&B £21·50–£25, B&B (double) £33–£44; HB
weekly £150–£185; L £6·50, D £10·50; WB (£47·50);
dep.

DYMCHURCH Kent. Map 27E4

Chantry Sycamore Gdns, TN29 0LA ☎(0303)
873137.
*Small hotel with sea views and large garden. From
A259 Hythe road take first left after Ship Inn into
Sycamore Gdns.*
🛏6 bedrs, 5 en suite, 1 ba; TV; tcf 🏨TV, dogs;
P 10, coach; child facs ✗LD 9. Resid & Rest lic
£ B&B £15–£21, B&B (double) £30–£38; HB weekly
£128–£157·50; D £6; WB (£42); [10% V]; dep.

EARL STERNDALE Derbyshire. Map 24C4

Fernydale Farm Buxton, SK17 0BS ☎(029883)
236. *Farm.* Joan Nadin
Sleeps 4
£ B&B from £15, D £10

EARSHAM Suffolk. Map 25E1

Earsham Park Farm Harleston Road, Bungay,
NR35 2AQ ☎(0986) 892180. *Farm.* Mrs Bobbie
Watchorn
Sleeps 6, ns ⮑
£ B&B from £16

Symbols (full details on p. 4)

🛏 information about bedrooms	nr no restaurant service	*Farms*
🏨 facilities at hotels	✗ languages spoken	⋔ dogs accepted
✗ information about meals	[V] RAC vouchers accepted	⮑ (4) children accepted (min. age)

EAST BARKWITH Lincolnshire.   Map 25A5

The Grange Torrington Lane, Nr Wragby, LN3 5RY ✆ (0673) 858249. *Farm.* Anne Stamp
Sleeps 6, ns ☎
£ B&B from £15, D from £8

EASTBOURNE East Sussex.   Map 27C2

Bay Lodge (Acclaimed)   61 Royal Par, BN22 7AQ ✆ (0323) 32515.
Attractive, detached seafront hotel with a large sun lounge, overlooking the Redoubt Gardens. Take the A22 to the seafront, turn right towards the pier and hotel is 200 yards on the right. Open Mar–mid-Oct.
➤ 12 bedrs, 9 en suite, 2 ba; TV; tcf 📶 TV, ns; G 2 (£3); no children under 7 ✗ LD 6, nr lunch. Resid & Rest lic
£ B&B £16–£21; B&B (double) £37–£53; HB weekly £147–£174; D £7; [10% V Mar–Jun, Sept & Oct]
cc Access, B'card/Visa; dep.

Beachy Rise (Acclaimed)   20 Beachy Head Rd, BN20 7QN ✆ (0323) 639171.

Pretty Victorian house, restored and modernised with attractive garden and sun terrace. From A259 Brighton to Eastbourne road take B2103 signed Beachy Head. Guest house is about 1 mile on right.
➤ 6 bedrs, 4 en suite, 1 ba; TV; tcf 📶 dogs, ns; child facs ✗ LD midday, nr lunch. Resid lic
£ B&B (double) £28–£40; HB weekly £138–£170
cc Access, B'card/Visa; dep.

Flamingo (Acclaimed)   20 Enys Rd, BN21 2DN ✆ (0323) 21654.
➤ 12 bedrs, 12 en suite; TV; tcf 📶 children over 8 ✗ LD 4.30, nr lunch. Resid lic
cc Access, B'card/Visa; dep.

Hanburies (Acclaimed)   4 Hardwick Rd, BN21 4HY ✆ (0323) 30698.
Elegant detached hotel in a quiet tree-lined road. Situated in the town centre opposite St Peters and St Saviors Church, off South St. Open Feb–Dec.
➤ 12 bedrs, 9 en suite, 1 ba; TV; tcf 📶 ns; P 3; children over 12 ✗ LD 6.30, nr lunch. Rest lic
£ B&B £18·50–£20·50; HB weekly £138–£160; D £7·50; WB (£44); [10% V]; dep.

Mandalay (Acclaimed)   16 Trinity Trees, BN21 3LE ✆ (0323) 29222.
Entrance to car park in Lismore Rd opposite Debenham's side entrance.
➤ 12 beds, 12 en suite; TV; tcf 📶 ns; P 20; child facs

Alfriston   16 Lushington Rd, BN21 4LL ✆ (0323) 25640.
A modern hotel in the centre of Eastbourne. Follow the A22 into town, continue into Grove Rd, left into South St, then first left and first right. Open Mar–Nov.
➤ 13 bedrs, 9 en suite, 2 ba; TV; tcf 📶 TV, ns; U 2 (£3), coach; no children under 5, child facs ✗ nr Mon–Sat lunch, Sun dinner. Resid lic
£ B&B £16·50–£17·50; D £5; dep.

Courtlands   68 Royal Par, BN22 7AQ ✆ (0323) 26915.
Family-run hotel on the seafront opposite the Redoubt fortress.
➤ 12 bedrs, 1 en suite, (4 sh), 5 ba; tcf 📶 TV; P 1 (£1), U 1 (£2); child facs ✗ LD 6, bar meals only lunch. Resid & Rest lic
£ B&B £16; D £7 cc Access, Amex, B'card/Visa.

Falcondale   5 South Cliff Av, BN20 7AH ✆ (0323) 643633.
Small hotel in a quiet tree-lined avenue. Situated just off King Edward's Parade. Open Apr–Oct
➤ 6 bedrs, 4 en suite, 2 ba; TV; tcf 📶 dogs; no children under 8 ✗ LD 6.15, nr lunch. Resid lic
£ B&B £15–£18; HB weekly £127–£138; D £7; dep.

Gilder   1 Marine Par, BN21 3DX ✆ (0323) 21818.
➤ 8 bedrs, 4 en suite, 1 ba; TV; tcf 📶 TV; P 2 (£3) ✗ LD 6, nr Mon–Sat lunch, Sun dinner. Resid lic
cc Access, Amex, B'card/Visa; dep.

Meridale   91 Royal Par, BN22 7AE ✆ (0323) 29686
➤ 8 bedrs, 2 ba; TV; tcf 📶 TV, dogs; no children ✗ LD 6.30, nr lunch. Unlic

Oakwood   28 Jevington Gdns, BN21 4HN ✆ (0323) 21900 Fax: (0323) 411663
Edwardian house retaining several original features. Take A22 to Eastbourne Station roundabout, take second exit to end of Grove Rd and continue over crossroads. Grange Rd is 6th on the left. Hotel is behind Grand Hotel. Open Mar–Dec.

Please tell the manager if you chose your hotel through an advertisement in the guide.

En suite rooms
En suite rooms may be bath or shower rooms. If you have a preference, remember to state it when booking a room.

ENGLAND

15 bedrs, 4 en suite, 3 ba; TV; tcf
⌂TV, dogs, ns; child facs ✗LD 6, nr lunch.
£ B&B £13–£21; HB weekly £95–£149; [10% V
Nov–Mar, 5% V Apr, May & Oct]; dep.

Sherwood   7 Lascelles Terr, BN21 4BJ ✆(0323)
24002.
*Follow signs to town centre west and Devonshire
Park Theatre. Hotel opposite theatre.*
13 bedrs, 7 en suite, 2 ba; TV; tcf ⌂TV, dogs, ns;
coach; child facs ✗LD 9 am, nr lunch. Resid lic
£ B&B £14·50–£19·50, B&B (double) £27–£38; HB
weekly £120–£150; [5% V Oct–Mar]; dep.

Sovereign View   93 Royal Par, BN22 7AE
✆(0323) 21657.
*Fork left at Willingdon roundabout past Gen.
Hospital cross 2 sets of lights, and turn left into road
immediately before seafront. House 200 yards on
left. Hotel is opposite the pier. Open Apr–Sep.*
7 bedrs, 2 en suite, 2 ba; TV; tcf ⌂TV; no
children under 12 ✗LD 4, nr lunch. Resid lic
£ B&B (double) £30–£34; HB weekly £125–£137;
[5% V Apr, May & Sept]

Stirling House   5 Cavendish Pl, BN21 3EJ
✆(0323) 32263.
Hotel is opposite the pier.
21 bedrs, 11 en suite, 3 ba; TV; tcf ⌂TV, ns;
coach; no children under 5 ✗LD midday, nr lunch.
Resid lic
£ B&B £16, B&B (double) £30–£34; HB weekly
£99–£135; [5% V]; dep.

EAST CLANDON   Surrey.   Map 27A4

Clandon Manor Farm   Back Lane, Guildford,
GU4 7SA ✆(0483) 222357/222765
Fax: (0483) 223585. *Farm.* Sally Grahame or Joan
Haines
Sleeps 8, ⌂ (12)
£ B&B from £10.50–£12.50

EAST GRINSTEAD   West Sussex.   Map 27B4

Acorn Lodge (Acclaimed)   Turners Hill Rd, RH19
4LX ✆(0342) 23207. *Hotel.*

Cranfield Lodge   Maypole Rd, RH19 1HW
✆(0342) 321251 or 410371 Fax: (0342) 321251.
*Family-run hotel in quiet position close to town
centre. Maypole Rd is off A22 London Rd.*
23 bedrs, 12 en suite, (2 sh), 4 ba; TV; tcf
⌂TV, dogs; P 12, U 1, G 2; coach ✗nr lunch.
Resid lic
£ B&B £27–£35, B&B (double) £42–£48; HB weekly
£200–£250; D £10·92; WB (£30); [5% V Dec–Mar
w/e] **cc** Access, Amex, B'card/Visa; dep.

EAST HOLME   Dorset.   Map 29E4

Priory Farm   Wareham, BH20 6AG ✆(0929)
552972. *Farm.* Mrs Goldsack
Sleeps 6, ns ⌂
£ B&B from £13–£15

EASTWOOD   Nottinghamshire.   Map 24D4

Sun Inn   Market Pl, NG16 3NR ✆Langley
Mill (0773) 712940
*Well-established hotel adjacent to the D H Lawrence
centre.*
15 bedrs, 12 en suite, 1 ba; tcf ⌂TV, dogs; P 12,
G 2, coach; child facs ✗LD 8, nr Sun dinner
£ B&B £19–£22·50, B&B (double) £31–£33;
L £4·50, D £5·25; WB

EBBERSTON   North Yorkshire.   Map 23F4

Foxholm   YO13 9NJ ✆Scarborough (0723)
85550. *Hotel.* Open March–Nov.
9 bedrs, 6 en suite, (2 sh), 3 ba; tcf ⌂TV, dogs;
P 12, U 2, G 2 ✗LD 5, nr lunch. Resid & Rest lic
£ B&B £20–£22, B&B (double) £36–£40; HB weekly
£184–£190; D £8; WB (£82 3 nights)

ECCLESHALL   Staffordshire.   Map 24B3

Glenwood   Croxton, ST21 6PF (063 082) 238
*Leave M6 at junction 14 or 15, follow signs to
Eccleshall, then take B5026 to Woore.*
3 bedrs, 1 en suite, 1 ba; TV; tcf ⌂TV, dogs, ns;
P 6; child facs ✗Breakfast only. Unlic
£ B&B £12; WB (£80); [10% V] **cc** Access, B'Card/
Visa; dep.

EDINGLEY   Nottinghamshire.   Map 24E4

New Manor Farm   Greaves Lane, Newark, NG22
8BJ ✆(0623) 883044. *Farm.* Mrs Debbie Tunnicliffe
Sleeps 6, ⌂ ⌂ ns
£ B&B from £13·50, D £6·50

EDINGTON   Wiltshire.   Map 26B4

Hillside Farm   Westbury, BA13 4PG ✆(0380)
830437. *Farm.* Carol Mussell
Sleeps 4, ⌂ ns
£ B&B from £12–£14

Using RAC discount vouchers
Please tell the hotel when booking if you plan to
use an RAC discount voucher (see end of guide)
in part payment of your bill. Only one voucher
will be accepted per party per stay. Discount
vouchers will only be accepted in payment for
accommodation, not for food.

ELLESMERE Shropshire. Map 30F7

Elson House Farm Elson, SY12 9EZ ☎(069 175)
276. *Farm.* Merie Sadler
Sleeps 6, ☎
£ B&B from £12·50

ELY Cambridgeshire. Map 25B1

Hill House Farm 9 Main Street, Coveney, CB6
2DJ ☎(0353) 778369. *Farm.* Hiliary Nix
Sleeps 6, ns ☎
£ B&B from £15

EMBOROUGH Somerset. Map 29D6

Redhill Farm Nr Bath, BA3 4SH ☎(076 121)
294. *Farm.* Jane Rowe
Sleeps 6, ☎ns
£ B&B on application

EMSWORTH Hampshire. Map 26E2

Jingles (Acclaimed) 77 Horndean Rd,
PO10 7PU ☎(0243) 373755.
*Nicely furnished and decorated, family-run hotel on
Emsworth to Rowlands Castle road (B2148).*
🛏13 beds, 4 en suite, 3 ba; tcf 🅟TV, dogs, ns;
P 13, coach; child facs ✕LD 6, nr Mon–Sat lunch.
Resid lic
cc Access, B'card/Visa; dep.

Merry Hall (Acclaimed) 73 Horndean Rd, PO10
7PU ☎(0243) 372424.

Please tell the manager if you chose your hotel
through an advertisement in the guide.

Discount vouchers

RAC discount vouchers are at the end of the
guide. Establishments with a [V] shown at the end
of the price information will accept them in part
payment for accommodation bills on the full,
standard rate, not against bargain breaks or any
other special offers. Please note the limitations
shown in the entry: w/e for weekends, w/d for
weekdays, and which months they are accepted.

---

*Family-run hotel with sun lounge overlooking large
attractive garden. From Emsworth follow B2148
towards Horndean. Hotel on left 1 mile past
Emsworth station. Putting.*
🛏10 bedrs, 7 en suite, (3 sh); TV; tcf 🅟TV; P 12,
coach; child facs ✕LD 7.30, nr Sat, Sun, dinner
Fri. Resid & Rest lic
£ B&B £32·50–£35, B&B (double) £48; [10% V Jan,
Dec] **cc** Access, B'card/Visa; dep.

Chestnuts 55 Horndean Rd, PO10 7PU ☎(0243)
372233.
*On B2148 about 1 mile N of village centre.
Swimming pool.*
🛏4 bedrs, 3 ba 🅟TV, dogs, ns; P 8; child facs
✕Breakfast only. Unlic
£ B&B (double) £25–£30; dep.

Queensgate 80 Havant Rd, PO10 7LH ☎(0243)
371960/377766.
On the A259 Havant Rd.
🛏10 bedrs, (8 sh), 2 ba; TV; tcf 🅟TV, dogs; P 12,
coach ✕Resid lic
£ B&B £19·50, B&B (double) £34·50; [5% V]

ENDON Staffordshire. Map 24B4

Hollinhurst Farm Park Lane, Stoke-on-Trent, ST9
9JB ☎(0782) 502633. *Farm.* Sandra Clowes
Sleeps 6, 🐦ns ☎
£ B&B from £10, D £6·50

EPSOM Surrey. Map 27A5

Epsom Downs (Acclaimed) 9 Longdown Rd,
KT17 3PT ☎(0372) 740643 Fax: (0372) 723259.
*Recently refurbished hotel in quiet suburban area.
From Upper High St Longdown Rd is a left turn.*
🛏15 bedrs, 13 en suite, (2 sh); TV; tcf
🅟TV, dogs; P 17, coach; child facs ✕LD 9
£ B&B £65, B&B (double) £71; L £8·50, D £17·50;
WB (£23) **cc** Access, Amex, B'card/Visa, Diners.

ERLESTOKE Wiltshire. Map 26B4

Longwater Lower Road, Nr Devizes, SN10 5UE
☎(0380) 830095. *Farm.* Pam Hampton &
Sleeps 6, 🐦ns ☎
£ B&B from £16, D £10

Emsworth (Hampshire)

ETCHINGHAM   East Sussex.   Map 27C3

Little Grandturzel Fontridge Lane, TN19 7DE
☎(0435) 882279. *Farm*. Norma Hawke
Sleeps 6, ☎
£ B&B from £14–£18, D £8

ETWALL   Derbyshire.   Map 24C3

Blenheim House (Acclaimed)   56 Main St, DE6
6LP ☎(028 373) 2254.
*Attractive conversion of listed farmhouse and
buildings in village centre.*
⇔7 bedrs, 5 en suite, 1 ba; TV; tcf

EVERCREECH   Somerset.   Map 29D6

♟ ♟ Pecking Mill Inn   A371, BA24 6PG
☎(0749) 830336
*A characterful 16th century inn with a modern
extension; one mile SW of village, on A371. Closed
25 Dec.*
⇔6 bedrs, 6 en suite; TV; tcf 🏠dogs; P23; child
facs ✕LD 10
cc Access, Amex, B'card/Visa, Diners; dep.

EXETER   Devon.   Map 29A4

Park View (Acclaimed)   8 Howell Rd, EX4 4LG
☎(0392) 71772 or 53047.
*Charming Grade II listed Georgian hotel with a
beautifully maintained garden. Overlooking park.
From M5 follow B3183 into city centre to clock tower
roundabout. Take 3rd exit, turn left at end into
Howell Rd. Hotel 200 yards on right.*
⇔15 bedrs, 7 en suite, (2 sh), 4 ba; TV; tcf
🏠TV, dogs, ns; P 6, coach; child facs ✕Breakfast
only. Unlic
£B&B £16–£28 **cc** Access, B'card/Visa; dep.

Braeside   21 New North Rd, EX4 4HF ☎(0392)
56875.
⇔8 bedrs, (3 sh), 1 ba; TV; tcf 🏠TV, dogs, ns;
children over 2 ✕LD 5.30, nr lunch. Unlic

Cre-Ber   32 Heavitree Rd, EX1 2LQ ☎(0392)
76102. *Guest House*.

Regents Park   Polsloe Rd, EX1 2NU ☎(0392)
59749.
⇔11 bedrs, 3 ba; tcf 🏠TV, dogs; P 16 ✕Breakfast
only. Unlic
£B&B £15, B&B (double) £29; dep.

En suite rooms
En suite rooms may be bath or shower rooms.
If you have a preference, remember to state it
when booking a room.

Rowhorne House   Rowhorne, Whitestone, EX4
2LQ ☎(0392) 74675. Open Mar–Oct.
*Leave Exeter for Whitestone village, follow sign to
Rowhorne. Rowhorne House is 2 miles along on left,
marked on white gate.*
⇔3 bedrs, 2 ba; tcf 🏠TV; P 4 ✕nr lunch. Unlic
£ B&B £11; HB weekly £112; [10% V]; dep.

Telstar   77 St David's Hill, EX4 4DW ☎(0392)
72466.
*Situated between St David's station and city centre.
Closed Xmas & New Year.*
⇔16 bedrs, 3 en suite, (4 sh), 2 ba; TV; tcf 🏠TV,
dogs; P 7, coach ✕Dinner by arrangement. Unlic
£B&B £12–£20, B&B (double) £24–£32; HB weekly
£110–£140

Trees Mini   2 Queen's Cres, York Rd, EX4 6AY
☎(0392) 59531.
*Small family run hotel overlooking a tree-lined green.
From High St continue into Sidwell St and York Rd
is on left.*
⇔12 bedrs, 1 en suite, 3 ba; TV; tcf 🏠TV, ns;
coach; child facs ✕LD 8, nr lunch. Unlic
£ B&B £14–£15, B&B (double) £24–£26; D £6; dep.

Mill Farm   Kenton, EX6 8JR ☎(0392)
832471. *Farm*. Delia Lambert
Sleeps 15, ☎
£ B&B from £12

EXFORD   Somerset.   Map 29A6

Ashott Barton   Minehead, TA24 7NG ☎(064 383)
294. *Farm*. Mrs Jackie Thorne
Sleeps 5
£ B&B from £12, D from £7

Edgcott House   Nr Minehead, TA24 7QG ☎(064
383) 495. *Farm*. Gillian Lamble
Sleeps 6, 🐎 ☎
£ B&B from £14–£17, D £8·50

EXHALL   Warwickshire.   Map 26C8

Glebe Farm   Alcester, B49 6EA ☎(0789)
772202. *Farm*. John and Margaret Canning
Sleeps 5, 🐎 ☎
£ B&B from £13·50

EXMOUTH   Devon.   Map 29B3

Carlton Lodge (Acclaimed)   Carlton Hill, EX8 2AJ
☎(0395) 263314.
*Detached, modernised hotel 300 yards from beach.
From seafront turn left between Pavilion and
swimming pool into Carlton Hill.*
⇔6 bedrs, 4 en suite, 1 ba; TV; tcf
🏠dogs, P 12; child facs ✕LD 10
£ B&B £21–£25, B&B (double) £32–38; HB weekly
£135–£160; L £5, D £7; WB (£42·50); [5% V Nov–
Mar] **cc** Access, B'card/Visa; dep (summer).

Blenheim   39 Morton Rd, EX8 1BA ✆ (0395) 264230.
🛏6 bedrs, 1 ba; TV; tcf 🏠 TV, dogs, P 1; child facs
✕LD 4.45, nr lunch. Resid lic
cc Access, B'card/Visa; dep.

St. Aubyns   11 Hartley Rd, EX8 2SG ✆ (0395) 264069. *Guest House.*

Maer Farm   Maer Lane, EX8 5DD ✆ (0395) 263651. *Farm.* Avril Skinner
Sleeps 6, ns 🐴
£ B&B from £12–£16

EYNSFORD   Kent.   Map 27B5

Castle   High St, DA4 0AB Farningham ✆ (0322) 863162. *Inn.*
🛏4 bedrs, (1 sh), 1 ba 🏠 P 40; no children under 8
✕LD 9, bar snacks only Sun

Home Farm   Riverside, Dartford, DA4 0AE
✆ (0322) 866193. *Farm.* Mrs Sarah Alexander
Sleeps 6, ns 🐴 (4)
£ B&B from £15

FAKENHAM   Norfolk.   Map 25D3

Old Coach House   Thursford, NR21 0BD ✆ (0328)
878273. *Farm.* Mrs Ann Green   ♿
Sleeps 8, 🐴 🐕 ns
£ B&B from £14, D £6

FALMOUTH   Cornwall.   Map 28C2

Chellowdene (Acclaimed)   Gyllyngvase Hill, TR11
4DN ✆ (0326) 314950.
*Attractive white-walled hotel close to the beach.
Situated just off Cliff Rd and Seafront. Open Apr 28–
3 Oct.*
🛏6 bedrs, 6 en suite; TV; tcf 🏠 ns; P6; children
over 13 ✕nr lunch. Unlic
£ B&B (double) £28; HB weekly £140–£175; [10% V
Apr, May]

Hawthorne Dene (Acclaimed)   12 Pennance Rd,
TR11 4EA ✆ (0326) 311427.
*Follow straight through Falmouth on A39. Turn right
at Greenlawns Hotel onto Pennance Rd. Open
Easter–Oct.*
🛏10 bedrs, 10 en suite; TV; tcf
🏠 ns; P 10 ✕nr lunch. Resid lic
£ B&B £14–£17; HB weekly £124–£149; dep.

Rathgowry (Acclaimed)   Gyllyngvase Hill,
TR11 4DN ✆ (0326) 313482.
🛏10 bedrs, 10 en suite; TV; tcf 🏠 dogs; P 10; child
facs ✕LD 6, nr lunch. Resid lic
£ B&B £11·50–£16·50; HB weekly £100–£135; dep.

Trevaylor (Acclaimed)   8 Pennance Rd, TR11
4EA ✆ (0326) 313041.

*Former gentleman's residence recently refurbished
and offering magnificent views of Falmouth Bay.
Turn right at second roundabout on beach road and
hotel is 100 yards on the right.*
Open Apr–Oct
🛏8 bedrs, 7 en suite, (1 sh); TV; tcf
🏠 P 8 ✕LD 6.30, nr lunch. Resid lic
£ B&B (double) £24–£28; HB weekly £112–£126;
dep.

Cotswold House   49 Melvill Rd, TR11 4DF
✆ (0326) 312077.
*From Falmouth follow signs for Princess Pavilion
and docks. Hotel 100 yards from Pavilion.*
🛏10 bedrs, 8 en suite, (1 sh); TV; tcf
🏠 P 10, coach; no children under 5 ✕LD 8, nr
lunch. Resid lic
£ B&B £16·50; HB weekly £256–£280; [5% V]; dep.

Dolvean   50 Melvill Rd, TR11 4DQ ✆ (0326)
313658.
*Victorian hotel with fully modernised facilities. On the
main town centre road close to station. Open Etr–
Oct.*
🛏14 bedrs, 7 en suite, 2 ba; tcf 🏠 TV, dogs, ns;
P 18, U 1 (75p), G 3 (75p); no children under 3
✕LD 7, nr Mon–Sat lunch, Sun dinner. Resid lic
£ B&B £13·20–£22, HB weekly £110–£165
cc Access, B'card/Visa; dep.

Dunmede   11 Melvill Rd, TR11 4AS ✆ (0326)
313429.
*Situated 190 metres from Castle Beach, close to the
Falmouth Hotel.*
🛏6 bedrs, 1 ba; TV 🏠 TV, dogs; P 3; no children
under 5 ✕LD 4.30, nr lunch. Resid lic
£ B&B £11; HB weekly £79; D £5; [10% V]; dep.

Using RAC discount vouchers
Please tell the hotel when booking if you plan to
use an RAC discount voucher (see end of guide)
in part payment of your bill. Only one voucher
will be accepted per party per stay. Discount
vouchers will only be accepted in payment for
accommodation, not for food.

Gyllyngvase House Gyllyngvase Rd, TR11 4DJ ✆(0326) 312956.
Attractive small hotel in its own grounds. Gyllngvase is off the seafront Cliff Rd.
⇥15 bedrs, 12 en suite, 2 ba; TV ฦTV, dogs; P 15, coach; child facs ✗LD 7, nr lunch. Resid lic £B&B £15·50–£29, B&B (double) £35; HB weekly £142–£159; dep.

Penty Bryn 10 Melvill Rd, TR11 4AS ✆(0326) 314988.
Follow main road nearly to docks, and Melville Rd, is on the right just before the Falmouth Hotel.
⇥7 bedrs, 4 en suite, (1 sh), 1 ba; TV; tcf ฦTV, dogs (small); P 1; child facs ✗Bar meals only, Resid lic
£B&B £13·50 **cc** Access, B'card/Visa; dep.

FAREHAM Hampshire. Map 26E2

Avenue House (Acclaimed) 22, The Avenue, PO14 1NS ✆(0329) 232175.

Former private residence converted in 1988 and retaining private home feel. Surrounded by mature gardens. Situated close to Fareham town centre on A27 Southampton Rd. From M27 take junctions 9 or 11 and follow A27 signs.
⇥10 bedrs, 10 en suite; TV; tcf ฦdogs; P 12; child facs ✗Breakfast only. Unlic
£B&B £29–£40; B&B (double) £39–£49; WB; [10% V] **cc** Access, Amex, B'card/Visa.

Discount vouchers

RAC discount vouchers are at the end of the guide. Establishments with a [V] shown at the end of the price information will accept them in part payment for accommodation bills on the full, standard rate, not against bargain breaks or any other special offers. Please note the limitations shown in the entry: w/e for weekends, w/d for weekdays, and which months they are accepted.

FARINGDON Oxfordshire. Map 26D6

Bowling Green Farm Stanford Road, SN7 8EZ ✆(0367) 240229 Fax (0367) 242568. *Farm*. Della Barnard
Sleeps 6, ns ⭗
£ B&B from £12–£17

FARMBOROUGH Avon. Map 29D6

Barrow Vale Farm Bath, BA3 1BL ✆(0761) 70300. *Farm*. Cherilyn Mary Langley
Sleeps 6, ns ⭗ (3)
£ B&B from £12

FARRINGTON GURNEY Avon. Map 29D7

Cliff Farm Bristol, BS18 5TS ✆(076 121) 274. *Farm*. Judy Candy
Sleeps 5, ns ⭗ (7)
£ B&B from £14

FAR SAWREY Cumbria. Map 22F4

West Vale (Acclaimed) Nr Hawkshead, LA22 0LQ ✆Windermere (096 62) 2817.

Traditional stone-built Lakeland house on edge of village with superb open views to Grizedale Forest and Coniston Fells. Situated 3 miles from Hawkshead on B5285 to Windermere ferry.
⇥8 bedrs, 7 en suite, 1 ba; tcf ฦTV, P8; children over 7 ✗LD4, nr lunch. Resid lic
£B&B £15–£17; HB weekly £147–£161; dep.

FAVERSHAM Kent. Map 27B5

Leaveland Court Leaveland, ME13 0NP ✆(023 374) 596. Mrs Corrine Scutt
Sleeps 9, ⭗ ⇱ ns
£ B&B from £16.50

Weekend breaks

Please consult the hotel for full details of weekend breaks; prices shown are an indication only. Many hotels offer mid week breaks as well.

Symbols (full details on p. 4)

⇥ information about bedrooms	nr no restaurant service	*Farms*
ฦ facilities at hotels	ℜ languages spoken	⇱ dogs accepted
✗ information about meals	[V] RAC vouchers accepted	⭗ (4) children accepted (min. age)

FILEY North Yorkshire.   Map 25A9

Southdown   The Beach, YO14 9LA
☎Scarborough (0723) 513392. *Hotel.*

FLAMBOROUGH Humberside.   Map 25A8

The Grange   Bempton Lane, Bridlington, YO15
1AS ☎(0262) 850207. *Farm.* Joan Thompson
Sleeps 6, 🛏 ☻
£ B&B from £10

FOLKESTONE Kent.   Map 27E4

Argos   6 Marine Ter, CT20 1PZ ☎(0303) 54309.
⇥9 bedrs, (1 sh), 3 ba 🏠TV; children over 3
✕LD 8, nr lunch. Resid lic

Beaumont   5 Marine Ter, CT20 1PZ ☎(0303)
52740. *Guest House.*

Belmonte   30 Castle Hill Av, CT20 2RE ☎(0303)
54470.

Gresham   18 Clifton Cres, The Leas, CT20 2EP
☎(0303) 53906. Fax: (0303) 220746.
*From town centre approach seafront on The Leas
head towards the west end of Leas and road leads
to Clifton Cres.*
⇥14 bedrs, 7 en suite, 3 ba; TV; tcf 🏠TV, dogs, ns;
P3, coach; child facs ✕Resid & Rest lic
£B&B £16–£22; HB weekly £143–£163; L £5, D £6
[10% V] **cc** Access, B'card/Visa; dep.

Wearbay   23 Wear Bay Cres, CT19 6AX ☎(0303)
52586.
*From M2 travel straight through roundabouts until
sea, and Wear Bay is last turning on the right before
harbour.*
⇥11 bedrs, 11 en suite; TV; tcf 🏠TV, dogs;
U (£1·50), coach; child facs ✕LD 11, Resid & Res
lic
£B&B £21, B&B (double) £40; HB weekly £196–
£202·65; L £9, D £9 **cc** Access, Amex, B'card/Visa,
Diners; dep.

Westward Ho   13 Clifton Cres, CT20 2EL ☎(0303)
52663.
*Victorian hotel situated in the Leas area of
Folkestone, just past the bandstand.*

⇥12 bedrs, 11 en suite, 1 ba; TV; tcf 🏠lift, TV,
dogs; coach ✕LD 4, nr lunch. Resid lic
£B&B £17·50–£20; HB weekly £132–£145; D £5;
[10% V Oct–May] **cc** Access, B'card/Visa; dep.

FORDHAM Essex.   Map 27D7

Kings Vineyard   Fossetts Lane, CO6 3NY
☎(0206) 240377. *Farm.* Mrs Inge Tweed
Sleeps 6, ns ☻ (2)
£ B&B from £13, D £6

FOWEY Cornwall.   Map 28D2

Carnethic House (Highly Acclaimed)   Lambs
Barn, PL23 1HQ ☎(072 683) 3336.
*Situated on the main B3269 road into Fowey,
directly opposite 'Welcome to Fowey' sign.
Swimming pool, tennis, putting. Open Feb–Nov.*
⇥8 bedrs, 5 en suite, (2 sh), 2 ba; TV; tcf 🏠dogs,
ns; P 20; child facs ✕LD 8, nr lunch. Resid lic
£B&B £23–£30; B&B (double) £36–£50; HB weekly
£180–£225; WB (£55); [10% V] **cc** Access, Amex,
B'card/Visa, Diners; dep.

FRAMPTON Dorset.   Map 29D4

Wessex Barn   DT2 9NB ☎Maiden Newton (0300)
20282.
*Picturesque 16th century thatched guest house.
From A37 Dorchester road turn left on A356.
Wessex Barn is 1 mile down on the right next to
petrol station. Closed Dec.*
⇥5 bedrs, 1 en suite, 1 ba 🏠TV, dogs, NS; P 5,
G 2 coach; no children under 12 ✕LD 9am, nr
Sun. Dinner by arrangement. Rest lic
£B&B £15–£18; L £2·95, D £7·50; dep.

FRESSINGFIELD Suffolk.   Map 25E1

Elm Lodge Farm   Chippenhall Green, Eye, IP21
5SL ☎(037 986) 249. *Farm.* Sheila Webster
Sleeps 6, 🛏 ☻
£ B&B from £13, D £8

Hillview Farm   Nr Eye, IP21 5PY ☎(037 986)
443. *Farm.* Mrs Rose Tomson   ♿

Sleeps 6, ⊞ ☎ (8)
£ B&B from £13, D £7·50

FRINTON-ON-SEA   Essex.   Map 27E7

Montpellier (Highly Acclaimed)   2 Harold Grove,
☎(025 56) 4462.
Recently refurbished hotel close to sea front.
⊨12 bedrs, 12 en suite, 1 ba
£ B & B £32·50–£34·50, B&B (double) £50–£54

FRITH COMMON   Worcestershire.   Map 26B9

Hunthouse Farm   between Tenbury Wells and
Bewdley, WR15 8JY ☎(029 922) 277. *Farm.* Chris
and Jane Keel
Sleeps 6, ☎ (8)
£ B&B from £14

FROGMORE   Devon.   Map 28G2

Globe Inn   Nr Kingsbridge, TQ7 2NR ☎(0548)
531351
⊨6 bedrs, 2 en suite; 2 ba; TV; tcf 📺TV, dogs;
P 20, coach; child facs ✕LD 9.30
cc Access, Amex, B'card/Visa, Diners; dep.

FROME   Somerset.   Map 29E6

Keyford Elms   92 Locks Hill, BA11 1NG ☎(0373)
63321.
*Attractive stone-built house on edge of town. Take
Bath road, west from centre, straight over mini
roundabout, then 3rd turning left (signed Maiden
Bradley). Turn left at traffic lights.*
⊨8 bedrs, 4 en suite, 2 ba; TV; tcf 📺TV, dogs;
P 35, coach; child facs ✕LD 9.30, nr Mon lunch.
Resid & Rest lic

Using RAC discount vouchers
Please tell the hotel when booking if you plan to
use an RAC discount voucher (see end of guide)
in part payment of your bill. Only one voucher
will be accepted per party per stay. Discount
vouchers will only be accepted in payment for
accommodation, not for food.

£ B&B £17–£27, B&B (double) £26·50–£38; HB
weekly £150–£220; L £6·50, D £9·50; WB; [10% V
w/e]   **cc** Access, B'card/Visa; dep.

FYLINGTHORPE   North Yorkshire.
Map 23F5

Croft Farm   Whitby, YO22 4PW ☎(0947)
880231. *Farm.* Pauline Featherstone
Sleeps 6, ns ☎ (5)
£ B&B from £12·50

GALMPTON   South Devon.   Map 28G2

Burton Farm   Kingsbridge, TQ7 3EY ☎(0548)
561210. *Farm.* David and Anne Rossiter
Sleeps 14, ns ☎
£ B&B from £11, D £6·50–£7

GARBOLDISHAM   Norfolk.   Map 25D1

Ingleneuk (Highly Acclaimed)   Hopton Rd, Diss,
IP22 2RQ ☎(095381) 541.
*Large modern bungalow set in 10 acres of part-
wooded grounds with a stream. Single level
accommodation with south-facing patio. On the
B111, one mile S of Garboldisham village at junction
with A1066.*
⊨11 bedrs, 10 en suite, 1 ba; TV; tcf 📺dogs, ns;
P 20; child facs ✕LD midday, nr lunch, Sun dinner.
Resid lic
£ B&B £18–£26, B&B (double) £29·50–£39·50; HB
weekly £166–£241; WB (£47·50 2 nights D, B&B);
[5% V]   **cc** Access, B'card/Visa; dep.

GARSTANG   Lancashire.   Map 22F2

Stirzakers Farm   Barnacre, Preston, PR3 1GE
☎(0995) 603335. *Farm.* Ruth Wrathall
Sleeps 6, ⊞ ☎
£ B&B from £12–£14

GILSLAND   Cumbria.   Map 23A7

Howard House Farm   Carlisle, CA6 7AN ☎(069
72) 285. *Farm.* Elizabeth Woodmass
Sleeps 6, ☎
£ B&B from £11·50, D £7·50

Frogmore (South Devon) ———————

THE GLOBE INN
Frogmore, Nr Kingsbridge, South Devon TQ7 2NR. Tel: Kingsbridge 531351
A small family run inn at the head of Frogmore Creek on the A379 Kingsbridge to
Dartmouth road. Double room £28 to £32 per night.

GISLINGHAM   Suffolk.   Map 25D1

Old Guildhall (Highly Acclaimed)   Mill St, nr Eye,
IP23 8JT ☎ Mellis (037 983) 361.

*15th century thatched hotel with traditional exposed
beams and lovely gardens. Situated off the B113
opposite the village school. Billiards. Open Feb–
Dec.*
⇔5 bedrs, 5 en suite; TV; tcf 🏠dogs, NS; P 6; child
facs ✗ LD 9, nr lunch. Resid & Rest lic
£ B&B £37·50, B&B (double) £45; HB weekly £175;
D £9; WB (£60); dep.

GLAISDALE   North Yorkshire.   Map 23E5

The Grange   Whitby, YO21 2QW ☎ (0947)
87241. *Farm.* Heather Kelly
Sleeps 6, 🐕 ☎
£ B&B from £12, D £6

GLASTONBURY   Somerset.   Map 29D6

🏆 🏆 **Red Lion**   West Pennard, BA6 8NN
☎ (0458) 32941
*A 17th-century stone-built inn on A361, 3 miles out
of town. Bedrooms in converted stone barn to one
side.*

Cradlebridge   BA16 9SD ☎ (0458) 31827.
*From Glastonbury head S on the A39, take second
right turn after Moorlands factory, farm sign on left
in ⅓ mile. Closed Xmas.*
⇔2 bedrs, 2 en suite; TV; tcf
🏠dogs; P6 ✗ LD noon, nr lunch. Unlic
£ B&B £14–£17·50; B&B (double) £25–£30; dep.

Dower House   Butleigh, BA6 8TG
☎ Baltonsborough (0458) 50354.
*Comfortable old Georgian farmhouse with large
garden. From Glastonbury take road to Butleigh (3⅓
miles S), turn right opposite Rose and Portcullis inn,
farm is 200 yards down lane on left.*
⇔3 bedrs, 1 en suite, 2 ba; tcf 🏠 TV, ns; P 4;
child facs ✗ LD 5.30, nr lunch. Unlic
£ B&B £15, B&B (double) £28; HB weekly £147;
[10% V Feb–Apr, Sept–Nov]; dep.

Hawthorns   Northload St, BA6 9JJ ☎ (0458)
31255.
⇔12 bedrs, (2 sh), 2 ba 🏠 TV, dogs; coach; child
facs ✗ LD 9.15. Resid & Rest lic
cc Access, Amex, B'card/Visa, Diners; dep.

Tor Down   Ashwell La, BA6 4BG ☎ (0458) 32287

GLOSSOP   Derbyshire.   Map 24C5

Wind in the Willows (Highly Acclaimed)
Derbyshire Level, off Sheffield Rd, SK13 9PT
☎ (0457) 868001. Fax: (0457) 853354.

*Early Victorian country house with elegant rooms
and unspoilt views overlooking the Peak District
National Park. From A57 Manchester to Sheffield
road turn right at the Royal Oak Moorfield road, and
hotel is on right.*
⇔8 bedrs, 8 en suite; TV; tcf 🏠 P 12 ✗ nr lunch.
Resid lic
£ B&B £48–£65, B&B (double) £58–£85
cc Access, Amex, B'card/Visa.

Hotel Winston   34 Norfolk St. ☎ (045 74) 5449.

Symbols (full details on p. 4)

⇔ information about bedrooms	nr no restaurant service	*Farms*
🏠 facilities at hotels	🗣 languages spoken	🐕 dogs accepted
✗ information about meals	[V] RAC vouchers accepted	☎ (4) children accepted (min. age)

GLOUCESTER Gloucestershire. Map 26B7

Gilbert's (Acclaimed) Gilbert's La, Brookthorpe, GL4 0UH ☎ (0452) 812364.

400 year old house beautifully restored and modernised. Now a Grade II listed building. Gilberts Lane is opposite Brookthorpe petrol station, north of bridge over M5, on A4173.
4 bedrs, 4 en suite; TV; tcf ⋔ P 6; child facs ✗Breakfast only. Unlic
£ B&B £19–£30, B&B (double) £38–£43; dep.

Lulworth (Acclaimed) 12 Midland Rd, GL1 4UF ☎ (0452) 21881.
Close to city centre opposite Gloucester Park. Closed 25 Dec.–1 Jan.
8 bedrs, 2 en suite, 3 ba; TV; tcf ⋔ TV, dogs; P 14; child facs ✗ Breakfast only. Unlic
£ B&B £13–£16, B&B (double) £26–£32

Rotherfield House (Acclaimed) 5 Horton Rd, GL1 3PX ☎ (0452) 410500.

Elegant, detached Victorian property in its own grounds, completely renovated recently. Follow signs for city centre and Royal Hospital. Hotel situated at first junction off London Rd.
13 bedrs, 8 en suite, 2 ba; TV; tcf ⋔ TV, dogs, ns; P 11; child facs ✗ LD 7.30, nr lunch Fri–Sun. Rest lic
£ B&B £16·95–£26·95, B&B (double) £35·95; L £7·25, D £7·25; WB (£49·24); [10% V] cc Access, Amex, B'card/Visa, Diners; dep.

Pembury 9 Pembury Rd ☎ (0452) 21856.
Interesting old house, airy and light. Take Stroud road out of Gloucester, at first roundabout turn left, then left again.
11 bedrs, 5 en suite, (3 sh), 1 ba; TV; tcf ⋔ TV, ns; P 8, G 2, coach; child facs ✗ Breakfast only. Unlic

£ B&B £15–£25, B&B (double) £26–£36; WB (£12–£15 pp low season); [10% V low season]; dep.

Westville   255 Stroud Rd, GL1 5JZ
℡(0452)301228.
⋈6 bedrs, 2 en suite, 2 ba; TV; tcf �📺TV, dogs; P 5; child facs ✗LD 11am, nr Mon–Sat lunch, Sun dinner. Unlic

GOATHLAND   North Yorkshire.   Map 23E4

Heatherdene (Acclaimed)   Nr Whitby YO22 5AN
℡Whitby (0947) 86334.
Small family run country house hotel surrounded by open moorland with breathtaking views. Located midway between village church and shops. Open Apr–Oct.
⋈7 bedrs, 4 en suite, 1 ba; TV; tcf ⏟ns; P 10
✗LD 7, nr lunch. Resid Rest lic
£ B&B £13·50–£16·50; dep.

GODALMING   Surrey.   Map 26F4

Meads   65 Meadow Row, GU7 3HS ℡ (048 68) 21800.
Situated on A3100 ⅓ mile out of Godalming.
⋈15 bedrs, 4 en suite, (5 sh), 3 ba; TV; tcf ⏟dogs; P 15; child facs ✗LD 6.30, nr lunch, Fri–Sun dinner. Resid & Rest lic
£ B&B £24–£38, B&B (double) £38–£45; D £9; [10% V w/e]

GODMANSTONE   Dorset.   Map 29D4

Watcombe Farm   Dorchester, DT2 7AD ℡(0300) 341295. *Farm.* Tim Mills
Sleeps 6, ⋔ ns ⌷
£ B&B from £13, D £8·50

GORLESTON-ON-SEA   Norfolk.   Map 25F2

Squirrel's Nest (Acclaimed)   7, Avondale Rd, NR31 6DJ ℡(0493) 662746.
Family-run hotel with sea views. From A12, turn right at second set of lights past hospital, then left at end of road.
⋈9 bedrs, 9 en suite, 1 ba; TV; tcf ⏟TV, dogs; P 5, coach; child facs ✗LD 9.30, nr Mon Lunch, Resid & Rest lic

£ B&B £20–£30; HB weekly £160–£225; D £7·95; WB; [10% V w/d] **cc** Access, Amex, B'card/Visa.

Balmoral   65 Avondale Rd, NR31 6DJ ℡Gt Yarmouth (0493) 662538.
Take A12 from London, A47 from Norwich, follow Gorleston signs and turn off at old railway bridge.
⋈9 bedrs. 2 en suite, (4 sh), 1 ba; TV; tcf ⏟TV, dogs; child facs ✗LD 4, nr Mon–Sat lunch, Sun dinner. Resid lic
£ B&B £15–£22; HB weekly £95–£140; WB (£36 3 nights); dep.

GOSPORT   Hampshire.   Map 26C2

Bridgemary Manor   Brewers Lane, PO13 0JY
℡ Fareham (0329) 232946 Fax: (0329) 220392.
From A27 at Fareham follow A32 Gosport road, turn right into Camp Rd before level crossing and left into Braemar Rd. Brewers Lane is at end.
⋈11 bedrs, 4 en suite, 2 ba; TV; tcf ⏟P 45, coach; child facs ✗LD 10
£ B&B £30, B&B (double) £45; HB weekly £345; L £8·50, D £10·50; [10% V] **cc** Access, B'card/Visa

GRAFTON   Herefordshire.   Map 31C8

Grafton Villa Farm   Hereford, HR2 8ED ℡ (0432) 268689. *Farm.* Jennie Layton
Sleeps 6, ⋔ ⌷ ns
£ B&B from £12·50, D £8·50

GRANGE MILL   Derbyshire.   Map 24C4

Lydgate Farm   Aldwark, Wirksworth, DE4 4HW
℡ (062 985) 250. *Farm.* Joy Lomas
Sleeps 6, ns ⌷
£ B&B from £13–£14

Please tell the manager if you chose your hotel through an advertisement in the guide.

En suite rooms
En suite rooms may be bath or shower rooms. If you have a preference, remember to state it when booking a room.

Middle Hills Farm   DE4 4HY ✆(062 988)
368. *Farm*. Mrs Linda Lomas
Sleeps 6, ☎ ✝
£ B&B from £12

GRANGE-OVER-SANDS   Cumbria.
Map 22F3

Elton (Highly Acclaimed)   Windermere Rd, LA11
6EQ (053 95) 32838.
*Family-run hotel in Victorian stone-built building.
From Main Street turn left up Windermere Road to
hotel a short way on left.*
⇝7 bedrs, (5 sh); TV; tcf

Corner Beech   Methven Ter, Kents Bank Rd,
LA11 7DP ✆(053 95) 33088.
*Family run guest house overlooking the Bay. Follow
signs to Grange, take coast road to fire station, and
Corner Beach is 25 metres on the right. Open Jan–
Oct.*
⇝9 bedrs, 2 ba; TV; tcf 🛈TV, dogs, ns; child facs
✗nr lunch; Resid lic
£B&B £12·50; HB weekly £115; [5% V]

Holm Lea   90 Kentsford Rd, LA11 7BB ✆(053 95)
32545.
*Small guest house in a quiet position overlooking
Morecambe Bay. Situated just past Kents Bank
station. Open Mar–Oct.*

⇝6 bedrs, 2 ba; tcf 🛈TV, dogs; P 5; child facs
✗LD 5, nr lunch. Unlic
£B&B £12; HB weekly £113; WB £32 (2 nights HB);
[5% V]

GRANTHAM   Lincolnshire.   Map 24F3

Lanchester (Acclaimed)   84 Harrowby Rd, NG31
9DS ✆(0476) 74169.
*Beautifully maintained Edwardian town house with
guest accommodation in the middle two floors. Take
B1174 into High St/St Peters Hill, turn onto St
Catherine Rd, right at grass triangle into Harrowby
Rd.*
⇝3 bedrs, 1 en suite, 1 ba; TV; tcf 🛈TV, ns; P 3;
G 1, U 1; child facs ✗LD noon, nr lunch, nr dinner
Sat & Sun. Unlic
£B&B £16–£22·50, B&B (double) £26–£35; HB
weekly £161–£206·50; dep.

Garden   86 Harrowby Rd, NG31 9AF ✆(0476)
62040

Hawthornes   51 Cambridge St, NG31 9EZ
✆(0476) 73644.
*Leave A1 and enter Grantham centre. Hawthorne
situated off London Rd, 100 yards from Isaac
Newton statue.*
⇝3 bedrs, 1 ba; TV; tcf 🛈TV, ns; child facs
✗LD 4. Unlic
£B&B £16–£18, B&B (double) £28–£30; [5% V
Oct–May]; dep.

Symbols (full details on p. 4)

⇝ information about bedrooms	nr no restaurant service	*Farms*
🛈 facilities at hotels	✸ languages spoken	✝ dogs accepted
✗ information about meals	[V] RAC vouchers accepted	☎ (4) children accepted (min. age)

Grange Over Sands (Cumbria)

The Elton Hotel
*Windermere Road, Grange Over Sands,
Cumbria LA11 6EQ.   Tel: 05395 32838*
**The Elton Hotel is a family run hotel, fast building
a reputation on friendliness, comfort, high quality
cuisine and value for money.**
Why not try a special 3-day break in this peaceful
setting.

RAC
Highly
Acclaimed

GRAPPENHALL Cheshire. Map 24A5

Kenilworth 2 Victoria Rd, WA4 2EN ☎Warrington (0925) 62323.
Large Victorian house in prominent corner position. Situated on A50 S of Warrington (2 miles). M6 junction 20, M6 junction 19 2¼ miles.
⇔16 bedrs, 16 en suite, 1 ba; TV; tcf ⟨TV, dogs; P18; child facs ✗Breakfast only. Unlic
£ B&B £25, B&B (double) fr £45; WB cc Access, B'card/Visa; dep.

GRASMERE Cumbria. Map 22F5

Bridge House (Highly Acclaimed) Stock Lane, LA22 9SN ☎(09665) 425.
Former Victorian private residence, built of local stone and standing in beautiful mature garden. Take A591 to Grasmere, and Stock Lane is a turning off. Open mid-Mar–Mid Nov.

⇔12 bedrs, 10 en suite, 1 ba; TV; tcf ⟨P20; no children under 5 mths ✗LD 7, nr lunch. Resid & Rest lic
£B&B £23–£30; HB weekly £200–£230; D£12 cc Access, B'card/Visa; dep.

Two Ben Place LA22 9RL ☎(09665) 581.
Small guest house with secluded garden and lovely views. Take A591 to Grasmere, avoiding village, and keep straight on to RC church. Turn right up lane to second gate. Open Etr–Nov.
⇔3 bedrs, (3 sh); tcf ⟨TV; P6; child facs ✗Breakfast only; Unlic
£B&B £16–£18, B&B (double) £30–£34; dep.

GRASSINGTON North Yorkshire. Map 23B3

🍸🍸Black Horse Garrs La, BD23 5AT ☎(0756) 752770.
Stone-built former coaching inn on edge of market square.
⇔11 bedrs, 11 en suite; TV; tcf ⟨TV, dogs; coach ✗LD9.30, bar meals only
£B&B £24·50–£32·50, B&B (double) £38·50–£46·50; WB cc B'card/Visa; dep.

GRAVESEND Kent. Map 27C5

Sunnyside 3 Sunnyside, off Windmill St, DA12 1LG ☎(0474) 365445.

GREAT BRICKHILL Buckinghamshire. Map 26F7

Duncombe Arms 32 Lower Way, MK17 9AG ☎(0525) 261226.
Small village centre inn with garden and patio. Situated 4 miles S of Bletchley, off A5 at Kelly's Kitchen roundabout. Putting.
⇔4 bedrs, 4 en suite, 1 ba; TV; tcf ⟨P 11, coach; child facs ✗LD 10, nr Sun dinner.
£B&B £32–£35, B&B (double) £45–£48; HB weekly £276·50–£297·50; L£7·50, D£7·50 cc Access, B'card/Visa; dep.

GREAT DRIFFIELD East Yorkshire. Map 24F8

Kelleythorpe YO25 9DW ☎(0377) 42297. *Farm.* Tiffy Hopper
Sleeps 6, 🐴 🐕
£ B&B from £11, D £8

GREAT HUCKLOW Derbyshire. Map 24C5

The Hall Tideswell, Buxton, SK17 8RG ☎(0298) 871175. *Farm.* Angela Whatley
Sleeps 6, ns 🐕 (5)
£ B&B from £15, D £10

GREAT RYBURGH Norfolk. Map 25D3

Highfield Farm Fakenham, NR21 7AL ☎(032 878) 249. *Farm.* Mrs E Savory
Sleeps 6, 🐕 (10)
£ B&B from £12·50, D £7·50

GREAT WITLEY Worcestershire. Map 26B8

Hillhampton Farm Nr Worcester, WR6 6JJ ☎(0299) 896604. *Farm.* Mrs Gail Johnson
Sleeps 2, ns 🐕 (8)
£ B&B from £12–£14, D £10

GRINTON IN SWALEDALE North Yorkshire. Map 23C4

Bridge Nr Richmond, DL11 6HH ☎Richmond (N Yorks) (0748) 84224.
Situated 10 miles W of Richmond on B6270. Fishing. Open Mar–Oct.
⇔9 bedrs, 3 en suite, (3 sh), 2 ba; tcf ⟨TV, dogs; P 25, coach ✗LD6.30, nr lunch
£B&B £19·50, B&B (double) £38; HB weekly £185; D£8·50; dep.

GUILDFORD Surrey.   Map 26F4

Blanes Court Albury Rd, GU1 2BT ☎(0483) 573171.
🚭22 bedrs, 13 en suite, 3 ba; TV; tcf 🛉TV, dogs; P20, coach; child facs ✕Breakfast only. Resid lic cc Access, Amex, B'card/Visa; dep.

Carlton 36 London Rd, GU1 2AF ☎(0483) 576539 or 575158 Fax: (0483) 34669.
Situated 3 mins walk from London Rd station, and close to High St. Billiards.
🚭36 bedrs, 13 en suite, (6 sh), 7 ba; TV; tcf 🛉TV; P 50, coach; child facs ✕LD8.15, nr lunch. Resid & Rest lic
£B&B £26–£36, B&B (double) £40–£46; HB weekly £217–£287; D£5 cc Access, Amex, B'card/Visa; dep.

GUISBOROUGH Cleveland.   Map 23E5

🏆 🏆 **Fox & Hounds** Slapewath, TS14 6PX ☎(0287) 32964.
Typical white-painted inn with some very well-furnished bedrooms.
🚭7 bedrs, 7 en suite; TV; tcf

GULWORTHY Devon.   Map 28F3

Rubbytown Farm Tavistock, PL19 8PN ☎(0822) 832493. *Farm.* Mary Steer
Sleeps 7, ns ⛌
£ B&B from £14, D from £7

GUNNISLAKE Cornwall.   Map 28F3

Hingston Country House (Acclaimed) St Anns Chapel, PL18 9HB ☎Tavistock (0822) 832468.
Beautiful country house in grounds overlooking Tamar Valley. Built in late Georgian times with elegant accommodation. Situated between Tavistock and Callington on A390, ¼ mile from Gunnislake Station. Putting.
🚭10 bedrs, 8 en suite, 1 ba; TV; tcf 🛉TV, dogs, ns; P12; child facs ✕LD8. Rest lic
£B&B £22·50–£29·50, B&B (double) £37–£48; HB weekly £204·75–£274·75; L£3·95, D£11·75; WB (£56·25); [10% V w/d] cc Access, B'card/Visa; dep.

Discount vouchers
RAC discount vouchers are at the end of the guide. Establishments with a [V] shown at the end of the price information will accept them in part payment for accommodation bills on the full, standard rate, not against bargain breaks or any other special offers. Please note the limitations shown in the entry: w/e for weekends, w/d for weekdays, and which months they are accepted.

HALIFAX West Yorkshire   Map 40C2

Fleece Inn (Acclaimed) Elland Rd, Bakisland, HX4 0DJ ☎(0422) 822598 Fax: (0422) 824460.
A listed 18th century building of great character high above Ryburn Valley with extensive views. From exit 22, M62 turn left into Ripponden, then right at traffic lights and up hill for 1 mile.
🚭4 bedrs, 4 en suite; TV; tcf 🛉P60, coach; child facs ✕LD 10.30
£B&B £35 (w/e £25) B&B double £45

HAILSHAM East Sussex.   Map 27C3

The Stud Farm Bodle Street Green, BN27 4RJ ☎(0323) 833201. *Farm.* Philippa and Richard Gentry
Sleeps 6, ⛌
£ B&B from £14, D £8

HALESWORTH Suffolk.   Map 25F1

Broad Oak Farm Bramfield, IP19 9AB ☎(098 684) 323. *Farm.* Mrs Pat Kelmsley
£ B&B from £13, D from £8

HALTWHISTLE Northumberland.   Map 23A7

Ashcroft NE49 0DA ☎(0434) 320213.
Situated 150 yards off A69 close to railway station. Closed 2 wks Xmas.
🚭6 bedrs, 3 ba 🛉TV, ns; P 12; child facs ✕Breakfast only; Unlic
£B&B £13–£15, B&B (double) £24–£25

White Craig Farm Shield Hill, NE49 9NW ☎(0434) 320565. *Farm.* Isobel Laidlow ♿
Sleeps 6, ns ⛌ (10)
£ B&B £15·50–£17·25

HANBURY Worcestershire.   Map 26C9

Upper Hollowfields Farm Redditch, B96 6RJ ☎(052 784) 461. *Farm.* Janette Terry
Sleeps 6, ⛌
£ B&B from £14–£16

HARBERTON Devon.   Map 29A3

Foales Leigh Totnes, TQ9 7SS ☎(0803) 862365. *Farm.* Carol Chudley
Sleeps 6, ⛌
£ B&B from £10, D £8

HARDINGHAM Norfolk.   Map 25E2

Hall Farmhouse High Common, Norwich, NR9 4AE ☎(0953) 851113. *Farm.* Karen Finch
Sleeps 6, ⛌
£ B&B from £15, D £9

HARROGATE North Yorkshire. Map 23D3

Glenayr (Highly Acclaimed) 19 Franklin Mount, HG1 5EJ ☎(0423) 504259.

A comfortable Victorian house set in a peaceful, tree-lined avenue close to the town centre. Situated 100 yards past Conference Centre on Kings Rd. Turn right into Franklin Mount, hotel is halfway up on right.
⊨6 bedrs, 5 en suite, 1 ba; TV; tcf ♠P4; child facs ✕LD 5, nr lunch. Resid lic
£B&B £17·50–£19·50, B&B (double) £40–£45; HB weekly £175–£210; WB (£55 2 nts HB); [5% V Nov–Mar]; dep.

Shannon Court (Highly Acclaimed) 65 Dragon Av, HG1 5DS ☎(0423) 509858.

Charming Victorian house retaining many original features yet with all modern facilities. Situated off A59 between Knaresborough Rd and Ripon Rd. Closed Xmas.
⊨8 bedrs, 8 en suite; TV; tcf ♠TV, dogs, P 3, child facs ✕LD midday, nr lunch. Resid lic
£B&B £18–£22·50, B&B (double) £36–£45; HB weekly £175–£200; WB (£25); [5% V]; dep.

Abbey Lodge (Acclaimed) 31 Ripon Rd, HG1 2JL ☎(0423) 569712.

Tastefully converted Victorian house with well-cared for gardens. Situated ¼ mile N of town centre on A61 ring road.
⊨20 bedrs, 14 en suite, 2 ba; TV; tcf ♠dogs, ns; P 21; coach; child facs ✕LD 8.30, nr lunch. Resid & Rest lic
£B&B £19, B&B (double) £36, D £9·50; WB (£26); [5% V Oct–Apr]; dep.

Arden House (Acclaimed) 69/71 Franklin Rd, HG1 5EH ☎(0423) 509224.

Ashley House (Acclaimed) 36–40 Franklin Rd, HE1 5EE (0423) 507474 or 560858.

Elegant hotel with comfortable accommodation, situated 3 mins from Conference Centre. From town centre turn right into Strawberry Dale Ave, then left into Franklin Rd.
⊨17 bedrs, 11 en suite, 2 ba; TV; tcf ♠TV, dogs, ns; P 4; coach; child facs ✕LD 12 noon, nr lunch. Resid lic
£B&B £18·75–£25, B&B (double) £32–£46; D£10·50 cc Access, B'card/Visa; dep.

Aston (Acclaimed) 7–9 Franklin Mount, HG1 5EJ ☎(0423) 564262.

Comfortable hotel in quiet leafy street close to shops. Second street on right after Conference Centre.
⊨16 bedrs, 14 en suite, 1 ba; TV; tcf ♠TV, dogs, ns; P 10, coach; child facs ✕LD midday, nr lunch.
£ B&B £22–£24, D £10·50; WB (£30 HB); [10% V] cc Access, B'card/Visa; dep.

Cavendish (Acclaimed) 3 Valley Dr, HG2 0JJ ☎(0423) 509637 Fax: (0423) 504429.
Small, recently reburbished hotel overlooking Valley Gdns. From Pump Rooms Museum, first hotel on the drive.

12 bedrs, 12 en suite; TV; tcf TV, dogs; child facs LD 8.30. Resid & Rest lic
£ B&B £22–£28, B&B (double) £48–£60; D £8·50; WB (£15) **cc** Access, B'card/Visa; dep.

Delaine (Acclaimed) 17 Ripon Rd, HG1 2JL. (0423) 567974.
Victorian house set in pleasant gardens, recently modernised but retaining many original features. Leave Harrogate on A61 Ripon Rd and hotel is on crest of the hill about 200 yards past Royal Hall and next to Cairn Hotel.
11 bedrs, 6 en suite, 2 ba; TV; tcf TV; P 12; no children under 2 LD mid afternoon, nr lunch, Resid lic
£ B&B £18–£25; WB (£70); [10% Nov–Feb]; dep.

Grafton (Acclaimed) 1–3 Franklin Mount, HG1 5EJ (0423) 508491.

With conference centre on left, cross traffic lights and take third turning on right into Franklin Mount.
17 bedrs, 13 en suite, 3 ba; TV; tcf TV, dogs; P 2, coach; child facs LD 4, Resid & Rest lic
£ B&B £20·50–£23–50, B&B (double) £36–£42; L £6·50, D £9·50 **cc** Access, Amex, B'card/Visa, Diners; dep.

Rosedale (Acclaimed) 86 Kings Rd, HG1 5JX (0423) 566630.

A late Victorian villa/town house with stripped pine hall and original fireplaces. Recently refurbished.
8 bedrs, 7 en suite, (1 sh); TV; tcf ns; P 8; children over 5 LD 6.30, nr lunch. Resid lic
£ B&B £25, B&B (double) £40; HB weekly £197·75 **cc** Access, B'card/Visa; dep.

Scotia House (Acclaimed) 66 Kings Rd, HG1 5JR (0423) 504361.

Small hotel offering comfortable accommodation, ideally situated opposite Conference Centre.
14 bedrs, 10 en suite, (1 sh), 2 ba; TV; tcf TV, dogs, ns; P 8, coach; no children under 7 LD 6, nr lunch. Resid & Rest lic
£ B&B £25–£28, HB weekly £195–£216; D £10; WB (£30 HB); [5% V Nov–Mar & w/e] **cc** Access, B'card/Visa; dep.

Wharfedale House (Acclaimed) 28 Harlow Moor Drive, HG2 0JY (0423) 522233.
From tourist office go to Valley Gdns entrance, turn left then right. Follow Valley Dr into Harlow Moor Dr.
8 bedrs, 8 en suite; TV; tcf dogs, ns; P 3, coach; child facs meals by arrangement only, ns; Resid lic
£ B&B £24, B&B (double) £42; HB weekly £207 by arrangement, D £10; WB (Oct–May); [10% V] dep.

Alexa House 26 Ripon Rd, HG1 2JJ (0423) 501988.
Solid detached house in mellow stone built in 1830. Situated on A61 Leeds to Ripon Rd, immediately after town centre on N side. Closed Xmas & New Year.

Please tell the manager if you chose your hotel through an advertisement in the guide.

13 bedrs, 11 en suite (1 sh), 1 ba; TV; tcf TV; P14; child facs Breakfast only. Resid lic
£ B&B £21; WB (£37·80); dep.

Craigleigh 6 West Grove Rd, HG1 2AD (0423) 64064. *Guest House.*
£ B&B £25–£30; HB weekly £196–£224; [10% V]

Gillmore 98 Kings Rd, HG1 5HH (0423) 503699.
Small family-run hotel close to Conference Centre. Kings Rd is a turning off Ripon Rd.
22 bedrs, 6 en suite, 6 ba; TV; tcf TV, dogs, ns; P10, coach; child facs LD5, nr lunch. Resid lic
£ B&B £18–£22·50, B&B (double) £32–£35; HB weekly £160–£175; [5% V]; dep.

Hadleigh 33 Ripon Rd, HG1 2JL (0423) 522994.
Attractive creeper-covered stone-built house. Situated on A59 out of Harrogate, halfway down Ripon Rd hill on left.
6 bedrs, 6 en suite; TV; tcf ns; P 8, G 2, no children under 12 LD 7, nr lunch. Resid & Rest lic
£ B&B £22–£25, D £9·50; [5% V] **cc** Access, B'card/Visa; dep.

Lamont House 12 St Mary's Walk, HG2 0LW (0423) 567143.
Small hotel in quiet residential area. Turn left off Cold Bath Rd then first right into St Marys Walk. Closed Xmas.
9 bedrs, 2 en suite, 2 ba; TV; tcf dogs; child facs LD 4, nr Sun & lunch.
£ B&B £16–£18, B&B (double) £30–£50

Mrs Murray's 67 Franklin Rd, HG1 5EH (0423) 505857. *Guest House.*

Princes 7 Granby Rd, HG1 4ST (0423) 883469.
Just off York/Knaresborough Rd on edge of The Stray.

8 bedrs, 4 en suite, (3 sh), 1 ba; TV; tcf TV, ns; no children under 3, child facs LD 9, nr lunch. Rest lic. dep.

Roan 90 Kings Rd, HG1 5JX (0423) 503087.
Follow signs to Conference Centre and guest house is nearby.
7 bedrs, 3 en suite, 1 ba; tcf TV, ns; no children under 7 LD 4.30, nr lunch. Unlic
£ B&B £15, B&B (double) £28; [5% V]; dep.

HARROW Greater London (Middx). Map 27A6

Lindal (Highly Acclaimed) 2 Hindes Rd, HA1 1SJ 081-863-3164.

Tastefully refurbished Edwardian style house in central situation off Station Rd in town centre.
21 bedrs, 18 en suite, 1 ba; TV; tcf dogs, ns; P 18 LD 8.45, nr lunch Fri–Sun dinner.
£ B&B £33–£43, B&B (double) £45–£53; D £12·75 **cc** Access, B'card/Visa; dep.

Crescent Lodge (Acclaimed) 58–62 Welldon Cres, HA1 1QR 081-863-5491/5163.
Hotel in a quite residential area with rear garden. By train from Euston to Harrow & Wealdstone, by underground to Harrow-on-the-Hill.
21 bedrs, 9 en suite, 5 ba; TV; tcf TV, ns; P8, coach; child facs LD am, nr lunch. Fri–Sun dinner. Unlic
£ B&B £26–£42, B&B (double) £44–£54, HB weekly £280–£476; dep.

Weekend breaks
Please consult the hotel for full details of weekend breaks; prices shown are an indication only. Many hotels offer mid week breaks as well.

En suite rooms
En suite rooms may be bath or shower rooms. If you have a preference, remember to state it when booking a room.

Symbols (full details on p. 4)		
information about bedrooms	nr no restaurant service	*Farms*
facilities at hotels	languages spoken	dogs accepted
information about meals	[V] RAC vouchers accepted	(4) children accepted (min. age)

Central 6 Hindes Rd, HA1 1SJ ☎ 081-427 0893

Hindes 8 Hindes Rd, HA1 1SJ ☎ 081-427 7468. *Small, homely hotel near High Street and 15 mins from M1 and Wembley Stadium. Nearest underground Harrow-on-the-Hill.* ⊨13 bedrs, 1 en suite, 3 ba; TV; tcf 🛱TV, ns; P 6, coach; child facs ✕Breakfast only. Unlic £B&B £28, B&B (double) £38 **cc** Access, B'card/Visa; dep.

HARTEST Suffolk.   Map 27D8

Caravel Pear Tree Farm, Bury St Edmunds, IP29 4EG ☎ (0284) 830217. *Farm.* Mrs Rachel White Sleeps 4 £ B&B from £13·50

HASTINGS AND ST LEONARDS East Sussex.   Map 27C3

Eagle House (Highly Acclaimed) 12 Pevensey Rd, St Leonards, TN38 0JZ ☎ (0424) 430535.

Victorian family house furnished in period style with a large garden. Situated adjacent to St Leonards shopping centre off London Rd, near Warrior Square station. ⊨23 bedrs, 20 en suite, 2 ba; TV; tcf 🛱dogs; P 11; child facs ✕LD 8.30. Resid & Rest lic £B&B £27–£31, B&B (double) £38–£45; HB weekly £237·65–£262·15; L £8·95, D £14·95; WB (£58 Jan–May, £67·90 Oct–Dec); [10% V] **cc** Access, Amex, B'card/Visa, Diners.

Norton Villa (Acclaimed) Hill Street, TN34 3HU (0424) 428168.

Harrow (Middlesex)

Hastings (Sussex)

Listed Victorian guest house with panoramic views over the sea and harbour, set in the cliffs below the castle. Situated in the Old Town by St Clements Church. Turn up No Through Rd into Hill St and Norton Villa is above George St.
⋈4 bedrs, 3 en suite, (1 sh); TV; tcf ⋔TV, dogs, ns; P5; children over 8 ✗Breakfast only. Unlic
£B&B £16–£20; [5% V w/d]; dep.

Argyle 32 Cambridge Gdns, TN34 1EN ✆(0424) 421294.
Situated off A21 to city centre, via Cambridge Road into Cambridge Gdns.
⋈8 bedrs, 3 en suite, 1 ba; tcf ⋔TV, ns; coach; no children under 4 ✗Breakfast only. Unlic
£B&B £13, B&B (double) £24; HB weekly £77.

Beechwood 59 Baldslow Rd, TN34 2EY ✆(0424) 420078.
Small, late Victorian hotel with unrivalled views of Alexandra Park. Take A2101 to traffic lights at railway viaduct, turn left and first left again.
⋈10 bedrs, 3 en suite, 1 ba; TV; tcf ⋔TV, dogs, ns; P6, coach; child facs ✗LD 6
£B&B £12–£23, B&B (double) £22–£35; HB weekly £150–£210; L£5, D£7; [5% V Sep–May]; dep.

French's 24 Robertson St. ✆(0424) 421195 Tx: 957141.
Traditional oak-panelled wine bar with comfortable rooms. Central position in main shopping and business area, only 300 yards from pier and promenade.
⋈4 bedrs, 4 en suite; TV ⋔dogs; coach; no children under 8
£B&B £40–£45, B&B (double) £58–£65; L£5–£12, D£15; WB (£66 2 nts) **cc** Access, Amex, B'card/Visa, Diners.

Gainsborough 5 Carlisle Par, TN34 1JG ✆(0424) 434010.
Early Victorian town house situated on the sea front. Set on A259 200 yards from the pier. Closed Xmas.
⋈12 bedrs, 8en suite, (1 sh), 1 ba; TV; tcf ⋔dogs, ns; child facs ✗LD 5, nr lunch, Resid & Rest lic
£B&B £13–£19; HB weekly £136·50–£178·50; [5% V] dep.

Waldorf Seafront, 4 Carlisle Par. TN34 1JG ✆(0424) 422185.
Small hotel in seafront position, adjacent to main A259 Folkestone to Brighton road.
⋈12 bedrs, 5 en suite, 2 ba; TV; tcf ⋔TV; coach; child facs ✗LD midday, nr lunch. Resid lic
£B&B £22, B&B (double) £28–£36; HB weekly £132–£157; dep.

HARTINGTON Derbyshire. Map 24C4

Wolfscote Grange Farm Nr Buxton, SK17 0AX ✆(0298) 84342. *Farm.* Jane Gibbs
Sleeps 6, ⋔ ⋗
£ B&B from £11–£12

HASFIELD Gloucestershire. Map 26B7

Little Colways GL19 4LE ✆(045 278) 250. *Farm.* Camilla Hope
Sleeps 4, ⋗
£ B&B from £12·50–£15

HASTINGLEIGH Kent. Map 27D4

Hazel Tree Farm Hassell Street, Ashford, TN25 5JE ✆(023375) 324. *Farm.* Christine Gorell Barnes
Sleeps 8, ⋗
£ B&B from £15–£16, D £7

HATHERN Leicestershire. Map 24D3

Leys Loughborough Rd, LE12 5JB ✆(0509) 844373.
Take junction 24 off M1, then follow A6 for 4 miles towards Leicester.
⋈5 bedrs, 2 ba; tcf ⋔TV, dogs; P 10; child facs ✗Breakfast only. Unlic
£B&B £13, B&B (double) £23 **cc** Access, B'card/Visa; dep.

HATT Cornwall. Map 28E3

Holland Toby Inn nr Saltash, PL12 6PJ ✆Saltash (0752) 844044.
From A38 take Callington road at Saltash Bridge. Hotel situated on right.
⋈28 bedrs, 28 en suite; TV; tcf ⋔dogs, ns; P 50, coach; child facs ✗LD 10

£ B&B £28·50, B&B (double) £38·50, L £10, D £10;
WB (£23·50) **cc** Access, Amex, B'card/Visa,
Diners; dep.

HAVERTHWAITE Cumbria. Map 22F4

⚑ ⚑ Dicksons Arms nr Ulverston, LA12 8AA
☎ Greenodd (022 986) 384.
*Two-storey, white-painted Lakeland inn on the
A590.*
⋈ 10 bedrs, 7 en suite, 1 ba; annexe 6 bedrs, 3
ba; TV; tcf 🅵 dogs; P 35, coach ✕ LD 10, bar
meals only lunch & Sun dinner
£ B&B £20–£28, B&B (double) £30–£39
cc Access, Amex, B'card/Visa.

HAWKHURST Kent. Map 27C3

Conghurst Farm TN18 4RW ☎ (0580)
753331. *Farm.* Mrs Rosemary Piper
Sleeps 6, 🐎 🐕 ns
£ B&B from £13·50, D £7·50

HAWKSHEAD Cumbria. Map 22F4

⚑ ⚑ Queens Head LA22 0NS ☎ (096 66) 271.
*Family-run 17th century inn of character in centre
of village.*
⋈ 10 bedrs, 6 en suite, 2 ba; TV; tcf 🅵 coach;
children over 10 ✕ LD 9.30, bar meals only lunch
£ B&B £23·50–£30, B&B (double) £39–£46; WB
£67 (3 nts); [5% V Nov–Mar w/d] **cc** Access, Amex,
B'card/Visa; dep.

⚑ ⚑ Red Lion The Square, LA22 0NS ☎ (096
66) 213.
*Stone-built 15th century inn in village centre.
Friendly, old-world atmosphere.*
⋈ 9 bedrs, 9 en suite; TV; tcf 🅵 TV; P 12, coach;
child facs

Greenbank Country House (Acclaimed) nr
Ambleside, LA22 0NS ☎ (096 66) 497.

*Former 17th century farmhouse with open fires and
views of surrounding fells.*
⋈ 10 bedrs, 5 en suite, 3 ba; tcf 🅵 TV, dogs, ns;
P 12; child facs ✕ LD 4, nr lunch. Resid lic
£ B&B £16–£20; HB weekly £150–£158; [5% V]

Ivy House (Acclaimed) LA22 0NS ☎ (096 66) 204.

*Attractive ivy-covered house, located in the centre
of Hawkshead opposite police station. Fishing.
Open Mar–Nov.*
⋈ 11 bedrs, 6 en suite, 2 ba; tcf 🅵 TV, dogs; P 16;
child facs ✕ nr lunch. Rest lic
£ B&B £17·25–£21·75, HB weekly £155·75–
£187·25; D £8·75; dep.

HAWORTH West Yorkshire. Map 23B2

Moorfield (Acclaimed) 80 West La, BD22 8EN
(0535) 43689.
*A detached Victorian residence set between the
village and moors with splendid views. Follow
Stanbury signs through Haworth. Open Feb to Dec.*
⋈ 6 bedrs, 5 en suite, 1 ba; TV; tcf 🅵 TV, ns; P 6;
child facs ✕ LD 4, nr lunch & Tue dinner. Resid &
Rest lic
£ B&B £15–£18, B&B (double) £26–£30; D £8·50
cc Access, B'card/Visa; dep.

Ferncliffe Hebden Rd, BD22 8RS ☎ (0535)
43405.
*Small hotel with magnificent views. From Keighley
take A629 towards Halifax for 2¼ miles. Turn right
to Haworth, take left fork A6033 to Hebden Bridge
and Oxenhope. Hotel 2 miles on left.*
⋈ 6 bedrs, 6 en suite; TV; tcf 🅵 TV, dogs; P 12,
coach; child facs ✕ LD 9, nr Sat lunch, Resid &
Rest lic
£ B&B £19–£21; HB weekly £192·50–£206·50;
L £6·50, D £8·95; WB (£55 Winter) **cc** B'card/Visa;
dep.

HAWNBY North Yorkshire. Map 23E4

Cringle Carr Farm Helmsley, YO6 5LT ☎ (043 96)
264. *Farm.* Susan Garbutt
Sleeps 5, 🐎
£ B&B from £12, D £8

Laskill Farm Nr Helmsley, YO6 5NB ☎ (043 96)
268. *Farm.* Sue Smith ♿
Sleeps 10, 🐕 🐎 (7)
£ B&B from £14, D £9

HAYLING ISLAND Hampshire. Map 26E2

Cockle Warren Cottage (Highly Acclaimed) 84
Church Rd, PO11 0NX

Traditional farmhouse-style building in a large garden on the sea front. Well-equipped, prettily decorated bedrooms.
➷5 bedrs, 5 en suite, 1 ba; TV; tcf
£B&B £30–£45; [10% V]

Rook Hollow (Acclaimed) 84 Church Rd, PO11 0NX ✆(0705) 467080 or 469620.
Attractive Victorian house completely modernised. Follow road across Hayling for 1 ¾ miles to first roundabout, turn left and hotel is immediately on left.
➷7 bedrs, 3 en suite, 1 ba; TV; tcf 📺TV, ns; P9 ✗LD 9, nr Fri–Sun. Resid lic
£ B&B £20–£23, B&B (double) £32–£50; [10% V Jan–Mar, Jun, Sep–Nov] cc Access, B'card/Visa, Diners; dep.

HEACHAM Norfolk. Map 25C3

St Annes 53 Neville Rd, PE31 7HB ✆(0485) 70021.
Period style guest house set back from the sea front, with comfortable accommodation. Turn into village at Norfolk Lavender farm on A149, turn right into Neville Rd from Station Rd. St Annes on corner of Neville Rd and Wilton Rd.
➷8 bedrs, 2 en suite, 2 ba; TV; tcf 📺TV, ns; P3; no children under 7 ✗LD 10 am, nr lunch. Resid & Rest lic
£ B&B £13–£16, D£7; dep.

HEADCORN Kent. Map 27D4

Bletchenden Manor Farm nr Ashford, TN27 9JB ✆(0622) 890228. *Farm.* John and Gill Waters Sleeps 3/4
£ B&B from £17·50

HELMSLEY North Yorkshire. Map 23E4

Beaconsfield Bondgate, YO6 5BW ✆(0439) 71346.
Elegantly furnished country house. From Black Swan in town square, guest house is 50 yards in Scarborough direction.
➷6 bedrs, 2ba; TV; tcf 📺P8; no children under 12 ✗Breakfast only. Unlic
£B&B £23, B&B (double) £38; dep.

HELPERBY North Yorkshire. Map 23D3

Thornton Manor YO6 2RH ✆(0423) 360648. *Farm.* Mrs Ann Hebblethwaite
Sleeps 6, ns ☎
£ B&B from £12, D £6·50

HELSTON Cornwall. Map 28C1

Hillsdale Polladras, Breage, TR13 9NT
✆Penzance (0736) 763334.
Modern hotel in peaceful countryside. Take B3302 from Helston, turn left into Carleen, right and right again. Badminton.
➷9 bedrs, 9 en suite; tcf 📺TV, dogs; P12, coach; child facs ✗nr lunch. Resid & Rest lic
£ B&B £16·65; HB weekly £113·85–£132·25; dep.

Longstone Farm Trenear, TR13 0HG ✆(0326) 572483. *Farm.* Gillian Lawrance &
Sleeps 12, 🐴☎
£ B&B from £10·50, D £6

HEMEL HEMPSTEAD Herts. Map 26F6

Southville 9 Charles St, HP1 1JH ✆(0442) 51387.
Detached Victorian building close to town centre. At Magic Roundabout follow sign to Kodak House, pass entrance and take first left into Charles St. Second hotel on right.
➷19 bedrs, 6ba; TV; tcf 📺TV, dogs; P9, coach ✗Breakfast only. Unlic
£B&B £18·50–£26, B&B (double) £33–£39; [10% V] cc B'card/Visa; dep.

HENLEY-IN-ARDEN Warwicks. Map 26C8

Ashleigh House (Highly Acclaimed) Whitley Hill, B95 5DL ✆(0564) 792315.

An Edwardian country house elegantly furnished with antiques, set in gardens with magnificent views. On B4095 Warwick road 1 mile from A34 traffic lights.
➷10 bedrs, 10 en suite; TV; tcf 📺TV, dogs, ns; P11; no babies ✗Breakfast only. Unlic
£B&B £35–£45, B&B (double) £45–£55; [5% V 2+ nights] cc Access, B'card/Visa; dep.

Lapworth Lodge (Acclaimed) Bushwood La, Lapworth, B94 5PJ ✆(0564) 783038.

Large Georgian red brick country house in 2 acres of grounds set in lovely countryside. Formerly a farmhouse. Situated 2 miles N of Henley-in-Arden on A34, a turning off by The Little Chef.
7 bedrs, 7 en suite; TV; tcf ns; P 20; child facs Breakfast only. Unlic
£ B&B £30–£40, B&B (double) £40–£46
cc Access, B'card/Visa.

Spinney (Acclaimed)   Stratford Rd, Wootten Wawen, B95 6DG (0564) 792534.

Brick built 1920's house, extended and modernised, standing in large grounds. On A3400 5 miles N of Stratford and 3 miles S of Henley-in-Arden. Swimming pool, putting.
4 bedrs, 2 en suite, 1 ba; TV; tcf TV, dogs, ns; P 10; child facs Breakfast only. Unlic

Irelands Farm   Irelands Lane, Solihull, B95 5SA (0564) 792476.   *Farm*. Pamela Shaw
Sleeps 6, ns
£ B&B from £12–£20

HENLEY-ON-THAMES   Oxfordshire.
Map 26E5

Little Parmoor Farm   Frieth, RG9 6NL (0494) 881600.   *Farm*. Frances Emmett
Sleeps 6,
£ B&B from £16–£20

HENSTRIDGE   Somerset.   Map 29D5

Quiet Corner Farm   Templecombe, BA8 9RA (0963) 63045.   *Farm*. Mrs Pat Thompson
£ B&B from £16

Toomer Farm   Templecombe, BA8 0PH (0963) 250237.   *Farm*. Ethelend Doggrell
Sleeps 6,
£ B&B from £12–£15

HEREFORD   Hereford & Worcester
(Herefordshire).   Map 31D8

Collins House (Highly Acclaimed)   19 St Owens St, HR1 2JB (0432) 272416 Fax: (0432) 341867.

A Georgian town house dating from 1722, retaining all its original features and with an Edwardian dining room. Lovely walled garden. Situated opposite town hall in city centre.
4 bedrs, 4 en suite; TV; tcf P 4 LD 9.30. Resid & Rest lic
£ B&B £65, B&B (double) £90; HB weekly £455; L £15·95, D £25 cc Access, Amex, B'card/Visa, Diners.

Hopbine   Roman Rd, HR1 1LE (0432) 268722. *Situated ½ mile from centre of Hereford towards Leominster on A49. Turn right opposite Beefeater onto A4103, continue to second crossroads. Hotel on left.*
12 bedrs, 3 en suite, 5 ba; TV; tcf TV, dogs, ns; P 30; child facs LD 6, nr lunch. Resid & Rest lic
£ B&B £16–£20, B&B (double) £28–£32; HB weekly £150·50–£192·50; D £7·50; [5% V]; dep.

Dinedor Court   HR2 6LG (0432) 73481/ 870481.   *Farm*. Rosemary Price
Sleeps 6,
£ B&B from £12·50

Sink Green Farm   Rotherwas, HR2 6LE (0432) 870223.   *Farm*. Mrs Helen Jones
Sleeps 6, ns
£ B&B from £14, D £9·50

HERNE BAY   Kent.   Map 2745

Beauvalle   92 Central Parade, CT6 5JJ (0227) 375330.

HERSTMONCEUX   East Sussex.   Map 29C3

Cleavers Lyng   Church Rd, nr Hailsham, BN27 1QJ (0323) 833131.
Family-run hotel dating from 1580 with oak-beams and inglenook fireplace. Located 2 miles off A271 towards Herstmonceux Church. Closed 24–31 Dec.
8 bedrs, 4 ba; tcf TV, dogs; P 15; child facs LD 7.30, nr lunch. Resid & Rest lic
£ B&B £15·25–£17·25; HB weekly £150–£175·50; [5% V]; dep.

HETHERSGILL Cumbria.   Map 22F6

Newpallyards, Carlisle, CA6 6HZ ✆ (022 877) 308 (0228) 577308 [1991]. *Farm.* Georgina Elwen ♿
Sleeps 12, �`🐕` ♿
£ B&B £14–£18, D £8·50

HEWISH Avon.   Map 29C7

Kara BS24 6RQ ✆ Yatton (0934) 834442.
🛏5 bedrs, 2 ba; TV; tcf 🏠 TV, dogs; P 5; child facs

HEXHAM Northumberland.   Map 23B7

Westbrooke Allendale Rd, NE46 2DE ✆ (0434) 603818.
Family run Victorian hotel on outskirts of town. Allendale Rd is off Hencotes and Battle Hill.
🛏11 bedrs, 3 en suite, (2 sh), 2 ba; TV; tcf 🏠 TV, dogs, ns; P 4, coach; child facs ✗ LD 8.30. Club lic
£ B&B £18–£20, B&B (double) £35–£45; HB weekly £179–£196; L £5, D £10; [5% V] **cc** Access, B'card/Visa; dep.

HIGH BENTHAM North Yorkshire.   Map 23A3

Fowgill Park Farm, Nr Lancaster, LA2 7AH ✆ (052 42) 61630. *Farm.* Shirley Metcalfe
Sleeps 4, 🐕 ♿
£ B&B from £9·50–£12, D £6·50

Lane House Farm, Nr Lancaster, LA2 7DJ ✆ (05242) 61479. *Farm.* Betty Clapham
Sleeps 6, 🐕 ♿
£ B&B from £12, D £7

HIGHER WYCH Cheshire.   Map 24A3

Mill House, Malpas, SY14 7JR ✆ (0948) 73362. *Farm.* Chris and Angela Smith
Sleeps 5, ns ♿
£ B&B from £11, D £6

HIGHWORTH Wiltshire.   Map 26C6

Ashen Copse Farm Coleshill, Nr Swindon, SN6 7PU ✆ (0367) 240175. *Farm.* Pat Hoddinott
Sleeps 6, ns ♿
£ B&B from £13–£16

HIGH WYCOMBE Bucks.   Map 26F6

Clifton Lodge (Acclaimed)   210 West Wycombe Rd, (A40), HP12 3AR ✆ (0494) 440095.

Situated 2 miles from M40 and 1 mile from High Wycombe on A40 towards Oxford/Aylesbury. Sauna.
🛏31 bedrs, 17 en suite, (2 sh), 4 ba; TV; tcf 🏠 TV, dogs, ns; P 24, coach; child facs ✗ LD 9.15, lunch by arrangement only. Rest lic
£ B&B £28–£44, B&B (double) £48–£62; HB weekly £196–£308; L £7·50, D £9·95; [5% V w/e]
cc Access, Amex, B'card/Visa, Diners.

Drake Court London Rd, HP11 1BT ✆ (0494) 23639.
Situated on A40 London Rd about 1 mile from M40 and ¾ mile from town centre. Swimming pool.
🛏20 bedrs, 3 en suite, (3 sh), 4 ba; TV; tcf 🏠 TV; P 30, coach ✗ LD 8.30
£ B&B £25·30–£40, B&B (double) £39·10–£50; L £6·50, D £8·50; [10% V w/e] **cc** Access, Amex, B'card/Visa, Diners.

HILGAY Norfolk.   Map 25C2

Crosskeys Riverside (Highly Acclaimed)   nr Downham Market, PE38 0LN ✆ Downham Market (0366) 387777.

Once a coaching inn, now a small, quiet country hotel with a large riverside garden. Just off the A10, 2 miles S of Downham Market. Follow Holgay sign. Fishing.
5 bedrs, 5 en suite; TV; tcf dogs, ns; P 10; child facs LD 8.30 nr Mon–Sat lunch, Sun dinner. Resid & Rest lic
£ B&B £29·10, B&B (double) £42·55; L £9·30, D £9·30; WB (£54·25) **cc** Access, B'card/Visa; dep.

HIMBLETON Worcestershire. Map 26B8

Phepson Farm, Droitwich, WR9 7JZ (090 569) 205. *Farm.* David and Tricia Havard
Sleeps 10,
£ B&B from £13–£18

HINCKLEY Leicestershire. Map 23C2

Kings (Acclaimed) 13 Mount Rd, LE10 1AD
(0455) 637193 Fax: (0455) 636201.
Large red brick hotel with attractive garden. Follow sign for town centre then 'Hospital'. Hotel in same road.
7 bedrs, 7 en suite; TV; tcf dogs, ns; P 20, U 3, coach; child facs LD 9.30, nr Mon, Sat, Sun lunch & Sun dinner. Resid & Rest lic
£ B&B £54·50–£64·50, B&B (double) £64·50–£69·50; HB weekly £350–£370; L £10·50, D £16·50; WB (£45); [5% V] **cc** Access, Amex, B'card/Visa.

HOLBEACH Lincolnshire. Map 25B3

Crown 5 West End, PE12 1LW (0406) 23941.
8 bedrs, 5 en suite, 1 ba; TV; tcf dogs; P 20, coach; child facs
cc Access, B'card/Visa; dep.

HOLMBURY ST MARY Surrey. Map 27A4

Bulmer Farm Dorking, RH5 6LG (0306) 730210. *Farm.* Gill Hill
Sleeps 6,
£ B&B from £13

HOLMESFIELD Derbyshire. Map 24D5

Cordwell Farm Cordwell Valley, Nr Sheffield, S18 5WH (0742) 890303. *Farm.* Janet Biggin
Sleeps 6,
£ B&B from £12·50–£15

HOLMFIRTH West Yorkshire. Map 24C6

White Horse Jackson Bridge, HD7 7HF (0484) 683940.
'Last of the Summer Wine' inn run by family. Take A616 for 9 miles from Huddersfield towards Sheffield. After Jackson bridge, follow Scholes first right to inn.
5 bedrs, 2 ba; TV; tcf TV, P 12, U 2, coach;

child facs LD 9.45
£ B&B £17, B&B (double) £30; [10% V]; dep.

HOLNE Devon. Map 28G3

Church House Inn TQ13 7SJ Poundsgate (036 43) 208.
Traditional inn in centre of picturesque village.

Wellpritton Farm (Acclaimed) TQ13 7RX
Poundsgate (036 43) 273.
A small farm tucked away in the fold of hills, close to River Dart Country Park. From M5 near Exeter take A38 Plymouth road. Near Ashburton take second turn marked Princetown and Two Bridges for 3 miles. Turn left opposite AA phone box, and Wellpritton is first on right. Swimming pool, snooker. Closed 25–26 Dec.
4 bedrs, 3 en suite, 1 ba; tcf TV, ns; P 4; child facs nr lunch. Unlic
£ B&B £13–£15; HB weekly £119–£154; dep.

Dodbrooke Farm Michelcombe, Newton Abbot, TQ13 7SP (03643) 461. *Farm.* Judy Henderson
Sleeps 6, ns
£ B&B from £11–£12.50, D £6

Mill Leat Farm Ashburton, Newton Abbot, TQ13 7RZ (03643) 283. *Farm.* Dawn Cleave
Sleeps 6,
£ B&B from £12, D £5·50

HOLSWORTHY Devon. Map 28E4

Coles Mill (Acclaimed) EX22 6LX (0409) 253313.

Well-converted old watermill set in picturesque valley on outskirts of Holsworthy. On the S of town, at junction of A3072 and A388. Fishing. Open Mar–Oct
5 bedrs, 5 en suite; TV; tcf TV, ns; P 12; no children under 6 LD 5, nr lunch. Resid lic
£ B&B £15–£16·50, B&B (double) £25–£29; HB weekly £138–£150·10; dep.

Leworthy EX22 6SJ (0409) 253488.
Attractive period farm house on working farm, three miles south west of Holsworthy. Leave town by Bodmin Street, down hill, signposted North Tarverton. At cross-roads keep straight on; farm on

left, signposted. Putting, tennis, fishing, riding, snooker.
20 bedrs, 3 en suite, 2 ba; tcf TV, ns; P30, coach; no children under 4 LD6, nr lunch. Resid lic

Elm Park Bridgerule, EX22 7EL (028881) 231. *Farm.* Sylvia Lucas
Sleeps 14,
£ B&B from £10, D £6

The Barton Pancrasweek, EX22 7JT (028881) 315. *Farm.* Linda Cole
Sleeps 12, ns
£ B&B from £9–£10, D £6

Thorne Park EX22 7BL (0409) 253339. *Farm.* Mariene Heard
Sleeps 15,
£ B&B from £10, D £6·50

HOLT Norfolk. Map 25D3

Lawn's (Acclaimed) 26 Station Rd, NR25 6BS (0263) 713390.

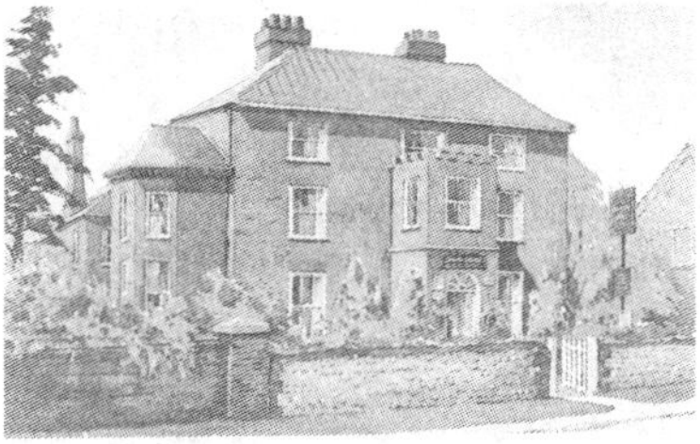

Elegant Georgian house with large rooms overlooking cricket pitch and walled gardens. Situated 50 yards from High St opposite Greshams junior school playingfields.
11 bedrs, 11 en suite; TV; tcf dogs, ns; P12, coach; child facs nr lunch, Resid & Rest lic
£ B&B £30, B&B (double) £55; HB weekly £250–£275; D £15; WB (£38); [5% V] **cc** Access, Amex, B'card/Visa.

HONEYCHURCH Devon. Map 28F4

Eastown Farm North Tawton, EX20 2AG (083 785) 279. *Farm.* Mrs Mary Pyle
Sleeps 6
£ B&B from £11, D from £6, Weekly bookings £ B&B & D £100

HONITON Devon. Map 29B4

Colestocks House (Highly Acclaimed) Colestocks, EX14 0JR (0404) 850633.

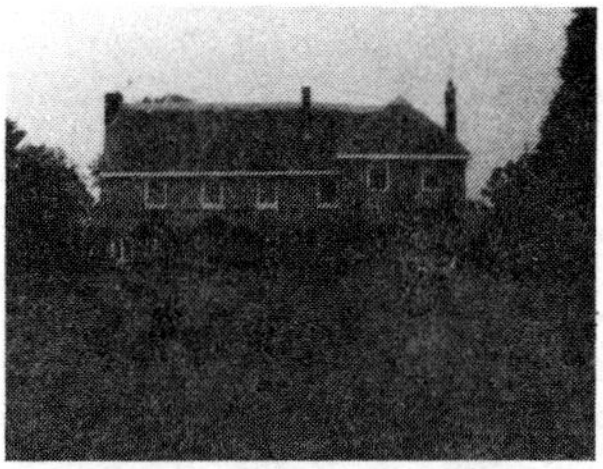

16th century, pink and thatched Grade II listed building with tranquil gardens in a peaceful hamlet. 4 miles W of Honiton and 2 miles N of A30 Honiton to Exeter road, between the villages of Feniton and Payhearbury. Putting.
9 bedrs, 9 en suite, TV; tcf P9; no children under 10 LD8, nr lunch. Resid & Rest lic
£ B&B £22·95–£29, B&B (double) £39·90–£55; HB weekly £189–£225; D £12·95; WB (£67 2 nights)
cc Access, B'card/Visa; dep.

HOOK Hampshire. Map 26E4

Cedar Court Reading Rd, RG27 9DB (0256) 762178.
Small guest house with delightful gardens. On B 3349, 1 mile N of Hook. 2 miles from junction 5 of M3.
6 bedrs, 1 ba; tcf TV; P6 Breakfast only. Unlic
£ B&B £17–£20, B&B (double) £30–£35; [5% V Jul–Aug]; dep.

HOPTON Derbyshire. Map 24C4

Henmore Grange Wirksworth, DE4 4DF (062 985) 420. *Farm.* John and Elizabeth Brassington
Sleeps 24,
£ B&B from £18–£27·50, D £10·50

Sycamore Farm Wirksworth, DE4 4DF (0629) 822466. *Farm.* Mrs Bridget Corbett
Sleeps 4, ns
£ B&B from £12

HORLEY Surrey. Map 27A4

Langshott Manor (Highly Acclaimed) Langshott, RH6 9LN (0293) 786680 Fax: (0293) 783905.
Superb Elizabethan manor house, elegantly decorated and furnished with taste and charm.

Using RAC discount vouchers
Please tell the hotel when booking if you plan to use an RAC discount voucher (see end of guide) in part payment of your bill. Only one voucher will be accepted per party per stay. Discount vouchers will only be accepted in payment for accommodation, not for food.

From A23 at Horley take Ladbroke Rd (Chequers Hotel roundabout) to Langshott. Manor is ¾ mile down Ladbroke Rd.
🛏5 bedrs, 5 en suite; TV 📺ns; P10; child facs ✕LD10. Resid & Rest lic
£B&B £84·50–£92·50, B&B (double) £104–£113·50; HB weekly £630–£693; L£15; [5% V] cc Access, Amex, B'card/Visa, Diners.

Cumberland House (Acclaimed) 39 Brighton Rd, RH6 7HH ☎(0293) 784379 Fax: (0293) 772001.

Situated on the A23 London to Brighton road 1 mile N of Gatwick Airport.
🛏12 bedrs, 7 en suite; TV; tcf 📺TV, dogs; P15 ✕LD8, Resid lic
£B&B £25–£33, B&B (double) £38–£46·50; L£5–£7, D£5–£8; [10% V] cc Access, Amex, B'card/Visa; dep.

Gainsborough Lodge (Acclaimed) 39 Massetts Rd, RH6 7DT ☎(0293) 783982. *Guest House.*

Massetts Lodge (Acclaimed) 28 Massetts Rd, RH6 7DE ☎(0293) 782738.

Family run Victorian guest house 5 mins from Gatwick but away from flight path. From M23, junction 9 take A23 north, at first roundabout take third exit, then second right signed Horley town centre. Massetts Lodge 600 yards on left.

🛏8 bedrs, 5 en suite, 2 ba; TV; tcf 📺ns; P10; child facs ✕LD8, nr lunch. Unlic
£B&B £21–£32, B&B (double) £32–£40; HB weekly £145·75–£169·75; [10% V] cc Access, Amex, B'card/Visa; dep.

Mill Lodge (Acclaimed) 25 Brighton Rd, RH1 6PP ☎Horley (0293) 771170. *Guest House.*
🛏8 bedrs, 2 en suite, 2 ba; TV; tcf 📺TV, dogs, ns; P35, U3; child facs ✕Dinner on request. Unlic
£B&B £23–£31, B&B (double) £31–£38; dep.

Lawns 30 Massetts Rd, RH6 7DE ☎(0293) 775571.
Situated just off A23/M23 4 miles from Gatwick Airport.
🛏7 bedrs, 7 en suite; TV; tcf 📺dogs, ns; P10 ✕Breakfast only. Unlic
£B&B (double) £39: [10% V] cc Access, B'card/Visa.

Melville Lodge 15 Brighton Rd, RH6 7HH ☎(0293) 784951.
From Gatwick follow A23 to Croydon-Redhill at roundabout with Gatwick Moat House Hotel. Turn right and Melville Lodge is on the left.
🛏5 bedrs, 2 ba; TV; tcf 📺TV, dogs, ns; P5; child facs
£B&B £20, B&B (double) £32–£35; dep.

Woodlands 42 Massetts Rd, RH6 7DS ☎(0293) 782994.
Attractive doublel-fronted detached house. Situated off A23, 1 mile N of Gatwick Airport. Closed 23 Dec–31 Dec.
🛏5 bedrs, 5 en suite, 1 ba; TV; tcf 📺NS; P20 (£1·50), U2; no children under 5 ✕Breakfast only. Unlic
£B&B £26, B&B (double) £36; [10% V]; dep.

HORNSEA Humberside (North Humberside). Map 25A7

Merlstead 59 Eastgate, HU18 1NB ☎(0964) 533068.
Small hotel close to sea front at Eastgate.
🛏5 bedrs, 3 en suite, 2 ba; TV; tcf 📺TV, dogs, ns; P4; child facs ✕LD7. Resid lic

£ B&B £24; B&B (double) £25–£35; HB weekly
£120–£165; [5% V]; dep.

HORRABRIDGE   Devon.   Map 28F3

Overcombe (Acclaimed)   nr Yelverton, PL20 7RN
Yelverton ✆ 0822 853501.
*Two semi-detatched houses combined and
extended, with panoramic views. Situated on A386
between Yelverton and Tavistock.*
⌗ 11 bedrs, 10 en suite, 1 ba; TV; tcf 🛎 TV, dogs;
P 10; child facs ✗ LD 7.15, nr lunch. Resid & Rest
lic
£ B&B £18–£23, B&B (double) £35–£41; HB weekly
£178–£205; L 6·50, D £10·50; WB (£53 2 nights HB
Oct–May); [5% V]   **cc** Access, B'Card/Visa; dep.

HORSHAM   West Sussex.   Map 27A3

Blatchford House (Acclaimed)   52 Kings Rd,
RH13 5PR ✆ (0403) 65317. *Guest House. Sauna.*

Horsham Wimblehurst   6 Wimblehurst Rd, RH12
2ED ✆ (0403) 62319. Fax: (0403) 211212.
*Victorian villa in a quiet residential area. Wimblehurst
Rd is a turning off the A24 opposite the Hop Picker
Pub.*
⌗ 14 bedrs, 11 en suite, (2 sh), 2 ba; TV 🛎 TV, ns;
P 14; child facs ✗ LD 6, nr lunch. Unlic
£ B&B £39·50–£49·50, B&B (double) £49·50–
£54·50; WB; [5% V w/e]   **cc** Access, B'card/Visa;
dep.

Goffsland Farm   Shipley, RH13 7BQ ✆ (0403)
730434. *Farm.* Mrs Carol Liverton
Sleeps 5, ⌖ 🐴
£ B&B from £12

HORSMONDEN   Kent.   Map 27C4

Pullens Farm   Lamberhurst Road, TN12 8ED
✆ (089 272) 2241. *Farm.* Sally Russell
Sleeps 6, ns ⌖
£ B&B from £14·50, D £10

HORTON   Dorset.   Map 26C2

Northill House (Acclaimed)   BH21 7HL ✆ (0258)
840407.

*Mid-Victorian house on Lord Shaftesbury's estate,
modernised and comfortable. Situated 7 miles N of
Wimborne off B3078 between Horton Inn and
Horton village. Open 14 Feb–20 Dec.*
⌗ 9 bedrs, 9 en suite; TV; tcf 🛎 ns; P 12; no
children under 8 ✗ LD 6. Resid lic
£ B&B £28; B&B (double) £52; HB weekly £233·10–
£245·70 **cc** Access, B'card/Visa; dep.

HORTON-CUM-STUDLEY   Oxfordshire.
Map 26E6

Studley Farmhouse   Arncott Road, Oxford, OX9
1BP ✆ (086735) 286. *Farm.* Mrs Jean Hicks   ♿
Sleeps 6, ns ⌖ (14)
£ B&B from £17·50

HORTON-IN-RIBBLESDALE   North
Yorkshire.   Map 23B3

Crown   nr Settle, BD24 0HF ✆ (072 96) 209.
*17th century beamed hotel standing on the Pennine
Way. 6 miles N of Settle on B6479 at the foot of
Penyghent.*
⌗ 10 bedrs, 1 en suite, (6 sh), 2 ba; tcf 🛎 TV, dogs;
P 20, coach; child facs
£ B&B £15·75–£19·80, B&B (double) £31·50–
£39·60; HB weekly £164·50–£183·50; D £8·25,
dep.

HOVE   East Sussex.   Map 27A2

Claremont House (Highly Acclaimed)   Second
Av, BN3 2LL ✆ Brighton (0273) 735161
Fax: (0273) 24764.
⌗ 12 bedrs, 12 en suite; TV; tcf 🛎 TV, dogs; child
facs ✗ LD 9.30, nr lunch. Resid & Rest lic
cc Access, Amex, B'card/Visa, Diners.

Albany   St Catherine Terr, Kingsway, BN3 2RR
✆ Brighton (0273) 773807.
*Small hotel with sea views, situated on Kingsway
close to King Alfred sports/entertainment complex,
1 mile from West Pier.*
⌗ 10 bedrs, 10 en suite; TV; tcf 🛎 dogs, ns; no
children under 8 ✗ LD 5, nr lunch & Sun dinner.
Resid lic
£ B&B £19·50–£29·50, B&B (double) £29·50–
£39·50; WB (£29·50); [10% V]   **cc** Access, B'card/
Visa; dep.

Cornerways   18 Caburn Rd, BN3 6EF ☎ Brighton (0273) 731882.
On the old Shoreham Rd (A27) near junction with Dyke Rd opposite 6th form college.
⊨11 bedrs, 1 en suite, 3 ba; TV; tcf 📺TV, dogs; coach; child facs ✕LD 2, nr lunch Sat & Sun dinner. Resid lic
£B&B £15; HB weekly £145; D £7 WB (Winter only); dep.

Croft   24 Palmeria Av, BN3 3GB ☎ Brighton (0273) 732860. Fax: (0273) 820775.
Small hotel recently refurbished, with patio garden. Situated N from Palmeira Square and the floral clock.
⊨11 bedrs, (2 sh), 2 ba; TV; tcf 📺TV, dogs; child facs ✕Breakfast only. Resid lic
£B&B £20–£22, B&B (double) £35–£38; [10% V]; dep.

HUBBERHOLME   North Yorkshire.
Map 24B8

Kirkgill Manor (Highly Acclaimed)   BD23 5JE
☎(075 676) 800. *Guest House.* Closed Dec.
⊨6 bedrs, 6 en suite, 1 ba; TV; tcf 📺dogs; P 12; child facs

HULL   Humberside (North Humberside).
Map 25A7

Earlsmere (Acclaimed)   76 Sunnybank, off Spring Bank West, HU3 1LQ ☎Hull City (0482) 41977
Tx: 592729 Fax: (0482) 214121.

⊨15 bedrs, 7 en suite, 2 ba; TV; tcf 📺TV, dogs; coach ✕LD6.30, nr lunch, Sun dinner. Resid lic
£B&B £18·40–£26·45; WB; dep.

Roseberry   86 Marlborough Ave, HU5 3JJ
☎(0482) 445256.
Follow signs to city centre to main traffic lights after station, take left fork into Springbank. Turn right at lights onto Prince's Ave and Marlborough Ave is 6th on the left.
⊨4 bedrs, 1 en suite, (3 sh), 1 ba; TV; tcf 📺TV; child facs ✕Breakfast only. Unlic
£B&B £17

HUNGERFORD   Berkshire.
Map 26D5

Marshgate Cottage (Acclaimed)   Marsh Lane RG17 0QX ☎(0488) 682307.
17th century thatched cottage with accommodation in linked units around central walled courtyard. From Hungerford High St turn into Church St, in ⅓ mile cross stream and turn immediately right into Marsh Lane. Cottage at end on right. Closed 25 Dec–24 Jan.
⊨9 bedrs, 7 en suite, 2 ba; TV; tcf 📺ns; P 8, G 2; no children under 5 ✕LD 7.30, nr lunch. Resid lic
£B&B £23·50–£33, B&B (double) £33–£45·50; [5% Nov–Apr] **cc** Access, B'card/Visa; dep.

HUNNINGHAM   Warwickshire.
Map 24D1

Snowford Hall   Nr Royal Leamington Spa, CV33 9ES ☎(0926) 632297. *Farm.* Rudi Hancock
Sleeps 6, ns ⚑
£ B&B from £12–£15, D £10–£12

HUNSTANTON   Norfolk.
Map 25C3

Sunningdale (Highly Acclaimed)   3 Avenue Rd, PE36 5BW ☎(0485) 532562.

Victorian building of local carrstone with delightful interior rooms and a classical dining room. Set 150 yards inland from Oasis sports and swimming centre on main promenade.
⊨11 bedrs, 11 en suite; TV; tcf 📺TV, dogs, ns; coach; no children under 7 ✕LD8, nr lunch. Resid & Rest lic
£B&B £25–£26·50, B&B (weekly) £40–£47; D £8·50 [10% V]; dep.

Deepdene (Acclaimed)   29 Avenue Rd, PE36 5BW ☎(04853) 2460.
Beautiful 83-year-old house built of local stone and brick with stained glass window. Take A149 from Kings Lynn to Hunstanton, cross over mini roundabout, next left down Sandringham Rd. Deepdene is 3rd turning on left. Indoor swimming pool, sauna, solarium, gymnasium, billiards. Closed Oct.
⊨9 bedrs, 1 en suite, 5 ba, TV; tcf 📺TV; P 12; child facs ✕LD 8, nr Sun lunch. Resid, Rest & Club lic
£B&B £22·50; HB weekly £252; dep.

Linksway (Acclaimed)   Golf Course Rd, Old Hunstanton PE36 6JE ☎(048 53) 2209.

Country house hotel in own quiet grounds overlooking golf course and sand dunes. Take coast road to old Hunstanton (A149), turn left signed golf course. Indoor swimming pool.
⇔15 bedrs, 15 en suite; TV; tcf 🏠P 15, coach; child facs ✕LD9.30, nr lunch Mon–Sat. Resid & Rest lic
£ B&B £27·50; D £9·95; [5% V]; dep.

HYDE Gtr Manchester. Map 24B5

Needhams Farm (Acclaimed) Uplands Rd, Werneth Low, Gee Cross, SK14 3AQ ☎061-368 4610
⇔6 bedrs, 3 en suite, 1 ba; TV; tcf 🏠dogs, ns; P 8, G 2; child facs ✕LD 10. Resid lic
£ B&B £15–£16·50; HB weekly £140–£150; WB; [5% V]; dep.

ILAM Derbyshire. Map 28F4

Beechenhill Farm Ashbourne, DE6 2BD
☎(033527) 274. *Farm.* Sue Prince
Sleeps 6, ns 🐄
£ B&B from £13

ILFORD Greater London (Essex). Map 27B6

Cranbrook 24 Coventry Rd, IG1 4QR ☎081-554 6544.
⇔16 bedrs, 11 en suite, (2 sh), 2 ba; TV; tcf 🏠TV, dogs; P 12, G 2, coach; child facs ✕LD 8, nr lunch. Resid lic
cc Access, Amex, B'card/Visa; dep.
(See advertisement under London)

Park 327 Cranbrook Rd, IG1 4UE ☎081-554 9616. Fax: 081-518 2700.
Situated on the A123 just S of junction with the A12 Gants Hill roundabout, ½ mile from M11, junction 3.
⇔21 bedrs, 12 en suite, (5 sh), 1 ba; TV; tcf 🏠TV, dogs, ns; P 23, coach; child facs ✕LD8.15, nr lunch & Fri, Sat & Sun dinner. Resid lic
£ B&B £27·50–£37, B&B (double) £37–£48; D £8
cc Access, B'card/Visa, CB, dep.

ILFRACOMBE Devon. Map 28F6

Avalon (Acclaimed) 6 Capstone Cres, EX34 9BT
☎(0271) 863325.
A completely refurbished Victorian hotel overlooking the sea. Follow signs to harbour, then turn left by Sandpiper pub.
⇔11 bedrs, 3 en suite, (1 sh), 2 ba; TV; tcf 🏠TV, ns; coach; child facs ✕LD 6. Resid lic
£ B&B £16·50, B&B (double) £27–£36; HB weekly £112–£127; D £6; WB (£39 3 nights B&B); [10% V]
cc Access, B'card/Visa; dep.

Cairngorm (Acclaimed) 43 St Brannocks Rd, EX34 8EH ☎(0271) 863911.

Detached Victorian hotel set in ¾ acres of grounds with extensive views of the sea and countryside. Situated on the A361 from Barnstaple, 1½ miles from Mullacott roundabout. Open Mar–Nov.
⇔8 bedrs, 8 en suite; TV; tcf 🏠dogs; P 12; child facs ✕LD 6, nr lunch. Resid lic
£ B&B £19–£22; HB weekly £168–£175; [10% V]
cc Access, B'card/Visa; dep.

Gables (Acclaimed) 1 Belmont Rd, EX34 8DR
☎(0271) 862475.
Grade II listed Victorian Gothic residence retaining many original features and set in a walled garden. Off A361 from Barnstaple. Turn left at War Memorial into Church Hill, then first left. Open Apr–28 Oct.
⇔8 bedrs, 8 en suite; TV; tcf 🏠TV, ns; P 10; no children under 5 ✕LD4, nr lunch. Resid lic
£ B&B £16, B&B (double) £32–£40; HB weekly £143·50–£164·50; [10% V]

Rosslyn (Acclaimed) 15 St Brannocks Rd, EX34 8EG ☎(0271) 862643.

Attractive terraced Victorian building, fully modernised yet retaining all its original features. Enter town on the A361 from Barnstaple, and Rosslyn is on the right 200 yards before traffic lights. Open Mar–Dec.
⊨5 bedrs, 1 en suite, 1 ba; tcf 📺TV, ns; U 1; child facs ✗LD 5, nr lunch. Resid lic
£B&B £14; HB weekly £140–£175; D £6; WB (£54 3 nights HB); [5% V Mar–May, Oct–Dec]; dep

Southcliffe (Acclaimed)   Torrs Park, EX34 8AZ ✆(0271) 862958. Open Mar–mid Sept.
Detached Victorian hotel with stained glass windows and terraced gardens. From Barnstaple turn left at 1st traffic lights, then left at 2nd traffic lights into Torrs Park. Hotel 400 metres on left.
⊨14 bedrs, 13 en suite, (1 sh); tcf 📺TV, ns; P 12; child facs ✗LD 6, nr lunch. Resid lic
£ HB weekly £153–£159; D £10; dep.

South Tor (Acclaimed)   Torrs Park, EX34 8AZ ✆(0271) 63750. Hotel. 1 Mar–30 Oct.
⊨12 bedrs, 12 en suite; tcf 📺TV; P 15, coach; no children under 6 ✗LD 6. Resid & Rest lic

Strathmore (Acclaimed)   57 St Brannocks Rd, EX34 8EQ ✆(0271) 862248.
Victorian building of local style, situated on A361 on outskirts of town opposite Park Court. Open Easter–end Sep.
⊨9 bedrs, 7 en suite, 2 ba; TV; tcf 📺dogs, P 7; child facs ✗LD 5, nr lunch. Resid & Rest lic
£B&B £15; HB weekly £159·50; WB (£42·50 3 nights B&B) cc Access, Amex, B'card/Visa, Diners; dep.

Trafalgar (Acclaimed)   Larkstone Terr, EX34 9NU ✆(0271) 862145.

Elegant Victorian hotel with magnificent views over the harbour and Bristol Channel. On the main Barnstaple to Combe Martin road.
⊨24 bedrs, 21 en suite, (3 sh), TV; tcf 📺dogs; P 7, coach; child facs ✗LD 7.30
£B&B £25–£27·50, B&B (double) £40–£54; HB weekly £150–£175; D £7·50; [10% V] cc Access, Amex, B'card/Visa, Diners; dep.

Wildercombe House (Acclaimed)   St Brannocks Rd, EX34 8EP ✆(0271) 862240.

Tastefully restored Victorian hotel with spacious accommodation. Situated just past the town sign on A361 Barnstaple road.
⊨11 beds, 11 en suite, 1 ba; TV; tcf 📺dogs; P 15; child facs ✗LD 5. Resid & Rest lic
£B&B £18·50–£20; HB weekly £170–£185; L £3·50; [10% V] cc Access, Amex, B'card/Visa, dep.

Avenue   Greenclose Rd, EX34 8BT ✆(0271) 863767.
Turn left at first traffic lights in Ilfracombe (off A361), and Greenclose Rd is on right.
⊨22 bedrs, 9 en suite, 4 ba, TV; tcf 📺TV, ns; P 10, coach; child facs ✗LD 7, Resid lic
£B&B £14–£18·50; HB weekly £140–£180; WB (£85 4 nights D, B&B); [5% V] cc Access, B'card/Visa; dep.

Beaufort   Torrs Park, EX34 8AY ✆(0271) 865483.
White-walled Victorian hotel close to the beach. Turn left at first traffic lights, in ¼ mile turn left again into Torrs Park. Swimming pool, solarium, gymnasium.
⊨14 bedrs, 12 en suite, 2 ba; TV; tcf 📺dogs, ns; P 25, coach; child facs ✗LD 8, nr lunch, Resid & Rest lic
£ B&B £15–£21; HB weekly £120–£160; WB (3 nights £30); [10% V except BH] cc Access, Amex, B'card/Visa; dep.

Collingdale   Larkstone Ter, EX34 9NU ✆(0271) 863770.
Small family hotel with 20 miles of uninterrupted sea views. From A361 follow road into High St, bear right where road divides, hotel ¼ mile on left. Open Mar–Oct.
⊨9 bedrs, 2 en suite, (1 sh), 2 ba; tcf 📺TV, dogs; child facs ✗LD 6.30, nr lunch. Resid & Rest lic

---

En suite rooms
En suite rooms may be bath or shower rooms. If you have a preference, remember to state it when booking a room.

£ B&B £15–£16; HB weekly £120–£135; D £6·50; dep.

Cresta   Torrs Park, EX34 8AY ✆ (0271) 863742.
Situated on the main seafront road, about 300 yards from first traffic lights in the town. Putting. Open May–Oct.
🛏31 bedrs, 17 en suite, 5 ba; tcf 👤lift, TV, dogs; P 28, coach; child facs ✗LD 7, Resid lic
£ B&B £16·50–£20·50, HB weekly £136·50–£161; [5% V] **cc** Access.

Earlsdale   51 St Brannocks Rd, EX34 8EQ ✆ (0271) 862496.
Small family hotel within walking distance of seafront. Situated on A361 from Barnstaple on left opposite Coach House Inn.
🛏10 bedrs, 5 en suite, 3 ba; TV 👤TV, dogs, P 10, coach; child facs ✗LD 6.30, nr lunch. Resid lic
£ B&B £10–£12·50; HB weekly £105–£125; [5% V]; dep.

Excelsior   Torrs Park, EX34 8AZ ✆ (0271) 862919.
Large stone house set in its own grounds. Turn left at first traffic lights on A361, left at next lights then left again. Open Apr–Oct.
🛏18 bedrs, 11 en suite, (1 sh), 2 ba; TV 👤TV, dogs; P 14, coach; child facs ✗LD 6.30, nr lunch. Resid lic.
£ B&B £15–£18; HB weekly £122–£145; dep.

Goodrest   45 St Brannocks Rd, EX34 8EH ✆ (0271) 863865.
Small hotel with good views on the A361 Barnstaple Rd.
🛏8 bedrs, 6 en suite, 1 ba; TV; tcf 👤dogs; P 8, coach; no children under 16 ✗LD 5, nr lunch. Resid & Rest lic
£ B&B £12, B&B (double) £28; HB weekly £119–£133; D £7·50 **cc** Access, B'card/Visa; dep.

Laston House   Hillsborough Rd, EX34 9NT ✆ (0271) 62627. *Hotel.*

Lympstone   14 Cross Park, EX34 8BJ ✆ (0271) 863038.
Situated in a quiet cul-de-sac off the Promenade. Open Mar–Oct.

🛏15 bedrs, 9 en suite, 2 ba; TV; tcf 👤TV, dogs; P 10, child facs ✗LD 5, nr lunch. Resid lic
£ B&B £13–£16; HB weekly £120–£135; D £6; WB (4 nights £47 B&B); dep.

Lyncott   56 St Brannocks Rd, EX34 8EQ ✆ (0271) 862425.
Family guest house close to Bicclescombe Park. Situated on A361 from Barnstaple on left. Open Mar 1–Oct 31.
🛏9 bedrs, 2 en suite, 3 ba; tcf 👤TV, dogs; P 7, U 1, child facs ✗LD 5, nr lunch. Unlic
£ B&B £10–£11·50; HB weekly £90–£105; D £4; [5% V]

Merlin Court   Torrs Park, EX34 8AY (0271) 862697. Open Mar–Nov.
🛏14 bedrs; TV; tcf 👤P 14, coach; child facs ✗LD 7, nr lunch. Resid lic
£ B&B £19–£21; HB weekly £168–£182 **cc** Access, B'card/Visa; dep.

Orion   16 St Brannocks Rd, EX34 8ZG ✆ (0271) 62410. *Guest House.*

St Brannocks House   61 St Brannocks Rd. EX34 8EQ ✆ (0271) 863873.
🛏20 bedrs, 8 en suite, 4 ba; TV; tcf 👤TV, dogs; P 20, coach; child facs ✗LD 6, bar snacks only lunch. Resid lic
£ B&B £13–£17; HB weekly £115–£147; D £6·50; WB (4 nights £68); [10% V] **cc** Access, B'card/Visa; dep.

Sunnyhill Country House   Lincombe, Lee, EX34 8LL ✆ (0271) 62953. *Hotel.*

Wentworth House   Belmont Rd, EX34 8DR ✆ (0271) 863048.
Victorian residence in attractive gardens. From A361 turn left into Church Hill by War Memorial, left into Belmont Rd. Open Apr–Xmas.
🛏10 bedrs, 3 en suite, 2 ba; tcf 👤TV, dogs; P 10; child facs ✗LD 6, nr lunch. Resid & Rest lic
£ B&B £12·50–£14·50, HB weekly £105–£126 **cc** Access, B'card/Visa; dep.

Westwell Hall   Torrs Park, EX34 8AZ ✆ (0271) 862792.
Large early Victorian house in its own grounds. Situated at top of Torrs Park. Billiards.
🛏10 bedrs, 10 en suite; TV; tcf 👤dogs, ns; P 12; no children under 6 ✗LD 8, nr lunch. Resid & Rest lic
£ B&B £20; HB weekly £154–£175; D £7·50; [5% V Oct–Mar]; dep.

INGLETON   North Yorkshire.   Map 24A8

Pines Country House (Highly Acclaimed)   near Carnforth, Lancs LA6 3HN ✆ Lancaster (05242) 41252.

Attractive country house hotel with sun terrace and magnificent views over the River Greta. Adjacent to A65 on edge of village.
🛏4 bedrs, 3 en suite, 1 ba; TV; tcf 📺TV, dogs, ns; P 14; child facs ✕LD 7.30
£ B&B £16–£18, HB weekly £185·50–£192; D £12·50; WB (£80 3 nights HB)

Oakroyd (Acclaimed)   Main St, Via Carnforth, LA6 3HJ ✆(05242) 41258.

Formerly the village rectory, close to White Scar Caves. Situated between Settle and Kirkby Lonsdale on A65 (junction 34 of M6).
🛏8 bedrs, 5 en suite, 2 ba; TV; tcf 📺TV, ns; P 8; coach; child facs ✕LD 7.30, nr lunch. Resid lic
£B&B £15, B&B (double) £30; HB weekly £145; D £8·50; [10% V]; dep.

Springfield (Acclaimed)   Main St, LA6 3HJ ✆(05242) 41280.
Detached Victorian villa in its own grounds with panoramic views. About 100 yards off A65 on the W end of Main St. Open 1 Jan–31 Oct.
🛏6 bedrs, 4 en suite, 1 ba; TV; tcf 📺TV, dogs; P 12; child facs ✕LD 5, nr lunch. Resid lic
£B&B £14–£16; HB weekly £140–£156; D £7·50; [5% V]; dep.

Langber   LA6 3DT ✆(052 42) 41587.
Small hotel set in large grounds. Turn off A65 between transport depot and Mason's Arms pub. Langber 1 mile on left. Closed 24 Dec–2 Jan.
🛏7 bedrs, 3 en suite, 2 ba; tcf 📺TV, dogs, ns; P 6, coach; child facs ✕LD 5, nr lunch. Unlic
£B&B £10·50–£14, B&B (double) £20·50–£27; HB weekly £92–£110; dep.

Gatehouse Farm   Far West House, Carnforth, LA6 3NR ✆(052 42) 41458/41307. Farm. Nancy Lund
Sleeps 7, 🐴🐂
£ B&B from £12, D £7

INGLEWHITE Lancashire.   Map 23A2

Park Head Farm   Nr Preston, PR3 2LN ✆(0995) 40352. Farm. Mrs Ruth Rhodes
Sleeps 6, 🐂 ns
£ B&B from £15

INSTOW Devon.   Map 29F5

Anchorage (Acclaimed)   The Quay, nr Bideford EX39 4HX ✆(0271) 860655

INWARDLEIGH Devon.   Map 28F4

Lower Oak Farm   Okehampton, EX20 3AS ✆(0837) 810412. Farm. Rosemary Banbury
Sleeps 8, 🐂
£ B&B from £10, D £7

IPPLEPEN Devon.   Map 29A3

Newhouse Barton   Newton Abbot, TQ12 5UN ✆(0803) 812539. Farm. Sue Stafford
Sleeps 6, ns 🐂 (3)
£ B&B from £12–£15, D £9

IPSWICH Suffolk.   Map 27E8

Anglesea (Acclaimed)   Oban St, IP1 3PH ✆(0473) 255630.
Refurbished Victorian house in quiet conservation area. From A45 follow signs to Ipswich West and North into Norwich Rd. Cross double mini-roundabout, first left into Anglesea Rd, and Oban St on right.
🛏7 beds, 7 en suite; TV; tcf 📺dogs; P 9; no children under 10 ✕LD 7.30, nr lunch. Resid lic
£B&B £38, B&B (double) £50; D £9·50 cc Access, Amex, B'card/Visa.

Highview House (Acclaimed)   56 Belstead Rd, IP2 8BE ✆(0473) 688659.
Attractive Victorian residence standing in large garden with panoramic views over Ipswich and surrounding countryside. Follow railway station signs into Willoughby Rd for 200 yards, turn right into Belstead Rd. Hotel 300 yards on right. Billiards.
10 bedrs, 7 en suite, 3 ba; TV; tcf 📺TV, dogs; P 12; no children under 7 ✕LD 8, nr lunch. Fri–Sun dinner by arrangement. Resid & Rest lic
£ B&B £28–£33, B&B (double) £39–£44; [10% V w/e] cc Access, B'card/Visa

Graham Court   Anglesea Rd, IP1 3PW ✆(0473) 53583. Hotel.

ISLE OF WIGHT

BRADING   Map 26D2

New Farm   Coach Lane, PO36 0JQ ✆(0983) 407371. Farm. Diane Morris   ♿
Sleeps 8, 🐴🐂
£ B&B from £12–£15

CARISBROOKE   Map 26D2

Great Park Farm   Betty Haunt Lane, PO30 4HR ✆(0983) 522945. Farm. Mrs Sheila Brownrigg
Sleeps 4, 🐂 (10)
£ B&B from £12–£15

FRESHWATER
Map 26D2

Blenheim House (Acclaimed)   Gate La, PO40 9QD ☎ Isle of Wight (0983) 752858.
Situated on main road out of Freshwater, 300 yards from the bay. Swimming pool. Open May–Oct.
⇔8 bedrs, 8 en suite, 2 ba; TV; tcf ⑥P6; no children under 6 ✗nr lunch
£ B&B £17·50; B&B (double) £33; HB weekly £175; dep.

MOTTISTONE
Map 26D2

Mottistone Manor Farm   Nr Newport, PO30 4ED ☎(0983) 740232. *Farm.* Anne Humphrey
Sleeps 6, ns ♨ (3)
£ B&B from £10–£12·50

NEWPORT
Map 26D2

Youngwoods Farm   Whitehouse Road, Porchfield, PO30 4LJ ☎(0983) 522170. *Farm.*
Judith Shanks
Sleeps 4, ns ♨ (8)
£ B&B from £11–£15

ROOKLEY
Map 26D2

Barwick   Rookley Farm Lane, Niton Road, PO38 3PA ☎(0983) 840787. *Farm.* Pamela Wickham
Sleeps 6, ♨
£ B&B from £12, D £6

RYDE
Map 26E2

Dorset   31 Dover Rd, PO33 2BW ☎ Isle of Wight (0983) 64327. *Swimming pool.*

Georgian   22 George St, PO33 2EW ☎ Isle of Wight (0983) 63989.

Briddlesford Lodge Farm   Wotton Bridge, PO33 4RY ☎(0983) 882239. *Farm.* Mrs Judi Griffin
Sleeps 6, ⛺♨
£ B&B from £10–£12

Hazelgrove Farm   Ashey, PO33 4BD ☎(0983) 63100. *Farm.* Sheila Curtis
Sleeps 6, ns ♨
£ B&B from £12–£15, D £6

SANDOWN
Map 26E2

Braemar (Highly Acclaimed)   5 Broadway, PO36 9DQ ☎ Isle of Wight (0983) 403358.

Late Victorian stone building situated on A3055 from Ryde to Ventnor, 100 yds before leisure centre.
⇔14 bedrs, 14 en suite, 2 ba; TV; tcf ⑥P12, coach; child facs ✗LD7.30, nr lunch. Resid & Rest lic
£ B&B £24; HB weekly £172–£218; D £8·95; WB (£55 HB); [10% V] **cc** Access, Amex, B'card/Visa, Diners; dep.

St Catherine's (Highly Acclaimed)   1 Winchester Park Rd. PO36 8HJ ☎ Isle of Wight (0983) 402392.

Former home of the Dean of Winchester, built in 1860 of Purbeck stone. Situated on the Ryde–Shanklin road on the corner of Winchester Park Rd. Closed 25 Dec–1 Jan.
⇔20 bedrs, 20 en suite; TV; tcf ⑥TV, ns; P 8, child facs ✗LD7, nr lunch. Resid & Rest lic
£ B&B £17·50–£20·50; HB weekly £159·25–£191·75; D £10 **cc** Access, B'card/Visa; dep.

Chester Lodge (Acclaimed)   7 Beachfield Rd, PO36 8NA ☎(0983) 402773.
Detached hotel facing the sea and close to shops. Set 300 yards up from the town on the right. Open Feb–Nov.
20 bedrs, 12 en suite, 3 ba; TV; tcf ⑥TV, dogs, ns; coach; no children under 4 ✗LD 6, nr lunch. Resid & Rest lic
£ B&B £13·80–£16·10; HB weekly £138–£150

SHANKLIN
Map 26E2

Apse Manor Country House (Highly Acclaimed) Apse Manor Rd, PO37 7NP ☎ Isle of Wight (0983) 866651.
⇔6 bedrs, 6 en suite; TV; tcf ⑥dogs; P 10; no children under 5 ✗LD7, nr lunch. Resid & Rest lic

Bay House (Highly Acclaimed)   8 Chine Av, Keats Green, PO37 6AN ☎(0983) 863180.
Indoor swimming pool, sauna, solarium.
⇔22 bedrs, 22 en suite, 1 ba; TV; tcf ⑥dogs, ns; P 25, G 2, coach; child facs ✗LD 7, nr lunch. Resid & Rest lic **cc** Access, B'card/Visa; dep.

Luccombe Chine (Highly Acclaimed)   Luccombe Chine, PO37 6RH ☎(0983) 862037.
Country house hotel set in 10 acres of grounds and looking out over Luccombe Bay. Situated on Shanklin–Ventnor Road.
⇔8 bedrs, 8 en suite; TV; tcf ⑥P 15; no children ✗LD 8, nr lunch. Resid & Rest lic

£ B&B £39–£45, B&B (double) £48–£60; HB weekly £210–252; D £11·50; WB (£27 Oct–Apr) cc Access, B'card/Visa; dep.

Osborne House (Highly Acclaimed) Esplanade, PO37 6BN **(**(0983) 862501.

A small Victorian seafront hotel in an elevated garden setting. Situated opposite clock tower. Open 1 Jan–Oct.
12 bedrs, 12 en suite, 2 ba; TV; tcf ns; children over 13 LD8, nr lunch, Sun dinner. Resid & Rest lic
£ B&B £26·50, B&B (double) £51; D £11·50
cc Access, B'card/Visa; dep.

Hambledon (Acclaimed) 11 Queens Rd, PO37 6AW **(**(0983) 862403 or 863651.
White-walled hotel with sea views, close to beach lift and shops. Set in central Shanklin.
11 bedrs, 11 en suite, 1 ba; TV; tcf TV, ns; P 8, coach, child facs LD 6.30, nr lunch. Resid lic

Pulboro (Acclaimed) 6 Park Rd, PO37 6AZ **(**(0983) 862740. Open 1 Feb–1 Dec.

17 bedrs, 11 en suite, 2 ba; TV; tcf P 7, coach; child facs LD 4, nr lunch. Resid lic
£ B&B £16–£24; HB weekly £135–£177; WB

Soraba (Acclaimed) 2 Paddock Rd, PO37 6NZ **(**(0983) 862367. Open 1 Jan–Nov.

Double-fronted detached house enclosed within walled gardens, with views of Shanklin Downs. Paddock Rd is off Highland Rd which is a turning off the A3020 into Shanklin.
6 bedrs, 3 en suite, 2 ba; TV TV, dogs, ns; P 4; child facs LD 3, nr lunch. Resid lic
£ B&B £12–£15; HB weekly £95–£131; D £6; WB (£34); [5% V Sept–May]; dep.

Aqua Esplanade, PO37 6BN **(**(0983) 863024.
The Aqua is opposite the beach and just past the Pier. Open Mar–Nov.
22 bedrs, 22 en suite, 4 ba; TV; tcf P 2, coach; child facs LD 6. Resid & Rest lic
£ B&B £19–£23; B&B (double) £36–£42; HB weekly £135–£185; L £7·50, D £12·50; WB (£45 D, B&B); [10% V] cc Access, B'card/Visa.

Shanklin (Isle of Wight)

Shanklin (Isle of Wight)

La Turbie   Culver Rd, PO37 6ER ☎(0983) 862767.
Hotel. Swimming pool. Open Mar–Nov.
🛏15 bedrs, 7 en suite, 3 ba; TV; tcf 📺TV; P 6,
coach; child facs
£B&B £11·50–£13·50; HB weekly £106·50–
£126·50

Overstrand   Howard Rd, PO37 6HD ☎Isle of
Wight (0983) 862100. *Private Hotel. Putting, tennis.*

Victoria Lodge   Alexandra Rd, PO37 6AF
☎(0983) 862361.
*Detached hotel set in wooded gardens. Turn off
Shanklin High St for theatre, hotel is last on the right.*
Open Apr–Oct.
🛏23 bedrs, 14 en suite, 2 ba; TV; tcf 📺ns; P 20,
coach; child facs ✕LD 6.30, nr lunch. Resid lic
£B&B £14–£19; HB weekly £115–£154, D £2;
[5% V Apr, May–Oct, Mon–Fri] **cc** Access, B'card/
Visa; dep.

*Originally built for a Victorian gentleman, converted
in 1975 to a small hotel. From Yarmouth ferry turn
right, cross over bridge and follow A3054 for about
2 miles. Turn left after Colwell Common into The
Avenue.* Closed Dec.
🛏7 bedrs, 5 en suite, 2 ba; TV; tcf 📺P 8; no
children under 5 ✕LD 1, nr lunch. Resid lic
£B&B £15·50, B&B (double) £37; HB weekly £127–
£157·50; [10% V]; dep.

Hermitage   Cliff Rd, PO39 0EW ☎Isle of Wight
(0983) 752518.
*Attractive hotel standing in sheltered, secluded
grounds, and overlooking Totland Bay. From
Yarmouth cross bridge and follow road to Totland.
Turn right at Broadway Inn, turn left at end of road
and follow towards Alum Bay. Swimming pool.*
Open 1 Mar–Oct.
🛏11 bedrs, 5 en suite, (1 sh), 2 ba 📺TV, dogs;
P 11; child facs ✕LD 5, nr lunch, Resid & Rest lic
£B&B £21–£23; HB weekly £200–£220

SHORWELL   Isle of Wight.   Map 26D2

North Court   PO30 3JG ☎(0983) 740415. *Farm.*
Christine Harrison
Sleeps 6, 🐾 ns 🐕
£ B&B from £14–£15

The Nodes   Alum Bay Rd, PO39 0HZ (0983)
752859 Fax: (0705) 201621.
*Lovely old country house set in 2¼ acres of
grounds. From Yarmouth go to Totland village,
follow Alum Bay signs, and Alum Bay Rd is a sharp
turn on left.*
11 bedrs, 10 en suite, 1 ba; TV; tcf 📺TV, dogs, ns;
P 15, coach; child facs ✕LD 3, nr lunch. Resid &
Rest lic
£ £15·50–£18·50; HB weekly £150–£189; D £8·50;
[10% V]; dep.

ST LAWRENCE   Isle of Wight.   Map 26E1

Lisle Combe   Bank End Farm, Undercliff Drive,
Ventnor, PO38 1UW ☎(0983) 852582. *Farm.* Hugh
and Judy Noyes
Sleeps 6, 🐕
£ B&B from £12·50

TOTLAND BAY   Map 26D2

Lismore (Acclaimed)   The Avenue, PO39 0DH
☎Isle of Wight (0983) 752025.

VENTNOR   Map 26E1

Hillside (Acclaimed)   Mitchell Ave, PO38 1DR
☎Isle of Wight (0983) 852271.

Ventnor's oldest and only thatched hotel with its own beautiful gardens. Situated out of Ventnor on B3327 to Newport road behind tennis courts.
⊯11 bedrs, 11 en suite; TV; tcf 🕅 dogs, ns; P 12, coach; children over 5 ✖ LD 7.30, nr lunch. Resid lic
£ B&B £16–£18; HB weekly £154–£175
cc Access, B'card/Visa; dep.

Richmond (Acclaimed)   Esplanade, PO38 1JX ☏ Isle of Wight (0983) 852496.
Small Victorian seafront hotel. Follow signs to Ventnor Esplanade.
⊯12 bedrs, 10 en suite, 2 ba; TV; tcf 🕅 TV, dogs, ns; coach; child facs ✖ LD 5.30. Resid & Rest lic
£ B&B £14·95–£17·45; HB weekly £135–£151·50
cc Access, B'card/Visa, Diners; dep.

Channel View   Hambrough Rd, PO38 1SQ ☏ Isle of Wight (0983) 852230.
⊯14 bedrs, (2 sh), 2 ba; tcf 🕅 TV, dogs, ns; coach; child facs ✖ LD 8.30. Resid & Rest lic   cc Access, B'card/Visa; dep.

Llynfi   23 Spring Hill, PO38 1PF ☏ Isle of Wight (0983) 852202.
Close to Ventnor town centre on one of main roads to Shanklin. Open Etr–Sept.
⊯10 bedrs, 7 en suite, 2 ba; TV; tcf 🕅 TV, ns; P 7; coach; child facs ✖ LD 6.30, nr lunch. Resid lic
£ B&B £14·50–£19; HB weekly £136–£170; [10% V]
cc Access, B'card/Visa; dep.

Macrocarpa   Mitchell Ave, PO38 1DW ☏ Isle of Wight (0983) 852428.
Stone built hotel in gardens overlooking sea. From Shanklin on A3055 take first right into Ventnor, then first right again.
29 bedrs, 29 en suite, TV; tcf 🕅 TV, ns; P 30, coach;

Please tell the manager if you chose your hotel through an advertisement in the guide.

Weekend breaks
Please consult the hotel for full details of weekend breaks; prices shown are an indication only. Many hotels offer mid week breaks as well.

---

child facs ✖ LD 8, nr lunch Sat, Sun, Resid & Rest lic
£ B&B £15·50–£33·50; HB weekly £126·50–£200·10; WB (£25); [10% V]   cc Access, B'card/Visa; dep.

Picardie   Esplanade, PO38 1JX ☏ Isle of Wight (0983) 852647.
Detached seafront hotel situated at opposite end of Esplanade to the Pier. Open Mar–end Oct.
⊯10 bedrs, 10 en suite, TV; tcf 🕅 TV, dogs, ns; child facs ✖ LD 4; nr lunch. Resid lic
£ B&B £15; HB weekly £135; D £8·50   cc Access, B'card/Visa; dep.

St Maur   Castle Rd. PO38 1LG ☏ Isle of Wight (0983) 852570.

Under Rock   Shore Rd, Bonchurch, PO38 1RF ☏ Isle of Wight (0983) 852714.

ISLES OF SCILLY
ST MARY'S

Brantwood (Highly Acclaimed)   Rocky Hill, TR21 0NW ☏ Scillonia (0720) 22531 Tx: 45117 Fax: (0736) 64293.
Situated 1 mile from Hugh Town along Telegraph Rd. Open May–Sept.
⊯4 bedrs, 4 en suite; TV; tcf 🕅 no children under 10 ✖ LD 6.30, nr lunch. Rest lic
£ HB weekly £378; D £14·50; [10% V May & Sept]
cc Access, Amex, B'card/Visa; dep.

ISLEWORTH   Greater London (Middlesex).
Map 27A5

Kingswood   33 Woodlands Rd, TW7 6NR ☏ 081-560 5614.
Family-run hotel near Heathrow Airport. Follow Hounslow High St towards Isleworth into London Rd, St John's Rd and sec o dyright into Woodlands Rd.
14 bedrs, 10 en suite, 4 ba; TV; tcf 🕅 TV; P 5; child facs ✖ Breakfast only. Resid & Rest lic
£ B&B £25–£30, B&B (double) £30–£40; [10% V]; dep.

IVEGILL   Cumbria.
Map 22F5

Streethead   Carlisle, CA4 0NG ☏ (069 74) 73327. *Farm.* Mrs Jeanette Wilson
Sleeps 6, ⛺ (7)
£ B&B from £11, D £6

IVYBRIDGE   Devon.
Map 28G2

Venn Farm   Ugborough, PL21 0PE ☏ (0364) 73240. *Farm.* Pat Stephens

Sleeps 12, ꜛ ns ఈ
£ B&B from £13·50, D £7

Marridge Farm   Ugborough, PL21 0HR
☎ (054882) 469. *Farm.* Fiona Winzer
Sleeps 6, ꜛ ఈ
£ B&B from £12·50

JACOBSTOWE   Devon.   Map 28F4

Higher Cadham Farm   Okehampton, EX20 3RB
☎ (083785) 647. *Farm.* John and Jenny King
Sleeps 7, ఈ (3)
£ B&B from £10·50, D £6

KELMSCOTT   Gloucestershire.   Map 26C6

Manor Farm   Nr Lechlade, GL7 3HJ ☎ (0367)
52620. *Farm.* Anne Amor
Sleeps 6, ns ఈ
£ B&B from £13, D from £8

KENDAL   Cumbria.   Map 23A4

Martindales (Acclaimed)   9–11 Sandes Ave,
LA9 4LL ☎ (0539) 24028. *Guest House.*
⇥ 8 bedrs, 8 en suite; TV; tcf 📺 TV, ns; P6, G1; no
children ✗ nr lunch. Resid lic
£ B&B £20, B&B (double) £33; dep.

Garnett House   Burneside, LA9 5SF ☎ (0539)
724542.
*Take A591 Kendal to Windermere and follow signs
to Burneside. Garnett House overlooks tennis
courts.*
⇥ 5 bedrs, 2 ba; TV; tcf 📺 P6; child facs ✗ LD 5,
nr lunch no Fri & Sun dinner. Unlic
£ B&B (double) £22–£23; D £5·50; dep.

Gateside Farm   Windermere Rd, LA9 55E
☎ (0539) 722036.
*Situated 2 miles from Kendal on A591, 9 miles from
M6 junction 36 following Windermere signs. Closed
Xmas.*
⇥ 5 bedrs, 2 ba; TV; tcf 📺 dogs; P6; child
facs ✗ LD 4.30, nr lunch, Fri dinner
£ B&B £15, B&B (double) £31; dep.

Plough Inn   Selside, LA8 9LD ☎ Selside
(053 983) 687.
*Situated 6 miles N of Kendal on A6, 10 miles from
M6 junction 39.*
⇥ 6 bedrs, 1 ba; tcf 📺 TV, P40, coach; child
facs ✗ LD9
£ B&B £17·50, B&B (double) £25. L £5–£7, D £6–
£10.

Patton Hall Farm   LA8 7DT ☎ (0539)
721590. *Farm.* Mrs Margaret Hodgson
Sleeps 6, ꜛ ఈ
£ B&B from £10·50, D from £4–£5

Riverbank House   Garnett Bridge, LA8 9AZ
☎ (053 983) 254. *Farm.* Julia Thom
Sleeps 6, ꜛ ns ఈ
£ B&B from £10–£11, D £6

KENILWORTH   Warwickshire.   Map 26D9

Nightingales   95 Warwick Rd, CV8 1HP ☎ (0926)
53594.
⇥ 12 bedrs, 12 en suite, 2 ba; TV; tcf 📺 TV, dogs,
ns; coach; child fac ✗ LD 9.30, nr lunch. Resid &
Rest lic
£ B&B £19, B&B (double) £35.

KESWICK   Cumbria.   Map 22F5

Allerdale House (Highly Acclaimed)   1 Eskin St,
CA12 4DH ☎ (076 87) 73891.

*Traditional stone built Victorian house with modern
comforts. Situated just off the Ambleside road, 5
mins from town centre. Closed Dec.*
⇥ 6 bedrs, 6 en suite; TV; tcf 📺 dogs, NS; P2; no
children under 6 ✗ LD 7, nr lunch. Resid lic
£ B&B £17·50; HB weekly £175; dep.

Dalegarth House (Highly Acclaimed)   Portinscale,
CA12 5RQ ☎ (076 87) 72817.
*Spacious Edwardian house in a sunny elevated
position, set in its own grounds. Take A66 towards
Cockermouth, turn left to Portinscale, and Dalegarth
is on left in village.*
⇥ 6 bedrs, 6 en suite; TV; tcf 📺 TV, NS; P12; no
children under 5 ✗ LD 5.30, nr lunch. Resid & Rest
lic
£ B&B £20–£22; HB weekly £190–£210; D £13·50
cc Access, B'card/Visa; dep.

Weekend breaks
Please consult the hotel for full details of weekend
breaks; prices shown are an indication only.
Many hotels offer mid week breaks as well.

En suite rooms
En suite rooms may be bath or shower rooms.
If you have a preference, remember to state it
when booking a room.

Gales Country House (Highly Acclaimed)
Applethwaite, CA12 4PL ☎ (07687) 72413.
Putting, bowling. Open Easter–Oct.
⋈ 13 bedrs, 12 en suite, 1 ba; tcf ⌂ TV, ns; P 12;
child facs ✕ LD 6, nr lunch. Resid lic **cc** Access,
B'card/Visa; dep.

Greystones (Highly Acclaimed)   Ambleside Rd,
CA12 4DP ☎ (07687) 73108.
*Quietly situated small hotel, opposite St John's
Church, 500 yards E of town centre.* Closed Dec–
Jan.
⋈ 9 bedrs, 8 en suite (1 sh), 2 ba; TV; tcf ⌂ ns; P 6,
U 2; no children under 8 ✕ LD 2, nr lunch or Mon
dinner. Resid lic
£ B&B £17·50, B&B (double) £29–£34; HB weekly
£231–£333.

Ravensworth (Highly Acclaimed)   29 Station
Street, CA12 5HH ☎ (076 87) 72476.

*Grand terraced residence built over 100 years ago
of traditional Lakeland slate. Close to town centre.*
⋈ 8 bedrs, 7 en suite; tcf ⌂ TV; P 5, coach; child
facs ✕ LD 7, nr lunch. Resid lic
£ B&B (double) £30–£36; HB weekly £154–£175;
D £7·50 **cc** Access, B'card/Visa, dep.

Shemara (Highly Acclaimed)   27 Bank St, CA12
5JZ ☎ (076 87) 73936.
*Family-run, refurbished guest house in the heart of
Keswick. On the A591 opposite car park.* Closed
Dec & Jan.
⋈ 7 bedrs, 7 en suite; TV; tcf ⌂ dogs, ns; P 7; no
children under 7 ✕ Breakfast only. Unlic
£ B&B (double) £32–£39; dep.

Stonegarth (Highly Acclaimed)   2 Eskin St,
CA12 4DH ☎ (07687) 72436.
*Bright and cheerful small hotel in convenient
position.*
⋈ 9 bedrs, 7 en suite, 1 ba; TV; tcf ⌂ dogs; P 9,
coach; no children under 3, child facs ✕ LD 6, nr
lunch. Resid & Rest lic
£ B&B £14·60, B&B (double) £34·50–£35·30; HB
weekly £165–£167·80; dep.

Swiss Court (Highly Acclaimed)   25 Bank St,
CA12 5JZ ☎ (07687) 72637.

Thornleigh (Highly Acclaimed)   23 Bank St,
CA12 5JZ ☎ (07687) 72863.
*On A591 in centre of Keswick, opposite Bell Close
car park.*

⋈ 6 bedrs, 6 en suite; TV; tcf ⌂ dogs, ns; P 3; no
children under 14 ✕ LD 4.30, nr lunch & Mon
dinner. Unlic
£ B&B (double) £34–£39; HB weekly £165–£185
cc Access, B'card/Visa; dep.

Acorn House (Acclaimed)   Ambleside Rd, CA12
4DL ☎ (07687) 72553.
*Large Georgian house standing in its own grounds
in a quiet situation. Set on the corner of Ambleside
Rd and Acorn St, just past church.* Closed Dec &
Jan.
⋈ 10 bedrs, 9 en suite, 1 ba; TV; tcf ⌂ ns; P 10, no
children under 8 ✕ Breakfast only. Resid lic
£ B&B (double) £30–£40 **cc** Access, B'card/Visa;
dep.

Charnwood (Acclaimed)   6 Eskin St, CA12 4DH
☎ (07687) 74111.
*Grade II listed, ornate Victorian house built of
Lakeland slate. Eskin St runs between Penrith Rd
and Ambleside Rd.*
⋈ 6 bedrs, 4 en suite, (1 sh), 2 ba; TV; tcf ⌂ ns; no
children under 5 ✕ LD 4, nr lunch. Resid & Rest
lic
£ B&B (double) £24–£32; HB weekly £124–£152;
D £6·50; dep.

Fell House (Acclaimed)   28 Stanger St, CA12 5JU
☎ (07687) 72669.
*Family-run guest house in small but spacious
Victorian house in central position.*
⋈ 6 bedrs, 2 en suite, 1 ba; TV; tcf ⌂ TV; P 4; child
facs ✕ LD 10am, nr lunch. Unlic
£ B&B £11·50–£14·50, B&B (double) £22–£32·50;
HB weekly £110–£138; dep.

Heights (Acclaimed)   Rakefoot La, Castlerigg,
CA12 4TE ☎ (07687) 72251.
*Attractive Victorian house in its own walled gardens
with spectacular lakeland views. Follow A591 out of
Keswick towards Grasmere for 1¼ miles, turn right
up signed lane.*
⋈ 13 bedrs, 8 en suite, 1 ba ⌂ TV, dogs; child facs
✕ LD am, nr lunch
£ B&B £19; HB weekly £185; D £9; [10%V]
cc Access, B'card/Visa; dep.

Silverdale   Blencathra St, CA12 4HT ☎ (07687)
72294.
*Detached Victorian building. Follow steep hill down
into Keswick, pass under old railway bridge and
take third turn on left.*
⋈ 12 bedrs, 7 en suite, 2 ba; tcf ⌂ TV, ns; P 5,
coach; no children under 5 ✕ LD 5, nr lunch. Resid
lic
£ B&B £13–£14·50; HB weekly £128–£155; D £7;
WB (£26); [5% V]; dep.

Greta View   2 Greta St, CA12 4HS ☎(07687) 73102.
Small central hotel overlooking River Greta. Situated on corner of A591 opposite river and park.
⇥6 bedrs, 3 en suite, 1 ba; TV; tcf ᴔTV, dogs; coach; child facs ✗LD 6.30, nr lunch. Resid lic
£ B&B £20, B&B (double) £35–£47; HB weekly £155·50–£193·50; D £7·50 **cc** Access, Amex, B'card/Visa; Diners; [5% V Oct–Jul]; dep.

Greystoke House   Leonard St, CA12 4EL ☎(076 87) 72603.
⇥6 bedrs, 2 en suite, (1 sh), 2 ba; TV; tcf ᴔTV, dogs, ns; P 4; no children under 5 ✗LD 4.30, nr lunch. Resid & Rest lic
£ B&B £15·50; D £6; dep.

Hazelgrove   4 Ratcliffe Pl, CA12 4DZ ☎(07687) 73391.
Attractive slate-built guest house. Turn left at St John's Church, then second right. Open Mar–Oct.
⇥4 bedrs, 2 en suite, (1 sh), 1 ba; TV; tcf ᴔTV, dogs, ns ✗LD 6.30, nr lunch. Unlic
£B&B (double) £22–£27; HB weekly £110–£136·50; D £6; dep.

Holmwood House   The Heads, CA12 5ER ☎(076 87) 73301.

Leonard's Field   3 Leonard St, CA12 4EJ ☎(076 87) 74170.
Small, quiet guest house. Turn left to top of Station St, turn right, first left and first right. Closed Xmas & Jan.
⇥8 bedrs, 1 en suite, (2 sh), 2 ba; TV; tcf ᴔdogs, ns; coach; no children under 5 ✗LD 4.30, nr lunch. Resid lic
£ B&B £12–£16·50; HB weekly £133–£164·50; [10% V Mar, May & Jun]; dep.

Sunnyside   25 Southey St, CA12 4EF ☎(07687) 72446.
Family-run, stone-built guest house. Turn left in Keswick at war memorial. Open Feb–Nov.
⇥8 bedrs, 3 ba; TV; tcf ᴔdogs, ns, P 8, child facs ✗Breakfast only (dinner in winter). Unlic
£B&B £11–£12; WB **cc** Access; dep.

> Please tell the manager if you chose your hotel through an advertisement in the guide.

KETTERING   Northamptonshire.   Map 24F1

Headlands   49 Headlands, NN15 7ET ☎(0536) 524624
Well-run small hotel close to town centre.
⇥13 bedrs, 6 en suite, 3 ba
£ B&B £17–£18; B&B (double) £28–£37.

KETTLEWELL   North Yorkshire.   Map 23B3

Langcliffe (Highly Acclaimed)   BD23 5RJ ☎(075676) 243.   &
Take B6160 from Skipton to Kettlewell, turn first right, then first left following police station signs. Open Feb–Dec.
⇥7 bedrs, 7 en suite; TV; tcf ᴔdogs, ns; P 7 ✗LD 7, nr lunch **cc** Access, B'card/Visa; dep.

Fold Farm   Skipton, BD23 5RJ ☎(075 676) 886.   *Farm.* Barbara Lambert
Sleeps 6, ns ⌖(10)
£ B&B from £12–£13

KEXBY   North Yorkshire.   Map 23E3

Ivy House Farm   Hull Rd, YO4 5LQ ☎York (0904) 489 368.

KEYNSHAM   Avon.   Map 29D7

Grasmere Court (Acclaimed)   22 Bath Rd, BS18 1SN ☎(0272) 862662.
Attractive detached Victorian house, situated on A4 between Bristol and Bath. Swimming pool.
⇥18 bedrs, 18 en suite; TV; tcf ᴔTV, ns; P 18; child facs ✗LD 7.30, nr lunch & Fri–Sun dinner. Resid & Rest lic
£B&B £27–£40, B&B (double) £40–£54; D £8·50; WB (£20); [5% V] **cc** Access, B'card/Visa; dep.

KIDDERMINSTER   Hereford & Worcester (Worcestershire).   Map 26B9

Cedars (Highly Acclaimed)   Mason Rd, DY11 6AL ☎(0562) 515595 Fax: (0562) 751103.
Charming Georgian property with quiet garden and fish pool. Some private patios. Follow ring road to Bridgenorth turnoff, then take first left turn at Doolittle & Dally. Closed Xmas & New Year.
⇥20 bedrs, 20 en suite; TV; tcf ᴔdogs, ns; P 23; coach; child facs ✗LD 8.30, nr lunch & Fri–Sun dinner. Resid lic

£ B&B £42·50–£47·50, B&B (double) £52–£56·50; D £11·50; WB (£70·60); [5% V] **cc** Access, Amex, B'card/Visa, Diners; dep.

KIDLINGTON   Oxfordshire.   Map 26D7

Bowood House (Highly Acclaimed)   238 Oxford Rd, OX5 1EB ✆ Oxford (0865) 842288 Fax: (0865) 841858.
Much extended and modernised 1930's house with new motel wing. On the A423 4 miles N of Oxford. Closed 24–31 Dec.
⇌22 bedrs, 20 en suite, 2 ba; TV; tcf 🛇ns; P 25; child facs ✗LD 8.30, nr Sun. Resid & Rest lic
£ B&B £32–£55, B&B (double) £60–£65; D £12·50; WB (£60 2 nights HB) **cc** Access, B'card/Visa; dep.
(*See advertisement under Oxford*)

KINGSBRIDGE   Devon.   Map 28G1

Sherford Down   Sherford, TQ7 2BA ✆ (0548) 531208. *Farm*. Mrs Heather Peters
Sleeps 6, ns ☞ (3)
£ B&B from £11

South Allington House   Chivelstone, TQ7 2NB ✆ (054851) 272. *Farm*. Barbara and Edward Baker
Sleeps 24, ns ☞
£ B&B from £13·50

KINGSDOWN   Kent.   Map 27F4

Blencathra   Kingsdown Hill, CT14 8EA ✆ (0304) 3737252.
⇌5 bedrs, 2 en suite, (2 sh), 2 ba; TV; tcf 🛇TV, ns; P 7 ✗ Breakfast only. Resid lic
£ B&B £14–£15, B&B (double) £30–£32; dep.

KINGSEY   Buckinghamshire.   Map 26E6

Foxhill Farm   Aylesbury, HP17 8LZ ✆ (0844) 291650. *Farm*. Mary-Joyce Hooper
ns ☞ (5)
£ B&B from £15–£17

KINGSLAND   Herefordshire.   Map 31C7

Bank Farm   Lugg Green, Leominster, HR6 9PY ✆ (056881) 638. *Farm*. Mrs Linda Crump
Sleeps 6, ☞ ns
£ B&B from £11, D £6

Holgate Farm   Leominster, HR6 9QS ✆ (056 881) 275. *Farm*. Mrs Jenny Davies
Sleeps 6, ns ☞ (10)
£ B&B from £12

KINGSLEY   Staffordshire.   Map 24B4

The Church Farm   Holt Lane, Stoke-on-Trent, ST10 2BA ✆ (0538) 754759. *Farm*. Mrs Jane Clowes
Sleeps 6, ns ☞
£ B&B from £11

KING'S LYNN   Norfolk.   Map 25C3

Russet House (Highly Acclaimed)   53 Goodwins Rd, Vancouver Ave, PE30 5PE ✆ (0553) 773098.

Victorian house built of warm russet bricks, nestling in lovely gardens. Closed 24 Dec–14 Jan.
⇌12 bedrs, 12 en suite; TV; tcf 🛇TV; dogs, ns; P 14, children over 3 ✗LD 7.30, nr lunch, Sun dinner
£ B&B £30–£39, B&B (double) £42–£65; D £11·50 **cc** Access, Amex, B'card/Visa, Diners.
(*See advertisement below*)

Havana (Acclaimed)   117 Gaywood Rd, PE30 2PU ✆ (0553) 772331.
Directly opposite King Edward VII High School.
⇌6 bedrs, 1 en suite, 1 ba; TV; tcf 🛇TV, ns; P 8 ✗ Breakfast only. Unlic
£ B&B £15, B&B (double) £24–£30; dep.

Beeches   2 Guannock Terr, PE30 5QT ✆ (0553) 766577. Closed Xmas & New Year.
⇌7 bedrs, 1 en suite, 2 ba; TV; tcf 🛇TV, dogs; P 2, coach; child facs ✗LD 4.30, nr lunch & Sun dinner. Resid & Rest lic

£ B&B £17–£20, B&B (double) £25–£32; L £4·50, D £6·25; dep.

Guanock   South Gates, PE30 5JG
☎(0553) 772959.
Small hotel with roof garden. From A10 or A47 follow town centre signs. Pass under South Gates, hotel immediately on right. Billiards.
⇌17 bedrs, 5 ba; TV; tcf 🛈TV, ns, G 10 (£1), coach; child facs ✗LD 5, bar meals only lunch & Fri & Sat dinner. Resid & Rest lic
£B&B £20, B&B (double) £30 **cc** Access, Amex, B'card/Visa.

Maranatha   115 Gaywood Rd, PE30 2PU
☎(0553) 774596.
Situated on B1145 opposite King Edward School.
⇌6 bedrs, 1 en suite, 2 ba; TV 🛈TV, dogs; P 6; child facs ✗LD 6, Resid lic
£ B&B £12–£15, B&B (double) £20–£25; HB weekly £112–£133; L £4, D £4; dep.

KINGSTON   Devon.   Map 28F2

Trebles Cottage (Acclaimed)   nr Kingsbridge, TQ7 4PT ☎Bigbury-on-Sea (0548) 810268.
Detached building dating back to 1801, set in large secluded grounds. From A28 Exeter road take B3210 for Ermington and Modbury. Follow signs for Kingston.
⇌5 bedrs, 5 en suite; TV; tcf 🛈dogs; P 10; no children under 12 ✗LD 4, nr lunch. Resid & Rest lic
£B&B £33–£36, B&B (double) £40–£48; HB weekly £225–£250; D £11·50; WB [5% V Oct–Mar]
cc B'card/Visa; dep.

KINGSTON UPON THAMES   Greater London (Surrey).   Map 27A5

Antoinette   26 Beaufort Rd, KT1 2TQ ☎081-546 1044. Tx: 928180 Fax: 081-547 2595
From M25, junction 9 follow A24 to Kingston. Hotel is on B3363.
⇌115 bedrs, 112 en suite, 1 ba; TV; tcf 🛈lift, dogs, ns; P80, coach; child facs ✗LD 9.15, nr lunch, Sat & Sun dinner. Resid & Rest lic
£ B&B £42, B&B (double) £48–£55; D £9

cc Access, B'card/Visa; dep.

Whitewalls   12 Lingfield Av, KT1 2TN ☎081-546 2719.
⇌7 bedrs, 3 en suite, (2 sh), 2 ba, TV; tcf 🛈TV; no children ✗Breakfast only. Unlic

KINGSWINFORD   West Midlands.   Map 24B1

♟ ♟ ♟ **Kingfisher**   Kidderminster Rd, Wall Heath, DV6 0EN ☎(0384) 273763 Fax: (0384) 277094.
A flamboyant thatched frontage identifies this popular modern inn on the A449.
⇌23 bedrs, 23 en suite; TV; tcf.

KIRKBY LONSDALE   Cumbria.   Map 23A4

Cobwebs (Highly Acclaimed)   Leck, Cowan Bridge, LA6 2HC ☎(052 42) 72141 Fax: (052 42) 72141.
Victorian house set in 4 acres of grounds, with log fires. From M6 junction 36 turn E onto A65. At Cowan Bridge turn left and Cobwebs is on the left. Open Mar–end Dec.
⇌5 bedrs, 5 en suite; TV; tcf 🛈TV, ns; P 20; no children under 12 ✗LD 7.30, nr Sun. Resid & Rest lic
£ B&B £30, B&B (double) £48; HB weekly £261; D £17·50; WB (£83 HB); [5% V exc Sat] **cc** Access, B'card/Visa; dep.

Capernwray House (Acclaimed)   Capernwray, LA6 1AE ☎(0524) 732363
Farmhouse set in area of outstanding natural beauty close to Lakes and Dales. From M6 junction 35 take B6254 to Over Kellet and quarries. Turn left at T junction into Over Kellet, at crossroads turn left, and house is 2 miles on right.
⇌3 bedrs, 3 en suite; 1 ba 🛈TV, NS; P5; no children under 5 ✗Breakfast only. Unlic
£ B&B (double) £34–£40; dep.

KIRKBY STEPHEN   Cumbria.   Map 23A5

Town Head House (Highly Acclaimed)   High St, CA17 4SH (07683) 71044 Fax: (07683) 72128.

Gracious part 18th and 19th century house offering spacious and elegant accommodation. Situated on A685 S of Kirkby Stephen town centre. Putting. Closed Xmas Day.
⋈6 bedrs, 6 en suite; TV; tcf 🏠dogs, ns; P10; no children under 12 ✗LD 7, nr lunch, Sun dinner. Resid & Rest lic
£ B&B £31–£39, B&B (double) £50–£58; HB weekly £275–£360; D £16·50; WB (£70 2 nights HB); [10%V] **cc** Access, B'card/Visa; dep.

The Thrang (Acclaimed)   Mallerstang, CA17 4JX
📞(07683) 71889.
Turreted Victorian rectory set among the high fells in peaceful, beautiful valley. From Kirkby Stephen take B6259 S for 6 miles through Nateby and hotel is 1 mile past Outhgill. Closed Xmas & New Year.
⋈7 bedrs, 4 en suite, 1 ba 🏠TV, dogs, ns; P7, coach; child facs ✗LD 7. Resid & Rest lic

£ B&B £19–£20; D £14; [10% V w/d] **cc** Access, B'card/Visa.

Winton Manor   CA17 4HL 📞(076 83) 71255. *Farm.* Mrs Jill Williamson
Sleeps 6, 🐴 🐄
£ B&B from £12·50, D £6

KIRKLINTON   Cumbria.   Map 22F6

Willow Hill Farm   Carlisle, CA6 6DD 📞(0228) 75201. *Farm.* Ida Tailford
Sleeps 6, 🐴 🐄
£ B&B from £11, D £6

KNARESBOROUGH   North Yorkshire.   Map 23D3

🏆 🏆 🏆 **Yorkshire Lass**   High Budge, Harrogate Rd, HG5 8DA 📞(0423) 862962.
Country inn with verandah in superb situation on River Nidd overlooking Nidd Valley.
⋈6 bedrs, 6 en suite; TV; tcf 🏠P32, coach ✗LD 10
£ B&B £30–£36, B&B (double) £40–£45; HB weekly £210–230, L £5, D £10; WB £32 (HB); [10% V]
cc Access, Amex, B'card/Visa

Newton House (Highly Acclaimed)   5–7 York Pl, HG5 0AD 📞Harrogate (0423) 863539 Fax (0423) 869614.

Grade II listed Georgian building of historic interest made of stone from Knaresborough Castle. 3 miles from A1 on A59, at last set of traffic lights before town.
🛏12 bedrs, 12 en suite; TV; tcf 🐾TV, dogs, ns; P10, coach; child facs ✕dinner by arrangement. Resid lic
£B&B £30–£35, B&B (double) £45–£60; WB (£50); [5% V w/d] **cc** Access, Amex, B'card/Visa.

Villa (Highly Acclaimed)   47 Kirkgate, HG5 8BZ
☎(0423) 865370
Recently refurbished small hotel with superb views over the River Nidd.
£ B&B £16·50–£27·50, B&B (double) £34–£38.

Ebor Mount   18 York Pl, HG5 0AA ☎Harrogate (0423) 863315.
Situated on A59, 4 miles from A1. Closed Xmas & New Year.
🛏8 bedrs, 7 en suite, (1 sh), 1 ba; TV; tcf 🐾dogs, ns; P8; no children under 5 ✕Breakfast only. Unlic
£ B&B £16·50–£35, B&B (double) £33–£45
cc Access, B'card/Visa; dep.

KNUTSFORD   Cheshire.   Map 30H3

Longview (Highly Acclaimed)   51–55 Manchester Rd, WA16 0LX ☎(0565) 2119. Fax: (0565) 52402.

Late Victorian property refurbished in period style with many antiques. From M6 junction 19 take A556 towards Northwich and Chester. Turn left at traffic lights, turn left at island in 1 ½miles, left again and 200 yard right. Situated on A50 overlooking Knutsford Heath. Closed Xmas & New Year.
🛏23 bedrs, 23 en suite; TV; tcf 🐾dogs; P35; child facs ✕LD8.45, lunch, dinner Sun by arrangement. Resid & Rest lic
£B&B £29–£42, B&B (double) £45–£50; L £8·50, D£11·75; WB (£65); dep.

LADOCK   Cornwall.   Map 28C2

Arrallas   Truro, TR2 4NP ☎(0872) 510379. *Farm.*
Mrs Barbara Holt
Sleeps 6
£ B&B from £12, D from £7

LANCING   West Sussex.   Map 27A2

🅿 🅿 **Sussex Pad**   Old Shoreham Rd, BN1 5RH
☎(0273) 454647.
Modernised period inn on the A27, opposite Shoreham airport, just below Lancing College.
🛏6 bedrs, 6 en suite; TV; tcf. 🐾dogs; P60; coach; child facs ✕LD 10
£ £39, B&B (double) £52; L £11·50, D £11·50; WB £60 **cc** Access, Amex, B'card/Visa.

LANDBEACH   Cambridgeshire.   Map 27B9

Manor Farm   CB4 3ED ☎(0223) 860165. *Farm.*
Vicki Hatley
Sleeps 6, 🐃 (3)
£ B&B from £14–£18

LANGFORD BUDVILLE Somerset.
Map 29B5

Orchard Haven Wellington, TA21 0QZ ☎ (0823) 672116. *Farm.* Mrs Jenny Perry-Jones
Sleeps 5, ns 🐾 (5)
£ B&B from £13

LANGPORT Somerset. Map 29C5

Hillards Farm (Highly Acclaimed) High St, Curry Rivel, TA10 0EY ☎ (0458) 251737.
Grade II listed building of great charm and character.
🛏5 bedrs, 3 en suite, 1 ba 📺TV, ns; P 15, G 2; no children ✕ Breakfast only. Unlic

LANGWITH Nottinghamshire. Map 24D4

Blue Barn Farm Mansfield, NG20 9JD ☎ (0623) 742248. *Farm.* June Ibbotson
Sleeps 6 + cot, 🐴 🐾
£ B&B from £12

LANHYDROCK Cornwall. Map 28D2

Treffry Farm Bodmin, PL30 5AF ☎ (0208) 74405. *Farm.* Pat Smith
Sleeps 6, ns 🐾 (6)
£ B&B from £15, D £7·50

LAUNCESTON Cornwall. Map 28E4

Hurdon Farm PL15 9LS ☎ (0566) 772955.
An 18th-century listed stone farmhouse set in picturesque surroundings. Leave A30 bypass at signs for Launceston on roundabout, take first left to Scarne Industrial Estate, take second right to Trebullet, Hurdon is first right. Open May–Oct.
🛏6 bedrs, 4 en suite, 1 ba 📺TV, ns; P 6; child facs ✕LD 4.30, nr lunch, Sun dinner. Unlic
£ B&B £12–£14·50; HB weekly £110–£127; dep.

LAVENHAM Suffolk. Map 27D8

Weaners Farm Bears Lane, Sudbury, CO10 9RX ☎ (0787) 247310. *Farm.* Tim and Hazel Rhodes
Sleeps 6, ns 🐾 (12)
£ B&B from £12·50–£17

LAXTON Nottinghamshire. Map 24E4

Manor Farm Moorhouse Road, Newark, NG22 0NU ☎ (0777) 870417. *Farm.* Mrs Pat Haigh
Sleeps 6, 🐴 ns 🐾
£ B&B from £12, D £6

LEAMINGTON SPA Warwickshire.
Map 26D9

Buckland Lodge 35 Avenue Rd, CV31 3PG ☎ (0926) 23843. *Hotel.*

Langport (Somerset)

Grade II listed building of historical and architectural interest, full of olde worlde charm, with a wealth of oak and elm panelled walls, beamed ceilings, large open fireplaces, creating intimate and homely atmosphere. Brochure on request.

Charnwood House   47 Avenue Rd, CV31 3PF
☎(0926) 831074.
Follow signs for public library, art gallery and museum. Closed Xmas.
⇥6 bedrs, 2 en suite, (1 sh), 2 ba; TV; tcf 📺TV, ns; P 3, coach; ✕LD midday, nr lunch & Fri–Sun dinner. Unlic
£ B&B £14–£28, B&B (double) £26–£38; HB weekly £120–£222; [5% V] cc Access, B'card/Visa; dep.

Milverton House   1 Milverton Terr, CV32 5BE
☎(0926) 428335. *Hotel.*
⇥11 bedrs, 7 en suite; 2 ba; TV; tcf 📺P 5; child facs ✕LD 5, nr lunch. Resid lic.

LEEDS West Yorkshire.   Map 23D2

Aragon (Acclaimed)   250 Stainbeck La, LS7 2PS
☎(0532) 759306.

Converted late Victorian mill owner's property set in an acre of tranquil gardens. From city centre follow A61 to Harrogate signs. Turn left at second roundabout 1 mile after interchange, into Stainbeck Lane. Closed Xmas & New Year.
⇥14 bedrs, 10 en suite, 2 ba; TV; tcf 📺dogs; P 24; child facs ✕LD 6, nr lunch RS Fri–Sun. Resid & Rest lic
£ B&B £23·40–£33·92, B&B (double) £35·30–£44·27; D £7·45 cc Access, Amex, B'card/Visa, Diners.

Pinewood (Acclaimed)   78 Potternewton La, LS7 3LW ☎(0532) 622561.
Large Victorian house set in pleasant gardens in a quiet residential area. On B6159, 600 yards E of junction with A61. Closed 21 Dec–6 Jan.
⇥10 bedrs, 6 en suite, (2 sh), 1 ba; TV; tcf 📺TV ✕LD 10 a.m., nr lunch, Fri–Sun dinner. Resid lic
£ B&B £25–£31, B&B (double) £38–£46; D £9
cc Access.

Broomhurst   12 Chapel La, Cardigan Rd, LS6 3BW ☎(0532) 786836.
Follow signs to city centre, Ilkley and Airport. At Headingley sign turn onto Cardigan Rd, then Chapel Lane in 600 yards.
⇥11 bedrs, 2 en suite, (1 sh), 2 ba; TV; tcf 📺TV; P 5; no children under 6 ✕LD 9am, nr lunch, nr dinner Fri–Sun. Resid lic
£ B&B £17·50–£27, B&B (double) £27–£35·50; HB weekly £150·50–£217; D £7

Clock   317 Roundhay Rd, LS8 4HT ☎(0532) 490304 or 488501.
Set on the A58 two miles from the city centre.
⇥24 bedrs, 15 en suite, 3 ba; TV; tcf 📺TV; P 24, coach; child facs ✕LD 7.30 nr Sat & Sun
£ B&B £15–£20, B&B (double) £27–£34·50; L £2·50–£4·95, D £4·95; dep.

Merevale   16 Wetherby Rd, Oakwood, LS8 2QD
☎(0532) 658933.
Situated on the Wetherby road, close to Roundhay Park and Oakwood Clock.
⇥14 bedrs, 5 en suite, 1 ba; TV; tcf 📺TV, ns; P 6, coach; child facs ✕LD midday, nr lunch, Fri–Sun dinner. Unlic
£ B&B £17–£25, B&B (double) £30–£39; [5% V]
cc Access, B'card/Visa; dep.

LEEK Staffordshire.   Map 24B4

Brook House Farm   Cheddleton, ST13 7DF
☎(0538) 360296. *Farm.* Elizabeth Winterton
Sleeps 10, 🐴 ⛵   ♿£ B&B from £12–£15, D £7

LEGSBY Lincolnshire.   Map 25A5

Bleasby House   Market Rasen, LN8 3QN ☎(0673) 842383. *Farm.* Janet Dring
Sleeps 5, 🐴 ⛵
♿£ B&B from £14–£17, D £6·50–£8·50

LEICESTER Leicestershire.   Map 24E2

💷 💷 **Red Cow**   Hinckley Rd, Leicester Forest East, LE3 3PG ☎(0533) 387878 Fax: (0533) 387878.
Attractive old thatched pub with separate modern bedroom block. On A47 on west side of Leicester Forest East.
⇥31 bedrs, 31 en suite; TV; tcf 📺dogs; P 120, coach; child facs ✕LD 10.30
£ B&B £38 (w/e £19), B&B (double) £46; L £9, D £9 cc Access, Amex, B'card/Visa, Diners.

Burlington   Elmfield Av, LE2 1RB ☎(0533) 705112. Fax: (0533) 550548.
⇥18 bedrs, 11 en suite, (4 sh), 1 ba; TV; tcf 📺P 23, coach ✕LD 7.30, nr lunch & Sat & Sun dinner. Resid lic cc Access, B'card/Visa.

Daval   292 London Rd, Stoneygate, LE2 2AG
☎(0533) 708234.
Set on the A6 Leicester/Market Harborough Rd, about 1 ½ miles from the city centre. 🍴 Es
⇥14 bedrs, 1 en suite, (8 sh), 2 ba; TV 📺TV, dogs; P 16, coach ✕LD 7, nr lunch, Fri–Sun dinner. Resid lic
£ B&B £18·50, B&B (double) £30; D £7·50 [10% V w/e].

Old Tudor Rectory   Main St, Glenfield, LE3 8DG
☎(0533) 320220 Fax: (0533) 876002. Closed 1 wk
Xmas.
⇔18 bedrs, 16 en suite, (2 sh); TV; tcf ♠dogs; P35,
coach; child facs ✕LD 9.30, nr dinner Sun. Rest
lic
£ B&B £28·75–£33·35, B&B (double) £46–£51·75;
HB weekly £251–£281·36; L £8·75, D £8·75; [5% V]
cc Access, B'card/Visa.

Scotia   10 Westcotes Dr, LE3 0QR ☎(0533)
549200.
Large Victorian building quietly situated just off A46,
1 mile from city centre.
⇔16 bedrs, 5 ba; TV; tcf ♠dogs; P 5; child facs
✕LD 5.15, nr lunch, Fri–Sun dinner. Resid & Rest
lic
£B&B £20–£21, B&B (double) £34–£35; dep.

Stoneycroft   5–7 Elmfield Ave, LE2 1RB ☎(0533)
707605 Fax: (0533) 543788.
Large private hotel, 3 mins from the city centre.
Situated off the main London Rd.
⇔46 bedrs, 5 en suite, (14 sh), 8 ba; TV; tcf ♠TV;
P20, coach ✕LD 9.30, nr lunch & Sun dinner,
Resid & Rest lic
£B&B £22–£33, B&B (double) £28–£39; D £8·75;
WB (£20); [10% V] **cc** Access, B'card/Visa.

LEIGH SINTON   Worcestershire.   Map 26B8

Chirkenhill   Malvern, WR13 5DL ☎(0886)
32205. *Farm.* Mrs Sarah Wenden
Sleeps 6, ♠ns ⦵
£ B&B from £13

LELANT   Cornwall   Map 23B2

⚑ ⚑ **Badger Inn**   Fore St, TR26 3JT ☎(0736) 75
2181
Two-storey inn on corner of main street in village
centre. Attractive garden behind.
⇔6 bedrs, 4 en suite, 1 ba; TV; tcf
£ B&B £30, B&B (double) £39 **cc** Access, B'card/
Visa

LENHAM   Kent.   Map 27D4

Harrow Inn (Acclaimed)   Warren St, ME17 2ED
☎Maidstone (0622) 858727.
⇔7 bedrs, 4 en suite, 1 ba; TV; tcf ♠P 50; child facs
✕LD 10
cc Access, B'card/Visa.

LEOMINSTER   Hereford & Worcester
(Herefordshire).   Map 31H4

Withenfield (Highly Acclaimed)   South St,
HR6 8JN ☎(0568) 2011.

Part Georgian building, converted from cottages,
with fine Victorian conservatory. Situated on B436,
¼ mile past 30 mph sign into town from the S.
⇔4 bedrs, 4 en suite; TV; tcf ♠TV, ns; P 5; child
facs ✕LD 9.30 Resid lic
£B&B £39–£45, B&B (double) £56–£62; HB weekly
£263–£282; D £13·75; WB (£65–£75); [10% V]
cc Access, B'card/Visa.

Marsh   Eyton, HR6 0AG ☎(0568) 3952.

Wharton Bank Farm   Wharton Bank, HR6 0NX
☎(0568) 2575. *Swimming pool.*

LESBURY   Northumberland.   Map 21F2

Townfoot   Alnwick, NE66 3AZ ☎(0665)
830755. *Farm.* Deborah Philipson
Sleeps 6, ♠ ⦵
£ B&B from £15, D £7·50

LEWDOWN   Devon.   Map 28F4

Stowford House (Acclaimed)   Stowford,
EX20 4BZ ☎(056 683) 415.
A 250-year-old Georgian rectory with a beautiful
staircase, set in tranquil gardens. From A30 turn
right ¼ mile past Shell petrol station in Lewdown.
Hotel ¼ mile down the lane. Open Mar–Dec.
⇔6 bedrs, 4 en suite, 1 ba; TV; tcf ♠TV; P 8;
children by prior arrangement only ✕LD 9, nr
lunch. Resid & Rest lic
£B&B £17–£24·50, B&B (double) £34–£46; HB
weekly £160–£212·50; D £14; dep.

LEYSTERS   Herefordshire.   Map 31C8

The Hills Farm   Leominster, HR6 9HP ☎(056 887)
205. *Farm.* Jane Conolly
Sleeps 4, ♠ ⦵
£ B&B from £15–£19, D £9·50

LICHFIELD   Staffordshire.   Map 24C2

Oakleigh House (Highly Acclaimed)   25 St Clad's
Rd, WS13 7LZ ☎(0543) 262688.

Coppers End   Walsall Rd, Muckley Corner, WS14
0BG ☎Brownhills (0543) 372910.
Detached character house, formerly a police station,
in its own grounds in a rural setting. Situated on
A461 100 yards from Muckley Corner roundabout
with A5.

6 bedrs, 1 ba; TV; tcf TV, dogs, ns; P8, G2 (50p); child facs nr lunch & Fri–Sun dinner. Resid lic
£B&B £18·40–£21·85, B&B (double) £32·20–£37·95, D £8.63; dep.

LIFTON Devon. Map 28E4

Thatched Cottage (Acclaimed)   Sprytown, PL16 0AY (0566) 84224.

A 16th-century thatched cottage with a tastefully converted coach house, set in 2¼ acres. Situated 40 metres off the A30.
4 bedrs, 4 en suite; TV; tcf TV, ns; P16; no children under 12 LD 9.30. Resid & Rest lic
£ B&B £27·50; L £8·50, D £15·50; [5% V Jan–Mar]
cc Access, Amex, B'card/Visa; dep.

LINCOLN Lincolnshire. Map 24F5

D'Isney Place (Highly Acclaimed)   Eastgate, LN2 4AA (0522) 538881 Fax: (0522) 511321.
A Georgian and Victorian building with an acre of garden. Situated 100 yards E of cathedral.
18 bedrs, 18 en suite; TV; tcf TV, dogs, ns; P7, child facs Breakfast only. Unlic
£B&B £38–£46, B&B (double) £59–£68; WB (£23·50) cc Access, Amex, B'card/Visa, Diners; dep.

Minster Lodge (Highly Acclaimed)   3 Church La, LN2 1QJ (0522) 51322 Fax: (0522) 5132200.

A15 from Lincoln centre, 5 mins walk to cathedral and castle.
5 bedrs, 5 en suite; TV; tcf TV; P5; child facs Breakfast only. Resid lic
£B&B £42, B&B (double) £48 cc Access, B'card/Visa.

Brierley House (Acclaimed)   54 South Park, LN5 8ER (0522) 526945.

Victorian 3-storeyed house situated on the southern edge of Lincoln, immediately adjacent to South Common and municipal golf course. Closed 24 Dec–14 Jan.
11 bedrs, 6 en suite, 2 ba; TV TV; child facs LD 9am, nr lunch, Sun dinner. Resid lic
£ B&B £16–£18, B&B (double) £28–£32, HB weekly £137–£151; D £6·50; WB (£44); dep.

Carline (Acclaimed)   3 Carline Rd, LN1 1HN (0522) 530422.
Situated a short drive from the cathedral area. Closed 22 Dec–6 Jan.
12 bedrs, 8 en suite, (2 sh), 1 ba; TV; tcf dogs, ns; P8, no children under 5 Breakfast only. Unlic

Hollies   65 Carholme Rd, LN1 1RT (0522) 22419.

LISKEARD Cornwall. Map 28E3

Old Rectory Country House   St Keyne, PL14 4RL (0579) 42617.
8 bedrs, 7 en suite, 2 ba; TV; tcf dogs, ns; P40, coach; child facs LD 7.30 nr lunch. Resid lic
cc Access, B'card/Visa; dep.

Trewint Farm   Menheriot, PL14 3RE (0579) 47155 or 62237.
Farmhouse dating back to 1700, in peaceful surroundings. From Plymouth take A38 towards Liskeard, turn right to Menheriot by Hayloft Restaurant. Turn right by White Hart pub and Trewint is first farm on left.
3 bedrs, 3 en suite; tcf TV, ns; P5; child facs nr lunch. Unlic
£ B&B £11–£13; HB weekly £105–£112; D £7; dep.

Caduscott   East Taphouse, PL14 4NG (0579) 20262. Farm. Lindsay Pendray
Sleeps 6, ns
£ B&B from £11–£14, D £6

LITTLEHAMPTON West Sussex. Map 26F2

Colbern (Acclaimed)   South Terr, BN17 5LQ (0903) 714270.
An Edwardian terraced house overlooking the sea. Follow signs to seafront, turn right towards the river,

---

Using RAC discount vouchers
Please tell the hotel when booking if you plan to use an RAC discount voucher (see end of guide) in part payment of your bill. Only one voucher will be accepted per party per stay. Discount vouchers will only be accepted in payment for accommodation, not for food.

and hotel is opposite West Green car park. Solarium.

⇔9 bedrs, 9 en suite, 1 ba; TV; tcf ⋔TV; coach; child facs ✗LD 12 noon, nr lunch. Resid & Rest lic
£ B&B £20–£25, B&B (double) £40–£50; HB weekly £180–£211; [5% V] cc Access, Amex, B'card/Visa, Diners; dep.

Regency 85 South Terr, BN17 5LJ ☎(0903) 717707.
On seafront opposite the boating lake, near the river estuary.
⇔8 bedrs, (8 sh), 1 ba; TV; tcf ⋔TV; dogs ✗Resid lic
£B&B £18–£20, B&B (double) £32–£36
cc Access, B'card/Visa; dep.

Sharoleen 85 Bayford Rd, BN17 5HW ☎(0903) 713464.
⇔7 bedrs, 2 en suite, 2 ba; TV; tcf ⋔TV; ns; P 2, coach; child facs ✗LD 4, nr lunch. Unlic

LITTLE MARLOW Buckinghamshire.
Map 26F6

Monkton Farm SL7 3RF ☎(0494) 21082. Farm. Jane and Warren Kimber
Sleeps 6, ns ☎ (5)
£ B&B from £16

LITTLE SMEATON North Yorkshire.
Map 23D4

East Farm Northallerton, DL6 2HD ☎(060 981) 291. Farm. Rosemary Metcalf
Sleeps 5, ns ☎ (8)
£ B&B from £11·50–£13·50

LITTLE TORRINGTON Devon. Map 28F5

Smytham Manor EX38 8PU ☎Torrington (0805) 22110. Swimming pool, putting. Open 1 Mar–Oct.
⇔6 bedrs, 4 en suite, 1 ba; tcf ⋔TV; dogs; P 14; child facs ✗LD 9, nr lunch. Resid & Rest lic
£ B&B £11–£17; HB weekly £120–£160; D fr £6·50; [10% V] cc Access, B'card/Visa; dep.

LITTLE WENLOCK Shropshire. Map 24A2

Lower Huntington Farm Telford, TF6 5AP ☎(0952) 505804. Farm. Mrs Pauline Williamson
Sleeps 6, ☎   ☎£ B&B from £15

LIVERPOOL Merseyside. Map 30G3

Aachen 91 Mount Pleasant, L3 5TB ☎051-709 3477 or 1126.
Grade II listed building in the centre of Liverpool situated between Central Station and Metropolitan Cathedral. Billiards.
⇔17 bedrs, 4 en suite, (6 sh), 3 ba; TV; tcf ⋔TV,

dogs; P 2 (£2), G 2 (£2), coach; child facs ✗LD 9, nr lunch, Sat & Sun dinner
£B&B £18–£24, B&B (double) £30–£40; HB weekly £166·25; WB (£17); [10% V] cc Access, Amex, B'card/Visa, Diners; dep.

New Manx 39 Catherine St, L8 7NE ☎051-708 6171.
Edwardian style terraced house, 3 mins walk from Anglican Cathedral.
⇔12 bedrs, (3 sh), 2 ba; TV; tcf ⋔dogs; U12, coach; child facs ✗Breakfast only. Unlic
£B&B £12·50–£15; WB (£12); [10% V] cc Access, Amex, B'card/Visa, CB, Diners.

LIZARD Cornwall. Map 28C1

Mounts Bay House Penmenner Rd, TR12 7NP ☎(0326) 290305 or 290393.
Large Victorian house in spacious grounds. Take B3083 from Helston to Lizard village. Closed Nov.
⇔7 bedrs, 2 en suite, (5 sh), 1 ba; tcf ⋔TV, dogs; P 10; child facs ✗LD 6.30, nr lunch. Resid & Rest lic
£B&B £16·50–£22·50; HB weekly £160–£204; D £9; [10% V Dec–Jun, Oct] cc Access, B'card/ Visa; dep.

Parc Brawse House Penmenner Rd, TR12 7NR ☎(0326) 290466.
In Lizard village turn right after green and car park into Penmenner Rd. Hotel at end on right. Open Mar–Nov.
⇔6 bedrs, 2 en suite, (1 sh), 2 ba; tcf ⋔TV, dogs; P 6; child facs ✗LD 5.30, nr lunch. Resid & Rest lic
£B&B £12–£19·50; B&B (double) £24–£34; HB weekly £126–£171·50; D £8; [5% V Oct–May] cc Access, B'card/Visa; dep.

Penmenner House Penmenner Rd, TR12 7NR ☎(0326) 290370.
A small hotel overlooking Lizard lighthouse. In Lizard village turn right after the green into Penmenner Rd. Hotel on right where road ends.
⇔8 bedrs, 5 en suite, 2 ba; TV; tcf ⋔TV; P 12; child facs ✗LD 7.30. Resid lic
£B&B £19–£21; HB weekly £185·50–£199·50; [5% V] cc Access, B'card/Visa; dep.

LODDISWELL S. Devon. Map 28G2

Reveton Farm Kingsbridge, TQ7 4RY ☎(0548) 550265. Farm. Jaap and Anneke Star Starrenburg
Sleeps 4, ⋔ ☎
£ B&B from £10

Tunley Farm Kingsbridge, TQ7 4ED ☎(0548) 550279. Farm. Paul and Joy Harvey
Sleeps 6, ns ☎
£ B&B from £12

Crannacombe Farm   Hazlewood, Nr Kingsbridge, TQ7 4DX ✆(0548) 550256. *Farm.* Shirley Bradley
Sleeps 6, �*/*ns ☞
£ B&B from £13–£14·50, D £7

LONDON
Map 27A5

E18
Grove Hill   38 Grove Hill, South Woodford, E18 2JG ✆081–9893344 Fax: 081–530 5286.
Tudor-style hotel close to South Woodford underground station and just off A11.
🛏21 bedrs, 14 en suite, 3 ba; TV; tcf 📺TV, dogs; P8, G4; child facs ✗Breakfast only. Resid lic
£B&B £23–£32·20, B&B (double) £40·82–£47·15
cc Access, Amex, B'card/Visa; dep.

N4
Redland   418 Seven Sisters Rd, N4 2LX ✆081–800 1826 Tx: 265218 Fax: 081–800 8824.
Conveniently situated hotel overlooking Finsbury Park and close to Manor House underground station.
🛏24 bedrs, (2 sh), 6 ba; TV; tcf 📺TV, dogs; P9, coach; child facs ✗Breakfast only. Unlic

£B&B fr £30, B&B (double) £39·50   **cc** Access, Amex, B'card/Visa, Diners; dep.

N8
Aber   89 Crouch Hill, N8 9EG ✆081–3402847.
From junction of A1 with North Circular, A406, follow signs to Highgate or Muswell Hill and Crouch End (Hornsey).
🛏9 bedrs, 2 ba 📺TV, ns; no children under 2 ✗Breakfast only. Unlic
£B&B £16–£18, B&B (double) £30–£32; dep.

N10
Raglan Hall   8–12 Queens Av, Muswell Hill, N10 3NR ✆081–883 9836 Fax: 081–883 5002.
🛏48 bedrs, 48 en suite; TV; tcf 📺dogs; P8, coach; child facs ✗LD 10.45
cc Access, Amex, B'card/Visa, Diners.

NW2
Clearview House   161 Fordwych Rd, Cricklewood, NW2 3NG ✆081–452 9773.
Hotel near Kilburn underground station. Can be reached via No 16 bus (Victoria station) or No 16A from Oxford Street.
🛏6 bedrs, 2 ba; TV 📺TV; no children under 5 ✗Breakfast only. Unlic
£B&B £12; [V] dep.

Garth 72 Hendon Way, Cricklewood, NW2 2NL 081–455 4742

NW3

Seaford Lodge (Acclaimed) 2 Fellows Rd, NW3 3LP 071–722 5032 Fax: 071–586 8735.
Family run guest house in Victorian residence close to Chalk Farm underground station.
15 bedrs, 15 en suite; TV; tcf dogs; P3, coach; child facs Unlic
£ £50–£70, B&B (double) £75–£90; D £7·50; [10% V w/e] **cc** Access, B'card/Visa, Diners; dep.

Rosslyn House 2 Rosslyn Hill, NW3 1PH 071–431 3873.
£ B&B £42·50–£52·50

NW6

Dawson House 72 Canfield Gdns, NW6 3ED 071–624 0079.
Small hotel seven minutes walk from Finchley Road underground station.
15 bedrs, 7 en suite; 4 ba TV; no children under 6 Breakfast only. Unlic
£ B&B £19–£25, B&B (double) £29–£35; [10% V] dep.

London NW11

CENTRAL HOTEL

Private
Bathrooms
and Parking

35 Hoop Lane, Golders Green,
London, NW11 8BS

Tel: 081-458 5636 *Fax:* 081-455 4792

London (East)

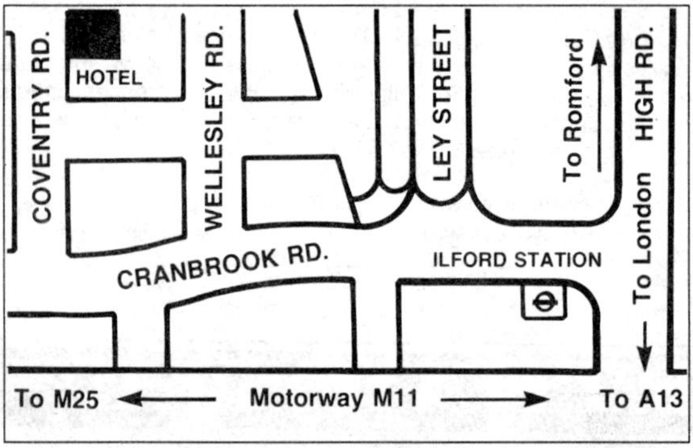
HOTEL
COVENTRY RD.
WELLESLEY RD.
LEY STREET
To Romford
HIGH RD.
CRANBROOK RD.
ILFORD STATION
To London
To M25
Motorway M11
To A13

The CRANBROOK HOTEL

24 Coventry Road, Ilford,
Essex IG1 4QR

081 554 6544
081 554 4765
081 518 2946
Fax:
081 518 1463

JACUZZI, BATH, PHONES IN MOST ROOMS.
SKY TV IN MOST ROOMS.
SOME SELF CATERING APARTMENTS.

Licensed Restaurant. 2 minutes to town centre. Underground 5 minutes. Minutes from M11 and M25. 20 minutes by train to London.

NW11

Croft Court (Highly Acclaimed)   44 Ravenscroft Av, Golders Green, NW11 8AY ☎081–458 3331. Fax: 081–455 9175. ✻ Fr, Po.
Recently refurbished hotel in own gardens. Not far from Golders Green station, between Finchley Rd & Golders Green Rd.
⇥20 bedrs, 20 en suite; TV; tcf ♟TV; P 3, coach; child facs ✖Breakfast only. Unlic
£ B&B £44–£49, B&B £59–£64; L £11·50, D £11·50; [10% V w/d] **cc** B'card/Visa; dep.

Central   35 Hoop La, Finchley Rd, Golders Green, NW11 8BS ☎081–458 5636 Fax: 081–455 4792. ✻ Fr, De.
Hotel near M1 and Golders Green underground station.
⇥36 bedrs, 18 en suite, 4 ba; TV ♟TV; P8 ✖Breakfast only. Unlic
£ B&B £35–£45, B&B £45–£65; [10% V] **cc** Access, Amex, B'card/Visa, Diners; dep.

Hazelwood House   865 Finchley Rd, Golders Green, NW11 8LX ☎081–458 8884.
⇥5 bedrs, 2 ba; TV ♟TV, dogs; P 6; children over 3 ✖Breakfast only. Unlic
£B&B £22–£26, B&B (double) £35–£40; [5% V Nov–Mar]; dep.

Regal   170 Golders Green Rd, NW11 8BB ☎081-455 7025.
⇥12 bedrs, 6 en suite, (6 sh), 1 ba; TV ♟TV, dogs; P 4 ✖Breakfast only. Unlic
cc Access, Amex, B'card/Visa.

SE3

Vanbrugh (Highly Acclaimed)   St John's Park, Blackheath, SE3 7TD ☎081–853 4051 Fax: 081 858 7387. ✻ De   ⟨&⟩
Large Victorian residence converted to a high standard in quiet residential area.
⇥30 bedrs, 30 en suite; TV; tcf ♟lift, TV; P16, coach; child facs ✖LD 9.30, nr lunch & Sun dinner. Resid lic
£ B&B £58–£65, B&B (double) £78–£110; D

£14·50; WB £31 (per day) **cc** Access, Amex, B'card/Visa; dep.

Clarendon (Acclaimed)   8–16 Montpelier Row, Blackheath, SE3 0RW ☎081–318 4321 Tx: 896367. ✻ Es.

Hotel facing Greenwich Park, four minutes from railway station, 20 minutes to central London.
⇥198 bedrs, 139 en suite, 12 ba; TV; tcf ♟lift, TV, dogs; P80, coach; child facs ✖LD 9.45
£B&B £40·15–£44, B&B (double) £65·50–£74·25; L £12, D £12 **cc** Access, Amex, B'card/Visa, Diners; dep.

Stonehall House   35–37 Westcombe Park Rd, Blackheath, SE3 7RE ☎081–858 8706.
Owner-run hotel close to Greenwich Park and Maze Hill station.
⇥27 bedrs, 11 en suite, 5 ba; TV ♟TV; coach ✖Breakfast only. Unlic
£ B&B £21, B&B (double) £32; [10% V] **cc** Access, B'card/Visa; dep.

SE9

Yardley Court (Acclaimed)   18 Court Yard, Eltham, SE9 5PZ ☎081–850 1850.
⇥9 bedrs, 5 en suite, 2 ba; TV; tcf ♟TV; P8 ✖Breakfast only. Unlic
cc Access, B'card/Visa; dep.

SE19

Crystal Palace Tower   114 Church Rd, SE19 2UB ☎081–653 0176. ✻ Fr.

London SW1

Large Victorian house retaining many original features, situated on A212.
11 bedrs, 5 en suite, (1 sh), 2 ba; TV TV, dogs; P 10, coach; child facs Breakfast only. Unlic
£B&B £18–£25, B&B (double) £30–£35; [5% V]**cc** Access, B'card/Visa; dep.

SW1

Caswell 25 Gloucester St, SW1V 2DB 071–834 6345. Fr.
Victorian terraced building just off Belgrave Road, close to Victoria Station.
18 bedrs, 7 en suite, 4 ba; tcf Breakfast only. Unlic
£ B&B £23–£34, B&B (double) £32–£63; dep.

Diplomat 2 Chesham St, Belgrave Sq, SW1X 8DT 071–235 1544. Tx: 926679 Fax: 071–259 6153.
Elegant Victorian house just off Belgrave Square.
27 bedrs, 27 en suite; TV; tcf lift, dogs; child facs

£ B&B £54·95–£64·95, B&B (double) £79·95–£95·95 **cc** Access, B'card/Visa; dep.

Easton 36–40 Belgrave Rd, SW1V 1RG 071–834 5938 Fax: 071–976 6560.
54 bedrs, 12 en suite, 12 ba; TV TV, ns; coach; child facs Breakfast only. Unlic
cc Access, Amex, B'card/Visa; dep.

Elizabeth 37 Eccleston Sq, SW1V 1PB 071–828 6812. Fr.
Hotel in square close to Victoria Station. Tennis.
37 bedrs, 19 en suite, (4 sh), 6 ba; TV TV, ns; coach; child facs Breakfast only. Unlic
£ B&B £30–£32, B&B (double) £46–£68.

Executive 57 Pont St, SW1X 0BD 071–581 2424. Tx: 9413498 Fax: 071–589 9456.
Victorian town house in street between Harrods and Sloane Square.
28 bedrs, 26 en suite; TV; tcf lift, dogs; child facs
£ B&B £54·95–£64·95, B&B (double) £79·95.

London SW3

Hamilton House 60 Warwick Way, SW1V 1SA
📞071–821 7113. Tx: 262433.
🛏40 bedrs, 25 en suite; 6 ba; TV 🏠ns; child facs
✕LD 9, nr lunch. Resid & Rest lic
£ B&B £35–£50, B&B (double) £48–£60; D £12;
[10% w/e] **cc** Access, B'card/Visa

Willett 32 Sloane Gdns, Sloane Sq, SW1W 8DJ
📞071–824 8415 Tx: 926678 Fax: 071–824 8415.
Restored Victorian town house in quiet tree-lined
street close to Sloane Square.
🛏18 bedrs, 14 en suite, 3 ba; TV; tcf 🏠dogs; child
facs ✕Breakfast only. Unlic
£B&B £54·95–£59·95, B&B (double) £59·95–
£69·95; dep.

Winchester 17 Belgrave Rd, SW1 1RB 📞071–828
2972.
🛏18 bedrs, 18 en suite; TV ✕Breakfast only. Unlic
cc Access,Amex, B'card/Visa, CB, Diners; dep.

SW3
Claverley (Acclaimed) 13 Beaufort Gdns,
SW3 1PS 📞071–589 8541.

Blair House 34 Draycott Pl. SW3 2SA 📞071–
581 2323 Fax: 071–823 7752. 🍴Es, lt.

Chelsea hotel convenient for Kings Road and
Sloane Square.
🛏18 bedrs, 9 en suite, (1 sh), 3 ba; TV; tcf 🏠dogs,
ns; coach; child facs ✕Breakfast only. Unlic
£ B&B £35–£52, B&B (double) £50–£65
cc Access, Amex, B'card/Visa, Diners; dep.

Knightsbridge 10 Beaufort Gdns, SW3 1PT
📞071–589 9271 Fax: 071–823 9692.
🛏20 bedrs, 9 en suite, (4 sh), 3 ba; TV; tcf 🏠TV;
child facs ✕LD 10.30, nr lunch. Resid lic
cc Access, Amex, B'card/Visa; dep.

SW5
Merlyn Court 2 Barkston Gdns, SW5 0EN 📞071–
370 1640.
Just off Cromwell and Earls Court Roads.
🛏17 bedrs, 12 ba 🏠dogs, ns ✕Breakfast only.
Unlic
£ B&B £20–£25, B&B (double) £28–£38; [10% V
Oct–Apr] **cc** B'card/Visa; dep.

SW7
Alexander (Highly Acclaimed) 9 Summer Place,
SW7 3EE 📞071-581 1591
Number Eight 8 Emperors Gate, SW7 4HH
📞071–370 7516 Tx: 925975 Fax: 071–373 3163.
Small private hotel in elegant South Kensington.
From Cromwell Road (A4) opposite Gloucester
Road underground station (Airport bus stop
nearby), turn up Grenville Place to Emperor's Gate.
🛏15 bedrs, 14 en suite, (1 sh), 1 ba; TV; tcf
🏠ns; coach; child facs ✕Breakfast only. Resid lic
£B&B £57·50–£69, B&B (double) £80·50–£92;
[5% V] **cc** Access, Amex, B'card/Visa, Diners; dep.

SW15
Lodge 52 Upper Richmond Rd, Putney, SW15
2RN 📞081-874 1598 Fax: 081-874 0910. *Billiards.*
🛏63 bedrs, 50 en suite, (13 sh), 3 ba; TV; tcf
🏠dogs, ns; P 35, coach; child facs ✕LD 8.30, nr
lunch & Sun dinner
cc Access, Amex, B'card/Visa, Diners; dep

SW19
Worcester House (Acclaimed) 38 Alwyne Rd,
Wimbledon, SW19 7AE 📞081-946 1300.
Hotel in residential area. From Wimbledon station
turn right. Past traffic lights, second turning on right
is Alwyne Road.
🛏9 bedrs, 9 en suite; TV; tcf ✕Breakfast only. Unlic
£ B&B £40·50–£47·50, B&B (double) £54·50–
£58·50.

Trochee   21 Malcolm Rd, Wimbledon, SW19 4AS
☎081–946 3924 Fax: 081–785 4058.
🛏17 bedrs, 3 ba; TV; tcf 📺TV; P 3, coach; child
facs ✗Breakfast only. Unlic
£B&B £32, B&B (double) £45; [5% V Sep–Mar]
cc Access, B'card/Visa; dep.

Trochee   52 Ridgway Pl, Wimbledon, SW19 4SW
☎081–946 1579 Fax: 081–785 4058.
🛏18 bedrs, 9 en suite, 3 ba; TV; tcf 📺TV; P 6,
coach; child facs ✗Breakfast only. Unlic
£B&B £32–£40, B&B (double) £45–£55; [5% V
Sep–Mar] **cc** Access, B'card/Visa; dep.

Wimbledon   78 Worple Rd, SW19 4HZ ☎081–946
9265.
Small family-run hotel. From Wimbledon station,
Wimbledon Hill, then left into Worple Road (B235)
to hotel on left.
🛏14 bedrs, 5 en suite, (6 sh), 2 ba; TV; tcf 📺TV, ns;
P 12; child facs ✗Breakfast only. Unlic
£B&B £38–£42, B&B (double) £48–£54
cc Access, B'card/Visa; dep.

W1

Georgian House (Acclaimed)   87 Gloucester Pl,
W1H 3PG ☎071–935 2211. Tx: 266079 Fax: 071–
486 7535. ✗ De.   ♿

Edward Lear   28 Seymour St, W1H 5WD ☎071–
402 5401 Fax: 071–706 3766.
Conveniently placed hotel, once home of Edward
Lear, near Marble Arch.
🛏31 bedrs, 4 en suite, (8 sh), 6 ba; TV; tcf 📺TV, ns;
child facs ✗Breakfast only. Unlic
£B&B £37·50–£39·50, B&B (double) £49·50–£54;
[10% V w/e & Dec–Feb] **cc** Access, B'card/Visa;
dep.
Recently refurbished hotel, walking distance of
Baker Street and Oxford Street.
🛏19 bedrs, 19 en suite; TV; tcf 📺lift, ns; no
children under 5 ✗Breakfast only. Resid lic
£ B&B £45, B&B £60 (double) **cc** Access, Amex,
B'card/Visa; dep.

Hart House   51 Gloucester Pl, W1H 3PE ☎071–
935 2288.

London SE3

Stonehall House Hotel

35/37 Westcombe Park Road, Blackheath, London SE3 7RE   Tel: 081-858 8706
Old fashioned, friendly and comfortable guest house with pleasant TV lounge and gardens.
20 minutes to London

London W2

CAMELOT HOTEL

**45–47 Norfolk Square,
London W2 1RX
Tel. 071-723 9118 & 071-262 1980
Fax: 071-402 3412**

A beautifully restored
townhouse of immense charm
and character perfectly located
a stroll away from Hyde Park,
Oxford Street and all transport
networks.
Every room has colour
television, radio, tea and coffee.
Central heating throughout and
lift.

**Excellent B&B
accommodation and super
value**

Family-run hotel in Georgian terrace close to Baker Street and Oxford Street.
🛏15 bedrs, 10 en suite, 2 ba; TV 🛦TV; coach; child facs ✗Breakfast only. Unlic
£B&B £25–£30, B&B (double) £45–£55; [10%V] cc Access, Amex, B'card/Visa; dep.

Montagu House   3 Montagu Pl, W1H 1RG ☎071–935 4632.
🛏18 bedrs, 1 en suite, (2 sh), 5 ba; TV; tcf 🛦TV, ns; coach; child facs ✗Breakfast only. Unlic
cc Access, B'card/Visa; dep.

W2

Byron (Highly Acclaimed)   36–38 Queensborough Terr, W2 3SH ☎071–723 3386 Tx: 266059 Fax: 071–723 3505. ✗ Fr, De, It, Es.
Refurbished hotel in listed building close to Hyde Park. Bayswater and Queensway underground stations nearby.
🛏42 bedrs, 42 en suite; TV; tcf 🛦lift, TV, ns; coach; child facs ✗Resid lic
£ B&B £70, B&B (double) £80–£95; [V] cc Access, Amex, B'card/Visa, Diners.

Pembridge Court (Highly Acclaimed)   34 Pembridge Gdns, W2 4DX ☎071–229 9977 Tx: 298363 Fax: 071–727 4982.

Gracious 19th century house now a friendly owner-run hotel close to Notting Hill Gate station.
🛏25 bedrs, 25 en suite; TV 🛦lift, dogs, ns; P 2; child facs ✗LD 11.15, nr lunch & Sun dinner. Resid & Rest lic
£ B&B £63·25–£92, B&B (double) £88·55–£126·50; WB £39 (Nov–Mar) cc Access, Amex, B'card/Visa, Diners; dep.

Camelot (Acclaimed)   45–47 Norfolk Sq, W2 1RX ☎071–262 1980 Tx: 268312. Fax: 071–402 3412.

Restored, Grade II listed Victorian town houses in garden square close to Paddington station.

London SW19

Trochee Hotel

21 Malcolm Road, Wimbledon SW19 4AS Tel: 081-946 1579/3924

★ Bed and English Breakfast ★ All rooms centrally heated with hand basin, colour TV, tea and coffee making facility and hairdryer ★ Many rooms have en suite bathroom and fridge.
★ Close to town centre and transport facilities. ★ Parking.

London W2

Parkwood HOTEL

4 Stanhope Place, Marble Arch, London W2 2HB
Tel: 071 402 2241 Fax: 071 402 1574

'A smart town house just a few steps from Hyde Park and the shops of Oxford Street. Quite stylish and comfortable bedrooms.'
Egon Ronay Hotel Guide

'Occupies one of the best locations for a good value hotel in London.'
Frommers England on $40 a day

'This gracious small hotel is only five minutes walk from Marble Arch yet in a quiet street of elegant porticoed houses which opens on to all the splendour of Hyde Park.'
London's Best Bed & Breakfast Hotels

⊨44 bedrs, 34 en suite, (5 sh), 1 ba; TV; tcf �r lift, TV; child facs ✗ Breakfast only. Unlic
£ B&B £35·50–£52, B&B (double) £70; [10% V Dec–Mar] **cc** Access, B'card/Visa; dep.

Mitre House (Acclaimed)   178–180 Sussex Gdns, Lancaster Gate, W2 1TU ☎ 071–723 8040
Tx: 914113 Fax: 071–402 0990.
Recently refurbished, family-run hotel just north of Hyde Park.
⊨70 bedrs, 67 en suite, 3 ba; TV �r lift, TV, ns; P 20, coach; child facs ✗ Breakfast only. Resid lic
£ B&B £50–£55, B&B (double) £60–£65 **cc** Access, Amex, B'card/Visa, Diners; dep.

Westland (Acclaimed)   154 Bayswater Rd, W2 4HP ☎ 071–229 9191 Tx: 94016297.
⊨45 bedrs, 45 en suite; TV; tcf �r lift, dogs; G 9; child facs ✗ LD 10.30, nr lunch & Sun dinner. Resid & Rest lic
cc Access, Amex, B'card/Visa, Diners.

> Please tell the manager if you chose your hotel through an advertisement in the guide.

Ashley   15 Norfolk Sq, W2 1RU ☎ 071–723 3375.
Hotel in attractive 19th-century garden square, close to Paddington station. Closed 24 Dec–3 Jan.
⊨16 bedrs, 8 en suite, (2 sh), 2 ba; TV; tcf �r TV, ns; coach ✗ Breakfast only.
£ B&B £19·50–£22, B&B (double) £36·60–£46; dep.

Commodore   50–52 Lancaster Gate, Hyde Park, W2 3NA ☎ 071–402 5291 Tx: 298928.
⊨89 bedrs, 89 en suite; TV; tcf �r lift, TV; coach; child facs ✗ LD midnight
cc Access, Amex, B'card/Visa, Diners; dep.

Dylan   14 Devonshire Ter, W2 3DW ☎ 071–723 3280.
Terraced hotel overlooking Queens Gardens. From Paddington station turn right into Praed Street then fourth turning on right is Devonshire Terrace.
⊨18 bedrs, 7 en suite, (4 sh), 3 ba; tcf �r TV; child facs ✗ Breakfast only. Unlic
£ B&B £25–£27, B&B (double) £35–£38; WB
cc Amex, B'card/Visa, Diners; dep.

Garden Court   30–31 Kensington Gdns Sq, W2 4BG ☎ 071–727 8304.

London W2

Hotel with garden in quiet square five minutes walk from Queensway and Bayswater underground station.
⇥38 bedrs, 12 en suite, (1 sh), 6 ba ⌂TV, ns; ✗ Breakfast only. Club lic
£ B&B £26–£38, B&B (double) £38–£50
cc Access, B'card/Visa; dep.

Kings 60–62 Queensborough Ter, W2 3SH ☎071–229 6848 Fax: (071) 792–8868. ☞ Es
Quiet but central hotel near Queensway and Bayswater stations.
⇥29 bedrs, 25 en suite, 4 ba; TV ⌂TV
✗ Breakfast only. Unlic
£ B&B £45, B&B (double) £55; [10%V] cc Access,

Amex, B'card/Visa, Diners; dep.
Norfolk Plaza 29–33 Norfolk Sq, W2 1RX ☎071–723 0792. *Hotel.*

Parkwood 4 Stanhope Pl, W2 2HB ☎071–402 2241 Fax: 071–402 1574.
Charming four-storey, terraced house conveniently located for the West End. Near Marble Arch Underground station.
⇥18 bedrs, 12 en suite, 3 ba; TV; tcf ⌂TV, ns; child facs ✗ Breakfast only. Unlic.
£ B&B £38·50–£42, B&B (double) £52·50–£57; [10% V, Nov–Apr] cc Access, B'card/Visa; dep.

Slavia 2 Pembridge Sq, W2 4EW ☎071–727 1316
Telex: 917458.

Situated in an elegant Victorian Square, well served by trains and buses and very close to Portobello Rd Market. Nearest Underground Notting Hill Gate.
🛏31 bedrs, 31 en suite 🛗lift, TV, dogs; P 1 (£6), coach; child facs ✗Breakfast only.
£B&B £28–£42, B&B (double) £40–£57 [V], WB.
cc Access, Amex, B'card/Visa, Diners; dep.

Tregaron 17 Norfolk Sq, Hyde Park, W2 1RU ✆071–723 9966.
Hotel in attractive 19th-century garden square, close to Paddington station. Closed 24 Dec–3 Jan.
🛏17 bedrs, 7 en suite, (2 sh), 3 ba; TV; tcf 🛗TV, coach ✗Breakfast only. Unlic
£B&B £19·50–£22, B&B (double) £36·60–£46; dep.

Coburg 129 Bayswater, W2 ✆071–221–2217
Awaiting inspection.

W3

Acton Park 116 The Vale, W3 7JT ✆081–743 9417 Fax: 081–743 9417.
Hotel next to park. From Shepherds Bush Underground station turn right and catch a bus or walk down Uxbridge Road which runs on to the Vale.
🛏21 bedrs, 21 en suite; TV; tcf 🛗lift, TV, dogs; P 15, coach; child facs ✗LD 9.30
£B&B £45·43 (w/e £39·85), B&B (double) £56·95; [10% V]; L£7·50, D £10 **cc** Access, Amex, B'card/Visa, Diners; dep.

W5

Grange Lodge 50 Grange Rd, Ealing, W5 5BX ✆081–567 1049. 🍽 Fr
Hotel with own garden, situated ten minutes walk to Ealing Broadway Underground station.
🛏18 bedrs, 8 en suite, 2 ba; TV 🛗TV, dogs; P 8; child facs ✗Breakfast only. Unlic
£B&B £25–£32, B&B (double) £36–£43; [5% V w/e].

W8

Observatory House (Acclaimed) 37 Hornton St, W8 7NR ✆071–937 1577 Tx: 914972 Fax: 071–938 3585.

Observatory House was built in the 1880s by the same craftsman who built the Albert Hall. Four minutes walk from High St Kensington Underground past the Town Hall.
🛏25 bedrs, 25 en suite; TV; tcf 🛗ns; child facs ✗Breakfast only. Unlic
£B&B £57·40–£62·90, B&B (double) £80·40–£89·90 **cc** Access, Amex, B'card/Visa, Diners; dep.

Apollo 18–22 Lexham Gdns, W8 5JE 071–835 1133 Telex 264189 Fax: 071-370 4853.🍽 Fr, De, It, Es, Po
Hotel in Victorian terrace near Earls Court and Gloucester Rd stations. Take A4 from the West. Near Cromwell Road. Closed Xmas.
🛏59 bedrs, 50 en suite, 6 ba, TV 🛗lift, TV, WB
£ B&B £30–£44, B&B (double) £45–£55, WB
cc Access, Amex, B'card/Visa, Diners.

Atlas 24–30 Lexham Gdns, W8 5JE ✆071–385 1155 Telex 264189 Fax: 071-370 4853. 🍽 Fr, De, It, Es, Po.
Sister to Apollo next door, small bar and separate lounge. Near Earls Court and Gloucester Rd Underground stations. Closed Christmas.
🛏64 bedrs, 45 en suite, 8 ba, TV 🛗lift, TV
£ B&B £30–£44, B&B (double) £54–£63; [5% V]; WB
cc Access, Amex, B'card/Visa, Diners.

W9

Colonnade 2 Warrington Cres, W9 1ER ☎071–286 1052 Tx: 298930 COLADE G Fax: 071–286 1057. ✗ Fr, De, Es, It.
A luxuriously refurbished Victorian Hotel near to Paddington Station and Warwick Ave Underground station.
🛏49 bedrs, 49 en suite; TV; tcf 🎬lift, dogs, ns; P 4 (£7), G 5; child facs ✗LD 10pm
£B&B £60·50–£66, B&B (double) £82·50–£93·50; L £5, D £12·50 [5% V Mar–Oct, w/e; 10% V Oct–Mar]; cc Access, Amex, B'card/Visa, Diners; dep.

W14

Centaur 21 Avonmore Rd, W14 8RP ☎071–603 5973. ✗ De, Fr, It, Es.
Family run hotel, close to Kensington and Knightsbridge shopping centres. Nearest underground station Kensington Olympia.
🛏12 bedrs, 12 en suite, 3 ba, TV 🎬TV, P, child facs
£B&B £32, B&B (double) £48

WC1

Academy (Highly Acclaimed) 17–21 Gower St, WC1E 6HG ☎071–631 4115. Telex 24634, Fax (071) 636–3442l. ✗ Fr, De.

A recently refurbished Georgian building with a library and patio garden. Close to the British Museum. Near Goodge Street underground station.
🛏32 bedrs, 22 en suite, 5 ba, TV 🎬child facs ✗LD 12pm
£ B&B £72·95–£79·95, B&B (double) £85–£98, L £12·50, D £15·50, WB cc Access, Amex, B'Card/Visa, Diners

Crescent 49–50 Cartwright Gdns, WC1H 9EL ☎071–387 1515. ✗ It, Fr.
An early nineteenth century hotel situated on a private square in Bloomsbury. Four tennis courts.
🛏29 bedrs, 1 en suite, (3 sh), 6 ba; TV; tcf 🎬TV; child facs ✗Breakfast only. Unlic
£B&B £26–£29, B&B (double) £40–£55 cc B'card/Visa; dep.

Haddon Hall 39–40 Bedford Pl, WC1B 5JT ☎071–636 2474. *Hotel.*

LONDON AIRPORT Heathrow. Map 27A5

Shepiston Lodge 31 Shepiston Rd, Hayes, UB3 1LJ ☎081–573 0266 Fax: 081–569 2279. *Guest House.*
🛏13 bedrs, (7 sh), 2 ba; TV; tcf 🎬TV, dogs; P12 ✗Breakfast only. Unlic
£ B&B £26·50–£29·50, B&B (double) £38·50–£42·50 cc Access, Amex, B'card/Visa.

LONGDOWN Devon. Map 29A4

Goose Farm Exeter, EX6 7SB ☎(039281) 515. *Farm.* Janet Popham
Sleeps 6, 🐂
£ B&B from £10, D £16

LONG HANBOROUGH Oxfordshire. Map 26E6

The Old Farmhouse Station Hill, OX7 2JZ ☎(0993) 882097. *Farm.* Vanessa Maundrell
Sleeps 4, ns 🐂 (12)
£ B&B from £14

LONGHOPE Gloucestershire. Map 31D8

New House Farm Aston Ingham Lane, GL17 0LS ☎(0452) 830484. *Farm.* Mrs Elizabeth Beddows
Sleeps 6, 🐕🐂
£ B&B from £14, D £8

LONG ITCHINGTON Warwickshire. Map 24D1

Newfields Shakers Lane, Rugby, CV23 8QB ☎(0926) 632207. *Farm.* Rosemary Reeve
Sleeps 4, 🐕 ns 🐂
£ B&B from £15–£22

LONGSDON Staffordshire. Map 24B4

Bank End Farm Motel Leek Old Road, Stoke-on-Trent, ST9 9QJ ☎(0538) 383638. *Farm.* Joanne Robinson
Sleeps 16, 🐕🐂 ♿£ B&B from £13–£18, D £10

LONGSLEDDALE Cumbria. Map 23A4

Murthwaite Farm Kendal, LA8 9BA ☎(053 983) 634. *Farm.* Nancy Waine
Sleeps 6, ns
£ B&B from £10–£11, D from £5

LOOE Cornwall. Map 28E2

Polraen (Highly Acclaimed) Sandplace, Morval, PL13 1PJ ☎(050 36) 3956.

Take A38 towards Liskeard turn left at B3252 signed Widegates, Sandplace Looe. Follow Looe signs and hotel at junction of A387 and B3254.
⋈5 bedrs, 5 en suite, 1 ba; TV; tcf 📺dogs; P28; child facs ✕LD 7
£ £25–£27, B&B (double) £44–£48; L £6·95, D £13; [5% V except Jul & Aug] cc Access, B'card/Visa; dep.

Bodrigan Hannafore Rd, PL13 2DD ✆(05036) 2065.

Coombe Farm Widegates, PL13 1QN ✆Widegates (05034) 223.
By Widegates village on the B3253 between Looe and Hessenford. Swimming pool. Open Mar–Oct.
⋈9 bedrs, 1 en suite, 2ba; TV; tcf 📺TV, dogs, ns; P12; no children under 5 ✕LD 7.30, nr lunch. Resid & Rest lic
£B&B £14·50–£18·50; HB weekly £160–£186; D£9·50; dep.

Deganwy Station Rd, PL13 1HL ✆(05036) 2984.
⋈10 bedrs, 1 en suite, 2ba; TV; tcf 📺TV, dogs; P6; child facs ✕LD 10am, nr lunch. Resid lic

Panorama Hannafore Rd, West Looe, PL13 2DE ✆(05036) 2123.
Situated in West Looe opposite the Banjo Pier. Open Mar–Nov.
⋈11 bedrs, 6 en suite, 1 ba; TV; tcf 📺TV, dogs; P8, coach; child facs ✕LD 9.30. Resid lic
£B&B £15–£24; HB weekly £135–£189; D£7;

[5% V Apr, May, Sept, Oct] cc Access, B'card/Visa; dep.

Pixies Holt Shutta Rd, East Looe, PL13 1JD ✆(05036) 2726.
Detached chalet-style hotel. Turn into road next to The Globe pub, hotel 150 metres ahead. Closed Nov–Feb.
⋈7 bedrs, 3 en suite, 1 ba; TV; tcf 📺TV; P8; no children under 10 ✕Breakfast only. Resid lic
£B&B £11–£20 cc Access, Amex, B'card/Visa; dep.

LORTON Cumbria.   Map 22E5

Low Hall (Acclaimed)   Lorton Vale, CA13 0RE ✆(0900) 826654.
17th-century farmhouse with many oak beams and exposed stone walls, in a secluded setting. Turn off A66 onto A5086 towards Egremont, at crossroads turn left. Hotel signed 1 mile on right. Then $\frac{1}{3}$ mile up track into fields. Open Easter–end Oct.
⋈6 bedrs, 3 en suite, (3 sh), 1 ba; tcf 📺TV, dogs, NS; P10; no children under 10 ✕LD 2.30, nr lunch. Resid lic
£B&B (double) £42–£46; HB weekly £234·50–£248·50 cc Access, B'card/Visa; dep.

Hope Farm Cockermouth, CA13 9UD ✆(0900) 85226. *Farm.* Sheila Harwood   ♿
Sleeps 6, 🐾 ☂ (12)
£ B&B from £14, D £6

LOSTWITHIEL Cornwall. Map 28D3

🍷 🍷 Royal Oak Duke St, PL22 1AH
☎(0208) 872552
Sympathetically modernised 13th century inn situated in town centre.
🛏6 bedrs, 4 en suite, 1 ba; TV; tcf 🐾dogs; P 20; no children
£ B&B £26·95, B&B (double) £46·20; L £5, D £8
cc Access, Amex, B'card/Visa; dep.

LOUGHBOROUGH Leics. Map 24D3

De Montfort 88 Leicester Rd, LE11 2AQ ☎(0509) 216061.
Family-run, comfortable hotel, on the A6 Leicester side of the town centre.
🛏9 bedrs, 3 ba; TV; tcf 🐾TV; coach; child facs
✗LD 4, nr lunch, Fri–Sun dinner. Resid lic
£ B&B £17·50, B&B (double) £30; HB weekly £143; D £6; [10% V] **cc** Access, B'card/Visa.

Sunnyside 5 The Coneries, LE11 1DZ ☎(0509) 216217.
Situated adjacent to GPO 5 mins from the town centre.
🛏11 bedrs, 2 ba; TV; tcf 🐾TV; P6, G3; no children under 5. ✗LD 4, nr lunch, Sat & Sun dinner. Unlic
£ B&B £16, B&B (double) £30 **cc** Access, B'card/Visa.

LOUTH Lincolnshire. Map 25A5

Priory (Acclaimed) Eastgate, LN11 9AJ. ☎(0507) 602930.
Enchanting Gothic building in a lovely garden just five minutes walk from town centre.
🛏12 bedrs, 9 en suite, (3 sh), 1 ba; TV; tcf 🐾TV; P 25, coach; child facs ✗LD 8.30, nr lunch, Sun dinner. Resid & Rest lic **cc** Access, B'card/Visa.

LOWESTOFT Suffolk. Map 25F2

Lodge (Highly Acclaimed) London Rd, Pakefield, NR33 7AA ☎(0502) 69805. *Hotel.*

Albany (Acclaimed) 400 London Rd South, NR33 0BQ ☎(0502) 574394.
🛏7 bedrs, en suite, 3 ba; TV; tcf 🐾TV, ns; P 1, coach; child facs ✗LD 1pm. Resid & Rest lic
cc Access, B'card/Visa; dep.

Rockville House (Acclaimed) 6 Pakefield Rd, NR33 0HS ☎(0502) 581011.
Semi-detached Victorian villa, quietly situated close to the sea. Turn right off A12(N) 1 mile from water tower. Hotel immediately after No Entry signs on right in Pakefield Rd
🛏8 bedrs, 3 en suite, 2 ba; TV; tcf 🐾ns; child facs
✗LD 10 am, nr lunch. Resid lic
£ B&B £16·50–£30, B&B (double) £28·50–£39; HB weekly £153–£175; [5% V Oct–Apr w/e]
cc Access, B'card/Visa; dep.

Katherine 49 Kirkley Cliff Rd, NR33 0DF ☎(0502) 567858. *Solarium.*

Kingsleigh 44 Marine Pde, NR33 0QN ☎(0502) 572513.
Situated on the sea front about 10 mins from the station. Closed Xmas.
🛏6 bedrs, 1 ba; TV; tcf 🐾dogs, ns; P3; no children under 3 ✗Breakfast only. Unlic
£ B&B £16–£18, B&B (double) £26–£28; [5% V]

Seavilla 43 Kirkley Cliff Rd, NR33 0DF ☎(0502) 574657.
Red-brick, family-run hotel facing the sea. Cross over bridge into Lowestoft, take A12 towards Ipswich, hotel about 500 yards on right past pier.
🛏9 bedrs, 4 en suite, 2 ba; TV; tcf 🐾TV; P3; no children ✗LD 12 noon, nr lunch. Resid lic.
£ B&B £18·40, B&B (double) £28–£36·80; HB weekly £148–£159·85; D £6 **cc** Access, B'card/Visa; dep.

LOW HAWSKER North Yorkshire. Map 23F5

Hall Farm Whitby, YO22 4LE ☎(0947) 880239. *Farm.* Mary E Sedman
Sleeps 5, ns 🐖 (8)
£ B&B from £11

LOW OXNOP North Yorkshire. Map 23C4

Oxnop Hall Gunnerside, Richmond, DL11 6JJ ☎(0748) 86253. *Farm.* Annie Porter
Sleeps 6, 🐖 (5)
£ B&B from £13–£17, D £9·50

LUDLOW Shropshire. Map 31H5

Church Inn (Acclaimed) Church St, Buttercross, SY8 1AP ☎(0584) 872174.
Inn standing on ancient site in Ludlow with history dating back seven centuries. In the centre of Ludlow in front of the church.
🛏9 bedrs, 9 en suite; TV; tcf 🐾dogs; child facs ✗LD 9.30
£ B&B £25, B&B (double) £38; L £2·95–£5·95, D £2·95–£8·95 **cc** Access, B'card/Visa; dep.

Cecil Sheet Rd, SY8 1LR ☎(0584) 2442.
Two-storey modern building of attractive appearance. In residential area of town.
🛏10 bedrs, 2 en suite, 2 ba; tcf 🐾TV, dogs, ns; P 11, G 1, coach; child facs ✗LD 9 a.m. Resid & Rest lic **cc** Access, B'card/Visa; dep.

Haynall Villa Little Hereford, SY8 4BG ☎(058 472) 589. *Farm.* Mrs Rachel Edwards
Sleeps 6, 🐕 🐖
£ B&B from £12, en suite extra, D £7·50

The Barn Farm Leinthall, Starkes, SY8 2HP
☎(056 886) 388. *Farm*. Sylvia Price
Sleeps 6 + cot, ☃ ⚲
£ B&B from £13, D £8

LUTON Bedfordshire. Map 27A7

Ambassador (Acclaimed) 31 Lansdowne Rd,
LU3 1EE ☎(0582) 451656.
*Impressive Edwardian property with ornate folly
tower, set in its own grounds. Leave Luton town
centre on Bedford Rd (A6). Lansdowne Rd is
second on left after lights.*
⊨14 bedrs, 14 en suite; TV; tcf �📶TV, dogs; P 20
✗LD 8.45. Resid lic
£B&B £51·75, B&B (double) £66·70; cc B'card/
Visa.

LYDFORD Devon. Map 28F4

Dartmoor Inn (Acclaimed) EX20 4AY ☎(082 282)
221.
*Family-run inn dating back to 16th century. On main
A386 halfway between Tavistock and Okehampton.*
⊨3 bedrs, 3 en suite, 1 ba; TV; tcf �📶dogs, ns; P50,
coach; no children ✗LD 9.55
£ B&B £25, B&B (double) £40 **cc** Access, B'card/
Visa, Diners; dep.

LYDGATE Greater Manchester. Map 24B6

Higher Quick Farm Oldham, OL4 4JJ ☎(0457)
872424. *Farm*. Annis Heathcote
Sleeps 6, ☃ ns
£ B&B from £14–£16

LYME REGIS Dorset. Map 29C4

White House (Acclaimed) 47 Silver St, DT7 3HR
☎(029 74) 3420.
*Georgian house with small flower garden, and fine
views of Dorset coastline. Situated on A3070
Axminster/Lyme Regis road about 50 metres from
junction with A3052. Open Etr–Oct.*
⊨7 bedrs, 7 en suite; TV; tcf �📶dogs; P6; children
over 10 ✗Breakfast only. Resid lic
£B&B (double) £27–£34; dep.

LYMPSTONE Devon. Map 29B4

Gulliford Farm Nr Exmouth, EX8 5AQ ☎(0392)
873067. *Farm*. Mrs June Hallett
Sleeps 6, ns ☃
£ B&B from £12·50–£15

LYNDHURST Hampshire. Map 26D3

Knightwood Lodge (Acclaimed) Southampton
Rd, SO43 7BU ☎(0703) 282502 Fax: (0703)
283730.

*Turn of the century lodge overlooking open forest.
Situated on the A35 ¼ mile from centre of Lyndurst
towards Southampton. Sauna.*
⊨12 bedrs, 12 en suite, 1 ba; TV; tcf �📶ns; P12; no
children under 5 ✗LD 8, nr lunch, Sun dinner.
Resid lic.
£ B&B £26–£32, B&B (double) £38–£48; [10% V
Nov–Mar] **cc** Access, Amex, B'cardVisa, Diners;
dep.

Ormonde House (Acclaimed) Southampton Rd
SO43 7BT ☎(042 128) 2806 Fax: (042 128) 3775.
⊨13 bedrs, 13 en suite; TV; tcf �📶dogs; P 15; child
facs ✗Breakfast only. Unlic
cc Access, B'card/Visa; dep.

LYNMOUTH Devon. Map 28G6

Countisbury Lodge (Acclaimed) 6 Tors Park,
EX35 6NB ☎Lynton (0598) 52388.

Former Victorian vicarage peacefully secluded and with much charm and character. Situated off A39 directly opposite a private drive.
8 bedrs, 7 en suite, 1 ba; tcf TV, dogs, ns; P8; child facs LD 5, nr lunch. Resid & Rest lic
£ B&B £14·50–£19, B&B (double) £33–£42; HB weekly £161–£166 cc Access, B'card/Visa; dep.

East Lynn House (Acclaimed)   17 Watersmeet Rd, EX35 6EP Lynton (0598) 52540.
Situated just off A39 in the centre of Lynmouth village.
8 bedrs, 5 en suite, (3 sh); TV; tcf dogs, ns; P 4, G 8; no children under 8 LD 8.30, nr lunch. Resid & Rest lic
£ B&B (double) £38–£40; HB weekly £168–£182; D £9·50; WB; [5% V] cc Access, B'card/Visa; dep.

Heatherville (Acclaimed)   Tors Park, EX35 6NB Lynton (0598) 52327.
Detached stone house built over 100 years ago, overlooking the River Lyn. Situated on narrow lane 150 yards along Tors Rd, which is off A39. Open Etr–Oct.
8 bedrs, 4 en suite, 2 ba; TV; tcf TV, ns; P8; no children under 7 LD 5.30, nr lunch. Resid & Rest lic
£ B&B £17; HB weekly £162–£174; WB (£49 HB); dep.

LYNTON Devon.   Map 28G6

Gordon House (Highly Acclaimed)   31 Lee Rd, EX35 6BS (0598) 53203.
Gracious Victorian building with many attractive period features, sympathetically restored. On right side of road running through Lynton towards Valley of Rocks. Open Mar–Nov.
7 bedrs, 7 en suite, 1 ba; TV; tcf TV, dogs, ns; P7; child facs LD 7, nr lunch. Resid lic
£ B&B £18–£21; HB weekly £172–£193; D £9; WB (£26 HB); [10% V] dep.

Millslade (Highly Acclaimed)   Brendon, EX35 6PS Brendon (059 87) 322. Fishing, riding.

Alford House (Acclaimed)   3 Alford Terr, EX35 6AT (0598) 52359.

Grade II listed Georgian style building in a prominent position overlooking Lynton. Access off Station Rd.
7 bedrs, 7 en suite, 1 ba; TV; tcf TV, ns; no children under 9 LD 4, nr lunch. Resid lic
£ B&B £23–£25, B&B (double) £35–£42; HB weekly £145–£165; WB (£50); [5% V] cc Access, B'card/Visa; dep.

Gable Lodge (Acclaimed)   35 Lee Rd, EX35 6BS (0598) 52367.
9 bedrs, 6 en suite, 1 ba; TV; tcf dogs; P8; no children under 12 LD 5, nr lunch. Resid & Rest lic

Hazeldene (Acclaimed)   27 Lee Rd, EX35 6BP (0598) 52364.
9 bedrs, 9 en suite; TV; tcf TV, dogs, ns; P8; no children under 5 LD 5, nr lunch. Resid lic
cc Access, Amex, B'card/Visa; dep.

Ingleside (Acclaimed)   Lee Rd, EX35 6HW (0598) 52223.
Situated on private road off Lee Rd between Town Hall and Methodist Church. Open Mar–Nov.
7 bedrs, 7 en suite; TV; tcf ns; P 10; no children under 5 LD 5.30, nr lunch. Rest lic
£ B&B £21–£23, B&B (double) £38–£42; HB weekly £210–£214; [5% V] cc Access, B'card/Visa; dep.

Kingford House (Acclaimed)   Longmead, EX35 6DQ (0598) 52361.
8 bedrs, 4 en suite, 2 ba; tcf TV, dogs; P8; child facs LD 5.15, nr lunch. Resid lic

Waterloo House (Acclaimed)   Lydiate La, EX35 6AT (0598) 53391.

Longmead House   Longmead, EX35 6DQ (0598) 52523.
Situated on fringe of village on road to Valley of Rocks, overlooking Hollerday Hill. Open Mar–Oct.
9 bedrs, 4 en suite, 1 ba; TV; tcf TV, dogs, ns; P 8 LD 3, nr lunch. Resid lic
£ B&B £14, B&B (double) £29–£31; HB weekly £142–£152; dep.

Mayfair   Lynway, EX35 6AY (0598) 53227.
9 bedrs, 6 en suite, (3 sh); TV; tcf dogs, ns; P 10, coach; child facs LD 5, nr lunch. Resid lic
£ B&B £21–£23, B&B (double) £36–£46; HB weekly £162–£183; WB cc Access, B'card/Visa; dep.

St Vincent   Castle Hill, EX35 6JA ☎(0598) 52244.
◢6 bedrs, 2 en suite, 1 ba; tcf ⋔TV; P 3; child
facs ✗LD 4.30, nr lunch. Resid & Rest lic

LYTHAM ST ANNES   Lancs.   Map 22F2

Endsleigh (Acclaimed)   315 Clifton Drive South,
FY8 1HN ☎(0253) 725622.
*Situated on main Preston to Blackpool road in
centre of St Annes, 2¼ miles S of Blackpool.*
◢16 bedrs, 15 en suite, 1 ba; TV; tcf ⋔ns; P 9;
child facs ✗LD 4, nr lunch. Rest lic
£ B&B £16·75; HB weekly £125–£135.

Strathmore (Acclaimed)   305 Clifton Dr South FY8
1HN ☎(0253) 725478.
*On the main Preston to Blackpool road opposite the
GPO.*
◢10 bedrs, 8 en suite, 1 ba; TV; tcf ⋔P 10; no
children ✗LD midday, nr lunch. Resid lic
£ B&B £15·75–£17·75; HB weekly £131·25–
£138·25; dep.

MACCLESFIELD   Cheshire.   Map 24B5

Moorhayes House   27 Manchester Rd, SK10 2JJ
☎(0625) 33228.
*Attractive 1930s detached property in mature
garden situated on left of A523 going N from
Macclesfield to Stockport, ¼ mile from town centre.*
◢9 bedrs, 5 en suite, 2 ba; TV; tcf ⋔dogs,
ns; P 13 ✗Breakfast only. Unlic
£ B&B £26–£38, B&B (double) £46·50–£50; dep.

MACCLESFIELD FOREST   Cheshire.
Map 24B4

Hardingland Farm   SK11 0ND ☎(0625)
425759. *Farm.* Anne Read
Sleeps 6
£ B&B from £12·50–£17·50, D £9

MADELEY   Staffordshire.   Map 24A4

♛ Wheatsheaf Inn at Onneley   Barhill Road,
Onneley, CW3 9QF ☎(0782)751581 Fax:(0782)
751499. ✗ Fr, Es.
*18th century country inn next to golf course, six
miles west of Newcastle-under-Lyme.*
◢5 bedrs, 5 en suite: TV; tcf ⋔dogs; P 150,
coach; child facs ✗LD 9.30, bar meals only Mon–
Sat lunch
£ B&B £37–£42, B&B (double) £42–£52; D £12·95;
WB £42; [10% V] **cc** Amex, B'card/Visa.

MAIDENHEAD   Berkshire.   Map 26F5

Clifton   21 Crauford Rise, SL6 7LR ☎(0628)
23572.
On A308 near Marlow.
◢12 bedrs, 12 en suite, 3 ba; TV; tcf ⋔TV; P 10,
coach; child facs ✗ LD 8, nr lunch
£ B&B £26·45, B&B (double) £44; dep.
cc Access, B'card/Visa.

MAIDEN NEWTON   Dorset.   Map 26A2

Maiden Newton House (Highly Acclaimed)
DT2 0AA ☎(0300) 20336 Tx: 417182 ENEL G.

*Romantic Tudor house in 11 acres of garden.
Situated in village centre next to Post Office. Fishing.
Open 15 Feb–30 Dec.*
◢6 bedrs, 6 en suite; TV ⋔TV, dogs, ns; P 10;
children over 12 ✗LD 8, nr lunch. Resid & Rest
lic
£ B&B £44–£69, B&B (double) £100–£130; D £25;
WB (£66 HB); [5% V] **cc** Access, B'card/Visa;
dep.

MAIDSTONE   Kent.   Map 27C4

Carval   56 London Rd, ME16 8QL ☎(0622)
762100.
◢9 bedrs, 4 en suite, 2 ba; TV; tcf ⋔ns; P 9; no
children under 5 ✗Breakfast only. Resid lic
cc Access, Amex, B'card/Visa, Diners; dep.

Howard   22 London Rd, ME16 8QL ☎(0622)
758778.
*Situated on the A20 London Road at the start of
the one-way system.*

16 bedrs, 3 ba; TV, tcf dogs; P 15; children over 1½ ✗ Breakfast only. Resid & Rest lic
£ B&B £18, B&B (double) £32.

Kingsgate 85 London Rd, ME16 0DX ✆ (0622) 753956.
From town centre follow signs for M20 to London. London Road is past MFI.
17 bedrs, (4 sh), 2 ba; TV; tcf TV, ns; P 17, G 2; child facs ✗ LD 10am, nr lunch, Sun dinner. Resid lic
£ B&B £29–£32, B&B (double) £40–£43; HB weekly £245–£266; [10% V] **cc** Access, Amex, B'card/ Visa, Diners .

MALHAM Yorkshire. Map 23B3

Miresfield Farm Skipton, BD23 4DA ✆ (072 93) 414. *Farm.* Vera Sharp
Sleeps 30, ns
£ B&B from £17–19, D £8

MALDON Essex. Map 27D6

Swan 73 High St, CM9 7EP ✆ (0621) 853170.
Take the A12 on to the A414.
6 bedrs, (2 sh), 2 ba; TV TV; P 25, U 1 (£1·50); coach; child facs ✗ LD 9
£ B&B £24, B&B (double) £38; HB weekly £200; L £4·50; D £5·50; [5% V] **cc** Access, Amex, B'card/ Visa.

MALMESBURY Wiltshire. Map 26B6

Manor Farm Corston, SN16 0HF ✆ (0666) 822148. *Farm.* Mrs Ross Eavis
Sleeps 10,
£ B&B from £12

Stonehill Farm Charlton, SN16 9DY ✆ (0666) 823310. *Farm.* Mrs Edna Edwards

Sleeps 6,
£ B&B from £13

MALTON North Yorkshire. Map 23E3

Greenacres (Highly Acclaimed) Amotherby YO17 0TG ✆ (0653) 693623.

MALVERN Hereford & Worcester (Worcestershire). Map 26B8

Sidney House (Acclaimed) 40 Worcester Rd, WR14 4AA ✆ (0684) 574994.
Elegant grade II listed building with panoramic views of the Cotswolds. Situated alongside the main Worcester Road (A449), 150 yards from Great Malvern town centre.
8 bedrs, 4 en suite, (1 sh), 1 ba; TV; tcf TV, dogs, ns; P 9; child facs ✗ Resid & Rest lic
£ B&B £17–£35; B&B (double) £36–£46; D £15; WB; [5% V] **cc** Access, Amex, B'card/Visa; dep.

Mellbreak 177 Wells Rd, WR14 4HE ✆ (068 45) 561287.
Grade II listed building set in large garden. Situated 2 miles south of Great Malvern on A449 near junction of B4209 to Upton on Severn.
4 beds, (3 sh), 1 ba; TV; tcf TV, dogs, P 4; child facs ✗ LD 4, nr lunch
£ B&B £14; D £8·50; dep.

MANCHESTER Gtr Manchester. Map 24B6

Horizon (Acclaimed) 69 Palatine Rd, West Didsbury, M20 9LJ ✆ 061-445 4705.
18 bedrs, 11 en suite, (7 sh); TV; tcf TV; dogs, NS; P 20, coach; no children under 5 ✗ LD 4, nr lunch. Resid & Rest lic

Manchester (Greater Manchester)

Manchester

£ B&B £23, B&B (double) £35; D £7; WB £20; [5% V] **cc** Access, B'card/Visa; dep.

Ebor 402 Wilbraham Rd, Chorlton-cum-Hardy, M21 1UA 061-881 1911. Closed Xmas & New Year.
16 bedrs, 1 en suite, (3 sh), 3 ba; TV; tcf TV; P 20, coach; no children under 4 LD 5·30, nr lunch, Fri–Sat dinner. Resid lic
£ B&B £20–£26, B&B (double) £31–£36; HB weekly £164·50–£201·50; [10% V w/e]; dep.

Imperial 157 Hathersage Rd, M13 0HY 061-225 6500.
Recently refurbished hotel close to Manchester Royal Infirmary. Situated 1½ miles S of city centre.
27 bedrs, 20 en suite, 4 ba; TV; tcf TV; P 30, coach; child facs LD 8.30, nr lunch. Resid & Rest lic
£ B&B £24–£30, B&B (double) £38; D £9·50; [5% V] **cc** Access, Amex, B'card/Visa, Diners; dep.

New Central 144 Heywood St, M8 7PD 061-205 2169.
Take Cheetham Hill Rd to Northern Hospital 1½ miles from city. Heywood St first on left past hospital.
10 bedrs, (5 sh), 2 ba; TV; tcf TV, dogs; P 5, U 5 LD 8.30, nr lunch, Sat & Sun dinner. Resid & Rest lic
£ B&B £19·50, B&B (double) £32·75; D £5; [10% V w/e]; dep.

MARAZION Cornwall. Map 28B2

Chymorvah-Tolgarrick (Acclaimed) TR17 0DQ (0736) 710497.

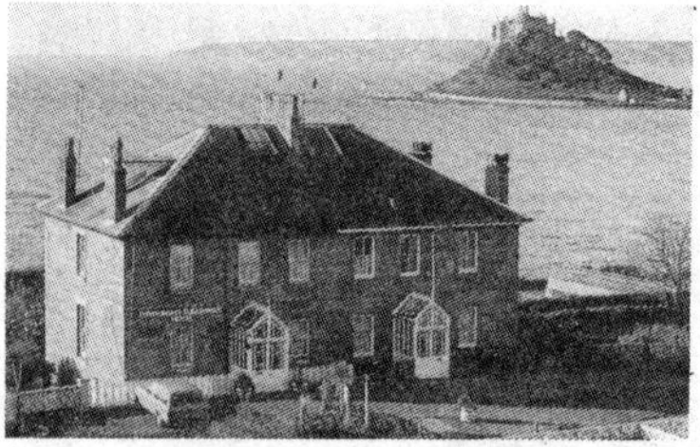

Victorian family house of local stone with access to private beach. Situated at E end of Marazion. Turn off Penzance–Helston road (A394) down private drive towards sea; signposted. Closed mid–end Dec.
9 bedrs, 9 en suite; 1 ba; TV; tcf dogs, ns; P 12, coach; child facs LD 6. Unlic
£ B&B £15–£18; B&B (double) £30–£48; HB weekly £145–£212; L £5, D £7·90; [5% V Oct–Easter] **cc** Access, Amex, B'card/Visa; dep.

MAPPLETON Derbyshire. Map 24C4

Little Park Farm Ashbourne, DE6 2BR (033529) 341. *Farm.* Joan Harrison
Sleeps 6, (3)
£ B&B from £10–£12

MARCH Cambridgeshire. Map 25B2

Olde Griffin High St, PE15 9EJ (0354) 52517.
21 bedrs, 19 en suite, 2 ba; TV; tcf TV; P 60, coach; child facs LD 9.30
cc Access, B'card/Visa.

MARGATE Kent. Map 27E5

Beachcomber 3 Royal Esplanade, Westbrook, CT9 5DL Thanet (0843) 221616.
Small hotel overlooking Westbrook Bay. Cross over bridge into Westbrook, Turn left immediately at foot of bridge, and sharp right down Westbrook Gardens into Royal Esplanade.
15 bedrs, (5 sh), 3 ba TV; ns; P 1, coach; child facs LD 4, nr lunch. Resid & Rest lic
£ B&B £15·50–£16·50; HB weekly £125–£140; D £8, dep.

Charnwood 20 Canterbury Rd, Westbrook, CT9 5BW. Thanet (0843) 224158.
Victorian terraced building close to beaches. Situated on A28, on left from Canterbury.
8 bedrs, (3 sh), 2 ba; tcf TV; coach; child facs LD 4, nr lunch. Resid lic
£ B&B £15–£18; B&B (double) £28–£34; HB weekly £110–£120; [5% V] **cc** Access, B'card/Visa; dep.

MARDEN Kent. Map 27C4

Great Cheveney Farm Great Cheveney, Tonbridge, Kent TN12 9LX (0622) 831207. *Farm.* Diana Day
Sleeps 4, ns
£ B&B from £14

Tanner House Tanner Farm, Goudhurst Road, Tonbridge, TN12 9ND (0622) 831214. *Farm.* Lesley Mannington

Sleeps 6, ns ☙
£ B&B from £16·50, D £12

MARGARET RODING   Essex.   Map 27E7

'Greys'   Ongar Road, Nr Great Dunmow, CM6
1QR ☎ (024 531) 509. *Farm.* Mrs Joyce Matthews
Sleeps 6, ns ☙ (10)
£ B&B from £12·50

MARK   Somerset.   Map 29C6

Northwick Farm   Highbridge, TA9 4PG ☎ (027
864) 228. *Farm.* Mrs Geraldine Hunt
Sleeps 6, ☙ (5) ✝
£ B&B from £14–£16, D £7·50

MARLBOROUGH   Wiltshire.   Map 26C5

Merlin   36–39 High St, SN8 1LW ☎ (0672) 52151.
Situated opposite Post Office.
▰16 bedrs, 14 en suite, 1 ba; TV; tcf ✿ dogs;
coach ✗ LD 9.30
£ B&B £30–£35, B&B (double) £40–£45; L £10,
D £15; [5% V] **cc** Access, B'card/Visa.

Bayardo Farm   Clatford Bottom, SN8 4DU
☎ (0672) 515225/515166. *Farm.* Mrs Shirley Bull
Sleeps 6, ✝ ns ☙ (8)
£ B&B from £13, D from £9

MARPLE BRIDGE   Cheshire.   Map 24B5

Shire Cottage   Ernocroft Farm, Stockport, SK6
5NT ☎ (0457) 866536 or 061-427 2377. *Farm.*
Monica Sidebottom   ♿
Sleeps 6, ☙
£ B&B from £12–£16

MARSTON   Lincolnshire.   Map 24F3

Gelston Grange   Grantham, NG32 2AQ ☎ (0400)
50281. *Farm.* Janet Sharman
Sleeps 6, ns ☙ (5)
£ B&B from £13·50, D £8

MARSTON MONTGOMERY   Derbyshire.
Map 24C3

Waldley Manor   Nr Doveridge, DE6 5LR ☎ (0889)
590287. *Farm.* Anita Whitfield
Sleeps 6, ns ☙
£ B&B from £11–£15

MARTOCK   Somerset.   Map 29D5

🐾 White Hart   East St, TA12 6JQ ☎ (0935) 82205
Stone-built coaching inn.
£ B&B £19·10, B&B (double) £33·60; L £4·25,
D £7·50 **cc** Access, B'card/Visa.

MARTON   Cheshire.   Map 24B4

Sandpit Farm   Messuage Lane, Macclesfield
SK11 9HS ☎ (0260) 224254. *Farm.* Irene Kennerley
Sleeps 6, ✝ ns ☙ (2)
£ B&B from £10

MARY TAVY   Devon.   Map 28F3

Wringworthy Farm   Tavistock, PL19 9LT
☎ (082281) 434. *Farm.* Mrs B Anning
Sleeps 6, ☙
£ B&B from £13

MASHAM   North Yorkshire.   Map 23C4

Bank Villa   Nr Ripon, HG4 4DB ☎ Ripon (0765)
89605.
*Listed stone-built Georgian house at the southern
entrance to Masham on A6108. Open Easter–Oct.*
▰7 bedrs, (4 sh), 1 ba; TV; dogs; children over 5
✗ LD midday, nr lunch. Resid & Rest lic
£ B&B £17, B&B (double) £29; HB weekly £175;
D £12; dep.

Haregill Lodge   Ellingstring, Ripon, HG4 4PW
☎ (0677) 60272. *Farm.* Mrs Rachel Greensit
Sleeps 6, ✝ ☙
£ B&B from £11–£13, D from £7

MATLOCK   Derbyshire.   Map 24D4

Parkfield (Acclaimed)   115 Lime Tree Rd, DE4
3NP ☎ (0629) 57221.

Jackson Tor   76 Jackson Rd, DE4 3JQ ☎ (0629)
582348.
*Stone built house with exposed beams. From
roundabout in Matlock, go up Bank Rd, take
second left into Smedley St. At All Saints Church
turn right up Farm Green into Jackson Rd.*
▰26 bedrs, (1 sh), 7 ba; TV ✿ P 20, coach; child
facs ✗ LD 5 (8.30 Fri & Sat), nr lunch Mon--Sat,
dinner Sun. Resid & Rest lic
£ B&B £16–£18; B&B (double) £30–£34; D £7; dep.

Packhorse   Tansley, DE4 5LF ☎ (0629) 582781.
*Take A615 Alfreton to Matlock Rd, turn right at
Tansley village.*
▰5 bedrs, 2 ba; tcf ✿ TV, ns; P 20; no children
under 3 ✗ Breakfast only. Unlic
£ B&B £15, B&B (double) £25; dep.

MAULDS MEABURN   Cumbria.   Map 23A6

Meaburn Hill Farm   Meaburn Hill, Penrith, CA10
3HN ☎ (093 15) 205. *Farm.* Ruth Tuer
Sleeps 6, ✝ ns ☙
£ B&B from £12, D £6·50

MAWGAN PORTH Cornwall.   Map 28C2

Trenance Farm House   Trenance, TR8 4BY ☎St Mawgan (0637) 860515.

White Lodge   Nr Newquay, TR8 4BN ☎St Mawgan (0637) 860512.
⇔15 bedrs, 10 en suite, 2 ba; TV; tcf 🛉dogs; P 15; coach; child facs ✗LD 7.30, nr lunch. Resid & Rest lic.

MAWNAN SMITH Cornwall.   Map 28C1

Trebah Farm   Falmouth, TR11 5JZ ☎(0326) 250295. *Farm.* Jean Kessell
Sleeps 4, ns ⇖
£ B&B from £9·50

MAXSTOKE Birmingham.   Map 24C1

Maxstoke Priory   Coleshill, B46 2QW ☎(0675) 462117. *Farm.* Mrs Penny Tyacke
Sleeps 6, 🛉 ns ⇖
£ B&B from £17–£22

MAXWORTHY Cornwall.   Map 28E4

Wheatley Farm   Launceston, PL15 8LY ☎(056681) 232. *Farm.* Valerie Griffin
Sleeps 12, ⇖
£ B&B from £12–£18, D £8

MELKSHAM Wiltshire.   Map 26B5

Regency (Acclaimed)   10 Spa Rd, SN12 7NS ☎(0225) 702971 or 705772.
Grade II listed Regency style building located in town centre 200 yards from Town Hall.
⇔11 bedrs, 6 en suite, (3 sh), 2 ba; TV; tcf 🛉dogs; coach; child facs ✗LD 8, nr lunch. Resid & Rest lic
£ B&B £18–£28, B&B (double) £28–£38; HB weekly £196–£216; D £12 **cc** Access, B'card/Visa; dep.

Frying Pan Farm   Broughton, Gifford Road, SN12 8LL ☎(0225) 702343. *Farm.* Barbara Pullen
Sleeps 5, ns ⇖ (2)
£ B&B from £12·50

MELLS Somerset.   Map 29E6

Mells Green Farm   Nr Frome, BA11 8QF ☎(0373) 812259. *Farm.* Judy Turner
Sleeps 6, 🛉 ⇖
£ B&B from £10

MELTON MOWBRAY Leics.   Map 24E3

Westbourne House   11A–15 Nottingham Rd, LE13 0NP ☎(0664) 69456.
Situated on the Nottingham Road just outside town centre. Closed Xmas & New Year.

⇔16 bedrs, 3 ba; TV 🛉TV, dogs, ns; P 16; coach; child facs ✗LD 7.30, nr lunch, Sun dinner. Resid lic.
£ B&B £16·50–£18, B&B (double) £29–£33; dep.

MENHENIOT Cornwall.   Map 28E3

Tregondale Farm   Liskeard, PL14 3RG ☎(0579) 42407. *Farm.* Stephanie Rowe
Sleeps 6, ns ⇖ (6)
£ B&B from £11, D £6·50

MEVAGISSEY Cornwall.   Map 28D2

Mevagissey House (Acclaimed)   Vicarage Hill, PL26 6SZ ☎(0726) 842427.
Georgian country house with large windows and panoramic views to harbour and sea beyond. Take B3273 past caravan park on beach, turn left at crossroads, first right then first right down long drive to Mevagissey House. Open Mar–Oct.
⇔6 bedrs, 4 en suite, 1 ba; TV; tcf 🛉P 12; no children under 7 ✗LD 5. Resid lic
£ B&B £20–£25, B&B (double) £32–£42; HB weekly £192–£213; WB **cc** Access, B'card/Visa; dep.

Sharksfin (Acclaimed)   The Quay, PL26 6TL ☎(0726) 843241.
Situated on harbour in centre of quay. Open Feb–Nov.
⇔11 bedrs, 4 en suite, (7 sh), 1 ba; TV; tcf 🛉coach; child facs ✗LD 9.50. Rest lic
£ B&B £21–£26, B&B (double) £30–£36; L £6, D £8; [10% V] **cc** Access, Amex, B'card/Visa, Diners; dep.

Headlands   Polkirt Hill, PL26 6UX ☎(0726) 843453.
Small hotel with magnificent coastal views. Follow one-way system through village and climb up towards Port Mellon. Hotel on right in ¼ mile. Open Mar–Oct.
⇔14 bedrs, 8 en suite, 2 ba; TV 🛉TV, dogs; P 11; child facs ✗LD 7, nr lunch. Rest lic
£ B&B £14–£22; HB weekly £161–£217; D £10; dep.

Ship Inn   Fore St, PL26 6TU ☎(0726) 843324. *Inn.*

Treleaven   PL26 6RZ ☎(0726) 842413.
From B3273 St Austell road turn right at foot of hill into Mevagissey. Swimming pool, putting. Open Jan–mid Dec.
⇔6 bedrs, 6 en suite; TV; tcf 🛉P 8; child facs ✗LD 7.30, nr lunch, Sun dinner
£ B&B (double) £32–£44; HB weekly £145–£220; D £7; [5% V Oct–May] **cc** Access, B'card/Visa; dep.

Valley Park   Valley Park, PL26 6RS ☎(0726) 842347.

Kerryanna Guest House   Treleaven Farm, PL26 6RZ ☎(0726) 843558. *Farm.* Linda Hennah

Sleeps 12, 🔁 (5) ns
£ B&B from £18, D £10

MIDDLESBROUGH Cleveland. Map 23D5

Grey House (Highly Acclaimed) 79 Cambridge
Rd, Linthorpe, TS5 5NL ✆ (0642) 817485.

Edwardian building on corner site with rose garden
and flower borders.
🛏8 bedrs, 8 en suite, 1 ba; TV; tcf 📺 dogs;
P 10 ✕ LD 7 nr lunch. Unlic
£ B&B £27, B&B (double) £36.

MIDDLETON-IN-TEESDALE Co Durham.
Map 23B5

Grassholme Farm Lunedale, Barnard Castle,
DL12 0PR ✆ (0833) 40494. Farm. Mrs Alison Sayer
Sleeps 6, 🔁 🐕
£ B&B from £9·75, D £4·75

Greengates Lunedale, DL12 0NV ✆ (0833)
40447. Farm. Mary Body
Sleeps 6, 🔁 🐕
£ B&B from £11, D £6

Wythes Hill Farm Lunedale, CL12 0NX ✆ (0833)
40349. Farm. Mrs J Dent
Sleeps 6, 🔁 🐕
£ B&B from £11, D £6

MIDDLETON-ON-SEA West Sussex.
Map 27A2

Ancton (Acclaimed) Ancton La, PO22 6NH
✆ (0243) 692482.

MILTON COMMON Oxfordshire. Map 26E6

Three Pigeons ✆ Milton (0844) 279247.
Attractive inn with real pub atmosphere, situated
near junction 7 of M40 on the A329 to Thame.
🛏3 bedrs, 3 en suite; TV; tcf 📺 TV, P 50; child
facs ✕ LD 10
£ B&B £28·75, B&B (double) £46; L £4·50, D £4·50;
[5% V] cc Access, Amex, B'card/Visa, Diners.

MILTON KEYNES Buckinghamshire.
Map 26F7

Linford Lodge (Highly Acclaimed) Wood Lane,
Great Linford, MK14 5AZ ✆ (0908) 605879.

Much extended seventeenth-century farmhouse.
Take A4146 north from Milton Keynes centre for
about 2 miles, then take first right turn signed Great
Linford/Giffard Gate. Cross over mini roundabout
into Wood Ln. Indoor Swimming pool.
🛏 9 bedrs, 6 en suite; 1 ba; TV; tcf 📺 TV; P 40,
coach; child facs ✕ LD 10.30, nr Sun, lunch Sat.
Rest lic
£ B&B £43·45–£52·95, B&B (double) £57–£74;
L £16, D £11·50; [5% V] cc Access, Amex, B'card/
Visa, Diners.

MILTON UNDER WYCHWOOD
Oxfordshire. Map 26C7

Hillborough (Highly Acclaimed) The Green, OX7
6JH ✆ (0993) 830501.
Mellow Cotswold-stone late Victorian house facing
the village green. Situated off A361 Burford to
Chipping Norton, and off A424 Burford to Stow on
the Wold. Closed Jan.
🛏10 bedrs, 10 en suite; TV; tcf 📺 dogs; ns; P 15;
child facs ✕ LD 9.30, nr Sun dinner. Resid & Rest
lic
cc Access, Amex, B'card/Visa, Diners; dep.

MINEHEAD Somerset. Map 29B6

Alcombe House (Highly Acclaimed) Bircham Rd,
Alcombe, TA24 6BG ✆ (0643) 705130.
🛏6 bedrs, 4 en suite, 1 ba; TV; tcf 📺 TV, dogs; P 6
✕ LD 8.15, nr lunch. Resid & Rest lic
cc Access, B'card/Visa; dep.

Dorchester (Highly Acclaimed) The Avenue TA24
5AZ ✆ (0643) 702052.

Attractive stone building in tree lined avenue.
Situated on the main road between the shops and
sea front.
🛏9 bedrs, 9 en suite; TV; tcf 📺 ns; P 9, coach; child
facs ✕ LD 9, Resid & Rest lic
£ B&B £19–£22, B&B (double) £40–£45; HB weekly
£140–£150; D £8·50; WB (£80) cc Access, B'card/
Visa; dep.

Mayfair (Highly Acclaimed) The Avenue,
TA24 5AY ✆ (0643) 702052.
Family run hotel of charm and elegance in a
delightful Victorian building. Situated on the main
avenue between the shops and sea front. Open Etr–
Nov.

🛏16 bedrs, 16 en suite; TV; tcf 🏠ns; P14, coach; child facs ✗LD6.30, Resid lic
£B&B £19–£22, B&B (double) £40–£45; HB weekly £140–£150; D£8·50; WB (£80) dep.

Carbery (Acclaimed)   Western La, The Parks, TA248BZ ☎(0643) 702941.

A detached hotel set in its own peaceful sunny garden with open views of hills and Exmoor located 80 yards off Western Lane and The Parks junction. Open Mar–Oct.
🛏7 bedrs, 6 en suite, 1 ba; TV; tcf 🏠ns; P8; children over 14 ✗LD7, nr lunch, Resid lic
£ £22; HB weekly £160; dep.

Gascony (Acclaimed)   50 The Avenue, TA245BB ☎(0643) 705939.
Located in The Avenue on the corner of Tregonwell Road. Open Mar–Oct.
🛏13 bedrs, 13 en suite, 1 ba; TV; tcf 🏠 dogs; P14; no children under 5 ✗nr lunch. Resid lic
£B&B £19·50; HB weekly £148; [5%V] **cc** Access, B'card/Visa.

Marshfield (Acclaimed)   Tregonwell Rd, TA245DU ☎(0643) 702517.
A small family run hotel in a pleasant tree-lined road close to the sea front. Follow signs on A39 for sea front, hotel on left on entering one-way system. Open Mar–Dec.
🛏12 bedrs, 7 en suite, 3 ba; tcf 🏠TV, dogs, ns; P7; child facs ✗LD 6.30, nr lunch. Resid & Rest lic
£B&B £13; HB weekly £119; D £6·50; dep.

Marston Lodge (Acclaimed)   St Michael's Rd, North Hill, TA245JP ☎(0643) 702510.
Large detached Edwardian house set in one acre of lovely gardens. Follow the road to North Hill, and the hotel is on the right near St Michael's Church. Open Feb–Dec.
🛏12 bedrs, 12 en suite; TV; tcf 🏠ns; P7; no children under 5 ✗LD7. Resid & Rest lic
£B&B £15–£19·50; HB weekly £165–£189; L£6, D£9·50 **cc** Access, B'card/Visa; dep.

Poplars (Acclaimed)   10 Townsend Rd, TA245RG ☎(0643) 704289.

Late Victorian house of character close to the sea and Exmoor. Situated on A39 in Minehead.
🛏6 bedrs, 3 en suite, 1 ba; TV; tcf 🏠NS; P6, TV, dogs, no children under 9 ✗LD 4, nr lunch. Rest lic
£B&B £15·50, B&B (double) £30–£34; HB weekly £154–£168; D £12·50; dep.

Woodbridge   12 The Parks, TA248BS ☎(0643) 704860.
🛏10 bedrs, 3 en suite, 1 ba; tcf 🏠TV, dogs; P5, U2, coach; child facs ✗LD6, nr lunch. Resid & Rest lic.

Binham Farm   Old Cleeve, TA24 6HX ☎(0984) 40222. *Farm.* Mrs S Bigwood
Sleeps 6, 🐴 ns 🐕
£ B&B from £12

Hindon Farm   TA24 8SM ☎(0643) 705244. *Farm.* Penny and Roger Webber
Sleeps 6, 🐴 🐕
£ B&B from £13·50, D £8·50

Tivington Farm   TA24 8SU ☎(0643) 702468. *Farm.* Mrs Fiona Dyer
Sleeps 6, 🐕 ns
£ B&B from £13

MINSTEAD   Hampshire.   Map 26D3

Acres Down Farm   Nr Lyndhurst, SO43 7GE ☎(0703) 813693. *Farm.* Mrs Annie Cooper   ♿
Sleeps 6, 🐕
£ B&B from £11

MINSTER LOVELL   Oxfordshire.   Map 26D6

Hill Grove Farm   Crawley Road, OX8 5NA ☎(0993) 703120. *Farm.* Mrs Katharine Brown
Sleeps 4, ns 🐕
£ B&B from £13·50–£16

MOLASH   Kent.   Map 27D4

Drylands Farm   Nr Canterbury, CT4 8HP ☎(023 374) 205. *Farm.* Martin and Sally Holmes
Sleeps 6, 🐕 ns
£ B&B from £18, D £13·50

MOLESWORTH Cambridgeshire. Map 25A1

Cross Keys Inn Huntingdon, PE11 0QF
☎ Bythorn (080 14) 283.
*Situated 100 yards off the A604 between
Huntingdon and Kettering. Follow signs for
Molesworth village.*
🛏9 bedrs, 9 en suite; TV; tcf 📺 dogs; P50
✗ LD 10.30
£ B&B £19·25, B&B (double) £30·50; L £5·75,
D £5·75; dep.

MONKOKEHAMPTON Devon. Map 28F4

Seldon Farm Winkleigh, EX19 8RY ☎ (0837)
810312. *Farm.* Mary Case
Sleeps 6, 🐾 ⛄
£ B&B from £11, D £7

MONK SOHAM Suffolk. Map 27E8

Monk Soham Hall Woodbridge, IP13 7EN ☎ (072
882) 358. *Farm.* Geoffrey and Gay Clarke 🔥
Sleeps 6, 🐾 ns ⛄ (12)
£ B&B from £16, D £8·50

MORCHARD BISHOP Devon. Map 29A4

Wigham Farm (Highly Acclaimed) Wigham,
EX17 6RJ ☎ (036 37) 350.

*A 16th Century Devon longhouse on a 30-acre farm
which supplies all fresh produce. Situated off the
A377 Exeter/Barnstaple Road. Swimming pool,
billiards.*
🛏5 bedrs, 5 en suite; TV; tcf 📺 NS; P5; no children
✗ nr lunch. Resid lic
£ B&B and dinner (double) £72–£106.

MORDIFORD Herefordshire. Map 31D8

Orchard Farm Nr Hereford, HR1 4EJ ☎ (0432)
73253 or 870253. *Farm.* Mrs Majorie Barrell
Sleeps 6, 🐾 ⛄
£ B&B from £12, D from £8

MORECAMBE Lancashire. Map 22F3

Beach Mount (Highly Acclaimed) 395 Marine Rd
East, LA4 5AN ☎ (0524) 420753. Open Mar–Oct.
🛏26 bedrs, 22 en suite, 2 ba; TV; tcf 📺 TV, dogs;
P6, child facs ✗ LD7, nr lunch. Resid lic

£ B&B £16·50–£19·50, B&B (double) £30–£36; HB
weekly £129–£147 **cc** Access, Amex, B'card/Visa,
Diners; dep.

Prospect (Highly Acclaimed) 363 Marine Rd, LA4
5AQ ☎ (0524) 417819.

*Small hotel on the seafront. Turn left at Morecambe
Promenade, and hotel is on the left. Open Easter–
Nov.*
🛏14 bedrs, 14 en suite, 1 ba; TV; tcf 📺 dogs;
coach; child facs ✗ LD 3, nr lunch. Rest lic
£ B&B £17–£20, B&B (double) £30–£35; HB weekly
£115–£125; WB £53 **cc** B'card/Visa; dep.

Warwick (Highly Acclaimed) 394 Marine Rd East,
LA4 5AN ☎ (0524) 418151.
*Hotel on sea front with fine views of the Bay and
Lakeland hills. Situated on the seafront (A589 from
Lancaster) just 300 metres West of the slipway or
400 metres East of the Town Hall.*
🛏23 bedrs. 11 en suite, 3 ba; TV; tcf 📺 TV, dogs;
coach; child facs ✗ LD7, nr lunch. Resid lic
£ B&B £16·50–£20·50; HB weekly £150–£164;
D £8; [5% V] **cc** Access, Amex, B'card/Visa, dep.

Ashley (Acclaimed) 371 Marine Rd East, LA4
5AH ☎ (0524) 412034.
*Sea front hotel close to the town centre, overlooking
Morecambe Bay and the Lake District. Situated at
the east end of the Promenade. Closed 24 Dec–
1 Jan.*
🛏13 bedrs, 11 en suite, 1 ba; TV; tcf 📺 P5, U1,
coach; child facs ✗ LD3, nr lunch. Resid lic
£ B&B £17–£18, B&B (double) £32–£34; HB weekly
£140–£147; WB (£63) **cc** Access, B'card/Visa;
dep.

New Hazelmere (Acclaimed) 391 Marine Rd
East, LA4 5AN ☎ (0524) 417876.
*Stone built hotel with unrestricted views of the Bay
and Lakeland Hills. Situated on Morecambe
seafront. Open May–Oct.*
🛏18 bedrs, 18 en suite, TV; tcf 📺 TV, dogs; P3,
coach; child facs ✗ LD5.30, nr lunch. Resid lic
£ B&B £15; HB weekly £135; [5% V]

Wimslow (Acclaimed) 374 Marine Rd East, LA4
5AH ☎ (0524) 417804.
*Situated on the sea front opposite new seabreak.
Open Feb–Nov.*

13 bedrs, 13 en suite, tcf ⌂ ns; P5, G6; coach ✗ LD4.30, nr lunch. Resid & Rest lic £B&B £13·23–£13·80; HB weekly £112·70–£118·45; D£6 **cc** Access, B'card/Visa; dep.

Carr Garth 18 Bailey La, Heysham Village, LA3 2PS ✆(0524) 51175.
A listed 17th-century house in a walled garden. Turn right off A589 at Strawberry Gardens Hotel. Open Easter–mid Oct.
10 bedrs, 2 ba; tcf ⌂TV, dogs; P8; child facs ✗LD4, nr lunch. Unlic
£B&B £12, B&B (double) £21; HB weekly £88–£97; dep.

Ellesmere 44 Westminster Rd, LA4 4JD ✆(0524) 411881.
5 bedrs, 1 ba; TV; tcf ⌂TV, ns; child facs ✗LD 5.15, nr lunch. Unlic

Stresa 96 Sandylands Prom, LA3 1DP ✆(0524) 412867.
9 bedrs, 2 ba; tcf ⌂TV ✗nr lunch. Unlic
cc Access; dep.

York Lancaster Rd, LA4 5QR ✆(0524) 418226.

MORETONHAMPSTEAD Devon.
Map 28G4

Cookshayes (Acclaimed) 33 Court St, TQ13 8LG ✆(0647) 40374.

Mid Victorian villa standing in one acre of ornamental gardens. Take B3212 Moreton-hampstead to Princetown road. Situated on the edge of Moretonhampstead Moorland town. Putting Open Mar–Oct.
8 bedrs, 6 en suite, 2 ba; TV; tcf ⌂dogs, ns; P15; no children under 7 ✗nr lunch. Resid lic
£B&B £18, B&B (double) £31–£39; HB weekly £175–£203; WB £23·50 (HB); [10% V May–Sep] **cc** Access, B'card/Visa; dep.

Great Sloncombe Farm Newton Abbot, TQ13 8QF ✆(0647) 40595. *Farm.* Mrs Trudie Merchant
Sleeps 6, ⌂ ☎
£ B&B from £13, D from £7

Wooston Farm Newton Abbot, TQ13 8QA ✆(0647) 40367. *Farm.* Mary Cuming
Sleeps 6, ⌂ ☎
£ B&B from £11–£13, D £7

MORETON-IN-MARSH Gloucestershire.
Map 26C7

Moreton House (Acclaimed) High St, GL56 0LQ ✆(0608) 50747.

Attractive Cotswold stone house, family run and owned by the same family for almost 100 years. Located at the junction of A44 and A429.
12 bedrs, 5 en suite, 2 ba; TV; tcf ⌂dogs, ns; P5, coach; child facs ✗LD8, nr Thu. Resid & Rest lic
£B&B £18·50, B&B (double) £34–£44; L £3·50
cc Access, B'card/Visa; dep.

MORETON PINKNEY Northamptonshire.
Map 26E8

Barewell Fields Daventry, NN11 6SQ ✆(029 576) 754. *Farm.* Margaret Lainchbury
Sleeps 5, ns ☎(7)
£ B&B from £13, D £5–£8

MORTEHOE Devon.
Map 28F6

Baycliffe Chapel Hill, EX34 7DZ ✆Woolacombe (0271) 870393.

MOTTRAM ST ANDREW Cheshire.
Map 24B4

Goose Green Farm Oak Road, Nr Macclesfield, SK10 4RA ✆(0625) 828814. *Farm.* Dyllis Hatch

---

Sleeps 6, ⛌
£ B&B from £15

MOUSEHOLE Cornwall. Map 28B1

Tavis Vor The Parade, TR196PR ☎Penzance
(0736) 731306.
From Penzance go through Newlyn, and Tavis Vor is first property in Mousehole on the left.
⇥7 bedrs, 3en suite, 1 ba; tcf ⌂TV, dogs; P7, coach ✗nr lunch, Resid & Rest lic
£ B&B £18·60; B&B (double) £41·20; HB weekly £151·20; D £9·50, dep.

MUCH COWARNE Herefordshire.
Map 31C8

Paunceford Court Nr Bromyard, HR7 4JQ
☎(0432) 820208. *Farm.* Jenny Keenan
Sleeps 4, ⛌
£ B&B from £12, D £7

MUCKLETON Shropshire. Map 24A3

New Farm Nr Shawbury, Telford, TF6 6RF
☎(0939) 250358. *Farm.* Glen Evans
Sleeps 6, ns ⛌
£ B&B from £15–£20, D £8

MUDDIFORD North Devon. Map 28F6

Home Park Lower Blakewell, EX31 4ET ☎(0271)
42955. *Farm.* Mrs Mari Lethaby
Sleeps 10
£ B&B from £12·50, D from £6

MULLION Cornwall. Map 28C1

Henscath House Mullion Cove, TR12 7EP
☎(0326) 240537.
⇥6 bedrs, 4en suite, 1 ba; tcf ⌂TV; P8; child facs
✗LD6.30, nr lunch. Resid lic

Polhormon Farm Porhormon Lane, Helston,
TR12 7JE ☎(0326) 240304. *Farm.* Alice Harry
Sleeps 8, ⛏⛌
£ B&B from £12

MUNGRISDALE Cumbria. Map 22F6

🍺 🍺 **Mill Inn** CA11 0XR ☎(07687) 79632.
Picturesque 16th century inn beside a river. Fishing.
⇥7 bedrs, 3en suite, (1 sh), 1 ba; tcf ⌂TV, dogs;
P20; coach ✗LD4, bar meals only lunch
£ B&B £15·50–£16·50; B&B (double) £31–£39;
D £9·75; WB **cc** B'card/Visa, dep.

Near Howe (Acclaimed) Near Howe, CA11 0SH
☎(07687) 79678. *Snooker.*
⇥7 bedrs, 5en suite, 1 ba; tcf ⌂TV, dogs; P10;
child facs ✗LD5, nr lunch & Sun dinner. Resid lic

MURTON North Yorkshire. Map 23E3

Dray Lodge (Acclaimed) Moor La, YO1 3UH
☎(0904) 489591 Fax: (0904) 488587.

⇥10 bedrs, 8 en suite, 2 ba; TV; tcf ⌂TV, dogs, ns;
P20, coach; child facs ✗LD8, nr Mon-Sat lunch
£ B&B £26·45–£29·90; HB weekly £215–£246;
[5% V] **cc** Access, B'card/Visa; dep.

MYLOR BRIDGE Cornwall. Map 28C2

Penmere Rosehill, TR11 5LZ ☎Falmouth (0326)
74470.
⇥6 bedrs, 3 ba; TV; tcf ⌂ns; P6; child facs
✗Breakfast only. Unlic.

NANTWICH Cheshire. Map 24A4

Henhull Hall Welshmans Lane, CW5 6AD
☎(0270) 624158. *Farm.* Philip and Joyce Percival
Sleeps 4, ns ⛌
£ B&B from £15

Poole Bank Farm Poole, CW5 6AL ☎(0270)
625169. *Farm.* Caroline Hocknell
Sleeps 5, ⛌
£ B&B from £12

Stoke Grange Farm Chester Road, CW5 6BT
☎(0270) 625525. *Farm.* Georgina West
Sleeps 6, ⛏ns ⛌
£ B&B from £15

NASEBY Northamptonshire. Map 24F1

Woolleys Farm Welford Road, NN6 7DP ☎(0858)
575310. *Farm.* Heather Jeffries
Sleeps 2, ⛏ ⛌
£ B&B from £14, D £5

NASTEND Gloucestershire. Map 26B6

Nastend Farm Nr Stonehouse, GL10 3RS
☎(0453) 822300. *Farm.* Jackie Guilding
Sleeps 6, ⛌
£ B&B from £12–£15, D £8

NEAR SAWREY Cumbria. Map 22F4

Garth (Acclaimed) LA22 0JZ ☎Hawkshead
(09666) 373.

7 bedrs, 2 en suite, 3 ba; TV; tcf ⛬TV, dogs; P12; no children under 5 ✗LD5, nr lunch, nr Tue dinner. Resid & Rest lic

High Green Gate (Acclaimed)   LA22 0LF
☎Hawkshead (09666) 296. Open Apr–Oct & Xmas–New Year.
6 bedrs, 2 en suite, 1 ba ⛬TV, dogs; P7, coach; child facs ✗LD 5, nr lunch. Unlic
£B&B £13·75–£16·50; HB weekly £137·50–£148·50; D£8; dep.

Sawrey House (Acclaimed)   LA22 0LF
☎Hawkshead (09666) 387. Open Mar–Nov.

11 bedrs, 7 en suite, 2 ba; tcf ⛬TV, dogs; P15; child facs ✗LD4, nr lunch. Resid & Rest lic
£B&B £18·75; HB weekly £180–£200; dep.

NEEDHAM MARKET   Suffolk.   Map 27D8

Pipps Ford (Acclaimed)   IP68LJ ☎Coddenham
(044979) 208. 🍽 Fr, De.   ♿

Private road from roundabout where A140 meets A45. Swimming pool. Closed 17 Dec–9 Jan.
3 bedrs, 3 en suite, annexe 3 bedrs, 3 en suite; tcf ⛬TV, ns, P12; no children under 5 ✗LD5, nr lunch & Sun dinner. Resid lic
£B&B £15–£30, B&B (double) £42–£52; HB weekly £240; D £15·50

NEWCASTLE UPON TYNE   Tyne & Wear. Map 23C7

Chirton House (Acclaimed)   46 Clifton Rd, NE4 6XH ☎091-273 0407.

Please tell the manager if you chose your hotel through an advertisement in the guide.

An imposing Victorian building set in its own grounds in a quiet street. Close to Newcastle General Hospital.
11 bedrs, 5 en suite, 2 ba; TV ⛬TV, dogs, ns; P11; child facs ✗LD6, Resid & Rest lic
£B&B £20–£30, B&B (double) £34–£42; HB weekly £170–£230; D£7·50; WB (£15); [5% V]

Portland   134 Sandyford Rd, NE2 1DD ☎091-232 7868.

NEWHAVEN   East Sussex.   Map 27B2

Old Volunteer   1 South Rd, BN9 9QL ☎(0273) 515204.
Situated opposite the Police station. Closed Xmas–New Year.
16 bedrs, 4 en suite, (1 sh), 3 ba; TV; tcf ⛬dogs; child facs ✗Breakfast only. Unlic
£B&B £16·50–£30, B&B (double) £28–£40; dep.

NEWINGTON   Kent.   Map 27E4

Beachborough Park   Nr Folkestone, CT18 8BW
☎(0303) 275432. *Farm.* Gordon and Jan Wallis
Sleeps 10, 🐂 🐑
£ B&B from £17·50–£25, D from £12·50

NEWLYN EAST   Cornwall.   Map 28C3

Shepherds Farm   Newquay, TR8 5NW
☎(087254) 340/502. *Farm.* Heather Harvey   ♿
Sleeps 8, 🐂 🐑
£ B&B from £11.50–£14, D £7

NEWNHAM BRIDGE   Worcestershire.
Map 24A1

Lower Doddenhill Farm   Nr Tenbury Wells, WR15 8NU ☎(058 479) 223. *Farm.* Clifford and Joan Adams
Sleeps 6, ns 🐑 (6)
£ B&B from £13–£14

NEWPORT PAGNELL   Buckinghamshire
Map 26F8

Thurstons   90 High St, MK16 8EH ☎(0908) 611377.
Small hotel close to the city, and 4 mins drive from M1 junction 14.
8 bedrs, 8 en suite; TV; tcf ⛬ns; P12; child facs ✗Breakfast only. Resid lic
£B&B £25–£38, B&B (double) £35–£48

NEWQUAY Cornwall. Map 28C3

Porth Enodoc (Highly Acclaimed) 4 Esplanade Rd, Pentire, TR7 1PY ✆(0637) 872372.
Small hotel overlooking Fistral Bay and the golf course, away from town centre. Follow signs to Pentire in Newquay, fork right into Esplanade Rd, and hotel is next to cliff edge. Open Easter–30 Oct.
⇔16 bedrs, 16 en suite, 1 ba; TV 🛏TV; ns; P16; child facs ✗LD 5, nr lunch. Resid lic
£ B&B £15·50–£18; HB weekly £106–£146; D£6·50; [5% V Easter–27 May, late Sep–Oct]; dep.

Arundell 86 Mount Wise, TR7 2BS ✆(0637) 872481.
Indoor swimming pool, billiards, sauna, solarium.
⇔37 bedrs, 26 en suite, 5 ba; TV; tcf 🛏TV, dogs; P32, U8, coach; child facs ✗LD6, nr lunch. Resid lic
cc Access, Amex, B'card/Visa; dep.

Copper Beech 70 Edgcumbe Av, TR7 2NN ✆(0637) 873376.
Hotel is opposite bowling green and park, 5 mins from sea front and beaches. Open Easter–Oct.
⇔15 bedrs, 12 en suite, (2 sh), 2ba; tcf 🛏TV, ns; P15; coach; child facs ✗LD6, nr lunch. Resid lic
£B&B £16·10–£18·40; HB weekly £126·50–£160.

Fistral Beach Esplanade Rd, Pentire, TR7 1QA ✆(0637) 850626.
Seafront hotel with panoramic views. Follow signs to Pentire, turn right into Esplanade Rd, and hotel is on right. Indoor swimming pool, billiards. Open Feb–Nov & Xmas.
⇔16 bedrs, 16 en suite; TV; tcf 🛏TV, dogs, ns; P14, coach; child facs ✗LD 6. Resid & Rest lic
£ B&B £25–£35, B&B (double) £40–£55; HB weekly £140–£160; L£6, D£10; WB £56 (3 nights)
cc Access, B'card/Visa; dep.

Jonel 88–90 Crantock St, TR7 1JW ✆(0637) 875084.
⇔12 bedrs, (2 sh), 2 ba; TV 🛏TV; P7, coach; child facs ✗LD 4.30, nr lunch. Resid lic

Kellsboro 12 Henver Rd, TR7 3BJ ✆(0637) 874620. *Indoor swimming pool.*

Links Headland Rd, TR7 1HN ✆(0637) 873211.

Pendeen 7 Alexandra Rd, Porth, TR7 3ND ✆(0637) 873521.

Philema Esplanade Rd, Pentire, TR7 1PY ✆(0637) 872571 Fax: (0637) 873188.

Recently extended and refurbished hotel overlooking golf course and beach. Follow signs to Pentire and hotel is at end of Pentire Road. Indoor swimming pool, sauna, solarium.
⇔37 bedrs, 32 en suite, 5 ba; TV; tcf 🛏 dogs; P32; coach; child facs ✗LD7.30. Resid & Rest lic
£B&B £18·50–£28; HB weekly £120–£190; D£7·50
cc Access, B'card/Visa; dep.

Priory Lodge 30 Mount Wise, TR7 2BH ✆(0637) 874111. *Swimming pool, sauna, solarium.*
⇔26 bedrs, 23 en suite, 1 ba; TV; tcf 🛏TV, dogs, ns; P28, coach; child facs ✗LD 7.30, Resid & Rest lic.

Quies 84 Mount Wise TR7 2BS ✆(0637) 872924.
Centrally situated hotel with pretty garden. Set on the right of the one-way system just past the large public car park. Open Mar–Dec.
⇔10 bedrs, 7 en suite, (2 sh), TV; tcf 🛏TV, dogs; coach; child facs ✗LD 7.30, nr lunch. Resid lic
£B&B £14–£22; HB weekly £115·50–£163·50; [10% V exc Jul & Aug] **cc** Access, B'card/Visa; dep.

Rolling Waves Alexandra Rd, Porth, TR7 3NB ✆(0637) 873236.
Turn right at mini-roundabout on Henver Rd, follow St Columb Porth sign. Turn sharp corner on Alexandra Rd and hotel is on the right. Closed Xmas.
⇔10 bedrs, 3 en suite, 2 ba; tcf 🛏TV, dogs, ns; P10; coach; child facs ✗LD6.30, nr lunch. Resid lic
£B&B £19·20–£22·65; HB weekly £138–£160; D£7·50; WB (£37·96); [5% V exc Jul–Sept]
cc B'card/Visa; dep.

Wheal Treasure 72 Edgcumbe Av, TR7 2NN ✆(0637) 874136.

Windward Alexandra Rd, Porth, TR7 3NB ✆(0637) 873185.
Newly designed and upgraded hotel in its own grounds. Located 1 mile along B3276 from its junction with A392. Open Easter–Oct.
⇔14 bedrs, 14 en suite, TV; tcf 🛏TV, ns; P14; child facs ✗LD6.30, nr lunch. Resid lic
£B&B £15–£25; HB weekly £133; WB £19 (HB); [5% V May, Jun, Sep & Oct]

Manuels Farm TR8 4NY ✆(0637) 873577. *Farm.*
Mrs Jean Wilson
Sleeps 12, 🐾 ns 🚭
£ B&B from £11–£14, D £7

Newquay (Cornwall)

NEWTON ABBOT Devon. Map 29A3

Hazelwood House (Acclaimed) 33a Torquay Rd,
TQ12 2LW ☎(0626) 66130.
*Light, imposing pre-war building with wood-
panelled dining room.*
🛏7 bedrs, 5 en suite, 2 ba; TV; tcf 🛗dogs; P 6,
coach; child facs ✗Resid lic
£B&B £25·50–£33, B&B (double) £37·50–£44;
[10% V] cc Access, B'card/Visa.

Lamorna Ideford Coombe, TQ13 0AR ☎(0626)
65627.
*Leave A380 at Ideford Combe on the B3195. Hotel
400 yards on left. Indoor swimming pool.*
🛏7 bedrs, 2 ba; TV; tcf 🛗TV, ns; P 10; child facs
✗Breakfast only. Resid & Club lic
£B&B £16–£18, B&B (double) £26–£28.

Narracombe Farm Ilsington, TQ13 9RD ☎(0364)
661243. *Farm.* Sue Wills
Sleeps 6, 🐎 ☞
£ B&B from £13

New Cott Farm Poundsgate, TQ13 7PD
☎(03643) 421. *Farm.* Margaret Phipps   ♿
Sleeps 8, ns ☞ (3)
£ B&B from £13–£14, D £8

NINFIELD East Sussex. Map 27C3

Moonshill Farm The Green, TN33 9LN ☎(0424)
892645.
🛏6 bedrs, 3 en suite, 1 ba; TV; tcf 🛗TV, dogs; P6;
child facs ✗Breakfast only. Unlic.
£ B&B from £13–£16

NORBURY Staffordshire. Map 24B2

Oulton House Farm Nr Stafford, ST20 0PG
☎(0785) 284264. *Farm.* Mrs Judy Palmer
Sleeps 6, ☞
£ B&B from £15, D £8

NORTHALLERTON North Yorkshire.
Map 23D4

Alverton (Acclaimed) 26 South Par, DL7 8SG
☎(0609) 776207.
*Large Victorian residence recently modernised but
retaining character. Situated at the S. end of town
centre between market place and station.*
🛏5 bedrs, 3 en suite, 1 ba; TV; tcf 🛗TV, dogs; P 4;
child facs ✗LD 5, Unlic
£B&B £16; B&B (double) £30; HB weekly £145;
D £6·95; [5% V]; dep.

Station 2 Boroughbridge Rd, DL7 8AN ☎(0609)
772053.

Situated 6 miles from A1 and 7 miles from A19.
🛏10 bedrs, 3 ba; TV; tcf 🛗dogs, ns; P 20, coach;
child facs.

Windsor 56 South Par, DL7 8SL ☎(0609)
774100. ☝ Fr, De.
*Victorian terraced house in tree-lined road. Pass
town sign into Northallerton, turn left at T junction,
past station and turn into third exit at traffic island.
Hotel 100 yards on left. Closed 25 Dec–4 Jan.*
🛏6 bedrs, 2 ba; TV; tcf 🛗TV, dogs; child facs
✗LD 4, nr lunch & Sun dinner. Resid lic
£B&B £18, B&B (double) £29; D £7·75; dep.

NORTHAMPTON Northamptonshire.
Map 26E8

Poplars (Acclaimed) Cross St, Moulton, NN3 1RZ
☎(0604) 643983.

*17th century farm house set in a conservation area.
Just off the A43 about 4 ½ miles NE of Northampton.*
🛏21 bedrs, 15 en suite, 2 ba; TV; tcf 🛗TV, dogs,
coach; P 21; child facs ✗LD 6.30, nr lunch & Sat,
Sun dinner. Resid lic
£B&B £16–£30, B&B (double) £30–£45; HB weekly
£185; D £10; WB (£16); [5% V w/d] cc Access,
B'card/Visa.

Simpson's 13 Leicester Par, Barrack Rd, NN2
6AA ☎(0604) 32127.
🛏10 bedrs, 5 en suite, 2 ba; TV; tcf 🛗G 2; child
facs ✗Breakfast only. Resid lic
cc Access, B'card/Visa.

NORTH BOVEY Devon. Map 28G4

Blackaller House (Acclaimed) TQ13 8QY
☎Moretonhampstead (0647) 40322.

*Devon longhouse in a secluded riverside setting.
Follow B3212 to Moretonhampstead, take first left*

after crossroads signed North Bovey. Open Apr–
Oct.
6 bedrs, 4 en suite, 1 ba TV, dogs, ns; P 12; no
children under 6 Breakfast only. Resid lic
£ B&B £17–£20, B&B (double) £43–£47
cc Access, Amex, B'card/Visa; dep.

NORTH NEWINGTON Oxfordshire.
Map 26D8

Mill House Nr Banbury, OX156AA Banbury
(0295) 730212. *Swimming pool.*

NORTH NIBLEY Gloucestershire. Map 29E8

Burrows Court (Acclaimed) Nibley Green,
Dursley, GL116AZ Dursley (0453) 546230.
*18th century former weaving mill and owner's
house, set in an acre of garden. Swimming pool.*
Closed New Year.
8 bedrs, 8 en suite; TV; tcf P 20; no children
under 5 LD 8.30, nr lunch. Resid lic
£ B&B £26–£34, B&B (double) £31–£47; HB weekly
£189–£220; D £12·50; WB cc Access, B'card/Visa;
dep.

Black Horse Inn GL116DT (0453) 546841.
6 bedrs, 4 en suite, 1 ba; TV; tcf dogs, ns;
P 30, coach; child facs LD9.30, nr Sun & Mon
dinner
cc Access, Amex, B'card/Visa; dep.

NORTH ORMSBY Lincolnshire. Map 25A5

Abbey Farm Louth, LN11 0TJ (0472)
840272. *Farm.* Marory Findlay
Sleeps 6,
£ B&B from £12–£15, D £8–£10

NORTH OTTERINGTON North Yorkshire.
Map 23D4

Wellfield House Farm Northallerton, DL7 9JF
(0609) 772766. *Farm.* Dorothy Hill
Sleeps 6,
£ B&B from £11, D £8

NORTH PETHERTON Somerset.
Map 29C5

Quantock View House Bridgwater Rd, JA66PR
(0278) 663309.
*Small family-run guest house. Situated on A38
between Bridgwater and North Petherton.*
4 bedrs, 1 en suite, (1 sh), 1 ba; TV; tcf TV,
dogs; P5; child facs LD3, nr lunch. Unlic
£ B&B £11–£12·50; HB weekly £105–£119; [5% V].

NORTH TAWTON Devon. Map 27F4

Oaklands Farm EX20 2BQ (0837)
82340. *Farm.* Winifred Headon
Sleeps 6,
£ B&B from £10, D £5·50

NORTON CUCKNEY Nottinghamshire.
Map 24D4

Norton Grange Farm Nr Mansfield, NG20 9LP
(0623) 842666. *Farm.* Jackie Palmer
Sleeps 6, ns
£ B&B from £12

NORWICH Norfolk. Map 25E2

Belmont (Highly Acclaimed) 60–62 Prince of
Wales Rd, NR1 1LT (0603) 622533.

Cavalier (Highly Acclaimed) 244 Thorpe Road,
NR1 1TP (0603) 34291 Fax: (0603) 31744.
*Situated 1 mile from city centre on A47 towards
Great Yarmouth.*
21 bedrs, 19 en suite, 2 ba; TV; tcf TV, dogs;
P30, coach; child facs LD 9.30, nr Sun dinner,
Rest & Club lic
£ B&B £33–£38, B&B (double) £45–£60; L £6·95,
D £9·95; [10% V w/e] cc Access, B'card/Visa.

Wedgewood House (Highly Acclaimed) 42 St
Stephens Rd, NR13RE (0603) 625730.
*Situated 200 yards past junction of A140 and A11,
opposite the Norfolk and Norwich Hospital.* Closed
Xmas & New Year.
11 bedrs, 8 en suite, 1 ba, TV; tcf ns; P7; child
facs LD midday, nr lunch. Unlic
£ B&B £15–£16·50, B&B (double) £32–£36; WB
(£28) cc Access, B'card/Visa; dep.

NOTTINGHAM Nottinghamshire. Map 24E3

Balmoral (Highly Acclaimed) 55 Loughborough
Rd, West Bridgford, NG2 7LA (0602) 455020 or
818588 Fax: (0602) 455683.
*Situated 500 yards S of Trent Bridge on A60.
Snooker.*
33 bedrs, 27 en suite, (8 sh); TV; tcf TV; P35
LD7.30, nr lunch & Fri-Sun dinner. Resid lic
£ B&B £26·50–£34·50, B&B (double) £46–£53;
[5% V] cc Access, B'card/Visa.

Fairhaven (Acclaimed) 19 Meadow Rd, Beeston
Rylands, NG91JP (0602) 227509. Open 1 Jan–24
Dec.
10 bedrs, 3ba TV, ns; P 12, coach; child facs
LD midday, nr lunch & Fri, Sat & Sun dinner.
Resid lic
£ B&B £16–£19·50, B&B (double) £24–£29; D £7;
dep.

Crantock 480 Mansfield Rd, Sherwood, NG5 2EL
(0602) 623294.
Large white building with annexe.
20 bedrs, 14 en suite, 3ba; TV; tcf dogs, ns;
P 70, coach; child facs LD 9.30, nr lunch, Sun
dinner, Resid & Rest lic
£ B&B £24–£39, B&B (double) £38–£49; L £7,
D £12; [5% V]; dep.

P & J 227 Derby Rd, Lenton, NG7 2DP
☎(0602) 783998.
*Large family run Victorian hotel. Situated on A52 ½
mile from city centre.*
☎20 bedrs, 8 en suite, (2 sh), 3 ba; TV; tcf 🅣TV,
dogs; ns; P 10; child facs ✗LD 9, nr lunch & Fri–
Sun dinner. Resid & Rest lic
£B&B £22–£32, B&B (double) £37–£45; (WB £18);
[10% V] **cc** Access, Amex, B'card/Visa; dep.

Park 7 Waverley St NG7 4HF ☎(0602) 786299
Fax: (0602) 424358.
*From city centre follow signs for Mansfield up hill
to traffic lights. Turn left, and left at next lights. Hotel
down hill on left.*
☎27 bedrs, 17 en suite, (8 sh), 3 ba; TV; tcf 🅣TV,
dogs, ns; coach ✗LD 11
£B&B £48, B&B (double) £58; HB weekly £350;
L £8·50, D £12·50; WB (£35); [5% V] **cc** Access,
Amex, B'card/Visa; dep.

Royston 326 Mansfield Rd, NG5 2EF ☎(0602)
622947.
☎14 bedrs, 9 en suite, (1 sh), 2 ba; TV; tcf 🅣TV, ns;
P 20, coach; child facs ✗Breakfast only. Unlic
£B&B £28, B&B (double) fr £40; WB (£26 per night);
[10% V Oct–Apr]

NUNEATON Warwickshire. Map 24D1

Ambion Court (Highly Acclaimed) The Green,
Dadlington, CV13 6JB ☎(0455) 212292 Fax: (0455)
213141. ✗ Fr
£ B&B £30–£45; [10% V w/e]

NUNNINGTON North Yorkshire. Map 23E4

Sunley Court York, YO6 5XQ ☎(043 95)
233. *Farm.* Mrs Joan Brown
Sleeps 6, 🐾 🔥
£ B&B from £12, D £7

OAKLEY Buckinghamshire. Map 23E4

New Farm Oxford Road, Aylesbury, HP18 9UR
☎(0844) 237360. *Farm.* Binnie Pickford
Sleeps 6, 🔥 (6)
£ B&B from £14–£17

ODDINGLEY Worcestershire. Map 26B8

Wessex House Farm Trench Lane, Droitwich,
WR9 7NB ☎(0905) 772826 or (090 569) 234. *Farm.*
Gwen Jackson
Sleeps 6 + cot, ns 🔥
£ B&B from £12, D £5–£6

OFFHAM East Sussex. Map 27B3

Ousedale House Lewes, BN7 3QF ☎(0273)
478680. *Farm.* Roland and Brenda Gough
Sleeps 6, ns 🔥
£ B&B from £18, D £9

Nottingham (Nottinghamshire)

Nuneaton (Warwickshire)

OLD Northamptonshire. Map 26EA

Wold Farm Northampton, NN6 9RJ ✆ (0604)
781258. *Farm.* Anne Engler &
Sleeps 10, ♀ ☞
£ B&B from £15, D £10

OLD BYLAND North Yorkshire. Map 23E4

Manor Farm Helmsley, York, YO6 5LG ✆ (043 96)
247. *Farm.* Joyce Garbutt
Sleeps 5, ☞
£ B&B from £12, D £8

Valley View Farm Helmsley, York, YO6 5LG
✆ (043 96) 221. *Farm.* Sally Robinson
Sleeps 12, ♀ ☞
£ B&B from £16–£18, D £9·50

OLD SODBURY Avon. Map 29D7

Dornden (Acclaimed) Church La, BS17 6NB
✆ Chipping Sodbury (0454) 313325. ✿ Es.

*Former Vicarage in beautiful gardens with lovely
views. From M4, junction 18, take A46 towards
Stroud. Turn left at A452, then right at Dog Inn. At
T junction turn right to hotel on right. Tennis. Closed
Xmas & New Year.*
⇔ 9 bedrs, 5 en suite, 2 ba; TV ⌂ TV, dogs; P; child
facs ✕ LD3, nr lunch. Unlic
£ B&B £23–£32, B&B (double) £38–£45; WB
(£18.50 per night); [5% V]; dep.

OLLERTON Nottinghamshire. Map 24E4

Old Rectory Main St, Kirton, NG22 9LP
✆ Mansfield (0623) 861540 Fax: (0623) 860751.
Closed 24 Dec–5 Jan.
⇔ 10 bedrs, 2 en suite, (1 sh), 3 ba; tcf ⌂ TV; P 15,
coach; child facs ✕ LD 6.30, nr lunch. Resid & Rest
lic
£ B&B £21, B&B (double) £21–£47·50 **cc** Access,
B'card/Visa; dep.

OMBERSLEY Worcester. Map 26B8

Eden Farm Nr Droitwich, WR9 0JY ✆ (0905)
620244. *Farm.* Mrs Ann Yardley
Sleeps 6, ♀ ☞
£ B&B from £14, D £10

ORFORD Suffolk. Map 27F8

King's Head Front St, IP12 2LW ✆ (0394) 450271.
*Charming old inn situated in the village square. Take
B1078 from A12; signposted to Orford Castle.*
⇔ 6 bedrs, 2 ba; TV; tcf ⌂ dogs; P 70, G 1 ✕ LD9
£ B&B (double) £34–£36; L £8, D £10;
WB; [5% V w/d] **cc** Diners; dep.

OTLEY West Yorkshire. Map 23C2

Old Hall Farm Clifton, LS21 2HE ✆ (0943)
463972. *Farm.* Sue Adams
Sleeps 6, ns ☞ (10)
£ B&B from £13

OTTERY ST MARY Devon. Map 29B4

Venn Ottery Barton (Acclaimed) EX11 1RZ
✆ (0404) 812733.
*Much extended Tudor house with fine views in
village of Venn Ottery. Take A3052 to Newton
Poppleford where turn north to Venn Ottery.*
⇔ 16 bedrs, 1 en suite, 3 ba; tcf ⌂ TV, dogs; P 20;
child facs ✕ LD7, bar meals only lunch. Resid lic
£ B&B £18–£24, B&B (double) £32–£44; HB weekly
£150·50–£192·50; D £10·50; WB (£21·50 3 nts)
cc Access, B'card/Visa; dep.

Claypits Farm East Hill, EX11 1QD ✆ (0404)
814599. *Farm.* Jayne Burrow
Sleeps 6, ns ☞ (3)
£ B&B from £13, D from £7

Home Farm Escot, EX11 1LU ✆ (0404)
850241. *Farm.* Dorren Turl
Sleeps 6, ☞
£ B&B from £11–£14

Pitt Farm EX11 1NL ✆ (0404) 812439. *Farm.*
Susan Hansford
Sleeps 16, ☞
£ B&B from £13, D from £7

OUSTON Co Durham. Map 23C6

Low Urpeth Farm Chester Le Street, DH2 1BD
✆ (091) 410 2901. *Farm.* Hilary Johnson
Sleeps 6, ☞
£ B&B from £12·50–£15

OVER ALDERLEY Cheshire. Map 24B5

Lower Harebarrow Farm Macclesfield, SK10
4SQ ✆ (0625) 24128. *Farm.* Mrs Beryl Leggott
Sleeps 3, ☞
£ B&B from £14·50

OVER WHITACRE Birmingham. Map 24C1

Monwode Lea Farm Coleshill, B46 2NR ✆ (0675)
81232. *Farm.* Mollie Callwood
Sleeps 5, ns ☞ (5)
£ B&B from £15, D £7·50

OXFORD Oxfordshire. Map 26D6

Chestnuts (Highly Acclaimed) 45 Davenant Rd, OX2 8BU ☎(0865) 53375.
Modernised house in quiet road off Woodstock Road to north of city.
⊨4 bedrs, 4 en suite; TV; tcf 📺 P 4; no children under 12 ✕Breakfast only. Unlic.
£ B&B £24–£28, B&B (double) £44–£54; [5% V Oct–Mar]

Cotswold House (Highly Acclaimed) 363 Banbury Rd, OX2 7PL ☎(0865) 310558.

Cotswold stone building on A423 in north of city. Well furnished with much antique oak.
⊨6 bedrs, 6 en suite, TV; tcf 📺 NS; P6; children over 6 ✕Breakfast only. Unlic
£ B&B £24–£27, B&B (double) £44–£50.

Gables (Highly Acclaimed) 6 Cumnor Hill, OX2 9HA ☎(0865) 862153. ✗ Fr.

Pink-washed modern house in quiet residential area. From city centre take Botley Rd for 1·8 miles west. Closed 23–27 Dec.
⊨6 bedrs, 5 en suite, 2 ba; TV; tcf 📺 TV, dogs; P6 ✕Breakfast only. Unlic
£ B&B £17–£18, B&B (double) £34–£36; dep.

Tilbury Lodge (Highly Acclaimed) 5 Tilbury La, Eynsham Rd, Botley, OX2 9NB ☎(0865) 862138.

Purpose-built hotel in quiet country lane, 2 miles W of city centre. Leave A34 ring road at Botley roundabout towards city. Turn right at lights and right again up B4044. Tilbury Lane on right.
⊨8 bedrs, 8 en suite; TV; tcf 📺 ns; P8, G1; no children under 6 ✕Breakfast only. Unlic
£ B&B £27–£30, B&B (double) £45–£60; dep.

Courtfield (Acclaimed) 367 Iffley Rd, OX4 4DP ☎(0865) 242991.
An individually designed house in a tree-lined road to SE of city centre. On A423 Henley road.
⊨6 bedrs, 4 en suite, 1 ba 📺 TV, ns; P6, G2; no children under 3 ✕Breakfast only. Unlic
£ B&B £24–£32, B&B (double) £36–£42; [10% V Oct–Apr 2 nts or more]; dep. cc Access, B'card/Visa.

River (Acclaimed) 17 Botley Rd, OX2 0AA ☎(0865) 243475.
Family-run hotel west of city beside River Thames at Osney Bridge. Closed 21 Dec–2 Jan.
⊨24 bedrs, 17 en suite, (2 sh), 2 ba; TV; tcf 📺 TV, ns; P25; child facs ✕LD7.30, nr Mon–Sat lunch & Sun dinner
£ B&B £33–£45, B&B (double) £50–£55; D £10 cc Access, B'card/Visa; dep.

Ascot 283 Iffley Rd, OX4 4AQ ☎(0865) 240259.
Guest house half a mile from city centre reached via A4158.
⊨6 bedrs, 3 en suite, 1 ba; TV; tcf 📺 TV, ns; P2; child facs. ✕Breakfast only. Unlic

Oxford (Oxfordshire)

£ B&B £20–£30, B&B (double) £32–£45
cc Access, B'card/Visa; dep.

Bedford House   19 Polstead Rd, OX2 6TW
📞(0865) 54107.
Guest house in quiet road off main Woodstock Road, one mile from city centre.
🛏5 bedrs, 2 ba; TV; tcf 📺TV, dogs;
P2 ✕Breakfast only. Unlic
£ B&B £17–£18; [10% V Jan-Mar]; dep.

Bravalla   242 Iffley Rd, OX4 1SE 📞(0865) 241326.
Family-run guest house south east of city centre, reached via A4158.
🛏5 bedrs, 4 en suite, (1 sh), TV; tcf 📺TV, dogs;
P4, child facs ✕Breakfast only. Unlic
£ B&B £20–£30, B&B (double) £30–£40; [V]
cc Access, B'card/Visa; dep.

Brown's   281 Iffley Rd, OX4 4AQ 📞(0865) 246822. *Guest House.*

Conifer   116 The Slade, Headington OX3 7DX
📞(0865) 63055.
From London, turn left at first traffic lights in Headington into Windmill Road, then The Slade. Swimming pool.
🛏8 bedrs, 3 en suite, 1 ba; TV; tcf 📺ns; P8; child facs ✕Breakfast only. Unlic
£ B&B £20, B&B (double) £30–£40 **cc** Access, B'card/Visa; dep.

Galaxie   180 Banbury Rd, OX2 7BT 📞(0865) 515688.
Turn-of-the century, double fronted hotel in north of city.

🛏34 bedrs, 23 en suite, (6 sh), 6 ba; TV 📺lift, TV, dogs; P34, coach ✕Breakfast only. Unlic
£ B&B £28–£42, B&B (double) £42–£54; WB £28; [5% V w/e] **cc** B'card/Visa.

Kings   363 Iffley Rd, OX4 4DP 📞(0865) 241363.
Guest House.
🛏5 bedrs, 2 en suite, (1 sh), 1 ba; TV; tcf 📺TV, ns; P6; child facs ✕Breakfast only. Unlic

Melcombe House   227 Iffley Rd, OX4 1SQ
📞(0865) 249520.
Family-run Victorian house, south east of city centre. Closed Xmas.
🛏9 bedrs, 1 en suite, (1 sh); 2 ba; TV; tcf 📺dogs; P6; ✕Breakfast only. Unlic
£ B&B £16–£18, B&B (double) £30–£40; dep.

Pickwick   17 London Rd, Headington OX3 7SP📞(0865) 750487. *Private Hotel.*
🛏14 bedrs, 9 en suite, 4 ba; TV; tcf 📺TV, dogs, ns; P14; coach, child facs ✕Breakfast only. Unlic

Pine Castle   290 Iffley Rd, OX4 4AE 📞(0865) 241497.
Family-run guest house in south east of city. Closed Xmas
🛏6 bedrs, (1 sh), 1 ba; TV; tcf 📺TV, dogs, ns; P4; child facs ✕Breakfast only. Unlic
£ B&B £18–£21; B&B (double) £35–£40; WB (£16 per nt. 2 nts min). **cc** Access, B'card/Visa; dep.

Portland House   338 Banbury Rd, OX2 7PR
📞(0865) 52076.

Conveniently placed guest house on main approach road from north.
5 bedrs, 1 en suite, (1 sh), 3 ba; TV; tcf dogs; P 4, G 1 (£2) Breakfast only. Unlic
£ B&B £17–£18, B&B (double) £30–£40

Willow Reaches   1 Wytham Street, OX1 4SU
(0865) 721545 Fax: (0865) 251139.
Family run hotel just off Abingdon Road to south of city centre.
9 bedrs, 9 en suite; TV; tcf TV; P 6, G 3; child facs LD 6, nr lunch. Resid & Rest lic
£ B&B £36, B&B (double) £48; D £15 **cc** Amex, B'card/Visa, Diners; dep.

Windrush   11 Iffley Rd, OX4 1EA (0865) 247933.
Guest house a short way down the Iffley Road from the roundabout at eastern end of the High Street.
8 bedrs, 2 ba; ns; child facs Breakfast only. Unlic
£ B&B £17·50–£21, B&B (double) £28·50–£35; dep.

Mead Close   Forest Hill, OX9 1EB (086 77) 2248. *Farm.* Audrey Dunkley
Sleeps 5,
£ B&B from £13, D from £7·50

PADSTOW   Cornwall.   Map 28D3

Green Waves (Highly Acclaimed)   Trevone Bay, PL28 8RD (0841) 520114. *Private Hotel.* Open Apr–Sep.
20 bedrs, 15 en suite, 4 ba; TV; tcf dogs; P 15, no children under 4 LD 7, nr lunch. Resid lic
£ B&B £15–£20; HB weekly £120–£150; dep.

Woodlands (Highly Acclaimed)   Treator, PL28 8RU (0841) 532426.

Agreeable hotel in rural setting near beaches and golf courses. From Padstow take B3276 ¾ mile to Trevone Road. Open Mar–Oct.
9 bedrs, 9 en suite; TV; tcf , dogs, ns; P 15; child facs LD 5, nr lunch. Resid & Rest lic
£ B&B £23·50–£25·50, B&B (double) £43–£47; D £8; WB £78 (HB); [5% V Mar–May, Sept–Oct]; dep.

Old Mill (Acclaimed)   Little Petherick, PL27 7QT Rumford (0841) 540388.

A 16th century, listed corn mill, in gardens beside a stream, carefully converted to retain its original charm and character. In Little Petherick village on A389 Wadebridge–Padstow road.
6 bedrs, 6 en suite; tcf. TV, dogs, ns; P 8; no children under 14 LD 6, nr lunch. Resid & Rest lic
£ B&B (double) £37–46; HB weekly £188–£219; D £9·50; dep.

Bay House   Porthcothan Bay, PL28 8LW (0841) 520472.
Modern purpose-built hotel on coast road overlooking beach and sea. Open Apr–Nov.
16 bedrs, 4 ba TV, ns; P 14; child facs LD 4, nr lunch. Resid lic
£ B&B £15–£17; HB weekly £114–£143; D £7; dep.

Dower House   Fentonluna La, PL28 8BA (0841) 532317.
From main road follow sign for 'Fentonluna – Parish Church'. Open March–end Nov.
8 bedrs, 5 en suite, 1 ba; tcf TV, dogs; P 9; child facs LD 6, nr lunch. Resid & Rest lic
£ B&B £18–£26·50, B&B (double) £28–£46; HB weekly £150–£210; D £11; dep.

Tregea 16 High St, PL28 8BB ☎(0841) 532455. Hotel.

PAIGNTON Torbay. Devon.   Map 29A3

Channel View (Acclaimed) 8 Marine Par, Sea Front, TQ3 2NU ☎(0803) 522432. Closed New Year.
🛏12 bedrs, 12 en suite; TV; tcf 📺TV; P12, coach; ✕LD 2, nr Sun dinner. Resid & Rest lic
£B&B (double) £25–£36; HB weekly £165; D£5·50
cc Access; dep.

Hotel Retreat (Acclaimed) 43 Marine Dr, TQ3 2NS ☎(0803) 550596.
A family run hotel pleasantly situated in a delightfully secluded garden opposite a sandy beach. Situated midway along the one-way system. Open Easter–Sep.
🛏13 bedrs, 5 en suite, (1 sh), 3 ba; TV; tcf 📺TV, dogs; P13; child facs ✕LD6, nr lunch. Resid lic
£B&B £16–£20, B&B (double) £32–£40; HB weekly £144–£185 cc Access, B'card/Visa; dep.

St. Weonards (Acclaimed) 12 Kernou Rd, TQ4 6BA ☎(0803) 558842.

Well-sited, attractive Victorian terraced hotel. Turn right off Esplanade just before the Festival Hall.
🛏8 bedrs, 4 en suite, 2 ba; tcf 📺TV, ns; P2, no children under 10. ✕LD 4.30, nr lunch. Resid lic
£B&B £13–£18; HB weekly £120–£135; dep.

Sealawn (Acclaimed) 20 Esplanade Rd, TQ4 6BE ☎(0803) 559031.
Tastefully furnished Victorian building situated on the seafront between Paignton Pier and the Festival Hall. Solarium.
🛏14 bedrs, 14 en suite; TV; tcf 📺TV, ns; P 14, coach; child facs ✕LD 5.30, nr lunch. Resid & Rest lic
£B&B £21–£27, B&B (double) £32–£44; HB weekly £147–£189; [10% V Oct–May]; D £6; dep.

Sea Verge (Acclaimed) Marine Dr, Preston, TQ3 2NJ ☎(0803) 557795. Closed Dec.
🛏12 bedrs, 5 en suite, 2 ba; TV; tcf 📺TV; P14; no children ✕LD5, nr lunch. Resid lic.

Bayview 6 Cleveland Rd, TQ4 6EN ☎(0803) 557400.
Modern hotel close to the seafront. Turn off Esplanade opposite Festival Theatre. Putting, billiards.

Beresford Adelphi Rd, TQ4 6AW ☎(0803) 551560. Closed Xmas & New Year.
🛏8 bedrs, 4 en suite, 2 ba; tcf 📺TV; P3; child facs ✕LD 10 am, nr lunch. Resid lic
£B&B fr £14.

Blue Seas 4 St Andrews Rd, TQ4 6HA ☎(0803) 558348.
Small hotel, quietly situated. Turn off Esplanade into Sands Rd, then second on the left. Open Mar–Oct.

ENGLAND

12 bedrs, 3 en suite, 2 ba; tcf TV, dogs; P 10, coach; child facs nr lunch, Resid lic
£ B&B £10·95–£15; HB weekly £109·55–£117·95; WB (£30 2 nights); [10% V Mar–Jun]; dep.

Florida 9 Colin Rd, Preston, TQ3 2NR (0803) 551447.
9 bedrs, 2 en suite, 2 ba; TV; tcf TV, dogs; P 4, coach; child facs LD 6, nr lunch. Unlic.

Palm Sands 21 Morin Rd, Preston, TQ3 2PL (0803) 523226.
Situated one road back from the seafront, overlooking Preston Beach at Paignton. Open Easter–Nov.
7 bedrs, 2 en suite, 2 ba; TV; tcf TV; P7; child facs. LD 6, nr lunch Resid lic
£ B&B £13–£15, B&B (double) £22–£26; HB weekly £80–£95; dep.

Sattva 29 Esplanade, TQ4 6BL (0803) 557820.
Attractive white-walled hotel on the seafront, located opposite the pier. Open Mar–Oct.
20 bedrs, 13 en suite, 2 ba; TV; tcf lift, TV, ns; P 12, coach; child facs LD 5.30, nr lunch. Resid lic
£ B&B £20–£28, HB weekly £120–£170; [5% V Mar–May, Sept & Oct]. **cc** Access, B'card/Visa; dep.

Sunnybank 2 Cleveland Rd, TQ4 6EN (0803) 525540.
12 bedrs, 2 en suite, (2 sh), 2 ba; tcf TV, dogs, ns; P 7, coach; no children under 3; child facs LD 3, nr lunch. Resid & Rest lic
cc Access; dep.

Torbay Sands 16 Marine Par, Preston, TQ3 2NU (0803) 525568.
Family run hotel with panoramic views, situated on Preston seafront.
14 bedrs, 9 en suite, 2 ba; TV; tcf TV, dogs; P 6, coach; child facs LD 4; Resid lic
£ B&B £12–£15; HB weekly £95–£120; D £5; [10% V Oct–May] **cc** Access, B'card/Visa; dep.

PAINSWICK Gloucestershire. Map 26B6

Damsels Farm GL6 6UD (0452) 812148. *Farm.* Michele Burdett
Sleeps 6,
£ B&B from £13·50–£16·50, D £15·50

PAPPLEWICK Nottinghamshire. Map 24E4

Forest Farm Mansfield Road, NG15 8FL (0602) 632310. *Farm.* Mrs E J Stubbs
Sleeps 5, (2) ns
£ B&B from £12·50, D £5

PAR Cornwall Map 28D2

Elmswood House 73 Tehidy Rd, Tywardreath, PL24 2QD (072681) 4221.
6 bedrs, 3 en suite, 1 ba; TV TV; P8; child facs LD noon, nr lunch. Resid lic

PATELEY BRIDGE North Yorkshire. Map 23C3

Roslyn House King St, HG3 5AT (0423) 711374.

Talbot High St, HG3 5AL (0423) 711597.
Listed late 17th century building in the centre of picturesque Pateley Bridge. Open Feb–Oct.
8 bedrs, 5 en suite, 1 ba; tcf TV, dogs; P 7 LD 6, nr lunch. Resid lic
£ B&B £16–£18·50, B&B (double) £26–£32; HB weekly £150·50–£178; WB (£40); dep.

PENCOMBE Herefordshire. Map 31C8

Hennerwood Farm Bromyard, HR7 4SL (0885) 400245. *Farm.* Anita Thomas
Sleeps 6, ns
£ B&B from £12, D £8

PENCRAIG Hereford & Worcester (Herefordshire). Map 31H3

Harbour HR9 6HR Llangarron (098 984) 359.

PENDEEN   Cornwall.   Map 28B1

Trewellard Manor Farm   Penzance, TR19 7SU
☎(0736) 788526. *Farm*. Mrs Marion Bailey
Sleeps 6, ns ⛌
£ B&B from £12–£15

PENRITH   Cumbria.   Map 23A6

Grotto (Acclaimed)   Yanwath, CA10 2LF ☎(0768)
63288.

*18th century grey stone house in attractive gardens
in a rural setting. Take the B5320 Eamont Bridge
to Pooley Bridge Rd, and after 1 mile turn right at
Yanwath. House is 300 yards from main road.*
🛏6 bedrs, 4 en suite, 1 ba; TV; tcf �📺P20, U4;
child facs ✗LD7.30, nr lunch. Resid & Rest lic
£B&B £20; HB weekly £200; [10% V] **cc** Access,
B'card/Visa.

Woodlands House (Acclaimed)   Wordsworth St,
CA11 7QY ☎(0768) 64177.

*A small hotel with a library of maps for walkers,
nature lovers and sightseers. Wordsworth St is off
Drovers Lane, a turn off the A6.*
🛏8 bedrs, 6en suite, 1 ba; TV; tcf �📺TV, NS; P10;
U1; child facs ✗LD4, nr lunch, Wed & Sun dinner.
Resid lic
£B&B £15–£18, B&B (double) £28–£33; HB weekly
£152–£172; D £7.50; dep.

Using RAC discount vouchers
Please tell the hotel when booking if you plan to
use an RAC discount voucher (see end of guide)
in part payment of your bill. Only one voucher
will be accepted per party per stay. Discount
vouchers will only be accepted in payment for
accommodation, not for food.

Barco   Carleton Rd, CA11 8LR ☎(0768) 63176.

Limes Country   Redhills, Stainton, CA11 0DT
☎(0768) 63343.
*From M6 junction 40 travel W along A66 for ¼ mile,
turn left by Little Chef and follow road to the right
for ¼ mile. The Limes is on the right.*
🛏6 bedrs, 3 en suite, 2 ba; tcf �📺TV; P7; child
facs ✗LD 3, nr lunch. Resid lic
£ B&B £14–£20, B&B (double) £24–£35; HB weekly
£140–£180; WB (£17·50 Oct–Mar) **cc** B'card/Visa.

Voreda View   2 Portland Pl, CA11 7QN ☎(0768)
63395.
*A small family-run guest house. Follow signs for
town centre and town hall.*
🛏6 bedrs, 2 ba; TV; tcf �📺TV, dogs; P1, child facs
✗ Breakfast only. Unlic
£B&B £14–£18; B&B (double) £25–£30; [10% V
Sun]

PENRYN   Cornwall.   Map 28C2

Prospect House (Acclaimed)   1 Church Rd, TR10
8DA ☎(0326) 73198.

*Restored late Georgian house with walled rose
garden. Situated on the A39, 8 miles from Truro,
2 miles before Falmouth, opposite Volvo garage.*
🛏4 bedrs, 3 en suite, 1 ba; tcf �📺TV, dogs, ns; P3,
U1, G1; no children under 12 ✗LD 12 noon, nr
lunch. Unlic
£B&B £15–£20, B&B (double) £36–£40; HB weekly
£178·50–£248·50; [5% V Oct–Apr]; dep.

PENSFORD   Avon.   Map 29D7

Leigh Farm   Nr Bristol, BS18 4BA ☎(0761)
490281. *Farm*. Mrs Josephine Smart
Sleeps 6, ⛌
£ B&B from £14·50

The Model Farm   Norton Hawkfield, Bristol, BS18
4HA ☎(0272) 832144. *Farm*. Margaret Hasell
Sleeps 6, ns ⛌
£ B&B from £11

PENTON   Cumbria.   Map 22F5

Craigburn Farm   Catlowdy, Carlisle, CA6 5QP
☎(022877) 214. *Farm*. Jane and Jack Lawson

Sleeps 12, 🏨 ☕
£ B&B from £16, D £9

PENZANCE   Cornwall.   Map 28B2

Estoril (Highly Acclaimed)   46 Morrab Rd, TR18
4EX ✆ (0736) 62468.
*An elegant Victorian house, carefully modernised
yet retaining its period charm. Turn right off the
Promenade into Morrab Rd, hotel 150 yards on the
right. Open Feb–Dec.*
🛏10 bedrs, 10 en suite; TV; tcf 📺 P 4; ns; child
facs ✖ LD 7.30, nr Sunday lunch. Resid lic
£ B&B £23–£24; HB weekly £192·50–£220; D £10;
[10% V] **cc** Access, B'card/Visa; dep.

Tarbert (Highly Acclaimed)   11 Clarence St, TR18
2NU ✆ (0736) 63758.

*Listed Georgian building with exposed granite walls
and tranquil garden. Take Penzance by-pass
signposted Lands End, Turn left at second
roundabout, then right into Clarence St at
pedestrian precinct. Closed 1 Dec–14 Jan.*
🛏12 bedrs, 12 en suite, 1 ba; TV; tcf 📺 TV, ns; P 5;
no children under 7 ✖ LD 8, nr lunch. Resid lic
£ B&B £22·50–£25·50, B&B (double) £39–£51; HB
weekly £180–£216; WB (£55) **cc** Access, Amex,
B'card/Visa, Diners; dep.

Sea and Horses (Acclaimed)   6 Alexandra Terr,
TR18 4NX ✆ (0736) 61961.
*Travel along sea front towards Newlyn/Mousehole.
Situated 1 ¾ miles from station. Open mid Feb–mid
Nov.*
🛏11 bedrs, 8 en suite, (3 sh); TV; tcf 📺 P 11, G 1
(£2), child facs ✖ LD 6, nr lunch
£ B&B £16–£19; HB weekly £166–£185; D £8·95
cc Access, B'card/Visa; dep.

Alexandra   Alexandra Terr, TR18 4NX ✆ (0736)
62644.

Blue Seas   Regent Ter, TR18 4DW
✆ (0736) 64744.

Camilla House   12 Regent Terr, TR18 4DE
✆ (0736) 63771.
*Take seafront road off one-way system at railway
station, continue past harbour on to promenade
taking access road into terrace. Hotel 40 yards past
swimming pool.*
🛏8 bedrs, 4 en suite, 3 ba; TV 📺 TV, dogs, ns; P 6,
child facs ✖ LD a.m., nr lunch. Resid lic
£ B&B £14·50–£17·50, B&B (double) £29–£35; HB
weekly £135–£150; D £7; dep.

Carlton   Promenade, TR18 4NW ✆ (0736) 62081.
*Situated almost opposite corporation car park along
the sea front promenade. Open March–Oct.*
🛏10 bedrs, 8 en suite, 2 ba; TV; tcf 📺 TV, no
children under 12 ✖ Breakfast only. Rest lic
£ B&B £14–£15; [5% V] dep.

Carnson House   2 East Terr, TR18 2TD ✆ (0736)
65589.
*A charming 250-year-old hotel close to the harbour.
Situated on the main road approaching the town
centre from the E.*
🛏8 bedrs, 2 en suite, 1 ba; TV; tcf 📺 TV, ns; no
children under 10 ✖ LD 4, nr lunch. Resid lic
£ B&B £13·50-£15·50, B&B (double) £25–£34; HB
weekly £120–£162·50; D £7·50; [5% V] **cc** Access,
Amex, B'card/Visa, Diners; dep.

Dunedin   Alexandra Rd, TR18 4LZ ✆ (0736)
62652.
*Pleasant well-furnished Victorian house. Follow
seafront to Alexandra Rd, and Dunedin is on the
right.*
🛏9 bedrs, 8 en suite, (1 sh), TV; tcf 📺 TV, dogs; ns;
coach; no children under 3, child facs ✖ LD 4.30,
nr lunch. Resid lic
£ B&B £12–£14; HB weekly £124–£132; D £6; dep.

Georgian House   20 Chapel St, TR18 4AW
✆ (0736) 65664.
*Attractive family-run hotel situated in historic Chapel
St, which runs from the main shopping centre to the
preomenade and harbour.*
🛏12 bedrs, 6 en suite, 2 ba; TV; tcf 📺 TV, dogs;
P 11, child facs ✖ LD 8.30, nr lunch, dinner Sun.
Resid & Rest lic

£B&B £16·10–£20·70, B&B (double) £26–£34·50; D £7·50 **cc** Access, B'card/Visa; dep.

Keigwin Alexandra Rd, TR18 4LZ ✆ (0736) 63930.
Keep to coast road past station, cross swing bridge, and take second exit at mini roundabout. Hotel is 200 metres on the right. Closed Xmas.
⇥8 bedrs, 5 en suite, 1 ba; TV; tcf �📺child facs ✗LD 9 am, nr lunch. Resid lic
£B&B £10·50, B&B (double) £21–£31; HB weekly £105–£133; D £7 **cc** Access, B'card/Visa; dep.

Kimberley House 10 Morrab Rd, TR18 4EZ ✆ (0736) 62727.
Large Victorian house of charm and character situated between the main shopping street and the promenade. Closed January.
⇥9 bedrs, 3 ba; TV; tcf �📺TV; P 4, coach; no children under 5 ✗LD 5, nr lunch. Resid lic
£B&B £12–£13; HB weekly £114–£124; D £7 **cc** Access, B'card/Visa.

Lynwood 41 Morrab Rd, TR18 4EX ✆ (0736) 65871.
Comfortable family guest house close to Morrab Gardens. Morrab Rd lies between the Promenade and the A30.
⇥6 bedrs, 3 ba; TV; tcf �📺TV, dogs, ns; child facs ✗Breakfast only. Unlic
£B&B £11–£12, B&B (double) £21–£23; [5% V]. **cc** B'card/Visa; dep.

Mount Royal Chyandour Cliff, TR18 3LQ ✆ (0736) 62233.
Small hotel with uninterrupted coastal views, situated on old A30 road entering Penzance from the E. Open Apr–Oct.
⇥8 bedrs, 5 en suite, 2 ba; TV; tcf �📺TV, dogs, P 6, U 4 (£3); child facs ✗Breakfast only. Unlic
£B&B £24–£26; B&B (double) £34–£38; [10% V] dep.

Panorama Chywoone Hill, Newlyn, TR18 5AR ✆ (0736) 68498.

Pass the station, follow the harbour road along the promenade to Newlyn Bridge, cross over and continue up the hill. Hotel on the left.
⇥8 bedrs, 4 en suite, 1 ba; TV; tcf �📺TV, P 12, coach; no children under 3 ✗LD 4, nr lunch. Resid lic
£ B&B £16–£19; D £9; HB weekly £166-£186; [5% V] **cc** Access, Amex, B'card/Visa, Diners; dep.

Penmorvah Alexandra Rd, TR18 4LZ ✆ (0736) 63711 or 60100.
Small, quiet hotel set in a lovely tree-lined avenue, 350 yards from the main promenade.
⇥10 bedrs, one en suite; TV; tcf �📺dogs; coach; child facs ✗LD 6, nr lunch. Resid lic
cc Access, Amex, B'card/Visa; dep.

Southern Comfort Alexandra Ter, Sea Front, TR18 4NX ✆ (0736) 66333. *Hotel.*

Trevelyan 16 Chapel St, TR18 4AW ✆ (0736) 62494.
Turn left into Chapel St at the top of the town centre. Hotel halfway down on left. Closed Xmas.
⇥8 bedrs, 1 en suite, (6 sh), 2 ba; TV; tcf ⏏TV; P 6, coach; child facs ✗LD midday, Resid lic
£B&B £11–£12; HB weekly £115–£120; D £6; dep.

Trewella 18 Mennaye Rd, TR18 4NG ✆ (0736) 63818.
Attractive guest house between the Promenade and the old A30. Open Mar–Oct.
⇥8 bedrs, 2 en suite, (1 sh) 1 ba; tcf ⏏TV, dogs, no children under 3 ✗LD l2 noon, nr lunch. Resid lic
£B&B £10·25–£12·75, HB weekly £106·75–£124·25; [5% V Mar–Jun, Sept & Oct 3 or more days]; dep.

Woodstock 29 Morrab Rd, TR18 4EZ ✆ (0736) 69049.
A charming granite-built Victorian house situated off the seafront. Turn right at Strollers Restaurant.
⇥5 bedrs, (1 sh), 2 ba; TV; tcf ⏏TV; ✗Breakfast only. Unlic

Penzance (Cornwall)

£ B&B £9·50–£13·50; [10% V Oct, Nov, Jan, Feb] **cc** Access, Amex, B'card/Visa, Diners; dep.

PERRANPORTH Cornwall. Map 28C2

Villa Margarita Country (Acclaimed) Bone Mill Rd, Bolingey, TR6 0AS ☎ Truro (0872) 572063.
A colonial villa set in pretty gardens in a peaceful valley within sight and sound of the sea. From A3075 turn towards Perranporth at Perranzubuloe Church/White House Inn crossroads. Hotel is nearly a mile on right. Swimming pool.
🛏 7 bedrs, 5 en suite, (2 sh), 1 ba; tcf 🏠 TV; P 8; no children under 8 ✕ LD 5, nr lunch. Resid lic
£ B&B £18·50, B&B (double) £34–£37; HB weekly £176–£185; dep.

Beach Dunes Ramoth Way, Reen Sands, TR6 0BY ☎ Truro (0872) 572263 Fax: (0872) 572263.
Indoor swimming pool, squash.
🛏 10 bedrs, 6 en suite, 1 ba; TV; tcf 🏠 dogs, ns; P 16; no children under 3 ✕ LD 7.30, bar meals only lunch. Resid & Rest lic
cc Access, B'card/Visa; dep.

Cellar Cove Droskyn Way, TR6 0DS ☎ Truro (0872) 572110. *Swimming pool.*
🛏 14 bedrs, 4 en suite, 4 ba; TV; tcf 🏠 TV, dogs; P 20, coach; child facs ✕ LD 12 noon, nr lunch. Resid & Rest lic
cc Access, B'card/Visa; dep.

Fairview Tywarnhayle Rd, TR6 0DX ☎ Truro (0872) 572278.
Detached Victorian house with views across the porth. Drive up Cliff Rd to the top, and Tywarnhayle Rd is on the left. Open Mar–Oct.
🛏 15 bedrs, 1 en suite, (4 sh), 3 ba; tcf 🏠 TV, dogs, ns; P 7, G 3, coach; child facs ✕ nr lunch. Resid & Rest lic
£ B&B £12·60–£14·50; HB weekly £110; D £5
cc Access, B'card/Visa; dep.

PETERBOROUGH Cambridgeshire. Map 25A1

Hawthorn House (Acclaimed) 89 Thorpe Rd, PE3 6JQ ☎ (0733) 40608.
A Victorian residence furnished and equipped to a high standard. Follow sign to city centre or district hospital.
🛏 8 bedrs, 8 en suite, TV; tcf 🏠 dogs, ns; P 11 ✕ LD 9, nr lunch or Fri–Sun dinner. Resid lic
£ B&B £38·25–£43·25, B&B (double) £43·25–£49·25; [10% V] **cc** Access, B'card/Visa, Diners; dep.

Thorpe Lodge (Acclaimed) 83 Thorpe Rd, PE3 6JQ ☎ (0733) 48759.
🛏 22 bedrs, 15 en suite, 2 ba; TV; tcf 🏠 TV, P 20; ✕ LD 9, nr lunch, Fri-Sun dinner. Resid & Rest lic
£ B&B £36·50–£48·50, B&B (double) £53–£64; D £10; WB **cc** Access, B'card/Visa; dep.

Aaron Park 109 Park Rd, PE1 2TR ☎ (0733) 64849.
Family run hotel in the city centre, 5 mins from the Queensgate Shopping Complex.
🛏 17 bedrs, 4 en suite, (7 sh), 3 ba; TV; tcf 🏠 TV, dogs, ns; P 10, coach ✕ LD 2 pm, nr lunch. Resid & Rest lic
£ B&B £22–£40, B&B (double) £38–£52; [10% V]
cc Access, B'card/Visa; dep.

Dalwhinnie Lodge 31 Burghley Rd, PE1 2QA ☎ (0733) 65968.
Situated ½ mile N of city centre just off A15.
🛏 17 bedrs, 2 en suite, (4 sh), 3 ba; TV; tcf 🏠 TV, dogs, ns; P 14, coach; child facs ✕ LD midday, nr lunch, Fri–Sun dinner. Resid lic
£ B&B £19–£27, B&B (double) £31–£39
cc Access, B'card/Visa.

PETERSFIELD Hampshire. Map 26E3

Brocklands Farm West Meon, GU32 1JN ☎ (073 086) 228/325. *Farm.* Sue Wilson ♿
Sleeps 6, 🐕 ns
£ B&B from £13–£15

PEVENSEY BAY East Sussex. Map 27C2

Napier The Promenade, BN24 6HD ☎ (0323) 768875.
Situated on the A259 between Bexhill and Eastbourne. Open Mar–Oct.
🛏 10 bedrs, 5 en suite, (3 sh), 1 ba; TV; tcf 🏠 TV, dogs, ns; P 5 ✕ LD 4·30, nr lunch. Resid lic
£ B&B £15–£17; HB weekly £110–£125; WB; [5% V Mar, Apr, Sept, Oct]; dep.

PILSLEY Derbyshire. Map 24D4

Shoulder of Mutton Inn Hardstoft, S48 8AF ☎ Chesterfield (0246) 850276.

PINKSMOOR Somerset. Map 29B5

Pinksmoor Millhouse Wellington, TA21 0HD ☎ (0823) 672361. *Farm.* Mrs Nancy K M Ash
Sleeps 6, 🐕 ns 🐴
£ B&B from £15, D £10·50

PLYMOUTH Devon. Map 28F2

Georgian House (Highly Acclaimed) 51 Citadel Rd, The Hoe PL1 3AU ☎ (0752) 663237. Closed Xmas–mid Jan.
🛏 12 bedrs, 12 en suite, 1 ba; TV; tcf 🏠 TV, dogs; child facs ✕ LD 9, nr lunch & Sun dinner

£ B&B £28–£30, B&B (double) £38–£40
cc Access, Amex, B'card/Visa, Diners; dep.

Alexander   20 Woodland Terr, Greenbank Rd,
Greenbank, PL4 8NL ✆ (0752) 663247.
Situated on Greenbank Rd near the hospitals.
🛏 7 bedrs, (5 sh), 1 ba; TV; tcf 📺 TV, ns; P 7, coach;
child facs ✕ LD 12 noon. Resid & Rest lic
£ B&B £11–£15; HB weekly £140; D £6 cc B'card/
Visa; dep.

Benvenuto   69 Hermitage Rd, Mannamead, PL3
4RZ ✆ (0752) 667030.
*Small comfortable guest house. Travel N through
Mutley Plain shopping area, at Hyde Park Rd, first
right and hotel is on the right.*
🛏 8 bedrs, (2 sh), 2 ba; tcf 📺 TV, dogs; child
facs ✕ LD 4, nr lunch. Resid lic
£ B&B £12·50, B&B (double) £22; dep.

Bowling Green   9 Osborne Pl, Lockyer St, PL1
2PU ✆ (0752) 667485.
*Follow signs to city centre, then the Hoe, and turn
left into Lockyer St.* Closed Xmas.
🛏 12 bedrs, 7 en suite, (5 sh); TV; tcf 📺 TV, dogs;
U 4 (£2); child facs ✕ Breakfast only. Unlic
£ B&B £20–£27, B&B (double) £28–£38; WB
cc Access, B'card/Visa; dep.

Carnegie   172 Citadel Rd, The Hoe, PL1 3BD
✆ (0752) 225158.
🛏 8 bedrs, 1 en suite, (3 sh), 2 ba; TV; tcf 📺 TV;
child facs ✕ LD 6.30, nr lunch. Resid lic
cc Access, Amex, B'card/Visa, Diners; dep.

Devonia   27 Grand Par, West Hoe, PL1 3DQ
✆ (0752) 665026.
*Follow seafront signs and Devonia is first guest
house on left.* Closed Jan.
🛏 6 bedrs, (5 sh), 1 ba; TV; tcf 📺 dogs ✕ Breakfast
only. Unlic
£ B&B £15–£20, B&B (double) £30–£35; dep.

Dudley   42 Sutherland Rd, Mutley, PL4 6BN
✆ (0752) 668322.

*Situated half-way between Mutley Plain and the
railway station opposite the Royal Eye Infirmary.*
🛏 6 bedrs, 1 ba; TV; tcf 📺 TV, dogs; coach ✕ LD 9
am, nr lunch. Unlic
£ B&B £14, B&B (double) £24; HB weekly £122
cc Access, B'card/Visa; dep.

Gables End   29 Sutherland Rd, Mutley, PL4 6BW
✆ (0752) 220803.
🛏 7 bedrs, 2 ba; TV; tcf 📺 TV, dogs, ns;
G 5 ✕ LD 3, nr lunch & Sun dinner. Unlic

Glendevon   20 Ford Park Rd, Mutley, PL4 6RB
✆ (0752) 663655. *Hotel.*

Headland   1a Radford Rd, West Hoe, PL1 3BY
✆ (0752) 660866.

Lockyer House   2 Alfred St, The Hoe, PL1 2RP
✆ (0752) 665755.
🛏 6 bedrs, 1 ba; TV 📺 TV; children over 8 ✕ LD 1,
nr lunch. Resid lic

Merville   73 Citadel Rd, The Hoe, PL1 3AX
✆ (0752) 667595.
Situated in road parallel to the Hoe.
🛏 10 bedrs, 2 ba; TV; tcf 📺 TV, dogs, ns; ✕ LD 12
noon, nr lunch & Sat–Sun dinner. Resid lic
£ B&B £11, B&B (double) £24; D £6; dep.

Oliver's   33 Sutherland Rd, Mutley, PL4 6BN
✆ (0752) 663923.
🛏 6 bedrs, 4 en suite, 1 ba; TV; tcf 📺 ns; P 3; no
children under 11 ✕ LD 9, nr lunch & Sun dinner.
cc Access, Amex, B'card/Visa, Diners; dep.

Phantele   176 Devonport Rd, Stoke, PL1 5RD
✆ (0752) 561506.
*From A38 take A386 to Stoke, and guest house is
¼ mile past shop. Do not turn right for Torpoint.*
Closed Xmas.
🛏 6 bedrs, 2 en suite, 2 ba; tcf 📺 TV, ns; child
facs ✕ LD 4, nr lunch. Resid lic
£ B&B £10·50–£15·50, B&B (double) £20–£26; HB
weekly £94·50–£114; dep.

Plymouth (Devon)

Riviera   8 Elliott St, The Hoe, PL1 2PP ✆(0752) 667379. *Hotel.*

Russell Lodge   9 Holyrood Pl, The Hoe, PL1 2BQ ✆(0752) 667774.
1 min walk from the Drake Memorial statue on the Hoe Promenade. Open Mar–Oct.
🛏8 bedrs, 2 en suite, (6 sh), 2 ba; TV; tcf 🛉TV, ns; P3, child facs ✗Breakfast only. Resid lic £B&B £16–£18, B&B (double) £32–£35; [5% V 2 nights min]   **cc** Access, Amex, B'card/Visa, Diners; dep.

St James   49 Citadel Rd, The Hoe, PL1 3AU ✆(0752) 661950.
From A38 follow signs to city centre and Hoe, and Citadel Rd runs parallel with Esplanade.

Swinton   43 Sutherland Rd, Mutley, PL4 6BN ✆(0752) 660887. *Private Hotel.*

Trillium   4 Alfred St, The Hoe, PL1 2RP ✆(0752) 670452.
Family run guest house close to the city centre, Barbican and ferry.
🛏7 bedrs, 3 en suite, (2 sh), 1 ba; TV; tcf 🛉TV; P3; child facs ✗ nr lunch. Resid lic £ B&B £16–£20; D £9·50

Victoria Court   62 North Rd East, PL4 6AL ✆(0752) 668133.
Follow city centre signs to railway station and into North Rd East. Closed Xmas–New Year.
🛏14 bedrs, 7 en suite, 2 ba; TV; tcf 🛉TV; P6, coach; child facs ✗LD7, nr lunch. Rest lic £B&B £18–£28, B&B (double) £30–£42; D £8·50; [10% V w/e Oct–Apr]   **cc** Access, B'card/Visa.

POLBATHIC   Cornwall.   Map 28E2

Old Mill House   Torpoint, PL11 3HA ✆St Germans (0503) 30596.

A 300-year-old mill overlooking the river. Follow A38 over Tamar Bridge for about 8 miles to Trerulefoot roundabout. Take left exit and continue for 2 miles. Mill on left.
🛏8 bedrs, 2 ba; tcf 🛉TV, dogs, ns; P12, coach; child facs ✗LD8, nr lunch. Resid & Rest lic £B&B £10–£12, HB weekly £100–£150; D £6; [10% V]; dep.

Hendra Farm   Torpoint, PL11 3DT ✆(05035) 225. *Farm.* Mrs A Hoskin
Sleeps 6, ns 🛏
£ B&B from £10

POLPERRO   Cornwall.   Map 28E2

Landaviddy Manor   Landaviddy Lane, PL13 2RT ✆(0503) 72210.

Lanhael House   Langreek Rd, PL13 2PW ✆(0503) 72428.
17th century house with beamed ceilings, situated down Langreek Rd, a turning oppostie Crumple Horn Inn. Swimming pool. Open Mar–Oct.
🛏6 bedrs, 2 en suite, (1 sh), 2 ba 🛉TV, ns; P6; no children under 14 ✗Breakfast only. Unlic £B&B £18–£20, B&B (double) £29–£32; dep.

Mill House   Mill Hill, PL13 2RP ✆(0503) 72362. *Hotel.*

Penryn House   The Coombes, PL13 2RG ✆(0503) 72157. *Hotel.*

POLZEATH   Cornwall.   Map 28D3

White Lodge   Old Polzeath, PL27 6TJ ✆Trebetherick (020886) 2370.
A pleasant hotel situated on high ground. Open mid Jan–Dec.
🛏9 bedrs, 3 en suite, 4 ba; TV; tcf 🛉TV, dogs, ns;

P 15; child facs ✕LD 10, lunch by arrangement. Resid lic
£ B&B £15–£20; HB weekly £140–£192·50; L £4, D £9; WB; dep.

PONTRILAS Herefordshire. Map 31D7

Rowlestone Court Hereford, HR2 0DW ✆ (0981) 240322. *Farm*. Mrs Margaret Williams
Sleeps 5
£ B&B from £13

POOLE Dorset. Map 26C2

Sheldon Lodge (Acclaimed) 22 Forest Rd, Branksome Park, BH13 6DA ✆ Bournemouth (0202) 761186.
Attractive hotel with light and airy rooms. Follow Bournemouth road signs, not Poole, to Frizzel Insurance building at Westbourne. Billiards, solarium.
⍻14 bedrs, 14 en suite; TV; tcf ♠TV dogs, ns; P 10, coach; child facs ✕LD 7, nr lunch. Resid lic
£ B&B £22–£24; HB weekly £210–£224; D £9; dep.

Avoncourt 245 Bournemouth Rd, Parkstone, BH14 9HX ✆ (0202) 732025.
Situated on A35 between Poole and Bournemouth. Closed mid Dec–Jan.
⍻6 bedrs, (2 sh), 1 ba; TV; tcf ♠TV; P 6, U 1, coach; child facs ✕LD 10 am, nr lunch. Resid lic
cc Access, B'card/Visa; dep.

Bays 82 Bournemouth Rd, Parkstone, BH14 0HA ✆ Parkstone (0202) 740116.
A small, convenient guest house on the A35 between Bournemouth and Poole. Closed Jan.
⍻6 bedrs, 1 en suite, (1 sh), 1 ba; TV; tcf ♠TV, dogs, ns; P 8; no children under 5 ✕ Breakfast only. Unlic
£ B&B £15–£17; dep.

Lewina Lodge 225 Bournemouth Rd, Parkstone, BH14 9HU ✆ Parkstone (0202) 742295.

PORLOCK Somerset. Map 29A6

Lorna Doone (Acclaimed) High St, TA24 8PS ✆ (0643) 862404.

Built by Byron's nephew, the Earl of Lovelace, in 1886, an attractive white-walled hotel. On the A39 in the centre of Porlock village.
⍻13 bedrs, 7 en suite, 3 ba; TV; tcf ♠TV, dogs; P 8, coach ✕LD 9, nr lunch. Resid & Rest lic
£ B&B £15–£16·50; L £5·50, D £7·50; [5% V except BH] cc Access, B'card/Visa; dep.

PORTESHAM Dorset. Map 29D3

Millmead (Acclaimed) DT3 4HE ✆ Abbotsbury (0305) 871432.
A family-run, sympathetically extended Victorian hotel with country house atmosphere situated on B3157 on edge of village of Portesham, midway between Weymouth and Bridport.
⍻8 bedrs, 5 en suite, (3 sh), 1 ba; TV ♠dogs, NS; P 20; no children under 10 ✕LD 7.30. Resid & Rest lic
£ B&B £19·50–£30·25; HB weekly £203·50–£275; L £7·50, D £11·50; [5% V except June–Sept] cc Access, B'card/Visa; dep.

PORT ISAAC Cornwall. Map 28D3

Bay 1 The Terrace, PL29 3SC ✆ Bodmin (0208) 880380.
Small hotel in prominent position overlooking the sea. Take B3267 from Wadebridge to Port Isaac, hotel is on cliff top opposite main public car park. Open Easter–Oct.
⍻10 bedrs, 3 en suite, (1 sh), 2 ba ♠TV, dogs; P 10, coach; child facs ✕LD 9, nr lunch. Resid & Rest lic
£ B&B £15·50–£23·50; HB weekly £161–£190; D £7; WB (£57.50 3 nights); dep.

Fairholme 30 Trewetha La, PL29 3RW ✆ Bodmin (0208) 880397.

Using RAC discount vouchers
Please tell the hotel when booking if you plan to use an RAC discount voucher (see end of guide) in part payment of your bill. Only one voucher will be accepted per party per stay. Discount vouchers will only be accepted in payment for accommodation, not for food.

Small family-run guest house situated on main road through village, on the corner of a private road called Lundy. Open Etr–Oct.
⇴6 bedrs, 2 en suite, 2 ba; TV; tcf �📺TV, dogs, ns; P 7; child facs ✕nr lunch. Resid lic
£B&B £12–£17·50, B&B (double) £24–£32; HB weekly £133–£164; D £7·50; [5% V Mar–May w/d]
cc Access, B'card/Visa; dep.

St Andrews The Terrace, PL29 3SG ☎Bodmin (0208) 880240.
⇴13 bedrs, 6 en suite, 3 ba; tcf �📺TV, dogs, ns; P 12; child facs ✕LD 8. Resid & Rest lic

PORTSMOUTH AND SOUTHSEA Hampshire. Map 26E2

Seacrest (Highly Acclaimed) 12 South Par, PO5 2JB ☎(0705) 733192 Fax: (0705) 832523.
Part of an early Victorian terrace on picturesque sea front. Follow signs for sea front; hotel is opposite the Pyramids.
⇴27 bedrs, 27 en suite; TV; tcf �📺lift, dogs, ns; P 8, coach; child facs ✕LD 4, nr lunch. Resid lic
£ B&B £30–£35, B&B (double) £42–£48; HB weekly £180–£210; D £10·50; [10% V Nov–Apr, 7 days]
cc Access, B'card/Visa; dep.

Hamilton House (Acclaimed) 95 Victoria Rd North, PO5 1PS ☎(0705) 823502. ✵ Fr.
From M275, at end of dual carriageway take first left at roundabout, follow road past church, across 3 roundabouts. Road now Victoria Road North, hotel on right.
⇴8 bedrs, 3 en suite, 1 ba; TV; tcf �📺TV; coach; child facs ✕nr lunch. Unlic
£B&B £12·50–£14; HB weekly £119–£129·50; [10% V Nov–Feb]; dep.

Rock Gardens (Acclaimed) Clarence Rd, PO5 2LQ ☎(0705) 833018.
Small family run hotel in a quiet residential area. Clarence Rd runs parallel with South Parade, 5 mins from the pier.
⇴15 bedrs, 8 en suite, (6 sh), l ba; TV; tcf �📺TV, dogs, ns; P 6; child facs ✕LD 6, nr lunch. Resid lic
£ B&B £20–£25, B&B (double) £30–£36; HB weekly £110–£125; D £7

Turret (Acclaimed) Clarence Par, PO5 2HZ ☎(0705) 291810.
Small hotel with distinctive turret.
⇴13 bedrs, 7 en suite, 3 ba; TV; tcf ⏚TV; no children under 4 ✕Breakfast only.
£ B&B £30, B&B (double) £40–£50 **cc** Access, Amex, B'card/Visa; dep.

Westfield Hall (Acclaimed) 65 Festing Rd, PO4 ONQ ☎(0705) 826971 Fax: (0705) 870200.

Detached hotel near sea front. All bedrooms with satellite TV and video channel. Five ground-floor bedrooms. From sea front turn left into St. Helen's Parade, opposite South Parade Pier, to fourth road on left, first past canoe lake.
⇴17 bedrs, 14 en suite, 3 ba; TV; tcf ⏚TV; P 12, coach; no children under 5 ✕LD 6, nr Mon–Sat lunch, Sun dinner. Resid lic
£ B&B £22–£34, B&B (double) £41–48; HB weekly £177–£198; WB (low season); [10% V low season]
cc Access, B'card/Visa; dep.

Abbeville 26 Nettlecombe Av, PO4 0QW ☎(0705) 826209

Amberley Court 97 Waverley Rd, PO5 2PL ☎(0705) 735419. *Guest House.*

Annaley 63 Clarendon Rd, PO5 2JX ☎(0705) 825525. Fax: (0705) 296829.
Small comfortable guest house, on road running parallel with the sea front.
⇴8 bedrs, 3 ba; TV; tcf ⏚TV, dogs; child facs ✕LD 7.30, nr lunch, Fri–Sun dinner. Unlic
£ B&B £15, B&B (double) £28; HB weekly £126; [5% V]; dep.

Aquarius Court 34 St Ronan's Rd, PO4 0PT ☎(0705) 822872.
Small friendly guest house 5 mins from South Parade Pier.
⇴12 bedrs, 2 ba; TV; tcf ⏚TV, P 5, coach; child facs ✕LD 4.30, Resid lic
£ B&B £13–£14; HB weekly £115–£125; L £5, D £5·50; [10% V]; dep.

Ashwood 10 St Davids Rd, PO5 1QN ☎(0705) 816228. Closed Xmas & New Year.
⇴6 bedrs, 2 ba; TV; tcf ⏚TV ✕Breakfast only. Unlic. dep.

Birchwood 44 Waverley Rd, PO5 2PP ☎(0705) 811337. *Guest House.*
⇴5 bedrs, 2 en suite, 1 ba; TV; tcf ⏚TV, dogs, ns; coach; child facs ✕LD 3, nr lunch. Resid lic

Bristol 55 Clarence Par, PO5 2HX ☎(0705) 821815.
Clarence Parade lies alongside Southsea Common.

◄13 bedrs, 11 en suite, 2 ba; TV; tcf 🛉TV; P 7, coach; child facs ✗Breakfast only. Resid lic
£ B&B £15·50–£32, B&B (double) £31–£42
cc Access, B'card/Visa; dep.

Collingham 89 St Ronan's Rd, PO4 0PR ✆(0705) 821549.
Going E along seafront, pass South Parade Pier and Canoe Lake, turn left at Festing Rd, then left and left again and Collingham is next left.
◄6 bedrs, 2 ba; tcf 🛉TV, dogs, ns; coach; child facs ✗Breakfast only. Unlic.
£ B&B £12·50; [10% V]

Dolphins 10 Western Par, PO5 3JF ✆(0705) 820833 or 820823.
Comfortable hotel overlooking the sea and Southsea Common. Situated opposite Clarence Pier.
◄32 bedrs, 19 en suite, (2 sh), 5 ba; TV; tcf 🛉TV, dogs; coach; child facs ✗LD9.50, nr lunch, dinner Sun. Resid & Rest lic
£ B&B £22–£30, B&B (double) £36–£42; HB weekly £200–£260; WB (£20–£28 B&B); [10% V Jan–Apr & Nov] **cc** Access, Amex, B'card/Visa, Diners; dep.

Dorcliffe 42 Waverley Rd, PO5 2PP ✆(0705) 828283.

Attractive guest house situated inland from South Parade Pier. Follow Burgoyne Rd to roundabout, cross over into Waverley Rd, and Dorcliffe is 100 yds on right, opposite park.
◄7 bedrs, 2 ba; tcf 🛉TV, dogs, ns; coach; child facs ✗LD4.30, nr lunch, Resid lic
£B&B £11–£14; HB weekly £102–£111; dep.

Gainsborough House 9 Malvern Rd, PO5 2LZ ✆(0705) 822604.
Long-established guest house, 2 mins from the seafront. From the Pyramids Leisure Centre, Florence Rd is opposite, and Malvern Rd is the second turning off. Closed Xmas–New Year.
◄7 bedrs, 2 ba; tcf 🛉TV, ns; no children under 3 ✗Breakfast only. Unlic
£B&B £12–£13·50; dep.

Goodwood House 1 Taswell Rd, Southsea, PO5 2RG ✆(0705) 824734. ✸ Fr.
From sea front opposite South Parade Pier, turn up Clarendon Rd, over roundabout then third turning on right into Worthing Rd, first right into Taswell Rd. Closed 24 Dec–1 Jan.
◄8 bedrs, (4 sh), 2 ba; TV; tcf 🛉ns; child facs ✗LD 6, nr lunch. Resid lic
£ B&B £11–£14; B&B (double) £20–£28; HB weekly £102–£120; D £7

Southsea (Hampshire)

Saville   38 Clarence Par, PO5 2EU ☎(0705) 822491. ✗ Ar, De.
Well placed hotel on sea front opposite the D-Day museum and overlooking gardens. Billiards.
⌘45 bedrs, 21 en suite, 8 ba; TV; tcf 🎧 lift, TV, dogs; G 4, coach; child facs ✗LD noon, nr lunch (& dinner low season). Resid lic
£ B&B £19–£28, B&B (double) £30–£40; HB weekly £145–£190; D £7; [10% V] **cc** Access, Amex, B'card/Visa, Diners; dep.

Upper Mount House   The Vale, Clarendon Rd, PO5 2EQ ☎(0705) 820456.
From D-Day museum go north to shopping precinct. Turn right at T junction; The Vale is first turning on right.
⌘11 bedrs, 10 en suite, 1 ba; TV; tcf 🎧 dogs, ns; P 9, coach; child facs ✗LD 6, nr lunch. Resid lic
£B&B £19–£28, B&B (double) £30–£46; HB weekly £120–£160; D £6·75; WB £17; [V Oct–May] **cc** Access, B'card/Visa; dep.

Victoria Court   29 Victoria Rd North, PO5 1PL ☎(0705) 820305.
Hotel under refurbishment.

POULSHOT   Wiltshire.   Map 26C5

Poulshot Lodge Farm   Devizes, SN10 1RQ ☎(0380) 828255. *Farm.* Diana Hues
Sleeps 5, ⌷ ♙
£ B&B from £15

POYNINGS   East Sussex.   Map 27B3

Manor Farm   Nr Brighton, BN45 7AG ☎(0273) 857371. *Farm.* Mrs Carol Revell
Sleeps 8, ns ⌷
£ B&B from £15, D £6·50

PRESTON   Lancashire.   Map 23A2

Tulketh (Highly Acclaimed)   209 Tulketh Rd, PR2 1ES ☎(0772) 728096.

A fine Edwardian building with a magnificent stained glass window. Modern bedroom extension. From A59 take A5085 (A583) towards Blackpool for 3.2 miles. Turn left into Tulketh Road (after 2nd rail bridge) at traffic lights. Closed 24 Dec–1 Jan.
⌘12 bedrs, 11 en suite, (1 sh), 2 ba; TV; tcf 🎧 TV,

P 12; child facs ✗LD 7·30, nr lunch. Resid & Rest lic
£B&B £26–£36, B&B (double) £38–£46; WB £19; [5% V on 2 nts] **cc** Access, B'card/Visa, dep.

Fulwood Park   49 Watling St Rd, Fulwood, PR2 4EA ☎(0772) 718067. *Hotel.*   ♿

PRESTON BROCKHURST   Shropshire.
Map 24A3

Grove Farm   Shrewsbury, SY4 5QA ☎(093 928) 223. *Farm.* Mrs Janet Jones
Sleeps 6, ns ⌷ (5)
£ B&B from £14

PULLOXHILL   Bedfordshire.   Map 26F7

Pond Farm   7 High Street, MK45 5HA ☎(0525) 712316. *Farm.* Judy Tookey
Sleeps 6, ⌷
£ B&B from £13·50–£18, D £8·50

RADFORD   Avon.   Map 29D6

Old Malt House   Timsbury, BA3 1QF ☎Timsbury (0761) 70106.
From A367 (Bath) take B135 for about 4 miles. Follow signs to Radford Farm and Shire Stables. Closed Xmas.
⌘10 bedrs, 10 en suite; TV; tcf 🎧P 40, coach; children over 3 ✗LD 8.30, nr lunch
£B&B £29–£30·50, B&B (double) £48–£51; HB weekly £234·50–£252; D £11·75; WB (£68 2 nts HB); [5% V] **cc** Access, Amex, B'card/Visa, Diners; dep.

RADFORD SEMELE   Warwickshire.
Map 26D8

Hill Farm   Lewis Road, Leamington Spa, CV31 1UX ☎(0926) 337571. *Farm.* Rebecca Gibbs
Sleeps 12, ⌷
£ B&B from £12–£15, D £10

Sharmer Farm   Fosse Way, Leamington Spa, CV31 1XH ☎(0926) 612448. *Farm.* Nora Ellis
Sleeps 8, ⌷
£ B&B from £13–£18

Using RAC discount vouchers
Please tell the hotel when booking if you plan to use an RAC discount voucher (see end of guide) in part payment of your bill. Only one voucher will be accepted per party per stay. Discount vouchers will only be accepted in payment for accommodation, not for food.

RAMSGATE   Kent.   Map 27F5

Goodwin View   19 Wellington Cres, CT11 8JD
☎(0843) 591419.
*From A253 follow signs to Ramsgate harbour, travel
up Madeira Walk into Wellington Cres. Goodwin
View almost opposite bandstand.*
⇌13 bedrs, 3 en suite, 3 ba; TV; tcf 📺TV; coach;
no children under 3 ✗LD3, nr lunch Mon–Sat &
Sun dinner. Resid lic
£B&B £19–£25, B&B (double) £34–£44·50; HB
weekly £154–£205; L £7·50, D £7·50; dep.

St Hilary   21 Crescent Rd, CT11 9QU ☎Thanet
(0843) 591427.
*Small hotel within walking distance of beaches.
Follow ferry sign onto B2504, at mini-roundabout
turn into West Cliffs Rd, and take second left.*
⇌7 bedrs, (3 sh), 1 ba 📺TV, ns; children over 4
✗LD3, nr lunch. Resid lic
£B&B £14–£16, B&B (double) £24–£28; HB weekly
£68–£80; WB (£20); [10% V w/d Sept–Jul]
cc Access, B'card/Visa; dep.

RAVENGLASS   Cumbria.   Map 22E4

St Michael's   Muncaster, CA18 1RD
☎(06577) 362.

RAWTENSTALL   Lancs.   Map 33B4

Lindau   131 Haslingden Old Rd, nr Rossendale,
BB4 8RR ☎(0706) 214592.

REDHILL   Surrey.   Map 27A4

Ashleigh House   39 Redstone Hill, RH1 4BG
☎(0737) 764763.
*A family-run Edwardian hotel, situated on A25 500
yards from Redhill station. Swimming pool. Closed
Xmas.*
⇌9 bedrs, 1 en suite, (2 sh), 2ba 📺TV;
P9 ✗Breakfast only. Unlic
£B&B £22–£24, B&B (double) £36–£44; dep.

REDMILE   Leicestershire (Notts).   Map 24E3

Peacock Farm (Acclaimed)   NG13 0GQ ☎(0949)
42475.   ♿
*Follow signs to Belvoir Castle, and Peacock Farm
is ⅓ mile out of village. Indoor swimming pool.
Snooker.*
⇌10 bedrs, 6 en suite, 2 ba; TV; tcf 📺TV, ns; P40,
coach; child facs ✗LD 8.30, nr Tues–Fri & Sun,
nr lunch Mon & Sat. Rest lic
£B&B £16·50, B&B (double) £28–£34; D £14·50;
[10% V] **cc** Access, B'card/Visa; dep.

REDRUTH   Cornwall.   Map 28C2

Lyndhurst   80 Agar Rd, TR15 3NB ☎(0209)
215146.
⇌8 bedrs, 4 en suite; 1 ba; tcf 📺TV; P8;
child facs ✗LD midday. nr lunch. Unlic
£B&B £11, B&B (double) £26; HB weekly £90; dep.

REIGATE   Surrey.   Map 27A4

Cranleigh (Acclaimed)   41 West St,
RH29BL☎(0737) 223417 Fax:(0737) 223734.
*Small friendly hotel with attractive garden, on the
main A25 1 mile from M25 junction 8. Swimming
pool, putting.*
⇌10 bedrs, 7 en suite, 2ba; TV; tcf 📺TV; P6; child
facs ✗LD9, nr lunch, Fri–Sun dinner. Resid & Rest
lic
£B&B £44–£59, B&B (double) £55–£65; D£14;
[10% V w/e, 5% V w/d] **cc** Access, Amex, B'card/
Visa, Diners; dep.

RIBDEN   Staffordshire.   Map 24B3

Tenement Farm   Nr Oakamoor, Stoke-on-Trent,
ST10 3BW ☎(0538) 702333. *Farm.* Mrs J Miller
Sleeps 6, ⌒ ✝
£ B&B from £15

RICHMOND   North Yorkshire.   Map 23C4

Whashton Springs Farm   DL11 7JS ☎(0748)
2884. *Farm.* Fairlie Turnbull
Sleeps 16, ⌒ (5)
£ B&B from £16–£20, D £9·50

RICHMOND-UPON-THAMES   Greater
London (Surrey).   Map 27A5

Richmond Gate (Highly Acclaimed)   Richmond
Hill, TW106RP ☎081-940 0061.
⇌51 bedrs, 51 en suite; TV 📺P60, coach; child
facs ✗Breakfast only
cc Access, Amex, B'card/Visa, CB, Diners.

Kew   339 Sandycombe Rd, TW93NA ☎081-948
2902.

RIEVAULX   North Yorkshire.   Map 23E4

Barn Close Farm   Helmsley, YO6 5HL ☎(043 96)
321. *Farm.* Joan Milburn   ♿
Sleeps 6, ⌒ ✝
£ B&B from £10–£12, D £8

RINGWOOD   Hampshire.   Map 26C2

Moortown Lodge (Highly Acclaimed)   244
Christchurch Rd, BH24 3AS ☎(0425) 471404.

189

ENGLAND

Charming Georgian country house situated on the edge of the New Forest, once part of the Gladstone estate. 1 mile from Ringwood town centre on B3347. Closed 24 Dec–14 Jan.
6 bedrs, 5 en suite, 1 ba; TV; tcf ns; P 8; child facs LD 8.30, nr lunch, dinner Sun. Resid & Rest lic
£ B&B £28–£37, B&B (double) £50–£54; HB weekly £217–£322; D £11·25; WB (£62 2 nights HB)
cc Access, Amex, B'card/Visa; dep.

RIPE East Sussex. Map 27B3

Manor Farm Nr Lewes, BN8 6AP (032 183) 425. *Farm.* Peter Benning
Sleeps 10,
£ B&B from £18, D £7·50

RIPLEY Derbyshire. Map 24D4

Britannia 243 Church St, Waingroves, DE5 9TF (0773) 43708.
7 bedrs, 1 en suite, 2 ba; tcf TV, dogs; P 10, coach; child facs LD midday, nr lunch. Unlic.

RIPON North Yorkshire. Map 23D3

Crescent Lodge 42 North St, HG4 1EN (0765) 2331.
11 bedrs, 3 ba; TV; tcf TV, ns Breakfast only. Resid lic.

ROCK Worcestershire. Map 26B9

Bullockhurst Farm Nr Bewdley, DY14 9SE (029922) 305. *Farm.* Margaret Nott
Sleeps 4, ns
£ B&B from £13

RODMELL East Sussex. Map 27B3

Barn House Lewes, BN7 3HF (0273) 477865. *Farm.* Ian and Bernadette Fraser
Sleeps 13
£ B&B from £23

ROSS-ON-WYE Hereford & Worcester (Herefordshire). Map 31C8

Arches Country House (Acclaimed) Walford Rd, HR9 5PT (0989) 63348.
Georgian style hotel in ⅓ acre of lawned gardens. Take B4228 from Ross town centre for ¼ mile, and The Arches is on the left.
6 bedrs, 2 en suite, 2 ba; TV; tcf TV, dogs, ns; P 10; child facs Breakfast only.
£ B&B £16–£18; B&B (double) £29–£36; [5% V]; dep.

Edde Cross House (Acclaimed) Edde Cross St, HR9 7BZ (0989) 65088.
Listed Georgian town house in a central location with river views. Approach from A40 via High St or Wilton Rd. Open Feb–Nov.
5 bedrs, 2 en suite, l ba; TV; tcf NS; no children under 10 Breakfast only. Unlic
£ B&B £16–£18, B&B (double) £32–£48; dep.

Ryefield House (Acclaimed) Gloucester Rd, HR9 5NA (0989) 63030.
7 bedrs, 4 en suite; TV; tcf TV, dogs, ns; P 10; child facs nr lunch & Sun dinner. Resid & Rest lic.

Brookfield House Overross, HR9 7AT (0989) 62188.
Entering the town from the M50–A40 dual carriageway, Brookfield is at the foot of the hill before the Renault garage. Closed Dec.
8 bedrs, 3 en suite, 3 ba; TV; tcf dogs; P 12; child facs Breakfast only. Resid lic
£ B&B £15, B&B (double) £27–£30; [5% V]
cc Access, B'card/Visa.

Radcliffe Wye St, HR9 7BS (0989) 63895.
From Market Place head towards Hereford on A40 to Swan Hotel, turn right and sharp left into Wye St.
6 bedrs, 1 en suite, 2 ba TV, ns; child facs LD 5.30, nr lunch, Sun dinner. Resid lic
£ B&B £14, B&B (double) £24–£30; HB weekly £130–£150; [10% V Oct–Jun w/d] dep.

Sunnymount Ryefield Rd, HR9 5LU (0989) 63880.
Family-run hotel in secluded position. Take the Gloucester road A40 past the Chase Hotel, then take second turn on left. Closed 21–31 Dec.
9 bedrs, 6 en suite, 1 ba TV, ns; P 7; child facs LD 5, nr lunch & Wed dinner. Resid & Rest lic
£ B&B £16–£29, B&B (double) £33–£44; HB weekly £195; D £10·50; [10% V Nov–May] cc Access, B'card/Visa.

Vaga House Wye St, HR9 7BS (0989) 63024.
Guest House.

White Lion Wilton, HR9 6AQ (0989) 62785

Aberhall Farm   St Owens Cross, Hereford, HR2
8LL ✆(098 987) 256. *Farm.* Freda Davies
Sleeps 6, ns ⛺ (10)
£ B&B from £11·50–£14, D £7·50

Upper Pengethley Farm   HR9 6LL ✆(0989)
87687. *Farm.* Sue Partridge
Sleeps 3, 🐾 ns ⛺
£ B&B from £12·50

ROTHERHAM   South Yorkshire.   Map 24D5

Regis   1 Hall Rd, S60 2BP ✆(0709) 376666.
*Take A631 to Bawtry, turn left at traffic lights into
Moorgate. In 1 ¼ miles turn right into Hall Rd.
Billiards.*
🛏12 bedrs, 4 en suite, 2 ba; TV; tcf 📺TV, dogs, P7,
G1, coach ✗LD 8.30, nr lunch, Fri–Sun dinner.
Resid lic
£ B&B £20–£29, B&B (double) £34–£40.

ROTTINGDEAN   East Sussex.   Map 27B2

Braemar House   Steyning Rd, BN2 7GA
✆Brighton (0273) 304263.
*Turn off A259 coast road into Rottingdean High St,
and Steyning Rd is first turn on the right.*
🛏16 bedrs, (2 sh), 3 ba 📺TV, dogs;
coach ✗Breakfast only. Unlic
£ B&B £12–£13.

ROWTON   Shropshire.   Map 24A2

Church Farm   Wellington, Telford, TF6 6QY
✆(0952) 770381. *Farm.* Virginia Evans
Sleeps 6, 🐾 ns ⛺
£ B&B from £11–£15, D £7·50

ROXTON   Bedfordshire.   Map 26F8

Church Farm   Bedford, MK44 3EB ✆(0234)
870234. *Farm.* Janet Must
Sleeps 6, 🐾 ⛺
£ B&B from £14

RUGBY   Warwickshire.   Map 26D9

Avondale   16 Elsee Road, CV21 3BA ✆(0788)
78639.
*Small Victorian guest house, situated close to the
parish church.*
🛏4 bedrs, 1 en suite, 2 ba; TV; tcf 📺TV, dogs; P 6,
G 2 ✗LD3, nr lunch. Unlic
£ B&B £18–£25, B&B (double) £32–£36; [5% V]

RUISLIP   Middlesex.   Map 27A6

Barn   West End Rd, HA4 6JB ✆(0895) 636057
Tx: 892514 Fax: (0895) 638379.
*Hotel based around a listed 17th century farmhouse
and barn set in 2 acres of landscaped gardens.*
🛏66 bedrs, 66 en suite; TV; tcf 📺TV, dogs, ns;
P 60, coach; child facs; con 60 ✗LD 9.30, nr Sun
dinner
cc Access, Amex, B'card/Visa, Diners.

RUSTINGTON   West Sussex.   Map 27A2

Kenmore   Claigmar Rd, BN16 2NL
✆(0903) 784634.
🛏6 bedrs, 3 en suite, 1 ba; TV; tcf 📺dogs; P 6;
child facs ✗Breakfast only. Unlic

RYE   East Sussex.   Map 27D3

Jeakes House (Highly Acclaimed)   Mermaid St,
TN31 7ET ✆(0797) 222828 Fax: (0797) 225758.
*Beautiful listed building dating from 1689 situated
in the heart of the Old Town.*
🛏11 bedrs, 9 en suite, 2 ba; TV; tcf 📺dogs,
ns; child fac ✗Breakfast only. Unlic
£ B&B £20, B&B (double) £36–£48; [10% Nov–
Mar]**cc** Access, B'card/Visa; dep.

Old Vicarage (Highly Acclaimed)   15 East St,
TN31 7JY ✆(0797) 225131.

Rye (East Sussex)

RAC
Highly
Acclaimed

Mermaid Street, Rye, East Sussex. TN31 7ET
Telephone Rye (0797) 222828 Fax: (0797) 222623

Beautiful listed building built in 1689. Set in
medieval cobblestoned street, renowned for its
smuggling associations. Breakfast – served in
eighteenth century galleried former chapel – is
traditional or vegetarian. Oak-beamed and
panelled bedrooms overlook the marsh and
roof-tops to the sea. Brass or mahogany
bedsteads, linen sheets and lace. En-suite
bathrooms, hot drinks trays, televisions and
telephones. Residential licence. Four poster
suite and family room available.
**Write or telephone for further details to the
proprietors: Mr & Mrs F Hadfield**

Georgian townhouse with rooms furnished in elegant period style, and panoramic views over Romney Marsh. Follow town centre signs and enter old town by Landgate Arch which leads to High St. East St is first on the left.
⊨4 bedrs, 4 en suite; Tv; tcf 🏠dogs ✕LD9, nr lunch. Resid & Rest lic
£ B&B £39–£44; B&B (double) £56–£64; HB weekly £259–£287; D £12 **cc** Access, B'card/Visa, Diners; dep.

Aviemore   28 Fishmarket Rd, TN31 7LP ✆ (0797) 223052.
Georgian house situated below the town on the A259 opposite recreation ground.
⊨8 bedrs, 2 ba; TV; tcf 🏠TV; coach, child facs ✕Dinner by prior arrangement. Resid lic
£ B&B £15–£18, B&B (double) £28–£32; HB weekly £147–£161; dep.

Cliff Farm   Iden Lock, Nr Rye, TN31 7QE ✆ Iden (07978) 331.
Farm close to Royal Military Canal about 2 miles north of Rye. Open Mar–Oct.
⊨3 bedrs, 1 ba; tcf 🏠TV; dogs; P6; child facs ✕Breakfast only. Unlic
£B&B (double) £12–£13·50.

Using RAC discount vouchers

Please tell the hotel when booking if you plan to use an RAC discount voucher (see end of guide) in part payment of your bill. Only one voucher will be accepted per party per stay. Discount vouchers will only be accepted in payment for accommodation, not for food.

Old Borough Arms   The Strand, TN31 7DB ✆ (0797) 222128.
A family-run hotel partly built on the old town wall, at the foot of the famous Mermaid St.
⊨9 bedrs, 9 en suite; TV; tcf 🏠TV, dogs, P2, coach ✕LD7. Resid lic
£B&B £22, B&B (double) £36–£50 **cc** Access, B'card/Visa.

SAFFRON WALDEN   Essex.   Map 27B8

Duddenhoe End Farm   CB11 4UU ✆ (0763) 838258. Farm. Peggy Foster
Sleeps 4, ns ⌂ (10)
£ B&B from £14pp (sharing double room)

Parsonage Farm   Arkesden, Essex CB11 4HB ✆ (0799) 5550306. Farm. Daniele Forster
Sleeps 4/6, 🐕 ⌂
£ B&B from £13

Rockells Farm   Duddenhoe End, CB11 4UY ✆ (0763) 838053. Farm. Mrs Tineke Westerhuis ঙ
Sleeps 6, 🐕 ⌂
£ B&B from £14, D £6

ST AGNES   Cornwall.   Map 28C2

Penkerris   Penwinnick Rd, (B3277), TR5 0PA ✆ (087 255) 2262.
Attractive Edwardian house in its own grounds. At the Chiverton Cross roundabout on A3 take B3277 into St Agnes. Penkerris is the first house on the right after town sign.
⊨5 bedrs, 1 en suite, 3 ba; TV; tcf 🏠TV, dogs; P8; child facs ✕LD morning, lunch and dinner on request only. Resid & Rest lic
£B&B £15–£20, B&B (double) £20–£30; HB weekly £105–£140; D £6·50; WB; [10% V exc high season]; dep.

Porthvean   Churchtown, TR5 0QP ✆ (087 255) 2581.
Original 18th-century hostelry with beams, in the centre of town opposite the parish church. Open Mar–Dec.
⊨6 bedrs, 5 en suite, 1 ba; TV; tcf 🏠ns; P6; child facs ✕LD9, nr lunch. Resid & Rest lic

£B&B £24·15–£31·05, B&B (double) £48·30–£55·20; [10% V exc Aug] **cc** Access, B'card/Visa.

St Agnes   Churchtown, TR5 0QP ✆ (087 255) 2307.
On the main road through St Agnes opposite the church.
🛏5 bedrs, 3 en suite, 1 ba; TV, tcf 📺TV, dogs; P60, coach; child facs ✗LD10
£B&B £18·50–£27·50, B&B (double) £33–£45; L£6, D£10; [5% V Oct–Jun] **cc** Access, B'card/Visa; dep.

ST ALBANS   Hertfordshire.   Map 27A6

Ardmore House   54 Lemsford Rd. ✆ (0727) 59313 or 61411.
Lovely old house set in large garden. Lemsford Rd runs between Sandpit Lane and Hatfield Rd.
🛏24 bedrs, 17 en suite, (2 sh), 1 ba; TV; tcf 📺dogs; P25; child facs ✗LD8, nr lunch, Fri–Sun dinner. Resid lic
£B&B £28·75–£43·70, B&B (double) £36·80–£49·45; dep. **cc** Access, B'card/Visa.

Haven   234 London Rd, AL1 1JQ ✆ (0727) 40904 Tx: 266020 Fax: (0727) 62750.
Modern hotel on city outskirts. Situated 2¼ miles N M25 junction 22.
🛏43 bedrs, 43 en suite; TV; tcf 📺TV, dogs; coach; child facs ✗LD9·30
£B&B £66, B&B (double) £83·50–£88·50; L£10, D£11; WB (£94·50 2 nts HB); [10% V Mon–Thur] **cc** Access, Amex, B'card/Visa, Diners.

Melford   24 Woodstock Rd North, AL1 4QQ ✆ (0727) 53642.
🛏12 bedrs, 4 en suite, 3 ba; tcf 📺TV, dogs, ns; P12, child facs ✗Breakfast only. Resid lic
£B&B £24·15–£43·70, B&B (double) £36·80–£46; WB; dep.

ST AUSTELL   Cornwall.   Map 28D2

Nanscawen House (Highly Acclaimed)   Prideaux Rd, St Blazey PL24 2SR ✆ (0726) 814488.

Beautiful Georgian house with luxury accommodation. Enter St Blazey on A390 and turn right after railway opposite Texaco garage. Hotel ¾ mile on right. Swimming pool. Closed Xmas & New Year.

🛏3 bedrs, 3 en suite; TV; tcf 📺NS; P6; no children under 12 ✗LD midday, nr lunch. Unlic
£B&B £30–£45, B&B (double) £55; HB weekly £297·50; D£15 **cc** Access, B'card/Visa; dep.

Alexandra   52 Alexandra Rd, PL25 4QN ✆ (0726) 74242.
Small hotel situated on rising ground close to the town centre on the A390 Liskeard Rd. Closed 24–31 Dec.
🛏14 bedrs, 4 en suite, 3 ba; TV; tcf 📺TV, dogs; P16, coach; child facs ✗LD5, nr lunch. Resid lic
£B&B £14–£20; HB weekly £130–£149; [5% V Jul–Sep] **cc** Access, Amex, B'card/Visa; dep.

Lynton House   48 Bodmin Rd, PL25 5AF ✆ (0726) 73787.
White-walled Victorian house situated on the A391 from Bodmin.
🛏5 bedrs, 1 ba 📺TV; P6 ✗Breakfast only. Resid lic
£B&B £11; dep.

Selwood House   60 Alexandra Rd, PL25 4QN ✆ (0726) 65707.
Follow A390 into town past three set of traffic lights, take third exit off next roundabout (signed Bodmin), cross over lights and hotel is ¼ mile on the left. Closed New Year.
🛏11 bedrs, 11 en suite; TV; tcf 📺TV, dogs, P13, coach; child facs ✗LD7, nr lunch. Resid & Rest lic
£B&B £27·50–£31·50; B&B (double) £51–£58; HB weekly £249–£280; D£9; [5% V] **cc** Access, Amex, B'card/Visa, Diners; dep.

ST EVAL   Cornwall.   Map 28C3

Bedruthan House   Bedruthan Steps, PL27 7UW ✆ St Mawgan (0637) 860346.
Situated on the B3276 between Mawgan Porth and Porthcothan opposite NT Bedruthan Steps. Closed Nov & Xmas.
🛏5 bedrs, 2 ba 📺TV, P12; children over 3 ✗LD9. Resid & Rest lic
£B&B £12–£14, HB weekly £115·50–£130; dep.

ST IVES   Cornwall.   Map 28B2

Dean Court (Highly Acclaimed)   Trelyon Av, TR26 2AD ✆ Penzance (0736) 796023.
A granite house in its own grounds overlooking St Ives Bay, with spacious accommodation. Situated on the seaward side of the main road into St Ives past the Tregenna Castle Hotel and golf course. Open Mar–Oct.
🛏12 bedrs, 12 en suite; TV; tcf 📺P12; children over 14 ✗nr lunch. Resid lic
£B&B £25–£32; HB weekly £180–£220; [5% V Mar–May, Sep & Oct]; dep.

WHEN FORD SAY THEY CARE...

When you buy a Ford, you begin a partnership with one of the world's greatest vehicle manufacturers, and you can be assured of lasting attentive service – proof that Ford cares.

Ford Dealers are trained by Ford to offer the fullest range of services, to both vehicle and customer, in the pursuit of customer satisfaction. Workshops are fully-equipped with the most sophisticated equipment demanded by today's technologically advanced vehicles, and are supported by Ford's massive European Parts Operation.

The purchase of a new Ford now includes a year's free vehicle membership of the RAC, and Ford also offers a range of Extra Cover optional warranties, and most Dealers also offer a Lifetime Guarantee on numerous repairs.

...THEY MEAN IT

Blue Mist   6 The Warren, TR26 2EA ✆ (0736) 795209.
Small hotel right on the water's edge. From the station, go down steps at exit and turn left. Open Easter–end Oct.
🛏9 bedrs, 8 en suite, 1 ba; TV; tcf 📶P 4 (£2, May to Sep); coach; children over 4 ✕LD 5, nr lunch. Unlic
£ B&B £15·40–£22·27, B&B (double) £30·80–£44·54; HB weekly £138·05–£144·65 **cc** Access, B'card/Visa; dep.

Dunmar   1 Pednolver Terr, TR26 2EL ✆ (0736) 796117.
Family run notel with delightful sea views. Fork left at Porthminster Hotel into Albert Rd, and hotel is 200 yards along.
🛏17 bedrs, 12 en suite, (5 sh), 5 ba; TV; tcf 📶TV, dogs, ns; P 25, coach; child facs ✕LD 8. Resid & Rest lic
£ B&B £14·50–£20; HB weekly £136·50–£182; L £4·50, D £6; WB (£40) **cc** Access, B'card/Visa.

Hollies   Talland Rd, TR26 2DF ✆ Penzance (0736) 796605.
Follow Trelyon Ave to Porthminster Hotel, fork left then turn left at Pete's Gym. Hollies is third on right.
🛏9 bedrs, 9 en suite; TV; tcf 📶TV; P 12, ns; child facs ✕LD 9 am, nr lunch. Resid lic
£ B&B £16–£20; HB weekly £130–£180; [10% V Sept–May]; dep.

Longships   2 Talland Rd, TR26 2DF ✆ Penzance (0736) 798180.
Granite built hotel with magnificent views. From Lelant and Carbis Bay take the left fork at Porthminster Hotel, follow road round to the left at Pete's Gym, and Longships is on Talland Rd.
🛏24 bedrs, 24 en suite; TV; tcf 📶TV, dogs; P 18, coach; child facs ✕LD 7. Resid & Rest lic
£ B&B £14·50–£20; HB weekly £129–£187; L £3·50, D £6; [5% V] **cc** Access, B'card/Visa; dep.

Lyonesse   Talland Rd, TR26 2DF ✆ Penzance (0736) 796315.
Fork left at Porthminster Hotel into Albert Rd, left again at Porthminster Terr and Talland Rd. Open Mar–Oct.
🛏15 bedrs, 15 en suite; TV; tcf 📶TV, ns; P 10, coach; child facs ✕LD 6.30, nr lunch. Resid lic
£ B&B £18–£25.

En suite rooms
En suite rooms may be bath or shower rooms. If you have a preference, remember to state it when booking a room.

Porth Dene   Primrose Valley TR26 2ED ✆ (0736) 796713.
Turn right off main road into St Ives, then right into Primrose Valley Hill, turning left at the bottom and left again. Open Apr–Oct.
🛏6 bedrs, 4 en suite, (1 sh), 1 ba; TV; tcf 📶TV; P 5; child facs ✕Breakfast only. Resid lic
£ B&B £12–£14; dep.

Primrose Valley   Primrose Valley, TR26 2ED ✆ Penzance (0736) 794939.
Well-positioned hotel beside Porthminster Beach. From A3074 pass St Ives Motor Co, take steep right turning down Primrose Valley signed to beach. Open Mar–Nov.
🛏11 bedrs, 6 en suite, 2 ba; TV; tcf 📶TV, ns; P 12; child facs ✕LD 7. Resid & Rest lic
£ B&B £16–£25; HB weekly £137·50–£210; D £7·50; dep.

St Margaret's   3 Parc Av, TR26 2DN ✆ Penzance (0736) 795785.

St Merryn   Trelyon, TR26 2PF ✆ Penzance (0736) 795767. *Putting.*

ST JUST-IN-PENWITH   Cornwall.
Map 28B2

Boswedden House   Cape Cornwall, TR19 7NJ ✆ Penzance (0736) 788733.
Early 19th-century former captain's home. From St Just take road to Cape Cornwall to big white house in 1 mile on right. Indoor swimming pool. Open Mar–Nov.
🛏8 bedrs, 7 en suite, 1 ba 📶TV, dogs, ns; P 7; child facs ✕LD 12 noon, nr lunch. Resid lic
£ B&B £11·50–£12·50; HB weekly £107–£121; dep.

ST JUST-IN-ROSELAND   Cornwall.
Map 28C2

Rose-da-Mar (Acclaimed)   TR2 5JB ✆ St Mawes (0326) 270450.

Small hotel with river and country views in an area of outstanding natural beauty. Pass through village of Sticker, just off St Austell to Truro road, follow signs to St Mawes and at crcss roads in St Just in Roseland turn right along B3289 for 500 yards. Open Apr–Oct.

8 bedrs, 5 en suite, 2 ba, tcf ‎fr‎ TV, dogs; P 9; children over 11 ✕ LD 6.30, nr lunch. Resid & Rest lic
£ B&B £21, B&B (double) £37–£48; HB weekly £214·99–£254·23; D £13·50; dep.

ST LEONARDS-ON-SEA   East Sussex

See HASTINGS.

SALCOMBE   Devon.   Map 28G2

Lyndhurst (Highly Acclaimed)   Bonaventure Rd, TQ8 8BG ✆ (054 884) 2481.
Small, friendly hotel with informal atmosphere and glorious views across the water. On entering Salcombe take first left, first right and first left leading into Bonaventure Rd. Open Jan–Nov.
8 bedrs, 8 en suite; TV; tcf ‎fr‎ NS; P 4; no children under 7 ✕ LD 4, nr lunch. Resid & Rest lic
£ B&B £18·50–£22; HB weekly £196–£210; dep.

Devon Tor   Devon Rd, TQ8 8HJ ✆ (054 884) 3106.
Private Hotel.

Old Porch House   Shadycombe Rd, TQ8 8DJ ✆ (054 884) 2157 Fax: (054 884) 3750.
17th-century property, the oldest house in Salcombe. Enter Salcombe on A381, turn first left past Mayflower garage, turn left before large church and hotel is on right. Closed 23–28 Dec.
8 bedrs, 6 en suite, 1 ba; TV; tcf ‎fr‎ TV, dogs; P 10; child facs ✕ Breakfast only. Resid lic
£ B&B (double) £35–£50; dep.

Penn Torr   Herbert Rd, TQ8 8HN ✆ (054 884) 2234.
Small comfortable hotel, not far from Salcombe harbour. Open Easter–Oct.
10 bedrs, 5 en suite, 1 ba; tcf ‎fr‎ TV; P 10; no children under 4 ✕ Breakfast only. Unlic
£ B&B £16·50–£21.

Terrapins Inn   Buckley St, TQ8 8DD ✆ (054 884) 2861 Fax: (054 884) 2265.
Friendly and attractive hotel with some marvellous views. Follow the hill down into Salcombe, and Terrapins is along the second road on the left past the parish church. Open Mar–Nov & winter weekends.
7 bedrs, 7 en suite, 1 ba; TV; tcf ‎fr‎ dogs; child facs ✕ LD 9, nr lunch.
£ B&B £21·85–£30·90, B&B (double) £33·45–£56·70; HB weekly £190·75–£255; D £9·50; WB (£87·75 3 nights HB Winter); [10% V w/d Mar–Jun & Oct, & Winter w/e]; dep.

Torre View   Devon Rd, TQ8 8HJ ✆ (054 884) 2633.

Detached residence with commanding estuary and sea views. On entering Salcombe on A381, pass a sharp corner and ⅓ mile later bear left into Devon Rd. Open Feb–Nov.
8 bedrs, 5 en suite, 2 ba; tcf ‎fr‎ TV, ns; P 4; child facs ✕ LD 6, nr lunch. Resid lic
£ B&B £23–£29, B&B (double) £39–£46; HB weekly £179–£199; D £8; [5% V Feb–20 May]; dep.
cc Access, B'card/Visa.

SALFORDS   Surrey.   Map 27A4

Mill Lodge (Acclaimed)   25 Brighton Rd, RH1 6PP ✆ (0293) 771170.
Small red-brick hotel 7 mins from Gatwick Airport. Situated on A23 between Redhill and Horley immediately by footbridge.
8 bedrs, 2 en suite, 2 ba; TV; tcf ‎fr‎ TV; P 34, U 3 ✕ Breakfast only. Unlic
£ B&B £25, B&B (double) £36; dep.

SALISBURY   Wiltshire.   Map 26C3

Byways (Acclaimed)   31 Fowler's Rd, SP1 2QP ✆ (0722) 28364 Fax: (0722) 322146.
From city centre follow Milford St leading into Milford Hill, and Fowlers Rd is first on the right. Billiards.
20 bedrs, 14 en suite, 2 ba; TV; tcf ‎fr‎ dogs, ns; P 15, coach; child facs ✕ LD 7, nr lunch. Resid & Rest lic
£ B&B £16–£25, B&B (double) £30–£40; HB weekly £175–£210; D £8·50; WB (£30); [10% V exc Sat]
cc Access, Amex, B'card/Visa, Diners; dep.

Glen Lyn   6 Bellamy La, Milford Hill, SP1 2SP ✆ (0722) 327880.
A large Victorian house in a quiet cul de sac at the top of Milford Hill, a continuation of Milford St.
7 bedrs, 4 en suite, 1 ba; TV; tcf ‎fr‎ ns; P 7; no children under 12 ✕ Breakfast only. Unlic
£ B&B £16–£20, B&B (double) £28–£34; [10% V]; dep.

Hayburn Wyke   72 Castle Rd, SP1 3RL ✆ (0722) 412627.
Family-run Victorian hotel ⅓ mile N of Salisbury on A345 by the park.
6 bedrs, 2 en suite, 1 ba; TV; tcf ‎fr‎ TV, dogs, ns; P 6, G 1, child facs ✕ Breakfast only. Unlic
£ B&B £18–£23, B&B (double) £29–£36; [5% V]

Holmhurst   Downton Rd, SP2 8AR ✆ (0722) 323164.
Small guest house off the A338 Ringwood Rd.
8 bedrs, 5 en suite, 1 ba ‎fr‎ TV, ns; P 8, G 1, coach; no children under 5 ✕ Breakfast only. Unlic
£ B&B £15–£32, B&B (double) £28–£32.

Leena's   50 Castle Rd SP1 3RL ✆ (0722) 335419.
From city centre proceed along Castle St to Castle Rd, and Leena's is on the left at the first junction.

6 bedrs, 3 en suite, 1 ba; TV; tcf TV, ns; P6; child facs ✕ Breakfast only. Unlic
£ B&B £17–£22, B&B (double) £27·50–£36; [5% V].

Old Mill Town Path, West Harnham, SP2 8EU
(0722) 27517.
7 bedrs, (1 sh), 2 ba; tcf TV; P 15, coach; children over 5 ✕ LD 10
cc Access, Amex, B'card/Visa, Diners; dep.

Richburn 23 Estcourt Rd, SP1 3AP (0722) 325189.
Victorian guest house with homely service. Enter Salisbury on A30, take third turning off St Marks roundabout into Estcourt Rd which runs parallel with Churchill Way ring road.
10 bedrs, 2 en suite, 2 ba; tcf TV, dogs, ns; P 10, coach; child facs ✕ Breakfast only. Unlic
£ B&B £15, B&B (double) £24–£34; dep.

SANDHURST Gloucestershire. Map 26B7

Brawn Farm Gloucester, GL2 9NR (0452) 731010. *Farm.* Sally Williams
Sleeps 4,
£ B&B from £16

SANDY Bedfordshire. Map 26A8

Highfield Farm SG19 2AQ (0767) 682332. *Farm.* Margaret Codd
Sleeps 6, ns
£ B&B from £13·50

SAXMUNDHAM Suffolk. Map 27F9

Park Farm Sibton, IP17 2LZ (072 877) 324. *Farm.* Margaret Gray
Sleeps 6, ns
£ B&B from £12, D £7·50

SCARBOROUGH N. Yorkshire. Map 24F9

Pickwick Inn Huntriss Row, YO11 2ED
(0723) 375787.
Busy inn on edge of pedestrianised area. Well-furnished bedrooms some with partial sea views.
11 bedrs, 11 en suite; TV; tcf Lift ✕ LD 10.15
£ B&B £24–£30, B&B (double) £40–£60; HB weekly £188–£209; L £5·95, D £9; WB
cc Access, Amex, B'card/Visa, Diners; dep.

Bay (Highly Acclaimed) 67 Esplanade, South Cliff, YO11 2UZ (0723) 373926. *Hotel.*

Premier (Highly Acclaimed) 66 Esplanade, South Cliff, YO11 2UZ (0723) 361484.
A spacious Victorian property, full of character and with many original features. Situated on the seafront opposite the Italian Gardens. Open Mar–Dec.
19 bedrs, 19 en suite, TV; tcf lift, dogs, ns; P14; child facs ✕ LD 6, nr Mon–Sat lunch, Sun dinner. Resid & Rest lic

£ B&B £28–£30, B&B (double) £52–£56; HB weekly £210–£224; D £10; WB (£50 2 nts); dep.

Anatolia (Acclaimed) 21 West St, YO11 2QR
(0723) 360864
£ B&B £11–£15

Crawford (Acclaimed) 8/9 Crown Terr YO11 2BL
(0723) 361494.
A pleasant, white-walled Georgian hotel with comfortable accommodation. From St Andrews Church on Ramshill Rd turn into Albion Rd, then take first left and first right. Open Apr–Nov.
21 bedrs, 19 en suite, 2 ba; TV; tcf lift, dogs; coach; child facs ✕ LD 6.30, nr lunch. Resid lic
£ B&B £17; HB weekly £143·50; D £9; [5% V Jul–Aug] cc Access, B'card/Visa; dep.

Glen Grant (Acclaimed) 18 West Sq, YO11 1UY
(0723) 364291. *Hotel.*
17 bedrs, 6 en suite, 3 ba; TV; tcf dogs; child facs ✕ LD 7, nr Mon–Sat lunch. Resid lic
cc Access, Amex, B'card/Visa; dep.

Parade (Acclaimed) 29 Esplanade, YO11 2AQ
(0723) 361285
Recently refurbished hotel on sea front opposite Spa lift. Open Mar–Dec.
18 bedrs, 16 en suite, 1 ba
£ B&B £19·50–£22; HB weekly £168–178·50

Parmella (Acclaimed) 17 West St, South Cliff, YO11 2QN (0723) 361914.
A former gentleman's Victorian residence, tastefully converted and retaining many original features. Follow signs to Southcliff and Esplanade and West St runs parallel with Esplanade. Open Mar–Nov.
15 bedrs, 10 en suite, (1 sh), 2 ba; TV; tcf TV, ns; child facs ✕ LD 5
£ B&B £15–£18; HB weekly £129·50–£147; [5% V Apr–Jun, Sep–Nov]; dep.

Geldenhuis 143 Queen's Par, YO12 7HU
(0723) 361677.
Hotel occupying superb seafront position, situated on the North Cliff near the indoor bowling centre. Open Easter–Oct.
30 bedrs, 9 en suite, 7 ba; tcf TV; P25; child facs ✕ LD 6, nr lunch. Resid & Rest lic
£ B&B £19·55; B&B (double) £36·80; HB weekly £128·80; D £5; [5% V]; dep.

Glenville 8 Blenheim St, North Bay, YO12 7HB
(0723) 372681.
Agreeable small hotel set between North Bay and South Bay.
9 bedrs, 2 ba; tcf TV; child facs ✕ LD 7, nr lunch. Resid lic
£ B&B £12·75–£16·25; HB weekly £105–£133; WB (£40); dep.

Paragon 123 Queen's Par, YO12 7HU ✆(0723) 372676.
Well-situated hotel overlooking the North Bay, set on the clifftop road.
⇌15 bedrs, 15 en suite, 2 ba; TV; tcf 📺 ns; coach ✕LD 6.30, nr lunch. Resid lic
£B&B £21–£23, B&B (double) £34–£38; HB weekly £196–£210; WB (£44) cc Access, B'card/Visa; dep.

Saint Margaret's 16 Weydale Ave, YO12 6AX ✆(0723) 373717.
⇌21 bedrs, 8 en suite, 2 ba; TV; tcf 📺 TV, dogs; P 8, coach; child facs ✕LD 6.30, bar meals only lunch. Resid lic
cc Access, B'card/Visa; dep.

Scalby Manor Burniston Coast Rd, YO13 0DA ✆(0723) 375716.
Victorian 'Queen-Anne'-style house just off the coast road north from Scarborough.
⇌11 bedrs, 7 en suite, 2 ba; TV; tcf
£B&B £20; HB weekly £96–£120.

Sefton 18 Prince of Wales Terr, South Cliff, YO11 2AL ✆(0723) 372310.
A comfortable hotel set behind Esplanade. Follow signs for South Bay. Open Mar–Oct.
⇌16 bedrs, 5 en suite, 6 ba; tcf 📺 lift, TV, ns; coach; children over 10 ✕LD 6. Resid lic
£B&B £13·50; HB weekly £108·50; dep.

Valley Lodge 51 Valley Rd, YO11 2LX ✆(0723) 375311.

West Lodge 38 West St, YO11 2QP ✆(0723) 500754.
Large Victorian semi-detached house with gardens and patio. From the town centre cross over Valley

Bridge then take third turning on the left into West St.
⇌7 bedrs, 1 en suite, 1 ba; TV; tcf 📺 TV; coach; child facs ✕LD 2, Resid lic
£B&B £10, B&B (double) £20–£25; HB weekly £87·50–£105; D £4·50; [10% V mid Sep–Jun]; dep.

Weydale Weydale Av, YO12 6BA ✆(0723) 373393.
Family run hotel in superb position overlooking North Bay. Situated adjacent to Peasholm Park. Open Mar–Oct.
⇌26 bedrs, 13 en suite, 3 ba; TV; tcf 📺 TV, dogs, ns; P 10, coach; children over 3 ✕LD 5.30, nr lunch
£B&B £14–£17; HB weekly £133–£161; [5% V exc Jul–Aug]

SCARISBRICK Lancashire. Map 30C7

Sandy Brook Farm Wyke Cop Road, Southport, PR8 5LR ✆(0704) 880337. *Farm.* Mrs W E Core ♿ Sleeps 16, ☎
£ B&B from £13

SCILLY ISLES

See ISLES OF SCILLY

SEASCALE Cumbria. Map 22E4

Cottage (Highly Acclaimed) Black How CA20 1LQ ✆(094 67) 28416.

SEATON Cornwall. Map 28E2

Blue Haven Looe Hill, PL11 3JQ ✆Downderry (05035) 310.

Scarborough (Yorkshire)

Scarborough (North Yorkshire)

Small hotel with magnificent views. In Seaton turn right to Looe Hill, and hotel is about 300 yards on right.
⊨7 bedrs, 5 en suite, 1 ba; TV; tcf 🎤TV, dogs, P6; child facs ✕LD6.30. Resid lic
£B&B £12–£14; HB weekly £119·50–£134·50; L£3, D£8; [5%V] **cc**Access, B'card/Visa; dep.

SEATON Devon. Map 29C4

Mariners (Acclaimed) East Walk, Esplanade, EX12 2NP ☎(0297) 20560.
A small private hotel in a superb seafront position directly on the front. Open Mar–Dec.
⊨10 bedrs, 10 en suite; TV; tcf 🎤TV, dogs, ns; P10; child facs ✕LD midday, nr lunch. Resid & Rest lic
£B&B £20·50–£24·50, B&B (double) £33–£37; HB weekly £132–£156; D£8·50 **cc**Access, B'card/Visa; dep.

SENNEN Cornwall. Map 28A2

Sunny Bank Seaview Hill, TR19 7AR ☎(0736) 871278.
On A30, 8 miles W of Penzance and 1¼ miles E of Lands End. Closed Dec.
⊨11 bedrs, (2 sh), 2 ba; tcf 🎤TV, dogs; P20; child facs ✕LD7, nr lunch. Resid & Rest lic
£B&B £11–£16; HB weekly £115–£150; dep.

SEVENOAKS Kent. Map 27B4

Moorings 97 Hitchen Hatch La, TN13 3BE ☎(0732) 452589.
Take exit 5 off M25, turn right on to A21 at Riverhead. Continue to railway bridge and turn left into Hitchen Hatch La.
⊨19 bedrs, 2 en suite, (4 sh), 2 ba; TV; tcf 🎤TV,

Discount vouchers

RAC discount vouchers are at the end of the guide. Establishments with a [V] shown at the end of the price information will accept them in part payment for accommodation bills on the full, standard rate, not against bargain breaks or any other special offers. Please note the limitations shown in the entry: w/e for weekends, w/d for weekdays, and which months they are accepted.

---

dogs; P22, coach; child facs ✕nr lunch, Fri–Sun dinner. Resid lic
£B&B £30–£45, B&B (double) £40–£60; [10%V] **cc** Access, B'card/Visa; dep.

SHABBINGTON Buckinghamshire. Map 26F7

Manor Farm Aylesbury, HP18 9HJ ☎(0844) 201103. *Farm.* Joan Bury ♿
Sleeps 6, ⚐
£ B&B from £15–£20

SHAWBURY Shropshire. Map 30A8

New Farm (Acclaimed) Muckleton, Telford, TF6 6RJ ☎(0939) 250358.

Modern farmhouse on 70 acre farm situated 1 mile off A53 near Shawbury.
⊨4 bedrs, 3 en suite, 1 ba; TV; tcf 🎤TV, ns; P10; no children under 1 ✕nr lunch, dinner Fri, Sat & Sun only. Unlic
£B&B £15–£18, D£8; [10% V]; dep.

SHEERNESS Kent. Map 27D5

Victoriana 103–109 Alma Rd, ME12 2PD ☎(0795) 665555.
From the town clock tower continue for ¾ mile on right, turn into Alma Rd by Napier public house.
⊨20 bedrs, 8 en suite, 3 ba; TV; tcf 🎤TV, dogs; P8, coach; child facs ✕LD9.30. Resid lic
£B&B £16·50–£30, B&B (double) £32–£40; L£9, D£9; WB **cc**Access, B'card/Visa; dep.

SHEFFIELD South Yorkshire. Map 24D5

Etruria House 91 Crookes Rd, Broomhill S10 5BD ☎(0742) 662241.
Situated 200 yards from the traffic lights at Broomhill.

---

11 bedrs, 7 en suite, 2 ba; TV; tcf 📺 TV, dogs; P 10, G 1; child facs ✕ LD 7, nr lunch. Unlic £ B&B £22–£27, B&B (double) £35–£40 **cc** Access, B'card/Visa; dep.

Lindum   91 Montgomery Rd, Nether Edge, S7 1LP ☎ (0742) 552356.
From city centre follow A625 Eccleshall Rd, turn left at Summerfield St and continue to Montgomery Rd. Closed 24 Dec–1 Jan.
12 bedrs, 1 en suite, 2 ba; TV; tcf 📺 TV, dogs, ns; P 4; child facs ✕ Resid lic
£ B&B £15·50–£25, B&B (double) £31–£35.

Millingtons   70 Broomgrove Rd, S10 2NA ☎ (0742) 669549.
Follow signs for A625 out of the city centre on Eccleshall Rd, turn into Broomgrove Rd, hotel about 1⅓ miles from the city.

Westbourne House   25 Westbourne Rd, Broomhill, S10 2QQ ☎ (0742) 660109.

SHELSLEY   Worcestershire.   Map 26B9

Church House   Beauchamp, Nr Worcester, WR6 6RA ☎ (0886) 812393.   *Farm.* Gill and Arthur Moore Sleeps 4, 🐾 ☺
£ B&B from £14–£16, D £9·50

SHENINGTON   Oxfordshire.   Map 26D8

Sugarswell Farm   Banbury, OX15 6HW ☎ (029 588) 512.   *Farm.* Rosemary Nunneley Sleeps 6, ns
£ B&B from £17–£27, D £14

SHEPTON MALLET   Somerset.   Map 29D6

Belfield   34 Charlton Rd, BA4 5PA ☎ (0749) 344353.
From town centre take Paul St which leads into Charlton Rd.
6 bedrs, 2 en suite, 2 ba; TV; tcf 📺 ns; P 6 ✕ Breakfast only. Rest lic
£ B&B £15·50–£17, B&B (double) £30–£36.

SHERINGHAM   Norfolk.   Map 25E4

Beacon (Highly Acclaimed)   1 Nelson Rd, NR26 8BT ☎ (0263) 822019.

Small hotel with panoramic views over the town and countryside, set in a prime cliff top position on the east side of Sheringham. Open May–Sep.
7 bedrs, 3 en suite, 2 ba; tcf 📺 TV, ns; P 6; children over 16 ✕ LD 6, nr lunch. Resid & Rest lic
£ HB weekly £165 **cc** Access, B'card/Visa; dep.

Fairlawns (Highly Acclaimed)   26 Hooks Hill Rd NR26 8NL ☎ (0263) 824717.

Victorian house with attractive lawned gardens, and individually styled bedrooms. Turn into Holt Rd opposite the police station and take second left into Vicarage Rd. At T junction turn immediately into cul-de-sac. Open Easter–Oct.
5 bedrs, 5 en suite; tcf 📺 TV; P 6; no children under 14 ✕ LD midday, nr lunch, Sun dinner. Resid lic
£ B&B £22·50, B&B (double) £37; HB weekly £158; WB £49.

Melrose (Acclaimed)   9 Holloway Rd, NR26 8HN ☎ (0263) 823299.

Comfortable Victorian hotel extensively improved recently. From the roundabout on the A149 coast road take Holloway Rd for 100 yds.
10 bedrs, 5 en suite, 2 ba; TV; tcf 📺 TV, dogs; P 10; child facs ✕ LD noon, nr lunch. Resid & Rest lic
£ B&B £15·50–£21; HB weekly £152·50–£177·50; D £7·50; [5% V excl Jul–Aug] **cc** Access, B'card/Visa; dep.

SHIFNAL   Shropshire.   Map 24A2

Old Bell   Church St. ☎ Telford (0952) 460475.

SHILTON   Warwickshire.   Map 24D1

Park Farm   Spring Road, Barnacle, Coventry, CV7 9LG ☎ (0203) 612628.   *Farm.* Linda Grindal

Sleeps 4, ns ☡ (12)
£ B&B from £15, D £9

SHOTTLE Derbyshire. Map 24D4

Dannah Farm Bowmans Lane, Belper, DE5 2DR
☎ (077 389) 273 630. *Farm.* Joan Slack &
Sleeps 18, ns ☡
£ B&B from £12–£18, D from £10·50

SHREWLEY Warwickshire. Map 26C9

Shrewley House (Highly Acclaimed) Hockley Rd,
CV35 7AT ☎ (092 684) 2549

*A grade II listed Georgian farmhouse dating back
to the 17th-century, set in 1¼ acres of garden and
surrounded by the beautiful Warwickshire
countryside. Situated on the B4439 just NW of
Warwick, off the A41.*
⇥7 bedrs, 7 en suite; TV; tcf 🛉TV, dogs; P 20, G 2;
child facs ✕LD 8. Meals by arrangement
£ B&B £28–£35, B&B (double) £35–£45

SHREWSBURY Shropshire. Map 31A7

Abbots Mead (Highly Acclaimed) 9–10 St Julians
Friars ☎ (0743) 235281. *Hotel.*

Haughmond Farm, SY4 4RW ☎ (0743)
77244. *Farm.* Pearl Teece
Sleeps 6, ns ☡
£ B&B from £12·50

SIDDINGTON Cheshire. Map 24B5

The Golden Cross Farm Nr Macclesfield, SK11
9JP ☎ (0260) 224358. *Farm.* Hazel Rush
Sleeps 6, ns ☡
£ B&B from £12

SIDMOUTH Devon. Map 29B4

Groveside (Acclaimed) Vicarage Rd, EX10 8UQ
☎ (0395) 513406.

*Detached Victorian brick building with spacious
accommodation. Take B3175 to Sidmouth, hotel is
about 1¼ miles on the left past the police station.*
Open Apr–Oct.
⇥8 bedrs, 3 en suite, 2 ba; TV; tcf 🛉TV, ns; P 8; no
children under 3 ✕LD 4, nr Mon–Sat lunch, Sun
dinner. Unlic
£ B&B £12·65–£16·45; HB weekly £133·40–£165;
dep.

Willow Bridge (Acclaimed) 1 Millford Rd, EX10
8DR ☎ (0395) 513599.
⇥7 bedrs, 5 en suite, 1 ba 🛉TV, dogs, ns; P 7; no
children under 5 ✕LD 6, nr lunch. Rest lic.

Canterbury House Salcombe Rd, EX10 8PR
☎ (0395) 513373.
*Detached Georgian house with many original
features. Salcombe Rd is a turning off Sidford Rd
opposite the cinema.* Open Mar–Nov.
⇥8 bedrs, 5 en suite, 1 ba; TV; tcf 🛉TV, dogs; P 6;
child facs ✕LD 4.30, nr lunch. Resid lic
£ B&B £15·50–£18·50; HB weekly £140–£165;
D £5·50; [5% V]; dep.

Higher Weston Farm, EX10 0PH ☎ (0395)
513741. *Farm.* Shirley Macfadyen &
Sleeps 6, ns ☡ (5) 🐾
£ B&B from £10–£15

Lower Pinn Farm Peak Hill, EX10 0NN ☎ (0395)
513733. *Farm.* Elizabeth Tancock
Sleeps 6, 🐾 ☡
£ B&B from £12–£17

Pinn Barton Farm Pinn Lane, Peak Hill, EX10
0NN ☎ (0395) 514004. *Farm.* Betty Sage
🐾 ☡
£ B&B from £12

SIMONSBATH Somerset. Map 28G5

Emmetts Grange Farm Emmetts Grange, TA24
7LD ☎ (064 383) 282. *Farm.* Julia Brown
Sleeps 6, 🐾 ☡
£ B&B from £16·50–£19, D £11

Gallon House, Minehead, TA24 7JY ☎ (064383)
283. *Farm.* Trudy Hawkins
Sleeps 6, 🐾 ☡
£ B&B from £12·65–£14·95, D £6·90

Shrewley (Warwickshire)

Shrewley House and Cottages
Shrewley, near Warwick CV35 7AT
Tel: (0926 84) 2549
Listed Georgian farmhouse, overlooking beautiful open
countryside, set amidst 1½ acres of gardens. Delightfully furnished,
all rooms en-suite, some with king-sized 4 poster beds.

SISSINGHURST   Kent.   Map 27C3

Sissinghurst Castle Farm   Cranbrook, TN17
2AB ✆(0580) 712885.   *Farm*. James and Pat
Stearns
Sleeps 6, ☖
£ B&B from £16·50–£21, D from £10

SKEGNESS   Lincolnshire.   Map 25B4

South Lodge   147 Drummond Rd, PE25 3BT
✆(0754) 5057.

SKIPTON   North Yorkshire.   Map 24B8

Skipton Park (Acclaimed)   2 Salisbury St, BD23
1NQ ✆(0756) 700640.
*Small hotel offering luxury bedrooms and friendly
service, on corner of Gargrave Road (A65).*
🛏7 bedrs, 7 en suite; TV; tcf 🛗Breakfast only.
Unlic
£B&B £35, B&B (double) £40.

Highfield   58 Keighley Rd, BD23 2NB ✆(0756)
793182.
*Situated 1 mile from town centre on the A629 road
to Keighley and Bradford.*
🛏11 bedrs, 8 en suite, 1 ba; TV; tcf 🛗TV,
dogs ✕LD6, nr lunch & Sun dinner. Rest lic
£B&B £17–£18 **cc** Access, B'card/Visa; dep.

Craven Heifer Farm   Grassington Road, BD23
3LA ✆(0756) 793732.   *Farm*. Dorothy Hundsdoerfer
Sleeps 6, ☖
£ B&B from £10–£13, D £8   ♿

SLALEY   Northumberland.   Map 23B7

Rye Hill Farm   Nr Hexham, NE47 0AH ✆(0434)
673259.   *Farm*. Elizabeth Courage
Sleeps 15, 🐎☖
£ B&B from £13–£16, D £9

SLEAFORD   Lincolnshire.   Map 25A4

Cross Keys (Acclaimed)   Cross Key Yard ✆(0529)
305463 Fax: (0529) 414495.
*Former pub, rebuilt and refurbished, and situated
in a quiet picturesque mews. Opposite the parish
church and next to the Market Square in Eastgate.*
🛏12 bedrs, 6 en suite, 2 ba; TV; tcf 🛗TV, ns; P7,
coach; child facs ✕LD 8, nr Sun & Sat dinner
£B&B £22–£28, B&B (double) £32–£40; L£4·95,
D£5·95; WB£26; [5% V w/e] **cc** Access, B'card/
Visa; dep.

SLOUGH   Berkshire.   Map 26F5

Colnbrook Lodge   Bath Rd, Colnbrook SL3 0NZ
✆(0753) 685958.
*Situated in the village of Colnbrook close to the
Punchbowl pub.* Closed Xmas & New Year.

🛏8 bedrs, 2 en suite; 2 ba; TV; tcf 🛗TV; P12,
coach; child facs ✕Breakfast only. Resid lic
£B&B £25–£38, B&B (double) £35–£48; WB
£17·50; [10% V] **cc** Access, B'card/Visa; dep.

SOHAM   Cambridgeshire.   Map 27C9

Brook House (Acclaimed)   49 Brook St, CB7 5AD
✆(0353) 721522.
🛏16 bedrs, 14 en suite, 1 ba; TV; tcf 🛗dogs, ns;
P100, coach ✕LD9, nr Sat lunch & Sun dinner
cc Access, B'card/Visa.

SOLIHULL   West Midlands.   Map 24C1

Cedarwood House (Acclaimed)   347 Lyndon Rd,
Sheldon, B92 7QT ✆021-743 5844
*Substantial brick-built house, quietly located in a
residential area. From Birmingham on A45 turn first
left after main traffic lights in Sheldon into Lyndon
Rd.*
🛏5 bedrs, 5 en suite; TV; tcf 🛗TV, dogs; P5, no
children under 3 ✕Breakfast only. Unlic
£B&B £30–£40, B&B (double) £40–£50; [5% V
w/d]; dep.

Richmond House   47 Richmond Rd, Olton, B92
7RP ✆021-707 9746.
🛏14 bedrs, 14 en suite; TV; tcf 🛗dogs, ns; P30,
coach; child facs ✕LD 10
cc B'card/Visa.

SOMERTON   Somerset.   Map 29D5

Lynch Country House (Highly Acclaimed)
4 Behind Berry, TA11 7PD ✆(0458) 72316
Fax: (0458) 74370.

*Late 18-century country house with exotic lake and
wildlife sanctuary in the grounds. Situated between
Yeovil and Glastonbury.*
🛏10 bedrs, 10 en suite; TV 🛗dogs, ns; P15; child
facs ✕LD 9·30, nr lunch. Rest lic
£B&B £30–£60, B&B (double) £50–£90; L£10,
D£18·50; WB; [5% V w/d] **cc** Access, B'card/Visa

Church Farm   School La, Compton Dundon,
TA11 6PE ✆(0458) 72927.
🛏7 bedrs, 7 en suite; TV; tcf 🛗dogs; P7; no
children under 4 ✕LD5, nr lunch. Resid lic.

Lower Farm   Kingweston, TA11 6BA ☎(0458)
223237. *Farm*. Mrs Jane Sedgman
Sleeps 5
£ B&B from £18·50

SOUTHAMPTON   Hampshire.   Map 26D3

Dormy (Acclaimed)   21 Barnes La, Sarisbury,
Warsash, SO3 6DA ☎Locks Heath (0489) 572626.
*Late Victorian house sympathetically converted to
a small hotel. Leave M27 at exit 8, follow signs to
Fareham and A27 and turn right on brow of hill
opposite Bat and Ball pub. Hotel about 1 mile on
right.*
🛏10 bedrs, 7 en suite, (1 sh), 1 ba; TV; tcf 🛎TV,
P18 coach; child facs ✗LD7, nr lunch, Fri–Sun
dinner. Unlic
£B&B £20–£32, B&B (double) £40–£46; [10% V
w/e]; dep.

Hunters Lodge (Acclaimed)   25 Landguard Rd,
Shirley, SO1 5DL ☎(0703) 227919.
*Family-run hotel with pleasant accommodation.
From railway station take Commercial Rd into Hill
Lane, and Landguard Rd is fourth on the left.
Closed Xmas & New Year.*
🛏17 bedrs, 7 en suite, (3 sh), 2 ba; TV; tcf 🛎TV,
dogs, ns; P17, U4, coach; child facs ✗nr lunch
& Fri–Sun dinner. Resid lic
£B&B £23·58, B&B (double) £42·50; D£7; WB £16
cc Access, B'card/Visa; dep.

Banister House   Banister Rd, Banister Park, SO1
2JJ ☎(0703) 221279.
*A personally-run hotel about 1 mile NE of
Southampton centre, just off A33 Winchester road.
Closed Xmas.*
🛏23 bedrs, 5 en suite, (9 sh), 6 ba; TV; tcf 🛎dogs;
P14; child facs ✗LD 7.45, nr lunch & Fri–Sun
dinner. Resid lic
£B&B £21–£26·50, B&B (double) £30·50–£35;
[5% V] cc Access, B'card/Visa; dep.

Earley House   46 Pear Tree Av, Bitterne, SO2 7JP
☎(0703) 448117.
🛏10 bedrs, 6 en suite, 2 ba; tcf 🛎TV, dogs, ns;
P35; child facs ✗nr lunch. Resid lic
£B&B £25, B&B (double) £45; HB weekly £162·50;
D£8; [10% V]

Landguard Lodge   21 Landguard Rd SO1 5DL
☎(0703) 636904
*Take Hill Ln from station to common, and
Landguard Rd is the fourth turning on the left.*
🛏13 bedrs, 1 en suite, 3 ba; TV; tcf 🛎TV; P4; no
children under 5

Linden   51 The Polygon, SO1 2BP ☎(0703)
225653.
In the city centre close to railway and coach station.

🛏12 bedrs, 3 ba; TV; tcf 🛎TV, ns; P7, coach; child
facs ✗Breakfast only. Unlic
£B&B £12·50–£13·50; [5% V]; dep.

Nirvana   386 Winchester Rd, Bassett, SO1 7DH
☎(0703) 790087.
*Small tudor style hotel 2 miles from city centre. Take
the Avenue towards Winchester, turn left into
Winchester Rd, and hotel is ½ mile on right opposite
shops.*
🛏21 bedrs, 8 en suite, 4 ba; TV; tcf 🛎dogs; P21,
coach; child facs ✗LD8.45, nr lunch & Fri–Sun
dinner. Resid lic
£B&B £24–£26, B&B (double) £38–£40; HB weekly
£235; [5% V] cc Access; B'card/Visa; dep.

Villa Capri   50–52 Archers RD S01 2LU ☎(0703)
632800.
Situated by Southampton Football Club. Sauna.
🛏14 bedrs, 11 en suite, 2 ba; TV; tcf 🛎TV, dogs;
coach; child facs ✗Unlic
£B&B £12·10–£15; D£4·50 cc Access, B'card/
Visa; dep.

SOUTH BRENT   Devon.   Map 28G3

Coombe House (Acclaimed)   North Huish, TQ10
9NJ ☎Gara Bridge (054 882) 277.

*Georgian-style farmhouse offering a high standard
of country house accommodation. At Avonwick pub
turn right on Ugborough Rd, take first left and third
right. Signed. Open 1 Mar–15 Dec.*
🛏4 bedrs, 4 en suite; tcf 🛎TV; P10; no children
under 5 ✗Breakfast only. Resid lic
£B&B £25; [5% V]; dep.

West Cannamore Farm   Wrangaton, TQ10 9HA
☎(0364) 72250. *Farm*. Mrs P E Wakeham   ♿
Sleeps 9, 🐎🐂
£ B&B from £11·50, D£6

Weekend breaks
Please consult the hotel for full details of weekend
breaks; prices shown are an indication only.
Many hotels offer mid week breaks as well.

SOUTHEND-ON-SEA Essex.   Map 27D6

Ilfracombe (Highly Acclaimed)   11 Wilson Rd,
SS1 1HG ✆(0702) 351000.
*Family-run hotel set in a conservation area halfway
between Westcliff Station and Southend Central
Station.*
⊨14 bedrs, 14 en suite; TV; tcf ⋔TV; coach; child
facs ✗LD 7.30. Resid lic
£B&B £28·75–£35·65, B&B (double) £42·55–
£49·45; HB weekly £297·10; WB (£28·75); [5% V]
cc Access, Amex, B'card/Visa, Diners; dep.

Argyle   12 Cliff Town Par, SS1 1DP ✆(0702)
339483.
*Small hotel on the cliffs facing the sea, opposite
Southend bandstand. Closed Xmas.*
⊨11 bedrs, (1 sh), 3 ba; TV; tcf ⋔TV; no children
under 5 ✗nr dinner. Resid & Rest lic
£B&B £17–£20; dep.

The Bay   187 Eastern Esplanade, SS1 3AA
✆(0702) 588415.
*Seafront hotel situated at Thorpe Bay. From
Southend centre follow seafront east towards
Shoeburyness for about 1 mile.*
⊨9 bedrs, 2 en suite, 2 ba; TV; tcf ⋔TV, dogs, ns;
P 3; child facs ✗Breakfast only. Unlic
£B&B £15–£18, B&B (double) £25–£30; dep.

Mayflower   6 Royal Terr, SS1 1DY ✆(0702)
340489.
⊨24 bedrs, 4 en suite, 5 ba; TV ⋔TV, dogs; child
facs ✗Breakfast only. Unlic
£B&B £18–£30, B&B (double) £32–£40.

Regency   18 Royal Terr, SS1 1DU ✆(0702)
340747

Terrace   8 Royal Terr, SS1 1DY ✆(0702) 348143.
*Small hotel overlooking the sea. At Pier roundabout
turn up Pier Hill and into Royal Terrace.*
⊨9 bedrs, 2 ba; tcf ⋔TV, dogs; coach; no children
under 5 ✗Breakfast only. Resid lic
£B&B £16, B&B (double) £28; dep.

SOUTH HUISH South Devon.   Map 28G1

South Huish Farm   Kingsbridge, TQ7 3EH
✆(0548) 561237. *Farm.* David and Jill Darke
Sleeps 6, ⛧
£ B&B from £11, D £7

SOUTH LOPHAM Norfolk.   Map 25E1

Malting Farm   Bio Norton Road, Diss, IP22 2HT
✆(037 988) 201. *Farm.* Cynthia Huggins
Sleeps 6, ns ⛧
£ B&B from £13

SOUTH MOLTON Devon.   Map 28G5

Heasley House   Heasley Mill, EX36 3LE ✆North
Molton (059 84) 213.

*Fine old residence with pleasant views, just inside
Exmoor National Park. Situated 5 miles N of South
Molton. Open Mar–Oct.*
⊨8 bedrs, 5 en suite, 2 ba ⋔TV, dogs, ns; P 11;
child facs ✗LD 6, nr lunch. Resid & Rest lic
£B&B £16–£17·50; HB weekly £170–£180; D £8·50
cc Access, B'card/Visa; dep.

Greenhills Farm   West Amstey, EX36 3NU ✆(039
84) 300. *Farm.* Mrs Gillian Carr
Sleeps 5
£ B&B from £11, D from £4

Headgate Farm   Twitchen, EX36 1BD ✆(059 84)
481. *Farm.* Mrs Judy Hayes
Sleeps 4, ⛧⛨ ns
£ B&B from £14, D £8

Sheepwash Farm   Molland, EX36 3NN ✆(076 97)
276. *Farm.* Rosalind Hayes
Sleeps 6, ⛧
£ B&B from £14, D £9

West Trayne   Georgenympton, EX36 4JE ✆(076
95) 2534. *Farm.* Phyl Rawle
Sleeps 6, ⛨⛧ (10)
£ B&B from £10·50, D from £6

SOUTHPORT Merseyside.   Map 30D7

Merlwood (Acclaimed)   22 Portland St, PR8 1HU
✆(0704) 531247.

*Large Victorian house with spacious
accommodation set in a town centre position. Open
Mar–Oct.*
⊨6 beds, 2 en suite, 2 ba; TV; tcf ⋔TV; P 8; no
children under 5 ✗LD 3, nr lunch. Unlic
£B&B £12–£16, HB weekly £105–£119; WB;
[10% V]; dep.

Ambassador   13 Bath St, PR9 0DP ✆(0704)
43998/30459. Closed Jan 1–15.
⊨8 bedrs, 8 en suite, 2 ba; TV; tcf ⋔dogs, ns; P 6;
no children under 4 ✗LD 7. Resid lic
£B&B £30; HB weekly £165; L £3, D £9 cc Access,
B'card/Visa; dep.

Brae-Mar   4 Bath St, PR9 0DA ✆(0704) 535838

Crimond   Knowsley Rd, PR9 0HN ✆(0704)
536456

Small family hotel with many facilities. Knowsley Rd runs parallel with the Promenade. Indoor swimming pool, sauna.
⇔17 bedrs, 17 en suite; TV; tcf 🐾dogs, ns; P 25, child facs ✗LD 8.30, nr lunch.
£B&B £37, B&B (double) £58; D £10; WB (£40 2 nights); [5% V] cc Access, Amex, B'card/Visa, Diners; dep.

Fairways 106 Leyland Rd, PR9 0DQ ☎(0704) 542069.
Follow along Promenade to end of boating lake, take right turn into Leyland Rd and hotel is three blocks down on the left. Open Feb–Nov.
⇔9 bedrs, 4 en suite, 3 ba; TV; tcf 🐾TV, P 10, coach; child facs ✗LD 6, nr lunch. Resid lic
£B&B £15–£19, B&B (double) £30–£34; dep.

Lake 55 Promenade PR9 0DY ☎(0704) 530996.
Set in the centre of the Promenade.
⇔21 bedrs, 20 en suite; 1 ba; TV; tcf 🐾TV, dogs, ns; P 14, coach; no children under 5 ✗LD 4, nr Mon–Sat lunch, Sun dinner. Resid lic
£B&B £20–£21, B&B (double) £35·60–£37·60; HB weekly £147·20; D £7; [10% V Oct–Easter]
cc B'card/Visa; dep.

Lyndhurst 101 King St, PR8 1LQ ☎(0704) 537520.
Small friendly guest house. Situated adjacent to Lord St 150 yards from the town hall.
⇔7 beds, 3 ba; TV; tcf 🐾TV; P 3, coach; children over 5 ✗LD midday, nr lunch. Resid lic
£B&B £13, HB weekly £116; D £5; dep.

Oakwood 7 Portland St, PR8 1LJ ☎(0704) 531858.
⇔8 bedrs, 4 en suite, 2 ba; TV; tcf 🐾TV, ns; P 10; no children under 4 ✗nr lunch. Resid lic

Rosedale 11 Talbot St, PR8 1HP ☎(0704) 530604.
Comfortable hotel in central situation. From the Promenade take Eastbank St and turn right into Talbot St.
⇔10 bedrs, 6 en suite, 2 ba; TV; tcf 🐾P 8, coach; child facs ✗LD 4, nr lunch. Resid lic
£B&B £14–£16; HB weekly £110–£130; [5% V Oct–Apr]; dep.

Sidbrook 14 Talbot St, PR8 1HP ☎(0704) 530608.
Family-run hotel with pleasant garden, 2 mins away from Tourist Information Centre. Sauna, solarium. Closed Xmas & New Year.
⇔10 bedrs, 7 en suite, 1 ba; TV; tcf 🐾P 10, coach; child facs ✗LD 5, nr lunch. Resid & Rest lic
£B&B £15–£18; HB weekly £90–£145; D £5·50 cc Access, B'card/Visa; dep.

Sunningdale 85 Leyland Rd, PR9 0NJ ☎(0704) 538673.

Detached house in its own spacious grounds. Leyland Rd is a turning off Albert Rd (A565).
⇔14 bedrs, 13 en suite, 1 ba; TV; tcf 🐾dogs, ns; P 10, coach; child facs ✗LD 4.30, nr lunch. Resid lic
£B&B £18–£20, B&B (double) £38; HB weekly £168–£182; D £7 cc Access, B'card/Visa; dep.

White Lodge 12 Talbot St, PR8 1HP ☎(0704) 536320.
Centrally located small hotel, 5 mins from coach and train stations, off East Bank St.
⇔9 bedrs, 3 en suite, (1 sh), 2 ba; tcf 🐾TV; P 6, coach; child facs ✗LD 6, nr lunch. Resid lic
£B&B £13–£18; HB weekly £120–£135; [10% V]; dep.

Whitworth Falls 16 Latham Rd, PR9 0JL ☎(0704) 530074.
Family-run hotel close to the Promenade, near Marine Lake.
⇔14 bedrs, 8 en suite, 3 ba; TV; tcf 🐾TV, dogs; P 9, coach; child facs ✗LD 9, nr lunch. Resid lic
£B&B £13·50; HB weekly £120; L £4, D £6; [5% Nov–May]; dep.

Windsor Lodge 37 Saunders St, PR9 0HJ ☎(0704) 530070.
⇔12 bedrs, 1 en suite, 3 ba; TV; tcf 🐾TV, P 10, coach; child facs ✗LD morning, nr lunch. Resid & Rest lic.

SOUTHSEA Hampshire

See PORTSMOUTH and SOUTHSEA.

SOUTHWELL Nottinghamshire. Map 24E4

Upton Fields (Acclaimed) Upton Rd, NG25 0QA ☎(0636) 812303.

Wood panelled, York stone house with inlaid gallery staircase and large garden. Halfway between Southwell and Upton on the A612.
⇔5 bedrs, 5 en suite; TV; tcf 🐾TV, dogs, ns; P 5, G 1; no children under 3, child facs ✗Breakfast only. Unlic

£ B&B £25, B&B (double) £45; WB (£40); [5% V Nov–Mar]

SOUTH WALSHAM Norfolk. Map 25F3

Old Hall Farm Norwich, NR13 6DS ☎(060 549) 271. *Farm.* Veronica and Richard Dewing ♿ Sleeps 6, ns ☻
£ B&B from £12–£16

SPALDING Lincolnshire. Map 25A3

Stables (Highly Acclaimed) Cowbit Rd PE11 2RJ ☎(0775) 767290 Fax: (0775) 767716.
Tastefully converted farm buildings, now a small motel. Situated on the A1073 Spalding to Peterborough Rd, ¾ mile from Spalding centre, on the Banks of the River Welland.
⇥11 bedrs, 11 en suite, 2 ba; TV; tcf ⋔dogs, ns; P20, coach; child facs ✗LD 9·30, nr Sun dinner. Resid & Rest lic

£ B&B £29·50–£46·50, B&B (double) £35–£80; HB weekly £308–£360; L £3·50, D £9·50; WB (£55); [5% V] **cc** Access, Amex, B'card/Visa, Diner.

STAFFORD Staffordshire. Map 24B3

Leonards Croft 80 Lichfield Rd, ST17 4LP ☎(0785) 223676.
Take A34 from town centre, hotel on left at foot of railway bridge. Putting. Closed Xmas & New Year.
⇥12 bedrs, 4 ba; tcf ⋔TV, dogs; P12; child facs ✗LD 9, nr lunch. Resid lic
£ B&B £16·50.

STAINES Surrey. Map 27A5

Angel 24 High St, TW19 5NT ☎(0784) 452509 Fax: (0784) 458336.
Former coaching inn in central position opposite Debenhams.
⇥11 bedrs, 2 ba; tcf ⋔TV, dogs; P 50, coach; child facs ✗LD 9, nr Sun dinner

Southwell (Nottinghamshire)

Symbols (full details on p. 4)

⇥ information about bedrooms
⋔ facilities at hotels
✗ information about meals
nr no restaurant service
⁑ languages spoken
[V] RAC vouchers accepted
Farms
ᵀ dogs accepted
☻ (4) children accepted (min. age)

Weekend breaks
Please consult the hotel for full details of weekend breaks; prices shown are an indication only. Many hotels offer mid week breaks as well.

En suite rooms
En suite rooms may be bath or shower rooms. If you have a preference, remember to state it when booking a room.

£B&B £30, B&B (double) £42; L£8, D£8; [5% V]
cc Access, Amex, B'card/Visa; dep.

Swan Inn   The Hythe, TW183JB ✆(0784) 452494
or 454471 Fax:(0784) 461593.
Close to Staines Bridge where A30 meets A320.
🛏6bedrs, 2ba; TV; tcf 🏠dogs; coach ✖LD 10
£B&B £33, B&B (double) £47; L£9·50, D£9·50
cc Access, Amex, B'card/Visa, Diners; dep.

STAINTONDALE   North Yorkshire. Map 23F4

Island Farm   Scarborough, YO13 0EB ✆(0723)
870249/870675. *Farm.* Mary Clarke
Sleeps 6, 🐴 ns 🐕
£ B&B from £12, D £7

STANFORD RIVERS   Essex.   Map 27B6

New House Farm   Mutton Row, Nr Ongar, CM5
9QH ✆(0277) 362132. *Farm.* Mrs Beryl Martin   &
Sleeps 10, 🐕
£ B&B from £15

STANNERSBURN   Northumberland.
Map 23B7

🍺 **Pheasant**   Falstone, Hexham, NE48 1DD
✆Bellingham (0660) 40382.
*Stone-built inn dating back 350 years, set in rural
surroundings amidst fine scenery.*
🛏11 bedrs, 2 en suite, 2 ba; TV; tcf 🏠dogs, ns;
P40, coach; child facs ✖LD 9; bar meals only
Mon–Sat lunch
£B&B £18–£24, B&B (double) £34–£42; HB weekly
£176·40–£186·40, L£7·50, D£10·50; WB £24 (HB);
dep.

STANTON HEATH   Shropshire.   Map 24A3

Longley Farm, Shawbury, SY4 4HE ✆(0939)
250289. *Farm.* Sue Clarkson   &
Sleeps 6, 🐴 🐕
£ B&B from £11–£15, D from £5

STANTON-UPON-HINE
HEATH   Shropshire.   Map 24A3

The Sett   Shrewsbury, SY4 4LR ✆(0939)
250391. *Farm.* Brenda and Jim Grundey   &
Sleeps 14, 🐴 ns 🐕
£ B&B from £18, D £10

STAPE   North Yorkshire.   Map 23E4

Seavy Slack   Pickering, YO18 8HZ ✆(0751)
73131. *Farm.* Anne Barrett
Sleeps 6, 🐴 🐕
£ B&B from £12, D from £8

STARBOTTON   N. Yorkshire.   Map 23B3

Hilltop (Highly Acclaimed)   nr Skipton, BD23 5HY
✆Kettlewell (075 676) 321.

*Listed building owned by present family since the
early 1600s. Beautifully situated with fine views. On
B6160 16 miles N of Skipton. Open Mar–Nov.*
🛏5 bedrs, 5 en suite; TV; tcf 🏠ns; P6; child
facs ✖LD 6, nr lunch. Resid & Rest lic
£ B&B (double) £48; D£14; [5% V exc Jun–Sep];
dep.

STAVELEY   Cumbria.   Map 23A4

Stockbridge Farm, Kendal, LA8 9LP ✆(0539)
821580. *Farm.* Mrs Betty Fishwick
Sleeps 11, 🐴 🐕
£ B&B from £10·50–£11·50

STEANE   Northamptonshire.   Map 26E7

Walltree House Farm   Brackley, NN13 5NS
✆(0295) 811235. *Farm.* Richard and Pauline
Harrison
Sleeps 16, 🐴 🐕
£ B&B from £17–£26

STEEPLE ASHTON   Wiltshire.   Map 26B4

Spiers Piece Farm   Nr Trowbridge, BA14 6HG
✆(0380) 870266. *Farm.* Jill Awdry   &
Sleeps 5, 🐕
£ B&B from £12·50

STEEPLE ASTON   Oxfordshire.   Map 26D7

Westfield Farm   The Fenway, OX5 3SS ✆(0869)
40591.
*Situated on A423 halfway between Banbury and
Oxford in the village of Steeple Aston. Riding.*
🛏6 bedrs, 6en suite; TV; tcf 🏠TV, dogs; P20;
child facs ✖Breakfast only. Unlic
£ B&B £28–£33, B&B (double) £41–£46;
[10% V w/e] **cc**Access, B'card/Visa; dep.

STEYNING   West Sussex.   Map 27A3

Nash Country (Acclaimed)   Horsham Rd, BN4
3AA ✆(0903) 814988.
*16th-century country house in large grounds and
with lovely views, on the B2135 off A283. Swimming
pool, tennis.*

4 bedrs, 1 en suite, 3 ba; TV; tcf TV, dogs, ns;
P10, coach Breakfast only
£ B&B £25, B&B (double) £40; [10% V].

Springwells High St, BN4 3GG (0903) 812446.
Swimming pool, sauna.
11 bedrs, 7 en suite, 2 ba; TV; tcf TV, dogs;
P6; child facs Breakfast only. Resid lic
cc Access, Amex, B'card/Visa, Diners.

ST HILARY Cornwall. Map 28B1

Ennys Penzance, TR20 9BZ (0736)
740262. *Farm.* Sue White
Sleeps 10,
£ B&B from £17−£20, D £11

ST MARTIN-BY-LOOE Cornwall. Map 28E2

Bucklawren Farm PL13 1NZ (05034)
738. *Farm.* Mrs Jean Henly
Sleeps 12,
£ B&B from £11−£15, D £7

ST MEWAN Cornwall. Map 28D2

Poltarrow Farm St Austell, PL26 7DR (0726)
67111. *Farm.* Judith Nancarrow
Sleeps 6,
£ B&B from £14, D £8

ST NEWLYN EAST Cornwall. Map 28C3

Degembris Farmhouse Newquay, TR8 5HY
(0872) 510555. *Farm.* Kathy Woodley
Sleeps 12,
£ B&B from £12−£14, D £7

STOCKBRIDGE Hampshire. Map 26D4

Carbery (Acclaimed) Salisbury Hill, SO20 6EZ
(0264) 810771.

*A fine old Georgian house situated in one acre of
gardens overlooking the River Test. Swimming pool.*
11 bedrs, 8 en suite, 1 ba; TV; tcf P12, coach;
child facs LD6, nr lunch. Resid lic
£ B&B £17·25−£25, B&B (double) £34·50−£40·25;
HB weekly £177·34−£230·34; dep.

Old Three Cups (Acclaimed) High St, SO20 6HB
(0264) 810527.

*15th-century coaching inn with beautifully kept
gardens. Situated halfway between Winchester and
Salisbury on the A30, in Stockbridge High St.
Closed Jan.*
8 bedrs, 3 en suite, 1 ba; TV P8 LD9.15, nr
Mon & dinner Sun. Resid & Rest lic
£ B&B £22−£32, B&B (double) £32−£42; L £6·75,
D £8; [5% V] cc Access, B'card/Visa; dep.

STOKE-ON-TERN Shropshire. Map 24A3

Stoke Manor Market Drayton, TF9 2DU (063
084) 222. *Farm.* Mike and Julia Thomas
Sleeps 6, ns
£ B&B from £20

STOKE PRIOR Herefordshire. Map 31C8

Great House Farm Leominster, HR6 0LG
(056882) 663. *Farm.* Shirley Bemand
Sleeps 6,
£ B&B from £11, D £7

STON EASTON Avon. Map 29D6

Midway House Bath, BA3 4DQ (076 121)
280. *Farm.* Mrs Jose Pullin
Sleeps 6, (2)
£ B&B on application

STOCKPORT Greater Manchester (Cheshire). Map 24B5

Ascot House 195 Wellington Rd North, SK4 2PB
061-432 2380 Fax: 061-443 1936.
*Recently modernised small hotel. Leave M63 at
junction 12, turn left onto A6, and hotel is on the
left towards Manchester.*
18 bedrs, 12 en suite, (6 sh), 3 ba; TV; tcf TV,
P20, coach; child facs LD7.15, nr lunch & Fri−
Sun dinner. Resid & Rest lic
£ B&B £25−£33, B&B (double) £38−£45; WB
cc Access, Amex, B'card/Visa.

STOURBRIDGE W. Midlands. Map 24B1

Limes 260 Hagley Rd, Pedmore, DY9 0RW
Hagley (0562) 882689.
Situated on A491, 1¼ miles outside Stourbridge.
11 bedrs, 2 ba; TV; tcf TV, dogs; P11, coach;
child facs LD7.15, nr lunch, Fri−Sun dinner.
Unlic
cc Access, B'card/Visa.

STOW-ON-THE-WOLD Gloucestershire. Map 26C7

Cross Keys Cottage (Acclaimed) Park St, GL54
1AQ Cotswold (0451) 31128.
3 bedrs, 1 en suite, 2 ba; TV; tcf TV, dogs; no

children under 7 ✗Breakfast only. Unlic

Limes (Acclaimed)   Tewkesbury Rd, GL54 1EN
✆Cotswold (0451) 30034.
*Large house situated in its own gardens. On the
A424 Evesham Rd.* Closed Xmas & New Year.
🛏5 bedrs, 3 en suite, (1 sh); TV 📺TV, dogs;
P5 ✗Breakfast only. Unlic
£B&B (double) £26–£32; dep.

Royalist   Digbeth St, GL54 1BN ✆Cotswold
(0451) 30670
🛏14 bedrs, 14 en suite; TV; tcf 📺P12; child facs;
con 25 ✗LD9, bar meals only lunch, Mon & Sun
dinner
£B&B £25–£35

STRAMSHALL Staffordshire.   Map 24C3

Stramshall Farm   Uttoxeter, ST14 5AG ✆(0889)
562363. *Farm.* Lynette Bailey
Sleeps 6, 🐓🐄
£ B&B from £10–£15

STRATFORD-UPON-AVON
   Warwickshire.   Map 26C8

Melita (Highly Acclaimed)   37 Shipston Rd, CV37
7LN ✆(0789) 292432.

*Imposing Victorian building once a family home with
delightful award-winning garden. Situated on the
A34 (Oxford side of town) close to Clopton Bridge.*
🛏12 bedrs, 12 en suite; TV; tcf 📺TV, dogs, ns;
P12, coach; child facs ✗Breakfast only
£B&B £27–£37, B&B (double) £45–£52; [5%V
Jan–May w/d] **cc** Access, B'card/Visa; dep.

Twelfth Night (Highly Acclaimed)   Evesham Pl,
CV37 6HT ✆(0789) 414595.
🛏7 bedrs, 5 en suite, (1 sh), 1 ba; TV; tcf 📺NS; P2,
G2, coach; no children under 5 ✗Breakfast only.
Unlic.

Ambleside (Acclaimed)   41 Grove Rd, CV37 6PB
✆(0789) 297239/295670.
🛏6 bedrs, 3 en suite, 1 ba; TV; tcf 📺TV, dogs, ns;
P20; child facs ✗Breakfast only. Unlic
£B&B £14–£16, B&B (double) £28–£40; [10%V]
cc Access, B'card/Visa; dep.

Avon View (Acclaimed)   121 Shipston Rd, CV37
7LW ✆(0789) 297542 Fax:(0789) 294550.
🛏10beds, 10en suite; TV; tcf 📺TV, ns; P12,
coach; children over 12 ✗Breakfast only. Resid lic
cc Access, Amex, B'card/Visa, Diners; dep.

Hardwick House (Acclaimed)   1 Avenue Rd,
CV37 6UY ✆(0789) 204307.

Stratford-upon-Avon (Warwickshire)

𝕸elita 𝕻rivate 𝕳otel

37 Shipston Road, Stratford-upon-Avon, CV37 7LN
Telephone: (0789) 292432

RAC
Highly Acclaimed

Built in 1888 as an imposing Victorian residence **'The Melita'** has been tastefully transformed into a beautifully appointed family run hotel. We offer our guests a very friendly welcome, cheerful service, excellent breakfasts and a high standard of accommodation.

Ample car parking is available. The theatre and town centre are only a pleasant five minute walk away. Therefore, whether touring the Heart of England or relaxing in our award winning garden, we feel sure you will enjoy your stay at **'The Melita'**.

Large attractive house set in a quiet, mature, tree-lined avenue. Situated off Stratford to Warwick Rd near St Gregory's Catholic Church. Closed Xmas.
⇥14 bedrs, 7 en suite, 4 ba; TV; tcf �📻 ns; P 12, coach; child facs ✕ Breakfast only. Unlic
£ B&B £15–£24; [10% V] cc Access, Amex, B'card/Visa; dep.

Nando's (Acclaimed)   18 Evesham Pl, CV37 6HT
☎ (0789) 204907.
A warm, comfortable guest house only minutes from the Royal Shakespeare Theatre. Set on the A422 Evesham side of town.
⇥21 bedrs, 7 en suite, 4 ba; TV �📻 TV, dogs, ns; P 7, coach; child facs ✕ LD 8. Unlic

Victoria Spa Lodge (Acclaimed)   Bishopton La, Bishopton, CV37 9QY ☎ (0789) 67985.
A comfortable, elegant Victorian house in peaceful surroundings overlooking the canal. On A34 at its junction with A46, 1½ miles N of Stratford.
⇥7 bedrs, 4 en suite, 2 ba; TV; tcf �📻 ns; P 12; child facs ✕ LD 4, nr lunch. Unlic
£ B&B £30–£35, B&B (double) £36–£42 cc Access, B'card/Visa; dep.

Virginia Lodge (Acclaimed)   12 Evesham Pl, CV37 6HT ☎ (0789) 292157.

Attractive Victorian house in the centre of town with individually designed bedrooms. Follow Evesham signs and Virginia Lodge is on the right.
⇥7 beds, 4 en suite, 2 ba; TV; tcf �📻 TV, dogs, ns; P 6, G 2 ✕ nr lunch. Resid lic

£ B&B £12–£14; [10% V]; dep.

Woodburn House (Acclaimed)   89 Shipston Rd, CV37 7LW ☎ (0789) 204453. *Hotel.*

Cymbeline House   24 Evesham Pl, CV37 6HT
☎ (0789) 292958.
⇥4 bedrs, 1 en suite, (2 sh), 1 ba; TV; tcf �📻 TV, dogs, ns; P 1, G 1 ✕ Breakfast only. Unlic.

Dylan   10 Evesham Pl, CV37 6HT ☎ (0789) 204819.
A 5 min walk from the town centre and Royal Shakespeare Theatre.
⇥5 bedrs, 4 en suite, TV; tcf �📻 dogs; P 3 ✕ LD 7, nr lunch, Sun dinner. Unlic
£ B&B £13–£19, B&B (double) £30–£38; HB weekly £151–£182.

Glenavon   Chestnut Walk, CV37 6HG ☎ (0789) 292588.
Situated in the road next to the Royal Shakespeare Theatre. Closed 24–31 Dec.
⇥15 bedrs, 4 ba �📻 TV, dogs, ns; coach; child facs ✕ Breakfast only. Unlic
£ B&B £12–£15; dep.

Marlyn   3 Chestnut Walk, CV37 6HG ☎ (0789) 293752.
Centrally situated close to Halls Croft and Holy Trinity Church. Closed Xmas.
⇥8 bedrs, 2 ba; tcf �📻 TV ✕ Breakfast only. Unlic
£ B&B £16, B&B (double) £30; dep.

Parkfield   3 Broad Walk, CV37 6HS ☎ (0789) 293313.
⇥6 bedrs, 4 en suite, 2 ba; TV; tcf �📻 dogs, ns; P 6, coach; children over 6 ✕ Breakfast only. Unlic
cc Access, B'card/Visa; dep.

Penryn   126 Alcester Rd, CV37 9DP ☎ (0789) 293718.
Small hotel close to Ann Hathaway's Cottage, situated on the A422.
⇥8 bedrs, 5 en suite, 1 ba; TV; tcf �📻 dogs, ns; P 8, coach; child facs ✕ Breakfast only. Unlic

---

Stratford-upon-Avon (Warwickshire)

£ B&B £18–£30, B&B (double) £28–£40; WB **cc** Access, B'card/Visa; dep.

Penshurst 34 Evesham Pl, CV37 6HT ✆ (0789) 205259.
⊨ 7 bedrs, 2 en suite, 2 ba; tcf 🛗 ns; P 3, coach; child facs ✗ LD 12 noon. Resid lic

Ravenhurst 2 Broad Walk, CV37 6HS ✆ (0789) 292515.
⊨ 7 bedrs, 3 en suite, 2 ba; TV; tcf 🛗 ns; coach ✗ Breakfast only. Resid lic **cc** Access, Amex, B'card/Visa, Diners; dep.

STRETTON GRANDISON Herefordshire.
Map 31C8

Moor Court Farm Nr Ledbury, HR8 2TR ✆ (053 183) 408. *Farm.* Elizabeth Godsall
Sleeps 6, �](🐕 ✗)
£ B&B from £12–£16, D £8

STROUD Gloucestershire. Map 26B6

Downfield (Acclaimed) 134 Cainscross Rd, GL5 4HN ✆ (0453) 764496.
An imposing Georgian house set back from the road. Situated on the A419. Closed Xmas & New Year.
⊨ 21 bedrs, 10 en suite, 3 ba; TV; tcf 🛗 TV, dogs; P 22, coach; child facs ✗ LD 8, nr lunch. Resid & Rest lic
£ B&B £18–£28, B&B (double) £32–£39; HB weekly £189; D £6; WB (£25 HB); [5% V] **cc** Access, B'card/Visa; dep.

Down Barn Farmhouse The Camp, GL6 7EY ✆ (0452) 812853. *Farm.* Anita Morley &
Sleeps 6, 🐕 🐈
£ B&B from £12

Wickridge Farm Folly Lane, GL6 8JT ✆ (0453) 764357. *Farm.* Gloria and Peter Watkins
Sleeps 4, 🐕 ns 🐈
£ B&B from £13–£16, D £9

STURMINSTER MARSHALL Dorset.
Map 29E4

Henbury Farm Dorchester Road, Wimborne, BH21 3RN ✆ (0258) 857306. *Farm.* Sue and Jonathan Tory
Sleeps 6, 🐈
£ B&B from £12·50–£15

STURMINSTER NEWTON Dorset.
Map 29E5

Holebrook Farm Lydlinch, DT10 2JB ✆ (0258) 817348. *Farm.* Sally and Charles Wingate-Saul &
Sleeps 11, 🐈
£ B&B from £14, D £9

SUMMERCOURT Cornwall. Map 28D2

Goonhoskyn Farm TR8 4PP ✆ (0872) 510226.
⊨ 3 bedrs, 1 ba; TV; tcf 🛗 TV, ns; P 4; no children under 6 ✗ nr lunch. Unlic.

SURBITON Surrey. Map 27A5

Amber Lodge 54 The Avenue, KT5 8JL ✆ 081-390 7360, 081-399 3058.

Pembroke Lodge 35 Cranes Park, KT5 8AB ✆ 081-390 0731.
Small, conveniently situated guest house close to Surbiton Station.
⊨ 10 bedrs, 2 en suite, (3 sh), 2 ba; TV; tcf 🛗 TV, dogs; P 10, U 1, G 1, coach; child facs ✗ Breakfast only. Unlic
£ B&B £25·30, B&B (double) £34·50; dep.

SUTTON Surrey. Map 27A5

Thatched House (Acclaimed) 135 Cheam Rd, SM1 2BD ✆ 081-642 3131. Fax: 081-770 0684.
Cottage-style house, thatched and completely modernised, with pretty gardens. Take A217 or A232 to Sutton.
⊨ 28 bedrs, 18 en suite, (1 sh). 4 ba; TV; tcf 🛗 TV, dogs; P 20; child facs ✗ LD 9, lunch and Sat–Sun dinner by arrangement. Resid & Rest lic
£ B&B £32·50–£47·50, B&B (double) £47·50–£62·50; D £12·75; [10% V w/e] **cc** Access, B'card/Visa; dep.

Dene 39 Cheam Rd, SM1 2AT ✆ 081-642 3170.
⊨ 28 bedrs, 12 en suite, (2 sh), 4 ba; TV; tcf 🛗 P 16; child facs ✗ Breakfast only. Unlic

Eaton Court 49 Eaton Rd, SM2 5ED ✆ 081-643 6766.
Situated 5 mins walk from Sutton Station. Closed Xmas & New Year.
⊨ 21 bedrs, 9 en suite, 2 ba; TV; tcf 🛗 TV, dogs; P 17, coach ✗ Breakfast only. Resid lic
£ B&B £30, B&B (double) £41; [10% V] **cc** Access, Amex, B'card/Visa.

Tara House 50 Rosehill, SM1 3EU ✆ 081-641 6142.
Situated opposite the leisure and tennis centre on the B317.
⊨ 13 bedrs, 7 en suite, 2 ba; TV; tcf 🛗 TV; P 14; no children under 2.

SUTTON-ON-SEA Lincolnshire. Map 25BE

Athelstone Lodge 25 Trusthorpe Rd, LN12 2LR ✆ (0507) 441521.
Friendly, welcoming hotel close to the sea front.
⊨ 7 bedrs, 3 en suite, 1 ba; tcf 🛗 TV, dogs; P 8; child facs ✗ LD 7, nr lunch. Resid lic
£ B&B £14–£15·50; HB weekly £216–£238; D £8; WB (£38); [5% V Mar–Jun, Sept & Oct]; dep.

SWAFFHAM Norfolk.   Map 25C2

Horse & Groom (Acclaimed)   40 Lynn St, PE37 7AY ✆ (0760) 721567.

SWANAGE Dorset.   Map 26C1

Havenhurst (Acclaimed)   3 Cranborne Rd, BH19 1EA ✆ (0929) 424224.
Pleasant guest house of charm and character standing in its own grounds. From Shore Rd, turn left into Victoria Ave, first left and first right.
🛏17 bedrs, 17 en suite; tcf 🛏TV, ns; P20, coach; child facs ✗LD4.30, nr lunch
£ B&B £17–£23·50; HB weekly £150–£186; WB £50 (2 nts); [10% V]; dep.

Sandringham (Acclaimed)   20 Durlston Rd, BH19 2HX ✆ (0929) 423076.
Small family-run hotel in a residential area. Follow signs for Durlston. Open Jan–Nov.
🛏11 bedrs, 9 en suite, 1 ba; tcf 🛏TV, dogs, ns; P8; child facs ✗LD 6.30, nr lunch. Resid & Rest lic.

Seychelles (Acclaimed)   Burlington Rd, BH19 1LR ✆ (0929) 422794.
From the town centre continue along sea front past Ocean Bay, and take second right turning opposite the Grand Hotel. Open May–Sept.
🛏9 bedrs, 6 en suite, 2 ba; TV; tcf 🛏ns; P9, child facs ✗LD6.30, nr lunch. Rest lic
£ B&B £16; D£10; [5% V May, Jun & Sept]; dep.

Bella Vista   14 Burlington Rd, BH19 1LS ✆ (0929) 422873.
Delightful property overlooking the bay. From Shore Rd continue into Ulwell Rd and turn right into Burlington Rd. Open Feb–Nov.
🛏6 bedrs, 5 en suite, 1 ba; tcf 🛏TV, ns; P6; no children under 2, child facs ✗Breakfast only. Rest lic
£ B&B (double) £32–£36: dep.

Chines   9 Burlington Rd, BH19 1LR ✆ (0929) 422457.
Family-run hotel opposite Swanage Bay. From Shore Rd continue into Ulwell Rd and turn right into Burlington Rd. Open Apr–Nov.
🛏12 bedrs, 8 en suite, 2 ba; TV; tcf 🛏TV, ns; P10, coach; child facs ✗LD5, nr lunch. Resid lic
£ B&B £17·50; HB weekly £150–£176; dep.

Eversden   5 Victoria Rd, BH19 1LY ✆ (0929) 423276. *Hotel.*

Firswood   29 Kings Rd, BH19 9HF ✆ (0929) 422306.
Small informal hotel close to the sea front. Kings Rd is opposite the steam railway. Closed Xmas.
🛏6 bedrs, 2 en suite, 2 ba; TV; tcf 🛏TV, ns; P7; no children under 5 ✗LD5, nr lunch
£ B&B £12·50, HB weekly £130; D£7

Glenlee   6 Cauldon Av, BH19 1PQ ✆ (0929) 425794. *Hotel.*

Monsal   32/34 Victoria Ave BH19 1AP ✆ (0929) 422805.
A small family run hotel close to the beach, situated on the main Wareham road opposite King George's Field. Solarium.
🛏11 bedrs, 7 en suite, 2 ba; TV; tcf 🛏TV, dogs, ns; P12, coach; child facs ✗LD 6.30. Resid & Rest lic
£ B&B £14·38–£24·15, HB weekly £131·10–£194·35; D£5·75; [5% V w/d] cc Access, B'card/Visa; dep.

Oxford   3–5 Park Rd, BH19 2AA ✆ (0929) 422247.
Small Victorian hotel, extensively modernised. Follow signs for the Pier and Durlston Country Park. Open Feb–Nov.
🛏14 bedrs, 6 en suite, 2 ba; TV; tcf 🛏TV, ns; coach; children over 5 ✗LD4, nr lunch. Resid & Rest lic
£ B&B £18–£19; HB weekly £175–£182; D£8; WB £48; [5% V]; dep.

St Michaels   31 Kings Rd, BH19 1HF ✆ (0929) 422064.
🛏6 bedrs, 3 en suite, 2 ba; TV; tcf 🛏dogs; P 5; no children under 5 ✗LD3, nr lunch. Resid lic
£ B&B (double) £28–£34; dep.

SYMONDS YAT Hereford & Worcester (Herefordshire).   Map 31D8

Saracens Head (Highly Acclaimed)   Symonds Yat East, HR9 6JL ✆ (0600) 890435.

Half-timbered inn on banks of the River Wye. From A40 take B4229 signposted Symonds Yat East. (Do not follow Symond Yat West signs—other side of river, 6 miles by road!)

10 bedrs, 7 en suite, 1 ba; tcf TV; P 25; child facs LD 9
£ D £9; WB £43; [5% V w/d excl. Summer]
cc Access, Amex, B'card/Visa, Diners; dep.

Garth Cottage (Acclaimed)   Symonds Yat East, HR9 6JL (0600) 890364. *Fishing.*
5 bedrs, 3 en suite, (1 sh), 2 ba; tcf TV; P 7; no children under 12 LD 9.30. Resid & Rest lic
cc Access, B'card/Visa; dep.

Woodlea (Acclaimed)   Symonds Yat West, HR9 5BL (0600) 890206.

Family-run Victorian country house hotel in secluded woodland setting overlooking Wye rapids. 1¼ miles from A40 at the end of the B4164. Swimming pool. Closed mid Dec–mid Feb.
9 bedrs, 5 en suite, 2 ba; tcf TV, dogs; P 10; child facs LD 7, nr lunch. Resid & Rest lic
£ B&B £18·50–£19·75; HB weekly £179–£199; D £10; WB **cc** Access, B'card/Visa; dep.

SWINHOPE   Lincolnshire.   Map 25A5

Hoe Hill   Nr Binbrook, LN3 6HX (047 283) 206. *Farm.* Erica Curd
Sleeps 6,

£ B&B from £12, D £10

SYDLING ST NICHOLAS   Dorset.
Map 29D4

Lamperts Farmhouse   11 Dorchester Road, Dorchester, DT2 9NU (030 03) 41790. *Farm.* Mrs R Bown
Sleeps 6,
£ B&B from £12·50, D £6·50

Stonegates House, Lamperts Farm, Dorchester, DT2 9NR (030 0341) 832. *Farm.* Mrs J E C Wareham
Sleeps 6
£ B&B from £12–£14

TARRINGTON   Herefordshire.   Map 31C8

Wilton Oaks   HR1 4ET (0432) 890212. *Farm.* Jean Phillips
Sleeps 6, ns
£ B&B from £12·50

TATTENHALL   Cheshire.   Map 30E8

Pheasant Inn   Higher Burwardsley, CH3 9DF (0829) 70434 Fax: (0829) 71097.
A 300-year-old timber and sandstone inn with smart bedrooms mostly in a converted barn. Magnificent views.
8 bedrs, 8 en suite; TV; tcf dogs; P 60; no children under 14 LD 9.30, bar meals only lunch
£ B&B £35, B&B (double) £45; HB weekly £256; L £6·50; D £12; WB; [5% V w/e] **cc** Access, Amex, B'card/Visa, Diners; dep.

Symbols (full details on p. 4)

information about bedrooms	nr no restaurant service	*Farms*
facilities at hotels	languages spoken	dogs accepted
information about meals	[V] RAC vouchers accepted	(4) children accepted (min. age)

Taunton (Somerset)

TAUNTON   Somerset.   Map 29C5

Meryan House (Highly Acclaimed)   Bishops Hull,
TA1 5EG ✆(0823) 337445.

*Delightful Georgian listed residence complete with
inglenooks and beamed ceilings. Situated first right
off A38 Exeter Rd past crematorium.*
🛏12 bedrs, 12 en suite; TV; tcf 📺TV, dogs, ns;
P 17; child facs ✗LD 8, nr lunch, Sun dinner. Resid
& Rest lic
£B&B £32–£36, B&B (double) £40–£45; HB weekly
£283–£290; [5% V Nov–Mar w/e] **cc** Access,
B'card/Visa; dep.

Old Manor Farmhouse (Acclaimed)   A361 Norton
Fitzwarren, TA2 6RZ ✆(0823) 289801.
🛏7 bedrs, 7 en suite, 1 ba; TV; tcf 📺P 12;
child facs ✗LD 6, nr lunch, Mon dinner. Resid lic
£B&B £30–£32, B&B (double) £40–£42; HB weekly
£273–£286 **cc** Access, B'card/Visa, Diners; dep.

Brookfield   16 Wellington Rd, TA1 4EQ ✆(0823)
272786.
🛏7 bedrs, 2 ba; TV; tcf 📺dogs, ns; P 7; child
facs ✗LD 3, nr lunch. Resid & Rest lic
£B&B £13–£15, B&B (double) £24–£28; HB weekly
£126–£140; D £5; dep.

White Lodge   81 Bridgwater Rd, TA1 2DU
✆(0823) 321112.
*Leave motorway at exit 25. Turn right at first
roundabout signed Taunton, take first left at next
roundabout, and hotel is signed.*
🛏40 bedrs, 40 en suite; TV; tcf 📺ns; P 100, coach;
child facs ✗LD 10·30
£B&B £27·50

Bushfurlong Farm   Isle Brewers, TA3 6QT
✆(04608) 219
From 1991 (0460) 281219. *Farm*. Michael and
Judith Glide
Sleeps 6, ns ☂
£ B&B from £15

TEBAY   Cumbria.   Map 23A5

Carmel House (Acclaimed)   Mount Pleasant CA10
3TH ✆(05874) 651.
*Large detached stone house, completely
refurbished to a high standard. From junction 38 of
the M6 follow Kendal signs for ¼ mile, hotel on the*

left before the phone box. Closed Xmas & New
Year.
🛏7 bedrs, 7 en suite; TV; tcf 📺TV; P 6;
child facs ✗Breakfast only. Unlic
£B&B £14·50–£16·50; dep.

TEDBURN ST MARY   Devon.   Map 29A4

🍺 **King's Arms**   EX6 6EG ✆(064 76) 224.
Small 17th century coaching inn in centre of village.
🛏8 bedrs, 1 en suite, (1 sh), 2 ba; TV; tcf 📺dogs;
P 50, coach; child facs; con 70 ✗LD 10, bar meals
only Mon–Sat lunch
£B&B £17·50, B&B (double) £27; L £4·95, D £8;
[5% V Mon–Wed] **cc** Amex, B'card/Visa.

TEIGNMOUTH   Devon.   Map 29B3

Cotteswold   Second Drive, Landscore Rd, TQ14
9JS ✆(0626) 774662. *Hotel. Swimming pool, sauna.*
🛏15 bedrs, 9 en suite, (1 sh), 3 ba; TV; tcf 📺dogs;
P 12, coach; child facs ✗LD 6. Resid lic

Glen Devon   3 Carlton Pl, TQ14 8AB ✆(0626)
772895.
*Follow road through Teignmouth to the Den Green
by the seafront. Hotel is behind cinema.*
🛏7 bedrs, 4 en suite, (1 sh), 1 ba; tcf 📺TV; P 5;
child facs ✗LD 5, nr Mon–Sat lunch & Sun dinner.
Resid & Rest lic
£B&B (double) £11–£12; HB weekly £90–£112;
[10% V excl Jul & Aug]; dep.

TELFORD   Shropshire.   Map 24A2

🍺 🍺 🍺 **Hundred House**   Norton TF11 9EE
✆(095 271) 353 Tx: 35815.
*Stylishly refurbished 18th-century inn with Tudor out-
buildings forming a rear courtyard. On main A442,
5 miles SE of Telford.*
🛏9 bedrs, 9 en suite; TV; tcf 📺dogs; P 30,
coach; child facs ✗LD 9.30
£B&B £59–£65; B&B (double) £65–£75; L £16·50,
D £16·50; WB £42·50 (HB); [V] **cc** Access, Amex,
B'card/Visa; dep.

TELSCOMBE   East Sussex.   Map 27B3

Stud Farm House   Lewes, BN7 3HZ ✆(0273)
302486. *Farm.* Tim and Nina Armour
Sleeps 8, 🐎 ☂
£ B&B from £13–£15, D from £6.50

TESTON   Kent.   Map 27C4

Court Lodge   Court Lodge Farm, The Street,
Maidstone, ME18 5AQ ✆(0622) 812570/
814200. *Farm.* Rosemarie Bannock
Sleeps 6, ns ☂
£ B&B from £14–£28, D £15

TETFORD Lincolnshire. Map 25A5

White Hart East Rd, nr Horncastle, LN9 6QQ
(065 883) 255.
Picturesque 16th century inn opposite the church.

TEYNHAM Kent. Map 27D7

Newlands Farm Sittingbourne, ME9 9JQ (0795)
522532. *Farm.* Mrs Fiona Boucher
Sleeps 4
£ B&B from £15

THAME Oxfordshire. Map 26E6

Essex House (Highly Acclaimed) Chinnor Rd,
OX9 3LS (084 421) 7567. Fax: (084 421) 6420.

16 bedrs, 14 en suite, 1 ba; TV; tcf
ns; P 20,coach LD 7, nr lunch, Sun dinner,
Resid & Rest lic
£ B&B £30–£40, B&B (double) £45–£55; D £11·95;
[10% V] cc Access, B'card/Visa; dep.

THAXTED Essex. Map 27C7

Farmhouse Inn Monk St (0371) 830864
Fax: (0371) 831196. lt.
*Original white-washed farmhouse with bedroom
extensions forming a small courtyard.*
11 bedrs, 11 en suite; TV; tcf dogs, ns; P 48,
coach; child facs LD 10
£B&B £42, B&B (double) £55; HB weekly £275;
L £7·50, D £7·50, WB £99; [10% V] cc Access,
Amex, B'card/Visa.

THELNETHAM Norfolk. Map 25E1

The Lodge Farm Weston Road, Diss, IP22 1JL
(0379) 898203. *Farm.* Mrs Christine Palmer
Sleeps 5, (10)
£ B&B from £14·50, D £7

THELBRIDGE Devon. Map 29A4

Stockham Farm Crediton, EX17 4SJ (0884)
860308. *Farm.* Mrs Carol Webber
Sleeps 8, ns
£ B&B from £10–£16, D from £6

THEYDON BOIS Essex. Map 27B6

Parsonage Farm House Abridge Rd CM16 7NN
(0378 81) 4242.
*15th-century farmhouse on the edge of Epping
Forest. Leave M25 at exit 26, follow signs for Epping
to roundabout, then take second exit signed
Theydon Bois. Farm house on left through village.*
6 bedrs, 2 en suite, 1 ba; TV; tcf NS; P 20;
child facs Breakfast only. Unlic
£ B&B £28, B&B (double) £45; [5% V]; dep.

THIRSK North Yorkshire. Map 23D4

Old Red House Station Rd, Carlton Miniott,
YO7 4LT (0845) 24383.
*Red-brick roadside pub on the A61 south west of
Thirsk.*
6 beds, 6 en suite; annexe 6 bedrs, 6 en suite;
TV dogs, ns; P 30, coach; child facs LD 9.30
£ B&B £16, B&B (double) £26; L £4·50, D £6·50
cc Amex, B'card/Visa.

THORALBY North Yorkshire Map 23B4

High Green House (Highly Acclaimed) DL8 3SU
(0969) 663420.
£ B&B fr £25·50; HB weekly fr £185·50

THORNTON CLEVELEYS Lancashire. Map 22F2

Victorian House (Highly Acclaimed) Trunnan Rd,
FY5 4HF (0253) 860619.
*Attractive house dating from 1876 and set in one
acre of mature gardens. Take the A585 to
Fleetwood from the M55.*
3 bedrs, 3 en suite; TV; tcf dogs; P 20; no
children under 6 LD 9.30, nr Sun & Mon lunch.
Rest lic
£ B&B £37·50, B&B (double) £57·50–£65; L £10,
D £15·50; WB; [5% V] cc Access, B'card/Visa.

Beachview 67–69 Beach Rd, FY5 1EG (0253)
854003.

THORNTON HEATH Surrey. Map 27B5

Cresta House 601 London Rd, CR4 6AY
081-684 3947.

Norfolk House 587 London Rd, CR4 6AY
081-689 8989 Fax: 081-689 0335.
*Located on A235 London Rd leading to A23 and
M25 (south)*
81 bedrs, 81 en suite, TV; tcf dogs; P 40,
coach; child facs LD 10
£ B&B £23–£61, B&B (double) £33–£72; L £8·50,
D £8·50; [10% V]

THORPENESS Suffolk.   Map 27F8

Dolphin   Pleace Pl, Nr Leiston ☎(0728) 452681.
£ B&B £12·50–£22·50; HB weekly £301–£402·50;
[10% V not w/e Jul–Aug]

TIBBERTON Worcestershire   Map. 26B8

Old House Farm   Droitwich, WR9 7NP ☎(090 565)
247. *Farm*. Pat Chilman
Sleeps 6, ⚑ ns ⛌
£ B&B from £13

TILEHURST Berkshire.   Map 26E5

Aeron   191 Kentwood Hill, RG3 6JE ☎ Reading
(0734) 424119 Fax: (0734) 451953.
*Well-equipped hotel close to Reading, situated just
off A329 Oxford/Reading Rd.*
⇔23 bedrs, 5 en suite, (1 sh), 6 ba; TV; tcf
📺 TV; dogs; child facs ✕LD 7.45, nr lunch, Fri–
Sun dinner. Rest lic
cc Access, B'card/Visa; dep.

TINTAGEL Cornwall.   Map 28D4

Belvoir House   Tregatta, PL34 0DY ☎Camelford
(0840) 770265.
*Situated on the B3263 Camelford to Tintagel Rd,
at Tregatta.*
⇔7 bedrs, 5 en suite, 1 ba; tcf 📺 TV, dogs, P 12; no
children under 1; child facs ✕ nr lunch. Resid lic
£B&B £11–£12; HB weekly £115·75–£122·75;
D £6·25; dep.

TIPTON ST JOHN Devon.   Map 29B4

Higher Coombe Farm   Sidmouth, EX10 0AX
☎(0404) 813385. *Farm*. Kerstin Farmer
Sleeps 5, ns ⛌
£ B&B from £11–£15, D £7

TIRLEY Gloucestershire.   Map 26B7

Town Street Farm   GL19 4HG ☎(045278)
442. *Farm*. Sue Warner
Sleeps 4, ⛌
£ B&B from £13–£16

TIVERTON Devon.   Map 29B5

Bridge (Acclaimed)   23 Angel Hill, EX16 6PE
☎(0884) 252804.
*An imposing 4-storey Victorian red brick town
house, retaining many original features. Situated
beside the River Exe in the centre of Tiverton.*
⇔10 bedrs; 2 en suite, 2 ba; TV; tcf 📺 TV, dogs, ns;
P 5, G 1; child facs ✕LD 6.30, nr lunch; Resid &
Rest lic
£ B&B £14·50–£17·50, B&B (double) £29–£35; HB
weekly £135–£165; D £7; [5% V]; dep.

Lodge Hill Farm   Ashley, EX16 5PA ☎(0884)
252907.
*Small guest house set in rolling countryside. 1 mile
S of Tiverton off A396 Tiverton to Bickleigh Rd.*
⇔9 bedrs, 7 en suite, 2 ba; TV; tcf 📺TV, dogs;
P 12, G 2; child facs ✕Breakfast only. Resid lic
£ B&B £13–£15; [10% V]

Great Bradley Farm   Withleigh, EX16 8JL
☎(0884) 256946. *Farm*. Mrs Sylvia Hann
Sleeps 4, ns ⛌ (7)
£ B&B from £12·50–£15, D from £8·50

Harton Farm   Oakford, EX16 9HH ☎(03985)
209. *Farm*. Mrs Lindy Head
Sleeps 6, ⚑ ns ⛌ (4)
£ B&B from £9–£11, D £5

Lower Collipriest Farm   EX16 4PT ☎(0884)
252321. *Farm*. Mrs Linda Olive
Sleeps 4, ns
£ B&B from £15, D £8

Newhouse Farm   Oakford, EX16 9JE ☎(03985)
347. *Farm*. Mrs Anne Boldry
Sleeps 6, ⛌
£ B&B from £11–£14·50, D £7

Quoit-at-Cross Farm   Stoodleigh, EX16 9PJ
☎(03985) 280. *Farm*. Mrs Linda Hill
Sleeps 6, ns ⛌
£ B&B from £12, D £7

TORPOINT Cornwall.   Map 28F2

Ap. Whitsand Bay   Portwinkle, PL11 3BU
☎(0503) 30276.
*Stone-built house in cliff-top grounds. Panoramic
sea views. Indoor swimming pool, golf, putting,
sauna, solarium, gymnasium. Open Mar–Jan 2.*
⇔30 bedrs, 26 en suite, 2 ba; tcf 📺TV, dogs, ns;
P 60, coach; child facs ✕LD 8.30
£ B&B £15–£20, B&B (double) £30–£40; D £12·50;
WB (£60 2 nts); [5% except May–Oct & w/e]; dep.

TORQUAY Devon.   Map 29A3

Glenorleigh (Highly Acclaimed)   26 Cleveland Rd,
TQ2 5BE ☎(0803) 292135.

*A detached Victorian hotel set in award-winning
gardens. Follow A380 to the traffic lights at Torre
Station. Turn right into Avenue Rd (A379) and first
left. Swimming pool, solarium. Open Jan–Oct.*

16 bedrs, 9 en suite, 4 ba; tcf ⓕTV, ns; P10, coach; child facs ✗LD6, nr Sat & Sun lunch. Resid lic
£B&B £16–£22; HB weekly £115–£190; WB (fr £45 2 nts); dep.

Haldon Priors (Highly Acclaimed) Meadfoot, Sea Rd TQ1 2LQ ✆(0803) 213365.
Attractive hotel set in its own grounds. From clock tower turn into Torwood St, at traffic lights turn right, up and over a hill, and hotel past small shop. Swimming pool. Open Easter–Oct.
8 bedrs, 7 en suite; tcf ⓕTV, ns; P7; child facs
£B&B £18–£28, B&B (double) £44–£62; [5% V]; dep.

Robin Hill (Highly Acclaimed) Braddons Hill Rd East, TQ1 1HF ✆(0803) 214518.

Elegant Victorian hotel standing in its own peaceful grounds. Recently refurbished throughout. From clock tower by inner harbour turn up Torwood St, take first left after museum. Closed mid Oct–mid Nov & 28 Dec–Jan.
18 bedrs, 18 en suite; TV; tcf ⓕP16; no children under 6 ✗LD6, nr lunch. Resid lic
£ B&B £20–£25; HB weekly £151–£183; dep.

Barn Hayes (Acclaimed) Maidencombe TQ1 4TR ✆(0803) 327980.
Attractive modern house commanding uninterrupted views from nearly every window. From A379 turn down lane opposite garage at Maidencombe, and Barn Hayes is ¾ mile on the left.
13 bedrs, 8 en suite, 2 ba; TV; tcf ⓕTV, dogs; child facs ✗LD 7·30. Resid & Rest lic
£B&B £14·50–£22; HB weekly £135–£198; WB (£40); [10% V] cc Access, B'card/Visa; dep.

Belmont (Acclaimed) 66 Belgrave Rd, TQ2 5HY ✆(0803) 295028.

Tastefully refurbished Victorian town house with much original character retained. Follow A380 into town, at T junction turn right.
11 bedrs, 7 en suite, 2 ba; TV; tcf ⓕTV, dogs, ns; P 4, coach; no children under 5; child facs ✗LD 5, nr lunch. Resid lic
£B&B £12–£20; HB weekly £105–£164; D£6; WB (£22) cc Access, B'card/Visa; dep.

Chesterfield (Acclaimed) 62 Belgrave Rd, TQ2 5HY ✆(0803) 292318.
An elegant Victorian building, recently refurbished to a high standard. Situated 500 yards from sea front.
11 bedrs, 6 en suite (1sh), 2 ba; TV; tcf ⓕTV, dogs; P3, child facs ✗LD4, nr lunch. Resid lic
£B&B £12–£17; HB weekly £99–£146
cc Access, B'card/Visa; [10% V Sep–Jun]; dep.

Concorde (Acclaimed) 26 Newton Rd, TQ2 5BZ ✆(0803) 22330. *Private Hotel. Swimming pool.*

Craig Court (Acclaimed) 10 Ash Hill Rd, TQ1 3HZ ✆(0803) 294400.
Attractive, small, south-facing hotel. From Castle Circus town hall take St Marychurch Rd, signed Babbacombe, and take first turn on right. Open Easter–Oct.
10 bedrs, 4 en suite, 3 ba; tcf ⓕTV; dogs; P8; child facs ✗LD9.30 am, nr lunch. Resid lic
£B&B £15–£18; HB weekly £140–£161; D£8; dep.

Cranborne (Acclaimed) 58 Belgrave Rd, TQ2 5HY ✆(0803) 298046.

White-walled hotel on the main road into Torquay. Belgrave Rd is a turning off A379 Torbay Rd. Closed Dec.
13 bedrs, 9 en suite, (1 sh), 2 ba; TV; tcf ⓕTV, ns; P3, coach; child facs ✗LD3, nr lunch. Resid lic
£B&B £13–£17·50; HB weekly £97–£130; [10% V exc Jul & Aug] cc Access, B'card/Visa; dep.

Cranmore (Acclaimed)   89 Avenue Rd, TQ2 5LH
✆ (0803) 298488.

Semi-detached hotel, built in 1910, on a level road to the seafront. Situated on A380. Turn right at Torre Station traffic lights, and hotel is about 200 yards on left.
🛏 8 bedrs, 4 en suite, 1 ba; TV; tcf 🏠TV, ns; P 4; child facs ✕ LD 4, lunch on request. Unlic
£ B&B £10–£12; HB weekly £108·50–£136·50
cc Access, B'card/Visa; dep.

Daphne Court (Acclaimed)   Lower Warberry Rd, TQ1 1QS ✆ (0803) 212011.
An elegant detached Victorian villa set in its own grounds. From the clock tower at the harbour take the seventh turning on the left off the Babbacombe Rd. Swimming pool. Open Mar–Oct.
🛏 16 bedrs, 16 en suite; TV; tcf 🏠TV, ns; P 15, coach; no children under 3, child facs ✕ LD 7.30, nr lunch
£ B&B £19–£25; HB weekly £150–£200; D £9; [5% V] **cc** B'card/Visa; dep.

Elmdene (Acclaimed)   Rathmore Rd, TQ2 6NZ
✆ (0803) 294940.
Follow signs to English Riviera Centre, turning right into Walnut Rd.
🛏 12 bedrs, 7 en suite, 1 ba; TV; tcf 🏠TV, dogs; P 12, coach; no children under 5 ✕ LD 6·45. Resid & Rest lic
£ B&B £15–£22; HB weekly £150·50–£160; L £3·50, D £7·50 **cc** Access, B'card/Visa.

Exmouth View (Acclaimed)   St Alban's Rd, Babbacombe, TQ1 3LJ ✆ (0803) 327307.
Modern detached hotel with a large car park. Head for model village then along Babbacombe Downs Rd into St Albans Rd.
🛏 32 bedrs, 19 en suite, 2 ba; TC; tcf 🏠TV, dogs; P 30, coach; child facs ✕ LD 6·30, nr lunch. Resid lic
£ B&B £10·95–£21·95; HB weekly £100·50–£177; [10% V] **cc** Access, B'card/Visa; dep.

Fairways (Acclaimed)   72 Avenue Rd, TQ2 5LF
✆ (0803) 298471.
Agreeable small hotel on the main route to Torquay. Turn right after Torre Station and Fairways is on the right.
🛏 7 bedrs, (2 sh), 1 ba; TV; tcf 🏠dogs, ns; P 7;

child facs ✕ LD 3, nr lunch. Unlic
£ B&B £12; HB weekly £120–£142; D £7; [5% V Nov–Apr] **cc** Access, B'card/Visa.

Glenwood (Acclaimed)   Rowdens Rd, TQ2 5AZ
✆ (0803) 296318.
Family-run hotel, recently completely refurbished. Turn right at Torre Station into Avenue Rd, and left just before second set of lights. Rowdens Rd is first turning on the left.
🛏 11 bedrs, 9 en suite, 1 ba; TV; tcf 🏠dogs; P 10, coach; no children under 5 ✕ LD 7·30, nr lunch. Resid lic
£ B&B £14·50–£25; HB weekly £119–£161; D £6
cc Access, B'card/Visa; dep.

Ingoldsby (Acclaimed)   1 Chelston Rd, TQ2 6PT
✆ (0803) 607497.

A former gentleman's residence standing in its own grounds, situated behind the Grand Hotel and station at the junction of Seaway Lane and Chelston Rd.
🛏 15 bedrs, 10 en suite, 1 ba; tcf 🏠TV; P 15, child facs ✕ LD 7. Resid lic
£ B&B £12·50–£17; HB weekly £102–£146; L £4·75, D £6·75; WB (£45) **cc** Access, B'card/Visa; dep.

Lindens (Acclaimed)   31 Bampfylde Rd, TQ2 5AY
✆ (0803) 212281.

Elegant Victorian building with comfortable, airy rooms overlooking large sunny garden. Bear right at Torre Station into Avenue Rd, take first left after next traffic lights.
🛏 7 bedrs, 7 en suite; TV; tcf 🏠TV, ns; P 7, coach; children over 10 ✕ LD midday, nr lunch. Unlic
£ B&B 15–£20; HB weekly £149–£184; [10% V exc Jun–Aug]; dep.

Lindum (Acclaimed)   Abbey Rd, TQ2 5NP
✆ (0803) 292795.

From seafront take Sheddon Hill exit at Belgrave Rd roundabout and continue to Abbey Rd junction. Open Easter–Oct.
⇰20 bedrs, 13 en suite, 2 ba; tcf TV, dogs; P 15, coach; child facs ✕LD 5·30, nr lunch. Resid lic
£B&B £10·50–£18·50; HB weekly £104·50–£154·50; [5% V Apr–Oct]; dep.

Mapleton (Acclaimed)   St Luke's Rd North, TQ2 5PD ☎(0803) 292389.

Small detached Victorian hotel, quietly situated in its own grounds. From seafront take Sheddon Hill, and St Lukes Rd is the second turning on the right.
⇰10 bedrs, 7 en suite, 2 ba; TV; tcf ns; P 7; children over 5 ✕LD 6·30, nr lunch. Resid & Rest lic
£B&B £13·75–£19; HB weekly £120–£161; D £6; WB (£54 3 nights) **cc** Access, B'card/Visa; dep.

Norwood (Acclaimed)   60 Belgrave Rd, TQ2 5HY ☎(0803) 294236.
Victorian building, tastefully refurbished to a high standard. Situated on the main road from Newton Abbot which leads into Belgrave Rd.
⇰12 bedrs, 8 en suite, 1 ba; TV; tcf TV, dogs, ns; P 3, coach; child facs ✕LD 3, nr lunch. Resid lic
£B&B £12·50; HB weekly £108–£152; WB (£37); [5% V excl Jul–Aug] **cc** Access, B'card/Visa; dep.

Patricia (Acclaimed)   Belgrave Rd TQ2 5HY ☎(0803) 293339.
A Victorian hotel offering a high standard of service, situated close to the English Riviera Conference Centre and the seafront.
⇰8 bedrs, 8 en suite, 2 ba; TV; tcf TV, dogs; P 3, coach; child facs ✕LD 7, Resid lic
£B&B £18–£22; HB weekly £168–£196; L £5, D £6; [10% V] **cc** Access, B'card/Visa; dep.

Rawlyn House (Acclaimed)   Rawlyn Rd, Chelston, TQ2 6PL ☎(0803) 605208.
A charming Victorian country house set in its own secluded grounds. Turn right at Torre Station into Avenue Rd, at second traffic lights turn right, and left past the shops. Rawlyn Rd is sharp right. Swimming pool. Open Apr–Oct & Xmas.
⇰17 bedrs, 12 en suite, 2 ba; TV, tcf ns; P 17, coach; child facs ✕LD 7.15, bar meals only lunch. Resid lic

£B&B £19–£26; HB weekly £144–£195; [5% V]

Red Squirrel Lodge (Acclaimed)   Chelston Rd, TQ2 6PU ☎(0803) 605496.

Large Victorian villa set in spacious gardens in a quiet road. Situated behind the Grand Hotel, off Seaway Lane.
⇰16 bedrs, 11 en suite, 2 ba; tcf TV, dogs, ns; P 12; children over 7 ✕LD 4, nr lunch. Resid lic
£B&B £14·50–£20; HB weekly £121–£155·65; WB £36; [10% V Oct–Apr] **cc** Access, B'card/Visa.

Seaway (Acclaimed)   Chelston Rd, TQ2 6PU ☎(0803) 605320.
Modernised Victorian residence, tastefully converted with fine sea views. Seaway Lane is behind the Grand Hotel, and Chelston Rd is a turning off.
⇰14 bedrs, 7 en suite, 2 ba TV; P 15, coach; child facs ✕LD 6·30. Resid lic
£B&B £16–£24; HB weekly £114–£160; L fr £2; D £5; [10% V] **cc** Access, B'card/Visa; dep.

Sherwood (Acclaimed)   Belgrave Road, TQ2 5HP ☎(0803) 294534.
Early Victorian building with lovely gardens. 200 yards from Torbay Sands, adjacent to Torre Abbey Gardens.
⇰55 bedrs, 46 en suite, 6 ba; TV; tcf TV, ns; P 25, coach; children's facs ✕LD 6·30, bar meals only lunch. Resid & Rest lic
£B&B £20–£28; HB weekly £156–£214; L fr £3, D £8; WB (£21); [5% V Oct–Apr] **cc** Access, B'card/Visa; dep.

Ascot House   7 Tor Church Rd, TQ2 5UR ☎(0803) 295142.
Family-run hotel with sea views, on main road to Torquay.
⇰9 bedrs, 2 en suite; (2 sh), 3 ba; TV; tcf TV, dogs, ns; P 10; child facs ✕nr lunch. Resid lic
£B&B £12·50–£15·50; HB weekly £133–£169·50; WB; [5% V Jan–May]; dep.

Ashwood   2 St Margaret's Rd, St Marychurch, TQ1 4NM ☎(0803) 328173.
⇰10 bedrs, 10 en suite, 1 ba; TV; tcf TV, dogs, ns; P 14, coach; child facs ✕LD 6·30, nr lunch. Resid lic
£B&B £12–£20; HB weekly £108–£156; D £6·50; WB; [5% V Sep–May] **cc** Access, B'card/Visa; dep.

Avron 70 Windsor Rd, TQ1 1SZ ☎(0803) 294182.
Open May–Sep.
⇌14 bedrs, 6 en suite, (2 sh), 2 ba; TV; tcf 🄵TV,
dogs; P 7; child facs ✕LD 6.30, nr lunch. Unlic
£HB weekly £98–£122; dep.

Briarfields 84–86 Avenue Rd, TQ2 5LF ☎(0803)
297844.
*Turn right at Torre Station into Avenue Rd, follow
sea front sign. Hotel ⅓ mile on right. Closed mid
Nov–mid Jan.*
⇌12 bedrs, 8 en suite (1sh); 1 ba, TV; tcf 🄵dogs,
ns; P 10, coach; child facs ✕LD3, nr lunch. Resid
lic
£B&B £14–£28, B&B (double) £22–£32; HB weekly
£115–£150; [10% V Jan–May]; dep.

Colindale 20 Rathmore Rd, TQ2 6NY ☎(0803)
293947.
*Situated on the edge of Torre Abbey Gardens, 200
yards from railway station. Open May–Dec*
⇌8 bedrs, 2 ba; tcf 🄵TV, ns; P 4; children over 4
✕LD pm, nr lunch. Rest lic.
£B&B £13–£14; HB weekly £123–£137; dep.

Courthouse Rock House Lane, Maidencombe,
TQ1 4SU ☎(0803) 328335.
*Historic, family-run country house hotel. Halfway
along Teignmouth to Torquay Rd (A379) Turn
towards sea at Maidencombe Cross, and hotel is
at foot of hill. Open Apr–Oct*
⇌14 bedrs, 6 en suite, 4 ba; tcf 🄵TV, dogs; P 10;
child facs ✕LD 7, nr lunch. Resid lic
£B&B £13·50–£16·50; HB weekly £140–£161;
[5% V Apr–Jun, Sep & Oct] cc Access, Amex,
B'card/Visa, Diners; dep.

Crowndale 18 Bridge Rd, TQ2 5BA ☎(0803)
293068.

Devon Court Croft Rd, TQ2 5UE ☎(0803)
293603.
*From Tor Abbey Sands proceed up Sheddon Hill.
Croft Rd is first on the left. Swimming pool. Open
Easter–Oct.*
⇌13 bedrs, 8 en suite, (2 sh), 3 ba; TV; tcf
🄵TV; P 14, coach; child facs ✕LD4, nr lunch.
Resid lic
£B&B £12–£20; HB weekly £98–£154; [10% V
Easter–May, Sept & Oct] cc Access, B'card/Visa;
dep.

Durlstone 156 Avenue Rd, TQ2 5LQ ☎(0803)
212307.
*Attractive small hotel. Turn right at Torre Station
traffic lights into Avenue Rd, and Durlstone is about
100 metres on the right.*
⇌6 bedrs, 1 ba; TV; tcf 🄵TV, dogs, ns; P6; child
facs ✕LD5, nr lunch. Unlic
£B&B £10–£12; HB weekly £97–£110; dep.

Hart Lea 81 St Marychurch Rd, TQ1 3HG ☎(0803)
312527. *Guest House.*

Melba House 62 Bampfylde Rd, TQ2 5AY
☎(0803) 292331. *Private Hotel.*

Olivia Court Braddons Hill Rd, TQ1 1HD ☎(0803)
292595.
*Turn left at clock tower, cross traffic lights and take
third on left. At top of hill on the right.*
⇌16 bedrs, 9 en suite, 3 ba; TV, tcf 🄵TV, dogs,
P3, child facs ✕LD7, nr lunch. Resid lic
£B&B £15–£31·50; HB weekly £133·50–£180;
D£7·50; WB (£38); [10% V Oct–Apr] cc Access,
B'card/Visa; dep.

Pencarrow 64 Windsor Rd, TQ1 1SZ ☎(0803)
293080.
Friendly family-run hotel.
⇌13 bedrs, 8 en suite, (5 sh), 1 ba; TV; tcf
🄵TV, dogs; P 7, coach; child facs ✕LD 5·50, nr
lunch. Resid lic
£B&B £13–£14; HB weekly £92–£129; WB;
[5% V]; dep.

Richwood 20 Newton Rd, TQ2 5QN ☎(0803)
293729.
*Comfortable small hotel, situated just past Torre
Station, on the right. Swimming pool.*
⇌21 bedrs, 14 en suite, 3 ba; TV; tcf 🄵TV, dogs,
ns; P 13, coach; child facs ✕LD 6.30, nr lunch.
Resid & Rest lic
£B&B £12–£21; HB weekly £84–£144; D £7; WB
(£44); [5% V] cc Access, B'card/Visa; dep.

St Kilda 49 Babbacombe Rd, TQ1 3SJ ☎(0803)
327238.
*Close to the cliff railway and Babbacombe Downs
on the main Babbacombe Rd. Open Easter–Oct.*
⇌25 bedrs, 17 en suite, 3 ba; tcf 🄵TV, dogs; P30,
coach; children over 2 ✕LD 6.30, nr lunch. Resid
lic
£ B&B £13·50–£16·50; HB weekly £102–£125;
dep.

Sandpiper Rowdens Rd, TQ2 5AZ ☎(0803)
292779.

Skerries 25 Morgan Av, TQ2 5RR ☎(0803)
293618.
*Off the one-way system from Castle Circus, parallel
with Union St.*
⇌12 bedrs, 2 ba; TV; tcf 🄵TV; P7, coach; child
facs ✕LD midday, nr lunch. Resid lic
£B&B £10·50–£14·50; HB weekly £98·50–£115·50;
[5% V exc Jul–Sept]; dep.

Southbourne 9 Cleveland Rd, TQ2 5BD ☎(0803)
297609.
*Family-run hotel in its own grounds. Turn right at
Torre Station traffic lights into Avenue Rd, then first
left into Cleveland Rd.*

≈20 bedrs, 17 en suite, 1 ba; TV; tcf 🛏TV, dogs; P15, coach; child facs ✕LD8, nr lunch. Resid & Rest lic
£B&B £15–£20; HB weekly £128; D£5; WB £38 (2 nights); [10% V Oct–Mar] **cc** Access, B'card/Visa; dep.

Torbay Rise   Old Mill Rd, TQ2 6HL ☎(0803) 605541.
Attractive hotel with sea and harbour views. Turn right at Torre Station, turn right at next set of lights, and Torbay Rise is at the top of the hill. Swimming pool. Open Easter–Oct.
≈15 bedrs, 13 en suite, 1 ba; tcf 🛏TV, dogs; P10; coach, child facs ✕LD midday, nr lunch. Resid lic
£B&B (double) £30–£48; HB weekly £140–£175; [5% V except Jul & Aug] **cc** Access, B'card/Visa dep.

Torcroft   28 Croft Rd, TQ2 5UE ☎(0803) 298292.
≈19 bedrs, 13 en suite, 2 ba 🛏TV, ns; P20, coach; child facs ✕LD 4, nr lunch. Resid lic

Trafalgar House   30 Bridge Rd, TQ2 5BA ☎(0803) 292486. *Hotel.*

Villa Marina   Cockington Lane, Livermead, TQ2 6QU ☎(0803) 605440.

White Gables   Rawlyn Rd, Chelston TQ2 6PQ ☎(0803) 605233.
From Torquay centre, follow signs for Cockington towards sea front, turn into Walnut Road, follow road past shops, turn left, then up and sharp right into Rawlyn Road. Swimming pool.
≈22 bedrs, 21 en suite, 1 ba; tcf 🛏TV; P20, coach; child facs ✕LD 4. Resid & Rest lic
£B&B £17–£23; HB weekly £117·50–£158; D £6; [5% V] **cc** Access, B'card/Visa; dep.

TOTNES   Devon.   Map 29A3

Great Court Farm   Weston Lane, TQ9 6LB ☎(0803) 862326. *Farm.* Janet Hooper
Sleeps 6, ns 🐾
£ B&B from £11–£13·50, D £7–£8

Higher Torr Farm   East Allington, TQ9 7QH ☎(0548) 52248. *Farm.* Susan Baker
Sleeps 6, 🐕 ns 🐾
£ B&B from £11, D £6

Weekend breaks
Please consult the hotel for full details of weekend breaks; prices shown are an indication only. Many hotels offer mid week breaks as well.

Please tell the manager if you chose your hotel through an advertisement in the guide.

TOTON   Nottinghamshire.   Map 24D3

Manor   Nottingham Rd, NG9 6EF ☎Long Eaton (0602) 733487.

TOTTENHILL   Norfolk.   Map 25C2

Oakwood House   PE33 0RH ☎King's Lynn (0553) 810256.
Picturesque Georgian hotel set in 2 acre gardens. On A10 4 miles S of King's Lynn just N of junction with A134.
≈10 bedrs, 8 en suite, 1 ba; TV; tcf 🛏dogs; P20; child facs ✕LD8.30, nr lunch. Resid & Rest lic
£B&B £23–£35, B&B (double) £28–£48; HB weekly £161–£280; D£7; WB £46–£64 **cc** Access, B'card/Visa; dep.

TOWERSEY   Oxfordshire.   Map 26E7

Upper Green Farm   Manor Road, OX9 3QR ☎(084 421) 2496. *Farm.* Majorie Aitken
Sleeps 5, ns
£ B&B from £15–£27

TREGONY   Cornwall.   Map 28D2

Tregonan   Truro, TR2 5SN ☎(087253) 249. *Farm.* Sandra Collins
Sleeps 6, 🐾
£ B&B from £10–£15

TRESILLIAN   Cornwall.   Map 28C2

Polsue Manor Farm   Truro, TR2 4BP ☎(087 2 52) 234. *Farm.* Geraldine Holliday
Sleeps 14, 🐕 🐾
£ B&B from £12·50, D £6·50

TREVALGA   Cornwall.   Map 28D4

Trehane Farm   Boscastle, PL35 0EB ☎(08405) 510. *Farm.* Mrs Sarah James
Sleeps 6, 🐕 ns 🐾 (12)
£ B&B from £13, D £6

TROTTON   Hants.   Map 26F3

Trotton Farm   Rogate, Nr Petersfield, GU31 5EN ☎(0730) 813618. *Farm.* Mrs G W Baigent
Sleeps 5, 🐾
£ B&B from £15

TROWBRIDGE   Wiltshire.   Map 29E6

Gordons   65 Wingfield Rd, BA14 9EG ☎(022 14) 2072.

TRURO   Cornwall.   Map 28C2

Marcorrie   20 Falmouth Rd, TR1 2HX ☎(0872) 77374.

12 bedrs, 6 en suite, (3 sh), 1 ba; TV; tcf
TV, dogs, ns; P 15; child facs ✕LD 5, nr lunch;
Resid & Rest lic
cc Access, B'card/Visa; dep.

TWO BRIDGES Devon.   Map 28F3

Cherrybrook (Acclaimed) PL20 6SP ☎Tavistock
(0822) 88260.
Farmhouse in middle of Dartmoor. Closed Xmas &
New Year.
7 bedrs, 7 en suite; 1 ba, TV; tcf dogs; P 12;
child facs ✕LD 7.15, nr lunch. Resid & Rest lic
£ B&B £21·50; HB weekly £210.

TWYNING Gloucestershire.   Map 26B7

Abbots Court Church End, Tewkesbury, GL20
6DA ☎(0684) 292515. *Farm.* Bernie Williams
Sleeps 15,
£ B&B from £13–£15, D £6·50

TYTHERINGTON Cheshire.   Map 24B5

Oldhams Hollow Farm Manchester Road,
Macclesfield, SK10 2JW ☎(0625) 424128. *Farm.*
Brenda Buxton
Sleeps 6,
£ B&B from £14·50

UCKFIELD East Sussex.   Map 27B3

Hooke Hall (Highly Acclaimed) 250 High St, TN22
1EN ☎(0825) 761578 Tx: 95228
Fax: (0825) 768025.

Discount vouchers

RAC discount vouchers are at the end of the
guide. Establishments with a [V] shown at the end
of the price information will accept them in part
payment for accommodation bills on the full,
standard rate, not against bargain breaks or any
other special offers. Please note the limitations
shown in the entry: w/e for weekends, w/d for
weekdays, and which months they are accepted.

*Elegant Queen Anne town house recently
refurbished. At northern end of High Street.* Closed
24–31 Dec.
6 bedrs, 5 en suite, (1 sh); TV; tcf P8; no
children under 12 ✕LD 9.30, nr lunch (dinner
residents only Sun–Thur). Resid & Rest lic
£ B&B £42·50–£65·50, B&B (double) £62·50–£100;
D £18·75 **cc** Access, B'card/Visa.

The Railands Isfield, TN22 5XG ☎(082 575)
492. *Farm.* Mrs Anne Fordham
Sleeps 6, ns
£ B&B from £17

UP-OTTERY Devon.   Map 29B4

Cleave Farm Honiton, EX14 9QT ☎(040 486)
226. *Farm.* Mrs Janette Curtis
Sleeps 6, ns
£ B&B from £12·50

Courtmoor Farm Honiton, EX14 9QA ☎(040486)
316. *Farm.* Mrs Sally Cooke
Sleeps 6,
£ B&B from £9·50, D £6·50

UPPER AFFCOT Shropshire.   Map 31E7

Travellers Rest Inn nr Church Stretton, SY6 6RL
☎Church Stretton (0694) 6275.

UPPINGHAM Leicestershire.   Map 24F2

Crown High St East, LE15 9PY ☎(0572)
822302.
*Refurbished, 17th century inn of great character in
town centre.*
7 bedrs, 7 en suite; TV; tcf dogs; P 20, coach;
child facs ✕LD 9.30, nr Sun dinner
£ B&B £30, B&B (double) £40, L £5, D £10
cc B'card/Visa; dep.

Two Bridges (Devon) _____

CHERRYBROOK HOTEL

Two Bridges, Yelverton, Devon PL20 6SP Tel: (0822) 88260

Old Dartmoor farmhouse in the middle of National Park now run as a comfortable licensed hotel. British Tourist
Authority commended. Bedrooms: 1 single, 3 double & 1 twin, 2 family rooms. Bathrooms: 7 private, 1 public.

Old Rectory (Highly Acclaimed)   Belton-in-Rutland, LE15 9LE ☎ Belton (057 286) 279 Fax: (057 286) 343.

Charming old house in 30 acres of parkland, 3½ miles W of Uppingham, just off A47. Follow signs to craft centre. Riding.
⊨6 bedrs, 6 en suite, 1 ba; TV; tcf ⌂TV, dogs, ns; P25, coach; child facs ✗LD 9. Resid & Rest lic
£ B&B £17·50–£20; HB weekly £132·50–£165; D £10.

Rutland House   61 High St, LE15 9QD ☎ (0572) 822497.
Hotel close to Town Hall in High Street. From Market Square go down High Street West.
£ B&B £25, B&B (double) £35.

UTTOXETER Staffordshire. Map 24C3

Hillcrest   3 Leighton Rd, ST14 8BL ☎ (0889) 564627.
Turn off the A518 onto the B5017 at the War Memorial, turn right in 600 metres and right again into Leighton Rd. Closed Xmas Day.
⊨7 bedrs, 7 en suite; TV; tcf ⌂TV, dogs, ns; P12, G 2; child facs ✗LD 4, nr lunch. Resid lic
£ B&B £14–£23, B&B (double) £32–£34; D £5–£6·50; [10% V] cc Access, Amex, B'card/Visa; dep.

VERYAN Cornwall. Map 28D2

Treverbyn House   Pendower Rd, TR2 5QL ☎ Truro (0872) 501201.
⊨4 bedrs, 2 ba ⌂TV; P 5–6; children over 7 ✗nr lunch. Resid & Rest lic
cc Access, Amex, B'card/Visa; dep.

VOWCHURCH Hereford & Worcester
(Herefordshire). Map 31C7

Croft Country House (Highly Acclaimed)   HR2 0QE ☎ Peterchurch (0981) 550226.

A charming small country house dating from the 18th century, with stripped pine, period furniture and panoramic views. Situated at the junction of B4348 and B4347.
⊨7 bedrs, 7 en suite, TV; tcf ⌂ns; P 12, G 2; children over 10 ✗LD 9, nr lunch Mon–Sat, dinner Sun. Resid & Rest lic
£ B&B £20 HB weekly £199·50; D £11·50; WB £59 (2 nts) cc Access, B'card/Visa; dep.

WADEBRIDGE Cornwall. Map 28D3

Hendra Country   St Kew Highway, PL30 3EQ ☎ (020 884) 343.
⊨5 bedrs, 4 en suite, 1 ba; TV; tcf ⌂TV, dogs, ns; P 10; child facs ✗LD 10, nr lunch. Resid lic.

WALKERINGHAM Nottinghamshire. Map 24E5

🍺 **Brickmakers Arms**   Fountain Hill Rd, DN10 4LT ☎ Gainsborough (0427) 890375.
Pleasant inn, converted from cottages and a barn, with spacious beer garden; on edge of quiet village.
⊨17 bedrs, 17 en suite; TV; tcf ⌂TV; P 20; child facs ✗LD 9.30, nr Mon–Sat lunch & Sun dinner
cc Access, Amex, B'card/Visa.

WALLINGFORD Oxfordshire. Map 26E6

North Farm   Shillingford Hill, OX10 8NB ☎ (086 732) 8406. *Farm.* Hilary Warburton
Sleeps 4/6, ns ⊠
£ B&B from £16·50

WALLASEY Merseyside. Map 30C7

Clifton   293 Seabank Rd, L45 5AF ☎ 051-639 6505. *Guest House.*

Sea Level   126 Victoria Rd, New Brighton, L45 9LD ☎ 051-639 3408.
⊨14 bedrs, 1 en suite, (2 sh), 3 ba; TV; tcf ⌂TV, dogs, coach; child facs ✗LD 11, nr lunch. Resid lic
cc Access, B'card/Visa; dep.

WALTHAM-ON-THE-WOLDS
Leicestershire Map 24E3

Royal Horseshoes Inn   LE14 4AJ ☎ (066 472) 289. Closed 25 & 26 Dec.
⊨4 bedrs, 4 en suite; TV; tcf ⌂P 45, coach ✗LD 9, nr Sun dinner
£ B&B £30, B&B (double) £53; WB £35 (HB); dep.

WANTAGE Oxfordshire. Map 26D6

Lyford Manor   Lyford, OX12 0EG ☎ (0235) 868204. *Farm.* Mary Pike

Sleeps 7, ns ☞
£ B&B from £14–£17

WARLEGGAN   Cornwall.   Map 28D3

Mennabroom   Bodmin Moor, PL30 4HE ☎(0208)
82272. *Farm.* Mrs Pamela Miller
Sleeps 6, ☞ (6)
£ B&B from £10, D £6

WARMINSTER   Wiltshire.   Map 29E6

Lane End Cottage (Acclaimed)   72 Lane End,
Corsley, BA12 7PG ☎Chapmanslade (037 388) 392.
Guest House.
⇔3 bedrs, 1 en suite, 1 ba; TV; tcf 📺TV, dogs, ns;
P 4, G 2; child facs ✕Breakfast only. Unlic.

WARRINGTON   Cheshire.   Map 30C8

Birchdale (Acclaimed)   Birchdale Rd, Appleton,
WA4 5AW ☎(0925) 63662. Fax: (0925) 860607.
*Two hundred year old mock Tudor property set in
its own large gardens. On the A49, 1 ⅓ miles from
the town centre, close to M6 & M56. Closed Dec
23–Jan 2.*
⇔16 bedrs, 7 en suite, 3 ba; TV; tcf 📺P 30; child
facs ✕LD 8, nr lunch, Fri–Sun dinner. Resid lic
£B&B £28–£36, B&B (double) £44–£52;
D £10·50 cc Access, B'card/Visa.

WARTON   Lancashire.   Map 22F3

Cotestones Farm   Sand Lane, Carnforth LA5
9NH ☎(0524) 732418. *Farm.* Gillian Close
Sleeps 6, ♠☞
£ B&B from £10

WARWICK   Warwickshire.   Map 26C8

North Leigh (Highly Acclaimed)   Five Ways Rd,
Hatton, CV35 7HZ Haseley Knob ☎(0926) 484203.
*Small 90-year old country house set in its own flower
garden surrounded by open country. Five miles NW
of Warwick on A4177 at Five Ways Island, follow
signs to Shrewley for ⅜ mile. Closed 15 Dec–mid
Jan.*
⇔6 bedrs, 6 en suite; TV; tcf 📺dogs, ns; P8
✕Dinner by arrangement. nr lunch. Unlic.
£ B&B £26–£33, B&B (double) £39–£45; D £13·50

Park Cottage (Highly Acclaimed)   113 West St,
CV34 6AH ☎(0926) 410319 Fax: (0926) 410319.
*An early 16th-century Grade II listed building
situated alongside the entrance drive to Warwick
Castle, offering completely refurbished
accommodation. Take A429 towards Warwick. Park
Cottage is 1 ⅓ miles on the right. Closed Xmas &
New Year.*
⇔5 bedrs, 5 en suite; TV; tcf 📺TV; ns; P8, U1; no
children under 12.

Croft (Acclaimed)   Haseley Knob, CV35 7NL
☎(0926) 484 447.
*A large family house set in picturesque
surroundings. Take the A4177 toards Balsall
Common and The Croft is 1 ⅓ miles on the right in
Haseley Knob village.*
⇔3 bedrs, 2 en suite, 2 ba; TV; tcf 📺TV, NS; P 8;
child facs ✕nr lunch. Unlic
£B&B £13–£18, D £7·50; [5% V Fri–Sun]; dep.

Avon   7 Emscote Rd, CV34 4PH ☎(0926) 491367.
*Family-run guest house close to the castle. Situated
on A445 Warwick to Leamington Spa Rd, opposite
the entrance to the park.*
⇔10 bedrs, (4 sh), 2 ba; tcf 📺TV, ns; P 6, G 1; child
facs ✕nr lunch, Sat & Sun dinner. Resid lic
£ B&B £13, B&B (double) £25–£26 cc B'card/Visa.

Westham   76 Emscote Rd, CV34 5QG ☎(0926)
491756.
*A fine Victorian house with most of its original
character intact. On the A445 ⅓ mile from Warwick
town centre opposite the Lord Nelson pub.*
⇔7 bedrs, 1 en suite, 2 ba; TV; tcf 📺TV; dogs, P6;
child facs ✕LD 9.30, nr lunch. Resid lic
£ B&B £15, B&B (double) £28–£32; dep.

WARWICK-ON-EDEN   Cumbria.   Map 22E6

🅟 🅟 Queens Arms   CA4 8PA ☎(0228) 60699.
*White-painted inn close to River Eden in quiet
village. Bedrooms in adjoining modern building.*
⇔8 bedrs, 8 en suite, TV; tcf 📺dogs; P 60; child
facs ✕LD 9.30
£ B&B £28, B&B (double) £36; L £6, D £10; WB £44
(2 nts) cc Access, Amex, B'card/Visa, Diners

WATCHET   Somerset.   Map 29B6

West Somerset   Swain St, TA23 0AB ☎(0984)
34434.
⇔12 bedrs, 3 en suite, 3 ba; TV; tcf 📺TV, dogs;
coach; child facs ✕LD 9.45
£ B&B £12·50; HB weekly £122·50, L £2·75,
D £7·50; [10% V] cc Access, B'card/Visa; dep.

WATFORD   Hertfordshire.   Map 27A6

The White House   29 Upton Rd, WD1 2EL
☎(0923) 37316 Tx: 8955439 Fax: (0923) 33109.
⇔89 bedrs, 89 en suite; TV; tcf 📺lift; dogs, ns;
P 45, coach; child facs ✕LD 9.45
£ B&B £60–£100, B&B (double) £80–£110; HB
weekly £465–£705; L £4·50, D £14·95; WB (£40)
cc Access, Amex, B'card/Visa; dep.

WEAVERHAM   Cheshire.   Map 24A4

Beechwood House   206 Wallerscote Road,
Northwich, CW8 3LZ ☎(0606) 852123. *Farm.* Janet
Kuypers   ♿
Sleeps 4, ns ☞

£ B&B from £11·50, D from £5·50

WEDMORE Somerset. Map 29C6

Yew Tree Country House (Acclaimed) Sand,
BF28 4XF ☎(0934) 712520.
From M5 junction 22 take B3139 to Wells, after 6
miles turn right at Hugh Sexey School. Continue for
1 ¼ miles and house is on right.
⇔5 bedrs, 5 en suite; TV; tcf ⋔TV; P10; child
facs ✗LD 7.15, nr lunch. Rest lic
£ B&B £25–£35, B&B (double) £39–£58; HB weekly
£136–£200; D £11·50; WB £19·50 **cc** Access,
B'card/Visa; dep.

WEETON Lancashire. Map 30C7

Swarbrick Hall Farm Singleton Road, Nr
Kirkham, PR4 3JJ ☎(0253 836465) 465. *Farm.* Mrs
Heather Smith
Sleeps 5, ☞
£ B&B from £15

WELLESBOURNE Warwickshire. Map 26C8

Little Hill Farm Warwick, CV35 9EB ☎(0789)
840261. *Farm.* Charlotte Hutsby
Sleeps 6, ✟ ns ☞
£ B&B from £13–£15

WELLINGBOROUGH Northamptonshire.
Map 26F9

Oak House 9 Broad Green, NN8 4LE ☎(0933)
71133.
Situated on the N of town just off the edge of the
town centre opposite the Cenotaph. Closed 24–31
Dec.
⇔13 bedrs, 12 en suite, (1 sh); TV; tcf ⋔TV, dogs;
P12; child facs ✗LD noon, nr lunch, Sat & Sun
dinner. Resid lic
£ B&B £30, B&B (double) £40; [5% V] **cc** Access,
B'card/Visa.

WELLINGTON Somerset. Map 29B5

Blue Mantle 2 Mantle St, TA21 8AW
☎(0823) 662000.
On approach to Wellington follow signs for Blue
Mantle. Swimming pool.
⇔9 bedrs, (1 sh), 2 ba; TV; tcf ⋔TV, dogs ✗LD 8,
nr Sun dinner. Rest lic

£ B&B £18, B&B (double) £30; L £3·50, D £8·50;
[10% V] **cc** Amex, B'card/Visa; dep.

Gamlins Greenham, TA21 0LZ ☎(0823) 672596.
Working farm offering rough shooting, coarse
fishing and swimming pool.
⇔4 bedrs, 1 en suite, 1 ba
£ B&B £16, B&B (double) £25–£30.

WELLS Somerset. Map 29D6

Bekynton (Acclaimed) 7 St Thomas St, BA5 2UU
☎(0749) 72222.

Stone-built period house with converted barn in one
of Wells' oldest streets. At the bottom of the Liberty
keep left after the pedestrian crossing lights, and
house is just past the Fountain Inn. Closed Xmas
& Boxing Day.
⇔9 bedrs, 3 en suite, 3 ba; TV; tcf ⋔ns; P6; no
children under 5 ✗Breakfast only. Unlic
£ B&B £17–£21, B&B (double) £31–£38; [5% V
Nov–May, w/d] **cc** Access, B'card/Visa; dep.

Tor 20 Tor St, BA5 2US ☎(0749) 72322.
⇔7 bedrs, 2 en suite, 2 ba; tcf ⋔TV, dogs, ns; P 12,
G 1, coach; child facs ✗LD 10 am. Unlic
£ B&B £16–£25, B&B (double) £32–£42; HB weekly
£164–£210; L £6, D £10; [5% V].

WEMBLEY Middlesex. Map 27A6

Brookside 32 Brook Ave, Wembley Park ☎081-
904 0019.
⇔13 bedrs, 3 ba; TV ⋔TV; dogs, ns; P 10, coach;
child facs ✗LD 2
£ B&B £23, B&B (double) £35; [10% V]; dep.

Elm Elm Rd, HA9 7JA ☎081-902 1764
Fax: 081-903 8365.
Comfortable hotel close to Wembley Central Station.
Situated behind the High St.

➤29 bedrs, 19 en suite, 5 ba; TV; tcf ♙dogs; P8, coach; child facs ✗Breakfast only. Unlic
£B&B £32–£42, B&B (double) £42–£52; dep.

WEOBLEY Hereford & Worcester
(Herefordshire).   Map 31D7

Tudor   Broad St, HR4 8SA ✆(0544) 318201.
Situated in the village centre, through a passage beside the Post Office. Closed New Year.
➤4 bedrs, 1 ba; tcf ♙TV, dogs, ns; P3; no children under 2, child facs ✗LD 7. Rest lic
£ B&B £15–£16·50, B&B (double) £26–£30; HB weekly £154–£175; D £10; [5% Nov–Mar]; dep.

Unicorn House   High St, HR4 8SL ✆(0544) 318230.
Charming building dating from 1412. Weobley is on a turning off A4112 and A480.
➤5 bedrs, 4 en suite, 1 ba; TV; tcf ♙TV, ns; coach; child facs ✗LD 10, Resid & Rest lic
£ B&B £16–£18, B&B (double) £40–£45; HB weekly £209·65; L £5·50, D £9·95; WB £60 HB; [5% V Sun & Wed] cc Access, Amex, B'card/Visa & Diners; dep.

WEST CHILTINGTON   West Sussex.
Map 27B3

New House Farm   Broadford Bridge Road, Nr Pulborough, RH20 2LA ✆(0798) 812215. *Farm.*
Alma Steele
Sleeps 6, ☎ (10)
£ B&B from £18–£22

WESTCLIFF-ON-SEA   Essex.   Map 27D6

West Park (Highly Acclaimed)   11 Park Rd, SS0 7PQ ✆Southend (0702) 330729 Fax: (0702) 338162.
Attractive small hotel in a quiet residential area. Park Rd is the second turning on the left off A13 Old London Rd.
➤21 bedrs, 17 en suite, (5 sh), 1 ba; TV; tcf ♙TV, dogs; P16, coach; child facs ✗LD 7, nr Sun. Resid & Rest lic
£ B&B £29–£32, B&B (double) £48–£51; L £4·50, D £10; WB; [5% V] cc Access, B'card/Visa.

Cobham Lodge (Acclaimed)   2 Cobham Rd, SS08EA ✆Southend (0702) 346438.
Delightfully situated seafront hotel with garden and terrace. On the A127 Southend road. Billiards.
➤30 bedrs, 23 en suite, 2 ba; TV; tcf ♙TV, ns; coach; child facs ✗LD6.30, nr lunch. Rest lic
£B&B £29·50, B&B (double) £38; HB weekly £180; D £8·50; WB £54 cc Access, B'card/Visa; dep.

Rose House   21–23 Manor Rd, SS07SR
✆Southend (0702) 341959.
Situated opposite Westcliff Station.
➤23 bedrs, 7 en suite, 4 ba; TV; tcf ♙TV, dogs;

P 9, coach; child facs ✗LD after breakfast, nr Mon–Sat lunch, Sun dinner. Resid & Rest lic
£ B&B £19·50–£22·50, B&B (double) £40–£45; D £6·95; [10% V 1 wk only] cc Access, B'card/Visa; dep.

WEST LULWORTH   Dorset.   Map 29E3

Newlands Farm   Wareham, BH20 5PU
✆(092941) 376. *Farm.* Mrs Lesley Simpson
Sleeps 6, ☎ ns
£ B&B from £16

WESTON-SUPER-MARE   Avon. Map 29C7

Braeside (Highly Acclaimed)   2 Victoria Park, BS23 2HZ ✆(0934) 626642.
Family-run hotel close to the seafront with magnificent views over Weston Bay and Brean Down. Between the Winter Gardens and Knightstone.
➤9 bedrs, 9 en suite; TV; tcf ♙dogs; child facs ✗LD6, nr Mon–Sat lunch, Sun dinner. Resid lic
£B&B £18–£20; HB weekly £147–£166; L £7·50 D £7·50; WB; dep.

Milton Lodge (Highly Acclaimed)   15 Milton Rd, BS23 2SH ✆(0934) 623161.
Small detached Victorian house restored to its original elegance with modern facilities. Follow signs to Milton and seafront north. Hotel on the right just past Ashcombe Rd traffic lights. Open Easter–Sept.
➤6 bedrs, 6 en suite; TV; tcf ♙TV, ns; P6; no children under 10 ✗LD4, nr Mon–Sat lunch, Sun dinner. Unlic
£B&B £21, B&B (double) £32; HB weekly £123–£134; dep.

Wychwood (Highly Acclaimed)   148 Milton Rd, BS23 2UZ ✆(0934) 627793.
Small family run hotel in pleasant area. On main approach road into town turn right at Mobil Garage. Hotel is ¾ mile on left. Swimming pool. Closed Xmas and New Year.
➤11 bedrs, 9 en suite, 2 ba; TV; tcf ♙dogs; P11; child facs ✗LD7, nr lunch. Resid lic
£B&B £19, B&B (double) £36; HB weekly £175; [5% V] cc Access, B'card/Visa; dep.

Ashcombe Court (Acclaimed)   2 Elmhyrst Rd, BS23 2SJ ✆(0934) 625104.
Family run hotel, tastefully decorated and furnished. On the Milton main approach road to town.
➤7 bedrs, 4 en suite, 3 ba; TV; tcf ♙TV, dogs, ns; P9, coach; child facs ✗LD 6, nr lunch Mon–Sat & dinner Sun. Unlic
£B&B £14–£17; HB weekly £85–£90; WB (£17); [5% V]; dep.

Accueil   193 Locking Rd, BS23 3HE ✆(0934) 626797.

🛏5 bedrs, 2 ba; TV; tcf 🛋TV, ns; P3; children over 7 ✗LD4, nr lunch

Baymead   19–23 Longton Grove Rd, BS23 1LS ☎(0934) 622951.
Situated at the top of the High St past the Playhouse Theatre.
🛏33 bedrs, 25 en suite, 3 ba; TV; tcf 🛋lift, TV, dogs; P6, coach; child facs ✗LD6.15, nr lunch Mon–Sat, dinner Sun. Resid lic
£B&B £15–£22, B&B (double) £30–£44; HB weekly £100–£160; L £5, D £5; dep.

Denewood   8 Madeira Rd, BS23 2EX ☎(0934) 620694.

L'Arrivee   75 Locking Rd, BS23 3DW ☎(0934) 625328.
🛏12 bedrs, 6 en suite, 1 ba; TV; tcf 🛋TV, dogs; P16; child facs ✗LD4.30, nr lunch

Newton House   79 Locking Rd, BS23 3DW ☎(0934) 629331.
Follow A370 into town, hotel on right past Taunton turn off. Closed 24 Dec–2 Jan.
🛏8 bedrs, 4 en suite, 2 ba; TV; tcf 🛋TV, dogs; P9, coach; child facs ✗LD midday, nr Mon–Sat lunch & Sun dinner. Resid lic
£B&B £15–£17·50, B&B (double) £30–£35; HB weekly £144–£161·50; [10% V Sept–Mar]
cc Access, Amex, B'card/Visa; dep.

Sandringham   1 Victoria Sq, BS23 1AA ☎(0934) 624891.

Shire Elms   71 Locking Rd, BS23 3DQ ☎(0934) 628605.

Vaynor   346 Locking Rd, BS22 8PD ☎(0934) 632332.
Situated on main road into town near Heron public house.
🛏3 bedrs, 1 ba 🛋TV, dogs; P3; child facs ✗LD4, nr lunch Mon–Sat, dinner Sun. Unlic
£B&B £10–£10·50; HB weekly £98–£101·50; [10% V Oct–May]; dep.

WESTON UNDERWOOD   Derbyshire.
Map 24D3

Parkview Farm   DE6 4PA ☎(0335) 60352. *Farm.*
Mrs Linda Adams
Sleeps 6, ns 🛇
£ B&B from £14–£18

WESTWARD HO!   Devon.
Map 28F5

Buckleigh Lodge (Acclaimed)   Bay View Rd, EX39 1BJ ☎Bideford (0237) 475988.
Large Victorian house in its own grounds overlooking the bay. Follow signs to Westward Ho from Bideford, after roundabout travel ¼ mile then turn left.

🛏6 bedrs, 2 en suite, 2 ba; TV; tcf 🛋TV, P7; child facs ✗LD5, nr lunch. Resid lic
£B&B £14–£17, B&B (double) £28–£34; D £7; [10% V]; dep.

WEST WOODBURN   Northumberland.
Map 23B8

Bay Horse   NE48 2RX ☎Bellingham (0434) 270218.
18th-century coaching inn on the A68 Darlington to Edinburgh. At the bottom of the hill in the village beside the River Rede.
🛏5 bedrs, (1 sh), 2 ba; TV; tcf 🛋P20; child facs ✗LD9
£B&B £18–£20, B&B (double) £32–£35; L £6, D £8·50; WB cc Access, B'card/Visa; dep.

WEYMOUTH   Dorset.
Map 29D3

Kenora (Acclaimed)   5 Stavordale Rd, Westham, DT4 0AD ☎(0305) 771215.

A Victorian gentleman's residence converted and adapted over the last 30 years. From Jubilee Clock at Esplanade turn down King St, take 2nd exit at Kings Island, cross bridge and take 2nd exit at Westham roundabout. Turn immediately left and right. Open 12 May–29 Sep.
🛏15 bedrs, 13 en suite, 1 ba; tcf 🛋TV; P21, coach; child facs ✗LD4.30, nr lunch. Resid & Rest lic
£B&B £14·50–£22·50, B&B (double) £29–£35; HB weekly £130–£153·50; D £7·50; dep.

Tamarisk (Acclaimed)   12 Stavordale Rd, DT4 0AB ☎(0305) 786514.
A brick and stone building in a quiet cul-de-sac close to the beach and harbour. Turn right at Jubilee Clock on Esplanade, cross over roundabout and bridge, second roundabout and then immediately left. Open Easter–Oct.

⋈16 bedrs, 12 en suite, 3 ba; TV; tcf ⊞TV; P 19, child facs ✗LD midday, nr lunch. Resid lic £B&B £15–£17; HB weekly £122–£139; dep.

Westwey (Acclaimed)   62 Abbotsbury Rd, DT4 0BJ ☎(0305) 784564.
⋈11 bedrs, 8 en suite, 2 ba; TV; tcf ⊞TV, ns; P 11, coach; no children under 6 mths, child facs ✗LD 6.30, nr lunch. Resid lic.

Bay View   35 The Esplanade, DT4 8DH ☎(0305) 782083.
⋈10 bedrs, 6 en suite, 1 ba; TV; tcf ⊞dogs; child facs ✗nr lunch & Sun dinner. Resid & Rest lic
cc Access, Amex, B'card/Visa; dep.

Beechcroft   128–129 The Esplanade, DT4 7EH ☎(0305) 786608.
Situated at the War Memorial end of the Esplanade. Open Apr–Sept.
⋈28 bedrs, 15 en suite, (7 sh), 6 ba; TV; tcf ⊞dogs; P 10, coach; child facs ✗LD 4, nr Mon–Sat lunch, Sun dinner. Resid & Rest lic
£B&B £13·28–£16·10; HB weekly £120·75–£138; D £5·75 cc Access, B'card/Visa; dep.

Birchfields   22 Abbotsbury Rd, DT4 0AE ☎(0305) 773255.
Small hotel close to town and beach on the main Bridport Rd.
⋈9 bedrs, 3 en suite, 2 ba; tcf ⊞TV, dogs; P 4, coach; child facs ✗LD 3, nr Mon–Sat lunch, Sun dinner. Resid lic
£B&B £12–£17; HB weekly £95–£122; [5% V Sep–Jun]; dep.

Cavendale   10 The Esplanade, DT4 8EB ☎(0305) 786960.
⋈9 bedrs, 2 ba; TV; tcf ⊞TV, dogs; child facs ✗LD 3.30, nr lunch, nr dinner Nov–Apr. Unlic.

Concorde   131 The Esplanade, DT4 7RY ☎(0305) 776900.
⋈17 bedrs, 3 en suite, (4 sh), 3 ba ⊞TV, dogs; P 4, coach; child facs ✗LD 7, nr Mon–Sat lunch, Sun dinner.

Greenhill   8 Greenhill, DT4 7SQ ☎(0305) 786026.
Turn right at Victoria Clock, cross over roundabout and bridge, and hotel is on right. Sauna, solarium.

Hazeldene   16 Abbotsbury Rd, DT4 0AE ☎(0305) 782579.
⋈7 bedrs, 3 ba; tcf ⊞TV; P 7, U 1, coach; no children under 5 ✗LD 2, nr lunch. Resid lic
£B&B £13–£16; HB weekly £75–£115; dep.

Kings Acre   140 The Esplanade, DT4 7NH ☎(0305) 782534.
Situated on Esplanade overlooking the beach and bay. Open mid Jan–Nov.
⋈13 bedrs, 5 en suite, (1 sh), 3 ba; TV; tcf ⊞TV, ns; P 9, coach; child facs ✗LD 3, nr lunch. Resid lic

£B&B £17–£30, B&B (double) £30–£44; HB weekly £133–£175 cc Access, B'card/Visa; dep.

Redcliff   18–19 Brunswick Terr, DT4 7SE ☎(0305) 784682.
Seafront hotel with uninterrupted views of the bay, situated on the Esplanade near the Pier Bandstand.
⋈15 bedrs, 3 en suite, 3 ba; TV; tcf ⊞TV; P 7 U 1, no children under 3 ✗LD 6, nr Mon–Sat lunch, Sun dinner. Resid lic
£ B&B £14·50–£18·50; HB weekly £146·50–£175; [5% V Mon–Fri]

Sandcombe   8 The Esplanade, DT4 4EB ☎(0305) 786833.
Small hotel with commanding views of Weymouth Bay and the harbour. Situated by the Ferry Terminal.
⋈9 bedrs, 2 ba; TV; tcf ⊞TV, ns; child facs ✗LD 6. Resid lic
£B&B £12–£17; HB weekly £120–£135; dep.

Sou'West Lodge   Rodwell Rd, DT4 8QT ☎(0305) 783749.
Family-run hotel, situated on the road to Portland. Closed Xmas & New Year
⋈9 bedrs, 6 en suite, 1 ba; TV; tcf ⊞TV, dogs; P 9; child facs ✗LD 3, nr lunch. Resid lic
£B&B £17·60–£22; HB weekly £140–£167; [10% V]; dep.

Sunningdale   52 Preston Rd, DT3 6QA ☎(0305) 832179.
Well-established hotel with extensive gardens, on the A353 1½ miles from seafront. Swimming pool, putting. Open Easter–Oct.
⋈20 bedrs, 10 en suite, (2 sh), 3 ba; TV; tcf ⊞TV, dogs; P 20, coach; child facs ✗LD 7, nr lunch. Resid & Rest lic
£B&B £17·75–£22, HB weekly £139–£177; D £5·25; WB £65 (3 nts); [5% V mid Sept–mid Jan]; dep.

WHEDDON CROSS   Somerset.   Map 29A6

Higherley   Nr Minehead, TA24 7EB ☎Timberscombe (064 3841) 582.
Set within the Exmoor National Park with panoramic views. In Wheddon Cross go over A396 and Higherley is ½ mile on the left.
⋈9 bedrs, (1 sh), 3 ba; TV ⊞TV, dogs; P 30, G 4; child facs ✗LD 8.30.
£B&B Prices on application. L £8, D £9·75; WB £48 [5% V Mon–Wed] cc Access, B'card/Visa; dep.

Cutthorne Farm   Luckwell Bridge, TA24 7EW ☎(064 383) 255. *Farm.* Ann Durbin
Sleeps 6, ⊞ ☺
£ B&B from £14·50, D £9·50

Little Brendon Hill   nr Minehead, TA24 7DG
☎(0643) 841556. *Farm*. Mrs Shelagh Maxwell
Sleeps 6
£ B&B from £13·50–£15·50

Little Quarme   Nr Minehead, TA24 7EA ☎(0643)
841249. *Farm*. Tammy and Bob Cody-Boutcher
Sleeps 4, ⛱ (3) ns
£ B&B from £12·65

WHIDDON DOWN   Devon.   Map 28F4

Fairhaven Farm   Gooseford, Okehampton, EX20
2QH ☎(0647) 23261. *Farm*. Mrs April Scott
Sleeps 6, ⛱ 🐓
£ B&B from £?

WHIMPLE   Devon.   Map 29B4

Middle Cobden Farm   Exeter, EX5 2PZ ☎(0404)
822276. *Farm*. Cathie Cottey
Sleeps 6, ⛱
£ B&B from £10–£13.50, D £6

WHITBOURNE   Worcester.   Map 31C8

Pixhill Farm   WR6 5ST ☎(0886) 21304. *Farm*.
Gail and Richard Bellville
Sleeps 3, ⛱
£ B&B from £10, D £8

WHITBY   North Yorkshire.   Map 23F5

Kimberley (Highly Acclaimed)   7 Havelock Pl,
YO21 3ER ☎(0947) 604125.
🛏9 bedrs, 5 en suite, 2 ba; TV; tcf 📺dogs, ns; no
children under 5 ✗LD 7, nr lunch. Resid lic
cc Access, B'card/Visa.

York House (Highly Acclaimed)   High Hawsker,
YO22 4LW ☎(0947) 880314.

*Small detached hotel in its own grounds, with
excellent facilities. From Whitby Take A171
Scarborough Rd, in 3 miles turn right after Hare and
Hound sign. Open Mar–Nov.*
🛏4 bedrs, 4 en suite, 2 ba; TV; tcf 📺NS; P 8; no
children ✗LD6.30, nr lunch. Resid lic
£B&B (double) £37; HB weekly £192·50; dep.

Corra Lynn (Acclaimed)   28 Crescent Ave, YO21
3EW ☎(0947) 602214.

*Attractive refurbished Victorian building set on
Whitby West Cliff on the corner of A174 and
Crescent Ave. Open Mar–Oct.*
🛏6 bedrs, 6 en suite; TV; tcf 📺TV, dogs; P 4; child
facs ✗LD3, nr lunch. Resid lic
£B&B £16·50–£19·50; HB weekly £185–£199; WB
(£52); dep.

Oxford (Acclaimed)   West Cliff, YO21 3EL ☎(0947)
603349.
*Situated on West Cliff promenade. Solarium. Open
Feb–Nov.*
🛏16 bedrs, 16 en suite, TV; tcf 📺lift; P 3, coach;
child facs ✗LD 5, nr lunch. Resid & Rest lic
£ B&B £26, B&B (double) £42; HB weekly £406;
D £9 **cc** Access, Amex, B'card/Visa, Diners; dep.

Seacliffe (Acclaimed)   North Promenade, YO21
3JX ☎(0947) 603139.
*Three-storey detached building in a prime seafront
position. Follow signs for West Cliff.*
🛏19 bedrs, 19 en suite, 1 ba; TV; tcf 📺TV, dogs,
ns; P 8, coach; child facs ✗LD9, nr lunch. Resid
& Rest lic
£B&B £37·50–£41·50, B&B (double) £47–£49;
D£11 **cc** Access, Amex, B'card/Visa, Diners; dep.

Sandbeck (Acclaimed)   2 Crescent Terr, West
Cliff, YO21 3EL ☎(0947) 604012.

Banchory   3 Crescent Terr, West Cliff, YO21 3EL
☎(0947) 603513.
🛏12 bedrs, 5 en suite, 2 ba; TV; tcf 📺dogs; P 3,
coach; child facs ✗LD4, nr lunch
£B&B £15–£20; B&B (double) £28–£38; HB weekly
£161; dep. **cc** Access, Amex, B'card/Visa, Diners.

Corner   3 Crescent Place, YO21 3HE ☎(0947)
602444.
*At the top of Kyber Pass bear left, first guest house
on the left.*
🛏11 bedrs, 2 ba; TV; tcf 📺TV; coach; child facs
✗LD 4, nr lunch. Resid lic
£ B&B £9–£14; dep.

Europa   20 Hudson St, West Cliff, YO21 3EP
☎(0947) 602251.
*On the West Cliff near to St. Hilda's Church and
sports field. Open Feb–Nov.*
🛏8 bedrs, 1 en suite, 3 ba; TV; tcf 📺TV, ns; no
children under 4 ✗LD 4, nr lunch. Unlic
£B&B £12; D £7; dep.

Glendale   16 Crescent Ave, YO21 3ED ☎(0947)
604242.
🛏7 bedrs, (1 sh), 2 ba; TV; tcf 📺TV, dogs; P 6;
child facs ✗LD4.30, nr lunch. Resid lic

Waverley   17 Crescent Ave, YO21 3ED ☎(0947)
604389.
*A small family hotel situated on the West Cliff close
to the Promenade. Open Mar–Oct.*

6 bedrs, 4 en suite, 2 ba; TV; tcf TV; no children under 3 LD 5.30, nr lunch. Resid lic
£ B&B £12·50–£14·50; HB weekly £112·50–£126·50; [10% V]; dep.

WHITCHURCH Hereford & Worcestershire (Herefordshire). Map 31D8

Crown HR9 6DB (0600) 890234.
An old inn, cream painted with red shutters, on a busy road.
5 bedrs, 5 en suite; TV; tcf TV, dogs; P 40, coach; child facs LD 9.45
£ B&B £25–£30, B&B (double) £40–£48; HB weekly £150–£170; L £6, D £8; WB £22 (2 nts); [10% V w/d]
cc Access, Amex, B'card/Visa, Diners; dep.

Portland HR9 6DB (0600) 890757. Closed Dec & Jan.
8 bedrs, (8 sh), 1 ba; TV; tcf TV, dogs, ns; P 8; child facs LD 6, nr lunch. Resid lic
£ B&B £15·50–£17·50; HB weekly £140–£155; dep.

WHITCHURCH Shropshire. Map 24A3

Bradeley Green Farm Tarporley Road, SY13 4HD (0948) 3442. *Farm.* Ruth Mulliner
Sleeps 6, ns
£ B&B from £15, D £7·50

WHITESTONE Devon. Map 29A4

Rowhorne House Rowhorne, EX4 2LQ Exeter (0392) 74675.

WHITLEY BAY Tyne & Wear. Map 23D7

York House (Acclaimed) 30 Park Parade, NE26 1DX 091-252 8313 & 251 3953.
Family-run hotel with good service and friendly atmosphere. The A193 passes Park Parade.
8 bedrs, 7 en suite, (1 sh); TV; tcf TV, dogs; U 2; child facs LD 6.45, nr Mon–Sat lunch & Sun dinner. Resid lic
£ B&B £18, B&B (double) £32; HB weekly £147
cc B'card/Visa; dep.

Cherrytree House 35 Brook St. NE26 1AF 091-251 4306.
4 beds, 1 en suite, (2 sh), 1 ba; TV; tcf TV, dogs; P 1, coach; child facs LD 4.50, nr lunch. Unlic.

Lindisfarne 11 Holly Ave, NE26 1ER 091-251 3954.
9 bedrs, 2 en suite, 2 ba; TV; tcf TV, dogs, ns LD 4, nr lunch. Resid lic
cc Access, B'card/Visa; dep.

White Surf 8 South Pde, NE2 2RG 091-253 0103.
Family-run guest house with modern facilities. Situated close to town centre and seafront promenade.

9 bedrs, 2 ba; TV TV, ns; P 7, G 1; coach; children over 1 LD 4.30, nr lunch. Unlic
£ B&B £12·50–£14·50; HB weekly £122·50–£136·50; [5% V Jul–Sep]

WHITTINGHAM Northumberland. Map 23C9

Dancing Hall Alnwick, NE66 4TB (066574) 660. *Farm.* Mrs Wendy Hyslop
Sleeps 5,
£ B&B from £12·50

Thrunton Farmhouse Alnwick, NE66 4RZ (066 574) 220. *Farm.* Phyllis Campbell
Sleeps 4, ns
£ B&B from £13–£14

WICKEN Cambridgeshire. Map 25B1

Spinney Abbey Ely, CB7 5XQ (0353) 720971. *Farm.* Valerie Fuller
Sleeps 6, ns (2)
£ B&B from £13

WIDECOMBE-IN-THE-MOOR Devon. Map 28G3

Higher Venton Farm Newton Abbot, TQ13 7TF (03642) 235. *Farm.* Mrs Betty Hicks
Sleeps 6,
£ B&B from £12, D £6

Lower Southway Farm TQ13 7TE (03642) 277. *Farm.* Dawn Nosworthy
Sleeps 6,
£ B&B from £9·50–£11, D £7

WIGAN Greater Manchester (Lancashire). Map 24A6

Aalton Court (Acclaimed) 23 Upper Dicconson St, WN1 2AG (0942) 322220.
Follow A49 N for Preston, turn left after Wigan Rugby ground. Turn fourth right into Dicconson Terrace and Upper Dicconson St is opposite.
6 bedrs, 6 en suite; TV; tcf TV; P 9; child facs LD 2, nr lunch. Resid lic
£ B&B £23, B&B (double) £35; WB £21; dep.

Charles Dickens 14 Upper Dicconson St, WN1 2AD (0942) 323263.
Small town centre hotel adjoining Wigan Market.
16 bedrs, 16 en suite; TV; tcf TV; dogs; P 9; coach; child facs LD 8.30, bar meals only Sun dinner
£ B&B £21, B&B (double) £30; L £3·65, D £5·65
cc Access, Amex, B'card/Visa.

WIGGLESWORTH   North Yorkshire.
Map 24B8

♟ ♟ ♟ Plough Inn   BD23 4RJ ☎(072 97) 243.
*Delightful 18th-century country inn, with beams and
open fires, set in beautiful countryside.*
🛏11 bedrs, 11 en suite; TV; tcf ♠TV; P50, coach;
child facs ✗LD9.30
cc Access, B'card/Visa, Diners.

WILLEY   Warwickshire.
Map 24D1

Manor Farm, Nr Rugby, CV23 0SH ☎(0455)
553143. *Farm.* Mrs Helen Sharpe
Sleeps 5, ns
£ B&B from £15, D £8

WILLITON   Somerset.
Map 29B6

Fairfield House   51 Long St, TA4 4QY ☎(0984)
32636.
*17th century hotel combining period charm with
modern comfort. Situated on Long St (A39) close
to the village centre. Open Mar–Oct.*
🛏5 bedrs, 5 en suite, tcf ♠TV; P 8–10; no children
under 11 ✗LD9, nr lunch. Rest lic
£B&B £23, B&B (double) £40; HB weekly £192·50;
D£11 **cc** Access, B'card/Visa; dep.

WIMBORNE MINSTER   Dorset.   Map 26C2

Beech Leas (Highly Acclaimed)   17 Poole Rd,
BH21 1QA ☎(0202) 841684.

*Grade II listed Georgian building, beautifully
restored, with small walled garden. Situated on
A349. Open Feb–Dec.*
🛏7 bedrs, 7 en suite, TV ♠ns; P9, child facs
✗LD9, nr lunch. Resid & Rest lic
£B&B £46·50–£66·50, B&B (double) £63·50–
£83·50; HB weekly £430·50–£570·50; D£15
cc Access, B'card/Visa.

Riversdale   33 Poole Rd, BH21 1QB ☎(0202)
884528.
🛏9 bedrs, (3 sh), 2 ba; TV; tcf ♠TV, dogs; P6; no
children under 3 ✗LD before 12 noon, nr lunch,
Sat & Sun dinner. Unlic

cc Access; dep.

WIMPSTONE   Warwickshire.   Map 26C8

Whitchurch Farm   nr Stratford-upon-Avon CV37
8NS ☎(0789) 450275. *Farm.* Mrs Joan James
Sleeps 6, ♋
£ B&B from £12, D £7·50

WINCHELSEA   East Sussex.   Map 27D3

Strand House   A259, TN36 4JT ☎Rye (0797)
226276.
*Reputed to go back to the early 1400's, Strand
House is one of the oldest houses in the district.
On A259 between Winchelsea and Rye.*
🛏10 bedrs, 10 en suite, TV; tcf ♠dogs, ns; P 15,
no children between 2–8 years ✗Breakfast only.
Resid lic
£B&B £18–£20, B&B (double) £26–£40; WB.

WINCHESTER   Hampshire.   Map ???

Harestock Lodge   Harestock Rd, SO22 6NX
☎(0962) 881870.
*Leave Winchester for Stockbridge on A272, follow
sign to Harestock, and hotel is 300 yards on right.
Swimming pool.*
🛏20 beds, 9en suite, (11 sh), 1 ba; TV; tcf ♠TV,
dogs; P26, coach; child facs ✗LD9.15. Resid &
Rest lic
£B&B £33–£38, B&B (double) £40–£47; HB weekly
£294–£329; [5% V] **cc** Access, Amex, B'card/Visa.

Kings Head   Hursley Village, SO21 2JW ☎(0962)
75208.

WINCHCOMBE   Gloucestershire.   Map 26B7

Postlip Hall Farm   Cheltenham, GL54 5AQ
☎(0242) 603351. *Farm.* Mrs Valerie Albutt
Sleeps 6
£ B&B from £12·50

Sudeley Hill Farm   GL54 5JB ☎(0242)
602344. *Farm.* Barbara Scudamore
Sleeps 6, ♋
£ B&B from £14

Discount vouchers
RAC discount vouchers are at the end of the
guide. Establishments with a [V] shown at the end
of the price information will accept them in part
payment for accommodation bills on the full,
standard rate, not against bargain breaks or any
other special offers. Please note the limitations
shown in the entry: w/e for weekends, w/d for
weekdays, and which months they are accepted.

WINDERMERE Cumbria.　　　Map 22F4

P P Albert　Queen's Sq, Bowness, LA23 3BY
☎(09662) 3241 Fax: (09662) 88067.
Family-run inn in centre of town.
⊷6 bedrs, 6 en suite; TV; tcf ⋔dogs; P5, coach;
child facs ✕LD 9.45
cc Access, B'card/Visa; dep.

Blenheim Lodge (Highly Acclaimed)　Brantfell Rd,
LA23 3AE **☎**(096 62) 3440.
*Attractive lakeland house set against National Trust
land at end of Dalesway footpath, with lake and
mountain views. Take lake road to Bowness, and
house is situated at top of Brantfell Rd.*
⊷11 bedrs, 9 en suite, 1 ba; TV; tcf ⋔TV, ns; P 14,
G 1; no children under 6 ✕LD 4, nr lunch. Resid
& Rest lic
£ B&B £16·50–£25, B&B (double) £36–£50; HB
weekly £189–£234; D £12; [10% V Thur]; dep.

Cranleigh (Highly Acclaimed)　Kendal Rd, LA23
3EW **☎**(09662) 3293.

*Once a Victorian merchant's house built of Lakeland
stone, only minutes from the lake. Turn left opposite
St. Martin's Church, then 300 yards on right. Open
Mar–Nov.*
⊷15 bedrs, 15 en suite; TV; tcf ⋔TV, ns; P 15; child
facs ✕LD 9, nr lunch. Resid & Rest lic
£B&B £31–£35, B&B (double) £42–£56; HB weekly
£190–£240; D £15; WB £60 (2 nts w/d); [10% V
Sun–Fri] **cc** Access, B'card/Visa; dep.

Fir Trees (Highly Acclaimed)　Lake Rd, LA23 2EQ
☎(09662) 2272.

*Elegant Victorian guest house of considerable
charm, furnished with antiques. Situated midway
between Windermere and Bowness.*
⊷7 bedrs, 7 en suite; TV ⋔P 9; child facs
✕Breakfast only. Unlic

£B&B £22·50–£26·50, B&B (double) £35–£43;
[10% V] **cc** Access, Amex, B'card/Visa; dep.

Glenburn (Highly Acclaimed)　New Rd, LA23 2EE
☎(09662) 2649.
*Attractive small hotel with comfortable
accommodation. Glenburn is 500 yds on the left
after Windermere shopping centre.*
⊷14 bedrs, 12 en suite, 1 ba; TV; tcf ⋔ns; P 16;
no children under 5 ✕LD 5, nr lunch. Resid lic
£B&B (double) £34–£54; HB weekly £179–£239;
WB **cc** Access, B'card/Visa; dep.

Glencree (Highly Acclaimed)　Lake Rd, LA23 2EQ
☎(09662) 5822.

*Traditional Lakeland stone-built house with many
original Victorian features. Close to stone clock
tower on main road. Open Feb–Nov.*
⊷5 bedrs, 5 en suite; TV; tcf ⋔ns; P8; children
over 7 ✕Breakfast only. Resid & Rest lic
£B&B (double) £39–£55; [5% V w/d] **cc** Access,
B'card/Visa; dep.

Hawksmoor (Highly Acclaimed)　Lake Rd, LA23
2EQ **☎**(09662) 2110.
*Century old ivy clad house surrounded by extensive
gardens and backed by private woodlands.
Situated $\frac{1}{3}$ mile in the direction of the lake, opposite
the Catholic church. Open Jan–Nov.*
⊷10 bedrs, 10 en suite; TV; tcf ⋔ns; P 12;
no children under 6 ✕LD 4, nr lunch. Resid lic
£ B&B £21–£27, B&B (double) £34–£50; HB weekly
£170–£205; dep.

Holly Park (Highly Acclaimed)　1 Park Rd, LA23
2AW **☎**(096 62) 2107.

*Handsome stone Victorian guest house in a quiet
area. Travel S through town, turn left along
Ellerthwaite Rd and left into Holly Rd. Open mid
Mar–Oct 31.*

⇔6 bedrs, 6 en suite; TV; tcf 🏠ns; P3; child facs ✖Breakfast only. Rest lic
£ B&B £22·50, B&B (double) £27–£34·50

St John's Lodge (Highly Acclaimed)   Lake Rd, LA23 2EQ ✆(096 62) 3078.
Victorian lakeland stone building, the original lodge to St John's Church. Situated half-way between Windermere and Bowness. Open Jan–end Nov.
⇔14 bedrs, 14 en suite, TV; tcf 🏠dogs, ns; P 12; no children under 3 ✖LD6, nr lunch. Resid lic
£B&B £16–£20; HB weekly £168–£187; D £9·50; WB £25 (HB); dep.

West Lake (Highly Acclaimed)   Lake Rd, LA23 2EQ ✆(096 62) 3020.
Semi-detached lakeland stone building with ivy clad walls. Situated half-way between Windermere and Bowness.
⇔8 bedrs, 8 en suite; TV; tcf 🏠TV, ns; P8; no children under 2 ✖nr lunch. Resid lic
£B&B (double) £32–£42; HB weekly £180–£205; dep.

Woodlands (Highly Acclaimed)   New Rd, LA23 2EE ✆(096 62) 3915.
Between Windermere and Bowness on the main A5074.
⇔11 bedrs, 9 en suite, 1 ba; TV; tcf 🏠ns; P11; children over 5 ✖LD 4, nr lunch. Resid lic
£B&B £16–£25; D £10 **cc** Access, B'card/Visa; dep.

Brendan Chase (Acclaimed)   College Rd, LA23 1BU ✆(096 62) 5638.
Family-run Edwardian guest house in a picturesque setting. Situated just off A591.
⇔8 bedrs, 4 en suite, 4 ba; TV; tcf 🏠TV, dogs, ns; P4; child facs ✖Breakfast only. Unlic
£B&B £12·50–£20; WB £80 (2 nts); [5% V]; dep.

Glenville (Acclaimed)   Lake Rd, LA23 2EQ ✆(096 62) 3371.
Traditional lakeland stone building standing in its own grounds. Half-way between Windermere and Bowness. Open Feb–Nov.
⇔9 bedrs, 6 en suite, 1 ba; TV; tcf 🏠ns; P12, coach; child facs ✖LD midday, nr lunch. Resid lic
£B&B £15–£19·50; dep.

Kirkwood (Acclaimed)   Prince's Rd, LA23 2DD ✆(096 62) 3907.
⇔8 bedrs, 3 en suite, 2 ba; TV; tcf 🏠dogs; P 1;

child facs ✖LD 6.30, nr lunch. Resid & Rest lic.

Montford (Acclaimed)   Prince's Rd, LA23 2DD ✆(096 62) 5671. *Guest House.*

Mylne Bridge (Acclaimed)   Brookside Lake Rd, LA23 2BX ✆(096 62) 3314.
Turn left at slate tower on Windermere to Bowness road, hotel on the right. Open Mar–Oct.
⇔10 bedrs, 7 en suite, 1 ba; TV; tcf 🏠dogs; P11; child facs ✖Breakfast only
£B&B £15·50–£18·50, B&B (double) £27–£36; [10% V]; dep.

Newstead (Acclaimed)   New Rd, LA23 2EE ✆(096 62) 4485.
Detached Victorian house in attractive gardens standing on left ½ mile towards Bowness from Windermere.
⇔7 bedrs, 7 en suite, TV; tcf 🏠ns; P 10 ✖Breakfast only. Unlic
£B&B (double) £30–£40; dep.

Oakthorpe (Acclaimed)   High St, LA23 1AF ✆(096 62) 3547.
Traditional lakeland stone building featuring a raised balcony. Turn off A591 at Rockside guest house, and Oakthorpe is 100 yds down Elleray road.
⇔19 bedrs, 7 en suite, (3 sh), 3 ba; TV; tcf 🏠dogs; P 19, coach; child facs ✖LD 8.30
£ B&B £18–£26; HB weekly £180–£220; D £14; WB £54 (2 nts) **cc** Access, B'card/Visa; dep.

Rockside (Acclaimed)   Ambleside Rd, LA23 1AQ ✆(096 62) 5343.
Stone and slate house of typical lakeland design. Turn second left after Windermere Hotel. Closed Xmas.
⇔14 bedrs, 10 en suite, 2 ba; TV; tcf 🏠ns; P 11, coach; child facs ✖Breakfast only. Unlic
£B&B £13·50–£18·50; WB (£13); [10% V w/d] **cc** Access, B'card/Visa; dep.

Rosemount (Acclaimed)   Lake Rd, LA23 2EQ ✆(096 62) 3739.
Comfortable small hotel situated on Lake Rd midway between Bowness and Windermere, opposite St John's Church.
⇔8 bedrs, 8 en suite; TV; tcf 🏠ns; P6, G3, coach; child facs ✖Breakfast only. Resid lic
£B&B £16·50–£21 **cc** Access, B'card/Visa; dep.

Windermere (Cumbria)

Wynbrook House (Acclaimed)   30 Ellerthwaite Rd, LA23 2AH ✆(096 62) 4932.
Friendly small guest house in Windermere town. Open Mar–Nov & 27 Dec–6 Jan.
6 bedrs, 3 en suite, (3 sh); TV; tcf ᴔTV, dogs, ns; P6; children over 8 ✗Breakfast only. Unlic
£B&B £15–£24, B&B (double) £23·50–£33·50; [10% V w/d]; dep.

Elim Bank   Lake Rd, LA23 2JJ ✆(096 62) 4810.
Hotel.

Field House   Kendal Rd, LA23 3EQ ✆(096 62) 2476.
7 bedrs, 1 en suite, 2 ba; TV; tcf ᴔdogs; P 7
✗Breakfast only. Unlic
cc Access, B'card/Visa; dep.

Green Gables   37 Broad St, LA23 2AB ✆(096 62) 3886.
Family-run guest house in pleasant location. Turn left off Bowness Rd after pedestrian crossing.
6 bedrs, 2 en suite, 2 ba; TV; tcf ᴔTV, ns; G 1
✗Breakfast only. Unlic
£B&B £12–£15, B&B (double) £22–£32; dep.

Lynwood   Broad St, LA23 2AB ✆(096 62) 2550.
Leave M6 at junction 36, and follow signs for Windermere.
11 bedrs, 4 en suite, 2 ba; TV; tcf ᴔns; P 2;
no children under 5 ✗Breakfast only. Unlic
£ B&B £12–£20, B&B (double) £20–£40; [10% V]; dep.

Melbourne   2 Biskey Howe Rd, LA23 2JP ✆(096 62) 3475. *Guest House.*

Oakfield   46 Oak St, LA23 1EN ✆(096 62) 5692.
A traditional lakeland stone house, situated in the fifth street on the left off A591.
5 bedrs, (1 sh), 1 ba; TV; tcf ᴔns; no children under 4 ✗LD 6, nr lunch. Resid lic
£B&B £12–£18; D £10; [10% V]; dep.

Thornleigh   Thornbarrow Rd, LA23 2EW ✆(096 62) 4203.
Lakeland guest house between Bowness and Windermere. Turn into Thornbarrow Rd off main road, and house is 50 yards on the left. Open Jan–Nov.
6 bedrs, (2 sh), 1 ba; TV; tcf ᴔTV; P 6, coach; child facs ✗Breakfast only. Unlic

£B&B £13–£16; [5% V] cc Access, B'card/Visa; dep.

WINDSOR Berkshire.   Map 13A3

Dorset (Highly Acclaimed)   4 Dorset Rd, SL4 3BA ✆(0753) 852669.
From M4 take A308 to Windsor, turn left into Clarence Rd at first roundabout, cross traffic lights. Dorset Rd is first on right.
5 bedrs, 5 en suite, TV; tcf ᴔP 7; children over 5 ✗Breakfast only. Resid lic
£B&B £50–£55, B&B (double) £60–£65 cc Access, Amex, B'card/Visa, dep.

Melrose House (Acclaimed)   53 Frances Rd SL4 3AQ ✆(0753) 865328.
Elegant Victorian town centre property. Follow High St from Castle into Sheet St, turn right into Frances Rd, and Melrose House is on right.
9 bedrs, 9 en suite; TV; tcf ᴔTV, dogs, ns; P 10; child facs ✗Breakfast only. Unlic
£ B&B £32–£36, B&B (double) £38–£42.

Clarence   9 Clarence Rd, SL4 5AE ✆(0753) 864436.
Follow road into Windsor and turn left at roundabout into Clarence Rd.
20 bedrs, 20 en suite, 1 ba; TV ᴔTV, dogs; P 2, coach; child facs ✗Breakfast only. Resid lic
£B&B £26–£28, B&B (double) £45–£47; [10% V]
cc Amex, B'card/Visa, Diners; dep.

WINSTER Derbyshire.   Map 24C4

Winster Hall   DE4 2DE ✆(062 988) 204.

WITHIEL FLOREY Somerset.   Map 29B6

Lower Eastcott Farm   Minehead, TA24 7OG ✆(03987) 293. *Farm.* Mrs Alison Nancekivell
Sleeps 6, ᴔ ns
£ B&B from £12, D £8

WIVELISCOMBE Somerset.   Map 29B5

Hurstone Farmhouse (Highly Acclaimed) Waterrow, TA4 2AT ✆(0984) 23441.
Lovely old country house over 400 years old, and re-built early this century. Situated ¼ mile off B3227 at Waterrow, 2¼ miles W of Wiveliscombe. Fishing.
5 bedrs, 5 en suite, TV; tcf ᴔTV, dogs, ns; P 8;

child facs ✕LD 10. Mon–Sat lunch by
arrangement. Resid & Rest lic
£ B&B £43–£48·50, B&B (double) £66–£75; HB
weekly £345–£378; L £9·50, D £15·50; WB £94
(2 nts HB) cc Access, Amex, B'card/Visa.

North Down Farm Taunton, TA4 2BL ✆(0984)
23730. *Farm.* Mrs Lucy Parker
Sleeps 6, ☎ ✿ ns
£ B&B from £12, D £6

WIX Essex. Map 27B2

New Farm (Acclaimed) Spinnels La, Manningtree,
CO11 2UJ ✆(0255) 870365.

*Modern farmhouse set in large gardens with play
area. From Wix village crossroads take Bradfield Rd
under A120 to top of hill, turn right, and house is
200 yds on left.*
🛏12 bedrs, 7 en suite, 2 ba; TV; tcf 🅿TV, dogs, ns;
P 12, coach; child facs ✕LD 5.30, nr lunch, Sun
dinner.
£ B&B £15·50–£18·50; HB weekly £145·65–
£164·55; D £7·50; [10% V] cc Access, B'card/Visa;
dep.

WOLSTON Warwickshire. Map 26D9

The Greenways Coalpit Lane, Coventry, CV8
3GB ✆(0203) 542098. *Farm.* Betty Gibbs
Sleeps 4, ns ☎ (5)
£ B&B from £12

WOMENSWOLD Kent. Map 27E4

Woodpeckers Country CT4 6HB ✆Canterbury
(0227) 831319.
*Charming Victorian house in 2¼ acres of gardens.
Swimming pool, snooker, putting.*
🛏12 bedrs, 7 en suite, (4 sh), 2 ba; TV; tcf 🅿TV,
dogs; P 60, coach; child facs
£ B&B £24; HB weekly £203; L £3·50, D £12·50;
WB £60; [5% V] cc Access, B'card/Visa.
(See advertisement under Canterbury)

WOODBURY Devon. Map 29B4

Higher Bagmores Farm Exeter, EX5 1LA
✆(0395) 32261. *Farm.* Myrtle Glanvill
Sleeps 6, ☎
£ B&B from £10

Lochinvar Shepherds Park Farm, Nr Exeter, EX5
1LA ✆(0395) 32185. *Farm.* Dorothy Glanvill
Sleeps 6, ✿ ☎
£ B&B from £12–£14

Rydon Farm Exeter, EX5 1LB ✆(0395)
32341. *Farm.* Sally Glanvill
Sleeps 6, ✿ ns ☎
£ B&B from £13

WOODSTOCK Oxfordshire. Map 26D7

Gorseland Boddington Lane, Nr North Leigh
OX8 6PU ✆(0993) 881895.
*From Woodstock take A4095 towards Witney, 1¾
miles past Long Harborough take first right turn after
Shepherdshall public house. Signed Roman Villa
and East End. Billiards. Open early Jul–late Sep &
most w/e June–Oct.*
🛏3 bedrs, 2 en suite, 1 ba; 🅿TV, NS; P 2, G 2;
child facs ✕LD 9, nr lunch, Mon–Wed dinner
£ B&B (double) £25–£30; HB weekly £125; [10% V].

WOODY BAY Devon. Map 28F5

The Red House (Acclaimed) EX31 4QX
✆Parracombe (05983) 255.
*Situated 3 miles W of Lynton on coastal road. Open
Apr–Oct.*
🛏6 bedrs, 4 en suite, 1 ba; TV; tcf 🅿TV, dogs;
P 10; no children under 4 ✕LD 6.30, nr lunch.
Resid lic
£ B&B (double) £33–£37; HB weekly £175–£190;
[5% V]; dep.

WOOLACOMBE Devon. Map 28F5

Sunnycliff (Highly Acclaimed) Mortehoe, EX34
7EB ✆(0271) 870597.
*Small quiet hotel beautifully situated above a sandy
cove and with sea views. Situated between
Mortehoe and Woolacombe.*
🛏8 bedrs, 8 en suite, 2 ba; TV; tcf 🅿ns; P 12;
no children ✕LD 6, nr lunch. Resid lic
£ B&B £22–£26, B&B (double) £39–£55; HB weekly
£176–£208; WB £57 (2 nts)

Caertref (Acclaimed) Beach Rd, EX34 7BT
✆(0271) 870361.
*A Victorian hotel, much improved in comfort over
the years. Situated on the left of the main road into
Woolacombe, next to the Methodist Chapel. Open
Easter–end Oct.*
🛏13 bedrs, 7 en suite, (1 sh), 2 ba; tcf 🅿TV, dogs;
P 12; child facs ✕nr lunch. Resid lic
£ B&B £12·50; HB weekly £120 cc Access, B'card/
Visa; dep.

Combe Ridge (Acclaimed) The Esplanade, EX34
7DJ ✆(0271) 870321.

Small hotel with magnificent views of Woolacombe Bay and Morte Point. On the seafront ¼ mile from the village. Open Apr–Sep.
📞8 bedrs, 5 en suite, 2 ba; TV; tcf 📺TV, dogs, ns; P7; child facs ✗LD 4.30, nr lunch. Resid lic.

WOOLER Northumberland. Map 21E2

Earle Hill Head Farm NE71 6RH ✆(0668) 81243. Farm. Sylvia Armstrong
Sleeps 6, 🐕 ⛺
£ B&B from £13–£14

WOOTTON BASSETT Wiltshire. Map 26C5

Angel 47 High St, SN4 7AQ ✆Swindon (0793) 852314.

Little Cotmarsh Farm Broad Town, Swindon, SN4 7RA ✆(0793) 731322. Farm. Mary Richards
Sleeps 6, ns ⛺
£ B&B from £12·50

WOOTTON WAWEN West Midlands. Map 24C1

Yew Tree Farm, Solihull, B95 6BY ✆(0564) 792701. Farm. Mrs Janet Haimes
Sleeps 6 + cot, 🐕 ⛺
£ B&B from £12–£15

WORCESTER Hereford & Worcester (Worcestershire). Map 26B8

Loch Ryan 119 Sidbury, WR5 2DH ✆(0905) 351143.
Situated on the A44 S of Worcester Cathedral.
📞13 bedrs, 3 en suite, 2 ba 📺TV, ns; coach; child facs ✗LD 8. Resid lic
£B&B £25–£30, B&B (double) £42–£50; L £8, D £8; [5% V]; dep.

Leigh Court WR6 5LB ✆(0886) 32275 (changing Spring '91 to (0886) 832275). Farm. Sally Stewart
Sleeps 6, 🐕 ⛺
£ B&B from £14–£21, D £11

WORKINGTON Cumbria. Map 22E5

Morven (Highly Acclaimed) Siddick Rd CA14 1LE ✆(0900) 602118.
Detached late Victorian house NW of town centre, with garden and large car park. Situated ¼ mile from Maryport Rd shopping centre.
📞6 bedrs, 4 en suite, 2 ba; TV; tcf 📺TV, dogs, ns; P 20; child facs ✗LD 4, nr lunch
£ B&B £16–£19, B&B (double) £30–£36; dep.

WORMELOW Nr Hereford. Map 31D8

Lyston Smithy HR2 8EL ✆(0981) 540625. Farm. Shirley Handy
Sleeps 6, 🐕 ⛺ (4) ns

£ B&B from £14

WROCKWARDINE Shropshire. Map 24A2

Church Farm Wellington, Telford, TF6 5DG ✆(0952) 244917. Farm. Mrs Jo Savage ♿
Sleeps 8, 🐕 ⛺
£ B&B from £18–£23, D £12

Wrockwardine Farm Nr Wellington, Telford, TF6 5DG ✆(0952) 242278. Farm. Mrs Margaret Carver
Sleeps 6, 🐕 ⛺
£ B&B from £12, D £8

WORTHING West Sussex. Map 27A2

Bonchurch House (Acclaimed) 1 Winchester Rd, BN11 4DJ ✆(0903) 202492.
Spacious end of terrace, red brick building, in picturesque setting just off A259, on the corner of Richmond Rd and Winchester Rd.
📞7 bedrs, 3 en suite, 1 ba; TV; tcf 📺TV, ns; P 4; no children under 4 ✗LD 4, nr lunch. Rest lic
£ B&B £13–£16; HB weekly £130–£145; D £7·50; dep.

Delmar (Acclaimed) 1 New Parade, BN11 2BQ ✆(0903) 211834.

Victorian building with uninterrupted Channel views. Opposite the Aquarena Swimming Pool in Brighton Rd.
📞13 bedrs, 7 en suite, 2 ba; TV; tcf 📺TV, ns; P 4; U 1 ✗LD 9 am, nr lunch. Resid lic
£ B&B £20·70–£22·43; HB weekly £228·83–£240·94 **cc** Access, B'card/Visa; dep.

Moorings (Acclaimed) 4 Selden Rd, BN11 2LL ✆(0903) 208882.

Victorian house, tastefully renovated and furnished, close to the beach. Just off A259 towards Brighton.

⋈8 bedrs, 8 en suite; TV; tcf 🏠ns; P 5; child facs ✗nr lunch. Resid & Rest lic
£B&B £19; B&B (double) £33; HB weekly £152; WB (£44); [5% V] **cc** Access, B'card/Visa; dep.

Mayfair   Heene Ter, BN11 3NS **☎**(0903) 201943.

Meldrum House   8 Windsor Rd, BN11 2LX **☎**(0903) 33808.
⋈7 bedrs, 1 ba; TV; tcf 🏠TV, ns ✗LD 4, nr lunch. Unlic
cc B'card/Visa; dep.

Osborne   175 Brighton Rd, BN11 2EX **☎**(0903) 35771.
Situated 1 mile out of town on Brighton coast road.
⋈8 bedrs, 2 en suite, 1 ba; TV; tcf 🏠TV, dogs, ns; children over 10 ✗Breakfast only. Resid lic
£B&B £13·50–£17 **cc** Access, Amex, B'card/Visa; dep.

WROXHAM   Norfolk.   Map 25E3

🍺 🍺 **King's Head**   Station Rd, Hoveton, NR12 8UR **☎**(0603) 782429.
Remodelled traditional pub on the bank of the River Bure in town centre.
⋈6 bedrs, 6 en suite; TV; tcf 🏠P 50, coach; child facs ✗LD 9.30
cc Access, Amex, B'card/Visa.

WYBUNBURY   Cheshire.   Map 24A4

Lea Farm   Wrinehill Road, Nantwich, CW5 7NS **☎**(0270) 841429. *Farm.* Allen and Jean Callwood
Sleeps 6, 🐾 ⛱
£ B&B from £11–£14, D £6

WYE   Kent.   Map 27D4

New Flying Horse Inn   Upper Bridge St, TN25 5AN **☎**(0233) 812297.
⋈10 bedrs, 4 en suite, 2 ba; TV; tcf 🏠dogs, ns; P 50, coach; child facs ✗LD 9.30
cc Access, Amex, B'card/Visa, Diners; dep.

WYFOLD   Berkshire.   Map 26E5

Neals Farm   Reading, RG4 9JB **☎**(0491) 680258. *Farm.* Bridget Silsoe   ♿
Sleeps 6, 🐾 ⛱
£ B&B from £15, D £8

YARMOUTH GREAT   Norfolk.   Map 25F5

Trotwood (Highly Acclaimed)   2 North Dr, NR30 1ED **☎**(0493) 843971.
Family-run hotel on sea front on north side of Britannia Pier.
⋈8 bedrs, 7 en suite, (1 sh), 1 ba; TV; tcf 🏠TV, dogs, ns; P 11; child facs ✗Breakfast only. Resid lic
£B&B £21–£37, B&B (double) £32–£42.

Georgian House (Acclaimed)   17 North Dr, NR30 4EW **☎**(0493) 842623.

Handsome seafront mansion, designed by Paxton Hood-Watson an Arts/Craft architect. Opposite Water Ways, north of Britannia Pier. Open Apr–Oct.
⋈ 25 bedrs, 15 en suite, 3 ba; TV; tcf 🏠P 24; no children under 5 ✗Breakfast only. Resid lic
£ B&B £21–£37, B&B (double) £30–£45; WB; dep.

Bradgate   14 Euston Rd, NR30 1DY **☎**(0493) 842578.
⋈5 bedrs, 5 en suite; TV; tcf 🏠dogs, ns; P 5; child facs ✗Breakfast only. Resid lic
cc Access, B'card/Visa.

Woburn   3 Sandown Rd, NR30 1EY **☎**(0493) 844661
£ B&B £12–£14; HB weekly £84–£98.

YELVERTON   Devon.   Map 28F3

🍺 🍺 **Burrator Inn**   Dousland, PL20 6NP **☎**(0822) 854370.

Harrabeer Country House (Acclaimed)
Harrowbeer La, PL20 6EA **☎**(0822) 853302.
Swimming pool.
⋈7 bedrs, 5 en suite, 1 ba; TV; tcf 🏠TV, ns; P 10; child facs ✗LD 8, nr lunch. Resid & Rest lic
cc Access, Amex, B'card/Visa, Diners.

Manor (Acclaimed)   Tavistock Rd, PL20 6ED **☎**(0822) 852099.

Greenwell Farm   Nr Meavy, Plymouth, PL20 6PY **☎**(0822) 853563. *Farm.* Bridget Cole
Sleeps 6, ⛱
£ B&B from £15·50, D from £8·50

YEOVIL   Somerset.   Map 29D5

Manor Farm   Chiselborough, Stoke-sub-Hamdon, TA14 6TQ **☎**(093588) 203.
⋈4 bedrs, 2 ba; TV; tcf 🏠TV; P 4; child facs ✗Breakfast only. Unlic.

Wyndham   142 Sherborne Rd, BA21 4HQ **☎**(0935) 21468.
Situated 5 miles from Sherborne on S side of A30. Closed Xmas.
⋈6 bedrs, 1 ba; TV; tcf 🏠TV; P 8; child facs ✗Breakfast only. Unlic
£B&B £15, dep.

YETMINSTER Dorset. Map 29D5

Manor Farmhouse High Street, Sherborne, DT9 6LF ✆(0935) 872247. *Farm.* Ann Partridge &
Sleeps 6, ns
£ B&B from £23, D £12·50

YORK North Yorkshire. Map 23E3

Arndale (Highly Acclaimed) 290 Tadcaster Rd, YO2 2ET ✆(0904) 702424.

A fine Victorian residence standing in one acre of walled gardens on the main A1036 opposite York racecourse. Closed Xmas and New Year.
⇔9 bedrs, 9 en suite; TV; tcf 🛉TV dogs, ns; P 20; no children under 7 ✕LD midday, nr lunch & Thur dinner. Resid lic
£ B&B (double) £45–£56; HB weekly £171·50–£280; WB £29·50 (HB); dep.

Acer (Acclaimed) 52 Scarcroft Hill, The Mount, YO2 1DE ✆(0904) 653839.

Small Victorian hotel close to York racecourse. Leave A64 at West York sign, follow to end of raecourse, turn left at next traffic lights. First left is Scarcroft Hill.
⇔6 bedrs, 6 en suite; TV; tcf 🛉TV, dogs; P 1, G 1 ✕LD 8, nr lunch. Resid lic
£ B&B £25–£30, B&B (double) £40–£50; D £7·50; [5% V] **cc** Access, B'card/Visa.

Avimore House (Acclaimed) 78 Stockton La, YO3 0BS ✆(0904) 425556.
Small, comfortable, family-run Edwardian hotel, situated 1 mile from York Minster on the NE side, just off Heworth Green.
⇔6 bedrs, 6 en suite; TV; tcf 🛉TV, ns; P 6; child facs ✕LD 10 am, nr lunch. Resid lic
£ B&B £17–£22, B&B (double) £30–£38; WB £20; [5% V Nov–Mar]; dep.

Barmby Moor (Acclaimed) Hull Rd, Barmby Moor, YO4 5EZ ✆Pocklington (0759) 302700.

Grade II former coaching inn converted into a small hotel and family run. On the A1079 on the edge of Barnby Moor village, 20 mins from York. Swimming pool.
⇔10 bedrs, 10 en suite; TV; tcf 🛉P 30, child facs ✕nr lunch. Resid & Rest lic
£ B&B £40, B&B (double) £48; HB weekly £224, D £12; [5% V w/d] **cc** Access, Amex, B'card/Visa; dep.

Bedford (Acclaimed) 108 Bootham, YO5 7DG ✆(0904) 624412.

A tastefully restored Victorian house with many original features. Situated on the A19 north of the city.
⇔14 bedrs, 14 en suite; TV; tcf 🛉TV; P 15; child facs ✕LD midday, nr lunch. Resid lic
£ B&B £24–£32, B&B (double) £34–£44; HB weekly £175–£280; WB **cc** Access, B'card/Visa; dep.

Curzon Lodge (Acclaimed)   23 Tadcaster Rd, Dringhouses YO2 2QG ✆(0904) 703157.
Attractive 17th century Grade II listed house and stables overlooking the racecourse. Situated between Chase Hotel and the Post House on A1036.
⌗10 bedrs, 10 en suite; TV; tcf ♨P 15; no children under 7 ✗Breakfast only. Unlic
£ B&B £27–£32, B&B (double) £42–£52; dep.

Derwent Lodge (Acclaimed)   Low Catton, YO4 1EA ✆(0759) 71468.

Large period country house dating from 1850, with some original oak beams and York stone fireplaces, and a large garden.
⌗6 bedrs, 4 en suite, 1 ba; TV; tcf ♨dogs, ns; P 8; no children under 8 ✗LD 4, nr lunch. Resid lic
£ B&B (double) £31–£35; HB weekly £273–£301; dep.

Fairmount (Acclaimed)   230 Tadcaster Rd, YO2 2ES ✆(0904) 638298 Telex: 557720 Fax: (0904) 627626.
Situated near York racecourse.
⌗10 bedrs, 8 en suite, 2 ba; TV; tcf ♨dogs, ns; P8, coach; child facs ✗LD 9, nr lunch. Resid & Rest lic
£ B&B £30, B&B (double) £50–£55; D £13·50
cc Access, B'card/Visa; dep

Fourposter Lodge (Acclaimed)   68 Barbican Rd, YO1 5AU ✆(0904) 651170.
A Victorian villa, lovingly restored and furnished.
⌗10 bedrs, 7 en suite, (2 sh), 1 ba; TV; tcf ♨dogs; P4, G2 ✗LD6, nr lunch. Resid lic
£B&B £22–£24, B&B (double) £33–£44; HB weekly £182–£217; [5%V Nov–Jan w/d]; dep.

Grasmead House (Acclaimed)   1 Scarcroft Hill, YO2 1DF ✆(0904) 629996.
Unusual building on a corner site with spacious accommodation. Situated off the Mount out from Micklegate Bar on Scarcroft Rd.
⌗6 bedrs, 6en suite; TV; tcf ♨TV, ns; P 1 ✗Breakfast only.
£B&B (double) £45 cc Access, B'card/Visa; dep.

Hazelwood (Acclaimed)   24 Portland St, Gillygate, YO3 7EH ✆(0904) 626548 Fax: (0904) 628032.
⌗15 bedrs, 10en suite, 3ba; TV; tcf ♨ns; P10;

child facs ✗LD midday, nr lunch & Sat/Sun dinner. Resid lic

Holgate Bridge (Acclaimed)   YO2 4BB ✆(0904) 635971.
Two Grade II listed buildings converted into a small hotel. On A59 close to junction with Blossom St and Micklegate Bar. Closed Xmas.
⌗14 bedrs, 11 en suite, 1 ba; TV; tcf ♨dogs; P 14, coach; child facs ✗LD 9, nr lunch. Resid lic
£B&B £18–£35, B&B (double) £35–£48; WB; [5% V July–Nov, 10% rest] cc Access, Amex, B'card/ Visa; dep.

Holmwood House (Acclaimed)   114 Holgate Rd YO2 4BB ✆(0904) 626183.

Listed Victorian town house, furnished with antiques and offering elegant accommodation. On the A59 10 mins from the city walls.
⌗10 bedrs, 10 en suite; TV; tcf ♨dogs, ns; P 10; no children under 8 ✗LD 11 am, nr lunch. Resid lic
£ B&B £35–£38, B&B (double) £45–£48; WB £65 (2 nts HB); [5% V Mon–Fri, Nov–Mar].

Le Petit (Acclaimed)   103 The Mount YO2 2AX ✆(0904) 647339.
⌗6 bedrs, 6 en suite, TV; tcf ♨coach; child facs ✗LD 10.15, nr Sun dinner. Lunch on request
£ B&B £50, B&B (double) £75; L £8·50, D £12; [10% V Nov–Mar] cc Access, B'card/Visa; dep.

Limes (Acclaimed)   135 Fulford Rd, YO1 4HE ✆(0904) 624548.
Small family-run hotel on the A19 about 1 mile from city centre.
⌗10 bedrs, 6en suite, 1ba; TV; tcf ♨ns; P, coach; child facs ✗LD6, nr lunch
£B&B £16–£28, B&B (double) £24–£44; [5% V] cc Access, Amex, B'card/Visa, Diners; dep.

Midway House (Acclaimed)   145 Fulford Rd, YO1 4HG ✆(0904) 659272.
Spacious, modernised Victorian villa set in its own grounds. From S take the main A19 through Fulford village. Hotel is within boundary sign.
⌗12 bedrs, 11 en suite, 1 ba; TV; tcf ♨ns; P 15, coach; child facs ✗LD8, nr lunch. Resid lic

£B&B £27–£40, B&B (double) £32–£45
cc Access, B'card/Visa.

Priory (Acclaimed)   126 Fulford Rd, YO1 4BE
📞(0904) 625280.

Situated on A19.
🛏20 bedrs, 20 en suite; TV; tcf 📺TV; P 24, coach;
child facs ✗LD 9.30, nr lunch. Resid & Rest lic
£B&B £20–£22; D £10; WB £60 (2 nights)
cc Access, Amex, B'card/Visa, Diners; dep.

Railway King (Acclaimed)   George Hudson St,
YO1 1JL 📞(0904) 645161.
Attractive hotel convenient for city centre.
🛏22 bedrs, 22 en suite; TV; tcf 📺P 6; child facs
✗Bar meals only Mon–Sat lunch
cc Access, Amex, B'card/Visa, Diners.

Skeldergate House (Acclaimed)   56 Skeldergate,
YO1 1DS📞(0904) 35521.

Abingdon   60 Bootham Cres, YO3 7AH 📞(0904)
621761.
*Guest house 5 mins walk from city centre. Just off
A19, Thirsk road.*
🛏8 bedrs, 5 en suite, 3 ba; TV; tcf 📺TV, ns; P 2;
child facs ✗Breakfast only. Unlic
£B&B £15–£17; [5% V]; dep.

Acres Dene   87 Fulford Rd, YO1 4BD
📞(0904) 637330.
*Situated on A19 S of city centre on the York–Selby
Rd. Open Easter–Oct.*
🛏6 bedrs, 2 en suite, 2 ba; TV; tcf 📺TV; P 4
✗Breakfast only. Unlic
£B&B £14–£15, B&B (double) £24–£28.

Ascot House   80 East Par, YO3 7YH 📞(0904)
426826. *Sauna.*
🛏10 bedrs, 10 en suite; TV; tcf 📺TV, dogs; P 10,
G 4; child facs ✗Breakfast only. Unlic

Beckett   58 Bootham Cres, YO3 7AH 📞(0904)
644728.
Situated on A19 close to the city centre.
🛏7 bedrs, 5 en suite, 1 ba; TV; tcf 📺TV; P 3,
coach ✗Breakfast only. Unlic.
£ B&B £12·50–£15; [5% Nov–Feb]; dep.

York (Yorkshire)

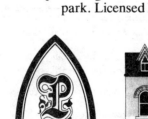

Beech House 6 Longfield Terr, YO3 7DJ ☎(0904) 634581.
⊭9 bedrs, 9 en suite; TV; tcf 🛉ns; P 5; no children under 5 ✗LD 3, nr lunch. Rest lic
cc Access, B'card/Visa; dep.

Bootham Bar 4 High Petergate, YO1 2EH ☎(0904) 658516.
An 18th century house within Bootham Bar, 100 yards from York Minster.
⊭9 bedrs, 9 en suite, 1 ba; TV; tcf 🛉child facs ✗nr dinner. Resid lic
£ B&B (double) £40–£58 cc Access, B'card/Visa; dep.

Cavalier 39 Monkgate, YO3 7PB ☎(0904) 636615.

Georgian listed building near city centre. Sauna.
⊭10 bedrs, 7 en suite, 3 ba; TV; tcf 🛉TV; P 4; child facs ✗LD3, nr lunch. Resid lic.

City 68 Monkgate, YO3 7PF ☎(0904) 622483.
Small guest house situated alongside the city walls, N of the Minster on the main NE exit via Monkbar into Monkgate.
⊭6 bedrs, 3 en suite, (3 sh); TV; tcf 🛉NS; P 5; no children under 5 ✗Breakfast only. Unlic
£ B&B £20–£22, B&B (double) £28–£38
cc Access, B'card/Visa; dep.

Crescent 77 Bootham, YO3 7DQ ☎(0904) 623216.
Georgian-style house, on the A19 N of the city centre.

York (Yorkshire)

Bootham Bar Hotel
4 High Petergate
York YO1 2EH
Telephone (0904) 658516

This hotel is a delightful 18th century building inside the city walls and 100 yards from York Minster.

The comfortable bedrooms have private facilities, colour TV, teamaking, radio and central heating.

Write to the resident proprietors Mr. and Mrs. J. Dearnley for brochure and tariff.

York (Yorkshire)

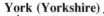

The Cavalier Private Hotel

THE CAVALIER PRIVATE HOTEL – is an early Georgian listed building recently refurbished to provide most comfortable accommodation.

The Hotel is ideally situated close to York's shopping centre and yet only yards from the ancient city walls and most of York's famous historical landmarks.

Double, twin or family rooms with en-suite. Two single and one double without shower/bathroom are available, all rooms having tea, coffee facilities and colour TVs. You can if you wish relax in our sauna for a small additional charge.

Evening meals can be arranged in our licensed dining room.

39 Monkgate, York YO3 7PB Tel: (0904) 636615

10 bedrs, 10 en suite, 2 ba; TV; tcf 📺 ns; P 4, coach; child facs ✗ LD midday, nr lunch & Sat/Sun dinner. Resid lic
£ B&B £15–£18, B&B (double) £28–£40; HB weekly £168–£203; D £9; WB £26 **cc** Access, Amex, B'card/Visa, Diners; dep.

Duke of Connaught Copmanthorpe Grange, Copmanthorpe ✆ Appleton Roebuck (090 484) 318.

Attractive modern hotel. From A64 turn into Appleton Roebuck, in 1½ miles hotel entrance is on left past large wood.
14 bedrs, 14 en suite; TV; tcf 📺 TV, dogs, ns; P 35; child facs ✗ LD 6. Resid lic
£ B&B £25, B&B (double) £42; HB weekly £200; L £4, D £9, WB £40; [10% V]; dep.

Farthings 5 Nunthorpe Av, YO2 1PF ✆ (0904) 653545.
Converted Victorian house with original features. Nunthorpe Ave is off Scarcroft Rd adjoining the A1036.
7 bedrs, 3 en suite, 2 ba; tcf 📺 TV ✗ Breakfast only. Resid lic
£ B&B (double) £26–£32; [10% V Nov–Mar]; dep.

Field House 2 St George's Pl, Tadcaster Rd, YO2 2DR ✆ (0904) 639572.

Fleece Bishop Wilton, YO4 1RU ✆ Bishop Wilton (075 96) 251.

Heworth 126 East Pde, YO3 7YG ✆ (0904) 426384.
From York inner ring road go to junction with Laverthorpe and on to East Parade.

6 bedrs, 3 ba; TV; tcf 📺 dogs, ns; P 1; G 1; child facs ✗ Breakfast only. Resid lic
£ B&B £11·50–£14·50; WB (£11); [5% V Nov–Apr]

Inglewood 7 Clifton Green, Clifton, YO3 6LH ✆ (0904) 653523.
Situated off A19.
7 bedrs, 2 en suite, 1 ba; TV 📺 P 3, G 2; no children under 3.

Linden Lodge 6 Nunthorpe Av, Scarcroft Rd, YO2 1PF ✆ (0904) 620107.
Victorian town house in quiet cul de sac. Take A1036 past racecourse, turn right at traffic lights, and take second right into Nunthorpe Ave.
12 bedrs, 2 en suite, 2 ba; TV; tcf 📺 TV, coach; child facs ✗ Breakfast only. Resid lic
£ B&B £15, B&B (double) £28; [10% V Oct–Nov, Jan–Mar w/d] **cc** Access, B'card/Visa; dep.

Marina Naburn, YO1 4RW ✆ (0904) 627365.
Converted village railway station just off A19 south of York. Open Mar–Nov.
8 bedrs, 3 en suite, (5 sh) 📺 TV; P 12; no children under 2 ✗ Breakfast only. Unlic
£ B&B £13–£14·50, B&B (double) £25–£32; dep.

Minster View 2 Grosvenor Terr, Bootham, YO3 7AG ✆ (0904) 655034.

St Denys St Denys Rd, YO1 1QD ✆ (0904) 622207.
11 bedrs, 11 en suite, 1 ba; TV; tcf 📺 TV, dogs; P 9, coach; child facs ✗ LD 4, nr lunch & Fri–Sun dinner. Resid lic.

St Raphael 44 Queen Anne's Rd, Bootham, YO3 7AF ✆ (0904) 645028.
Guest house in quiet cul-de-sac close to Minster.
8 bedrs, 2 en suite, 2 ba; TV; tcf 📺 dogs; child facs ✗ LD 4, nr lunch. Unlic
cc Access; dep.

Scarcroft 61 Wentworth Rd, YO1 1DG ✆ (0904) 633386
7 bedrs, 7 en suite
£ B&B £23–£25

ZELAH Cornwall. Map 28C2

Nanteague Farm Maranvose, TR4 9DH ☎(0872) 540351.
Farmhouse on 130-acre working farm set in glorious countryside overlooking lake. On main A30 two miles from Zelah opposite Nissan garage at top of hill. Swimming pool. Open end Mar–early Oct.
🛏4 bedrs, 4 en suite; 1 ba; TV; tcf 🅏TV, ns; P 8; child facs. ✗LD 4, nr lunch
£ B&B £12–£15; HB weekly £129·50–£150·50; [5% V Apr, May, Sept]; dep.

Shipdham (Norfolk)

SCOTLAND

ABERDEEN   Grampian (Aberdeenshire).
Map 19F1

Cedars (Acclaimed)   339 Great Western Rd, AB1 6NW ✆ (0224) 583225.
⊨ 13 bedrs, 4 en suite, (9 sh), 3 ba; TV 🛏 dogs, ns; P 14, coach; child facs ✗ Breakfast only. Unlic
£ B&B £25–£30, B&B (double) £36–£38 **cc** Amex; dep.

Fourways (Acclaimed)   435 Great Western Rd, AB1 6NJ ✆ (0224) 310218.
⊨ 7 bedrs, 6 en suite, 1 ba; TV, tcf 🛏 TV; P 7; child facs ✗ LD 4, nr lunch. Unlic

Bimini   69 Constitution St, AB2 1ET ✆ (0224) 646912.
Situated in the town centre near the beach.
⊨ 7 bedrs, 2 ba; TV; tcf 🛏 TV, ns; P 7; child facs ✗ Breakfast only. Unlic
£ B&B £14–£16, B&B (double) £24–£28 **cc** Access, B'card/Visa; dep.

Craiglynn   36 Fonthill Rd, AB1 2UJ ✆ (0224) 584050. Fax: (0224) 584050
An impressive granite Victorian building. Centrally situated, Fonthill Rd is a turning off Holburn St, A92.
⊨ 9 bedrs, 6 en suite, 2 ba; TV 🛏 TV, ns; P 7; child facs ✗ LD 7.30. Restrict lic
£ B&B £27–£35, B&B (double) £38–£46; D £12 **cc** Access, Amex, B'card/Visa, Diners.

Dunromin   75 Constitution St, AB2 1ET ✆ (0224) 647995.
⊨ 5 bedrs, 2 ba; TV; tcf 🛏 TV, dogs; child facs ✗ Unlic

Jays   422 King St, AB2 3BR ✆ (0224) 638295
From Holburn St, A92, turn into Union St and then King St.
⊨ 6 bedrs, 1 en suite, 1 ba; TV; tcf 🛏 TV, NS; P 8; no children under 5 ✗ Breakfast only. Unlic
£ B&B £15–£16, B&B (double) £26–£30; dep.

Discount vouchers

RAC discount vouchers are at the end of the guide. Establishments with a [V] shown at the end of the price information will accept them in part payment for accommodation bills on the full, standard rate, not against bargain breaks or any other special offers. Please note the limitations shown in the entry: w/e for weekends, w/d for weekdays, and which months they are accepted.

Klibreck   410 Great Western Rd, AB1 6NR ✆ (0224) 316115.
⊨ 6 bedrs, 2 ba; tcf 🛏 TV, ns; P 3 ✗ LD 2, nr lunch. Unlic

Strathboyne   26 Abergeldie Terr, AB1 6EE ✆ (0224) 593400.
Traditional granite hotel about ¾ mile from Bridge of Dee just off Holburn St.
⊨ 6 bedrs, 2 ba; TV; tcf 🛏 TV, dogs, child facs ✗ LD 5.30, nr lunch. Unlic
£ B&B £11·50–£12; HB weekly £119; dep.

ABERFELDY   Tayside (Perthshire).   Map 21A7

Guinach (Highly Acclaimed)   Urlar Rd, PH15 2ET ✆ (0887) 20251.

A small hotel built in 1900, and set in 3 acres of mature gardens. On the Crieff Rd just outside the town, on the right past the church.
⊨ 7 bedrs, 7 en suite; TV; tcf 🛏 dogs, ns; P 12; child facs ✗ LD 9·30; Restrict lic
£ B&B £29·50; L fr £7·50, D £17; WB £30 (HB); [10% V w/d May–Oct, any time Oct–Apr]; dep.

Balnearn   Crieff Rd, PH15 2BJ ✆ (0887) 20431.
⊨ 13 bedrs, 3 en suite, 3 ba; TV; tcf 🛏 TV, dogs; P 13; child facs ✗ LD 7.30, nr lunch. Unlic

Caber-Feidh   56 Dunkeld St, PH15 2AF ✆ (0887) 20342.
At the eastern end of Main St opposite corner to Palace Hotel, entrance in side street.
⊨ 6 bedrs, 2 ba; tcf 🛏 TV, dogs, ns; P 5, coach; child facs ✗ LD 8.30, nr lunch. Rest lic
£ B&B £11·50; HB weekly £129·50; D £5·50; WB (£70); [5% V w/d]

Nessbank House   Crieff Rd, PH15 2BJ, ✆ (0887) 20214.

6 bedrs, 4 en suite, 2 ba; TV; tcf TV, dogs, ns; P7, G2; child facs LD 8, nr lunch. Resid lic **cc** Access, B'card/Visa; dep.

ABERLEMNO Tayside. Map 21D7

Wood of Auldbar By Brechin, DD9 6SZ (030 783) 218. *Farm*. Jean Stewart
Sleeps 6, ns
£ B&B from £10, D from £6

AIRDRIE Lanarkshire. Map 21A3

Easter Glentore Farm Greengairs, ML6 7TJ (023 683) 243 *Farm*. Mrs Elsie Hunter
Sleeps 5
£ B&B from £12·50, D from £8

ANNAN Dumfries & Galloway (Dumfriesshire). Map 22E6

Ravenswood St John's Rd, DG12 6AW (046 12) 2158.
From Carlisle direction turn left at traffic lights in Annan, and hotel is 400 yards on right.
7 bedrs, 2 ba; tcf TV, dogs; child facs LD8, Resid & Restric lic
£ B&B £15, B&B (double) £26; D£6

ANNANWATER Dumfriesshire. Map 22E6

Corehead Farm Moffat, DG10 9LT (0683) 20973 *Farm*. Berenice C Williams
Sleeps 6, ns
£ B&B from £13, D £8

ANSTRUTHER Fife. Map 21D5

Royal 20 Rodger St, KY10 3DU (0333) 310581.
9 bedrs, 2 en suite, 2 ba; tcf TV; P4, coach LD8.30, nr Tue lunch & Mon–Wed dinner
£ B&B £17·50–£20·50, B&B (double) £29–£35; HB weekly £140–£175; L £6·50, D £6·50; dep.

ARBROATH Tayside (Angus). Map 21D6/7

Kingsley House 29 Market Gate, DD11 1AU (0241) 73933.
From A92 follow signs for harbour, then take first on the left. Billiards.
14 bedrs, 5 ba TV, dogs, coach; child facs LD7, nr lunch. Resid lic
£ B&B £12–£13, B&B (double) £22–£24; HB weekly £100; D£4; [10% V]; dep.

AUCHTERARDER Tayside (Perthshire). Map 21A5

Cairn Lodge (Highly Acclaimed) Orchil Rd, PH3 1LX (0764) 62634.
Small country house in its own gardens. Take the Auchterarder turn off the A9, then the A824. Putting.
5 bedrs, 5 en suite; TV; tcf P40, coach; child facs LD 9.30 (9 winter)
£ B&B £45–£65, B&B (double) £75–£85; L £10–£12·50, D£20; [5% V w/d] **cc** Access, Amex, B'card/Visa; dep.

AUCHTERMUCHTY Fife. Map 21B5

Ardchoille Farmhouse (Acclaimed) Woodmill Farm, KY14 7ER (0337) 28414. *Riding*.

AVIEMORE Highland (Inverness-shire). Map 19B1

Balavoulin (Highly Acclaimed) Grampian Rd, PH22 1RL (0479) 810672. Fax: (0479) 810672

Auchterarder (Tayside)

Family run hotel built in 1902 and sympathetically modernised. On main road through village next to Winking Owl restaurant.
⇥8 bedrs, 8 en suite; TV; tcf 🛗dogs, ns; P 10+, coach; child facs ✕LD 8.30, bar lunch only
£B&B (double) £36–£45; HB weekly £392–£455; D £9·95; [10% V] **cc** Access, B'card/Visa; dep.

Ravenscraig, Grampian Rd PH22 1RP ☎(0479) 810278
Situated at the north end of the main street.
⇥11 bedrs, 9 en suite, (2 sh) 1 ba; tcf 🛗TV, dogs, ns; P 12, coach; child facs ✕Breakfast only. Unlic
£B&B (double) £29–£34; [10% V Feb–Jun, Sep–Nov]; dep.

AYR Strathclyde (Ayrshire).   Map 20E2

Windsor (Highly Acclaimed)   6 Alloway Pl, KA7 2AA ☎(0292) 264689.
A comfortable small hotel in a residential area, close to beach and town centre. On the A719 at the foot of Millar Rd. Closed 21 Dec–4 Jan.
⇥10 bedrs, 6 en suite, 2 ba; TV; tcf 🛗TV, dogs; child facs ✕LD 7, nr lunch. Unlic
£B&B £18–£30, B&B (double) £32–£36; HB weekly £150–£164; D £8; WB £47 (HB) **cc** B'card/Visa; dep.

Parkhouse   1A Ballantine Dr, KA7 2RG ☎(0292) 264151.
Off the A79 going south from town centre, take first left after Safeways supermarket.
⇥5 bedrs, 2 ba; TV; tcf 🛗TV, ns; child facs
✕Breakfast only. Resid & Restrict lic
£B&B £20, B&B (double) £28; [10% V]

BALLACHULISH Highland (Argyll).   Map 20D7

Lyn Leven (Acclaimed)   West Laroch ☎(08552) 392.

⇥11 bedrs, 11 en suite, 1 ba; TV; tcf 🛗dogs, ns; P 12; child facs ✕LD 8, nr lunch. Restrict lic
£B&B (double) £26–£34; HB weekly £140–£155

BALLATER Grampian (Aberdeenshire).   Map 21C9

Moorside (Acclaimed)   Braemar Rd, AB3 5RL ☎(033 97) 55492.

A former Free Church of Scotland manse built in 1883, set in ¾ acre of lawns and garden. On the A93 Ballater to Braemar road 400 yards from village centre. Open Mar–Nov.
⇥9 bedrs, 9 en suite; TV; tcf 🛗dogs; P 10; child facs ✕LD 5, nr lunch & Sun dinner. Restrict lic
£B&B £21, B&B (double) £28; HB weekly £146
cc Access, B'card/Visa; dep.

Morvada (Acclaimed)   Braemar Rd, AB3 5RL ☎(033 97) 55501.
A traditional Scottish house set in its own grounds close to all amenities. Open May–Oct
⇥7 bedrs, 6 en suite, 1 ba; TV; tcf 🛗TV, dogs, ns; P 7 ✕Breakfast only. Restrict lic
£B&B (double) £30–£32

Aspen   44 Braemar Rd, AB2 5RQ ☎(033 97) 55486
⇥11 bedrs, 3 en suite; TV; tcf 🛗TV, dogs; P 20, coach; child facs ✕LD 8.30

Ballater   34 Victoria Rd, AB3 5QX ☎(033 97) 55346.
⇥16 bedrs, 4 ba; tcf 🛗TV; child facs ✕LD 7, nr lunch. Restrict lic

---

BARR Ayrshire.   Map 22B6

Glengennet Farm   Girvan, KA26 9TY ☎(046 586) 220 *Farm*. Vera Dunlop
Sleeps 4, ⌂ (12)
£ B&B from £11

BARRHILL Ayrshire.   Map 22B6

Blair Farm   Girvan, KA26 0RD ☎(046 582) 247
Farm. Mrs Elizabeth Hughes
Sleeps 6
£ B&B from £10–£12, D from £5

BEATTOCK Dumfriesshire.   Map 22E7

Cogries Farm   Moffat, DG10 9PP ☎(057 64) 320
Farm. Freda Bell
Sleeps 8, ns ⌂
£ B&B from £10·50, D £7

BEAULY Highland (Inverness-shire).   Map 18G2

Chrialdon (Acclaimed)   Station Rd, IV4 7EH ☎(0463) 782336.

On leaving Inverness take the A862 alongside the Beauly Firth to Beauly village.
⋈8 bedrs, 2 en suite, 4 ba; TV; tcf ⌂TV, dogs, ns; P30; child facs ✗LD8·30, nr lunch. Resid lic
£B&B £14–£18·50; HB weekly £185·50–£217; D£12·50; WB £45·50; dep.

Heathmount Station Rd, IV4 7EQ ☎(0463) 782411.
On the main road in the village near the Post Office. Open Feb–Nov.
⋈5 bedrs, 1 ba; TV; tcf ⌂TV, dogs, ns; P5; child facs ✗Breakfast only. Unlic
£B&B £12–£12·50; dep.

BIRNAM   Tayside (Perthside).   Map 21B6

Waterbury   Dunkeld, PH80BG ☎Dunkeld (03502) 324.
Victorian listed building with baronial tower, in the centre of the village next to St Mary's Church.
⋈6 bedrs, 2 ba; tcf ⌂TV, dogs, ns; P6, coach; child facs ✗LD 7.30, nr lunch. Restrict lic
£B&B £12–£12·50; HB weekly £122·50–£129·50; D£7; WB £34·50 (3 nts); [10% V]; dep.

BLAIRGOWRIE   Tayside (Perthshire).
                                                    Map 21B7

Rosebank House (Highly Acclaimed)   Balmoral Rd, PH10 7AF ☎(0250)2912.

Elegant Georgian house set in spacious gardens, on the A93 leaving Blairgowrie for Braemar. Open Jan–Oct.
⋈6 bedrs, 5en suite, 2ba ⌂TV; P12; children over 10 ✗LD 6, nr lunch. Restrict lic
£B&B £20–£22, B&B (double) £38–£40; HB weekly £172–£188; dep.

Glenshieling   Hatton Rd, PH10 7HZ ☎(0250) 4605.
Turn right off A93 past the petrol station out of Blairgowrie, then right again.
⋈7 bedrs, 3en suite, 3ba; TV; tcf ⌂dogs; P16, coach; child facs ✗LD8.30, nr lunch, Sun dinner. Restrict lic
£B&B £15·85–£19·80, B&B (double) £25·50–£44; HB weekly £170–£230; D£11·50; WB; [10% V exc Jul & Aug] **cc** Access, B'card/Visa; dep.

Ivy Bank House   Boat Brae, Rattray, PH107BH ☎(0250)3056.
Turn right off the A93 past the petrol station. Tennis.
⋈6 bedrs, 2ba; TV; tcf ⌂TV, dogs; P6; child facs ✗LD6, nr lunch. Unlic
£B&B £14·50; D£7; [10% V]

BOAT OF GARTEN   Highland (Inverness-shire).   Map 19B1

Moorfield House (Acclaimed)   Deshar Rd, PH24 3BN ☎(047983) 646.
A charming traditional house set in picturesque surroundings. Situated 5 miles N of Aviemore. Closed Nov.
⋈6 bedrs, 3en suite, 1 ba; tcf ⌂TV, dogs, ns; P10; child facs ✗LD4, nr lunch. Restrict lic
£B&B £14–£20; HB weekly £182–£224; dep.

BO'NESS   Central (West Lothian).   Map 21A4

Kinglass   Borrowstoun Rd ☎(0506) 822861.
Follow signs for Bo'ness from Edinburgh direction, turn right, first left and farm is 1½ miles down road.
⋈6 bedrs, 1 en suite, 3 ba; TV; tcf ⌂TV, dogs; P20, coach; child facs

BRAEMAR   Grampian (Aberdeenshire).
                                                    Map 21B8

Callater Lodge   9 Glenshee Rd, AB35YQ ☎(033 97) 41275.

BRIDGE OF EARN   Tayside (Perthshire).
                                                    Map 21B6

Rockdale   Dunning St, PH29AA ☎(0738) 812281.
A terraced property on three floors. Turn right opposite bowling green in the village centre.
⋈7 bedrs, 1 en suite, 2 ba; tcf ⌂TV, dogs ✗LD7, nr lunch. Restrict lic
£B&B £14, B&B (double) £25–£31; HB weekly £133–£152·95; [5% V]; dep.

CALLANDER   Central (Perthshire).   Map 20F5

Arden House (Acclaimed)   Bracklinn Rd, FK17 8EQ ☎(0877) 30235.

A large stone-built house peacefully situated in attractive gardens. Follow road to golf course and

Bracklinn Falls; last house on left. Putting. Open
Feb–Nov.
🛏8 bedrs, 6 en suite, 2 ba; tcf 📺TV, dogs, NS;
P 12; child facs ✗LD 7, nr lunch. Unlic
£B&B £12–£16; HB weekly £120–£145; [5% V
Feb–Nov]
Highland House (Acclaimed)   South Church St,
FK17 8BN ✆(0877) 30269.
*A charming Georgian house with magnificent views.
Follow signs for police station and library, and hotel
is on right.* Open Mar–Nov & Xmas–New Year.
🛏10 bedrs, 3 en suite, (1 sh), 2 ba; tcf 📺TV, dogs,
ns; child facs ✗LD 6, nr lunch. Restrict lic
£B&B £15; HB weekly £177–£190; D £12; dep.
Rock Villa (Acclaimed)   1 Bracklinn Rd, FK17 8EH
✆(0877) 30331.
*Beautifully situated house in its own large attractive
garden. Situated at the east end of Callander.*
🛏6 bedrs, 2 en suite, 1 ba; TV; tcf 📺TV, dogs; P 7;
child facs ✗LD 4, nr lunch. Unlic
£B&B £14, B&B (double) £24; dep.
Annfield House   18 North Church St, FK17 8EG
✆(0877) 30204.
*Large stone house situated off Main St, at the top
of North Church St.*
🛏8 bedrs, 2 ba; tcf 📺TV, dogs, ns; P 6
✗Breakfast only. Unlic
£B&B £11; dep.
Riverview House   Leny Rd, FK17 8AL ✆(0877)
30635.

CAMPBELTOWN Argyll.   Map 20C5

Machrimore   Southend, PA28 6RQ ✆(058 683)
256 *Farm.* Mrs E Taylor
Sleeps 6 + cot ☎
£B&B from £12, D £6

CARDROSS Strathclyde.   Map 20E4

Kirkton House (Highly Acclaimed)   Darleith Rd
G82 5EZ ✆(0389) 841951

*A south-facing converted farmhouse with feature
courtyard, with superb views of the Clyde. Follow
village signs for Kirkton Chapel, after ¼ mile turn
right into Kirkton House Drive.*
🛏6 bedrs, 4 en suite, 1 ba; TV; tcf 📺TV, dogs;
P 12; child facs ✗LD 7·30, nr lunch. Restrict lic
£B&B £19·50–£25, B&B (double) £33–£41; HB
weekly £182–£210; D £10·75; [5% V Nov–Mar]
cc Access, B'card/Visa; dep.

CARRBRIDGE Highland (Inverness-shire).   Map 19B2

Fairwinds (Acclaimed)   PH23 3AA ✆(047 984)
240.

*A former manse, traditionally stone built, extensively
modernised, with its own small loch. In the centre
of the village opposite the village car park.* Closed
2 Nov–mid Dec.
🛏5 bedrs, 5 en suite; TV; tcf 📺ns; P 8; child facs
✗LD 4, nr lunch. Resid lic
£B&B £20–£21, B&B (double) £36–£38; HB weekly
£180–£187; [5% V May–Jun, Sep–Oct] **cc** Access,
B'card/Visa; dep.

CLACKMANNAN Clackmannanshire.   Map 21A5

Gartfinnan Farm   FK10 3QA ✆(0259) 30349
Farm. Mrs Martha Warnock   ♿
Sleeps 4 ☎
£B&B from £10–£12

CLARENCEFIELD Dumfries & Galloway.   Map 22E6

Comlongon Castle (Acclaimed)   nr Annan, DG1
4NA ✆(0387) 87283.

*15th-century castle set in 50 acres of secluded
grounds. From A75 at Annan follow B724 to Castle
in Clarencefield. Fishing.* Open Mar–Dec.
🛏8 bedrs, 5 en suite; 4 ba; TV 📺ns; P 30
✗LD 8·15, nr lunch. Resid & Restrict lic
£B&B £27, B&B (double) £54–£90; HB weekly
£308; [5% V] **cc** Access, B'card/Visa; dep.

CONNEL Strathclyde (Argyll).   Map 20C6

Ards House (Acclaimed)   By Oban PA37 1PT
✆(0631) 71255

Situated ¼ mile past Connel Bridge on A85 heading towards Oban. Open Mar–Nov.
🛏8 bedrs, 3 en suite, 2 ba; tcf TV; P 10; no children under 12 ✕LD 8·15, nr lunch. Resid lic
£ B&B £20, B&B (double) £36–£46; D £10·50
cc Access, B'card/Visa.

Loch Etive (Acclaimed) PA37 1PH ☎(063 171) 400.

Old stone building, beautifully restored and upgraded, set in its own riverside gardens. Five miles from Oban on the A85 turn into Connel Bridge. Open Easter–Oct.
🛏6 bedrs, 4 en suite, 1 ba; TV; tcf dogs; P 8; child facs ✕LD 7·30, nr lunch. Resid lic
£ B&B £19·75–£22·25, B&B (double) £32·50–£37·50; HB weekly £164–£179·55; WB; [5% V]; dep.

COLMONELL Ayrshire. Map 22A7

Burnfoot Farm Girvan, KA26 0SQ ☎(046 588) 220/265 *Farm.* Grace and David Shankland
Sleeps 6, ns
£ B&B from £11, D £6

CONTIN Highland (Ross & Cromarty). Map 18F3

Coul House (Highly Acclaimed) IV14 9EY ☎Strathpeffer (0997) 21487 Fax: (0997) 21945.
Secluded country mansion in beautiful headland setting with forest and mountain views. By-pass

Cardross (Dunbartonshire)

Licensed Country Guest Accommodation at a

– GATEWAY to the HIGHLANDS –

NORTH OF THE RIVER CLYDE

RAC *Highly Acclaimed,* GUESTACCOM *Good Room Award,* STB *Commended* featured in the *Best B&B in World* and the 'WHICH' *Good B&B Guide*

GLASGOW AIRPORT
20/25 minutes by car
DUMBARTON, HELENSBURGH
each 4 miles

FOR BREAKS – an ideal base for LOCH LOMOND, TROSSACHS, ARGYLL HIGHLANDS and myriad other local attractions.
FOR BUSINESS – near GLASGOW (35 minutes by car or train) and in the CLYDE VALLEY, the luxury of friendly and personal service at both ends of the working day.
FOR STOP-OVER – a convenient break in the journey – between ENGLAND/BORDERS and WEST HIGHLANDS – and for the AIRPORT.

FEATURES: Family run; 19th Century converted farm around an attractive courtyard – in a tranquil rural setting above Cardross village; superb Clyde and Argyll views; paddock/stabling and large garden; desk, hairdryer, radio/alarm, shaverpoint, TV, telephone and tea/coffee facilities in all bedrooms, most with private bathrooms; guest lounge and dining rooms have informal and unpretentious ambience; home cooked dinners at oil lamplit tables.

KIRKTON HOUSE, CARDROSS

DUNBARTONSHIRE, G82 5EZ, SCOTLAND
YOUR HOSTS: STEWART & GILLIAN MACDONALD
– TEL: (0389) 841 951 –

Clarencefield (Dumfries)

Comlongon Castle

Clarencefield, Drumfries DG1 4NA, Scotland. Tel: 038 787 283

A magnificent Scottish Castle country house hotel set in 50 acres. Before dinner guests may take our candlelit tour of the medieval castle. *For brochure tel 038 787 283.*

*Inverness and follow A9 over Moray Firth bridge.
After 5 miles take second exit at roundabout on to
A835. Follow to Contin, and hotel ¼ mile up private
drive on the right. Putting.*
➤21 bedrs, 21 en suite; TV; tcf �📺TV, dogs; P40,
coach; child facs ✕LD9
£B&B £28·50–£43·50; B&B (double) £47–£67; HB
weekly £231–£329; L£3, D£18·50; WB £99 (3 nts);
[10%V] cc Amex, Diners; dep.

CRAIL Fife. Map 21D5

Caiplie House 53 High St, KY10 3RA ☎(0333)
50564.
On the A917, Crail High Street. Open Mar–Oct.
➤7 bedrs, 2ba; tcf �📺TV, dogs; child facs
✕LD4, nr lunch. Restrict lic
£B&B £11·50–£14·50; HB weekly £143·50–
£164·50; WB £61·50 (3 nts); dep.

CRAWFORD Strathclyde (Lanarkshire). Map 21A2

Field End The Loaning, ML12 6TN ☎(086 42)
276.
*Small guest house, situated opposite the church in
Crawford.*
➤5 bedrs, 2en suite, (1 sh), 1 ba; tcf
�📺TV, ns; P6; child facs ✕nr lunch. Unlic
£B&B £12; HB weekly £105–£125, Dfr£5; WB £20;
[10%V w/d]; dep.

CRIANLARICH Central (Perthshire). Map 20E6

Portnellan (Highly Acclaimed) FK208QS
☎(083 83) 284. Fax: (08383) 332
Fishing.
➤23 bedrs, 3 en suite, 11 ba; tcf �📺TV, P26, child
facs ✕Breakfast only, Unlic
£B&B £27, B&B (double) £42; [5%V] cc Access,
B'card/Visa; dep.

Glenardran FK20 8QS ☎(083 83) 236.
*A late Victorian stone house, situated on the A85
on the eastern edge of Crianlarich, ¼ mile from the
station.*
➤6 bedrs, 1 ba; TV; tcf �📺dogs; ns; P6; no children
under 5 ✕LD 6, nr lunch. Restrict lic
£B&B £16·50, B&B (double) £29–£33 cc Access,
B'card/Visa; dep.

CRIEFF Tayside (Perthshire). Map 21D5

Keppoch (Acclaimed) Perth Rd ☎(0764) 4341
*On the main A85 east of the town centre close to
the golf course. Open Feb–Jan.*
➤6 bedrs, 5 en suite, 1 ba; TV; tcf �📺TV, dogs, ns;
P15, coach; child facs

Heatherville 29 Burrell St, PH7 4DT ☎(0764)
2825.

➤5 bedrs, 1 en suite, 2 ba; tcf �📺TV, dogs;
P5 ✕LD midday, nr lunch. Restrict lic

Leven House Comrie Rd, PH7 4BA ☎(0764)
2529
Situated off the High St beside the War Memorial.
➤11 bedrs, 5 en suite, 2ba; tcf �📺TV, dogs, ns;
P10, U2, coach; child facs ✕LD7.30, nr lunch.
Restrict lic
£B&B £14–£20; HB weekly £150–£190; WB (£25
for 2 nights); dep.

Sydney Villa 57 Burrell St, PH7 4DG ☎(0764)
2757.
*Situated between petrol station and Strathearn
lighting centre on main entrance to town. Open
Feb–Dec.*
➤4 bedrs, 2ba; TV �📺TV, dogs, ns; P3; no children
under 14 ✕LD7, nr lunch. Restrict lic
£B&B (double) £24; D£5; dep.

Clathybeg Findo Gask, PH7 3PH ☎(073 873)
213 *Farm.* Mrs Jeanette Kinloch
Sleeps 5 + cot
£ B&B from £12, D from £7

CULLEN Grampian (Banffshire). Map 19D3

Bayview (Highly Acclaimed) 57 Seafield St AB5
2SV ☎(0542) 41031
Situated overlooking Cullen harbour. Closed Nov.
➤6 bedrs, 5 en suite, 1 ba; TV; tcf �📺child
facs ✕LD9
£B&B £24–£30, B&B (double) £40–£48
cc Access, B'card/Visa.

CULLODEN MOOR Highland (Inverness-shire). Map 19A2

Balaggan Farm By Inverness, IV1 2EL ☎(0463)
790213 *Farm.* Phyllis Alexander
Sleeps 5, 🐴 🐄
£ B&B from £11, D £7

CUPAR Fife. Map 21C5

Redlands (Highly Acclaimed) By Ladybank,
KY7 7SH ☎Ladybank (0337) 31091.
*A converted game keeper's house set in beautifully
landscaped gardens. From A91, follow Pitlessie
signs, cross level crossing, take first right and
Redlands is ¼ mile on right. Closed Feb.*
➤4 bedrs, 4 en suite; TV; tcf �📺P6; child facs
✕LD5, nr lunch. Resid & Restrict lic
£B&B £23·50, B&B (double) £39; HB weekly
£206·50; WB £91·50 (3 days); [10%V]; dep.

DALCROSS Highland (Inverness-shire). Map 19A2

Easter Dalziel Farm Inverness, IV1 2JL ☎(0667)
62213 *Farm.* Bob & Margaret Pottie

Sleeps 6, ⚡ ns ☜
£ B&B from £12–£18, D £8

DALRY   Strathclyde.   Map 20E3

🏆 🏆 **Dalry**   Kilbirnie Rd, KA24 5JS 📞(029 483) 5135
White-painted building situated in rural surroundings on the Kilbirnie road (A284).
🛏6 bedrs, 6 en suite; TV; tcf 🏠dogs, P 150, coach; child facs ✗LD 10
£ B&B £20–£25, B&B (double) £40–£45; L £5, D £8·50; [10% V] **cc** Access, Amex, B'card/Visa.

DAVIOT   Inverness-shire.   Map 19A2

Daviot Mains Farm   Nr Inverness, IV1 2ER 📞(046 385) 215   *Farm.* Margaret & Alex Hutcheson
Sleeps 8, ⚡ ns ☜ (3)
£ B&B from £12, D £7

DENNY   Central (Stirlingshire).   Map 21A4

Topps Farm (Highly Acclaimed)   Fintry Rd, FK6 5JF 📞(0324) 822471.
New chalet style farmhouse with superb views over Carron Valley. Travel due west out of Denny on B818 and hotel is 4 miles on right.
🛏8 bedrs, 8 en suite; TV; tcf 🏠TV, dogs; NS; P 15; coach; child facs ✗LD 8, nr Mon–Fri lunch. Restrict lic
£ B&B £22, B&B (double) £30; HB weekly £170; L £2·50, D £10

Lochend Farm   Carronbridge, FK6 5JJ 📞(0324) 822778   *Farm.* Jean Morton
Sleeps 6, ☜ (3)
£ B&B from £11–£12, D £8

DUMFRIES   Dumfries & Galloway (Dumfriesshire).   Map 22D6

Embassy (Acclaimed)   Newbridge, DG2 2EG 📞(0387) 720233.
About 2 miles from Dumfries on the A76.
🛏7 bedrs, 6 en suite, (1 sh); TV; tcf 🏠dogs; P 100, coach; child facs
£B&B £25, B&B (double) £40

DUNBAR   Lothian (East Lothian).   Map 21D4

Bay View (Acclaimed)   Bayswell Rd, EH42 1AB 📞(0368) 62778
Situated 2 mins from town centre overlooking the bay.
🛏6 bedrs, 1 en suite, 1 ba; TV; tcf 🏠dogs; coach; child facs ✗LD 9, nr lunch. Restrict lic
£ B&B £15–£19; HB weekly £168–£196; D £10; WB (£14) **cc** Access, B'card/Visa; dep.

Marine   7 Marine Rd, EH42 1AR 📞(0368) 63315.
🛏10 bedrs, 2 ba 🏠TV, dogs, ns; child facs ✗nr lunch. Unlic
£ B&B £12

Overcliffe   11 Bayswell Park, EH42 1AE 📞(0368) 64004.
Family-run guest house in attractive situation. Turn left at top of High St, then first right.
🛏5 bedrs, 3 ba; TV; tcf 🏠TV, dogs; child facs ✗LD 5, nr lunch. Restrict lic
£ B&B £12, B&B (double) £22; WB; dep.

St Beys   2 Bayswell Rd, EH42 1AB 📞(0368) 63571. *Guest House.*

Springfield   42 Belhaven Rd, EH42 1NH 📞(0368) 62502.
A 19th-century villa set in its own grounds, at the west side of Dunbar, near the parish church. Open Mar–Oct.
🛏5 bedrs, 2 ba; TV; tcf 🏠TV, dogs; P 7, child facs ✗LD 5, nr lunch. Restrict lic
£ B&B £15, B&B (double) £28; HB weekly £145, D £9 **cc** Access, B'card/Visa.

DUNDEE   Tayside (Angus).   Map 21C6

Beach House (Acclaimed)   22 Esplanade, Broughty Ferry 📞(0382) 76614 Fax: (0382) 480241.
Terraced house with patio garden overlooking the Tay Estuary. From the A930 turn off into Broughty Ferry centre, then head for Sandy beach.
🛏5 bedrs, 5 en suite, TV; tcf 🏠dogs, ns; child facs ✗LD 9, nr lunch. Restrict lic
£ B&B (double) £38–£44; D £8 **cc** Access, B'card/Visa.

Kemback 6 Mcgill St, DD4 6PH ☎(0382) 461273.
*From city centre follow one-way system to Victoria
St, branch first left after traffic lights.*
⇥9 bedrs, 2 ba; TV; tcf 🐾dogs; P 6, child facs
✗Breakfast only. Unlic
£B&B £15–£19, B&B (double) £25–£26; [5% V];
dep.

DUNOON Strathclyde (Argyll). Map 20D4

Cedars (Acclaimed) East Bay, PA23 8AF ☎(0369)
2425.
⇥13 bedrs, 13 en suite; TV; tcf 🐾TV; child facs
✗Breakfast only. Restrict lic
£ B&B £19, B&B (double) £34; [5% V] **cc** Access,
Amex, B'card/Visa, Diners

Rosscairn (Acclaimed) 51 Hunter St, Kirn, PA23
8JR ☎(0369) 4344.
*Small hotel in large mature gardens. Follow coast
road A815, turn up Kirkbrae beside church, then
right at crossroads into Hunter St.*
⇥11 bedrs, 11 en suite, tcf 🐾TV, ns; P 12
✗LD6, nr lunch. Unlic
£B&B £18–£20; HB weekly £155–£175; D £7·50;
[5% V]; dep.

DUNS Borders (Berwickshire). Map 21D3

Cockburn Mill TD11 3TL ☎(0361) 82811 *Farm.*
Mrs A M Prentice
Sleeps 5, ➥ns
£ B&B from £15, D £7

EDINBURGH Lothian (Midlothian). Map 21B4

Brunswick (Highly Acclaimed) 7 Brunswick St,
EH7 5JB ☎031-556 1238.
Georgian listed building convenient for city centre.
⇥10 bedrs, 10 en suite; TV; tcf 🐾ns; no children
under 2 ✗Breakfast only. Unlic
£B&B £20–£30, B&B (double) £36–£50; dep.

Cumberland (Highly Acclaimed) 1 West Coates,
EH12 5JQ ☎031-337 1198.

*A listed building dating back to the 19th-century.
Situated on A8, 2 mins from Haymarket Station.*
⇥9 bedrs, 8 en suite, 2 ba; TV; tcf 🐾P 14; child
facs ✗Breakfast only
£B&B £35–£40, B&B (double) £50–£60; [10% V
Oct–Apr] **cc** Access, Amex, B'card/Visa; dep.

Lodge (Highly Acclaimed) 6 Hampton Terr, West
Coates, EH12 5JD ☎031-337 3682.

*Elegant detached stone town house with fine
architectural features. Situated on A8 Edinburgh–
Glasgow Rd.*
⇥10 bedrs, 10 en suite, 1 ba; TV; tcf 🐾ns; P 10,
coach; child facs ✗LD8, nr lunch. Resid lic
£B&B £35–£45, B&B (double) £50–£60; D £9·50;
[10% V Oct–Mar] **cc** Access, B'card/Visa; dep.

Thrums (Highly Acclaimed) 14 Minto St, EH9
1RQ ☎031-667 5545.
*Two large Georgian houses with peaceful gardens
at rear. On the A7 in the city centre. Closed Xmas
& New Year.*
⇥14 bedrs, 12 en suite, 4 ba; TV; tcf 🐾dogs; P 13,
coach; child facs ✗LD8. Restrict lic
£B&B £22–£35, B&B (double) £39–£50; HB weekly
£315–£392; L £4, D £6·50; dep.

Allison House (Acclaimed) 15–17 Mayfield Gdns,
EH9 2AX ☎031-667 8049
⇥24 bedrs, 21 en suite, 4 ba; TV; tcf 🐾P 12; child
facs ✗Breakfast only. Restrict lic
cc Access, B'card/Visa; dep.

Arthurs View (Acclaimed) 10 Mayfield Gdns EH9
2BZ ☎031-667 3468

⇥12 bedrs, 8 en suite, (4 sh), TV; tcf
🐾dogs; P 10, coach; child facs ✗LD8·30
£B&B £18–£25, B&B (double) £50; L £5, D £12·50
cc Access, Amex, B'card/Visa; dep.

Ashdene House (Acclaimed) 23 Fountainhall Rd,
EH9 2LN ☎031-667 6026.

Victorian town house on three floors retaining many original features. Two mins drive from A7 and A701.
⋈5 bedrs, 5 en suite, TV; tcf �📺dogs, ns; no children under 2 ✗Breakfast only. Unlic
£ B&B (double) £28–£36

Ashlyn (Acclaimed)   42 Inverleith Row, EH3 5PY
☏031-552 2954.
Listed Georgian building retaining much of its original charm. From Princes St proceed to mini roundabout at Cannon Hills, turn left past Botanic Gardens.
⋈8 bedrs, 4 en suite, 2 ba; TV; tcf �📺dogs, ns; P 1, coach; no children under 7 ✗LD 5·30, nr lunch, Fri–Sun dinner. Unlic
£ B&B £16–£18, HB weekly £168–£189; WB (£15); [10% V Oct–Apr]; dep.

Boisdale (Acclaimed)   9 Coates Gdns, EH12 5LG
☏031-337 1134.
Listed Victorian terraced hotel at the west end of Princes St.

⋈10 bedrs, 10 en suite; TV; tcf ⏰TV, dogs; coach; child facs ✗LD 7, nr lunch, dinner by arrangement. Resid & Restrict lic
£B&B £20–£28, B&B (double) £40–£56; [10% V]; dep.

Buchan (Acclaimed)   3 Coates Gdns, EH12 5LG
☏031-337 1045/8047
Situated 200 yards W of Haymarket Station on road to airport.
⋈11 bedrs, 2 en suite, 3 ba; TV; tcf ⏰TV, dogs, child facs ✗Breakfast only. Unlic
£B&B £18, B&B (double) £34–£45; dep.

Dorstan (Acclaimed)   7 Priestfield Rd, EH16 5HJ
☏031-667 6721.
Victorian villa in a quiet residential area. Follow city centre signs.
⋈14 bedrs, 9 en suite, (3 sh), 3 ba; TV; tcf ⏰ns; P 7; child facs ✗LD 4, nr lunch. Unlic
£B&B £16–£20; D £10; [5% V Nov–Mar]; dep.

Galloway (Acclaimed)   22 Dean Park Cres, EH4 1PH ☏031-332 3672
Victorian townhouse in city centre, ½ mile from Princes St west end on Queensferry Rd.
⋈10 bedrs, 6 en suite, 2 ba; TV; tcf ⏰dogs; coach; child facs ✗Breakfast only. Unlic
£B&B £18–£28, B&B (double) £28–£38; [5% V]; dep.

Glenora (Acclaimed)   14 Rosebery Cres, EH12 5JY ☎031-337 1186.
A Georgian townhouse near the town centre, opposite Haymarket Station.
⇥10 bedrs, 10 en suite, 1 ba; TV; tcf TV, ns; child facs ✕Breakfast only. Resid lic
£B&B £25–£30, B&B (double) £40–£50; [5% V]
cc Access, B'card/Visa; dep.

Heriott Park (Acclaimed)   256 Ferry Rd, EH5 3AN ☎031-552 6628.
⇥6 bedrs, 2 en suite, 2 ba; TV; tcf TV, dogs, ns; coach ✕Breakfast only. Restrict lic
£B&B £16–£17; B&B (double) £26–£28; dep.

Lovat (Acclaimed)   5 Inverleith Terr, EH3 5NS ☎031-556 2745
Family-run hotel opposite the Botanical Gardens.
⇥7 bedrs, 7 en suite; TV; tcf dogs; child facs ✕Breakfast only. Unlic
£B&B £28, B&B (double) £42; HB weekly £250; WB (£25); [10% V]; dep.

Marvin (Acclaimed)   46 Pilrig St, EH6 5AL ☎031-554 6605.
A comfortable Georgian town house dating from 1790. From the GPO on Princes St take A900 to Leith Walk, at the third set of traffic lights turn left.
⇥7 bedrs, 4 en suite, 2 ba; TV; tcf ns; P6; child facs ✕Breakfast only. Unlic
£B&B (double) £23–£32; [5% V]; dep.

Newington (Acclaimed)   18 Newington Rd, EH9 1QS ☎031-667 3356.
Victorian stone-built house with period character. Set between the A7 and A68 routes into Edinburgh.
⇥8 bedrs, 3 en suite, (1 sh), 3 ba; TV; tcf TV, dogs, ns; P3, coach; child facs ✕LD8, nr lunch. Resid & Restrict lic
£B&B £20–£22, B&B (double) £29–£40; D £9·50.

Rockville (Acclaimed)   2 Joppa Pans, EH15 2HF ☎031-669 5418.
A Victorian detached house with panoramic views, between Portobello and Musselburgh.
⇥5 bedrs, 5 en suite; TV; tcf TV, dogs; P10, coach; child facs ✕LD9

£B&B £30–£45, B&B (double) £40–£60; L£4·50, D£6·50; WB (£20); [10% V Mon–Thu exc Jun–Aug]
cc Access, Amex, B'card/Visa, Diners.

Roselea (Acclaimed)   11 Mayfield Rd, EH9 2NG ☎031-667 6115

A well-appointed Victorian guest house, on the south side of the city centre.
⇥7 bedrs, 3 en suite; 2 ba; TV TV, dogs, ns; P3, coach ✕LD4, nr lunch, Fri–Sun dinner. Unlic
£B&B £13–£22, B&B (double) £24–£40; D£6·50; [5% V Oct–May]; dep.

Salisbury (Acclaimed)   45 Salisbury Rd, EH16 5AA ☎031-667 1264.

Comfortable Georgian house, carefully refurbished. Between A68 and A7 one mile S of Princes St.
⇥13 bedrs, 9 en suite, 4 ba; TV; tcf TV, dogs, ns; P12; child facs ✕Breakfast only. Resid lic
£B&B £15–£20, B&B (double) £30–£40; [5% V].

Stra'ven (Acclaimed)   3 Brunstane Rd North EH15 2DL ☎031-669 5580
⇥7 bedrs, 7 en suite; TV; tcf TV, NS; child facs ✕Breakfast only. Unlic
£B&B £15–£18, B&B (double) £30; dep.

Amaragua 10 Kilmaurs Terr, EH16 5DR ☎031-667 6775.
Haven 180 Ferry Rd, EH6 4NS ☎031-554 6559
Situated on the A902.
╫10 bedrs, 1 en suite, 2 ba; TV; tcf ᛜTV, dogs, ns; P8, coach; child facs ✕Breakfast only. Restrict lic
£B&B £18–£25, B&B (double) £30–£40; WB £30 (2 nts); dep.
Kariba 10 Granville Terr, EH10 4PQ ☎031-229 3773.
╫9 bedrs, 2 en suite, (5 sh), 2 ba; TV; tcf ᛜTV, dogs; P4, coach; child facs ✕Breakfast only. Unlic [10% V]; dep.
Kildonan Lodge 27 Craigmillar Park, EH16 5PE ☎031-667 2793.
Elegant Victorian house on the main A7 entry to the city. Situated near the Cameron Toll roundabout, on the right side going towards Princes St.
╫13 bedrs, 8 en suite, 2 ba; TV; tcf ᛜP12, child facs ✕LD 8.30, nr lunch. Restrict lic
£B&B £15–£25, B&B (double) £25–£35; D£8·50
cc Amex, B'card/Visa; dep.
Lindsay 108 Polwarth Terr, EH11 1NN ☎031-337 1580.
From Princes St turn west into Lothian Rd to Kings Theatre and turn right. Follow road to end.
╫8 bedrs, 1 en suite, 2 ba; TV; tcf ᛜdogs, ns; P6, coach; child facs ✕Breakfast only. Unlic
£B&B £15–£18, B&B (double) £32–£36; dep.
Lygon 4 Lygon Rd, EH16 5QE ☎031-667 1374.
Marchhall 14 Marchhall Cres, EH16 5HL ☎031-667 2743.
Turn first left after Royal Commonwealth Swimming Pool going south on A68 Dalkeith Rd.
╫13 bedrs, 2 en suite, (4 sh), 3 ba; TV; tcf ᛜTV, dogs; child facs ✕nr lunch
£B&B £17–£25, B&B (double) £34–£50; D£8·50; dep.
Shalimar 20 Newington Rd, EH9 1QS ☎031-667 2827.
╫9 bedrs, 4 en suite, (1 sh), 2 ba ᛜP2, coach ✕Breakfast only. Unlic

Sherwood 42 Minto St, EH9 2BR ☎031-667 1200.
Situated 1½ miles from city centre on A7 road south.
╫6 bedrs, 2 ba; TV; tcf ᛜdogs; P3 ✕Breakfast only. Unlic
£B&B (double) £20–£30; dep.
Southdown 20 Craigmillar Park, EH16 5PS ☎031-667 2410.
Situated on the main A7 into Edinburgh.
╫6 bedrs, (6 sh), 2 ba; TV; tcf ᛜTV, ns; P7, coach; child facs ✕Breakfast only. Unlic
£B&B £17·50–£25, B&B (double) £32–£40
Turret 8 Kilmaurs Terr, EH16 5DR ☎031-667 6704.
╫6 bedrs, 2 ba; TV; tcf ᛜTV; no children under 2 ✕Breakfast only. Unlic
£B&B £14–£16, B&B (double) £24–£30; [10% V]

ELGIN Grampian (Moray). Map 19C3

Park House (Highly Acclaimed) South St, IV30 1JB ☎(0343) 7695. Fax: (0343) 541594
Set at the west end of South St.
╫6 bedrs, 6 en suite; TV; tcf ᛜdogs; P30, coach; child facs ✕LD 9·30
£B&B £35, B&B (double) £52; HB weekly £300–£350; L£5·90, D£15 **cc** Access, B'card/Visa.
City 191–193 High St, IV30 1DJ ☎(0343) 547055.
At the west end of Elgin High St.
╫15 bedrs, 15 en suite; TV; tcf ᛜdogs; P10, coach; child facs ✕LD8, nr Sun
£B&B £25, B&B (double) £32; HB weekly £192·50; [10% V] **cc** Access, Amex, B'card/Visa.

FALKLAND Fife. Map 21B5

Covenanter (Acclaimed) The Square, KY7 7BU ☎(0337) 57224. Fax: (0337) 57272
Located at the village centre opposite the parish church.
╫4 bedrs, 4 en suite; TV; tcf ᛜP6; child facs ✕LD9
£B&B £35, B&B (double) £45; L£7, D£11·50; WB; [5% V] **cc** Access, Amex, B'card/Visa, Diners

Edinburgh (Lothian)

FORTINGALL   Tayside (Perthshire).   Map 20F6

Rose Villa (Highly Acclaimed)   Nr Aberfeldy,
PH15 2LL ☎ Kenmore (08873) 335. *Guest House.*

GALASHIELS   (Borders) Selkirkshire.
Map 21C3

Torwoodlee Mains   TD1 1UB ☎ (0896) 3377
Farm. Carolyn Timm
Sleeps 6, 🐎 ns ☃
£ B&B from £12, D from £9

GATEHOUSE-OF-FLEET   Dumfries &
Galloway (Kirkcudbrightshire).   Map 22C5/6

Bank o'Fleet   47 High St, DG7 2HR ☎ (05574)
302.
🛏5 bedrs, 2 ba; TV; tcf 🛎TV, dogs, coach;
child facs ✗ LD9
cc Access, B'card/Visa; dep.

Bobbin   36 High St, DG7 2HP ☎ (055 74) 229.
🛏7 bedrs, 1 en suite, 2 ba; tcf 🛎TV, dogs; P7,
coach; child facs ✗ LD4.30, nr Sun. Unlic
cc Access, B'card/Visa; dep.

GLASGOW   Strathclyde (Lanarkshire).
Map 20F4

Marie Stuart   46–48 Queen Mary Av, G42 8DT
☎ 041-424 3939.
*Small family-run hotel in serene surroundings
between Cathcart Road and Langside Rd.*
🛏31 bedrs, 9 en suite, 5 ba; TV; tcf 🛎TV, dogs;
P50, coach ✗ LD7, nr Sun, high tea only Sat pm.
Restrict lic
£ B&B £17–£38, B&B (double) £32–£46; L £3·95,
D £7·20; [5% V]; dep.

Smith's   963 Sauchiehall St, G3 7TQ ☎ 041-339
6363.
From Bath St turn right at Sauchiehall St, then left.
🛏33 bedrs, 7 ba; TV; tcf 🛎TV, dogs; coach
✗ Breakfast only. Unlic
£ B&B £18–£21, B&B (double) £27–£30; [5% V];
dep.

GRANTOWN-ON-SPEY   Highland (Moray).
Map 19B2

Ravenscourt House (Highly Acclaimed)   Seafield
Av, PH26 3JG ☎ (0479) 2286 Fax: (0479) 3260.

*Elegant Victorian house, formerly a manse, restored
and furnished in period style. Just off the main
square in the town centre.* Open Feb–Oct.
🛏9 bedrs, 8 en suite, 2 ba; TV; tcf 🛎TV, ns; P 10;
child facs ✗ LD9·30, nr lunch. Rest & Restrict lic
£ B&B £24–£31·50, B&B (double) £48–£53; HB
weekly £300–£318; D £19; [10% V]; dep.

Culdearn House (Acclaimed)   Woodlands Terrace
PH26 3JU ☎ (0479) 2106
*Elegant Victorian family home standing well back
from the road. Approaching from the south turn left
immediately after 30 mph sign.* Open Mar–Oct.
🛏9 bedrs, 9 en suite; TV; tcf 🛎P9
✗ LD 6, nr lunch. Resid lic
£ B&B £19·95–£25; HB weekly £194·65–£225
cc Access, B'card/Visa; [10% V]; dep.

Garden Park (Acclaimed)   Woodside Av, PH26
3JN ☎ (0479) 3235

*Victorian house dating from 1863 set in half an acre
of pretty gardens. On entering town from Aviemore
turn right at traffic lights, then left into Woodside Av.*
🛏6 bedrs, 6 en suite; tcf 🛎TV; P8
✗ LD7, nr lunch. Restrict lic
£ B&B (double) £35–£37; HB weekly £160–£165;
dep.

Kinross House (Acclaimed)   Woodside Av, PH26
3JR ☎ (0479) 2042.

*100-year-old granite villa standing in its own
grounds in a quiet residential avenue. Approaching
from south, turn right at traffic lights in main street,
and right again at first crossroads.* Open Mar–Oct.
🛏7 bedrs, 4 en suite, 2 ba; TV; tcf 🛎ns; P6;
no children under 5 ✗ LD5, nr lunch. Restrict lic
£ B&B £13·50–£14, B&B (double) £26–£32; HB
weekly £145–£163; D £8; dep.

Umaria Highland   Woodlands Terr, PH26 3JD
📞(0479) 2104.
🛏8 bedrs, 3 ba; tcf 📺TV, dogs, ns; P 8, coach; child facs ✗LD 4, nr lunch. Resid lic

---

GRETNA   Dumfries & Galloway.   Map 22F6

Surrone House (Highly Acclaimed)   Annan Rd, CA6 5DL 📞(0461) 38341.

Old farmhouse recently modernised with its character retained. Situated along the main street.
🛏6 bedrs, 5 en suite; 1 ba; TV; tcf 📺TV, dogs; P 14; child facs ✗LD 8, nr lunch. Restrict lic
£B&B £20, B&B (double) £34; D £5·75

HADDINGTON   Lothian.   Map 22C4

Browns (Highly Acclaimed)   1 West Rd, EH41 3RD
📞(062 082) 2254.

Georgian country house hotel with open views towards Lammermuir Hills, and furnished with

period pieces. Turn down Haddington Road at garage on corner, house on left in one mile.
🛏5 bedrs, 5 en suite, TV; tcf 📺ns; P 10, coach ✗LD 9, nr lunch Mon–Sat
£B&B £47·50, B&B (double) £62·50; L £14·50, D £19·50 **cc** Access, Amex, B'card/Visa; dep.

HAWICK   Borders (Roxburghshire).   Map 21C2

Drinkstone   TD9 7NY 📞(0450) 72895 *Farm.* Mrs Elizabeth Gray
Sleeps 5, 🐾 🦃 ns
£ B&B from £12, D £5

INNELLAN   Strathclyde (Argyll).   Map 20D4

Osborne (Acclaimed)   Shore Rd, PA23 7TJ
📞(036 983) 445.
Turn left from ferry and travel 3½ miles along Shore Rd. Hotel situated by Innellan Pier. Billiards.
🛏4 bedrs, 3 en suite, 1 ba; TV; tcf 📺TV, dogs; child facs ✗LD 9
£B&B £20; B&B (double) £33; HB weekly £170; L £5·50, D £10·50; [10% V Oct–Mar] **cc** Access, B'card/Visa; dep.

INVERGARRY   Highland (Inverness-shire).   Map 18F1

Ardgarry   Faichem, PH35 4HG 📞(08093) 226.
From A82 at Invergarry, take A87, continue 1 mile, turn right at Faichem sign. Bear left up hill to first entrance on the right.
🛏3 bedrs, 2 ba; tcf 📺TV, dogs, P 8; no children under 5 ✗LD 3, nr lunch. Unlic
£B&B (double) £21; HB weekly £112; dep.

Lundie View   Aberchalder, PH35 4HN 📞(080 93) 291
Guest house on A82 3½ miles north east of Invergarry.
🛏B&B £14–£20; HB weekly £60–£100

INVERNESS   Highland.   Map 19A2

Brae Ness (Acclaimed)   Ness Bank, IV24SF
℄ (0463) 712266.
*A Georgian house built in 1830 on the banks of the
River Ness. Follow signs from town centre to Dores
on B862, turn right to River Ness at church in Haugh
Rd then sharp left along Ness Bank. Open Feb–
Nov.*
⇌ 10 bedrs, 9 en suite, 1 ba; TV; tcf 🔥dogs, ns; P6;
child facs ✗ LD7, nr lunch. Resid, Restrict & Rest
lic
£ B&B £22–£29, B&B (double) £34–£47; HB weekly
£173–£215; D£10; [5% V mid Sep–25 May]

St Ann's House   37 Harrowden Rd, IV3 5QN
℄ (0463) 236157.
*A small family-run stone-built hotel built in 1880, with
attractive garden. Cross over Friar's Bridge and
Harrowden Rd is straight over the roundabout.
Open Nov–Sept.*
⇌ 6 bedrs, 6 en suite; TV; tcf 🔥TV, dogs, ns; P;
child facs ✗ LD4, nr lunch. Unlic
£ B&B £11–£12, B&B (double) £27·50–£30; dep.

Four Winds   42 Old Edinburgh Rd, IV2 3PG
℄ (0463) 30397.
⇌ 7 bedrs, 4 en suite, (3 sh), 2 ba; TV; tcf
🔥dogs; P15; child facs ✗ Breakfast only. Unlic

ISLE OF BUTE

ROTHESAY   Strathclyde (Bute).   Map 20D4

Ardyne (Highly Acclaimed)   38 Mount Stewart Rd,
PA20 9EB ℄ (0700) 542052 Fax: (0700) 545129
£ B&B £15–£18·50; HB weekly £135–£162·50;
[5% V]

St Ebba (Highly Acclaimed)   37 Mount Stuart Rd,
Craigmore, PA209EB ℄ (0700) 2683.

⇌ 12 bedrs, 11 en suite, 1 ba; TV; tcf 🔥TV, dogs,
ns; P5; child facs ✗ Breakfast only. Resid lic

ISLE OF COLL

ARINAGOUR   Strathclyde (Argyll).   Map 20A7

Tigh-na-Mara (Acclaimed)   PA78 6SY ℄ (08793)
354. *Putting, fishing.*

ISLE OF MULL

DERVAIG   Strathclyde.   Map 20A7

Druimard Country House (Highly Acclaimed)
Druimard, PA75 6QW ℄ (0688) 4345.
*A tastefully restored Victorian manse on peaceful
wooded hillside near the sea. Splendid views over
open country. Take B8073 west from Tobermory to
Dervaig for 8 miles, turn left after the church and
house is about ¾ mile on left. Open Easter–Oct*
⇌ 5 bedrs, 3 en suite, 1 ba; TV; tcf 🔥dogs; P20;
child facs ✗ LD9, nr lunch. Rest lic
£ B&B from £37·50, B&B (double) £50–£65; [10% V
Mar, Apr, Sep & Oct]; dep.

TOBERMORY   Strathclyde (Argyll).   Map 20B7

Harbour House (Highly Acclaimed)   59 Main St
℄ (0688) 2209.
⇌ 9 bedrs, 1 en suite, 3 ba; TV; tcf 🔥TV, dogs;
child facs ✗ LD8.15, nr lunch. Rest lic

JEDBURGH   Borders (Roxburghshire).
Map 44B4

Ferniehirst Mill Lodge (Acclaimed)   TD86PQ
℄ (0835) 63279. Fax: (0835) 63749

*Purpose-designed hotel set in 25 acres by the River
Jed amongst original mill buildings. Situated 2½
miles south of Jedburgh on main A68 Newcastle
road. Riding. Fishing.*
⇌ 11 bedrs, 8 en suite, 2 ba; tcf 🔥TV, dogs; P10,
G2; child facs ✗ nr lunch. Resid lic
£ B&B £15–£18·50; HB weekly £300–£325;
D£12·50; [5% V] **cc** Access, B'card/Visa; dep.

Froylehurst   Friars, TD8 6BN ℄ (0835) 62477.
*Leave Market Place by Exchange St, take first right
into Friars, third driveway on left in Friars, and
Froylehurst is first house on left after S bend. Open
Apr–mid Nov.*
⇌ 5 bedrs, 2 ba; TV; tcf 🔥TV; P6, G1; no children
under 5 ✗ Breakfast only. Unlic
£ B&B £13·50, B&B (double) £23; dep.

KELSO   Borders (Roxburghshire).   Map 21D2

Belford-on-Bowmont   Yetholm, TD5 8PY ℄ (057
382) 362 *Farm.* Alison M Johnson
Sleeps 6, 🐎 🐃
£ B&B from £11·50, D £6·50

Cliftonhill   TD5 7QE ✆(0573) 25028 *Farm.* Archie & Maggie Stewart
Sleeps 6, ⇗ ⛺
£ B&B from £12·50, D £6

Whitmuirhaugh   Sprouston, TD5 8HP ✆(0573) 24615 *Farm.* Patricia McCririck
Sleeps 5, ⛺⇗
£ B&B from £12, D £8

KILCHRENAN   Strathclyde (Argyll).
Map 20D6

Cuil Na Sithe (Acclaimed)   PA35 1HF ✆(086 63) 234. *Putting, tennis, fishing, boating, riding.*

KILLIECRANKIE   Tayside (Perthshire).
Map 21A7

Dalnasgadh House   PH165LN ✆(0796) 3237
Situated on the B8079 between Blairatholl and Pitlochry ¼ m from Killicrankie Pass and opposite RSPB. Open Easter–Oct.
⇤5 bedrs, 2 ba; tcf ฅTV, ns ✗Breakfast only. Unlic
£ B&B £14·50–£15, B&B (double) £25–£26

KINGSBARNS   Fife.
Map 21C5

Cambo House   St Andrews, KY16 8QD ✆(0333) 50313 *Farm.* Peter Erskine
Sleeps 2, ⛺
£ B&B from £25

KINGUSSIE   Highland (Inverness-shire).
Map 19B1

Craig an Darach   PH21 1JE ✆(0540) 661235
Fax: (0540) 661235.
A large stone-built house set in 3 acres of grounds. From A9 turn sharp right from slip road to Kingussie, and house drive is on right. Closed Nov–Dec.
⇤6 bedrs, 3 en suite, 1 ba; tcf ฅTV, dogs, NS; P10 ✗Breakfast only. Unlic
£ B&B £12–£15

KIRKBEAN   Dumfries & Galloway.
Map 22D6

Cavens (Highly Acclaimed)   DG28AA ✆(038 788) 234.
Charming old country mansion with a strong American history connection, set in lovely grounds. On the A710 signed Solway Coast road.
⇤6 bedrs, 6 en suite, TV; tcf ฅTV, dogs; P10; child facs ✗LD 7, nr lunch, Resid & Rest lic
£ B&B £25–£30, B&B (double) £40–£44; HB weekly £220; L fr £6 D£12, **cc** Access, B'card/Visa; dep.

KYLE OF LOCHALSH   Highland (Ross & Cromarty).
Map 18D2

Retreat   Main St, IV40 8BY ✆Kyle (0599) 4308.
Small comfortable guest house on the main street.
⇤13 bedrs, 3 ba; tcf ฅTV, NS; P 11, coach; no children under 12 ✗LD 5.30, nr lunch. Restrict lic
£ B&B £11·50–£15; D£7·50 **cc** Access, B'card/Visa.

LARBERT   Central (Stirlingshire).
Map 20E5

Wester Carmuirs Farm   FK5 3NW ✆(0324) 812459 *Farm.* Mrs Sheila Taylor
Sleeps 5, ⇗
£ B&B from £11

LARGS   Strathclyde (Ayrshire).
Map 20D3

Carlton   10 Aubrey Cres, KA30 8PR ✆(0475) 672313.
From seafront turn left after Information Centre. Open Easter–Oct.
⇤6 bedrs, 2 ba; tcf ฅTV, dogs, ns; P 6 ✗LD4·30, nr lunch. Unlic
£ B&B £12–£13, B&B (double) £22–£24; HB weekly £115·50–£122·50

LARKHALL   Strathclyde (Lanarks).
Map 21A3

Fleming Crest   Ayr Rd, ML92TZ ✆(0698) 791711.
Hotel 500 yards from junction 8 of M74, on A71 in Edinburgh direction. Snooker.
⇤8 bedrs, 1 en suite, 2 ba; TV; tcf ฅdogs; P 100, coach; child facs ✗LD 10
£ B&B £23, B&B (double) £34·50; L £2·50, D £5; WB; [10% V] **cc** Access, Amex, B'card/Visa.

LENNOXTOWN   Strathclyde (Dunbartonshire).
Map 20F4

Glazertbank   Main St, G65 7DJ ✆(0360) 310790.

LOCHINVER   Highland (Sutherland).
Map 18E5

Ardglas   Inver, IV27 4L1 ✆(057 14) 257
Guest House. Open Mar–Nov
£ B&B £11–£11·50

LOCKERBIE   Dumfriesshire.
Map 22E6

Nether Boreland   Boreland, DG11 2LL ✆(05766) 248 *Farm.* Marjorie Rae
Sleeps 6, ⇗
£ B&B from £12–£14, D £7

MOFFAT   Dumfries & Galloway (Dumfriesshire).
Map 22E7

Well View (Highly Acclaimed)   Ballplay Rd.
✆(0683) 20184.

An early Victorian whinstone house in ½ acre of mature gardens overlooking town and hills. On A708 out of Moffat turn left after fire station into Ballplay Rd. Well View is 150 metres on the right.
🛏 7 bedrs, 5 en suite, 1 ba; TV; tcf 🏠 dogs, ns; P8; child facs ✕ LD 8.30. Resid, Rest & Restrict lic
£ B&B £20–£37, B&B (double) £40–£68; HB weekly £210–£322; L £7·50, D £14; [5% V] **cc** Access, B'card/Visa; dep.

Arden House (Acclaimed) High St, DG10 9HG ☎ (0683) 20220.

A Georgian mansion with comfortable accommodation, situated in the main High St. Open Mar–Oct.
🛏 7 bedrs, 4 en suite, 2 ba; TV; tcf 🏠 dogs; P7
✕ LD 6.45, nr lunch. Unlic
£ B&B £14–£16, B&B (double) £25–£32; HB weekly £125–£150; dep.

Bridge (Acclaimed) Well Rd, DG10 9JT ☎ (0683) 20383.
🛏 9 bedrs, 3 en suite, 2 ba; TV; tcf 🏠 TV, dogs, ns; P8, coach; child facs ✕ LD7. Restrict lic

Merkland House (Acclaimed) Buccleuch Place, DG10 9AN ☎ (0683) 20957.
Attractive house standing in 2 acres of grounds. From A74 continue up one-way street, over crossroads, up hill and first right and right again into Buccleuch Place. Open Feb–Nov.
🛏 6 bedrs, 4 en suite (2 sh); TV; tcf 🏠 TV, dogs; P6; child facs ✕ Breakfast only. Unlic
£ B&B £14–£20; [10% V Wed & Thu, Feb, Oct–Nov]

Ivy Cottage High St, DG10 9HG ☎ (0683) 20279.
18th-century cottage with corbelled first floor windows, opposite the town hall.
🛏 4 bedrs, 1 ba 🏠 TV, dogs; no children under 12
✕ Dinner by arrangement. Unlic
£ B&B £14·50

Coxhill Farm Old Carlisle Rd, DG10 9QN ☎ (0683) 20471 *Farm.* Mrs Sandra Long
Sleeps 6, 🐴
£ B&B from £11, D £7

MONTROSE Tayside (Angus). Map 21D7

Linksgate 11 Dorward Rd, DD10 8SB ☎ (0674) 72273.

NAIRN Highland (Nairnshire). Map 19B3

Ardgour Seafield St, IV12 4HN ☎ (0667) 54230.
Situated just off the sea front. Open Mar–Oct.
🛏 10 bedrs, 3 ba; tcf 🏠 TV, dogs; P8, coach; child facs ✕ LD5. Unlic
£ B&B £13, B&B (double) £22–£24; HB weekly £107; dep.

NEWTON STEWART Dumfries & Galloway (Wigtownshire). Map 22B6

Auchenieck Farm DG8 7AA ☎ (0671) 2035
Farm. Margaret Hewitson
Sleeps 6, 🐴
£ B&B from £10·50–£11·50

Clugston Farm DG8 9BH ☎ (067 183) 338 *Farm.* Janet Adams ♿
Sleeps 6, 🐕 🐴 (5)
£ B&B from £12, D £5

OBAN Strathclyde (Argyll). Map 20C6

Foxholes (Acclaimed) Cologin, PA34 4SE ☎ (0631) 64982.

Family-run hotel in its own grounds. Take A816 south out of Oban, in 2 miles turn right then right again in ¾ miles. House in ¼ mile. Closed Nov–Feb.
🛏 7 bedrs, 7 en suite, TV; tcf 🏠 dogs; P7; no children under 5 ✕ LD 7, nr lunch. Restrict lic
£ HB weekly £200–£210; dep.

Please tell the manager if you chose your hotel through an advertisement in the guide.

Glenburnie (Acclaimed)   Esplanade, PA34 5AQ
☎(0631) 62089.

*Small family-run hotel with magnificent view over
Kerrera, Mull and Lismore. Situated in the quieter
part of the Esplanade. Open Apr–Sep.*
⇥15 bedrs, 9 en suite, 3 ba; TV; tcf 📶ns; P 10, U 1,
no children under 3 ✕Breakfast only. Unlic
£B&B £13·50–£14·50, B&B (double) £31–£50
cc Access, B'card/Visa; dep.

Ardblair   Dalriach Rd, PA34 5JB ☎(0631) 62668.
*Small hotel with magnificent views. Situated beside
the bowling green, swimming pool and tennis
courts. Open Easter & May–Oct.*
⇥16 bedrs, 11 en suite, 4 ba; tcf 📶TV; P 10,
coach; child facs ✕LD 5
£B&B £9–£13; HB weekly £96–£123; dep.

Craigvarran House   Ardconnel Rd, PA34 5DJ
☎(0631) 62686.
*Small guest house with panoramic views, situated
on Oban Hill off Rockfield Rd. Open mid Jan–mid
Dec*
⇥8 bedrs, 2 ba; tcf 📶TV, dogs, ns; P 10; child facs
✕LD6, nr lunch. Unlic
£B&B £11; HB weekly £119; dep.

Roseneath   Dalriach Rd, PA34 5EQ ☎(0631)
62929.
*A fine granite house with views, situated past
swimming pool and bowling green.*
⇥10 bedrs, 2 en suite, (4 sh), 2 ba; TV; tcf 📶TV, ns;
P 8, coach; no children ✕Breakfast only. Unlic
£B&B £12–£15, B&B (double) £24–£34; dep.

Sgeir-Mhaol   Soroba Rd, PA34 4JF ☎(0631)
62650.
*Family-run guest house in quiet part of town on the
A816 opposite the high school.*

⇥7 bedrs, 2 ba; tcf 📶TV, dogs; P 10; child facs
✕LD6, nr lunch. Unlic
£B&B (double) £24–£31

ONICH   Highland (Inverness-shire).   Map 20D7

Tigh-a-Righ   PH33 6SE ☎(085 53) 255.
*Situated on the main A82. Closed Xmas & New
Year.*
⇥6 bedrs, 3 en suite, 2 ba; tcf 📶TV, dogs, ns; P,
coach; child facs

PAISLEY   Strathclyde (Renfrewshire).
Map 20E4

Ashburn   Milliken Park Rd, Kilbarchan PA10 2DB
☎(05057) 5477
⇥6 bedrs, 2 en suite, 2 ba; TV; tcf 📶TV, dogs; P 7,
coach; child facs ✕LD 6·30. Restrict lic
£B&B £18·50–£25·50, B&B (double) £31–£44;
L £7, D £8·50; WB £46 (3 nts); [5% V w/e]
cc Diners; dep.

PERTH   Tayside (Perthshire).   Map 21B6

Clunie (Acclaimed)   12 Pitcullen Cres, PH2 7HT
☎(0738) 23625
⇥7 bedrs, 7 en suite; TV; tcf 📶dogs, ns; P 7;
child facs ✕LD 6, nr lunch. Unlic

Pitcullen (Acclaimed)   17 Pitcullen Cres, PH2 7HT
☎(0738) 26506 or 28265.
*Attractive guest house in residential area. On A94,
last guest house on left before leaving Perth.*
⇥6 bedrs, 2 en suite, 2 ba; TV; tcf 📶dogs, ns; P 6,
coach ✕LD 7, nr lunch & nr dinner Sat & Sun. Unlic
£B&B £15–£20, B&B (double) £26–£34; D £7; dep.

Rowanbank   3 Pitcullen Cres, PH2 7HT ☎(0738)
21421.
*A late Victorian town house about 1 mile from the
centre of Perth on A94.*
⇥4 bedrs, 2 en suite, 1 ba; TV; tcf
📶TV, dogs; P 7 ✕nr lunch. Unlic
£B&B (double) £25–£31; HB weekly £127–£152;
[5% V]; dep.

PITLOCHRY   Tayside (Perthshire).   Map 21A7

Balrobin (Highly Acclaimed)   Higher Oakfield,
PH16 5HT ☎(0796) 2901.

Oban (Argyll)

Foxholes Hotel
Cologin, Lerags, Oban, Argyll
Enjoy peace and tranquillity at 'Foxholes'. All rooms en-suite, colour
TV, teamaker, CH facilities. Good views all round. All food home
cooked to high standard. Dinner, bed and breakfast.   RAC acclaimed
Contact 0631 64982   ETB ♨♨♨

Fine Victorian country house in its own grounds, with panoramic views of Tummel Valley and hills. Turn into East Moulin Rd from Atholl Rd, then take second turn on left. Open Easter–Oct.
12 bedrs, 11 en suite, 2 ba; TV; tcf ♠ dogs, ns; P 12; no children under 10 ✕ LD 7.30, nr lunch.
£ B&B £20–£22, HB weekly £175–£215; [10% V mid May–Sept]; dep.

Knockendarroch House (Highly Acclaimed) Higher Oakfield, PH16 5HT ☎ (0796) 3473.
12 bedrs, 12 en suite; TV; tcf ♠ dogs: P 15, coach; child facs ✕ LD 7.30, nr lunch. Resid lic
cc Access, Amex, B'card/Visa, Diners.

Well House (Acclaimed)   11 Toberargan Rd, PH16 5HG ☎ (0796) 2239.
Small family-run hotel. From centre of Pitlochry go up Bonnethill Road and first right. Open Mar–Oct.
6 bedrs, 6 en suite; TV; tcf ♠ dogs, ns; P 6; child facs ✕ LD 6.30, nr lunch. Restrict lic
£ B&B (double) £29–£31; D £7 **cc** Access, B'card/Visa.

PRESTWICK   Strathclyde (Ayrshire).
Map 20E2

Kincraig (Acclaimed)   39 Ayr Rd, KA9 1SY ☎ (0292) 79480.
6 bedrs, 3 ba; TV; tcf ♠ TV, dogs; P 7; no children under 3 ✕ LD 6, nr lunch. Restrict lic
£ B&B £13; dep.

Fernbank (Acclaimed)   213 Main St, KA9 1SU ☎ (0292) 75027.
7 bedrs, 4 en suite, 2 ba ♠ TV, ns; P 7; children over 5 ✕ Breakfast only. Unlic

Braemar   113 Ayr Rd, KA9 1TN ☎ (0292) 75820.

ST ANDREWS   Fife.
Map 21C5

Albany (Acclaimed)   56 North St, KY16 9AH ☎ (0334) 77737
Elegant hotel overlooking the university. Follow A91 through traffic lights, and the Albany is 200 yards before Cathedral ruins.
12 bedrs, 5 en suite, 3 ba; TV; tcf ♠ dogs, ns; coach; child facs ✕ LD 6, Resid & Restric lic

£ B&B £12·50–£20, B&B (double) £25–£40, HB weekly £180–£220; L £3·50, D £7 **cc** Access, B'card/Visa; dep.

Amberside (Acclaimed)   4 Murray Park, KY16 AW ☎ (0334) 74644.
Small guest house set close to the Scores which leads to sands, sea and golf courses. Open Feb–Nov.
6 bedrs, 4 en suite, (1 sh) 1 ba; TV; tcf ♠ TV, dogs, ns; child facs ✕ Breakfast only. Unlic
£ B&B £16–£23, B&B (double) £30–£36; dep.

Argyle (Acclaimed)   127 North St, KY16 9AG ☎ (0334) 73387.
Substantial late Victorian stone-faced building close to shops and golf courses. Open Mar–Nov.
19 bedrs, 19 en suite; TV ♠ TV, dogs; no children under 2 ✕ Breakfast only. Resid lic
£ B&B £18–£22 **cc** Access, B'card/Visa; dep.

Arran House (Acclaimed)   5 Murray Park, KY16 9AW ☎ (0334) 74724 Fax: 0334 72072. Open Feb–Nov
6 bedrs, 3 en suite, 2 ba; TV; tcf ♠ TV ✕ Breakfast only. Unlic
£ B&B £15–£25, B&B (double) £25–£40; dep.

Beachway House (Acclaimed)   6 Murray Park, KY16 9AW ☎ (0334) 73319.
From A91 turn left into Murray Place and on to Murray Park. Open Mar–Dec
6 bedrs, 5 en suite, 1 ba; TV; tcf ♠ dogs; coach; child facs ✕ Breakfast only. Unlic
£ B&B £20–£24, B&B (double) £26–£34; [10% V]; dep.

Cadzow (Acclaimed)   58 North St, KY16 9AH ☎ (0334) 76933.
On the main street 200 yards from police station. Open Feb–Nov.
7 bedrs, 4 en suite, 2 ba; TV; tcf ♠ TV, dogs, ns; child facs ✕ Breakfast only. Unlic
£ B&B (double) £23–£36; dep.

Cleveden House (Acclaimed)   3 Murray Pl, KY16 9AP ☎ (0334) 74212.
Late Victorian stone-built house in central situation.
6 bedrs, 3 en suite, (1 sh), 2 ba ♠ TV, ns; child facs ✕ Breakfast only. Unlic
£ B&B £12–£18, B&B (double) £26–£38; [5% V Nov–Apr]

Craigmore (Acclaimed)   3 Murray Park, KY16 9AW ☎ (0334) 72142. *Guest House.*
6 bedrs, 5 en suite, 1 ba; TV; tcf ♠ TV, dogs; coach; child facs ✕ Breakfast only. Unlic

Hazelbank (Acclaimed)   28 The Scores, KY16 9AS ☎ (0334) 72466
10 bedrs, 10 en suite; TV; tcf ♠ dogs, ns; child facs ✕ Breakfast only. Restrict lic

Number Ten (Acclaimed)   10 Hope St, KY16 9HT
✆(0334) 74601.

Sporting Laird (Acclaimed)   5 Playfair Terr, KY16
9HX ✆(0334) 75906 Fax: (0334) 73881
Traditional listed Victorian building, situated at the
bottom of North St. Open Mar–Jan.
⇔9 bedrs, 9 en suite; TV; tcf �📺TV, dogs, ns; child
facs ✘LD 7. Resid, Rest & Restrict lic
£B&B £24–£28; HB weekly £225–£250; [5%V]
cc Access, B'card/Visa; dep.

West Park (Acclaimed)   5 St Mary's Pl, KY16 9UY
✆(0334) 75933.
In the centre of St Andrews, 5 mins from beach.
Open Mar–Dec
⇔5 bedrs, 3 en suite, (1 sh), 3 ba; TV; tcf 📺ns; child
facs ✘Breakfast only. Unlic
£B&B (double) £31–£37

Yorkston House (Acclaimed)   68–70 Argyle St,
KY16 9BV ✆(0334) 72019
Late 19th-century hotel, converted from two town
houses. Situated 800 yards in a western direction
from the tourist information centre.
⇔10 bedrs, 5 en suite, (1 sh), 2 ba; tcf 📺TV; child
facs ✘LD7, nr lunch. Restrict lic
££16–£20, B&B (double) £32–£44; HB weekly
£160–£200

SANDYHILLS Dumfries & Galloway
(Kirkcudbrightshire).   Map 22D5

Craigbittern House   nr Dalbeattie, DG5 4NZ.
✆(0387) 78247
Fine old Scottish baronial house with historic
atmosphere, situated in a two-acre garden. Take
A710 coast road out of Dumfries through New
Abbey and on to Sandyhills. Open Easter–Oct
⇔5 bedrs, 2 en suite, 2 ba; TV; tcf 📺TV; P 10;
child facs ✘LD 6, nr lunch. Resid & Restrict lic
£ B&B £13; B&B (double) £25–£32; HB (weekly)
£126–£154; dep.

SHETLAND ISLANDS

VIRKIE Mainland.   Map 19D9

Meadowvale (Acclaimed)   ✆Sumburgh (0950)
60240

SOUTH QUEENSFERRY   Lothian.
Map 21B4

🍺 **Hawes Inn**   Newhalls Rd, EH30 9TE ✆031-331
1990
Attractive 2-storey white-painted 16th century inn
with fine view of Forth Bridge.
⇔8 bedrs, 3 ba; TV; tcf 📺dogs, ns; P 50; child facs
✘LD 10
£B&B £35, B&B (double) £47·50; L£8·50, D£12;
[10%V w/e, also w/d Oct–Mar] **cc** Access, Amex,
B'card/Visa, Diners.

Please tell the manager if you chose your hotel
through an advertisement in the guide.

En suite rooms
En suite rooms may be bath or shower rooms.
If you have a preference, remember to state it
when booking a room.

Discount vouchers
RAC discount vouchers are at the end of the
guide. Establishments with a [V] shown at the end
of the price information will accept them in part
payment for accommodation bills on the full,
standard rate, not against bargain breaks or any
other special offers. Please note the limitations
shown in the entry: w/e for weekends, w/d for
weekdays, and which months they are accepted.

WALES

ABERCRAF Powys. Map 31E5

🍷 **Abercrave Inn** SA9 1XS ✆ (0639) 730460.
The river Craf runs through the garden of this traditional inn. Most bedrooms in motel-style building across road. Tennis.
🍴2 bedrs, 2 en suite; annexe 7 bedrs, 7 en suite; TV; tcf 📺P30, coach; con30.

ABERDYFI (ABERDOVEY) Gwynedd.
Map 31A4

Bodfor (Acclaimed) Bodfor Ter, LL350EA
✆ (0654) 767475 Fax: (0654) 767475.
Tall white Victorian building overlooking the Dovey Estuary and sandy beach. On the A493 main promenade in the centre of town.
🍴16 bedrs, 10en suite, (6 sh), 3ba; TV; tcf 📺dogs, ns; coach; child facs 🍴LD9.30. Resid & Rest lic
£ B&B £22–£26, B&B (double) £46–£50; HB weekly £145–£175; L £7·95, D£10·95; WB £56 (for 2, HB); [10% V Nov–Mar] **cc** Access, B'card/Visa; dep.

Cartref (Acclaimed) LL35 0NR ✆ (0654) 767273.
From centre of town, head N towards Tywyn Drive, and Cartref is opposite recreation ground.
🍴7 bedrs, 4en suite, 1 ba; TV; tcf 📺TV, dogs, ns; P8; no children under 3 🍴nr lunch. Unlic
£B&B £13, B&B (double) £30; HB weekly £154; dep.

Frondeg (Acclaimed) Copperhill St, LL35 0HT
✆ (0654) 767655.
🍴4 bedrs, 2 en suite, 1 ba; TV; tcf 📺TV, NS; P4; child facs 🍴LD 6, nr lunch. Unlic.

Tyddyn Rhys Farm LL35 0PG ✆ (0654) 72533
Farm. Mrs Mair Jones
Sleeps 6, 🐕 ns 🐴
£ B&B from £12

┌─────────────────────────────────────┐
│ **En suite rooms** │
│ En suite rooms may be bath or shower │
│ rooms. If you have a preference, │
│ remember to state it when booking a │
│ room. │
└─────────────────────────────────────┘

┌─────────────────────────────────────┐
│ **Weekend breaks** │
│ Please consult the hotel for full │
│ details of weekend breaks; prices │
│ shown are an indication only. Many │
│ hotels offer mid week breaks as well.│
└─────────────────────────────────────┘

ABERGYNOLWYN Gwynedd. Map 31A4

Dolgoch Falls (Acclaimed) Tywyn, LL36 9UW
✆ (0654) 782258.
Formerly a Welsh farmhouse, and parts of the original 400-year-old building form the dining room. Situated on the B4405 between Tywyn and the A487. Open Mar–Oct.
🍴6 bedrs, 3 en suite, 1 ba 📺TV, dogs, ns; P100; no children under 6 🍴LD8. Resid & Rest lic
£ B&B £17·95–£20·95; HB weekly £150·50–£171·50; D £8·95; WB £45·50 **cc** B'card/Visa; dep.

Tanycoed Ucha Tywyn, LL36 9UP ✆ (0654)
782228 *Farm.* Gweniona Pugh
Sleeps 6, 🐕 🐴
£ B&B from £10, D £6

ABERSOCH Gwynedd. Map 30F3

Llysfor LL53 7AL ✆ (075881) 2248.
🍴7 bedrs, 2ba; tcf 📺TV, dogs; P12; child facs 🍴LD 12 noon, nr lunch. Resid lic.

ABERYSTWYTH Dyfed. Map 31B4

Glyn Garth (Acclaimed) South Rd, SY231JS
✆ (0970) 615050.
A family run guest house situated next to the castle, and adjacent to South Promenade. Closed 24 Dec–2 Jan.
🍴10 bedrs, 6en suite, 1 ba; TV; tcf 📺TV, ns; U2; child facs 🍴Resid lic
£B&B £13·50–£25, B&B (double) £27–£36; [5%V Nov–Mar]

Shangri-La 36 Portland St, SY23 2DX ✆ (0970)
617659.
Situated 200 yards from the seafront, the second turning on the left.
🍴6 bedrs, 1 ba; TV 📺TV, dogs, ns; child facs 🍴Breakfast only. Unlic
£B&B £11, B&B (double) £24; dep.

BALA Gwynedd. Map 30F5

Pen Isa'r Llan Llanfor, LL23 7DW ✆ (0678)
520507.
Sauna, solarium, gymnasium, riding.
🍴6 bedrs, 3en suite, 1 ba; TV; tcf 📺dogs; P10; coach; child facs 🍴LD5, nr lunch. Resid & Rest lic`
cc Access, B'card/Visa; dep.

Plas Teg   45 Tegid St, LL23 7EN ☎(0678) 520268.

BARMOUTH   Gwynedd.   Map 31A4

Tal-y-Don   St Anne's Sq, High St, LL42 1DL
☎(0341) 280508.
*Stone building situated in the High St opposite
Woolworths.*
⇔7 bedrs, 2 ba; TV; tcf ⌂TV, dogs; coach
✗LD 9.15
£dep.

BEDDGELERT   Gwynedd.   Map 30E4

Sygun Fawr Country House (Acclaimed)   LL55
4NE ☎(076686) 258.
*Traditional Welsh granite manor house with many
original features. Situated on A498 Capelcurig to
Portmadog road. Hotel sign is beside village sign.
Sauna.*
⇔7 bedrs, 6 en suite, (1 sh), 1 ba; tcf ⌂TV, dogs;
P30; child facs ✗nr lunch. Resid & Rest lic
£B&B £15–£19; HB weekly £159–£183; D £9·50;
WB £52; [5% V].

BETWS-Y-COED   Gwynedd.   Map 30E5

Tyn-y-Celyn House (Acclaimed)   Llanrwst Rd,
LL24 0HD ☎(06902) 202.
*On A470, pi¼ mile N of A5/A470 junction. Open
Easter–Jan.*
⇔8 bedrs, 8 en suite; TV; tcf ⌂TV, dogs; P 10;
child facs ✗Breakfast only. Resid lic
£B&B £20–£30, B&B (double) £32–£40; [5% V];
dep.

BLAINA   Gwent.   Map 31D7

Chapel Farm   NP3 3DJ ☎(0495) 290888   *Farm.*
Mrs Betty Hancocks
Sleeps 8, ⌣
£ B&B from £13, D £7

BODEDERN   Gwynedd.   Map 30D3

Crown   Anglesey, LL65 3TU ☎Valley (0407)
740734.

⇔5 bedrs, (1 sh), 1 ba; TV ⌂dogs; P 50, coach;
child facs ✗LD9.

BODUAN   Gwynedd.   Map 30F3

Mathan Uchaf Farm   Pwllheli, LL53 8TU ☎(0758)
720487 *Farm.* Mrs Jean Coker
Sleeps 5, ⌁ ns ⌣
£ B&B from £12–£14, D £8

BORTH   Dyfed.   Map 31B4

Glanmor   SY24 5UP ☎(0970) 871689.
*A small family hotel overlooking Cardigan Bay.
Situated along Borth sea front's northern end.*
⇔7 bedrs, 2 ba; TV; tcf ⌂TV, dogs; P 6,
G2 ✗LD5. Resid lic
£B&B £14·50; HB weekly £150·15; L £4·95,
D £6·95; [10% V Oct–Jun w/d]; dep.

BRECON   Powys.   Map 31D6

Coach (Highly Acclaimed)   Orchard St, Llanfaes,
LD3 8AN ☎(0874) 3803.
*Follow the one-way system to traffic lights, turn left
over river bridge, and the Coach is 250 yards on
the right.*
⇔6 bedrs, 6 en suite; TV; tcf ⌂ns; P5 ✗LD 7.30,
nr lunch. Resid & Rest lic
£B&B £18–£20, B&B (double) £30–£32; dep.

Peterstone Court (Acclaimed)   Llanhamlach, LD3
7YB ☎Llanfrynach (0874 86) 666. *Swimming pool.*
⇔9 bedrs, 9 en suite; TV; tcf ⌂ns; P 25; child facs
✗LD 5.30, nr lunch. Resid lic.

BROAD HAVEN   Dyfed.   Map 31E1

Broad Haven (Acclaimed)   SA62 3JN ☎(0437)
781366.
*Large white-walled hotel right on the edge of a
magnificent beach, with lovely views. Situated 7
miles W of Haverfordwest on the seafront.
Swimming pool, solarium, billiards.*
⇔39 bedrs, 34 en suite, 1 ba; TV; tcf ⌂dogs, ns;

Betws-y-Coed (Gwynedd)

P 100, coach; child facs ✕ LD 8.30, nr Mon–Sat lunch
£B&B £22–£27, B&B (double) £34–£44; HB weekly £155–£185; D £6·50; WB; [10% V] cc Access, Amex, B'card/Visa; dep.
(See advertisement under Haverfordwest)

BRYNSIENCYN Gwynedd.   Map 30E4

Plas Trefarthen Anglesey, LL61 6SZ ☎(0248) 430379 *Farm.* Marian Roberts
Sleeps 14, ↿ ☡
£ B&B from £14–£16, D £7·50

CAERNARFON Gwynedd.   Map 30B4

Menai View North Rd, LL55 1BD ☎(0286) 4602.
Situated on the main Bangor road overlooking the Menai Strait.
⋈6 bedrs, 2 ba; TV; tcf ♠TV, dogs; coach; child facs ✕ LD 7, nr lunch. Resid & Rest lic
£B&B £14–£18, B&B (double) £24–£28; HB weekly £129·50–£143·50; D £6·50; [10% V]; dep.

CARDIFF South Glamorgan.   Map 31F6

Clare Court (Acclaimed) 46–48 Clare Rd, Grangetown CF1 7QP ☎(0222) 344839.

Small, family-run hotel, recently refurbished, and located a short walk from the main bus and railway stations.
⋈9 bedrs, 9 en suite; TV; tcf ♠TV, ns; child facs ✕ LD 7.45, nr lunch. Resid lic
£ B&B £22–£28, B&B (double) £32–£38; HB weekly £115–£140; [5% V] cc Access, Amex, B'card/Visa; dep.

Balkan 144 Newport Rd, CF2 1DT ☎(0222) 463673.
⋈14 bedrs, 6 en suite, 4 ba; TV; tcf ♠TV, ns; P 14; no children under 10 ✕ nr lunch. Unlic
£ B&B £16–£20, B&B (double) £28–£32.

Clayton 65 Stacey Rd, CF2 1DS ☎(0222) 492345.
⋈10 bedrs, (4 sh), 1 ba; tcf ♠TV, ns; P 6, coach; no children under 3 ✕ LD 12 noon, nr lunch, Sat & Sun dinner. Resid lic.

Domus 201 Newport Rd, CF2 1AJ ☎(0222) 473311.

Come off A48 Cardiff bypass at Cardiff East/Docks. Turn right onto A4161, follow city centre signs for 1½ miles, and guest house is on right. Open Jan 8–Dec 21.
⋈11 bedrs, 2 en suite, (5 sh), 2 ba; TV; tcf ♠TV, ns; U11, coach ✕ LD 8, nr lunch, Sat–Sun dinner. Resid lic
£ B&B £16–£21, B&B (double) £33–£36.

Imperial 132 Newport Rd, CF2 1DJ ☎(0222) 490032.
⋈27 bedrs, 1 en suite, (6 sh), 3 ba; TV ♠TV, dogs; P 15, G 4, coach; child facs ✕ LD 8, nr lunch. Resid & Rest lic
cc Access, B'card/Visa.

Tane's 148 Newport Rd, Roath, CF2 1AJ ☎(0222) 491755 & 493898.
An agreeable hotel close to the castle.
⋈9 bedrs, 2 ba; TV; tcf ♠TV, ns; P 10, coach; no children under 5 ✕ LD 7, nr lunch, Fri–Sun dinner. Resid lic
£ B&B £16, B&B (double) £28; HB weekly (5 nights) £110; WB £41 (2 nts); [5% V w/e]; dep.

Willows 128 Cathedral Rd, Pontcanna CF1 9LQ ☎(0222) 340881.
Keeping the castle on the right, cross river bridge, turn right at lights into Cathedral Rd.
⋈10 bedrs, 6 en suite, (2 sh), 2 ba; TV; tcf ♠TV, ns; P 10; child facs ✕Breakfast only. Resid lic
£ B&B £16·50–£21·50, B&B (double) £30–£34; WB £14; [5% V].

CARDIGAN Dyfed.   Map 31C3

Highbury House (Acclaimed) North Rd, SA43 1JU ☎(0239) 613403.
⋈6 bedrs, 3 en suite; 1 ba; TV; tcf ♠ns; child facs ✕ Breakfast only. Resid lic
cc Access, B'card/Visa.

Maes-y-Mor (Acclaimed) Gwbert Rd, SA43 1AE ☎(0239) 614929.
Small, friendly guest house opposite park, just off Aberystwyth Road.
£ B&B (double) £24–£30.

Brynhyfryd Gwbert Rd, SA43 1AE ☎(0239) 612861.
Situated 100 yards from the A487 on B4548.
⋈6 bedrs, 2 en suite, 2 ba; TV; tcf ♠TV ✕ LD 8. Unlic
£B&B £13; HB weekly £120–£134; [5% V].

CARMARTHEN Dyfed.   Map 31D3

Ty Mawr (Highly Acclaimed) Brechfa SA32 7RA ☎(0267) 202332 Fax: (0267) 202437.

A peaceful 16th-century stone building by the bridge over the River Marlais, with open log fires, plenty of beams and a river garden. Set 6 miles from Nantgaredig turn off A40, on B4310.
⇌5 bedrs, 4 en suite, 1ba; tcf ⌂dogs; P 40; child facs ✗LD 9.30, nr Mon
£ B&B £38, B&B (double) £58; HB weekly £350; L £8·50–£12·50, D £17; WB £77 (2 nts); [10% V Nov–Jun] **cc** Access, Amex, B'card/Visa; dep.

CHURCHSTOKE Powys. Map 31A6

The Drewin Farm Montgomery SY15 6TW
☎(0588) 620325 *Farm.* Mrs Ceinwen Richards
Sleeps 6, ⍓ ns ⌂
£ B&B from £12–£13, D £6–£7

COLWYN BAY Clwyd. Map 30D5

Cabin Hill (Acclaimed) College Av, Rhos-on-Sea, LL28 4NT ☎(0492) 44568.

Attractive hotel on level ground off the Promenade. College Ave is off Marine Drive. Open Mar–Oct.
⇌10 bedrs, 7 en suite, 2ba; TV; tcf ⌂TV; P 6, no children under 3 ✗LD5, nr lunch. Resid lic
£B&B £15–£18, B&B (double) £27·50–£33; HB weekly £115–£131; D £7; WB £49·50 (3 nts); dep.

Grosvenor 106–108 Abergele Rd, LL29 7PS ☎(0492) 531586.
On the main road through Colwyn Bay close to the Old Colwyn exit from A55. Open 7 Jan–20 Dec.
⇌18 bedrs, 2 en suite, 4ba; TV; tcf ⌂TV; dogs; P 14, coach; child facs ✗LD7; nr lunch. Resid & Rest lic
£B&B £14; HB weekly £120 **cc** B'card/Visa; dep.

Northwood 47 Rhos Rd, Rhos-on-Sea, LL28 4RS ☎(0492) 49931.
Small hotel off the Promenade, opposite Rhos Tourist Information Centre.

⇌13 bedrs, 10 en suite, 1 ba; TV; tcf ⌂TV, dogs, ns; P 11, coach; child facs ✗LD 6.30, nr lunch. Resid & Rest lic
£ B&B £13–£15·50; HB weekly £107–£139; D £8; WB £39·75 (2 nts); [5% V Oct–Apr] **cc** Access, B'card/Visa; dep.

Sunny Downs 66 Abbey Rd, Rhos-on-Sea LL28 4NU ☎(0492) 44256.
Family-run hotel between Colwyn Bay and Llandudno.
⇌15 bedrs, 15 en suite, 1 ba; TV; tcf ⌂TV, dogs, ns; P12, coach; child facs ✗ LD 6. Resid & Rest lic
£ B&B £17–£22; HB weekly £160; L £5, D £7; [5% V]; dep.

CORRIS Powys. Map 31A5

Dulas Valley Nr Machynlleth ☎(065 473) 688.

CRICCIETH Gwynedd. Map 30F4

Glyn-y-Coed Porthmadog Rd, LL52 0HL ☎(0766) 522870 Fax: (0766) 523341.
Situated on main A497 Portmadoc–Pwllheli Rd. Open Jan–Nov.
⇌9 bedrs, 9 en suite; TV; tcf ⌂TV, dogs; P 14, coach; child facs ✗LD4, nr lunch. Resid & Rest lic
£ B&B £16–£17; HB weekly £165–£170; dep.

Min-y-Gaer Porthmadog Rd, LL52 0HP ☎(0766) 522151.
Family-run hotel with commanding views. On A497 ¼ mile E of town centre. Open Mar–Oct.
⇌10 bedrs, 9 en suite, 1 ba; TV; tcf ⌂TV, dogs; P 12; child facs ✗LD4, nr lunch. Resid & Rest lic
£B&B £13–£17; HB weekly £130–£156; WB £44 (2 nts); [5% V excl. Aug]; dep.

Mor Heli Marine Ter, LL52 0EF ☎(0766) 522878.
A well established family-run hotel on the seafront.
⇌10 bedrs, 4 en suite, 3 ba; TV ⌂TV, dogs; coach; child facs
£ B&B £13·50; D £6·50.

Neptune Marine Ter, LL52 0EF ☎(0766) 522794.
Family-run hotel with superb views of Cardigan Bay.
⇌10 bedrs, 5 en suite, (1 sh), 4 ba; TV ⌂TV, dogs; coach; child facs ✗LD 6, nr lunch. Resid & Rest lic
£ B&B £13·50; D £6·50; [5% V].

CRICKHOWELL Powys. Map 31D6

Dragon House (Acclaimed) High St, NP8 1BE ☎(0873) 810362 Fax: (0873) 811868.
Approach Crickhowell on A40, turn left down High St. Hotel 100 yards on left.
⇌17 bedrs, 9 en suite, 2 ba; TV; tcf ⌂TV, ns; P16; child facs ✗LD8.30, nr lunch

£ B&B £15–£30; HB weekly £140–£175; WB (£40–£50); [10% V] **cc** Access, B'card/Visa; dep.

Stables (Acclaimed) Llangattock, NP8 1LE
℡ (0873) 810244.
Large farmhouse dating from 1580 with its own riding stables and 30 acres of grounds. Turn left at Vine Tree in town, follow through Llangattock to Chapel, turn right at Beaufort sign and cross canal. First drive on left. Riding.
⇝12 bedrs, 10 en suite, (2 sh); TV; tcf ਜTV, dogs; P50 ✕LD9
£ B&B £35, B&B (double) £45; L fr £6, D fr £10
cc B'card/Visa; dep.

CROESGOCH Dyfed. Map 31D1

Torbant Farm SA62 5JN ℡ (0348) 831276.
300-year old farmhouse with modern extensions, situated just S of A487, 1 mile E of Croesgoch. Open Easter–Oct.
⇝10 bedrs, 3 en suite, 3 ba; tcf ਜTV, dogs, ns; P40; child facs ✕ LD 6, nr lunch
£ B&B £12–£16; HB weekly £115–£140; D £8; [5% V Apr, May & Oct].

Trearched Farm SA62 5JP ℡ (0348) 831310.
Old farmhouse set in spacious grounds. Situated down a farm drive off A487 in village. Signed at lodge entrance. Open Feb–Nov.
⇝6 bedrs, 2 ba; tcf ਜTV; P10 ✕LD noon, nr lunch. Unlic
£ B&B £14–£15; HB weekly £132; dep.

CYNWYD Clwyd. Map 30F6

Pen-y-Bont Fawr Corwen, LL21 0ET ℡ (0490) 2226 *Farm.* Kay Culhane
Sleeps 10, ns ☞(5)
£ B&B from £13–£14, D £7

EARLSWOOD Gwent. Map 31E7

Parsons Grove Nr Chepstow, NP6 6RD
℡ (02917) 382 *Farm.* Gloria Powell
Sleeps 7, ⚐ ns ☞
£ B&B from £13

FELINFACH Powys. Map 31D6

Trehenry Farm Brecon, LD3 0LN ℡ (0874) 754312 *Farm.* Mrs Teresa Jones
Sleeps 6, ☞

£ B&B from £14, D £8

FISHGUARD Dyfed. Map 31D2

Gilfach Goch Farmhouse SA65 9SR ℡ (0348) 873871 *Farm.* June Devonald ⛨
Sleeps 15, ⚐ ☞
£ B&B from £14–£16, D from £7

GILWERN Gwent. Map 31D7

The Wenallt Farm Nr Abergavenny, NP7 0HP
℡ (0873) 830694 *Farm.* Janice Harris
Sleeps 16, ⚐ ☞
£ B&B from £12·65–£16·10, D £7·50–£8·50

GOODWICK Dyfed. Map 31D2

Siriole Quay Rd, SA64 0BS ℡ Fishguard (0348) 873203.
Small guest house on the coastal path with magnificent views. At the end of A40 just before Fishguard Bay Hotel. Closed Xmas Day.
⇝6 bedrs, 3 ba; tcf ਜTV, ns; no children under 6 ✕ Breakfast only. Unlic
£ B&B £11; dep.

GWAUN VALLEY Dyfed. Map 31D2

Tregynon Country Farmhouse (Acclaimed) nr Fishguard, SA65 9TU ℡ (0239) 820531.
An attractive 16th-century farmhouse perched on the edge of the spectacular Gwaun Valley. At junction of B4313/B4329, take B4313 to Fishguard, then take first right and first right again. Tregynon is 1¼ miles on left.
⇝8 bedrs, 8 en suite; TV; tcf ਜns; P; child facs ✕LD 8.45, lunch by arrangement. Resid & Rest lic
£ B&B (double) £59–£75; HB weekly £190–£240; D £12; WB fr £52–£66 (2 nts); dep.

GWEHELOG Gwent. Map 31D7

Tŷ-Gwyn Farm Usk, NP5 1RT ℡ (02913) 2878 *Farm.* Jean Arnett
Sleeps 6, ns ☞ (14)
£ B&B from £15, D £8·50

HARLECH Gwynedd. Map 30F4

Castle Cottage (Acclaimed) LL46 2YL ℡ (0766) 780479.

In the upper part of Harlech, 100 yards behind the Castle.
6 bedrs, 4 en suite, 1 ba; tcf TV, dogs, ns; child facs LD 9.30, nr lunch Mon–Sat. Resid & Rest lic
£ B&B £17, B&B (double) £37; L £8·75, D £13·50; WB (£27·50); [5% V] cc Access, B'card/Visa; dep.

St Davids (Acclaimed) LL46 2PT (0766) 780366.

Large comfortable hotel set in Snowdonia National Park with spectacular views. On Harlech's main road next to Coleg Harlech. Swimming pool, billiards, solarium.
58 bedrs, 58 en suite; TV; tcf lift, dogs; P60, coach; child facs LD8.30, nr lunch
£ B&B £15–£25; D £10; [10% V] cc Access, Amex, B'card/Visa, Diners; dep.

Byrdir High St, LL462YN (0766) 780316.

HAY-ON-WYE Powys.   Map 31C7

York House Hardwicke Rd, Cusop, HR3 5QX (0497) 820705.
Elegant, quiet house in lovely gardens, ½ mile from Hay-on-Wye car park on B4348.
5 bedrs, 3 en suite, 1 ba; TV; tcf NS; dogs; P6; no children under 8 LD4.30, nr lunch. Unlic
£ B&B £18–£28, B&B (double) £30–£40; HB weekly £154·35–£185·85; dep.

HOLYWELL Clwyd.   Map 30D6

Miners Arms Rhes-y-Cae, CH8 8JG Halkyn (0352) 780567.

JOHNSTON Dyfed.   Map 31E2

Redstock SA62 3HW (0437) 890287.

LAMPETER Dyfed.   Map 31C4

Bryncastell Farm Llanfair Road, SA48 8JY (0570) 422447 *Farm.* E A Beti and Sian Davies
Sleeps 4,
£ B&B from £12–£13, D £7

LANGLAND BAY West Glamorgan.
                                    Map 31E4

Wittenberg (Acclaimed) 2 Rotherslade Rd, SA3 4QN Swansea (0792) 369696.
A small, family-run hotel, 200 yards walk from Rotherslade Bay. Follow signs for Langland Bay, and hotel is first on right. Closed Xmas.
12 bedrs, 10 en suite, 2 ba; TV; tcf TV, ns; P12; no children under 5 LD 4, nr lunch. Resid lic
£ B&B £30, B&B (double) £40–£44; HB weekly £190–£204; WB (£60); [5% V w/d] cc Access, B'card/Visa; dep.

Brynteg 1 Higher La, SA3 4NS Swansea (0792) 366820.

LITTLE HAVEN Dyfed.   Map 31E1

Pendyffryn SA62 3LA Broad Haven (0437) 781337.
Follow B4341 coastal road towards Broad Haven for ½ mile into Little Haven. Hotel on left. Open Apr–end Sept.
7 bedrs, 2 en suite, (1 sh), 2 ba; TV; tcf ns; P6; no children under 4 Breakfast only. Rest lic
£ B&B (double) £26–£34; dep.

LITTLE MILL Gwent. Map 31E7

Pentwyn Farm Pontypool, NP4 0HQ ✆(049 528) 249 *Farm*. Stuart and Ann Bradley
Sleeps 6, ☞ (4)
£ B&B from £12, D £7

LLANBEDR Gwynedd. Map 30F4

🍴 🍴 P Victoria Inn LL45 2LD ✆(034 123) 213.
Stone-built 18th century inn in village centre.
Garden running down to River Artro.
🛏5 bedrs, 5 en suite; TV; tcf ⌂P 80, U 13, coach; child facs ✕LD 9
£ B&B £20·50, B&B (double) £38; HB weekly £123; WB £37·50 (2 nts) £54 (3 nts); WB **cc** Access, B'card/Visa.

LLANBERIS Gwynedd. Map 30E4

Lake View (Acclaimed) Tan-y-Pant, LL55 4EL ✆(0286) 870422.
Small hotel just outside Llanberis on A4068. Lovely lake views.

LLANDEGLA Clwyd. Map 30E7

Cae Madoc Farm Nr Wrexham, LL11 3BD ✆(097 888) 270 *Farm*. Mrs Del Crossley
Sleeps 6, 🐾 ns ☞
£ B&B from £2–£14, D £7

Saith Daran Farm Wrexham, LL11 3BA ✆(097 888) 685 *Farm*. Pat Thompson
Sleeps 4, ☞
£ B&B from £12–£14, D £7

LLANDEILO Dyfed. Map 31D4

Brynawel (Acclaimed) 19 New Rd SA19 6DD ✆(0558) 822925.
Turn of the century building, fully refurbished, on the A40 200 yards from police/fire/ambulance stations. Closed Xmas.
🛏5 bedrs, 3 en suite, 1 ba; TV; tcf ⌂P 7, coach; child facs ✕LD 7, nr Sun dinner. Mon–Thu dinner by arrangement. Rest lic
£ B&B £16–£21, B&B (double) £26–£30; [5% V Sun–Thu] **cc** Access, B'card/Visa.

LLANDELOY Dyfed. Map 31D1

Upper Vanley Farm (Acclaimed) Nr Solva ✆Croesgoch (034 83) 418.
🛏8 bedrs, 8 en suite, 1 ba; TV; tcf ⌂TV, dogs, ns; P 10, coach; child facs ✕LD 6, nr lunch. Unlic

LLANDOGO Gwent. Map 31E8

Brown's NP5 4TW ✆Dean (0594) 530262.
🛏5 bedrs, 3 en suite, 1 ba ⌂TV, dogs, ns; P 20, coach ✕LD 8. Rest lic

Sloop NP6 5TW ✆Dean (0594) 530291.
An 18th-century inn on the A466 Chepstow–Monmouth Rd in the village centre.
🛏4 bedrs, 4 en suite; TV; tcf ⌂dogs; P 40, coach; children over 11 ✕LD 10
£ B&B £25·50, B&B (double) £36–£44; L £7, D £7; [10% V] **cc** Access, Amex, B'card/Visa; dep.

LLANDOVERY Dyfed. Map 31D5

Llwyncelyn Chain Bridge, SA20 0EP ✆(0550) 20566.
Century-old stone building on the western edge of Llandovery.
🛏6 bedrs, 2 ba ⌂TV, ns; P 12; child facs ✕LD 7.30, nr lunch. Resid & Rest lic
£ B&B £16·80–£19·80, B&B (double) £29·60–£31·60; HB weekly £152·80–£180·80; D £10; WB (£26·64); dep.

LLANDRINDOD WELLS Powys. Map 31C6

Three Wells (Highly Acclaimed) Howey, LD1 5PB ✆(0597) 822484/824427.

A working farm overlooking a fishing lake in peaceful unspoilt countryside. Take A483 S of Llandrindod Wells to Howey Village, turn into village and follow up Chapel Rd ¼ mile to farm. Fishing. Riding.
🛏15 bedrs, 15 en suite; TV; tcf ⌂lift, TV, ns; P 20; no children under 10 ✕LD 6, nr lunch. Resid lic
£B&B £14–£19; HB weekly £130–£172; dep.

Charis (Acclaimed) Pentrosfa, LD1 5NL ✆(0597) 824732.
An Edwardian-style house with spacious first floor rooms, situated on the first turn after passing the 'welcome' sign from the South. Open Mar–Nov.
🛏4 bedrs, 4 en suite; tcf ⌂TV, dogs, ns; P 2; no children under 10 ✕LD 2.30, nr lunch. Unlic
£B&B £15, B&B (double) £36–£38; dep.

Griffin Lodge (Acclaimed) Temple St, LD1 5HF ✆(0597) 822432.
On A483 near town centre. Closed Xmas & New Year.
🛏8 bedrs, 5 en suite, 2 ba; TV; tcf ⌂TV, dogs; P 5 ✕LD 8.45, lunch by arrangement.
£B&B fr £15·50–£19·50, B&B (double) fr £27–£35; HB weekly £130·50–£157·50; L £5, D £8; [10% V] **cc** Access, B'card/Visa; dep.

LLANDUDNO Gwynedd. Map 30D5

Banham House (Acclaimed) 2 St Davids Rd, LL30 2UL (0492) 75680.
Attractive white house with black trim with beautiful garden. From the Promenade continue into Lloyd St, and St David's Rd is fourth on left.
8 bedrs, 6 en suite, 1 ba; TV; tcf TV, ns; child facs LD 7.30, lunch on request. Resid lic
£ B&B £14–£16; HB weekly £140–£154; L £4·50, D £6; [10% V Oct–Jun]; dep.

Britannia 15 (Acclaimed) Craig-y-Don Par, LL30 1BG (0492) 77185.
9 bedrs, 5 en suite, 2 ba; TV; tcf TV, dogs; child facs LD 5, nr lunch. Unlic.

Buile Hill (Acclaimed) St Mary's Rd, LL30 2UE (0492) 76972. Open Mar–Dec.
13 bedrs, 7 en suite, 2 ba; tcf TV, ns; dogs; P 6, coach; child facs LD 4.30, nr lunch. Resid lic
£ B&B £13·50–£19·50; HB weekly £112–£147; WB £35; [5% V]; dep.

Concord (Acclaimed) 35 Abbey Rd, LL30 2EH (0492) 75504.

Cornerways (Acclaimed) St David's Pl, LL30 2UG (0492) 77334.
From railway station turn left at traffic lights, then second on right. Open Easter–Oct.
6 bedrs, 6 en suite; TV; tcf ns; P 5; no children LD 4.30, nr lunch. Resid lic
£ B&B £23, B&B (double) £36; HB weekly £175; dep.

Kinmel (Acclaimed) Central Promenade, LL30 1AR (0492) 76171.
A family-run hotel with views over Llandudno Bay. Located on the seafront. Open Mar–Oct & Xmas period.
16 bedrs, 10 en suite, 3 ba; TV; tcf TV, dogs, ns; coach; child facs LD 7.30. Bar meals only lunch. Resid & Rest lic
£ B&B £15–£18; HB weekly £140–£160; L £4·50, D £5·50; [10% V Mar–May] **cc** Access; B'card/Visa; dep.

Lynwood (Acclaimed) Clonmel St, LL30 2LE (0492) 76613.
Clonmel St runs from the shopping centre to the Promenade. Open Feb–Nov.
26 bedrs, 20 en suite, 3 ba; TV; tcf ns; coach; child facs LD 7.30
£ B&B £22–£26, B&B (double) £39–£46; HB weekly £134–£165; L £3, D £6 **cc** Access, B'card/Visa; dep.

Mayfair (Acclaimed) 4 Abbey Rd, LL30 2EA (0492) 76170.

A small family-run hotel situated under the lee of the Great Orme on Abbey Rd near the shops. Open Easter–Nov.
12 bedrs, 9 en suite, 1 ba; TV; tcf TV, dogs; P 4; child facs LD 6, nr lunch. Rest lic
£ B&B £16·50; HB weekly £160; dep.

Mayville (Acclaimed) 4 St David's Rd, LL30 2UL (0492) 75406.

A small, family-run hotel in a residential area. St David's Rd is a turning off Lloyd St which comes off the High St.
6 bedrs, 4 en suite, 1 ba; tcf TV, ns; P 6; no children under 6 LD 5, nr lunch. Resid lic
£ B&B £24, B&B (double) £40; HB weekly £150; WB (£40); [5% V w/d]; dep.

Northgate (Acclaimed) Central Promenade (0492) 77701.
12 bedrs, 6 en suite, (1 sh), 2 ba; TV; tcf TV, dogs, ns, coach; child facs LD 6, nr lunch. Resid lic.

Orotava (Acclaimed) 105 Glen-y-Mor Rd, Penrhyn Bay, LL30 3PH (0492) 49780.
Brick built house from 1920's, situated on the Promenade about 1 mile from Rhos on Sea.
6 bedrs, 3 en suite; 1 ba; TV; tcf TV, ns; P 10; no children LD 6, nr Sun dinner. Rest lic
£ B&B £16·50–£19, B&B (double) £25–£30; L £3·95, D £6; [10% V] **cc** B'card/Visa; dep.

Warwick (Acclaimed) 56 Church Walks, LL30 2HL (0492) 76823.
Quietly situated small hotel overlooking terraced gardens. Turn off the Promenade by the pier into Church Walks. Closed Dec & Jan.
17 bedrs, 10 en suite, 2 ba; TV; tcf TV, dogs; coach; child facs LD 6.45, nr lunch. Resid & Rest lic

£ B&B £14–£17.50; HB weekly £126–£150; D £5·50; WB (£38); [5% V mid Sept–mid Jul]; dep.

White Court (Acclaimed)   2 North Parade, LL30 2LP ✆ (0492) 76719.
🛏16 bedrs, 4 en suite, 3 ba; TV; tcf 🅽ns; P 2, coach; child facs ✗LD 4.30, nr lunch. Resid lic **cc** Access, B'card/Visa; dep.

White Lodge (Acclaimed)   Central Promenade, LL30 1AT ✆ (0492) 77713.
Family-run Victorian-style hotel on the seafront, situated by the conference centre. Open Mar–Nov.
🛏12 bedrs, 12 en suite; TV; tcf 🅽TV; dogs, ns; P 12 ✗LD 7, nr lunch. Resid lic
£ B&B £17·50–£21·50; HB weekly £150·50–£175; [5% V Mar–Apr, Oct–Nov]; dep.

Wilton (Acclaimed)   South Parade, LL30 2LN ✆ (0492) 78343.
🛏14 bedrs, 12 en suite, 2 ba; TV; tcf 🅽dogs; child facs ✗LD 4.30, nr lunch. Resid lic

Brannock   36 St David's Rd, LL30 2UH ✆ (0492) 77483.

Brigstock   1 St David's Pl, LL30 2UG ✆ (0492) 76416.
Small hotel in quiet garden area. From railway station turn left at traffic lights, third right into St David's Rd and first right.
🛏9 bedrs, 3 en suite, 2 ba; TV; tcf 🅽TV, ns; P 6; no children under 6 ✗LD 5, nr lunch. Resid lic
£ B&B £11–£12; HB weekly £109–£116; D £6; WB; [10% V]; dep.

Carmel   17 Craig-y-Don Par, LL30 1BG ✆ (0492) 77643.
Small hotel with sea and mountain views, on the Promenade. Open Easter–mid Oct.
🛏10 bedrs, 5 en suite, 2 ba; TV; tcf 🅽TV, ns; P 6; no children under 4 ✗LD 1 pm, nr Mon–Sat lunch, Sun dinner. Unlic
£ B&B £10·50–£16; HB weekly £105–£122·50; D £5; dep.

Cleave Court   1 St Seiriol's Rd, LL30 2YY ✆ (0492) 77849.

Cumberland   North Par, LL30 2LP ✆ (0492) 76379.

Hen Dy   10 North Pde, LL30 2LP ✆ (0492) 76184.
🛏12 bedrs, 4 en suite, 3 ba; TV; tcf 🅽TV, dogs; child facs ✗LD 5.30, nr lunch. Resid & Rest lic **cc** Access, B'card/Visa; dep.

Karden   16 Charlton St, LL30 2AN ✆ (0492) 879347/899990.
Follow Llandudno sign to roundabout, turn left and first right.

🛏11 bedrs, 3 ba; tcf 🅽TV; coach; child facs ✗nr lunch. Resid lic
£ B&B £10·50–£13; [5% V Oct–May]; dep.

Kenmore   28 Trinity Ave, LL30 2SJ ✆ (0492) 77774.
Turn left at station traffic lights into Trinity Ave. Open Apr–Oct.
🛏10 bedrs, 3 en suite, 2 ba; TV; tcf 🅽TV, ns; P 5, child facs ✗LD 6, nr lunch. Resid lic
£ B&B £12·50–£15; HB weekly £114–£132; [10% V Apr–Jun & Oct]; dep.

Mayfield   19 Curzon Rd, Craig-y-Don, LL30 1TB ✆ (0492) 77427.

Minion   21 Carmen Sylva Rd, LL30 1EQ ✆ (0492) 77740.
Small hotel set in south-facing garden. Carmen Sylva Rd is off Mostyn Avenue. Open Apr–Oct.
🛏14 bedrs, 10 en suite, 1 ba; tcf 🅽TV, dogs; P 8 ✗LD 4, nr lunch. Resid lic
£ B&B £10–£12·50; HB weekly £108·50–£129·50; [5% V Apr & Oct]; dep.

Montclare   North Par, LL30 2LP ✆ (0492) 77061.
Situated opposite the Cenotaph on the Promenade. Open Mar–Nov.
🛏16 bedrs, 12 en suite, 1 ba; TV; tcf 🅽dogs, ns; coach; child facs ✗LD 4, nr lunch. Resid & Rest lic
£ B&B £13–£14·50; dep.

Rosaire   2 St Seiriols Rd, LL30 2YY ✆ (0492) 77677.
Edwardian house on level ground. From seafront turn into Lloyd St, left into St. Davids Rd, then turn next right. Open Mar–Oct.
🛏10 bedrs, 4 en suite, 2 ba; tcf 🅽TV, dogs, ns; P 6; no children under 3 ✗LD 4, nr lunch. Resid lic
£ B&B £10·50–£13·50; HB weekly £92–£149; [5% V]; dep.

St Hilary   Craig-y-Don Par, Promenade, LL30 1BG ✆ (0492) 75551.
A traditional Victorian hotel on the main Promenade. Open Jan–Nov.
🛏11 bedrs, 6 en suite, 3 ba; TV; tcf 🅽TV; child facs ✗LD 5.30, nr dinner Sun, lunch Mon–Sat. Rest lic
£ B&B (double) £24–£29; HB weekly £119–£136·50; L £4·50, D £4·50 **cc** Access, B'card/Visa; dep.

Seaclyffe   11 Church Walks LL30 2HG ✆ (0492) 76803

Seaforth   6 Neville Cres, Central Promenade, LL30 1AT ✆ (0492) 76784. *Snooker.*
🛏29 bedrs, 12 en suite, (5 sh), 2 ba.

Spindrift   24 St David's Rd, LL30 2UL ✆ (0492) 76490.

Friendly hotel on level ground. From seafront turn into St Georges Place, and St David's Rd is on the left. Closed Xmas.
⇔5 bedrs, 1 en suite, 1 ba; TV; tcf 📺dogs, ns; P4; no children under 10 ✕LD6, nr lunch. Unlic
£ B&B £16–£18, B&B (double) £28–£32; HB weekly £140–£154; WB (£12·50); [10% V min 2 nts]; dep.

Tilstone Carmen Sylva Rd, Craig-y-Don, LL301EQ ☎(0492) 75588.
Attractive hotel off main A55 to A470 link road, signed Post Craig-y-Don to Carmen Sylva Rd.
⇔7 bedrs, 2 ba 📺TV, ns; no children ✕LD12 noon, nr lunch. Resid & Rest lic
£B&B £12; HB weekly £115; dep.

Wedgwood 6 Deganwy Ave, LL30 2YB ☎(0492) 78016. *Private Hotel.*

Westbourne 8 Arvon Av, LL302DY ☎(0492) 77450.
⇔13 bedrs, 3en suite, 2ba; TV; tcf 📺TV, dogs; coach; child facs ✕LD4. Resid lic

Westdale 37 Abbey Rd, LL302EH ☎(0492) 77996.
A small family-run hotel on the level. Turn left at roundabout on Promenade, third right and first left. Open Mar–Oct.
⇔12 bedrs, 3en suite, 2ba; tcf 📺TV, dogs; P6; child facs ✕LD4.30, nr lunch. Resid lic
£B&B fr £11, B&B (double) fr £26; HB weekly fr £105.

LLANDYSSIL Powys.   Map 31A6

Gate Farm Montgomery, SY15 6LN ☎(068688) 625 *Farm.* Mrs Anwen Lloyd
Sleeps 6, ⊁⛺
£ B&B from £12, D £7

LLANERCHYMEDD Gwynedd.   Map 30D3

Llwydiarth Fawr Isle of Anglesey, LL71 8DF ☎(0248) 470321 *Farm.* Mrs Margaret Hughes ⅄
Sleeps 6/8, ns ⛺
£ B&B from £15, D £7·50

Tre'r Ddol Farm Isle of Anglesey, LL71 7AR ☎(0248) 470278 *Farm.* Ann Astley ⅄
Sleeps 8, ⊁⛺
£ B&B from £14, D £6·50

LLANFAGLAN Gwynedd.   Map 30E4

Cae'r Efail Caernarfon, LL54 5RE ☎(0286) 76226/2824 *Farm.* Mrs Mari Williams
Sleeps 6, ⛺
£ B&B from £12, D £6

LLANFAIR Dyfed.   Map 31C4

Pentre Farm, Lampeter, SA48 8LE ☎(0570) 45313 *Farm.* Eleri Davies

Sleeps 6, ⛺
£ B&B from £14, D £7

LLANFAIR WATERDINE Powys.   Map 31B7

Monaughty Poeth Nr Knighton, LD7 1TT ☎(0547) 528348 *Farm.* Jim and Jocelyn Williams
Sleeps 5, ⊁⛺(6)
£ B&B from £12·50

LLANFYLLIN Powys.   Map 30F6

Cyfie Farm (Acclaimed) Llanfihangel, SY22 5JE ☎(069184) 451.
A 17th-century Welsh longhouse with magnificent views and a pretty garden. From Llanfyllin take B4393, turn left in 4 miles to Llanfihangel. Bear right in village past cemetery, take first left and Cyfie is third farm on left.
⇔3 bedrs, 3 en suite; TV; tcf 📺TV, ns; P 8; child facs ✕LD 6, nr lunch. Unlic
£ B&B £15–£18; HB weekly £126–£156; dep.

LLANFWROG Clwyd.   Map 30D6

Bodangharad Ruthin, LL15 2AH ☎(082 42) 2370 *Farm.* Enid Jones
Sleeps 6, ⊁⛺
£ B&B from £10–£12, D £6

LLANGRANNOG Dyfed.   Map 31D3

Hendre Farm Llandysul, SA44 6AP ☎(023 9) 654342 *Farm.* Bethan Williams
Sleeps 6, ns ⛺
£ B&B from £11–£14, D from £6

LLANGYNHAFAL Clwyd.   Map 30E6

Tŷ Coch Farm Denbigh, LL16 4LN ☎(082 44) 423 *Farm.* Anne L Richards
Sleeps 5, ⛺
£ B&B from £9–£10, D £5

LLANIDLOES Powys.   Map 31B5

Dol-Llys Farm SY18 6JA ☎(05512) 2694 *Farm.* Olwen S Evans
Sleeps 6, ⛺
£ B&B from £10–£12

LLANRUG Gwynedd.   Map 30E4

Plas Tirion Farm Caernarfon, LL55 4PY ☎(0286) 673190 *Farm.* C H Mackinnon
Sleeps 8, ⛺
£ B&B from £13, D from £6

LLANTILIO Gwent.   Map 31D7

Little Treadam Crossenny, Abergavenny, NP7 8TA ☎(060 085) 326 *Farm.* Beryl Ford

Sleeps 6, ⚑ ⛺
£ B&B from £12, D £7

LLANWNDA Gwynedd.   Map 30E4

Tŷ Mawr Farmhouse   Saron, Caernarfon, LL54
5UH ✆ (0286) 830091 *Farm.* Carol Mills
Sleeps 6, ⚑ ns ⛺ (4)
£ B&B from £13–£15

LLANWRTHWL Powys.   Map 31C6

Dyffryn Farm   Llandrindod Wells, LD1 6NP
✆ (0597) 811017 *Farm.* Freddie Duffell
Sleeps 5, ⚑ ⛺
£ B&B from £15–£17·50, D £9·50

LLANWRTYD WELLS Powys.   Map 31C5

Lasswade House (Highly Acclaimed)   LD5 4RW
✆ (059 13) 515.

*A spacious Edwardian house set in magnificent
countryside with unrivalled views. Follow directions
to village railway station. Swimming pool.*
⇥7 bedrs, 7 en suite; TV; tcf 📺 dogs; ns; P 12; child
facs ✗LD8.30, nr lunch. Resid & Rest lic
£ B&B £32–£34, B&B (double) £50–£52; HB weekly
£230–£240; D £11·50; WB; [10% V Oct–Apr]
cc Access, B'card/Visa; dep.

MACHYNLLETH Powys.   Map 31A5

🍴 🍴 **White Lion**   Heol Pentrerhedyn, SY20 2ND
✆ (0654) 703455. Fax: (0654) 703746.
*Charming old coaching inn in the town centre on
the A487; the 'Inn by the Clock'.*
⇥9 bedrs, 6 en suite, 1 ba; TV; tcf 📺 dogs; P 45,
coach; child facs ✗LD9
£ B&B £20–£30, B&B (double) £37–£52; WB
£55·95 **cc** Access, Amex, B'card/Visa, Diners; dep.

Maenllwyd   Newton Rd, SY20 8EY ✆ (0654)
702928.
*From clock tower in town centre take Newtown/
Welshpool Rd, Maenllwyd is ⅓ mile on right.*
⇥8 bedrs, (1 sh), 2 ba; TV; tcf 📺 TV, dogs; P 10;
child facs ✗morning, nr lunch. Unlic
£ B&B £16·50–£18, B&B (double) £28–£30;
[10% V]
cc Access; B'card/Visa; dep.

MILFORD HAVEN Dyfed.   Map 31E1

Belhaven House   29 Hamilton Terr, SA73 3JJ
✆ (064 6) 695983. Fax: (0646) 690787.
*Family-run hotel with homely atmosphere, 200 yards
west of the town hall.*
⇥12 bedrs, 10 en suite, (1 sh), 1 ba; TV; tcf
📺 TV, dogs; P 8, coach; child facs ✗LD 10, nr
Mon–Sat lunch. Resid & Rest lic
£ B&B £18·35–£26·45, B&B (double) £34·50–
£41·40; HB weekly £176·30–£225·40; D £13;
[10% V] **cc** Access, Amex, B'card/Visa, Diners;
dep.

MOLD Clwyd.   Map 30E7

Old Mill (Acclaimed)   Melin y Wern, Denbigh Rd,
Nannerch CH7 5RH ✆ (0352) 741542
*A former stone water mill stables, sympathetically
converted and set in landscaped gardens. On the
A541 Mold to Denbigh Rd, 7 miles from Mold.*
⇥7 bedrs, 7 en suite; TV; tcf 📺 dogs, NS; P 20;
child facs ✗Breakfast only. Unlic
£ B&B £21·50–£28·60, B&B (double) £36; [10% V
Oct–Mar] **cc** Access, Amex, B'card/Visa; dep.

MONMOUTH Gwent.   Map 31E8

Queens Head Inn   St James St, NP5 3DL ✆ (0600)
2767

MONTGOMERY Powys.   Map 31A6

Little Brompton Farm   SY15 6HY ✆ (0686)
668371 *Farm.* Gaynor Bright
Sleeps 6, ⚑ ns ⛺
£ B&B from £12·50–£14·50, D from £7

MORFA NEFYN Gwynedd.   Map 20F3

Graeanfryn   Nr Pwllheli, LL53 6YQ ✆ (0758)
720455 *Farm.* Mrs Ellen Llewelyn   ♿
Sleeps 6, ns ⛺
£ B&B from £10–£12

MUMBLES West Glamorgan.   Map 31F4

Shoreline   648 Mumbles Rd, Southend, SA3 4EA
✆ Swansea (0792) 366233.

NEATH West Glamorgan.   Map 31E5

Europa   32–34 Victoria Gardens, SA11 3BH
✆ (0639) 635094.
Small, personally-run hotel in the town centre.

Weekend breaks

Please consult the hotel for full details of weekend
breaks; prices shown are an indication only.
Many hotels offer mid week breaks as well.

⋈12 bedrs, 2 ba; TV; tcf 📺TV; P 3 ✕Meals by arrangement. Bar meals. Resid lic
£ B&B £15, B&B (double) £27; [5% V] **cc** Access, B'card/Visa; dep

NEW QUAY Dyfed. Map 31C3

Park Hall (Highly Acclaimed) Cwmtydu SA44 6LG
📞(0545) 560306.

A former Victorian gentleman's residence, lovingly restored to its former glory and set in its own grounds with panoramic views of Cwmtydu Bay. A turning of the A487 Aberystwyth to Cardigan Rd.
⋈5 bedrs, 5 en suite; TV; tcf 📺TV; dogs, ns; P 20; no children under 12 ✕LD 8. Rest lic
£ B&B £25–£30; HB weekly £245–£280; L £2·95, D £8·50–£14·50 **cc** Access, Amex, B'card/Visa, Diners.

Ty Hen Farm (Acclaimed) Llwyndafydd 📞(0545) 560346.
18th-century farmhouse tastefully extended into converted farm buildings. From Llwyndafydd go up hill for 1 mile, take sharp right bend, then 'No Through Rd'. Entrance in 100 yds. Sauna, solarium, gymnasium, swimming pool. Closed mid Nov–mid Feb.
⋈5 bedrs, 5 en suite; TV; tcf 📺TV; dogs, NS; P 50; child facs ✕LD 4. Resid & Rest lic
£D £8; [10% V] **cc** Access; dep.

NEWTOWN Powys. Map 31B6

Lower Gwestydd SY16 3AY 📞(0686) 626718 *Farm.* Iris Jarman
Sleeps 6, ☌
£ B&B from £12–£14, D £6

PENARTH South Glamorgan. Map 31F6

Westbourne 8 Victoria Rd CF6 2EF 📞(0222) 707268.
A Victorian house set in mature gardens, situated opposite the station.
⋈8 bedrs, 3 en suite, 2 ba; TV; tcf 📺TV, dogs; P 4, coach; child facs ✕LD 8.30, nr Sat & Sun. Resid & Rest lic
£ B&B £17–£21, B&B (double) £29–£32; WB £39 (HB); [5% V] **cc** Access, Amex, B'card/Visa; dep.

PENIEL Clwyd. Map 30E6

College Farm Denbigh, LL16 4TT 📞(074 570) 276 *Farm.* Helen Parry   ♿
Sleeps 5, ↟ ns ☌
£ B&B from £11–£12, D £6·50

PENNAL Powys. Map 31A5

Gogarth Hall Farm Machynlleth, SY20 9LB
📞(0654) 791235 *Farm.* Mrs Deilwen Breese
Sleeps 6, ☌
£ B&B from £11·50–£13·50, D £6·50

PENTRE CELYN Clwyd. Map 30E6

Llainwen Ucha Ruthin, LL15 2HL 📞(097 888) 253 *Farm.* Elizabeth Parry
Sleeps 5, ↟ ☌
£ B&B from £10, D £6

PORTHCAWL Mid Glamorgan. Map 31F5

Collingwood 40 Mary St, CF36 3YA ✆(065 671) 2899. *Hotel.*

Oakdale 46 Mary St, CF36 3YA ✆(065 671) 3643.

Penoyre 29 Mary St, CF36 2YN ✆(065 671) 4550. *Mary St is between The Esplanade Hotel and the Grand Pavilion.*
⊨5 bedrs, 2 ba; TV; tcf �📺TV, dogs; child facs ✗LD5, nr lunch. Resid lic
£B&B £13–£14; HB weekly £130–£140; dep.

Summerfield 44 Esplanade Av, ✆(0656) 715685.

Villa 27 Mary St, CF36 3YN ✆(065 671) 5074. *Mary St is between The Esplanade Hotel and the Grand Pavilion.*
⊨8 bedrs, 3 en suite; 2 ba; TV; tcf �📺TV, ns; no children under 3 ✗LD1, nr lunch, Sat–Sun dinner. Unlic
£B&B £13, B&B (double) £22–£28; HB weekly £112–£154; dep.

PWLLHELI Gwynedd. Map 30F3

Yoke House Farm LL53 5TY ✆(0758) 612621 *Farm.* Annwen Hughes
Sleeps 4/6, ⏃
£ B&B from £10–£12

RHALLT Powys. Map 31A6

Gungrog House Welshpool, SY21 9HS ✆(0938) 553381 *Farm.* Eira Jones
Sleeps 6, ns ⏃
£ B&B from £13–£15, D £7

RHYL Clwyd. Map 30D6

Arncliffe 100 Crescent Rd, LL18 1LY ✆(0745) 53634. *Hotel.*

Pier 23 East Par, LL18 3AL ✆(0745) 350280. *Small, personally-run hotel directly opposite the Rhyl Floral Hall.*
⊨9 bedrs, 8 en suite, 1 ba; TV; tcf �📺TV, dogs; P3; child facs ✗nr Mon–Sat lunch, Sun dinner. Resid lic
£B&B £12–£16, B&B (double) £20–£30; HB weekly £90–£130; [10% V] **cc** Access, B'card/Visa; dep.

RHAYADER Powys. Map 31B5

Beili Neuadd LD6 5NS ✆(0597) 810211 *Farm.* Mrs Ann Edwards
Sleeps 6, ⯐⏃
£ B&B from £12–£13, D £8·50

RHYDLEWIS Dyfed. Map 31C3

Broniwan, Llandysul, SA44 5PF ✆(023 975) 261 *Farm.* Carole Jacobs
Sleeps 6, ⯐ns ⏃

£ B&B from £13·50, D from £7

RUTHIN Clwyd. Map 30D6

Bryn Awel Bontchel, LL15 2DE ✆(082 42) 2481 *Farm.* Beryl J Jones
Sleeps 5, ⯐⏃
£ B&B from £12, D from £7·50

SENNYBRIDGE Powys. Map 31D5

Brynfedwen Farm Trallong Common, Brecon, LD3 8HW ✆(087482) 505 (changing to (0874) 636505 in Spring 1991) *Farm.* Mrs Mary Adams ♿
Sleeps 6, ⏃
£ B&B from £14, D £6

Llwynneath Farm LD3 8HN ✆(087482) 641 (changing to (0874) 636641 in Spring 1991) *Farm.* Val Williams
Sleeps 5, ⯐⏃
£ B&B from £11

SPITTAL Pembrokeshire. Map 31D1

Lower Haythog Haverfordwest, SA62 5QL ✆(0437) 731279 *Farm.* Nesta Thomas
Sleeps 8, ⯐⏃
£ B&B from £12–£14, D from £7

ST ASAPH Clwyd. Map 30D6

Bach-y-Graig Tremeirchion, LL17 0UH ✆(074 5) 730627 *Farm.* Anwen Roberts
Sleeps 6, ns ⏃
£ B&B from £14, D £7·50

Rhewl Farm Waen, LL17 0DT ✆(0745) 582287 *Farm.* Eirlys Jones
Sleeps 6, ns ⏃
£ B&B from £10–£11, D £6·50

ST CLEARS Dyfed. Map 31D3

Black Lion ✆(0994) 230700. *Characterful old inn on A40. Billiards.*

ST DAVID'S Dyfed. Map 31C1

Alandale 43 Nun St, SA62 6NL ✆(0437) 720333.

Ramsey House Lower Moor, SA62 6RP ✆(0437) 720321. *Small hotel in its own attractive gardens, ½ mile from the town centre on the Porthclais road.*
⊨7 bedrs, 2 en suite, 2 ba; tcf �📺TV, dogs, ns; P9; no children under 5 ✗LD7, nr lunch. Resid & Rest lic
£B&B £15·95–£18·80, B&B (double) £27·60–£33; HB weekly £136·20–£157·20; D £9·70; WB (£40); [5% V Oct–Apr]; dep.

Redcliffe House 17 New St, SA62 6SW ✆(0437) 720389. Open Apr–Oct.

5 bedrs, 2 ba; TV; tcf TV; P 2; no children under 6 Breakfast only. Unlic £ B&B (double) £24.

Y Glennydd 51 Nun St, SA62 6NU (0437) 720576.
Welcoming guest house situated behind the Cathedral, next to the fire station on the one-way system. Open Mar–Dec.
10 bedrs, 3 en suite, 3 ba; TV; tcf TV; coach; child facs LD 8.45, nr lunch, Mon dinner. Rest lic £ B&B £13–£16; HB weekly £150·50–£168; D £9.

SAUNDERSFOOT Dyfed. Map 31E2

Bay View (Acclaimed) Pleasant Valley, Stepaside, SA67 8LR (0834) 813417.
A purpose-built hotel. Turn off A477 for Stepaside, turn left at flats and left again behind flats. Turn left in ⅓ mile at chapel. Swimming pool, putting. Open 1 Apr–Oct.
12 bedrs, 7 en suite, 3 ba; tcf TV; P 14; child facs LD 5, nr lunch. Resid & Rest lic £ B&B £12–£15·95; HB weekly £110–£140; dep.

Gower (Acclaimed) Milford Terr, SA69 9EL (0834) 813452.

Jalna (Acclaimed) Stammers Rd SA69 9HH (0834) 812282.

Small hotel situated on the level, 200 yards from beach and harbour. Follow through village, and turn right at junction past Post Office. Solarium. Closed Nov–Feb.
14 bedrs, 14 en suite; TV; tcf dogs; P 14; child facs LD6, nr lunch. Resid & Rest lic £ B&B £18–£20, B&B (double) £32–£36; HB weekly £142–£167; WB £42; [5% V Mar–May & Sep] **cc** Access, B'card/Visa; dep.

Merlewood (Acclaimed) St Brides Hill, SA69 9NP (0834) 812421.

Woodlands (Acclaimed) St Brides Hill, SA69 9NP (0834) 813338.
A family-run hotel commanding superb views across Carmarthen Bay. Situated on the B4316.
10 bedrs, 10 en suite; TV; tcf TV, ns; P 10, coach; child facs LD 8.30, nr lunch. Resid & Rest lic £ B&B £18, B&B (double) £32–£34; HB weekly £138–£145; WB (£40 2 nights) **cc** Access, B'card/Visa; dep.

Claremont St Brides Hill, SA69 9NP (0834) 813231.

Harbour Light 2 High St, SA69 9EJ (0834) 813496.

Malin House St Brides Hill, SA69 9NP (0834) 812344. *Indoor swimming pool.*
18 bedrs, 18 en suite, 1 ba; TV; tcf TV, ns; P 25, coach; child facs LD7, nr lunch. Resid lic **cc** Access, B'card/Visa.

Sandy Hill Tenby Rd, SA69 9DR (0834) 813165.
Converted farmhouse with a rural outlook. From Kilgetty roundabout take A478 Tenby Rd for 3 miles. Situated on the corner of Sandy Hill. Swimming pool. Open Mar–Sep.

St Clears (Dyfed)

Porthcawl (Mid Glamorgan)

5 bedrs, 2 ba; TV; tcf 🏠dogs; P8; no children under 3 ✗nr lunch. Resid lic
£B&B £12·50; HB weekly £119; [5% V except high season].

Springfield St Brides Hill, SA69 9NP ☎(0834) 813518.
5 bedrs, 2 en suite, 3 ba; tcf 🏠TV, dogs, ns; P6; child facs ✗Breakfast only. Resid lic.

SOLVA Dyfed.　　　　　　　　Map 31D1

Lochmeyler Farm (Highly Acclaimed) Pen-y-Cwm SA62 6LL ☎(0348) 837724.
Farm guest house on working farm 4 miles from Solva Harbour.
6 bedrs, 6 en suite; TV; tcf 🏠dogs; P; no children under 10
£ B&B fr £12; HB weekly £140–£150; [V].

SWANSEA West Glamorgan.　　　Map 31E4

Tredilion House (Highly Acclaimed) 26 Uplands Cres, Uplands, SA2 0PB ☎(0792) 470766.

Late Victorian town house, decorated and furnished in period style. On the main road to Gower (Port Eynon) opposite Upland Post Office behind the trees.
7 bedrs, 7 en suite; TV; tcf 🏠TV, dogs; P8, U 1 (£1); ✗LD noon, nr lunch. Resid lic
£B&B £31–£35, B&B (double) £45–£48; HB weekly £212–£290; D £11; WB £61; [5% V Fri–Sun]
cc Access, B'card/Visa; dep.

Alexander (Acclaimed) 3 Sketty Rd, Uplands, SA2 0EU ☎(0792) 470045.
7 bedrs, 6 en suite, 1 ba; TV; tcf 🏠TV, ns; no children under 2 ✗LD midday, nr Mon–Sat lunch, Sun dinner. Resid lic
cc Access, Amex, B'card/Visa, Diners; dep.

The Guest House (Acclaimed) 4 Bryn Rd, Brynmill, SA2 0AR ☎(0792) 466947.
Situated opposite St Helen's Rugby Ground.
£B&B £10.

Winston (Acclaimed) 11 Church La, Bishopston, SA3 3JT ☎Bishopston (044 128) 2074.
Small hotel in quiet, wooded surroundings. Indoor swimming pool, sauna, solarium, billiards.
19 bedrs, 8 en suite, (8 sh), 2 ba; TV; tcf 🏠TV, dogs; P20, coach; child facs ✗LD7.30, nr lunch. Resid lic

£ B&B £17–£25, B&B (double) £28–£44; D £8
cc Access, B'card/Visa; dep.

Coynant Farm Felindre, SA5 7PU ☎Ammanford (0269) 5640. *Riding.*

Crescent 132 Eaton Cres, Uplands, SA1 4QR ☎(0792) 466814.
Edwardian end-of-terrace house with original features. Set off B4118, first left after St James Church.
7 bedrs, 1 en suite, (4 sh), 1 ba; TV; tcf 🏠TV, dogs, ns; P 4; child facs ✗Breakfast only. Unlic
£B&B £15, B&B (double) £26; dep.

Tregare 9 Sketty Rd, Uplands, SA2 0EU ☎(0792) 470608. *Billiards.*

Uplands Court 134 Eaton Crescent, Uplands, SA1 4QS ☎(0792) 473046.

TALGARTH Powys.　　　　　　Map 31D6

Lodge Farm Brecon, LD3 0DA ☎(0874) 711244
Farm. Mrs Marion Meredith
Sleeps 6, �+ 🛏
£ B&B from £12, D £7

TENBY Dyfed.　　　　　　　　Map 31E2

Harbour Heights (Highly Acclaimed) The Croft, SA70 8AP ☎(0834) 2132.
8 bedrs, 8 en suite; TV; tcf 🏠no children under 8 ✗LD 9.30, nr lunch & Sun dinner. Resid & Rest lic
cc Access, Amex, B'card/Visa, Diners; dep.

Ripley St. Mary's (Acclaimed) St. Mary's St, SA70 7HN ☎(0834) 2837.

Small personally-run hotel 100 yards from seafront. Turn towards the harbour. Open Easter–Oct.
14 bedrs, 8 en suite, 3 ba; TV; tcf 🏠TV, dogs; coach; child facs ✗LD5, nr lunch. Resid lic
£B&B £16–£20; HB weekly £145–£170; [10% V]
cc Access, B'card/Visa; dep.

Tall Ships (Acclaimed) 34 Victoria St, SA70 2DY ☎(0834) 2055.
9 bedrs, 4 en suite, 3 ba; TV; tcf 🏠TV; coach; child facs ✗LD5, nr lunch. Resid lic
cc Access, B'card/Visa; dep.

Castle View   The Norton, SA70 8AA ☎ (0834) 2666.
⋈ 10 bedrs, 10 en suite, 2 ba; TV; tcf ⌂ TV, dogs; P 7; child facs ✗ LD 6.30, nr Sat lunch. Resid lic.

Myrtle House   St Mary's St, SA70 7HW ☎ (0834) 2508.
⋈ 8 bedrs, 5 en suite, 2 ba; TV; tcf ⌂ ns; coach; child facs ✗ LD 4, nr lunch. Resid lic
cc Access, B'card/Visa; dep.

Sea Breezes   18 The Norton, SA70 8AA ☎ (0834) 2753.
⋈ 17 bedrs, 10 en suite, (1 sh), 1 ba; TV; tcf ⌂ TV, ns; coach; child facs ✗ LD 4, nr lunch. Resid lic.

THREE COCKS   Powys.   Map 31C6

Old Gwernyfed Manor (Acclaimed)   Felindre, LD3 0SU ☎ (049 74) 376.

TINTERN   Gwent.   Map 31E8

Parva Farmhouse (Highly Acclaimed)   NP6 6SQ ☎ (0291) 689411.
£ B&B £28–£40; [10% V w/d].

Fountain Inn   Trellech Grange, NP6 6QW ☎ (0291) 689303.
⋈ 5 bedrs, 1 ba; TV; tcf ⌂ dogs; P 40, coach; child facs ✗ LD 10.

TREARDDUR BAY   Gwynedd.   Map 30D3

Highground   Off Ravenspoint Rd, LL65 2YY ☎ (0407) 860078. Closed 16 Dec–4 Jan.
⋈ 6 bedrs, 1 en suite, 2 ba; TV; tcf ⌂ ns; P 7; child facs ✗ LD 3, nr lunch. Resid lic
£ B&B £14·50–£19·50; HB weekly £168–£196; [10% V excl Jul–Sep] **cc** Access, B'card/Visa; dep.

Moranedd   Trearddur Rd, LL65 2UE ☎ (0407) 860324.
⋈ 6 bedrs, 2 ba; tcf ⌂ TV, dogs; P 10; child facs ✗ LD 5, nr lunch. Resid lic
£ B&B £12–£16.

TRECASTLE   Powys.   Map 31D5

Castle (Acclaimed)   Brecon LD3 8UH ☎ Sennybridge (087 482) 354.
⋈ 9 bedrs, 4 en suite, 2 ba; TV; tcf ⌂ dogs, ns; P 40, coach; child facs ✗ LD 9.30 nr lunch, Mon & Sun dinner

£ B&B £29·50–£34, B&B (double) £43–£48; HB weekly £175; L fr £4, D £7·50; WB £27·50; [5% V Oct–Jun] **cc** Access, B'card/Visa.

TREGARON   Dyfed.   Map 31C4

Neuaddlas ☎ (0974) 298905 *Farm*. Margaret Cutter   ⅊
⌂ ☞
£ B&B from £11·50–£14·50, D £6·50

TRETOWER   Powys.   Map 31D6

Tretower Court   NP8 1RF ☎ (0874) 730204.

TYWYN   Gwynedd.   Map 31A4

Arthur (Acclaimed)   Marine Par, LL36 0DE ☎ (0654) 711863.
£ B&B £24; [5% V].

WELSHPOOL   Powys.   Map 31A7

Tynllwyn   SY21 9BW ☎ (0938) 55175/3054.
⋈ 6 bedrs, 2 ba; TV; tcf ⌂ TV, dogs; child facs. ✗ LD 5.30, nr lunch. Resid lic.
£ B&B from £12, D £6·50

Moat Farm   SY21 8SE ☎ (0938) 553179 *Farm*. Gwyneth Jones
Sleeps 6, ☞ ns
£ B&B from £13, D £7

WHITLAND   Dyfed.   Map 31D3

Waungron   SA34 0QX ☎ (0994) 240682. *Inn*.

WOLFSCASTLE   Dyfed.   Map 31C2

Stone Hall (Acclaimed)   Welsh Hook, SA62 5NS ☎ (0348) 840212.

ISLE OF MAN

DOUGLAS   Map 22B2

Hydro   Queen's Promenade. ✆(0624) 76870.

Modwena   39 Loch Promenade ✆(0624) 75728.
⇌34 bedrs, 15 en suite, 6 ba; TV; tcf ᴦᴧlift, TV,
dogs; coach; child facs ✕LD 6.30. Resid lic
cc Access, B'card/Visa; dep.

PORT ERIN   Map 22A2

Regent House (Highly Acclaimed)   Promenade
✆(0624) 833454.

⇌8 bedrs, 6 en suite, 1 ba; TV; tcf ᴦᴧNS; child
facs ✕LD7, nr lunch. Unlic

RAMSEY   Map 22B3

Sulby Glen   ✆(0624) 897240. *Inn.*
⇌12 bedrs, 2 en suite, 2 ba; tcf
ᴦᴧTV; P30, U1, coach; child facs ✕LD8.30.

Sulby (Isle of Man)

Sulby Glen Hotel

Sulby, Isle of Man.   Telephone (0624) 89 7240

Proprietor: Rosemary Sayle

Situated on famous TT course, 3 miles from Ramsey. Ideal centre for shopping, business, golf or fishing. Open all year. Some rooms en-suite, own car park.

CHANNEL ISLANDS

GUERNSEY

CASTEL

Le Galaad (Acclaimed)   Rue des Francais ✆(0481)
57233. *Hotel. Putting.* Open Mar–Oct.
⇌12 bedrs, 12 en suite; TV; tcf ᴦᴧns; P14; child
facs ✕LD 6, nr lunch. Resid lic.

Wayside Cheer   Grandes Rocques ✆(0481)
57290. *Swimming pool.*
⇌33 bedrs, 20 en suite; 4 ba; tcf ᴦᴧ TV, dogs;
P30, coach; child fac ✕ LD7, bar meals only lunch

L'ANCRESSE

Lynton Park (Highly Acclaimed)   Hacse La
✆(0481) 45418. *Hotel. Putting.*
⇌15 bedrs, 14 en suite, 2 ba; TV; tcf ᴦᴧTV; P30,
coach; no children under 5 ✕LD9.15, bar meals
only Mon–Sat lunch. Resid & Rest lic
£B&B £28–£35·50; HB weekly £188·50–£238
cc Access, Amex, B'card/Visa, Diners; dep.

ST PETER PORT

Midhurst House (Highly Acclaimed)   Candie Rd
✆(0481) 24391.

⇌8 bedrs, 8 en suite; TV; tcf ᴦᴧU; no children
under 8 ✕LD7, nr lunch. Rest lic.

ST SAMPSONS

Ann-Dawn (Acclaimed)   Route des Capelles
✆(0481) 25606. *Private Hotel.*
£ B&B £17–£22; HB weekly £157·–£171·50; [5% V]

ST SAVIOURS

La Girouette Country House (Highly Acclaimed)
La Girouette ☎(0481) 63269 Fax: (0481) 63023.

🛏14 bedrs, 12 en suite; 1 ba; TV 🛗ns; P 20, coach;
no children under 5 ✗LD 7.30, nr Mon–Sat lunch.
Resid & Rest lic
£ B&B £18–£39; [10% V] **cc** Access, Amex,
B'card/Visa, dep.

JERSEY

BEAUMONT

Bryn-y-Mor Ronte de la Haule ☎(0534) 20295
Tx: 4192638 Fax: (05324) 35231

ST HELIER

Runnymede Court (Highly Acclaimed) 46
Roseville St, ☎(0534) 20044.

🛏57 bedrs, 57 en suite; 2 ba; TV; tcf 🛗lift, TV;
coach; no children under 3 ✗LD 7.30, nr lunch.
Resid lic
cc Access, B'card/Visa; dep.

Cornucopia (Acclaimed) Mont Pinel ☎(0534)
32646.
Well-equipped hotel with superb views.

Millbrook House (Acclaimed) Rue de Trachy,
Millbrook ☎(0534) 33036.
Peaceful period house in lovely gardens.
🛏27 bedrs, 27 en suite, 1 ba; TV; tcf 🛗TV, ns; P 20;
child facs ✗LD 7, nr lunch. Resid lic.

ST OUEN

Hotel des Pierres (Highly Acclaimed) Greve de
Lecq Bay ☎(0534) 81858 Fax: (0534) 85273. Open
Mar–Dec. ✗ Fr, De.
£ B&B £23–£28; HB weekly £175–£231.

ST PETER'S

Midvale St Peter's Valley ☎(0534) 42498.

ST SAVOURS

Willows Grand Vaux ☎(0534) 37267.

NORTHERN IRELAND

AGHADOWEY Co Londonderry. Map 32c4

Greenhill House 24 Greenhill Road, Coleraine,
BT51 4EU ✆(0265) 868241 *Farm.* Mrs Elizabeth
Hegarty
Sleeps 14, ᛧ ⛺
£ B&B from £16·50, D £10

Inchadoghill House 196 Agivey Road,
Coleraine, BT51 4AD ✆(0265) 868250/868232
Farm. Mamie and Ann McIlroy
Sleeps 6, ⛺
£ B&B from £12, D £6

AHOGHILL Co Antrim. Map 32C7

Neelsgrove Farm, 51 Carnearney Road,
Ballymena, BT42 2PL ✆(0266) 871225 *Farm.* Mrs
Margaret Neely
Sleeps 3, ᛧ ⛺
£ B&B from £12, D £6–£8

ANNACLONE Co Down. Map 32F7

The Moor Lodge 20 Ballynafern Road,
Banbridge, BT32 5AE ✆(08206) 71516 *Farm.*
Brigid and Jim McClory
Sleeps 9, ᛧ ⛺
£ B&B from £10·50, D £6

ARDKEEN Co Down. Map 32E8

Millview Farm 8 Abbacy Road, Newtownards,
BT22 1HH ✆(02477) 28030 *Farm.* Rachel Birch
Sleeps 4, ⛺
£ B&B from £10, D £6

ARMAGH Co Armagh. Map 32F6

Victoria Cloughfin, BT61 8HB ✆(0861) 525925
Farm. May Hanson
Sleeps 6, ᛧ ⛺
£ B&B from £11

BALLYGAWLEY Co Tyrone. Map 32E5

The Grange 15 Grange Road ✆(066 253) 8053/
266 *Farm.* Mrs Ella Lyttle
Sleeps 8, ᛧ ⛺
£ B&B from £10·50, D £6–£8

BALLYMARTIN Co Down. Map 32E8

Ashcroft 12 Ballykeel Road, Kilkeel, BT34 4PL
✆(06937) 62736
Farm. Esther Orr

Sleeps 9, ⛺
£ B&B from £10·50, D £5·50

Sharon Farmhouse, 6 Ballykeel Road, BT34 4PL
✆(06937) 62521
Farm. M. Bingham ♿
Sleeps 7, ᛧ ns ⛺
£ B&B from £10–£11, D £6

BALLYMENA Co Antrim. Map 32C7

Elm Tree House 62 Old Tullygarley Road
✆(0266) 48461 *Farm.* Heather Edmondson
Sleeps 6, ᛧ ⛺
£ B&B from £11, D £5

BALLYMONEY Co Antrim. Map 32C6

Ballynagashel House 30 Cregagh Road, BT53
8JN ✆(026 56) 41366 *Farm.* Mrs Barbara
Kirkpatrick
£ B&B from £12·50

Country Guest House 41 Kirk Road, BT53 8HB
✆(02656) 62620 *Farm.* Dorothy Brown ♿
Sleeps 8, ᛧ ⛺
£ B&B from £11, D £5

BALLYNAHINCH Co Down. Map 32D8

Cornerhouse 182 Dunmore Road, BT24 8QQ
✆(0238) 562670 *Farm.* Mrs Mary Rogan
Sleeps 6, ᛧ ⛺
£ B&B from £11, D £6–£8

BALLYNURE Co Antrim. Map 32D8

Farmhouse 98 Carrickfergus Road, Ballyclare,
BT39 9QP ✆(096 03) 52092 *Farm.* Mrs Mildred
Crawford
Sleeps 4
£ B&B £10·50

BALLYWALTER Co Down. Map 32E8

Greenlea Farm 48 Dunover Road, Newtownards,
BT22 2LE ✆(02477) 58218 *Farm.* Evelyn McIvor
Sleeps 10/12, ᛧ ⛺
£ B&B from £11, D £4·50–£6

BELLANALECK Co Fermanagh. Map 32E3

Broadmeadows Guest House Cleenish Island
Road, Enniskillen ✆(036582) 395 *Farm.* Liliann
McKibbin ♿
Sleeps 6, ᛧ ns ⛺
£ B&B from £11–£12, D £7

BELLARENA   Co Londonderry.   Map 32C5

Ballycarton Farm   Limavady, BT49 0HZ
☎(05047) 50216   *Farm*. Mrs Emma Craig
Sleeps 12, 🏠 🐕
£ B&B from £11, D from £6

BLANEY   Co Fermanagh.   Map 32E3

Lakeview Farm Guest House   Drumcrow,
Enniskillen ☎(036 564) 263   *Farm*. Mrs Jason
Hassard
Sleeps 12, 🐕
£ B&B from £11–£12, D £6–£8

Lough Erne House   St Catherines, Enniskillen
☎(036 564) 216   *Farm*. Mrs Hannah Bruce
Sleeps 8, 🏠
£ B&B £11

BOARDMILLS   Co Antrim.   Map 32E7

Bresagh Farm, 55 Bresagh Road, Lisburn, BT27
6TU ☎(0846) 638316   *Farm*. Mrs Elsie Girvin
Sleeps 4, ns 🐕 (12)
£ B&B from £12

BUNCRANA ROAD   Co Londonderry.
Map 32C4

Elagh Hall   ☎(0504) 263116   *Farm*. Elizabeth
Buchanan
Sleeps 9, 🏠 🐕
£ B&B from £11

BUSHMILLS   Co Antrim.   Map 32B6

Carnside Farm Guest House   23 Causeway
Road, Giants Causeway, BT57 8SU ☎(02657)
31337   *Farm*. Frances Lynch
Sleeps 15, 🏠 🐕
£ B&B from £11–£12, D £6·50–£7

Farmhouse   46 Castlecatt Road, BT57 8TN ☎(026
57) 31359   *Farm*. Mrs Kathleen Richmond
Sleeps 6
£ B&B £11

Hillcrest Country House   306 Whitepark Road,
BT57 8SN ☎(02657) 31577   *Farm*. M. C. McKeever
Sleeps 8, 🐕
£ B&B from £17·50, D from £8

Montalto Guest House   5 Craigaboney Road,
BT57 8XD ☎(02657) 31257   *Farm*. Mrs Dorothy
Taggart
Sleeps 6, 🏠 🐕
£ B&B from £13, D £8

White Gables   83 Dunluce Road, BT57 8SJ ☎(026
57) 31611   *Farm*. Mrs Ria Johnston
Sleeps 6, 🐕 (6)
£ B&B from £16, D £9

CARRICK FERGUS   Co Antrim.   Map 32D8

Beechgrove   412 Upper Road, Trooperslane,
BT38 8PW ☎(09603) 63304   *Farm*. Betta Barron
Sleeps 8, 🏠 🐕   ♿
5 B&B from £10·50; D £5

CARROWDORE   Co Down.   Map 32E8

Ernsdale   120 Mountstewart Road, Newtownards,
BT22 2ES ☎(0247) 861208   *Farm*. Dot McCullagh
Sleeps 6, 🏠 🐕
£ B&B from £11, D £7

CASTLEROCK   Co Londonderry.   Map 32C5

Carneety House   120 Mussenden Road, BT51
4TX ☎(0265) 848640   *Farm*. Mrs Carol Henry
Sleeps 6, 🏠 🐕
£ B&B from £12, D from £6

CHURCHILL   Co Fermanagh.   Map 32E3

Bayview Guest House   Tully, Enniskillen, BT74
7BW ☎(036564) 250   *Farm*. Mrs Dorothy Hassard
Sleeps 9, 🏠 ns 🐕
£ B&B from £10·50, D from £5

CLOUGHMILLS   Co Antrim.   Map 32C7

Breezemount   27 Ballylig Road, Dunloy,
Ballymena, BT44 9DS ☎(026563) 468   Mrs May
O'Mullan
Sleeps 6, 🐕
£ B&B from £11, D £6–£8

COLERAINE   Co Londonderry.   Map 32B6

Ballywatt   174 Ballybogey Road, BT52 2LP
☎(02657) 31627   *Farm*. Jean Brown   ♿
Sleeps 15, ns 🐕
£ B&B from £12, D £6

Camus House   27 Curragh Road, BT51 3RY
☎(0265) 42982   *Farm*. Mrs Josephine King
Sleeps 6, 🐕
£ B&B from £12·50–£15, D £8·50

Killeague House   Blackhill, BT51 4HJ ☎(0265)
868229   *Farm*. Margaret Moore
Sleeps 6, ns 🐕
£ B&B from £12, D £6

Traditional Farmhouse   31 Ballylagan Road,
BT52 2PQ ☎(0265) 822487   *Farm*. Mrs Joyce Lyons
Sleeps 6
£ B&B from £12

COMBER   Co Down.   Map 32E8

Trench Farm   35 Ringcreevy Road,
Newtownards, BT23 5JR ☎(0247) 872558   *Farm*.
Maureen Hamilton
Sleeps 6, 🐕
£ B&B from £12

COOKSTOWN Co Tyrone.   Map 32D6

The Piper's Cave 38 Cady Road ☎(06487)
63615 Mrs Jean Warnock
Sleeps 9, ⊩ ﹋
£ B&B from £11, D £6–£8

CRAIGAVON Co Armagh.   Map 32F6

Ivanhoe 10 Valley Lane, Waringtown, BT66 7SR
☎(0762) 881287 *Farm*. Mrs F Dewart
Sleeps 5/6, ﹋
£ B&B from £10, D from £2·50

CRANAGH Co Tyrone.   Map 32D4

New Chalet Farmhouse 254 Glenelly Road,
Omagh, BT79 8LS ☎(06626) 48334 *Farm*. Mr and
Mrs B Conway   &
Sleeps 8, ns ﹋
£ B&B from £10, D £5–£7

CRUMLIN Co Antrim.   Map 32E7

Crossroads 1 Largy Road ☎(08494) 52491/
52259 *Farm*. William and Vanessa Lorimer
Sleeps 8, ⊩ ﹋
£ B&B from £12, D £8

Hillvale Farm 11 Largy Road, BT29 4AH
☎(08494) 22768 *Farm*. Mrs Eileen Duncan
Sleeps 6, ⊩ ﹋
£ B&B from £12, D £6–£8

CULKY Co Fermanagh.   Map 32E3

Riverside Gortadrehid, Enniskillen ☎(0365)
22725 *Farm*. Mrs Mary Fawcett
Sleeps 12, ﹋
£B&B from £11·50–£12·50, D £7–£8

CUSHENDUN Co Antrim.   Map 32B8

The Villa 185 Torr Road, BT44 0PU ☎(026 674)
252 *Farm*. Mrs Catherine Scally
Sleeps 16, ⊩ ﹋
£ B&B from £11, D £6–£8

DONAGHADEE Co Down.   Map 32D9

Bridge House 93 Windmill Road, BT21 0NQ
☎(0247) 883348 *Farm*. Florence Logan
Sleeps 6, ﹋
£ B&B from £12

DOWNPATRICK Co Down.   Map 32F8

Havine Farm Guest House 51 Bally Donnell
Road, BT30 8EP ☎(039685) 242 *Farm*. Mrs Myrtle
Macauley
Sleeps 6, ⊩ ﹋
£ B&B from £11, D £4.50–£5·50

DROMORE Co Down.   Map 32E7

Sylvan Hill House 76 Kilntown Road, BT25 1HS
☎(0846) 692321 *Farm*. Mrs J Coburn
Sleeps 14, ⊩ ﹋
£ B&B from £14

The Maggimin 11 Bishopswell Road, BT25 1ST
☎(0846) 693520 *Farm*. Wilson and Rhoda Mark
Sleeps 8, ﹋
£ B&B from £12–£14, D £6–£8

Win-Staff 45 Banbridge Road, BT25 1NE
☎(0846) 692252 *Farm*. Mrs Esther Erwin
Sleeps 6, ⊩ ﹋
£ B&B from £12, D from £8·50

DRUMAHOE Co Londonderry.   Map 32C5

Killenan House 40 Killenan Road, BT47 3NG
☎(0504) 301710 *Farm*. Mrs Averil Campbell
Sleeps 10, ⊩ ﹋
£ B&B from £11, D £6–£8

DUNGANNON Co Tyrone.   Map 32E6

Creevagh Lodge Carland, BT70 3LQ ☎(086 87)
61342 *Farm*. Mr and Mrs Gilmour Nelson
Sleeps 16, ⊩ ﹋
£ B&B from £12, D £6–£8

Farm Bungalow Cohannon, 225 Ballynakelly
Road, BT71 6HJ ☎(08687) 23156 *Farm*. Jean
Currie
Sleeps 4, ⊩ ns ﹋
£ B&B from £10, D £6

Grange Lodge 7 Grange Road, BT71 7EJ
☎(08687) 84212/22458 *Farm*. Norah Brown
Sleeps 6, ⊩ ns ﹋(10)
£ B&B from £17·50, D £14

ENNISKILLEN Co Fermanagh.   Map 32E3

Dunrovin Skea, Arney ☎(036 582) 354 *Farm*.
Mrs Catherine Harron
Sleeps 8, ⊩ ﹋
£ B&B from £10–£12, D from £6

Lackaboy Farm Guest House Tempo Road,
BT74 6HR ☎(0365) 22488 *Farm*. Elma Noble
Sleeps 20, ⊩ ns ﹋
£ B&B from £12, D £6·50

FIVEMILETOWN Co Fermanagh.   Map 32E4

Al-Di-Gwyn Lodge 103 Clabby Road, BT75 0QY
☎(0365) 521298 *Farm*. Vera Gilmore   &
Sleeps 25, ⊩ ﹋
£ B&B from £12–£14, D £5–£8

FLORENCECOURT Co Fermanagh.
Map 32F3

Tullyhona House ✆(036 582) 452 *Farm*. Mrs
Rosemary Armstrong &
Sleeps 17, ⛺
£ B&B from £11, D £6–£8

GARVAGH Co Londonderry Map 32C6

Heathfield 31 Drumcroon Road, BT51 4EB
✆(026 65) 58245 *Farm*. Mrs Heather Torrens
Sleeps 4, ⛺⛺
£ B&B from £12

GLENARIFFE Co Antrim. Map 32B7

Dieskirt Farmhouse 104 Glen Road, BT44 0RG
✆(02667) 71308/71796 *Farm*. James and Kathleen
McHenry
Sleeps 10, ⛺
£ B&B from £9, D £6–£8

GLENAVY Co Antrim. Map 32E7

Ashmore 64 Main Street, Crumlin, BT29 4LP
✆(08494) 22773 *Farm*. Mrs Moira McClure
Sleeps 4, ⛺⛺
£ B&B from £10·50, D £6–£8

GORTACLARE Co Tyrone. Map 32D4

Greenmount Lodge 58 Greenmount Road,
Omagh, BT79 0YE ✆(0662) 841325 *Farm*. Mrs F
Louie Reid
Sleeps 15, ⛺ ns ⛺
£ B&B from £10·50–£11, D £7·50

GREYABBEY Co Down. Map 32E8

Abbey Farm 17 Ballywater Road, Newtownards,
BT22 2RF ✆(024774) 207 *Farm*. Mabel Hall
Sleeps 6, ⛺⛺
£ B&B from £10·50, D £6

Gordonall 93 Newtownards Road, Newtownards,
BT22 2QJ ✆(024774) 325 *Farm*. Billy and Angela
Martin
Sleeps 5, ⛺⛺
£ B&B from £10·50

HELEN'S BAY Co Down. Map 32D8

Carrig Gorm 27 Bridge Road, Bangor, BT19 1TS
✆(0247) 853680 *Farm*. Mrs Elizabeth Eves
Sleeps 6, ⛺ ns ⛺
£ B&B from £15

ISLANDMAGEE Co Antrim. Map 32D8

Hillview 30 Middle Road, Larne, BT40 3SL
✆(09603) 72581 *Farm*. Mrs Maureen Reid
Sleeps 6

£ B&B from £11–£13

KILKEEL Co Down. Map 32G7

Carginagh Lodge 195 Carginagh Road, Silent
Valley, BT34 4QA ✆(06937) 62085 *Farm*. Mrs Stella
Stronge
Sleeps 6, ⛺⛺
£ B&B from £9, D £6

Heath Hall 160 Moyadd Road, BT34 4HJ
✆(06937) 62612 *Farm*. Marie McGlue
Sleeps 8, ⛺⛺
£ B&B from £10·50, D £5–£6

Morne Abbey Guest House 16 Greencastle
Road, BT34 4DE ✆(06937) 62426 *Farm*. Annabel
Shannon
Sleeps 13, ns ⛺(1)
£ B&B from £11·50, D £7

Wyncrest 30 Main Road, Ballymartin, BT34 4NU
✆(06937) 63012 *Farm*. Mrs Irene Adair
Sleeps 10, ⛺
£ B&B from £13·50, D from £8·50

KILLADEAS Co Fermanagh. Map 32D3

Brindley Guest House Tully, Enniskillen
✆(03656) 28065 *Farm*. Olive and Deane Flood &
Sleeps 15, ⛺⛺
£ B&B from £12, D £8

Trevenna Enniskillen ✆(03656) 21500 *Farm*.
Bob and Evelyn Crowys
Sleeps 6
£ B&B from £10·50

KILLYLEA Co Armagh. Map 32E6

Heimat Polnagh Road, BT60 4NW ✆(0861)
568661 *Farm*. Doris McLoughlin
Sleeps ? ?, ⛺⛺
£ B&B from £10·50

LIMAVADY Co Londonderry. Map 32C5

Ballyhenry House 172 Seacoast Road, BT49
9EF ✆(05047) 22657 *Farm*. Mrs Rosemary Kane
Sleeps 8, ⛺
£ B&B from £12, D £6–£8

The Poplars 352 Seacoast Road, BT49 0LA
✆(050 47) 50360 *Farm*. Mrs H McCracken
Sleeps 10, ⛺⛺
£ B&B from £12, D £5

Whitehill 70 Ballyquin Road, BT49 9EY ✆(050 47)
22306 *Farm*. Mrs Maud McCormick
£ B&B from £11

LISBELLAW Co Fermanagh. Map 32E3

Aghnacarra House Carrybridge ✆(0365) 87077
Mrs Norma Ensor

Sleeps 17, ㄡ
£ B&B from £11–£12, D £5–£6

Mullaghkippin Farm   Derryharney, Enniskillen
☎(0365) 87419   *Farm*. Mrs Hazel Johnston
Sleeps 4
£ B&B £10–£11

Wilner Lodge   Carrybridge Road ☎(0365) 87045/
87522   *Farm*. Mrs Margaret Mulligan
Sleeps 8
£ B&B £9·50

LISBURN   Co Down.   Map 32E7

Brook Lodge   79 Old Ballynahinch Road, BT27
6TH ☎(0846) 638454   *Farm*. Mrs Dulibel Moore
Sleeps 8, ⚲ ns ㄡ
£ B&B from £12–£13, D £5

LISNASKEA   Co Fermanagh.   Map 32E4

Colorado House   102 Lisnagole Road ☎(03657)
21486   *Farm*. John and Eileen Scott
Sleeps 18, ⚲
£ B&B from £10–£12, D from £6

Mallard House   Drumany, BT92 0EU ☎(036 57)
21491   *Farm*. Mrs Jean McVitty
Sleeps 8, ㄡ
£ B&B from £10·50, D £6–£8

MOY   Co Tyrone.   Map 32E6

Muleany House   86 Gorestown Road, BT71 7EX
☎(08687) 84183   *Farm*. Mrs Mary Mullen
Sleeps 14, ⚲ ㄡ
£ B&B from £12, D £6–£8

MUCKAMORE   Co Antrim.   Map 32D7

The Old School House   106 Ballyrobin Road,
BT41 4TF ☎(08494) 28209   *Farm*. Jim and
Margaret Kelly   ♿
Sleeps 8, ⚲ ㄡ
♿**£** B&B from £12, D £7·50

NEWCASTLE   Co. Down.   Map 32B8

Brook Cottage (Acclaimed)   58 Bryansford Rd,
BT33 0LD ☎(039 67) 22204.
*Small but well-equipped hotel. Turn right at the end
of Main Street, Bryansford Road is on the left.
Snooker.*
⇔8 bedrs, 5 en suite, 2 ba; tcf ⌂TV; P 50, coach;
child facs ✗LD 9
cc Access, B'card/Visa, Diners; dep.

Maple Leaf Cottage   169 Bryansford Road ☎(039
67) 23500   *Farm*. Mr & Mrs Ronald Martin
Sleeps 7
£ B&B from £13

Old Town Farm   25 Corrigs Road, BT33 0JZ
☎(03967) 22740   *Farm*. Mrs Cissie Annett
Sleeps 6, ㄡ
£ B&B from £11, D from £6

NEWRY   Co Down.   Map 32F7

Ashton House   Omeath Road, Fathom Line
☎(0693) 62120   *Farm*. Mrs Bridget Heaney
£ B&B from £12

NEWTOWNARDS   Co Down.   Map 32E8

Ballycastle House   20 Mountstewart Road, BT22
2AL ☎(024774) 357   *Farm*. Margaret Deering
Sleeps 6, ⚲ ns ㄡ
£ B&B from £12·50

Beechill   Loughries Road, BT23 3RN ☎(0247)
817526   *Farm*. Mrs Joan McKee
Sleeps 6, ⚲ ㄡ
£ B&B from £12, D £8–£10

Brackney House   2 Green Road, Conlig, BT23
3PZ ☎(0247) 461423   *Farm*. Mrs Ann Thompson
Sleeps 8, ⚲ ㄡ
£ B&B from £13, D £6–£8

Burnside   26 Ballyblack Road, BT22 2AP ☎(0247)
812920   *Farm*. Mrs Jean Bartholomew
Sleeps 5, ⚲ ns ㄡ
£ B&B from £10, D from £6

Cuan Chalet   41 Milecross Road, BT23 4SR
☎(0247) 812302   *Farm*. Mrs Winifred Cochrane
Sleeps 4,
£ B&B from £12, D £6

Green Acres   5 Manse Road, BT23 4TP ☎(0247)
816 193   *Farm*. Mrs Dorothy Long
Sleeps 10,
£ B&B from £12·50, D £6–£8

PORTADOWN   Co Armagh.   Map 32E6

Greenacres   57 Red Lion Road ☎(0762) 352610
Farm. Florence Hampton
Sleeps 6, ⚲ ㄡ
£ B&B from £10

PORTBALLINTRAE   Co Antrim.   Map 32B6

Kenban   55 Bayhead Road, BT57 8SA ☎(026 57)
31534   *Farm*. Mrs Elizabeth Morgan
Sleeps 6,
£ B&B £12·50

PORTBRADDAN   Co Antrim.   Map 32B6

Danescroft   171 Whitepark Road, Bushmills,
BT57 8SS ☎(0267) 31586   *Farm*. Mrs Olga
Rutherford
⚲ ㄡ
£ B&B from £13–£15, D £7–£9

PORTRUSH Co Antrim. Map 32B6

Ardnaree 105 Dunluce Road, White Rocks, BT56 8NB ✆ (0265) 823407 *Farm.* Elsie Rankin
Sleeps 6, 🐴 ns ☎ (5)
£ B&B from £12·50–£13·50

Ballymagarry County House Leeke Road, BT56 8NH ✆ (0265) 823737 *Farm.* Mrs Alyson Leckey
£ B&B from £13·50

Islay-View 36 Leeke Road, Off Ballymagary Road, BT56 8NH ✆ (0265) 823220 *Farm.* Eileen Smith &
Sleeps 6, 🐴 ☎
£ B&B from £11·50

Loguestown Farm 59 Magheraboy Road, BT56 8NY ✆ (0265) 822742 *Farm.* Mrs Mary Adams
Sleeps 18, 🐴 ☎
£ B&B from £10·50, D £6–£8

Maddybenny Farmhouse 18 Maddybenny Park, Off Loguestown Road, BT52 2PT ✆ (0265) 823394
Farm. Rosemary White
Sleeps 6, 🐴 ☎
£ B&B from £12·50–£16

PORTSTEWART Co Londonderry. Map 32B6

118 Station Road BT55 7PU ✆ (0265 83) 2826
Farm. Mrs Vi Anderson
Sleeps 10, 🐴 ☎
£ B&B from £12–£15, D £6–£8

RATHFRILAND Co Down. Map 32F7

Rathglen Villa 7 Hilltown Road, BT34 5NA ✆ (08206) 38090 *Farm.* Mrs Madge Maginn
Sleeps 10, ☎
£ B&B from £11, D £7

STRABANE Co Tyrone. Map 32C4

Country House 38 Leckpatrick Road, Artigarvan, BT82 0HB ✆ (0504) 882714 *Farm.* Mrs Jean Ballantine
Sleeps 5, 🐴 ☎
£ B&B £10

STRAID Co Antrim. Map 32D8

Cairnview 69 Irish Road, Ballyclare, BT39 9NJ ✆ (09603) 52607 *Farm.* Mrs Jenny Bradford
Sleeps 6, 🐴 ☎
£ B&B from £10·50, D £5·50

TEMPLEPATRICK Co Antrim. Map 32D7

Toberagnee Farm, 54 Lylehill Road, BT39 0ES ✆ (08494) 32389 *Farm.* Mr and Mrs W. D. Hyde
Sleeps 6, 🐴 ☎
£ B&B from £12

WARRENPOINT Co Down. Map 32G7

Fern-Hill House 90 Clonallon Road, BT34 3QR ✆ (069 37) 72677 *Farm.* Pat and Patricia McCullough
£ B&B from £12

REPUBLIC OF IRELAND

The RAC does not currently inspect hotels in the Republic of Ireland. For the convenience of readers, and in order to make the Guide as comprehensive as possible, we include selected bed and breakfast accommodation throughout the Republic which has been visited and approved by Bord Fáilte. These premises are divided into Town, Country and Farm houses. Many will provide an evening meal, usually dinner but occasionally high tea, if notice is given.

Prices given for hotels in the Republic of Ireland are shown in Irish pounds (punts) and are those charged in 1990. Prices for 1991 may have increased.

ACHILL ISLAND Co. Mayo.

Mrs K. Sweeney Aquila, Sraheens ✆(098) 45163. *Country*. Open May–Sep
⇔4 bedrs, 2 en suite
£ B&B IR£12–£13

ADARE Co. Limerick.

Mrs M. Dundon Abbey Villa, Kildimo Rd ✆(061) 86113. *Town*.
⇔6 bedrs, 6 en suite
£ B&B IR£15·50

Mrs K. Glavin Castleview, Clonshire More, Croagh ✆(061) 86394. *Country*.
⇔4 bedrs, 3 en suite
£ B&B IR£15–£16; D IR£9·50

ADRIGOLE Co. Cork.

Mrs J. Crowley Forthill House ✆(027) 60034. *Farm*. Open Jun–Sep.
⇔5 bedrs
£ B&B (double) IR£20

ANNAGHDOWN Co. Galway.

Scott Family Corrib View Farm ✆(091) 91114. *Farm*. Open 15 Apr–15 Sep.
⇔4 bedrs, 1 en suite
£ B&B (double) IR£24–£29; D IR£12·50

ARDARA Co. Donegal.

Mr & Mrs M. Bennett Bayview Country House, Portnoo Rd ✆(075) 41145. *Country*. Open 1 Mar–15 Nov.
⇔7 bedrs, 7 en suite
£ B&B (double) IR£23; D IR£10

Vincent & Susan McConnell Rose Wood Country House, Killybegs Rd ✆(075) 41168. *Country*. Open 1 Mar–31 Oct.
⇔3 bedrs, 3 en suite
£ B&B IR£15, B&B (double) IR£23

ARKLOW Co. Wicklow.

Mrs A. Nuzum Ballykilty House, Coolgreany ✆(0402) 7111. *Farm*. Tennis. Open Mar–Oct.
⇔6 bedrs, 4 en suite
£ B&B IR£13–£15; D IR£10·50

ATHLONE Co. Westmeath.

Mrs N. Denby Shelmalier House, Cartrontroy, Retreat Rd ✆(0902) 72245. *Town*.
⇔7 bedrs, 6 en suite; tcf
£ B&B IR£15; D IR£10

BALLINA Co. Mayo.

Mrs M. Dempsey Whitestream House, Foxford Rd ✆(096) 21582. *Town*. Open Jan–Nov.
⇔6 bedrs, 5 en suite
£ B&B IR£13, B&B (double) IR£21–£23; D IR£10·50
cc B'card/Visa.

Mrs M O'Dowd Cnoc Breandain, Quay Rd ✆(096) 22145. *Country*. Open 1 May–30 Sep.
⇔4 bedrs, 3 en suite
£ B&B IR£13, B&B (double) IR£22; D IR£10

BALLINAKILL Co. Laois.

Mrs A. Dowling The Glebe. ✆(0502) 33368. *Country*. *Fishing*.
⇔4 bedrs
£ B&B (double) IR£32; D IR£15

BALLINAMORE Co. Leitrim.

Thomas Family Riversdale. ✆(078) 44122. *Farm*. *Fishing, indoor swimming pool, sauna, squash*.
⇔6 bedrs
£ B&B (double) IR£18; D IR£9

BALLYCONNEELY Co. Galway.

Mrs. C. Joyce Teach an Easard ✆(095) 23560. *Country*.
⇔4 bedrs, 4 en suite
£ B&B IR£26; D £11

BALLYSHANNON Co. Donegal.

Mrs R. McCaffrey Ardpatton House, Cavan Garden ✆ (072) 51546. *Farm. Riding.*
5 bedrs, 1 en suite
£ B&B IR£15, B&B (double) IR£24–£27; D IR£12
cc Access, B'card/Visa.
Mrs M.T. McGee Killeadan, Bundoran Rd ✆ (072) 51377 Fax: (072) 51207 *Country.* Open 1 Jun–31 Jul.
4 bedrs, 3 en suite
£ B&B IR£13–£14·50, B&B (double) IR£22–£25

BANDON Co. Cork.

Mrs E. Stone Milton House ✆ (023) 41388. *Farm.* Open Easter–Sep.
6 bedrs
£ B&B IR£20; D IR£9·50

BANTRY Co. Cork.

Mrs K. O'Donovan Ashling House, Cahir ✆ (027) 50616. *Country.* Open 1 Apr–15 Oct.
4 bedrs, 2 en suite
£ B&B IR£13·50–£15·50, B&B (double) £21–£25; D IR£10·50

BLARNEY Co. Cork.

Callaghan Family Ashlee Lodge, Tower ✆ (021) 385346. *Country.* Open Apr–Oct.
5 bedrs, 4 en suite
£ B&B (double) IR£22–£30

BLESSINGTON Co. Wicklow.

Miss E. Beattie Elbrook Manor, Kilbride ✆ (01) 582418. *Country.*
3 bedrs, 1 en suite
£ B&B (double) IR£20–£22; D IR£10

BOYLE Co. Roscommon.

Mrs E. Kelly Forest Park House, Carrick-on-Shannon Rd ✆ (079) 62227. *Country.*
8 bedrs, 4 en suite.
£ B&B (double) IR£21–£24; D IR£9·50
Mr & Mrs Mitchell Abbey House ✆ (079) 62385
6 bedrs, 5 en suite
£ B&B IR£13, B&B (double) IR£22–£24; D IR£10

BROADFORD Co. Clare.

Mrs N. O'Donnell Lake View House, Doon Lake ✆ (061) 73125
3 bedrs
£ B&B (double) IR£22

BRITTAS BAY Co. Wicklow.

Mrs P. Tighe Parkwood House, Jack White's Cross ✆ (0404) 7221. *Country.* Open Mar–31 Oct.
5 bedrs, 1 en suite
£ B&B IR£15–£19, B&B (double) IR£22–£25; D IR£10

BRUCKLESS Co. Donegal.

Mrs J. Evans Bruckless House ✆ (073) 37071. *Farm. Fishing.* Open Apr–Sep
5 bedrs
£ B&B IR£15; D IR£18

BRUREE Co. Limerick.

Mrs E. McDonogh Cooleen House ✆ (063) 90584. *Farm. Fishing.* Open May–Sep
4 bedrs
£ B&B (double) IR£22; D IR£11

BUNRATTY Co. Clare.

Mrs M. Browne Bunratty Lodge ✆ (061) 72402. *Country*
9 bedrs, 9 en suite
£ B&B IR£17, B&B (double) IR£26
Mrs M. Whyte Palm Lodge, Hurlers Cross ✆ (061) 364682. *Country.* Open Apr–Oct
5 bedrs, 5 en suite
£ B&B IR£14, B&B (double) IR£22

BURREN Co. Clare.

Mrs A. Martin Villa Maria, Leagh South ✆ (065) 78019. *Country.* Open 1 Feb–30 Nov.
5 bedrs, 3 en suite
£ B&B IR£13–£15, B&B (double) £21–£23; D IR£9·

BUTLERS BRIDGE Co. Cavan.

Mrs P. Mundy Ford House, Deredis ✆ (049) 31427. *Farm.* Open May–1 Oct.
6 bedrs
£ B&B IR£10; D IR£9.

CAHIR Co. Tipperary.

Butler Family Carrigeen Castle, Cork Rd ✆ (052) 41370. *Country.*
6 bedrs, 1 en suite
£ B&B IR£12·50; HT IR£9
Mrs B. Fitzgerald Ashling, Dublin Rd ✆ (052) 41601. *Country.*
5 bedrs, 3 en suite
£ B&B IR£16

CAHIRCIVEEN Co. Kerry.

Mrs B. Landers San Antoine, Valentia Rd ✆ (0667) 2521. *Town.*
6 bedrs, 6 en suite
£ B&B IR£16, B&B (double) IR£24; D IR£11

Mrs N. McKenna   Mount Rivers, Carhan Rd
☎(0667) 2509. *Town*. Open 1 Apr–30 Sep.
🛏 5 bedrs, 4 en suite
£ B&B IR£13–£15·50, B&B (double) IR £21–£24

Mrs A. Quill   Ard na Greine, Valentia Rd ☎(0667)
2281. *Town*. Open 1 Mar–30 Nov.
🛏 3 bedrs
£ B&B IR£9, B&B (double) IR£20; D IR£9

CARAGH LAKE   Co. Kerry.

Mrs H. Windecker   Carrig House ☎(066) 69104.
Country
🛏5 bedrs, 5 en suite

£ B&B (double) IR£38; D IR£16

CARLINGFORD   Co. Louth.

Mrs M. Woods   Viewpoint, Omeath Rd ☎(042)
73149. *Town*. Open Mar–Oct
🛏6 bedrs, 6 en suite; TV; tcf
£ B&B IR£15

CARLOW   Co. Carlow.

Mrs M. Quinn   The Locks, Milford ☎(0503) 46261.
Country. Fishing.
🛏6 bedrs, 1 en suite

£ B&B IR£12; D IR£8

CARRICK-ON-SUIR   Co. Tipperary.

Cedarfield House   Waterford Rd ☎(051) 40164.
Guest House.
🛏6 bedrs, 6 en suite; TV
£ B&B IR£23·50–£30; D IR£16·85

CASHEL   Co. Galway.

Mrs M. M. Cloherty   Glynsh House, Cashel Bay
☎(095) 32279
🛏10 bedrs, 9 en suite
£B&B IR£16–£18, B&B (double) IR£24–£48;
D IR£13 **cc** Access, B'card/Visa

CASHEL   Co. Tipperary.

Mrs M. Foley   Rahard Lodge, Kilkenny Rd ☎(062)
61052. *Farm*. Open Feb–Nov
🛏6 bedrs, 4 en suite
£ B&B IR£22–£26; D IR£12 **cc** B'card/Visa.

Mrs M. A. Kennedy   Thornbrook House,
Kilkenny/Dualla Rd ☎(062) 61480. *Country*.
🛏5 bedrs, 3 en suite
£ B&B IR£16, B&B (double) IR£22–£26.

Mrs E. Moloney   Ros-Guil House, Kilkenny/Dualla
Rd ☎(062) 61507 *Country. Tennis*. Open Apr–Oct
🛏5 bedrs, 3 en suite
£ B&B IR£16–£18, B&B (double) IR£22–£26

Mrs E. O'Brien   Knock Saint Lour House ☎(062)
61172. *Farm*. Open Apr–Oct
🛏8 bedrs, 4 en suite
£ B&B IR£14, B&B (double) IR£22–£26; D IR£11.

CASTLEBAR   Co. Mayo.

Mrs M. Moran   Lakeview House, Westport Rd
☎(094) 22374. *Country*.
🛏4 bedrs, 2 en suite
£ B&B fr IR£10; HT IR£7.

CASTLEBLAYNEY   Co. Monaghan.

Mrs M. Fleming   Lochbeg, Corracloughan ☎(042)
40664. *Country*.
🛏3 bedrs
£ B&B fr IR£12, B&B (double) IR£21–£24

CASTLECONNELL   Co. Limerick.

Mrs H. Wilson   Spa House ☎(061) 377171.
Country. Open Apr–Sep
🛏5 bedrs, 3 en suite
£ B&B (double) IR£22–£25

CASTLEISLAND   Co. Kerry.

O'Mahony Family   Beach Grove, Camp Rd
☎(066) 41217. *Farm*. Open 1 Apr–30 Sep
🛏5 bedrs, 2 en suite
£ B&B IR£12; D IR£10

CASTLEMAINE   Co. Kerry.

Mrs E. O'Connor   Tom & Eileen's Farm ☎(066)
67373. *Farm*. Open 1 Apr–31 Oct.
🛏5 bedrs, 1 en suite; tcf

£ B&B IR£13·50; D IR£10

CASTLETOWNBERE   Co. Cork.

Mrs M. Donegan   Realt-na-Mara ☎(027) 70101.
Country.
🛏5 bedrs, 3 en suite
£B&B IR£9·50–£10; D IR£9

CASTLETOWNSHEND   Co. Cork.

Mrs R. Vickery   Bow Hall ☎(028) 36114. *Town*.
🛏3 bedrs, 3 en suite
£ B&B IR£26; D IR£16

CHARLESTOWN   Co. Mayo.

Mrs J. Keane   Hawthorne House ☎(094) 54237.
Town. Open May–Sep
🛏5 bedrs
£ B&B (double) IR£21

Mrs C. O'Gorman   Ashfort, Airport Rd ☎(094)
54706. *Country*.
🛏5 bedrs, 4 en suite

£B&B IR£15, B&B (double) £22

CLAREMORRIS Co. Mayo.

Basil & Cora Judge Ashlawn, Brookhill ✆(094) 71415. *Country*.
⇴3 bedrs, 1 en suite
£ B&B IR£12–£13; DIR£6

CLIFDEN Co. Galway.

Mrs K. Hardman Mallmore House ✆(095) 21460. *Country*. Open Mar–Oct
⇴6 bedrs, 4 en suite
£ B&B IR£22–£24

Shanley-O'Toole Family Rose Cottage, Rockfield, Moyard ✆(095) 41082. *Farm. Fishing*.
⇴6 bedrs, 6 en suite; tcf
£B&B IR£24; DIR£12

CLONMEL Co. Tipperary.

Mrs T. O'Callaghan St Loman's, The Roundabout, Cahir Rd ✆(052) 22916. *Town*.
⇴3 bedrs, 1 en suite
£ B&B (double) IR£20–£26; D IR£10

Mrs B O'Connor New Abbey, Marlfield ✆(052) 22626. *Farm*. Open Apr–30 Sep.
⇴3 bedrs. 1 en suite
£ B&B (double) IR£22; DIR£10

Mrs O'Loughlin Old Grange, Knocklofty ✆(052) 38232. *Farm*
⇴3 bedrs
£ B&B IR£10, (double) IR£20; HT IR£6

Mrs J. Phelan Cluain Ard, Melview ✆(052) 22413. *Town*
⇴3 bedrs
£ B&B IR£9; HT IR£7.

Mrs S. Phelan Mullinarinka House ✆(052) 21374. *Farm, tennis*. Open Easter–Sep.
⇴5 bedrs
£ B&B (double) IR£24; DIR£12

Mrs M. Whelan Amberville, Glenconner Rd (off Western Rd) ✆(052) 21470. *Town*.
⇴5 bedrs, 2 en suite
£ B&B IR£12·50; DIR£9·50

CORK Co Cork.

Mrs N. Murray Roserie Villa, Mardyke Walk, off Western Rd ✆(021) 272958. *Town*.
⇴7 bedrs, 5 en suite; TV
£ B&B IR£15–£20; B&B (double) IR£22–£35
cc Access, Amex, B'card/Visa, Diners.

Mrs M. Reddy St Anthony's, Victoria Cross ✆(021) 541345. *Town*.
⇴6 bedrs
£ B&B IR£10·50

COROFIN Co. Clare.

Kelleher Family Fergus View, Kilnaboy ✆(065) 27606. *Farm. Fishing*. Open Apr–Sep
⇴6 bedrs, 3 en suite
£ B&B IR£14, B&B (double) IR£22–£26; DIR£10·50

John & Betty Kelleher Inchiquin View Farm, Kilnaboy ✆(065) 27731. *Farm. Fishing*. Open Mar–Oct
⇴5 bedrs, 2 en suite
£ B&B IR£14; DIR£10·50

COURTOWN HARBOUR Co Wexford.

Miss B. Kinsella Riverchapel House ✆(055) 25120
⇴7 bedrs
£B&B (double) IR£20; D IR£9

DINGLE Co Kerry.

Mrs R. Brosnan Drom House, Coumgaugh ✆(066) 51134. *Country*.
⇴3 bedrs, 3 en suite; TV
£ B&B (double) IR£22; D IR£12

Mrs M. Devane Lisdargan, Lispole ✆(066) 51418. *Farm*. Open 1 Jun–30 Sep.
⇴3 bedrs
£ B&B (double) IR£21; D IR£10.

Mrs A. Murphy Ard na Mara, Ballymore, Ventry ✆(066) 59072. *Country. Fishing*. Open 1 Mar–1 Dec
⇴5 bedrs, 4 en suite
£ B&B IR£12–£16, B&B (double) IR£21–£24

Mrs A. Neligan Duinin House, Conor Pass Rd ✆(066) 51335. *Country*. Open 1 Apr–31 Oct.
⇴5 bedrs, 4 en suite
£ B&B IR£14–£15, B&B (double) £22–£25

Mrs P. O'Connor Knocknahow ✆(066) 51449. *Farm*. Open Apr–Oct
⇴4 bedrs, 2 en suite
£B&B IR£12, B&B (double) £22–£23; HT IR£8.

Mrs C. O'Dowd Knockarrogeen West ✆(066) 51307. *Farm. Riding, swimming pool, tennis, golf*. Open Mar–Nov
⇴6 bedrs, 6 en suite
£B&B IR£16, B&B (double) IR£26; DIR£12
cc Access, Amex, B'card/Visa.

DONEGAL Co. Donegal.

Mrs E. Murray Glebe, Ballyshannon Rd ✆(073) 21223. *Town*. Open 1 May–30 Sep.
⇴4 bedrs, 3 en suite
£ B&B (double) IR£20–£22

DROGHEDA Co. Louth.

Mrs S. Dwyer Harbour Villa, Mornington Rd ✆(041) 37441. *Country. Tennis*.

🛏4 bedrs
£ B&B IR£14, B&B (double) IR£22; D IR£10

DRUMCLIFFE Co. Sligo.

McDonagh Family Westway ✆(071) 63178. *Farm*. Open 15 May–31 Aug.
🛏3 bedrs
£ B&B IR£13, B&B (double) IR£22; D IR£11

DRUMSHANBO Co. Leitrim.

Mrs M. Costello Forest View, Carrick Rd ✆(078) 41243. Open 1 Mar–30 Nov.
🛏5 bedrs, 1 en suite
£ B&B (double) IR£20–£22; D IR£9·50

DUBLIN CITY Co. Dublin.

Mrs N. Doran Wesley House, Anglesea Rd, Ballsbridge 4 ✆(01) 681201
🛏3 bedrs, 3 en suite; TV; tcf
£ B&B IR£18–£20, B&B (double) IR£30–£34; D IR£12·50

Mrs E. Kelly 17 Seacourt, St Gabriel's Rd, off Seafield Rd, Clontarf ✆(01) 332547.
🛏3 bedrs, 2 en suite
£ B&B (double) IR£24–£28

Mrs Mary Mooney Aishling House, 20 St Lawrence Rd, Clontarf ✆(01) 339097. Closed 24–31 Dec.
🛏9 bedrs, 7 en suite
£ B&B IR£20–£25, B&B (double) IR£24–£28

Mrs T. Ryan Parknasilla, 15 Iona Dr, Drumcondra 9 ✆(01) 305724
🛏4 bedrs, 2 en suite
£ B&B IR£14, B&B (double) IR£24–£28

DULEEK Co. Meath.

Mrs K. Sweetman Annesbrook ✆(041) 23293. *Country*. Open 15 May–15 Sep
🛏3 bedrs, 3 en suite
£ B&B IR£19·50, B&B (double) IR£33; D IR£12.50

DUNDALK Co. Louth.

Mrs M. Meehan Rosemount, Dublin Rd ✆(042) 35878. *Town*.
🛏6 bedrs, 3 en suite
£ B&B IR£15, B&B (double) IR£22–£24

DUNMORE EAST Co. Waterford.

Mrs M. Kent Foxmount Farm, Half-way House ✆(051) 74308. *Farm. Tennis, riding, snooker*. Open Apr–Oct
🛏6 bedrs
£ B&B IR£16, B&B (double) £26; D IR£12

ENNIS Co. Clare.

Mrs M. Duggan Woodquay House, Woodquay ✆(065) 28320. *Town*. Open Mar–Oct.
🛏4 bedrs, 1 en suite
£ B&B (double) £20–£22

Mrs T. O'Donohue Sanborn House, Edenvale, Kilrush Rd ✆(065) 24959. *Country*.
🛏4 bedrs
£ B&B IR£13; HT IR£7·50.

Mrs M. O'Loughlin Massabielle, Gaurus (Off Quin Rd) ✆(065) 29363. *Country*.
🛏5 bedrs, 4 en suite
£ B&B (double) IR£21–£24; D IR£11.

ENNISKERRY Co. Wicklow.

Mrs K. Lynch Cherbury, Monastery ✆(01) 828679. *Country*.
🛏3 bedrs, 3 en suite
£ B&B (double) IR£25.

FERNS Co. Wexford.

Mrs Betty Breen Clone House ✆(054) 66113. *Farm. Fishing, tennis*. Open Apr–Sep.
🛏4 bedrs, 3 en suite
£ B&B IR£15–£17, B&B (double) IR£24–£28; D IR£11.

GALWAY AND SALTHILL Co. Galway.

Mrs S. Davy Ross House, Whitestrand Av ✆(091) 67431. *Town*.
🛏4 bedrs, 2 en suite
£ B&B IR£15, B&B (double) IR£21–£24.

Mrs T. Cunningham La Salette, Grattan Park ✆(091) 65720. *Town*. Open Easter–Oct
🛏4 bedrs, 3 en suite
£ B&B (double) IR£22–£24

Mrs J. Maher Petra, Laurel Park, Newcastle ✆(091) 21844. *Town*. Open 1 Apr–30 Sep.
🛏4 bedrs, 1 en suite
£ B&B (double) IR£22–£24; D IR£10

Mrs M. Nolan Glencree, 20 Whitestrand Av, Lower Salthill ✆(091) 61061. *Town*.
🛏4 bedrs, 4 en suite
£ B&B (double) IR£24.

Mrs O. Connolly Seacrest, Roscam ✆(091) 57975. *Town. Indoor swimming pool*.
🛏6 bedrs, 5 en suite; tcf
£ B&B (double) IR£22–£26.

Tim & Carmel O'Halloran Roncalli House, 24 Whitestrand Av, Lower Salthill ✆(091) 64159. *Town*.
🛏6 bedrs, 6 en suite
£ B&B (double) IR£24.

Mrs B. Thompson Rock Lodge, Whitestrand Rd
☎(091) 63789. *Town.*
🛏6 bedrs, 5 en suite
£ B&B IR£12, B&B (double) IR£24

Mr & Mrs Dermot & Margaret Walsh De Sota,
54 Newcastle Rd ☎(091) 65064. *Town.*
🛏6 bedrs, 4 en suite
£ B&B (double) IR£21–£24.

GORESBRIDGE Co. Kilkenny.

Mrs C. Lawlor Mount Loftus ☎(0503) 75228.
Country. Open mid June–mid Sep
🛏3 bedrs, 1 en suite
£B&B IR£21–£25; D IR£10.

GRANGE Co. Sligo.

Mrs C. Anhold Horse Holiday Farm, Mount
Temple ☎(071) 66152. Fax: (071) 66400. *Farm.
Riding, sauna.* Open 15 Jan–15 Dec
🛏4 bedrs, 4 en suite

Mrs U. Brennan Armada Lodge, Mount Temple
☎(071) 63250. *Country. Sauna, tennis.*
🛏5 bedrs, 5 en suite
£ B&B IR£14–£15.

HEADFORD Co. Galway.

McDonagh Family Balrickard Farm ☎(093)
35421. *Farm.* Open Mar–Nov
🛏3 bedrs
£ B&B (double) IR£20–£25; D IR£10.

INVER Co. Donegal.

Mrs R. M. Boyd Cranny House ☎(073) 36010.
Farm. Open 1 Apr–31 Oct.
🛏3 bedrs, 1 en suite
£ B&B IR£12–£14; D IR£13·25.

KELLS Co. Meath.

Mrs P. Mullan Lennoxbrook, Carnacross ☎(046)
45902. *Farm. Fishing.*
🛏5 bedrs
£ B&B IR£14, B&B (double) IR£22; D IR£12.

KENMARE Co. Kerry.

Mrs P. Dignam Glendarragh ☎(064) 41436.
Farm. Sauna. Open Feb–15 Nov
🛏6 bedrs, 6 en suite
£ B&B IR£12, B&B (double) IR£24; D IR£10.

Mrs T. Hayes Ceann Mara, Killowen ☎(064)
41220. *Farm. Tennis, fishing, private beach.* Open
Apr–Oct
🛏6 bedrs, 5 en suite; tcf
£ B&B IR£14–£15; D IR£11.

O'Donnells of Ashgrove, Ashgrove ☎(064)
41228. *Country.* Open 1 Mar–31 Oct.
🛏4 bedrs, 3 en suite
£ B&B IR£11–£13, B&B (double) IR£20–£24;
D IR£10.

Mrs M. O'Mahoney The Arches, Blackwater
Bridge ☎(064) 82030. *Country.* Open Apr–Oct
🛏5 bedrs, 5 en suite
£ B&B IR£17, B&B (double) IR£25.

Mrs M. Whyte Riverside, Killarney Rd ☎(064)
41316. *Town.* Open Apr–Oct
🛏3 bedrs
£ B&B IR£11.

KILDARE Co. Kildare.

Mrs A. Winters St Mary's, Maddenstown,
Curragh ☎(045) 21243. *Farm.* Open Apr–Sep
🛏3 bedrs
£ B&B IR£20; D IR£9.

KILGARVAN Co. Kerry.

Eileen & Sean Dineen Glenlea Farmhouse
☎(064) 85314. *Farm. Fishing.* Open Feb–Nov
🛏8 bedrs, 4 en suite
£ B&B (double) IR£23; D IR£10·50.

Dineen Family Hawthorn Farm ☎(064) 85326.
Farm. Open 1 Apr–31 Oct.
🛏6 bedrs, 3 en suite
£B&B IR£23–£25; D IR£10·50.

Mrs J. McCarthy Sillerdane Lodge, Coolnoohill
☎(064) 85359. *Country. Swimming pool.*
🛏6 bedrs, 6 en suite
£B&B IR£14; D IR£10.

KILKENNY Co. Kilkenny.

Mrs M. T. Neary Tara Farm, off Freshford Rd
☎(056) 67619. *Farm.* Open 1 Apr–31 Oct.
🛏4 bedrs
£ B&B IR£22; D IR£9.

KILLALOE Co. Clare.

Miss E. Coppen Lantern House, Ogonnelloe,
Tuamgraney ☎(0619) 23034. *Country.* Closed Nov
🛏6 bedrs, 6 en suite
£ B&B IR£15, B&B (double) IR£28; D IR£10.

KILLARNEY Co. Kerry.

Mr & Mrs M. Beazley Carriglea House,
Muckcross Rd ☎(064) 31116. *Farm.* Open Easter–
Oct.
🛏9 bedrs, 6 en suite
£B&B IR£24–27; D IR£9·50.

Mrs M. Counihan Villa Marias, Aghadoe ☎(064)
32307. *Country.* Open Mar–Oct.

4 bedrs
£ B&B (double) IR£21.

Mrs P. Cronin St Ritas Villas, Mill Rd (off Muckcross Rd) ✆(064) 31517. *Town*.
5 bedrs, 4 en suite
£ B&B IR£14–£15, B&B (double) IR£21–£24

Hannah & Dan Daly Brookfield House, Coolgarrive, Aghadoe ✆(064) 32077. *Farm*. Open Mar–Oct.
6 bedrs, 1 en suite
£ B&B (double) IR£24; D IR£9·50.

Mrs N. Dineen Manor House, 18 Whitebridge Manor, Ballycasheen ✆(064) 32716. *Town*.
5 bedrs, 3 en suite
£ B&B IR£15, B&B (double) IR£22–£24; D IR£9·50.

Mrs T. Doona Hollybough House, Cappagh, Kilgobnet ✆(064) 44255. *Country*. Open Easter–Oct.
4 bedrs, 2 en suite
£ B&B IR£14·50–£15, B&B (double) IR£21; D IR£10 **cc** Access.

Mrs M. Geaney Pine Crest, Woodlawn Rd (off Muckcross Rd) ✆(064) 31721. *Town*.
5 bedrs, 3 en suite
£ B&B IR£15, B&B (double) IR£21–£23

Mrs K. Guerin Irish Cottage, Muckcross Rd ✆(064) 32443. *Town*.
5 bedrs, 1 en suite
£ B&B IR£14·50; D IR£10.

Mrs J. Horan Knockane Farm, Ballyfinnane, Farranfore ✆(066) 64324. *Farm. Riding, fishing*. Open 1 May–30 Sep.
3 bedrs, 1 en suite
£ B&B IR£12·50; D IR£12·50.

Mrs M.R. Kearney Gap View Farm, Firies (via Ballyhar) ✆(066) 64378. *Farm*. Open Easter–Oct.
6 bedrs, 2 en suite
£ B&B IR£10·50–£12; D IR£9·50.

Mrs K. McAuliffe Carrowmore House, Knockasarnett, Aghadoe ✆(064) 33520. *Country*. Open Apr–Oct.
5 bedrs, 4 en suite
£ B&B IR£14–£16.

Miss C. McSweeney Emerville House, Muckcross Dr, Muckcross Rd ✆(064) 33342. *Town*. Open Mar–Oct.
4 bedrs, (3 sh)
£ B&B (double) IR£22.

Mrs C. O'Brien Tara, Gap of Dunloe Rd ✆(064) 44355. *Country*. Open 1 Apr–31 Oct.
5 bedrs, 4 en suite
£ B&B IR£14·50, B&B (double) IR£21–£24; D IR£10.

Mrs N. O'Neill Alderhaven, Ballycasheen ✆(064) 31982. *Country*. Open 15 Mar–31 Oct.
5 bedrs, 4 en suite
£ B&B IR£16.

Mrs C. Spillane Beauty's Home, Tralee Rd ✆(064) 31567. *Country*.
3 bedrs, 2 en suite; TV; tcf
£ B&B IR£14–£16·50, B&B (double) IR£22–£27

Mrs E. Spillane Inveraray, Beaufort ✆(064) 44224. *Farm. Fishing, riding*. Open Feb–Nov.
6 bedrs, 4 en suite
£ B&B IR£21–£24; D IR£9

Mrs A. Teahan Fair Haven, Lissivigeen, Cork Rd ✆(064) 32542. *Country*.
6 bedrs, 5 en suite
£ B&B (double) IR£21–£24.

KILLORGLIN Co. Kerry.

Mrs M. Melia Ashling, Sunhill ✆(066) 61226. *Town*. Open Mar–Nov.
4 bedrs
£ B&B IR£10.

KILLYBEGS Co. Donegal.

Mrs E. O'Keeney Glenlee House, Fintra Rd ✆(073) 31026. *Country*.
5 bedrs, 5 en suite; tcf
£ B&B IR£15, B&B (double) IR£24; D IR£10.

KILTEGAN Co. Wicklow.

Mrs E.F. Jackson Beachlawn ✆(0508) 73171. *Farm*. Open 1 Mar–31 Oct.
4 bedrs
£ B&B (double) IR£22; D IR£10

KILTIMAGH Co. Mayo.

Mrs M. Carney Hillcrest, Kilkelly Rd ✆(094) 81112. *Country*. Open Apr–Sep.
4 bedrs, 2 en suite
£ B&B (double) IR£20–£21; D IR£9·50.

KINSALE Co. Cork.

Griffin Family Griffins, Hillside House, Camp Hill ✆(021) 772315. *Country*.
6 bedrs, 3 en suite
£ B&B IR£10–£13; D IR£9·50.

Mr & Mrs A. Moran-Salinger The Lighthouse, The Rock ✆(021) 772734
6 bedrs, 3 en suite
£ B&B IR£17, B&B (double) IR£27; D IR£10.

KNOCKFERRY Co. Galway.

Mr Des Moran Knockferry Lodge, Knockferry, Roscahill ✆(091) 80122. *Farm*. Open May–Oct.

10 bedrs, 10 en suite
£ B&B IRE£19, B&B (double) IRE£32; D IRE£13·50.

LAHINCH   Co. Clare.

Mrs B. Fawl   Mulcarr House, Ennistymon Rd
(065) 81123. *Town*. Open 17 Mar–31 Oct
4 bedrs, 3 en suite
£ B&B IRE£14·50; B&B (double) £22–£24.

LEENANE   Co. Galway.

Mrs B. Daly   Portfinn Lodge (095) 42265.
Country. Fishing. Open Apr–Sep.
4 bedrs, 4 en suite
£B&B (double) IRE£23; D IRE£12·75.
cc Access, B'card/Visa.

LIMERICK   Co. Limerick.

Mrs B. Boylan   Trelawne House, Ennis Rd (061)
54063. *Town*.
£ B&B IRE£15–£16·50, B&B (double) £22–£25

Mrs M. Collins   St Anthony's, 8 Coolraine Ter,
Ennis Rd (061) 52607. *Town*.
3 bedrs
£ B&B (double) IRE£19.

Mrs C. A. Gavin   Shannonville, Ennis Rd (061)
53690. *Town*. Open May–Sep.
3 bedrs
£ B&B (double) IRE£19.

Mrs K. O'Reilly   Erris House, Fairs Rd, Meelick
(051) 54605. *Country*. Open May–1 Oct.
4 bedrs, 2 en suite
£B&B IRE£21–£24.

LISTOWEL   Co. Kerry.

Mrs J. Groarke   Burntwood House (068) 21516.
Farm. Open 1 Apr–1 Oct.
6 bedrs, 4 en suite
£ B&B IRE£10; D IRE£12.

Mrs T. Keane   Whispering Pines, Bedford (068)
21503. *Country*.
4 bedrs
£ B&B (double) IRE£22–£26; D IRE£24.

Mrs N. O'Neill   Ashgrove House, Ballybunion Rd
(068) 21268. *Country*. Open Mar–Oct.
4 bedrs, 4 en suite
£ B&B IRE£16; B&B (double) £22–£32.

Mrs K. Stack   Tralee Rd, Ballygrennane (068)
21345. *Town*. Open Apr–Oct.
4 bedrs, 3 en suite
£ B&B (double) IRE£21–£31.

MALAHIDE   Co. Dublin.

Mrs M. Farelly   Lynfar, Kinsealy La (01) 463897.
Town. Open Feb–Oct.

4 bedrs
£ B&B IRE£15, B&B (double) IRE£24.

MALLOW   Co. Cork.

Mrs B. Copplestone   Dawna, Navigation Rd
(022) 21479. *Country*. Open Mar–Oct.
3 bedrs, 3 en suite
£ B&B IRE£15, B&B (double) IRE£25; D IRE£10.

MOUNTRATH   Co. Laois.

Frank & Rosemarie Kennan   Roundwood House
(0502) 32120. *Country*.
6 bedrs, 6 en suite
£ B&B IRE£30, B&B (double) IRE£46; D IRE£16 **cc**
Access, Amex.

MULLINAHONE   Co. Tipperary.

Mrs R.E. Sherwood   Killaghy Castle (052)
53112. *Farm*. Open mid Mar–mid Oct
4 bedrs, 2 en suite
£ B&B (double) IRE£45–£50; D IRE£14·50.

MULLINGAR   Co. Westmeath.

Mr & Mrs S. Casey   Hilltop, Navan Rd,
Rathconnell (044) 48958. *Country*.
5 bedrs, 5 en suite
£ B&B IRE£16, B&B (double) IRE£24; D IRE£11.

NAVAN   Co. Meath.

Mrs. M. Reilly   Gainstown House (046) 21448.
Farm. Open Apr–Oct.
4 bedrs
£ B&B IRE£14; D IRE£18.

NENAGH   Co. Tipperary.

Mrs K. Healy   Rathnaleen House, Golf Club Rd
(067) 32508. *Country*.
3 bedrs, 1 en suite
£ B&B IRE£14, B&B (double) IRE£22–£26; D IRE£10.

Mrs B. Lewis   Ballyartella Farmhouse (067)
24219. *Farm. Fishing*. Open Mar–Oct.
4 bedrs
£ B&B (double) IRE£22; D IRE£9.

Mrs G. McAuliffe   Avondale, Tyone (067)
31084. *Town*. Open Apr–Nov.
4 bedrs
£ B&B IRE£14; D IRE£10.

NEWBLISS   Co. Monaghan.

Mrs M. O'Grady   Glynch House (047) 54045.
Farm. Open Jan–mid Dec.
6 bedrs, 1 en suite
£ B&B IRE£16, B&B (double) IRE£26; D IRE£11.

NEWMARKET-ON-FERGUS Co. Clare.

Mrs P.O'Leary Weavers Lodge ☎(061) 71348. *Farm.*
4 bedrs, 1 en suite
£ B&B IR£11, B&B (double) IR£21; D IR£9

OUGHTERARD Co. Galway.

Mr & Mrs M. Healy Corrib Wave House, Portacarron ☎(091) 82147. *Farm.*
Open 1 Apr–15 Oct.
£ B&B IR£13–£1·50; D IR£11.

Mr & Mrs Lal Faherty Lakeland Country House, Portacarron ☎(091) 82121. *Country.* Open 2 Jun–mid Oct.
9 bedrs, 5 en suite
£ B&B IR£15; HT IR£7.

PALLASKENRY Co. Limerick.

Mrs M. Walsh Home Farm Stores ☎(061) 393142. *Town.*
4 bedrs
£ B&B IR£8·50; D IR£8.

PATRICKSWELL Co. Limerick.

Mrs C. Geary Carnlea, Caher Rd ☎(061) 27576. *Country.* Open Mar–Oct.
5 bedrs, 2 en suite
£ B&B IR£15, B&B (double) IR£21–£23.

PORTMARNOCK Co. Dublin.

Mrs M. Creane Robinia, 452 Strand Rd ☎(01) 462987. *Town.* Open Apr–Oct.
3 bedrs, 1 en suite
£ B&B IR£15, B&B (double) IR£24–£29.

Mrs A. Healy Pine Lodge, Coast Rd ☎(01) 460097. *Town.* Open 15 Mar–31 Oct.
5 bedrs, 1 en suite
£ B&B IR£27–£33.

RAMELTON Co. Donegal.

Mrs A. Campbell Ardeen ☎(074) 51243. *Town. Tennis.* Open 23 Mar–30 Sep.
4 bedrs
£ B&B IR£12 **cc** Amex

Mrs F. Scott The Manse ☎(074) 51047. *Town.*
Open 1 Apr–30 Sep.
4 bedrs
£ B&B (double) IR£26; D IR£12.

RATHDRUM Co. Wicklow.

Mrs E. O'Brien Abhainn Mor House, Corballis ☎(0404) 46330. *Country. Tennis.* Open Feb–Nov.
6 bedrs, 4 en suite

£ B&B IR£16–£18, B&B (double) IR£22–£25; D IR£10.

RIVERSTOWN Co. Sligo.

Mr & Mrs B. C. O'Hara Coopershill ☎(071) 65108 Tx: 40301 Fax: (071) 65466. *Farm.* Open 24 Mar–31 Oct.
6 bedrs, 6 en suite; tcf
£ B&B IR£38; D IR£16 **cc** Access, Amex, B'card/Visa.

ROSCOMMON Co. Roscommon.

Mrs D. Dolan Munsboro House, Sligo Rd ☎(0903) 26375. *Farm.* Open Mar–Nov.
4 bedrs
£ B&B (double) IR£22; D IR£11.

ROSCREA Co. Tipperary.

Mrs M. Fallon Cregganbell, Birr Rd ☎(0505) 21421. *Country.*
4 bedrs
£ B&B IR£10.

ROUNDSTONE Co. Galway.

Mrs M. King High Trees, Errisbeg East ☎(095) 35881. *Farm.* Open 1 Jun–30 Sep.
3 bedrs
£ B&B IR£10·50; D IR£10·50.

SKIBBEREEN Co. Cork.

Mrs R. O'Byrne Elysium Herb Farm, Lisheenroe, Castletownshend Rd ☎(028) 21325. *Tennis.* Open 1 May–31 Aug.
4 bedrs, 1 en suite
£ B&B IR£16–£17·50; D IR£10.

SLIGO Co. Sligo.

Mrs C. Carr St Martin's Cummeen, Strandhill Rd ☎(071) 60614. Open Feb–Nov.
5 bedrs, 5 en suite; TV
£ B&B IR£15, B&B (double) IR£22–£24.

Mrs L. Diamond Lisadorn, Lisnalurg ☎(071) 43417. *Country.*
5 bedrs, 5 en suite
£ B&B IR£13–£17·50, B&B (double) IR£27.

Mrs E. Fitzgerald Lough Gill Lodge, Green Rd, Cairns ☎(071) 60996. Open Apr–Sep.
3 bedrs, 1 en suite
£ B&B (double) IR£20–£22; HT IR£8.

Mrs D. MacEvilly Tree Tops, Cleveragh Rd (off Dublin Rd) ☎(071) 60160. *Town.*
6 bedrs, 4 en suite
£ B&B IR£14·50–£15·50, B&B (double) £22–£24.

Mrs A. McKiernan Glenwood, Carrowmore
☎(071) 61449. *Country*. Open Apr–Sep.
⊨4 bedrs, 2 en suite
£ B&B IR£15–£17, B&B (double) IR£22–£26;
D IR£11.

SNEEM Co. Kerry.

Mrs M. Teahan Derry East Farmhouse, Waterville
Rd ☎(064) 45193. Open Mar–Nov.
⊨4 bedrs, 1 en suite
£ B&B IR£15–£16; D IR£10.

SPIDDAL Co. Galway.

Mrs M. Feeney Cala n'Uisce, Greenhill ☎(091)
83324. *Country*. Open Apr–Oct.
⊨6 bedrs, 4 en suite
£ B&B IR£14·50; D IR£10.

Mrs V. Feeney Ardmor Country House, Greenhill
☎(091) 83145. *Country*. Open 1 Mar–30 Nov.
⊨8 bedrs, 7 en suite
£ B&B IR£13–£15, B&B (double) IR£21–£25;
D IR£12·50.

STROKESTOWN Co. Roscommon.

Cox Family Church View House ☎(078) 33047.
Farm. Open Feb–Nov.
⊨6 bedrs, 2 en suite
£ B&B IR£12·50–£14·50; D IR£10–£11.

SWORDS Co. Dublin.

Mrs H. Dwyer Greenogue House, Greenogue,
Kilsallaghan ☎(01) 350319.
⊨3 bedrs
£ B&B IR£24.

TIPPERARY Co. Tipperary.

Mr & Mrs J. Marnane Bansha House, Bansha
☎(062) 54194. Open Mar–Nov.
⊨7 bedrs
£ B&B (double) IR£22; D IR£10.

Mrs M. Merrigan Teach Gobnatan, Glen of
Aherlow Rd ☎(062) 51645. Open Mar–Oct.
⊨4 bedrs, 3 en suite
£ B&B IR£11–£12; D IR£10.

Mrs N. O'Dwyer Barronstown House, Emly Rd
☎(062) 55130. *Farm*. Open May–Nov.
⊨4 bedrs
£ B&B (double) IR£22; D IR£20.

Mrs M. O'Neill Villa Maria, Bohercrowe, Limerick
Rd ☎(062) 51557. Open Jun–Sep.
⊨3 bedrs
£ B&B IR£14, B&B (double) IR£21.

Mrs M. Quinn Clonmore, Cork–Galbally Rd
☎(062) 51637. *Country*. Open Apr–Oct.

⊨4 bedrs, 4 en suite
£ B&B IR£15, B&B (double) IR£22.

TRALEE Co. Kerry.

Mrs B. Fitzgerald Seaview House, Main Dingle
Rd, Annagh ☎(066) 21830. *Country*. Open Easter–
Oct.
⊨5 bedrs, 4 en suite
£ B&B IR£22–£26.

Mrs H. McCrohan Woodview, Caherslee, Ardfert
Rd ☎(066) 22872. Open Easter–Oct.
⊨3 bedrs
£ B&B IR£9.

Mrs M. McGrath Kerria, Listellick North
☎(066) 24451. *Country*. Open Easter–Oct.
⊨5 bedrs
£ B&B IR£14, B&B (double) IR£22–£25;
D IR£10·50.

Mrs C. Nealon The Gables, Listowel Rd
☎(066) 24396. *Town*. Open Jun–Sep.
⊨4 bedrs, 1 en suite
£ B&B IR£12·50, B&B (double) IR£21–£25.

Mrs O'Sullivan, Knockanish House, The Spa
☎(066) 36268. *Country*. Open Apr–Nov.
⊨6 bedrs, 5 en suite; tcf
£ B&B (double) IR£26–£30; D IR£10.

Misses N & K Prendergast Caheerslee House,
Caheerslee ☎(066) 22616. *Town*.
⊨5 bedrs
£ B&B IR£12.

VIRGINIA Co. Cavan.

Lake ☎(049) 47561. *Fishing*.
⊨13 bedrs, 6 en suite
£ B&B IR£17, B&B (double) IR£28; D IR£6·50.

WATERFORD Co. Waterford.

Mrs M. C. Fitzmaurice Blenheim House,
Blenheim Heights ☎(051) 74115. *Country*.
⊨6 bedrs, 6 en suite
£ B&B IR£14·50

Mrs A Forrest Ashbourne House, Slieverue
☎(051) 32037. *Farm*. Open Apr–Oct.
⊨7 bedrs, 4 en suite
£ B&B IR£14–£15·50, B&B (double) IR£22–£25;
D IR£9.

Gough Family Moat Farmhouse, Faithlegg,
Cheekpoint Rd ☎(051) 82166. *Farm*. Open 17 Mar–
31 Oct.
⊨3 bedrs
£ B&B IR£13; D IR£12.

WATERVILLE Co. Kerry.

Frank & Anne Donnelly Lake Lands House, Lake Rd ✆(0667) 4303. *Farm.*
📭5 bedrs
£ B&B IR£13·50; D IR£10.

WESTPORT Co. Mayo.

Mrs A. Cox Sea River House, Mayour, Kilmeena
✆(098) 26536. *Farm.* Open May–mid Oct.
📭6 bedrs, 1 en suite
£ B&B IR£13·50–£14·50; D IR£11.

Mrs M. O'Brien Rath a Rosa, Rossbeg
✆(098) 25348. *Farm.* Open 15 Mar–31 Oct.
📭4 bedrs, 3 en suite
£ B&B IR£16·50–£18; D IR£13.

O'Malley Family Seapoint Ho., Kilmeena
✆(098) 41254. *Farm.* Open Mar–Oct.
📭7 bedrs, 5 en suite
£ B&B IR£15–£18; D IR£10·50.

WEXFORD Co. Wexford.

Mrs E. Cuddihy Rathaspeck Manor ✆(053) 42661. *Farm.* Open 1 Jun–31 Oct.

📭7 bedrs, 7 en suite; TV
£ B&B (double) IR£36–£40; D IR£12.

Mr & Mrs Hayes Clonard Ho., Clonard Great
✆(053) 23141. Open 15 Apr–1 Nov.
📭9 bedrs, 9 en suite
£ B&B IR£16, B&B (double) IR£26–£28; D IR£11.

Mrs K. Mernagh Killiane Castle, Drinagh
✆(053) 58885. *Farm.* Open Easter–Oct.
📭8 bedrs, 1 en suite
£ B&B IR£15–£17; D IR£12.

WICKLOW Co. Wicklow.

Mrs P. Klaue Lissadell House, Ashtown ✆(0404) 67458. *Farm.* Open Mar–Nov.
📭4 bedrs, 2 en suite
£ B&B IR£24–£28; D IR£12.

YOUGHAL Co. Cork.

Miss S.O. Sullivan Shalamar, Ballyvergan East
✆(024) 93398. Open May–Sep.
📭4 bedrs, 1 en suite
£ B&B (double) IR£19–£21.

DISCOUNTS

Many hotels are prepared to offer readers of this Guide discounts on accommodation prices—which can be as much as £50 per visit at hotels offering 10% discounts, £25 per visit at others offering 5% discounts. These hotels are indicated by a [V] at the end of the price section of their entry. Use the vouchers opposite to obtain your discount. Only one voucher can be used per visit.

Discounts are given on the appropriate full tariff for the room and the date. Vouchers will not be accepted for week-end breaks, rooms occupied by children at a reduced rate or against other tariffs already discounted. Hotels usually do not offer discounts over Bank Holidays, at Christmas and Easter or when there are local events in progress, for instance Gold Cup week at Cheltenham or major conferences in Harrogate.

Hotels may limit the day of the week or the time of year the vouchers can be used; this may be weekdays or weekends depending on whether the hotel is mainly a business one or mainly a holiday one. When you book, please inform the hotel that you intend to use an RAC discount voucher in part payment of your bill. Then if there is any confusion over when discounts are offered it can be sorted out easily.

D I S C O U N T
V O U C H E R

10%

UP TO £50

off accommodation at hotels
Only one voucher per visit
(for conditions see over)

D I S C O U N T
V O U C H E R

5%

UP TO £25

off accommodation at hotels
Only one voucher per visit
(for conditions see over)

D I S C O U N T
V O U C H E R

10%

UP TO £50

off accommodation at hotels
Only one voucher per visit
(for conditions see over)

D I S C O U N T
V O U C H E R

5%

UP TO £25

off accommodation at hotels
Only one voucher per visit
(for conditions see over)

CONDITIONS

1. Vouchers are only accepted for hotel accommodation at full tariff rates for the room and season, not against already discounted tariffs such as week-end breaks.
2. Only one voucher accepted per person or party per stay.
3. Hotels should be informed that an RAC voucher is to be used in part payment when a room is booked.
4. A copy of this 1991 RAC Guide must be produced when the voucher is used.
5. This voucher is not valid after 31 October 1991.

CONDITIONS

1. Vouchers are only accepted for hotel accommodation at full tariff rates for the room and season, not against already discounted tariffs such as week-end breaks.
2. Only one voucher accepted per person or party per stay.
3. Hotels should be informed that an RAC voucher is to be used in part payment when a room is booked.
4. A copy of this 1991 RAC Guide must be produced when the voucher is used.
5. This voucher is not valid after 31 October 1991.

CONDITIONS

1. Vouchers are only accepted for hotel accommodation at full tariff rates for the room and season, not against already discounted tariffs such as week-end breaks.
2. Only one voucher accepted per person or party per stay.
3. Hotels should be informed that an RAC voucher is to be used in part payment when a room is booked.
4. A copy of this 1991 RAC Guide must be produced when the voucher is used.
5. This voucher is not valid after 31 October 1991.

CONDITIONS

1. Vouchers are only accepted for hotel accommodation at full tariff rates for the room and season, not against already discounted tariffs such as week-end breaks.
2. Only one voucher accepted per person or party per stay.
3. Hotels should be informed that an RAC voucher is to be used in part payment when a room is booked.
4. A copy of this 1991 RAC Guide must be produced when the voucher is used.
5. This voucher is not valid after 31 October 1991.